A Classroom Approach of

DIGITAL IMAGE PROCESSING

A Classroom Approach of

DIGITAL IMAGE PROCESSING

MUNESH CHANDRA TRIVEDI
Asst. Professor (IT)
Institute of Management Studies
Ghaziabad (NCR)

DR. SANJAY M. SHAH
Director
S.V. Institute of Computer Studies
Kadi (Gujrat)

KHANNA BOOK PUBLISHING CO. (P) LTD.

Publisher of Engineering and Computer Books

4C/4344, Ansari Road, Darya Ganj, New Delhi-110002
Phone : 011-23244447-48 **Mobile:** +91-9910909320
E-mail : contact@khannabooks.com
Website : www.khannabooks.com

Dear Readers,

To prevent the piracy, this book is secured with HIGH SECURITY HOLOGRAM on the front title cover. In case you don't find the hologram on the front cover title, please write us to at contact@khannabooks.com or whatsapp us at +91-99109 09320 and avail special gift voucher for yourself.

Specimen of Hologram on front Cover title:

Moreover, there is a SPECIAL DISCOUNT COUPON for you with EVERY HOLOGRAM.

How to avail this SPECIAL DISCOUNT:

Step 1: Scratch the hologram
Step 2: Under the scratch area, your "coupon code" is available
Step 3: Logon to www.khannabooks.com
Step 4: Use your "coupon code" in the shopping cart and get your copy at a special diccount
Step 5: Enjoy your reading!

Price: ₹ 550.00

ISBN: 978-93-80016-15-3

Digital Image Processing
by Dr. Munesh Chandra Trivedi

First Edition: 2010
Reprint (Revised): 2023, **2024**

Published by:
Khanna Book Publishing Co. (P) Ltd.
Visit us at: **www.khannabooks.com**
Write us at: **contact@khannabooks.com**
CIN: U22110DL1998PTC095547

Printed in India.

Munesh Chandra Trivedi

Dedicated to My Lovely Daughter

Saumya & Wife Alpna

Sanjay M. Shah

Dedicated to My Parents

PREFACE

Digital image processing is a subject that is an integral component of the ubiquitous soft computing paradigm. An in depth understanding and appreciations of the field requires some background knowledge of the image processing, mathematics and computer programming. This is a difficult task. The "Digital Image Processing" aims to achieve a balanced of these areas. Digital Image Processing is the discipline that attempts to provide methods to handle this complexity and enable us to produce reliable real time systems with maximum productivity.

This book is for students who have not had previous training in Digital Image Processing Technology, and is suitable for a one-semester course. This book covers syllabus of all India universities. This is also useful for a project based introducing course in Digital Image Processing in which both the students and the instructor can follow the chapters in the order given both in the lectures as well as in the project.

ACKNOWLEDGEMENT

At the various stages in the writing of this book, a number of people have given invaluable comments on the manuscript. In this regard, we owe a debt of gratitude to Dr. R.K. Bharadwaj, Director I.M.S. Ghaziabad, Dr. B.S. Agarwal, Director Vadu college of M.C.A. and Dr. N .N. Jani Professo & Director Kadi Sarva University, Gandhi Nagar (Gujrat).

We are also grateful to the Dr. S.S. Sarangedevot Director Department of Computer Science & I.T., J.R.N. Rajasthan Vidhyapeeth University, Udaipur for his encouragement at the very outset of this project. An excellent Support in writing this book was received from Dr. P. Gupta, Professor (Computer Science), I.I.T. Kanpur.

Just as one does not thank himself, expressing gratitude to one's wife in public is not a Hindu custom. For the wife is considered a part of the husband, and her co-authorship is Tacitly assumed in any book her husband writer? There is little doubt that without Alpana's help this book would not have been possible.

Munesh Chandra Trivedi

CONTENTS

1

INTRODUCTION TO IMAGE PROCESSING

1.1 WHAT IS AN IMAGE?

An image is an array, or a matrix, of square pixels (picture elements) arranged in columns and rows.

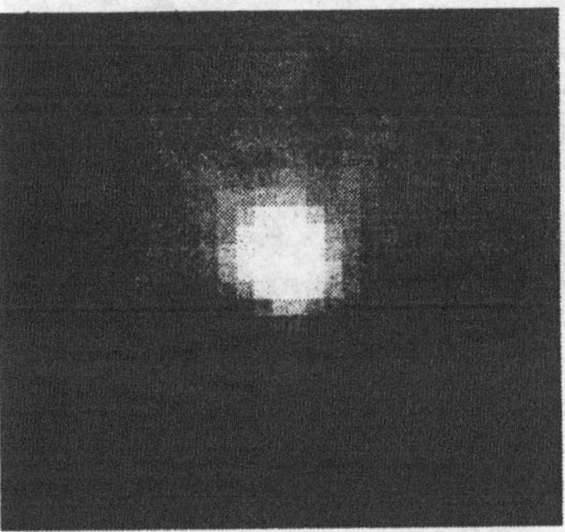

Fig. (1.1) An image – an array or a matrix of pixels arranged in columns and rows.

In a (8-bit) grey scale image each picture element has an assigned intensity that ranges from 0 to 255. A grey scale image is what people normally call a black and white image, but the name emphasizes that such an image will also include many shades of grey shown on fig. (1.2).

A normal grey scale image has 8 bit colour depth = 256 greyscales. A "true colour" image has 24 bit colour depth = $8 \times 8 \times 8$ bits = $256 \times 256 \times 256$ colours = ~16 million colours shown on fig. (1.3).

Some grey scale images have more grey scales, for instance 16 bit = 65536 greyscales. In principle three greyscale images can be combined to form an image with 281,474,976,710,656 greyscales. There are two general groups of 'images': vector graphics (or line art) and bitmaps (pixel-based or 'images'). Some of the most common file formats are:

Fig. (1.2) Each pixel has a value from 0 (black) to 255 (white). The possible range of the pixel values depend on the colour depth of the image, here 8 bit = 256 tones or grey scales.

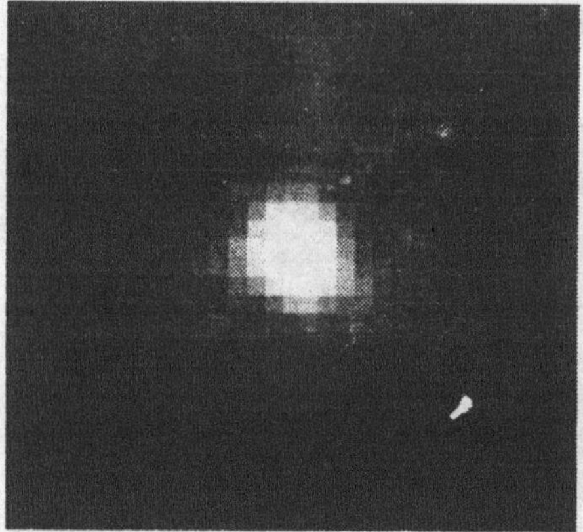

Fig. (1.3) A true-colour image assembled from three greyscale images coloured red, green and blue. Such an image may contain up to 16 million different colours.

- GIF — an 8-bit (256 colour), non-destructively compressed bitmap format. Mostly used for web. Has several sub-standards one of which is the animated GIF.
- JPEG — a very efficient (i.e. much information per byte) destructively compressed 24 bit (16 million colours) bitmap format. Widely used, especially for web and Internet (band-width-limited).
- TIFF — the standard 24 bit publication bitmap format. Compresses non-destructively with, for instance, Lempel-Ziv-Welch (LZW) compression.
- PS — Postscript, a standard vector format. Has numerous sub-standards and can be difficult to transport across platforms and operating systems.
- PSD — a dedicated Photoshop format that keeps all the information in an image including all the layers.

1.2 COLOURS FOR SCIENCE COMMUNICATION THE TWO MAIN COLOUR SPACES ARE RGB AND CMYK

1.2.1 RGB

The RGB colour model relates very closely to the way we perceive colour with the r, g and b receptors in our retinas. RGB uses additive colour mixing and is the basic colour model used in television or any other medium that projects colour with light. It is the basic colour model used in computers and for web graphics, but it cannot be used for print production.

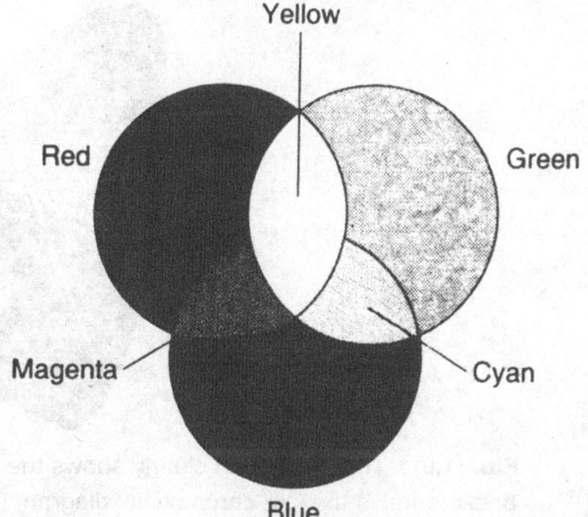

Fig. (1.4) The additive model of RGB. Red, green and blue are the primary stimuli for human colour perception and are the primary additive colours.

The secondary colours of RGB – cyan, magenta, and yellow – are formed by mixing two of the primary colours (red, green or blue) and excluding the third colour. Red and green combine to make yellow, green and blue to make cyan, and blue and red form magenta. The combination of red, green, and blue in full intensity makes white.

In Photoshop using the "screen" mode for the different layers in an image will make the intensities mix together according to the additive colour mixing model. This is analogous to stacking slide images on top of each other and shining light through them.

1.2.2 CMYK

The 4-colour CMYK model used in printing lays down overlapping layers of varying percentages of transparent cyan (C), magenta (M) and yellow (Y) inks. In addition a layer of black (K) ink can be added. The CMYK model uses the subtractive colour model.

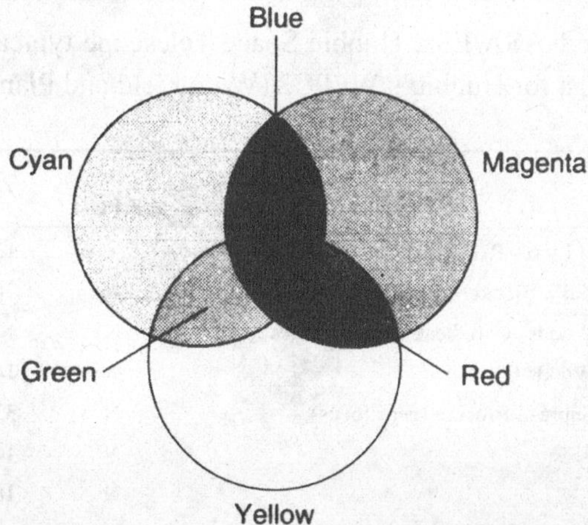

Fig. (1.5) The colours created by the subtractive model of CMYK don't look exactly like the colours created in the additive model of RBG most importantly, CMYK cannot reproduce the brightness of RBG colours. In addition, the CMYK gamut is much smaller than the RBG gamut. Courtesy of adobe.com.

1.2.3 Gamut

The range, or gamut, of human colour perception is quite large. The two colour spaces discussed here span only a fraction of the colours we can see. Furthermore the two spaces do not have the same gamut, meaning that converting from one colour space to the other may cause problems for colours in the outer regions of the gamuts.

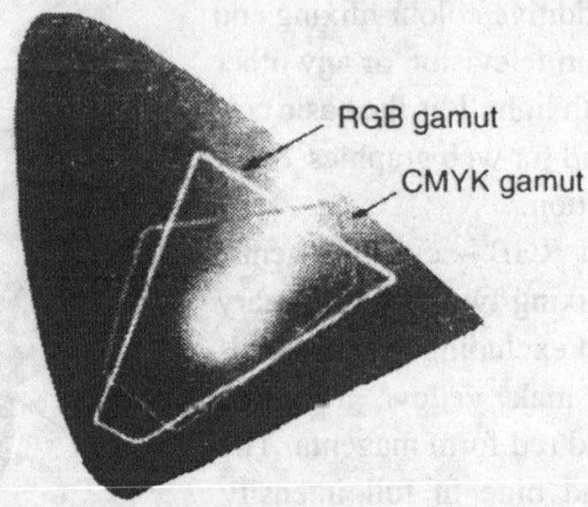

Fig. (1.6) This illustration clearly shows the different gamuts of the RBG and CMYK colour spaces. The background is the CIE chromaticity diagram (representing the whole gamut of human colour perception). Courtesy adobe.com

1.3 ASTRONOMICAL IMAGES

Images of astronomical objects are usually taken with electronic detectors such as a CCD (Charge Coupled Device). Similar detectors are found in normal digital cameras. Telescope images are nearly always greyscale, but nevertheless contain some colour information. An astronomical image may be taken through a colour filter. Different detectors and telescopes also usually have different sensitivities to different colours (wavelengths).

1.3.1 Filters

A telescope such as the NASA/ESA Hubble Space Telescope typically has a fixed number of well-defined filters. A filter list for Hubble's WFPC2 (Wide Field and Planetary Camera 2) camera is seen below.

Name	Type	Wheel	Slot	Notes	In WF/PC-1?	$\bar{\lambda}$(Å)	$\Delta\bar{\lambda}$(Å)	Peak T (%)	Peak λ (Å)
F122M	A	1	4	H Ly α - Red Leak	Y	1259	224.4	19.3	1240
F130LP	B	2	1	CaF2 Blocker (zero focus)	N	2681	5568.3	94.5	8852
F160AW	A	1	3	Woods A - redleak from pinholes	N	1471	457.2	10.1	1403
F160BW	A	1	2	Woods B	N	1446	457.1	12.1	1400
F165LP	B	2	2	Suprasil Blocker (zero focus)	N	3301	5533.2	95.4	5796
F170W	A	8	1	—	N	1666	434.6	30.7	1655
F185W	A	8	2	—	N	1899	297.4	25.9	1849
F218W	A	8	3	Interstellar feature	N	2117	367.9	21.1	2092
F255W	A	8	4	—	N	2545	408.2	14.8	2489
F300W	A	9	4	Wide U	N	2892	727.6	50.8	3760
F336W	A	3	1	WFPC2 U, Strömgren u	Y	3317	370.5	82.6	3447

F343N	A	5	1	Ne V	N	3427	23.5	9.3	3432
F375N	A	5	2	[OII] 3727 RS	Y	3732	24.4	19.5	3736
F380W	A	9	1	—	N	3912	694.8	65.0	3980
F390N	A	5	3	CN	N	3886	45.0	36.5	3886
F410M	A	3	2	Strömgren v	N	4086	147.0	70.4	4097
F437N	A	5	4	[OIII]	Y	4369	25.2	52.0	4368
F439W	A	4	4	WFPC2 B	Y	4283	464.4	68.2	4176
F450W	A	10	4	Wide B	N	4410	925.1	91.4	5060
F467M	A	3	3	Strömgren b	N	4663	166.4	75.3	4728
F469N	A	6	1	He II	Y	4694	25.0	52.4	4697
F487N	A	6	2	H β	Y	4865	25.9	58.6	4862
F502N	A	6	3	[OIII]	Y	5012	26.9	63.7	5008
F547M	A	3	4	Strömgren y (but wider)	Y	5446	486.6	91.3	5360
F555W	A	9	2	WFPC2 V	Y	5202	1222.6	94.6	5148
F569W	A	4	2	F555W generally preferred[a]	Y	5524	965.7	94.2	5310
F588N	A	6	4	He I & Na I (NaD)	Y	5893	19.0	91.4	5894
F606W	A	10	2	Wide V	Y	5767	1579.0	96.7	6186
F622W	A	9	3	—	Y	6131	935.4	95.6	6034
F631N	A	7	1	[OI]	Y	6306	30.9	85.7	6301
F656N	A	7	2	Hα	Y	6564	21.5	77.8	6562
F658N	A	7	3	[NII]	Y	6591	28.5	79.7	6591
F673N	A	7	4	[SII]	Y	6732	47.2	87.0	6732
F675W	A	4	3	WFPC2 B	Y	6714	889.5	97.3	6780
F702W	A	10	3	Wide B	Y	6940	1480.6	97.1	6538
F785LP	A	2	3	F814W generally preferred[a]	Y	9283	2096.1	91.7	9959
F791W	A	4	1	F814W generally preferred[a]	Y	7969	1304.6	95.9	8082
F814W	A	10	1	WFPC2 I	Y	8203	1758.0	94.8	8387
F850LP	A	2	4	—	Y	9650	1672.4	89.2	10028
F953N	A	1	1	[SIII]	N	9546	52.5	95.6	9528
F1042M	A	11	2	—	Y	10437	611.0	81.6	10139

Fig. (1.7) Filter list for Hubble's WFPC2 camera (Wide field and planetary camera 2). Filter names are to the left (names include approximate wavelength in nm) in column 1. Column 5 contains the physical property of the radiation the filter lets through. Column 7 is the central wavelength. The N's and W's are short for narrow and wide.

Filters can either be broad-band (Wide) or narrow-band (Narrow). A broad-band filter lets a wide range of colours through, for instance the entire green or red area of the spectrum. A narrow-band filter typically only lets a small wavelength span through, thus effectively restricting the transmitted radiation to that coming from a given atomic transition, allowing astronomers to investigate individual atomic processes in the object.

A filename such as 502nmos.fits indicates that the filter used has a peak at 502 nm. In the table below, you can see that this filter is a narrow bandwidth filter, i.e. it only lets radiation with wavelengths within a few nm of 502 nm through. Below is an example of an image composed from narrow-band exposures. This results in very sharply defined wisps of nebulosity since each exposure separates light from only some very specific physical processes and locations in the nebula.

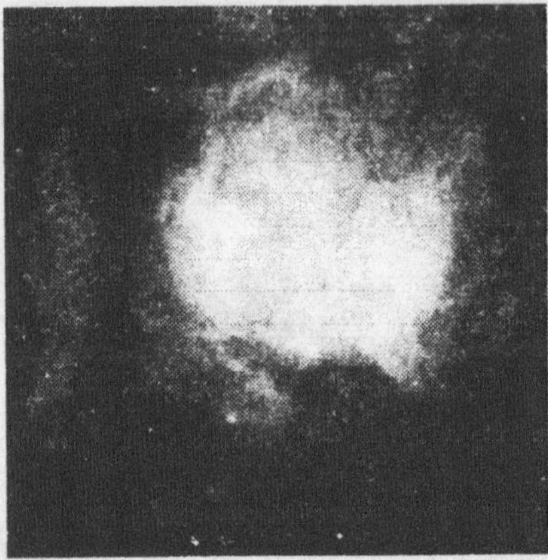

Fig. (1.8) Example of an image constructed from narrow-band exposures. Since the narrow-band exposures probe individual atomic transitions the result is an image that has very 'sharp' features.

Galaxies are often studied through broad-band filters as they allow more light to get through. Also the processes in a galaxy are more 'mixed' or complicated, result from the outputs of billions of stars and so narrow-band filters give less 'specific' information about the processes there.

Fig. (1.9) A broad-band image of the "Hyperactive galaxy NGC 7673".

A visual example of the different filters available onboard Hubble is seen in the following figure.

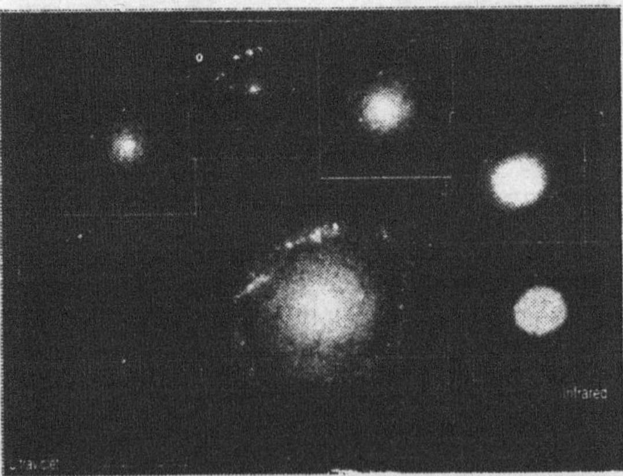

Fig. (1.10) An example of an image constructed from 7 broad-band filters all the way from ultraviolet (left) to inf ared (right).

A figure illustrating the process of stacking together different colour exposures is seen below.

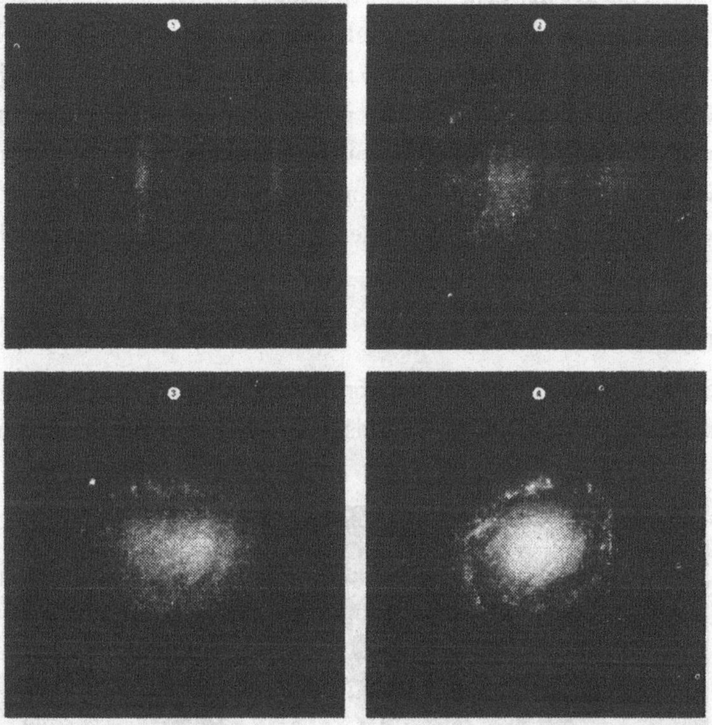

Fig. (1.11) An example of how a colour image is constructed from four broad-band filters (seen from the side in 1) : blue, green, yellow and red. When the images are overlaid (2 and 3) the resulting image (4) is a colour composite.

1.4 ASSIGNING COLORS TO DIFFERENT FILTER EXPOSURES

The astronomical images we see on the web and in the media are usually 'refined' or 'processed' as compared to the raw data that the astronomers work on with their computers. In 'pretty pictures' all art effects coming from the telescope or the detectors are for instance removed as they do not say anything about the objects themselves. It is very rare that images are taken with the sole intention of producing a 'pretty' colour picture. Most 'pretty pictures' are constructed from data that was acquired to study some physical process, and the astronomer herself probably never bothered to assemble the grey scale images to a colour image.

Natural Colour Images

It is possible to create colour images that are close to "true-colour" if three wide band exposures exist, and if the filters are close to the r, g and b receptors in our eyes. Images that approximate what a fictitious space traveller would see if he or she actually travelled to the object are called "natural colour" images.

To make a natural colour image the order of the colours assigned to the different exposures should be in "chromatic order", i.e. the lowest wavelength should be given a blue hue, the middle wavelength a green hue and the highest wavelength should be red.

Representative Colour Images

If one or more of the images in a data set is taken through a filter that allows radiation that lies outside the human vision span to pass – i.e. it records radiation invisible to us - it is of course not possible to make a natural colour image. But it is still possible to make a colour image that shows important information about the object. This type of image is called a representative colour image. Normally one would assign colours to these exposures in chromatic order with blue assigned to the shortest wavelength, and red to the longest. In this way it is possible to make colour images from electromagnetic radiation far from the human vision area, for example x-rays. Most often it is either infrared or ultraviolet radiation that is used.

Enhanced Colour Images

Sometimes there are reasons to not use a chromatic order for an image. Often these reasons are purely aesthetic, as is seen in the example below. This type of colour image is called an enhanced colour image.

Fig. (1.12) An example of an enhanced colour image (not in chromatic order) : Sometimes it is necessary to break the 'rules' for image processing. Here the hydrogen-alpha filter is coloured blue instead of the red colour it is in nature. This is an example of a so-called false-colour image, where the blue was chosen for aesthetic reasons.

You are the Judge

When processing raw science images one of the biggest problems is that, to a large degree, you are 'creating' the image and this means a colossal freedom within a huge parameter space. There are literally thousands of sliders, numbers, dials, curves etc. to twist and turn.

Speaking of right and wrong, there really are no wrong or right images. There are some fundamental scientific principles that should normally be observed, but the rest is a matter of aesthetics — taste. Chromatic ordering of the exposures is one of the important scientific principles.

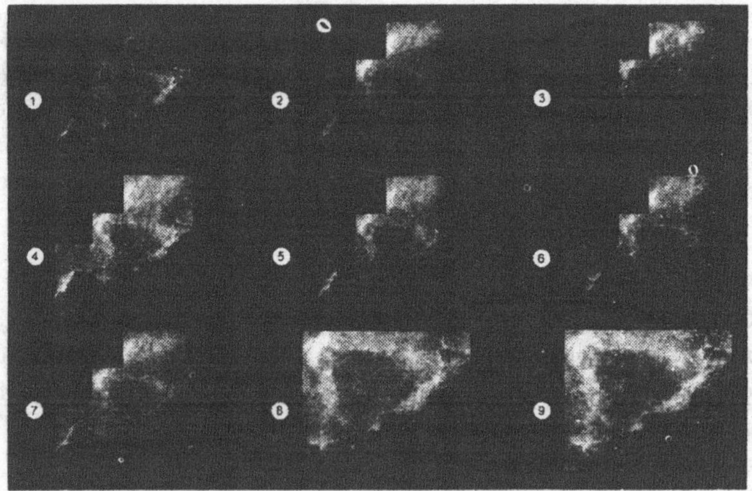

Fig. (1.13) Sequences in the production of a hubble space telescope image of Messier 17. First the individual exposure (taken through three different filters) : 1. 673n (sulphur) shown in red in the final image, 2. 656n (hydrogen, green), 3. 502n (oxygen, blue), 4. First colour composite attempt, 5. Improving, 6. Improving, 7. Improving, 8. Adjusting the composition and then, 9. Final colour and contrast adjustments for the final image.

■ 1.5 STRETCH FUNCTION

One particularly important aspect of image processing is the choice of the best stretch function. You choose which "stretch function" or representation to use in the Fits Liberator window.

A logarithmic representation of the pixel values tends to suppress the bright parts of the image, i.e. the stars, and to enhance the fainter part, e.g. nebulosity. This can be desirable if the 'faint stuff' needs 'a boost', but a logarithmic stretch function can also reduce the contrast in an image, producing a lower dynamic range as is seen in the example below.

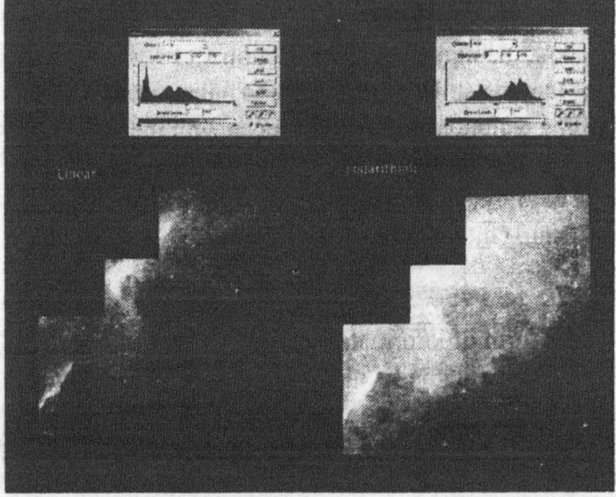

Fig. (1.14) The difference between two stretch functions. To the left is a linear representation of the pixels and to the right a logarithmic. It is seen that the log lowers the contrast too much and therefore is not the aesthetically desirable function to choose here.

1.6 IMAGE PROCESSING

Image processing is any form of information processing for which the input is an image, such as photographs or frames of video; the output is not necessarily an image, but can be for instance a set of features of the image. Most image-processing techniques involve treating the image as a two-dimensional signal and applying standard signal-processing techniques to it. Image processing holds the possibity of developing the ultimate machine that could perform the visual functions of all living beings.

1.6.1 Motivation and Perspective

A major portion of information received by a human from the environment is visual. Hence, processing visual information by computer has been drawing a very significant attention of the researchers over the last few decades. The process of receiving and analying visual information by human species is referred to as sight, perception or understanding. Similarly, the process of receiving and analysing visual information by digital computer is called digital image processing.

Two broad classes of techniques i.e. processing and analysis have evolved in the field of digital image processing and analysis. Processing of an image includes improvements in its appearance and efficient representation. So the fields consists of not only feature extraction , analysis and recognition of images, but also coding, filtering, enhancements and restoration. The entire process of image processingg and analysis and analysis starting from the receiving of visual information to the giving out of description of the scene, may be divided into three major stages which are also considered as major sub-areas and are given below :

(1) **Discretization and representation:** converting visual information into a discrete form, suitable for computer processing, approximating visual information to save storage space as well as time requirement in subsequent processing.

(2) **Processing:** improving image quality by filtering etc and compressing data to save storage and channel capacity during transmission.

(3) **Analysis:** extracting image features, quantifyig shapes, registration and recognition.

In the initial stage , the input is a scene (visual information), and output is corresponding digital image. In secondary stage, both the input and output are images where output is an improved version of the input. In final stage, the input is still an image but the output is a description of that image. In facts, potentials of image processing techniques came into focus with the advancements of large scale digital computer and with the journey to moon. In 1964 jet propulsion laboratory USA, images of moon are processed by Ranger. Since 1964, field has experianced growth , Rosenfield(1981),Rosenfield(1984) see the surveys in Computer Vision, Graphics and image processing.

1.6.2 Applications of Image Processing

Image processing is any form of information processing for which the input is an image, such as photographs or frames of video; the output is not necessarily an image, but can be for instance a set of features of the image. Most image-processing techniques involve treating the image as a two-dimensional signal and applying standard signal-processing techniques to it. The major applications of image processing are the following :

- Photography and printing
- Satellite image processing
- Machine Vision

- Medical image processing
- Face detection, feature detection, face identification
- Microscope image processing
- Car barrier detection

1.7 INTRODUCTION TO DIGITAL IMAGE PROCESSING

Digital image processing is the use of computer algorithms to perform image processing on digital images. Digital image processing has the same advantages over analog image processing as digital signal processing has over analog signal processing — it allows a much wider range of algorithms to be applied to the input data, and can avoid problems such as the build-up of noise and signal distortion during processing. The most common kind of digital image processing is digital image editing.

Image editing encompasses the processes of altering images, whether they be digital photographs, traditional analog photographs, or illustrations. Before digital scanners and cameras became mainstream, traditional analog image editing was known as photo retouching, using tools such as an airbrush to modify photographs, or editing illustrations with any traditional art medium. However, since the advent of digital images, analog image editing has become largely obsolete.

History : Many of the techniques of digital image processing, or digital picture processing as it was often called, were developed in the 1960s at the Jet Propulsion Laboratory, MIT, Bell Labs, University of Maryland, and a few other places, with application to satellite imagery, wirephoto standards conversion, medical imaging, videophone, character recognition, and photo enhancement. But the cost of processing was fairly high with the computing equipment of that era. In the 1970s, digital image processing proliferated, when cheaper computers and dedicated hardware became available. Images could then be processed in real time, for some dedicated problems such as television standards conversion.

As general-purpose computers became faster, they started to take over the role of dedicated hardware for all but the most specialized and compute-intensive operations. With the fast computers and signal processors available in the 2000s, digital image processing has become the most common form of image processing, and is generally used because it is not only the most versatile method, but also the cheapest.

An image is digitized to convert it to a form which can be stored in a computer's memory or on some form of storage media such as a hard disk or CD-ROM. This digitization procedure can be done by a scanner, or by a video camera connected to a frame grabber board in a computer. Once the image has been digitized, it can be operated upon by various image processing operations.

Image processing operations can be roughly divided into three major categories, Image Compression, Image Enhancement and Restoration, and Measurement Extraction. Image compression is familiar to most people. It involves reducing the amount of memory needed to store a digital image. Image defects which could be caused by the digitization process or by faults in the imaging set-up (for example, bad lighting) can be corrected using Image Enhancement techniques. Once the image is in good condition, the Measurement Extraction operations can be used to obtain useful information from the image.

Some examples of Image Enhancement and Measurement Extraction are given below. The examples shown all operate on 256 grey-scale images. This means that each pixel in the image is stored as a number between 0 to 255, where 0 represents a black pixel, 255 represents a white pixel and values in-between represent shades of grey. These operations can be extended to operate on colour images.

1.7.1 Digital Processing of Camera Images

Digital cameras generally include dedicated digital image processing chips to convert the raw data from the image sensor into a color-corrected image in a standard image file format. Images from digital cameras often receive further processing to improve their quality; a distinct advantage digital cameras have over film cameras. The digital image processing is typically done by special software programs that can manipulate the images in many ways. Many digital cameras also enable viewing of histograms of images, as an aid for the photographer to better understand the rendered brightness range of each shot.

Uses : Digital Image Processing allows the use of much more complex algorithms for image processing, and hence can offer both more sophisticated performance at simple tasks, and the implementation of methods which would be impossible by analog means.

In particular, digital image processing is the only practical technology for :

- Classification
- Feature extraction
- Pattern recognition
- Projection
- Multi-scale signal analysis

Some techniques which are used in digital image processing include:

- Principal components analysis
- Independent component analysis
- Self-organizing maps
- Hidden Markov models
- Neural networks

The examples below represent only a few of the many techniques available for operating on images.

1.7.2 Image Enhancement and Restoration

The image at the left of Figure 1.15 has been corrupted by noise during the digitization process. The 'clean' image at the right of Figure 1.15 was obtained by applying a median filter to the image.

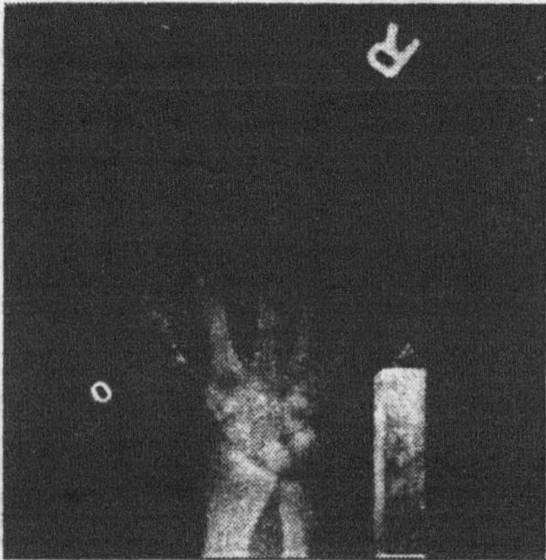

Fig. (1.15) Application of the median filter.

An image with poor contrast, such as the one at the left of Figure 1.16, can be improved by adjusting the image histogram to produce the image shown at the right of Figure 1.16.

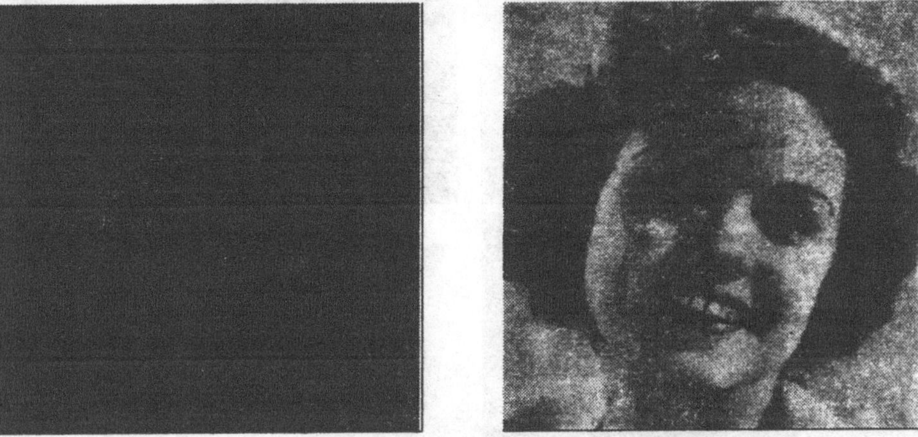

Fig. (1.16) Adjusting the image histogram to improve image contrast.

The image at the top left of Figure 1.17 has a corrugated effect due to a fault in the acquisition process. This can be removed by doing a 2-dimensional Fast-Fourier Transform on the image (top right of Figure 1.17), removing the bright spots (bottom left of Figure 1.17), and finally doing an inverse Fast Fourier Transform to return to the original image without the corrugated background bottom right of Figure 1.17).

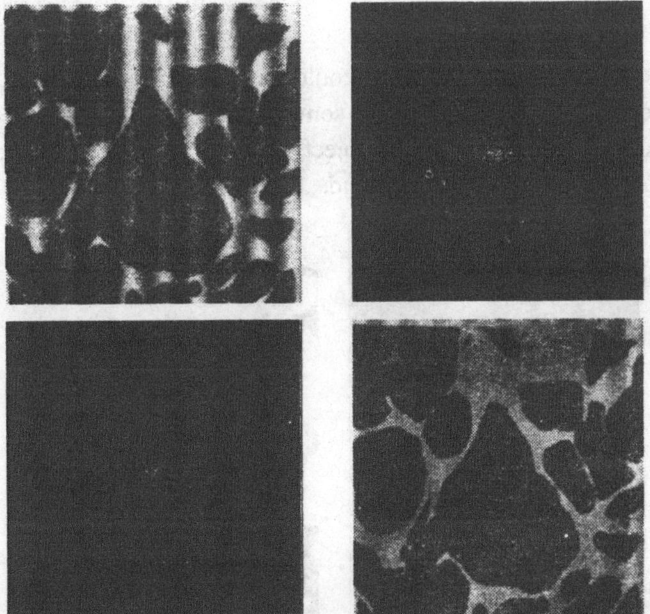

Fig. (1.17) Application of the 2-dimensional fast fourier transform.

An image which has been captured in poor lighting conditions, and shows a continuous change in the background brightness across the image (top left of Figure 1.18) can be corrected using the following procedure. First remove the foreground objects by applying a 25 by 25 grey scale dilation operation (top

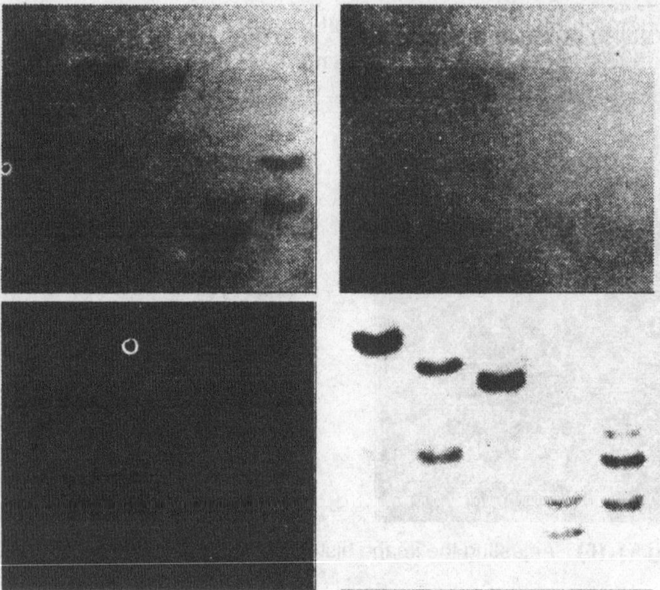

Fig. (1.18) Correcting for a background gradient.

right of Figure 1.18). Then subtract the original image from the background image (bottom left of Figure 1.18). Finally invert the colors and improve the contrast by adjusting the image histogram (bottom right of Figure 1.18).

Image Measurement Extraction

The example below demonstrates how one could go about extracting measurements from an image. The image at the top left of Figure 1.19 shows some objects. The aim is to extract information about the distribution of the sizes (visible areas) of the objects. The first step involves segmenting the image to separate the objects of interest from the background.

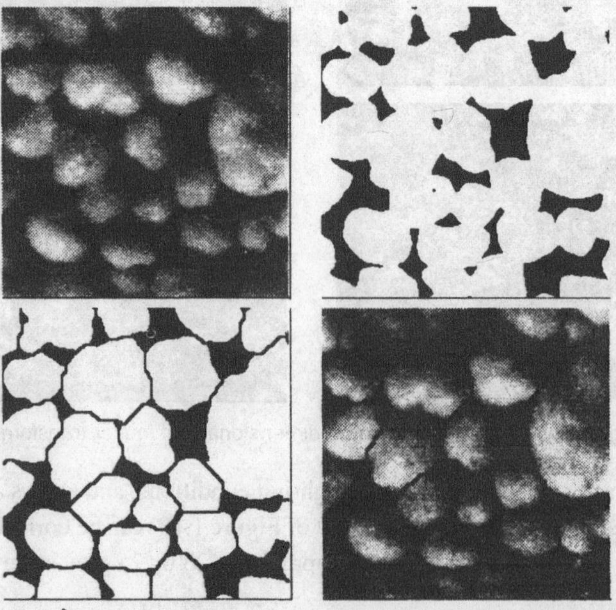

This usually involves thresholding the image, which is done by setting the values of pixels above a certain threshold value to white, and all the others to black (top right of Figure 1.19). Because the objects touch, thresholding at a level which includes the full surface of all the objects does not show separate objects. This problem is solved by performing a watershed separation on the image (lower left of Figure 1.19). The image at the lower right of Figure 1.19 shows the result of performing a logical AND of the two images at the left of Figure 1.19. This shows the effect that the watershed separation has on touching objects in the original image.

Finally, some measurements can be extracted from the image. Figure 1.20 is a histogram showing the distribution of the area measurements. The areas were calculated based on the assumption that the width of the image is 28 cm.

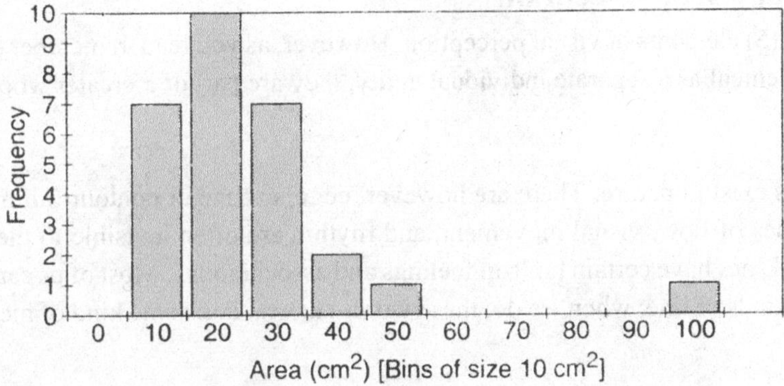

Fig. (1.20) Histogram showing the area distribution of the objects.

1.8 IMAGE PROCESSING COMPONENTS

Image processing components allow developers to transform, filter, convert color spaces and draw onto images. Many times, you can't control what the images look like as they come into your software application. They may come from various places and in various states of view ability. Your job as a programmer is not only to support the input of images, but to make them look their best once they arrive. Image processing components are available to handle a wide array of image enabling functions.

Whether you need to :

- Automatically trim a bitmap to remove blank space around the edges.
- Rotate the image.
- Change the orientation by flipping the image horizontally or vertically.
- Change brightness using gamma correction.
- Stretch the range of intensities.
- Change saturation.
- Halftone for display or printing.
- Sharpen or blur.
- Combine two images so that one appears to be an underlying texture of the other.
- Anti-alias the image.

1.9 VISUAL PERCEPTION

In psychology, visual perception is the ability to interpret visible light information reaching the eyes which is then made available for planning and action. The resulting perception is also known as eyesight, sight or vision. The various components involved in vision are known as the visual system.

1.9.1 Visual System

The visual system allows us to assimilate information from the environment to help guide our actions. The act of seeing starts when the lens of the eye focus an image of the outside world onto a light-sensitive membrane in the back of the eye, called the retina. The retina is actually part of the brain that is isolated to serve as a transducer for the conversion of patterns of light into neuronal signals. The lens of the eye focuses light on the photoreceptive cells of the retina, which detect the photons of light and respond by producing neural impulses. These signals are processed in a hierarchical fashion by different parts of the brain, such as the lateral geniculate nucleus, and the primary and secondary visual cortex of the brain.

1.9.2 Elements of Visual Perception

There are five (5) elements of visual perception. However, as you read, remember that although we are studying each element as a separate individual entity, they are part of a greater whole.

1. Line or Edge

Very few lines exist in nature. There are however, edge, outline or contour (all meaning roughly the same thing). Lines of flow, visual movement, and rhythm are often invisible to the eye but can be "seen" nonetheless. Lines have certain built-in feelings and associations... Most of us can find adjectives to describe various kinds of line; when we do, these words suggest that some kind of meaning resides in the lines.

Exercises :

- Find lines which are expressive, which convey a sensation in and of itself.
- Can you see music and rhythm in line? Can you sing it?

Look for :

- Auras
- Relationship between edge, volume and space
- Invisible or implied lines
- Visual movement
- Interrelationship of lines

Questions :

- What does line tell you about the way a tree grows?
- What does it tell you about its personality?

2. Shape

Shape is an area that stands out from the space next to it or around it because of a defined boundary or because of a difference of value, color, or texture. Shapes contain certain meanings within themselves, some readily recognizable, others more complex and less clear. Some common meanings ascribable to squares, for instance, are: perfection, stability, solidity, symmetry, self-reliance, and monotony. Every visual experience is embedded in a context of space and time. Just as the appearance of objects is influenced by that of neighboring objects in space, so also is it influenced by sights that preceded it in time.

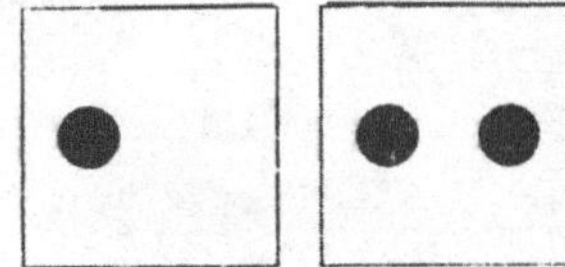

The dots within the squares illustrate :

- Shape relationships
- Energy fields
- Positive/negative space
- Tensions
- Balance

Exercises :

- Follow the interplay between shapes. Look for counterpoint, dance, rhythm, theme variations, tensions, conflict, and balance.
- See shapes as alive.
- Form follows function. Look at an object and study how its shape or shapes are directly a product of function.
- Walk through an area and watch the interplay of shapes. Note the relationship between three-dimensional shapes and the two-dimensional images of those shapes. Experience your own shape in relation to the shapes around you.

3. Color

Color is the visual response to the wavelengths of sunlight identified as red, green, blue, etc.; having the physical properties of hue, intensity (or saturation), and value. Color perception seems to involve the one hundred million rods and six and a half million cones in the retina at the back of the eye.

We are able to hear a single tone, but we almost never (without special devices) see a single color unconnected and unrelated to other colors. Colors present themselves in continuous flux, constantly related to changing neighbors and changing conditions. In no reliable sense can we speak of color "as it really is"; it is always determined by its context. The same color in two different contexts is not the same color. This means that the identity of a color does not reside in the color itself, but is established by relation.

Exercises :

- Look at the many colors; just look, do not name.
- Try to find as many colors as possible within a single color.
- Look at color combinations. See how adjacent colors affect or change each other. Remember that all color is relative and exists in context.
- What moods and emotions do colors convey to you? Find a color that produces strong emotion. Play it out. Stay with the emotion as long as possible. Analyze the experience but only do so after the initial impact is gone. Is it even possible to bring rational thought to the experience?
- Obtain a color wheel and experiment with the colors in various lighting.

4. Value

Value is the relative degree of light and dark. There are several types of light :

- Direct
- Reflected : (primary, secondary, tertiary, etc.)

- Absorbed
- Translucent
- Symbolic
- Inner
- Divine

Light is required for the eyes to observe shape, color, space, and movement; but light is more than just the physical cause of what we see.

The scale below shows a gradation from dark to light.

Each rectangle contains a single color, yet the eye makes it appear to change value from the left side to the right side.

Exercises :

- Look at sharp edges and rounded surfaces. Follow value change from the broadest, sharpest contrasts to the subtlest nuances, to the most gradual flow of one value into another.
- Watch the play of light and shadow.
- Follow reflected light through primary, secondary, tertiary reflections.
- See how light creates volume.
- See how light affects the way things grow.
- Study shadows. Look at edge, shape, flow and value.
- Look at how light clarifies shape. Look for light that dissolves shape.
- Try to see, feel, and experience the light within things (including people).
- Can you see, feel, know your own inner light?
- Draw a picture of a hen egg sitting on a sheet of white paper. Do it without using lines.
- Study a black and white photograph. Notice the shades of gray.

5. Texture

Texture is the surface character of a material that can be experienced through touch or the illusion of touch. The illusion of touch can be experienced visually. Light and shadow patterns on an object define its texture. So, visual texture really amounts to exploring light and shadow, value and contrasts. Physical touch can be experienced in the following ways:

hotcold	pressure	pain	hardness	resistance/pliability
texture	wetness	vibration	shape	flow & movement
weight	rough	smooth	jagged	

Exercises :

- Touch everything.
- Find something that you have never touched and "feel" it with your eyes first, then actually touch it. Compare the difference.
- Create various textures by drawing them.
- Do various textures convey emotions? Find something that creates a strong reaction mood-wise, emotion-wise, aesthetically. Do this with both visual and actual texture.

Concentrate on using the five elements of visual perception whenever you can. Through practice it will be possible to see more than you saw before. How can you use this knowledge in the art of camouflage? Can you see how you might be better able to hide from the untrained eye? Can you determine which colors/values/patterns might be the hardest to see in specific locations? Can you see that standard camouflage patterns can be picked out easily? What visual methods do the animals use to escape detection?

1.10 SAMPLING AND QUANTIZATION

A signal is defined as some variable which changes subject to some other independent variable. We will assume here, that the independent variable is time, denoted by t and the dependent variable could be any physical measurement-variable which changes over time - think for example of a time varying electric voltage. We will denote the generic measurement variable with x or $x(t)$ to make its time-dependence explicit. An elementary example of such a signal is a sinosoid. When we want to represent such a sinusoid in the digital domain, we have to do two things: sampling and quantization which are described in turn.

Sampling

The first thing we have to do, is to obtain signal values from the continuous signal at regular time-intervals. This process is known as sampling. The sampling interval is denoted as T_s and its reciprocal, the sampling frequency or sample-rate is denoted as f_s, where $f_s = 1/T_s$. The result of this process is just a sequence of numbers. We will use n as an index into this sequence and our discrete time signal is denoted as $x[n]$ – it is customary in DSP literature to use parentheses for continuous variables such as the time t and brackets for discrete variables such as our sample index n. Having defined our sampling interval T_s, sampling just extracts the signals value at all integer multiples of T_s such that our discrete time sequence becomes.

$$x[n] = x(n - T_s) \quad \text{...(1)}$$

Note that at this point (after sampling), our signal is not yet completely digital because the values $x[n]$ can still take on any number from a continuous range - that's why we use the terms discrete-time signal here and not digital signal. Figure 1.21 illustrates the process of sampling a continuous sinosoid.

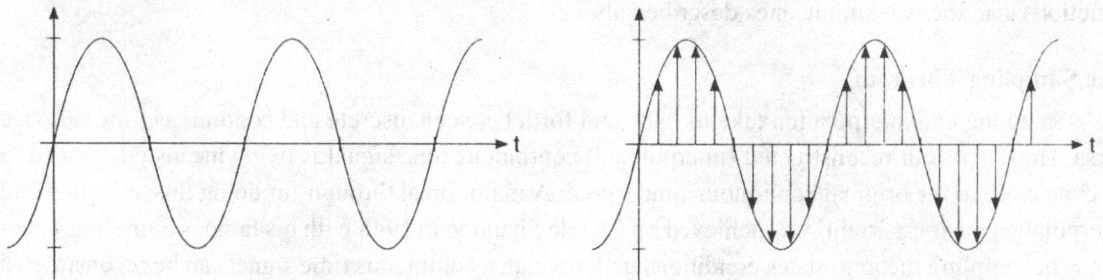

Fig. (1.21) Sampling a sinusoid - we measure the value of the signal at regular time-intervals.

Although it has been drawn in the right plot, the underlying continuous signal is lost in this process - all we have left after the sampling is a sequence of numbers. Those numbers themselves are termed samples in the DSP community - each such number is a sample in this terminology. This is different from what a musician usually means when talking about samples - musicians refer to a short recording of an acoustic event as sample. In this article we will use the DSP terminology. The question is: can we reconstruct the original continuous signal from its samples?

Interpolation

Whereas the continuous signal $x(t)$ is defined for all values of t, our discrete-time signal is only defined for times which are integer multiples of T_s. To reconstruct a continuous signal from the samples, we must somehow 'guess', what value the signal could probably take on in between our samples. Interpolation is the process of 'guessing' signal values at arbitrary instants of time, which fall - in general - in between the actual samples. Thereby interpolation creates a continuous time signal and can be seen as an inverse process to sampling. Ideally, we would want our interpolation algorithm to 'guess right' - that is: the continuous signal obtained from interpolation should be equal to the original continuous signal. The crudest of all interpolation schemes is piecewise constant interpolation - we just take the value of one of the neighboring samples as guessed signal value at any instant of time in between. The reconstructed interpolated function will have a stair step-like shape.

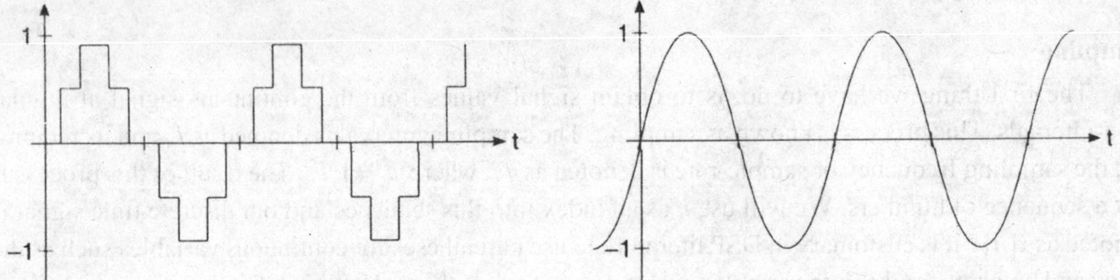

Fig. (1.22) Reconstructing the sinusoid from its samples via piecewise constant and linear interpolation.

The next better and very popular interpolation method is linear interpolation - to reconstruct a signal value we simply connect the values at our sampling instants with straight lines. Figure 1.22 shows the reconstructed continuous signals for piecewise constant and linear interpolation. More sophisticated interpolation methods such as higher order polynomial interpolation (quadratic, cubic, quartic, pentic, etc.), (windowed) sinc-interpolation exist as well - they will yield smoother and more faithful reconstructions than the two simple ones described above.

The Sampling Theorem

Sampling and interpolation take us back and forth between discrete and continuous time and vice versa. However - our reconstructed (interpolated) continuous time signal is by no means guaranteed to be even close to the original continuous time signal. A major breakthrough for doing this sampling and interpolation business 'right' was achieved by Claude Shannon in 1948 with his famous Sampling Theorem. The sampling theorem states conditions under which a continuous time signal can be reconstructed exactly from its samples and also defines the interpolation algorithm which should be used to achieve this exact reconstruction.

In loose terms, the sampling theorem states, that the original continuous time signal can be reconstructed from its samples exactly, when the highest frequency (denoted as fh) present in the signal (seen as composition of sinosoids) is lower than a half of the sampling frequency:

$$f_h < \frac{f_s}{2}$$

Half of the sample-rate is also often called the Nyquist frequency, in honor to Harry Nyquist who also contributed a lot to sampling theory. When this condition is met, we can reconstruct the underlying continuous time signal exactly by a process known as sinc-interpolation (the details of which are beyond the scope of this article). A subtle side-note: in some books, the above in equation is stated with a<= rather than a <= this is wrong: fh has to be strictly less than half the sample-rate because when you try to sample a sinusoid with frequency of exactly half the sampling frequency, you may be able to capture it faithfully (when the sample-instants happen to coincide with the maxima of the sinusoid), but when the sample-instants happen to coincide with the zero-crossings, you will capture nothing - for intermediate cases, you will capture the sinusoid with a wrong amplitude. Thus, perfect reconstruction is not guaranteed for fh = fs/2. When the above condition is not met, but we sample and reconstruct the signal anyway, an odd phenomenon occurs, widely known and quite often misunderstood.

Aliasing

According to the sampling theorem, the signal in figure 1.21 is sampled properly. As this particular signal is just a single sinosoid (as opposed to a composition of sinosoids), the highest frequency present in this signal is just the frequency of this sinosoid. The sampling frequency is 10 times the sinosoids frequency, that is :

$$f_h = \frac{f_s}{10} < \frac{f_s}{2}$$

To see it the other way around: 10 samples are taken from each period of the signal and this is more than enough to exactly reconstruct the underlying continuous time sinosoid. To make it more concrete, imagine the sinusoid has a frequency of 1Hz and the sample-rate was 10Hz (not really practical values for audio signals, but that doesn't matter for a general discussion). Now let's see what happens when we try to sample an 8Hz sinusoid at a sample rate of 10Hz. This is depicted in figure 1.23. The high frequency sinusoid at 8Hz produces a certain sequence of samples as usual. However,

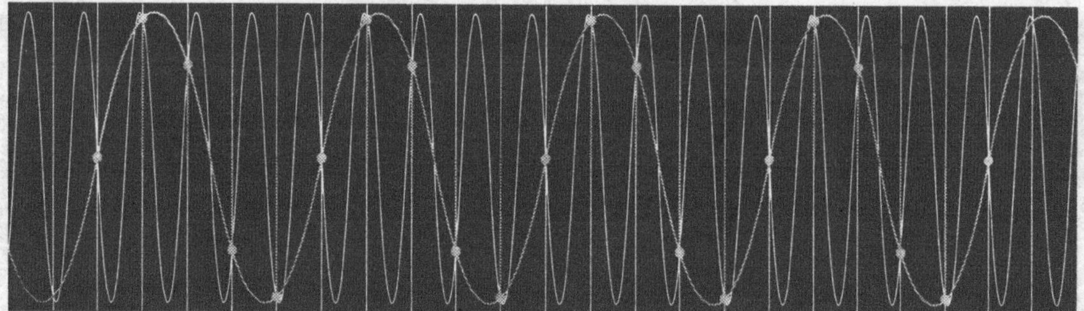

Fig. (1.23) Aliasing : the sinusoid at f = 8 Hz is aliased into another sinusoid at f = 2 Hz, at a sample rate f_s = 10 Hz because both produce the same sequence of samples.

There exists a sinusoid of frequency 2Hz which would give rise to the exact same sequence of samples and it is this lower frequency sinusoid which will be reconstructed by our interpolation algorithm. The general rule is: whenever we sample a sinusoid of a frequency f above half the sample-rate but below the sample rate, then its alias will appear at a frequency of

$$f' = f_s - f \text{ or } f' = \frac{f_s}{2} - (f - f_s/2)$$

where the second form makes it clear that we must reflect the excess of the signals frequency over the Nyquist frequency at the Nyquist frequency to obtain its alias. Figure 1.24 illustrates the process of reflecting at the Nyquist frequency for a signal with a spectrum that violates the condition of in equation 2 – this reflection is as sometimes termed as foldover. When the sinusoid is even above the samplerate, we will see it spectrally shifted into the band below half the sample-rate (which is called baseband).

Fig. (1.24) Aliasing from a spectral point of view : parts of the spectrum above the Nyquist frequency are reflected back into the basebond.

For even higher frequencies the whole thing repeats itself over and over - this explanation is probably a bit quirky, but figure 1.25 should give a fairly good intuition of which goes where and when we have to reflect. The fact that higher frequencies intrude into the spectrum which we want to capture calls for lowpass-filtering the continuous signal before we sample it. This is, what we need the so called Anti-Alias filters for. Without those filters, we would have our spectrum completely messed up with aliasing products of frequencies above the Nyquist frequency. Moreover, these alias products will in general not have any harmonic relationship to our signal to be captured, which makes them sonically much more annoying than harmonic distortion as we know them from analog equipment. Aliasing does not only occur when we want to capture analog.

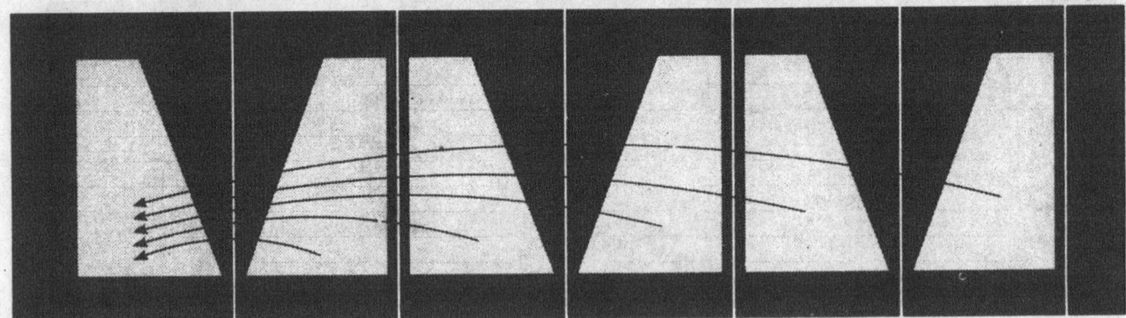

Fig. (1.25) If the original spectrum would have looked either one of the gray blocks, the resulting reconstructed spectrum would always look like the first gray block.

Signals which are not properly anti-alias filtered, but also when we generate signals inside the computer in the first place.

Quantization

After the sampling we have a sequence of numbers which can theoretically still take on any value on a continuous range of values. Because this range in continuous, there are infinitely many possible values for each number, in fact even uncountably infinitely many. In order to be able to represent each number from such a continuous range, we would need an infinite number of digits - something we don't have.

Instead, we must represent our numbers with a finite number of digits, that is: after discretizing the time-variable, we now have to discretize the amplitude-variable as well. This discretization of the amplitude values is called quantization. Assume, our sequence takes on values in the range between -1... + 1. Now assume that we must represent each number from this range with just two decimal digits: one before and one after the point. Our possible amplitude values are therefore: -1.0,-0.9, . . . ,-0.1, 0.0, 0.1, . . . , 0.9, 1.0. These are exactly 21 distinct levels for the amplitude and we will denote this number of quantization levels with Nq. Each level is a step of 0.1 higher than its predecessor and we will denote this quantization step size as q. Now we assign to each number from our continuous range that quantization level which is closest to our actual amplitude: the range -0.05... + 0.05 maps to quantization level 0.0, the range 0.05...0.15 maps to 0.1 and so on. That mapping can be viewed as a piecewise constant function acting on our continuous amplitude variable x. This is depicted in figure 6. Note, that this mapping also includes a clipping operation at ±1: values larger than 0.95 are mapped to quantization level 1, no matter how large, and analogous for negative values

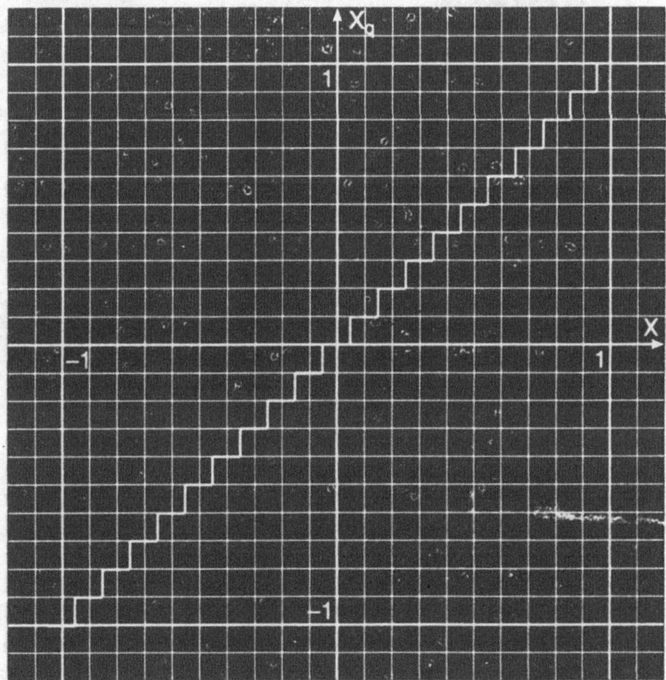

Fig. (1.26) Characteristic line of a quantizer - inputs from a continuous range X are mapped to discrete levels X_q.

Quantization Noise

When forcing an arbitrary signal value x to its closest quantization level xq, this xq value can be seen as x plus some error. We will denote that error as eq (for quantization error) and so we have:

$$x_q = x + e_q \quad \Leftrightarrow \quad e_q = x_q - x \qquad \ldots(3)$$

The quantization error is restricted to the range -q/2... + q/2 - we will never make an error larger than half of the quantization step size. When the signal to be sampled has no specific relationship to the sampling process, we can assume, that this quantization error (now treated as a discrete time signal eq[n]) will manifest itself as additive white noise with equal probability for all error values in the range -q/2...+q/2. Mathematically, we can view the error-signal as a random signal with a uniform probability density function between -q/2 and +q/2, that is:

$$p(e) = \begin{cases} \frac{1}{q} & \text{for } \frac{-q}{2} \le e < \frac{q}{2} \\ 0 & \text{otherwise} \end{cases} \quad \text{...(4)}$$

For this reason, the quantization error is often also called quantization noise. A more rigorous mathematical justification for the treatment of the quantization error as uniformly distributed white noise is provided by Widrow's Quantization Theorem, but we won't pursue that any further here. We define the signal-to-noise ratio of a system as the ratio between the RMS-value of the wanted signal and the RMS value of the noise expressed in decibels:

$$SNR = 20 \log_{10} \frac{x_{\text{rms}}}{e_{\text{rms}}} \quad \text{...(5)}$$

where the RMS value is the square root of the (average) power of the signal. Denoting the power of the signal as Px and the power of the error as Pe and using an elementary rule for logarithms, we can rewrite this as:

$$SNR = 10 \log_{10} \frac{P_x}{P_e} \quad \text{...(6)}$$

The power of the quantization error is given by the variance of the associated continuous random variable and comes out as:

$$P_e = \int_{-q/2}^{q/2} \frac{1}{q} e^2 \, de = \frac{q^2}{12} \quad \text{...(7)}$$

We take a sinusoid at unit amplitude as the wanted signal, this signal has a power of:

$$P_x = \frac{1}{2} \quad \text{...(8)}$$

Putting these expressions into equation 6, we obtain:

$$SNR = 10 \log_{10} \frac{6}{q^2} \quad \text{...(9)}$$

To reiterate, this equation can be used to calculate the SNR between an unit amplitude sinusoid and the quantization error that is made when we quantize the sinusoid with a quantization step size of q. In the discussion above, we used a step size of 0.1 - this was only for easy presentation of the principles. Computers do not represent numbers using decimal digits, instead they use binary digits - better known as bits. With b bits, we can represent distinct numbers. Because we want those numbers to represent the range between -1 and 1, we could represent quantization levels below zero and above zero - however, we have not yet represented the zero level itself. To do so, we 'steal' one binary pattern from the positive range - now we can only represent - 1 strictly positive levels. The step size is given by:

$$q = \frac{1}{2^{b-1}} \quad \text{...(10)}$$

Having all this machinery in place, we are now in the position to calculate the SNR for a quantization of the signal with b bits as:

$$SNR = 10 \log_{10} (6 . 2^{2b-2}) \qquad ...(11)$$

and as an easy rule of thumb:

$$SNR \approx 6 . b \qquad ...(12)$$

This says: each additional bit increases the signal-to-noise ratio by 6dB. The exact formula gives an SNR of roughly 98dB for 16 bits and an SNR of 146dB for 24 bits (as opposed to 96 and 144 for the thumb rule). Taking a sinusoid at full amplitude as reference signal is of course a rather optimistic assumption, because this is a signal with a quite high power.

Sampling and Quantization of Images

In sensing image brightness, or indeed depth, it is inevitable that the individual picture element (pixel) values will be subject to the corrupting effect of noise both at sensing and amplification of the resulting electronic signal. Thus if several measurements are taken of the same pixel intensity whilst viewing the same scene, there will be distribution of measured value about a mean intensity, . In most cases, this distribution can be approximated by a normal probability distribution function, , of standard deviation, $p(x)$, where x is the value of intensity, depth or other function.

$$p(x) = \frac{1}{\sqrt{(2\pi)}\,\sigma} e^{-1/2\left(\frac{x-\mu}{\sigma}\right)^2} \qquad ...(13)$$

where

$$\mu = \int_{\infty}^{\infty} xp(x)\, dx \qquad ...(14)$$

and

$$\sigma^2 = \int_{-\infty}^{\infty} (x-\mu)^2\, p(x)\, dx \qquad ...(15)$$

The pixel intensity stored in the digital framestore or computer is further quantised, i.e. it is stored as one of a finite number of digital values, typically 256 values when stored as a single byte. The effect of quantising the original analogue signal by analogue to digital conversion introduces a further source of inaccuracy, i.e. quantising error or loosely, quantising noise. This can be expressed with regard to the original digital signal in terms of the mean squared error signal,

$$\overline{c}^2 = \frac{q^2}{12} \qquad ...(16)$$

or the root mean square noise (cf),

$$\overline{c} = \frac{q}{\sqrt{12}} \qquad ...(17)$$

where q is the width of the region of uncertainty of the signal level. In designing a video input signal, it is desirable to equate the "noise" levels introduced by the quantisation and Gaussian noise effects. For a CCTV camera, 8-bit quantisation is certainly adequate, and in practice it is likely that only the first 6 bits are significant.

Because the computer can only store a finite number of measurements of image intensity etc., spatial sampling is also required. In effect the image on the camera "retina" is sampled according to a predefined grid, normally rectangular, which may be 512 by 512 elements to obtain TV quality for example. Each number in the sampled image then represents the average image irradiance over a small square or rectangular area. The effect of this tessellation of the image into the pixel elements will have further effects on the image data. In general, the optimum separation of the sampling pixels is related to the rate of transition of intensity of the image data by the sampling theorem, which states that

$$\text{pixel separation} \leq \frac{1}{2f_m} \qquad \ldots(18)$$

where f_m is the maximum frequency of intensity change in the original image, a function of the filtering introduced both by the optical and electronic pre-processing. If the sampling interval is too large with respect to the image function then the phenomenon of aliasing occurs. In this case, undersampling of the high frequency components results in spurious low frequency signals being generated, interacting with the real image and producing unusual effects. Figures 1.27, 1.28, 1.29, and 1.30, below, show the effect of increasing the sampling frequency and number of digital signal levels.

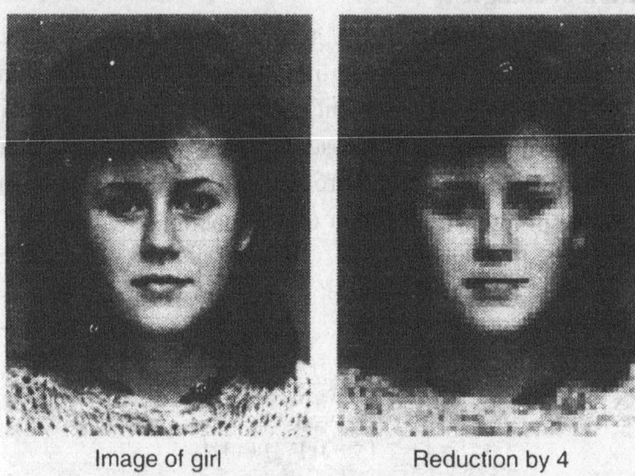

Image of girl   Reduction by 4

Fig. (1.27) The effects of sampling.

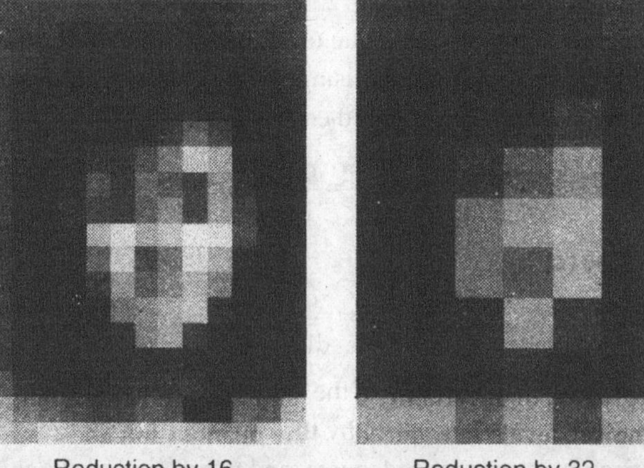

Reduction by 16   Reduction by 32

Fig. (1.28) The effects of sampling.

Image girl : 256 levels 8 levels

Fig. (1.29) The effects of quantisation.

4 levels 2 levels

Fig. (1.30) The effects of quantisation.

■ SUMMARY

- An image is an array, or a matrix, of square pixels (picture elements) arranged in columns and rows.
- Images of astronomical objects are usually taken with electronic detectors such as a CCD (Charge Coupled Device). Similar detectors are found in normal digital cameras.
- One particularly important aspect of image processing is the choice of the best stretch function. You choose which "stretch function" or representation to use in the Fits Liberator window.
- A logarithmic representation of the pixel values tends to suppress the bright parts of the image, i.e. the stars, and to enhance the fainter part, e.g. nebulosity. This can be desirable if the 'faint stuff' needs 'a boost', but a logarithmic stretch function can also reduce the contrast in an image, producing a lower dynamic range as is seen in the example below.
- Image processing is any form of information processing for which the input is an image, such as photographs or frames of video; the output is not necessarily an image, but can be for instance a set of features of the image.

- Digital image processing is the use of computer algorithms to perform image processing on digital images.
- Digital cameras generally include dedicated digital image processing chips to convert the raw data from the image sensor into a color-corrected image in a standard image file format. Images from digital cameras often receive further processing to improve their quality; a distinct advantage digital cameras have over film cameras.
- Visual perception is the ability to interpret visible light information reaching the eyes which is then made available for planning and action. The resulting perception is also known as eyesight, sight or vision. The various components involved in vision are known as the visual system.
- The visual system allows us to assimilate information from the environment to help guide our actions. The act of seeing starts when the lens of the eye focus an image of the outside world onto a light-sensitive membrane in the back of the eye, called the retina. The retina is actually part of the brain that is isolated to serve as a transducer for the conversion of patterns of light into neuronal signals.
- A signal is defined as some variable which changes subject to some other independent variable. We will assume here, that the independent variable is time, denoted by t and the dependent variable could be any physical measurement-variable which changes over time - think for example of a time varying electric voltage.

Review Questions

1. Watch the TV news, and see if you can observe any examples of image processing.
2. If your TV set allows it, turn down the colour as far as you can to produce a monochromatic display. How does this affect your viewing? Is there anything which is hard to recognize without colour?
3. Look through a collection of old photographs. How can they be enhanced, or restored?
4. For each of the following, list five ways in which image processing could be used:
   - Medicine _ astronomy
   - Sport
   - Music
   - Agriculture
   - Travel
5. Image processing techniques have become a vital part of the modern movie production process. Next time you watch a film, take note of all the image processing involved.
6. If you have access to a scanner, scan in a photograph, and experiment with all the possible scanner settings.
   (a) What is the smallest sized file you can create which shows all the detail of your photograph?
   (b) What is the smallest sized _le you can create in which the major parts of your image are still recognizable?
   (c) How do the colour settings affect the output?
7. If you have access to a digital camera, again photograph a fixed scene, using all possible camera settings.
   (a) What is the smallest file you can create?
   (b) How do the light settings effect the output?
8. Suppose you were to scan in a monochromatic photograph, and then print out the result. Then suppose you scanned in the printout, and printed out the result of that, and repeated this a few times. Would you expect any degradation of the image during this process? What aspects of the scanner and printer would minimize degradation?

9. Look up ultrasonography. How does it differ from the image acquisition methods discussed in this chapter? What is it used for? If you can, compare an ultrasound image with an x-ray image. How to they differ? In what ways are they similar?
10. If you have access to an image viewing program (other than Matlab) on your computer, make a list of the image processing capabilities it others. Can you find imaging tasks it is unable to do?
11. Type in the command

    >> help imdemos

    This will give you a list of, amongst other things, all the sample TIFF images which come with the Image Processing Toolbox. Make a list of these sample images, and for each image.
    (a) Determine its type (binary, grey scale, true colour or indexed colour),
    (b) Determine its size (in pixels)
    (c) Give a brief description of the picture (what it looks like; what it seems to be a picture of)
12. Pick a grey scale image, say camera man.tif or wombats.tif. Using the imwrite function, write it to files of type JPEG, PNG and BMP.
    What are the sizes of those _les?
13. Repeat the above question with
    (a) A binary image, (b) An indexed colour image, (c) A true colour image.
14. Open the grey scale image cameraman. if and view it. What data type is it?
15. Explain the Motivation and Perspective of image processing.
16. Explain the Applications of image processing.
17. Explain the Components of Image Processing System.
18. Explain the Element of Visual Perception and Visual System.
19. Explain a Simple Image Model
20. Explain the Sampling and Quantization.

□□□

2

IMAGE ENHANCEMENT IN SPATIAL DOMAIN

The principal objective of enhancement is to process an image so that the result is more suitable than the original image for a specific application. Thus, for example, a method that is quite useful for enhancing X-ray images may not necessarily be the best approach for enhancing pictures of Mars transmitted by a space probe. Regardless of the method used, however, image enhancement is one of the most interesting and visually appealing areas of image processing.

Image enhancement approaches fall into two broad categories:

- Spatial domain methods.
- Frequency domain methods.

The term spatial domain refers to the image plane itself, and approaches in this category are based on direct manipulation of pixels in an image. Frequency domain processing techniques are based on modifying the Fourier transform of an image. Enhancement techniques based on various combinations of methods from these two categories are not unusual.

There is no general theory of image enhancement. When an image is processed for visual interpretation, the viewer is the ultimate judge of how well a particular method works. Visual evaluation of image quality is a highly subjective process, thus making the definition of a "good image" an elusive standard by which to compare algorithm performance. When the problem is one of processing images for machine perception, the evaluation task is somewhat easier.

For example, in dealing with a character recognition application, and leaving aside other issues such as computational requirements, the best image processing method would be the one yielding the best machine recognition results. However, even in situations when a clear-cut criterion of performance can be imposed on the problem, a certain amount of trial and error usually is required before a particular image enhancement approach is selected.

■ 2.1 IMAGE ENHANCEMENT

Image enhancement is the improvement of digital image quality (wanted e.g. for visual inspection or for machine analysis), without knowledge about the source of degradation. If the source of degradation is known, one calls the process image restoration. Both are iconical processes, viz. input and outputs are images.

Many different, often elementary and heuristic methods are used to improve images in some sense. The problem is, of course, not well defined, as there is no objective measure for image quality. Here, we discuss a few recipes that have shown to be useful both for the human observer and/or for machine recognition. These methods are very problem-oriented: a method that works fine in one case may be completely inadequate for another problem.

Apart from geometrical transformations some preliminary grey level adjustments may be indicated, to take into account imperfections in the acquisition system. This can be done pixel by pixel, calibrating with the output of an image with constant brightness. Frequently space-invariant grey value transformations are also done for contrast stretching, range compression, etc. The critical distribution is the relative frequency of each grey value, the grey value histogram. Examples of simple grey level transformations in this domain are:

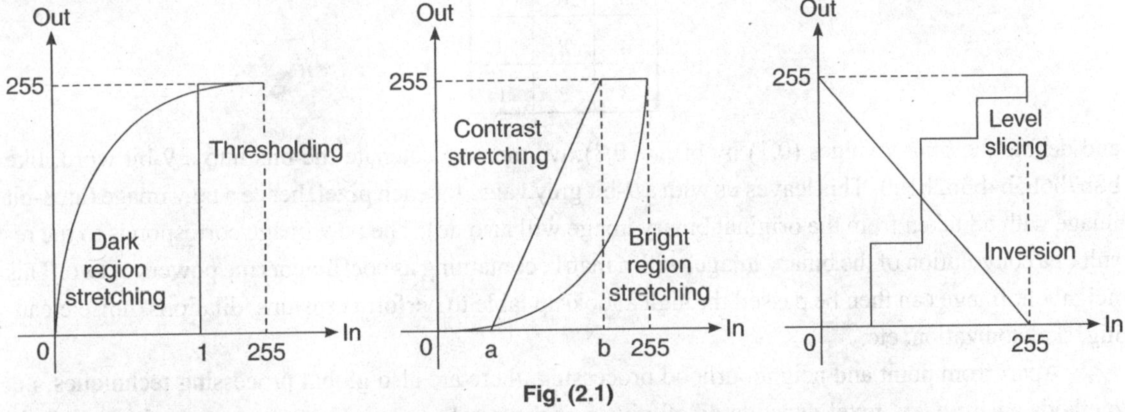

Fig. (2.1)

Grey values can also be modified such that their histogram has any desired shape, e.g flat (every grey value has the same probability). All examples assume point processing, viz. each output pixel is the function of one input pixel; usually, the transformation is implemented with a look-up table:

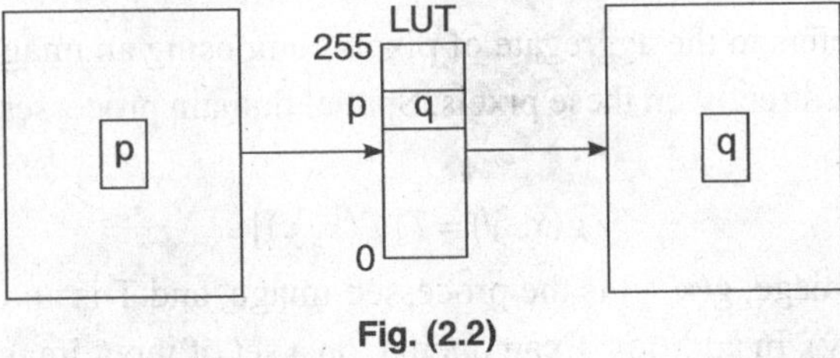

Fig. (2.2)

Physiological experiments have shown that very small changes in luminance are recognized by the human visual system in regions of continuous greyvalue, and not at all seen in regions of some discontinuities. Therefore, a design goal for image enhancement often is to smooth images in more uniform regions, but to preserve edges. On the other hand, it has also been shown that somehow degraded images with enhancement of certain features, e.g. edges, can simplify image interpretation both for a human observer and for machine recognition. A second design goal, therefore, is image sharpening. All these operations need neighbourhood processing, viz. the output pixel is a function of some neighbourhood of the input pixels:

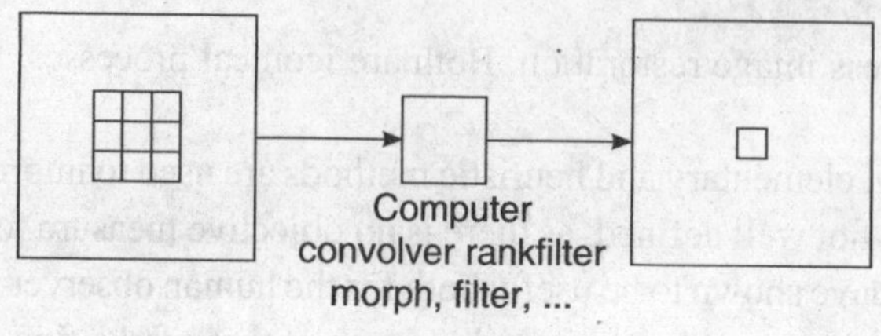

Fig. (2.3)

These operations could be performed using linear operations in either the frequency or the spatial domain. We could, e.g. design, in the frequency domain, one-dimensional low or high pass filters (Filtering), and transform them according to McClellan's algorithm to the two-dimensional case.

Here is a trick that can speed up operations substantially, and serves as an example for both point and neighbourhood processing in a binary image: we number the pixels in a neighbourhood like,

5	6	7
4	8	0
3	2	1

and denote the binary values (0,1) by bi (i = 0,8); we then concatenate the bits into a 9-bit word, like b8b7b6b5b4b3b2b1b0. This leaves us with a 9-bit grey value for each pixel, hence a new image (an 8-bit image with b8 taken from the original binary image will also do). The new image corresponds to the result of a convolution of the binary image, with a matrix containing as coefficients the powers of two. This neighbour image can then be passed through a look-up table to perform erosions, dilations, noise cleaning, skeletonization, etc.

Apart from point and neighbourhood processing, there are also global processing techniques, i.e. methods where every pixel depends on all pixels of the whole image. Histogram methods are usually global, but they can also be used in a neighbourhood.

■ 2.2 SPATIAL DOMAIN

The term spatial domain refers to the aggregate of pixels composing an image. Spatial domain methods are procedures that operate directly on these pixels. Spatial domain processes will be denoted by the expression

$$g(x, y) = T[f(x, y)]$$

where f(x, y) is the input image, g(x, y) is the processed image, and T is an operator on f, defined over some neighborhood of (x, y). In addition T can operate on a set of input images, such as performing the pixel-by-pixel sum of K images for noise reduction.

The principal approach in defining a neighborhood about a point (x, y) is to use a square or rectangular sub image area centered at (x, y), as Fig. 2.4 shows. The center of the sub image is moved from pixel to pixel starting, say, at the top left corner. The operator T is applied at each location (x, y) to yield the output, g, at that location. The process utilizes only the pixels in the area of the image spanned by the neighborhood. Although other neighborhood shapes, such as approximations to a circle, sometimes are used, square and rectangular arrays are by far the most predominant because of their ease of implementation.

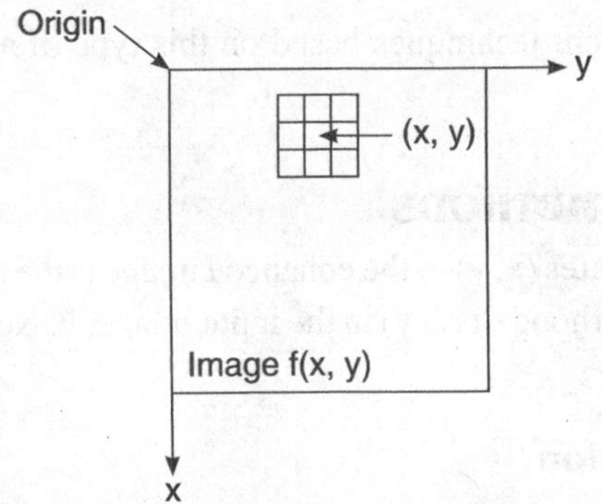

Fig. (2.4) A 3 * 3 neighbourhood about a point (*x, y*) in an image.

The simplest form of T is when the neighborhood is of size 1*1 (that is, a single pixel). In this case, g depends only on the value of f at (x, y), and T becomes a gray-level (also called an intensity or mapping) transformation function of the form

$$s = T(r)$$

where, for simplicity in notation, r and s are variables denoting, respectively, the gray level of f(x, y) and g(x, y) at any point (x, y). For example, if T(r) has the form shown in Fig. 2.2(a), the effect of this transformation would be to produce an image of higher contrast than the original by darkening the levels below m and brightening the levels above m in the original image. In this technique, known as contrast stretching, the values of r below m are compressed by the transformation function into a narrow range of s, toward black. The opposite effect takes place for values of r above m. In the limiting case shown in Fig. 2.2(b), T(r) produces a two-level (binary) image. A mapping of this form is called a thresholding function. Some fairly simple, yet powerful, processing approaches can be formulated with gray-level transformations. Because enhancement at any point in an image depends only on the gray level at that point, techniques in this category often are referred to as point processing.

Larger neighborhoods allow considerably more flexibility. The general approach is to use a function of the values of f in a predefined neighborhood of (x, y) to determine the value of g at (x, y). One of the principal approaches in this formulation is based on the use of so-called masks (also referred to as filters, kernels, templates, or windows). Basically, a mask is a small (say, 3*3) 2-D array, such as the one shown in Fig. 2.5, in which the values of the mask coefficients determine the nature of the process, such

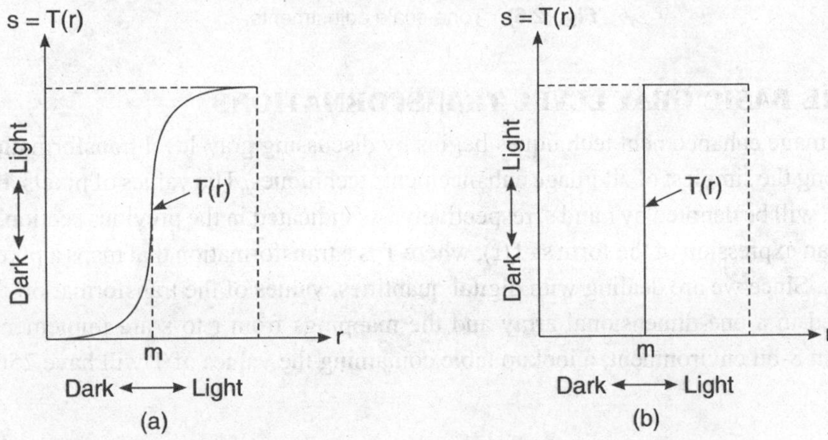

Fig. (2.5) Gray level transformation functions for contrast enhancement.

as image sharpening. Enhancement techniques based on this type of approach often are referred to as mask processing or filtering.

2.3 SPATIAL DOMAIN METHODS

The value of a pixel with coordinates (x, y) in the enhanced image is the result of performing some operation on the pixels in the neighbourhood of (x, y) in the input image, F. Neighbourhoods can be any shape, but usually they are rectangular.

2.3.1 Grey Scale Manipulation

The simplest form of operation is when the operator T only acts on a pixel neighbourhood in the input image, that is only depends on the value of F at (x, y). This is a *grey scale transformation* or mapping.

The simplest case is thresholding where the intensity profile is replaced by a step function, active at a chosen threshold value. In this case any pixel with a grey level below the threshold in the input image gets mapped to 0 in the output image. Other pixels are mapped to 255. Other grey scale transformations are outlined in figure 2.6 below.

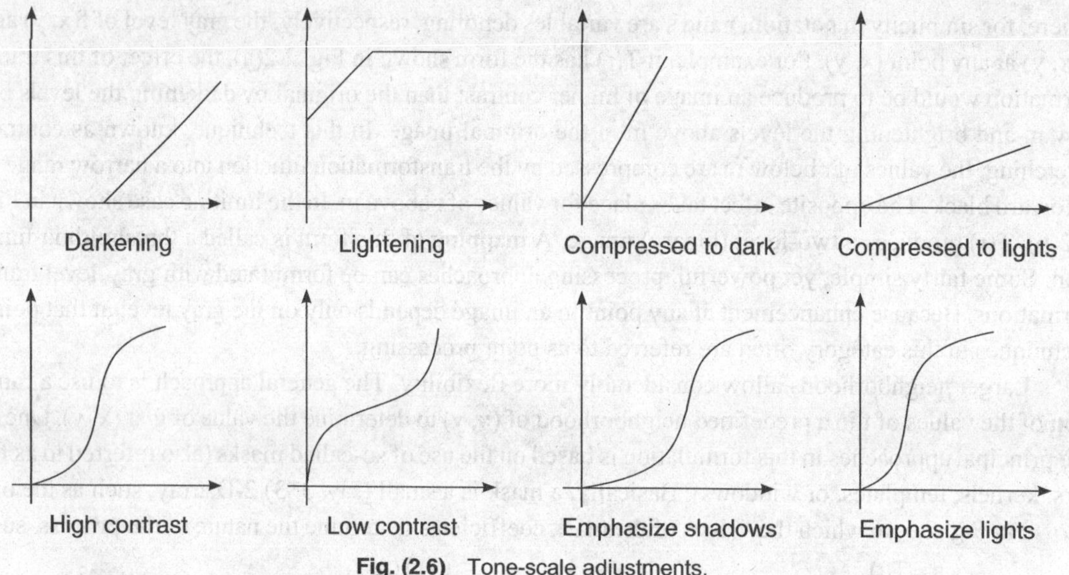

Fig. (2.6) Tone-scale adjustments.

2.4 SOME BASIC GRAY LEVEL TRANSFORMATIONS

The study of image enhancement techniques begins by discussing gray-level transformation functions. These are among the simplest of all image enhancements techniques. The values of pixels, before and after processing, will be denoted by r and s, respectively. As indicated in the previous section, these values are related by an expression of the form s=T(r), where T is a transformation that maps a pixel value r into a pixel value s. Since we are dealing with digital quantities, values of the transformation function typically are stored in a one-dimensional array and the mappings from r to s are implemented via table lookups. For an 8-bit environment, a lookup table containing the values of T will have 256 entries.

As an introduction to gray-level transformations, consider Fig. 2.7, which shows three basic types of functions used frequently for image enhancement: linear (negative and identity transformations), logarithmic (log and inverse-log transformations), and power-law (nth power and nth root transformations).The identity function is the trivial case in which output intensities are identical to input intensities. It is included in the graph only for completeness.

2.4.1 Image Negatives

The negative of an image with gray levels in the range [0, L-1] is obtained by using the negative transformation shown in Fig. 2.7, which is given by the expression

$$s = L - 1 - r \qquad ...(2.1)$$

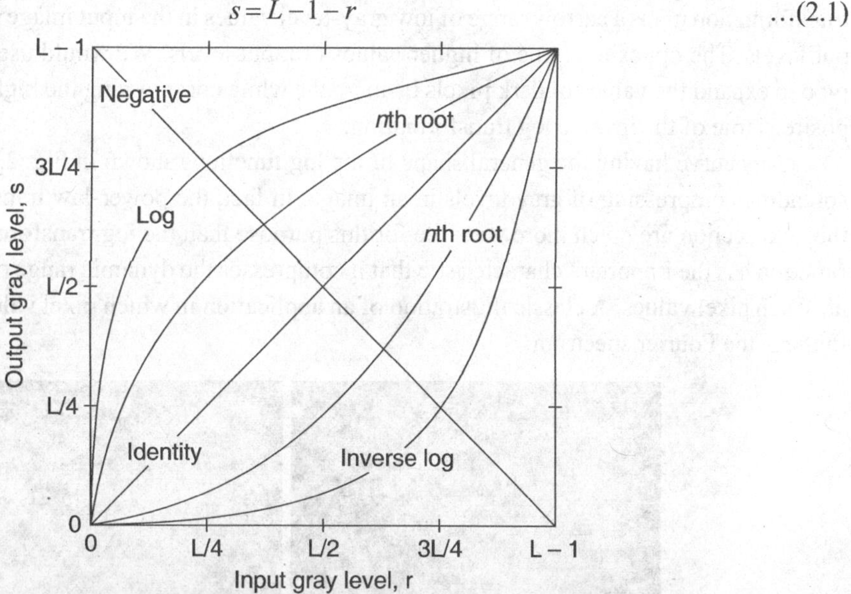

Fig. (2.7) Some basic gray-level transformation functions used for image enhancement.

Reversing the intensity levels of an image in this manner produces the equivalent of a photographic negative. This type of processing is particularly suited for enhancing white or gray detail embedded in

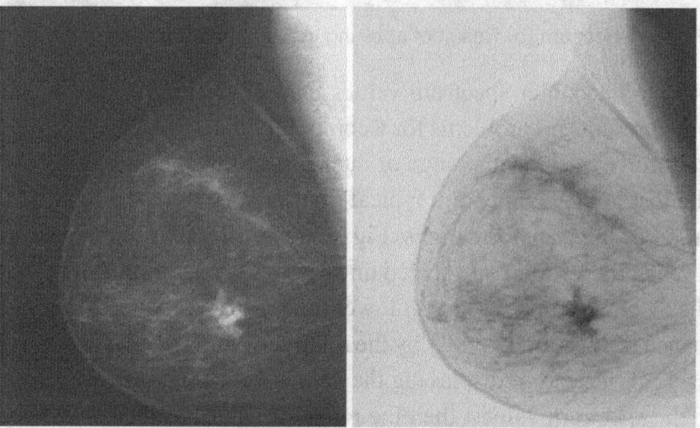

Fig. (2.8) (a) Original digital mammogram (b) Negative image obtained using the negative transformation in eq. 2.1

dark regions of an image, especially when the black areas are dominant in size. An example is shown in Fig. 2.8. The original image is a digital mammogram showing a small lesion. In spite of the fact that the visual content is the same in both images, note how much easier it is to analyze the breast tissue in the negative image in this particular case.

2.4.2 Log Transformations

The general form of the log transformation shown in Fig. 2.7 is

$$s = c \log (1 + r) \qquad \text{...(2.2)}$$

where c is a constant, and it is assumed that r>= 0. The shape of the log curve in Fig. 2.7 shows that this transformation maps a narrow range of low gray-level values in the input image into a wider range of output levels. The opposite is true of higher values of input levels. We would use a transformation of this type to expand the values of dark pixels in an image while compressing the higher-level values. The opposite is true of the inverse log transformation.

Any curve having the general shape of the log functions shown in Fig. 2.7 would accomplish this spreading/compressing of gray levels in an image. In fact, the power-law transformations discussed in the next section are much more versatile for this purpose than the log transformation. However, the log function has the important characteristic that it compresses the dynamic range of images with large variations in pixel values. A classic illustration of an application in which pixel values have a large dynamic range is the Fourier spectrum.

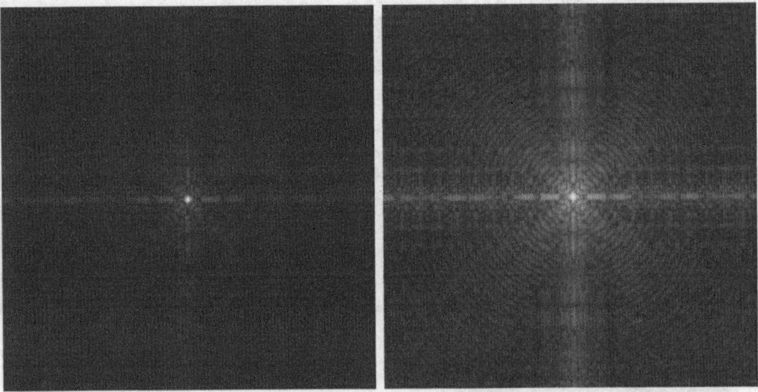

Fig. (2.9) (a) Fourier spectrum (b) Result of applying the log transformation given in eq. (2.2) with $c = 1$

It is not unusual to encounter spectrum values that range from 0 to or higher. While processing numbers such as these presents no problems for a computer, image display systems generally will not be able to reproduce faithfully such a wide range of intensity values. The net effect is that a significant degree of detail will be lost in the display of a typical Fourier spectrum.

As an illustration of log transformations, Fig. 2.9(a) shows a Fourier spectrum with values in the range 0 to 1.5*106.When these values are scaled linearly for display in an 8-bit system, the brightest pixels will dominate the display, at the expense of lower (and just as important) values of the spectrum. The effect of this dominance is illustrated vividly by the relatively small area of the image in Fig. 2.9(a) that is not perceived as black. If, instead of displaying the values in this manner, we first apply Eq. (2-2) (with c=1 in this case) to the spectrum values, then the range of values of the result become 0 to 6.2, a more manageable number. Figure 2.9(b) shows the result of scaling this new range linearly and displaying the spectrum in the same 8-bit display. The wealth of detail visible in this image as compared to a straight display of the spectrum is evident from these pictures. Most of the Fourier spectra seen in image processing publications have been scaled in just this manner.

2.4.3 Power-Law Transformations

Power-law transformations have the basic form

$$s = cr \qquad \text{...(2.3)}$$

where c and g are positive constants. Sometimes Eq. (3.2-3) is written as to account for an offset (that is, a measurable output when the input is zero). However, offsets typically are an issue of display calibration and as a result they are normally ignored in Eq. (2-3). Plots of s versus r for various values of g are shown in Fig. 2.10.

As in the case of the log transformation, power-law curves with fractional values of g map a narrow range of dark input values into a wider range of output values, with the opposite being true for higher values of input levels. Unlike the log function, however, we notice here a family of possible transformation curves obtained simply by varying g.As expected, we see in Fig. 2.10 that curves generated with values of g>1 have exactly the opposite effect as those generated with values of g<1. Finally, we note that Eq. (2-3) reduces to the identity transformation when c=g=1.

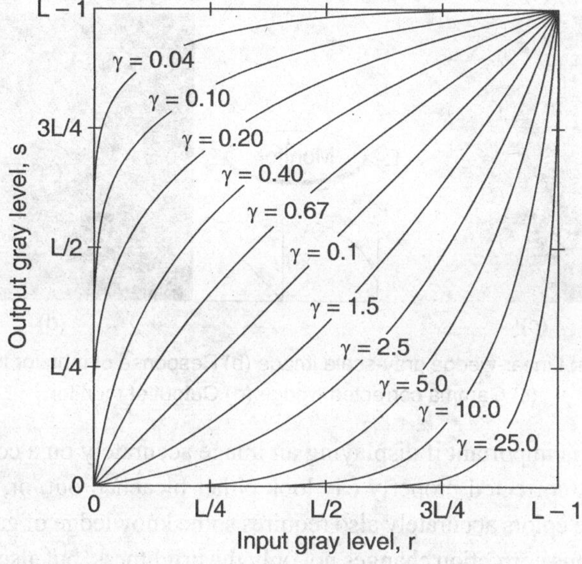

Fig. (2.10) Plots of the equation $s = cr^{\gamma}$ fromvarious values of g (c = 1in all cases).

A variety of devices used for image capture, printing, and display respond according to a power law. By convention, the exponent in the power-law equation is referred to as gamma [hence our use of this symbol in Eq. (2-3)].The process used to correct this power-law response phenomena is called gamma correction. For example, cathode ray tube (CRT) devices have an intensity-to-voltage response that is a power function, with exponents varying from approximately 1.8 to 2.5.With reference to the curve for g=2.5 in Fig. 2.10, we see that such display systems would tend to produce images that are darker than intended. This effect is illustrated in Fig. 2.10. Figure 2.11(a) shows a simple gray-scale linear wedge input into a CRT monitor. As expected, the output of the monitor appears darker than the input, as shown in Fig. 2.11(b). Gamma correction in this case is straightforward. All we need to do is preprocess the input image before inputting it into the monitor by performing the transformation the result is shown in Fig. 2.11(c).When input into the same monitor, this gamma-corrected input produces an output that is close in appearance to the original image, as shown in Fig. 2.11(d).A similar analysis would apply to other imaging devices such as scanners and printers. The only difference would be the device-dependent value of gamma.

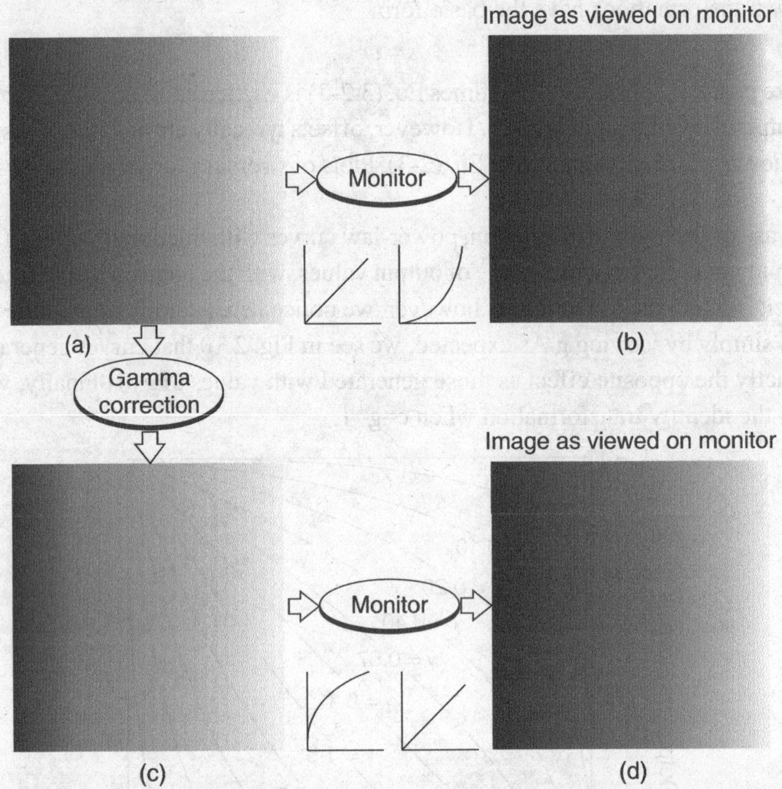

Fig. (2.11) (a) Linear-wedge gray-scale image (b) Response of monitor to linear wedge (c) Gamma corrected wedge (d) Output of monitor.

Gamma correction is important if displaying an image accurately on a computer screen is of concern. Images that are not corrected properly can look either bleached out, or, what is more likely, too dark. Trying to reproduce colors accurately also requires some knowledge of gamma correction because varying the value of gamma correction changes not only the brightness, but also the ratios of red to green to blue. Gamma correction has become increasingly important in the past few years, as use of digital images for commercial purposes over the Internet has increased. It is not unusual that images created for a popular Web site will be viewed by millions of people, the majority of whom will have different monitors and/or monitor settings. Some computer systems even have partial gamma correction built in. Also, current image standards do not contain the value of gamma with which an image was created, thus complicating the issue further. Given these constraints, a reasonable approach when storing images in a Web site is to preprocess the images with a gamma that represents an "average" of the types of monitors and computer systems that one expects in the open market at any given point in time.

In addition to gamma correction, power-law transformations are useful for general-purpose contrast manipulation. Figure 2.12(a) shows a magnetic resonance (MR) image of an upper thoracic human spine with a fracture dislocation and spinal cord impingement. The fracture is visible near the vertical center of the spine, approximately one-fourth of the way down from the top of the picture.

Since the given image is predominantly dark, an expansion of gray levels are desirable. This can be accomplished with a power-law transformation with a fractional exponent. The other images shown in the Figure were obtained by processing Fig. 2.12(a) with the power-law transformation function of Eq. (2-3). The values of gamma corresponding to images (b) through (d) are 0.6, 0.4, and 0.3, respectively (the value of c was 1 in all cases).We note that, as gamma decreased from 0.6 to 0.4, more detail became visible.

A further decrease of gamma to 0.3 enhanced a little more detail in the background, but began to reduce contrast to the point where the image started to have a very slight "washed-out" look, especially in the background. By comparing all results, we see that the best enhancement in terms of contrast and discernable detail was obtained with g=0.4.A value of g=0.3 is an approximate limit below which contrast in this particular image would be reduced to an unacceptable level.

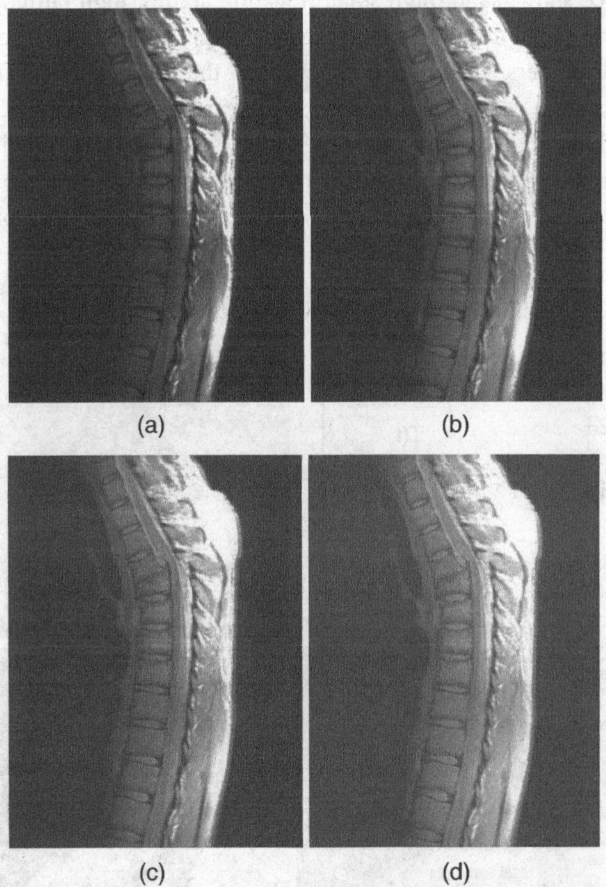

Fig. (2.12) (a) Magnetic resonance (MR) image of a fractured human spine, (b)-(d) Results of applying the transformation in eq. (2.3) with c = 1and g = 0.6, 0.4 and 0.3, respectively.

■ 2.5 PIECEWISE-LINEAR TRANSFORMATION FUNCTIONS

A complementary approach to the methods discussed in the previous three sections is to use piecewise linear functions. The principal advantage of piecewise linear functions over the types of functions we have discussed thus far is that the form of piecewise functions can be arbitrarily complex. In fact, a practical implementation of some important transformations can be formulated only as piecewise functions. The principal disadvantage of piecewise functions is that their specification requires considerably more user input.

2.5.1 Contrast Stretching

One of the simplest piecewise linear functions is a contrast-stretching transformation. Low-contrast images can result from poor illumination, lack of dynamic range in the imaging sensor, or even wrong setting of a lens aperture during image acquisition. The idea behind contrast stretching is to increase the dynamic range of the gray levels in the image being processed.

Contrast enhancement is only intended to improve the visual quality of a displayed image. It is a process generally required for all images because satellite based sensors with global coverage need to image a wide range of scenes , from very low radiance (oceans, low solar elevation angles, high latitudes etc) to very high radiance snow, sand, high solar elevation angles, high latitudes). Any one scene will generally have a radiance range much less than the full range. When such a scene is imaged and converted to 1 byte digital numbers (DN's), it uses less than the full quantization range (usually 0-255). When the image is displayed it will have low contrast, appearing quite dull, making visual interpretation difficult. Contrast stretching involves increasing the range (spreading or stretching) of data values to occupy the available image display range (usually 1 byte or 0-255). The result is displayed image with a greater level of contrast and so easier interpretability. Figure 2.13(a) shows a typical transformation used

Fig. (2.13) Contrast stretching (a) Form of transformation function, (b) A low-contrast image, (c) Result of contrast stretching, (d) Result of thresholding.

for contrast stretching. The locations of points Ar1, s1B and Ar2, s2B control the shape of the transformation function. If r1=s1 and r2=s2, the transformation is a linear function that produces no changes in gray levels. If r1=r2, s1=0and s2=L-1, the transformation becomes a thresholding function that creates a binary image, as illustrated in Fig. 2.13(b). Intermediate values of (r1, s1) and (r2, s2) produce various degrees of spread in the gray levels of the output image, thus affecting its contrast. In general, r1<= r2 and s1<= s2 is assumed so that the function is single valued and monotonically increasing. This condition preserves the order of gray levels, thus preventing the creation of intensity artifacts in the processed image.

Figure 2.13(b) shows an 8-bit image with low contrast. Thus, the transformation function stretched the levels linearly from their original range to the full range [0, L-1]. Finally, Fig. 2.13(d) shows the result of using the thresholding function defined previously, with r1=r2=m, the mean gray level in the image. The original image on which these results are based is a scanning electron microscope image of pollen, magnified approximately 700 times.

2.5.2 Gray-level Slicing

Highlighting a specific range of gray levels in an image often is desired. Applications include enhancing features such as masses of water in satellite imagery and enhancing flaws in X-ray images. There are several ways of doing level slicing, but most of them are variations of two basic themes. One approach is to display a high value for all gray levels in the range of interest and a low value for all other gray levels. This transformation, shown in Fig. 2.14(a), produces a binary image.The second approach,

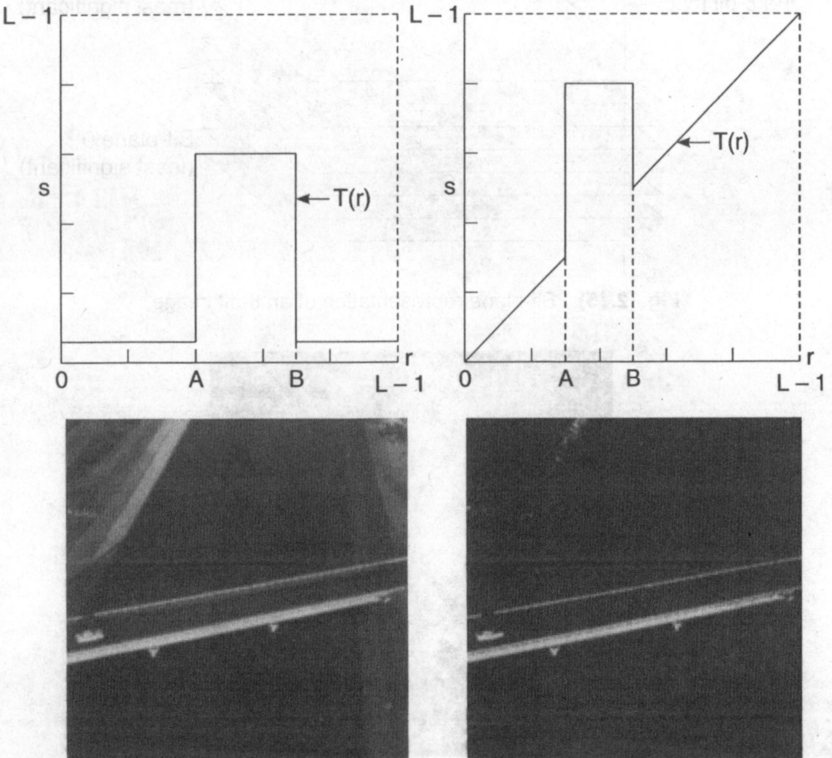

Fig. (2.14) (a) This transformation highlights range [A, B] of gray levels and reduces all others to a constant level, (b) This transformation highlights range [A, B] but preserves all other levels, (c) An image (d) Result of using the transformation (a).

based on the transformation shown in Fig. 2.14(b), brightens the desired range of gray levels but preserves the background and gray-level tonalities in the image. Figure 2.14(c) shows a gray-scale image, and Fig. 2.14(d) shows the result of using the transformation in Fig. 2.14(a).Variations of the two transformations shown in Fig. 2.14 are easy to formulate.

2.5.3 Bit-plane Slicing

Instead of highlighting gray-level ranges, highlighting the contribution made to total image appearance by specific bits might be desired. Suppose that each pixel in an image is represented by 8 bits. Imagine that the image is composed of eight 1-bit planes, ranging from bit-plane 0 for the least significant bit to bit plane 7 for the most significant bit. In terms of 8-bit bytes, plane 0 contains all the lowest order bits in the bytes comprising the pixels in the image and plane 7 contains all the high-order bits. Figure 2.15 illustrates these ideas, and Fig. 2.16 Shows the various bit planes for the image shown in Fig. 2.16. Note that the Higher-order bits (especially the top four) contain the majority of the visually significant data. The other bit planes contribute to more subtle details in the image. Separating a digital image into its bit planes is useful for analyzing the relative importance played by each bit of the image, a process that aids in determining the adequacy of the number of bits used to quantize each pixel. Also, this type of decomposition is useful for image compression.

In terms of bit-plane extraction for an 8-bit image, it is not difficult to show that the (binary) image for bit-plane 7 can be obtained by processing the input image with a thresholding gray-level transforma-

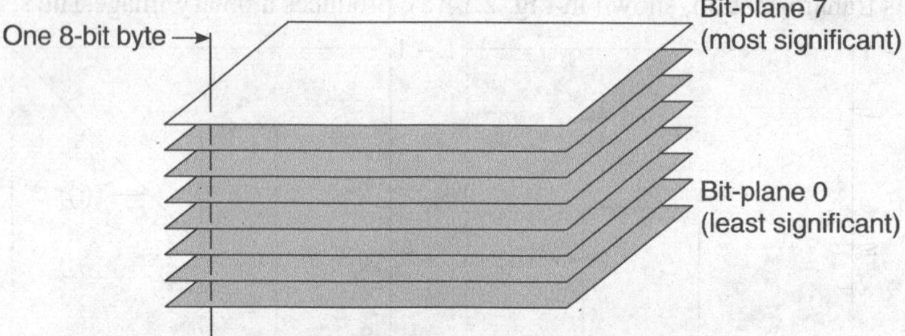

Fig. (2.15) Bit-plane representation of an 8-bit image.

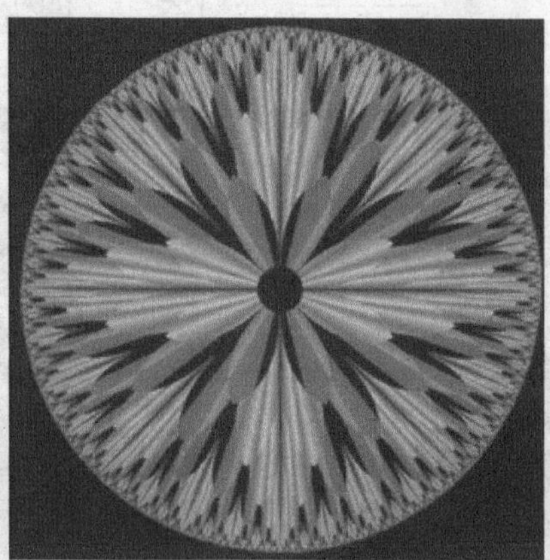

Fig. (2.16) An 8-bit fractal image (A fractal is an image generated from mathematical expressions).

tion function that (1) maps all levels in the image between 0 and 127 to one level (for example, 0); and (2) maps all levels between 129 and 255 to another (for example, 255).The binary image for bit-plane 7 in Fig. 2.16 was obtained in just this manner. It is left as an exercise to obtain the gray-level transformation functions that would yield the other bit planes.

■ 2.6 HISTOGRAM PROCESSING

The histogram of a digital image with gray levels in the range [0, L-1] is a discrete function h(rk)= nk, where rk is the kth gray level and nk is the number of pixels in the image having gray level rk. It is common practice to normalize a histogram by dividing each of its values by the total number of pixels in the image, denoted by n. Thus, a normalized histogram is given by p (rk) =nk/n, for k=0, 1, p, L-1. Loosely speaking, p (rk) gives an estimate of the probability of occurrence of gray level rk. Note that the sum of all components of a normalized histogram is equal to 1.

Histograms are the basis for numerous spatial domain processing techniques. Histogram manipulation can be used effectively for image enhancement. In addition to providing useful image statistics, we shall see that the information inherent in histograms also is quite useful in other image processing applications, such as image compression and segmentation. Histograms are simple to calculate in software and also lend themselves to economic hardware implementations, thus making them a popular tool for real-time image processing.

As an introduction to the role of histogram processing in image enhancement, consider Fig. 2.17, which is the pollen image of Fig. 2.17 shown in four basic gray-level characteristics: dark, light, low con-

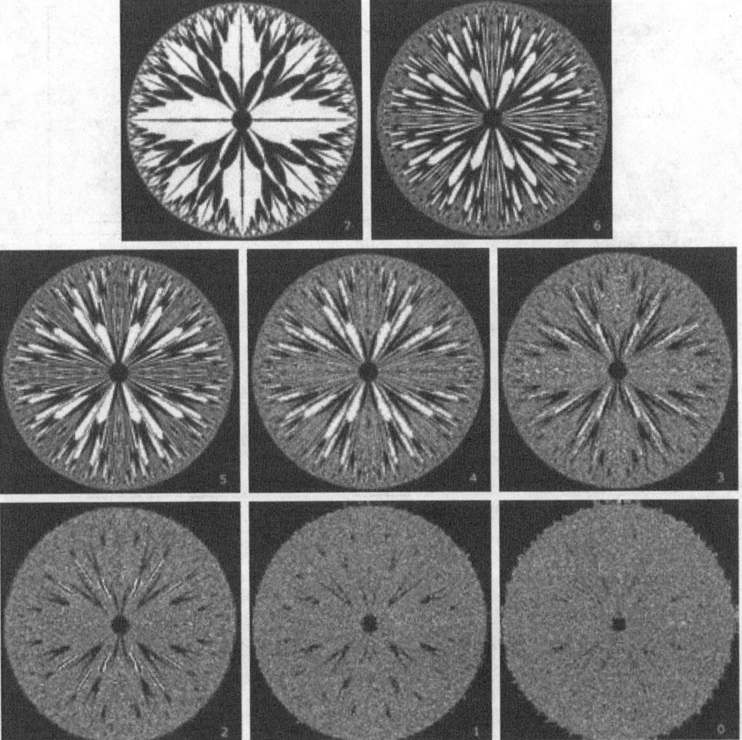

Fig. (2.17) The eight bit planes of the image in fig. (2.13). The number at the bottom, right of each image identifies the bit plane.

trast, and high contrast. The right side of the figure shows the histograms corresponding to these images. The horizontal axis of each histogram plot corresponds to gray level values, rk. The vertical axis corresponds to values of h(rk)=nk or p(rk)=nk/n if the values are normalized. Thus, as indicated previously, these histogram plots are simply plots of h(rk)=nk versus rk or p(rk)=nk/n versus rk.

We note in the dark image that the components of the histogram are concentrated on the low (dark) side of the gray scale. Similarly, the components of the histogram of the bright image are biased toward the high side of the gray scale. An image with low contrast has a histogram that will be narrow and will be centered toward the middle of the gray scale. For a monochrome image this implies a dull, washed-out gray look. Finally, we see that the components of the histogram in the high-contrast image cover a broad range of the gray scale and, further, that the distribution of pixels is not too far from uniform, with very few vertical lines being much higher than the others. Intuitively, it is reasonable to conclude that an im-

Fig. (2.18) Four basic image types : dark, light, low contrast, high contrast and their corresponding histograms.

age, whose pixels tend to occupy the entire range of possible gray levels and, in addition, tend to be distributed uniformly, will have an appearance of high contrast and will exhibit a large variety of gray tones. The net effect will be an image that shows a great deal of gray-level detail and has high dynamic range. It will be shown shortly that it is possible to develop a transformation function that can automatically achieve this effect, based only on information available in the histogram of the input image.

2.6.1 Histogram Specification

Convert the image so that it has a particular histogram as specified. First consider equalization transform of the given image:

$$y = f(x) = \int_0^x p_x(u)\, du$$

If the desired image were available, it could also be equalized:

$$y' = g(z) = \int_0^z p_x(u)\, du$$

where is the desired histogram. The inverse of the above transform is

$$z = g^{-1}(y')$$

Since the images and have the same equalized histogram, they are the same image and the over all transform from the given image to the desired image can be found as:

$$z = g^{-1}(y) = g^{-1}(f(x)) = h(x)$$

where $h(x) = g^{-1}(f(x))$ is the over all transform, and both and can be found from the corresponding histograms of the given image and the desired image, respectively.

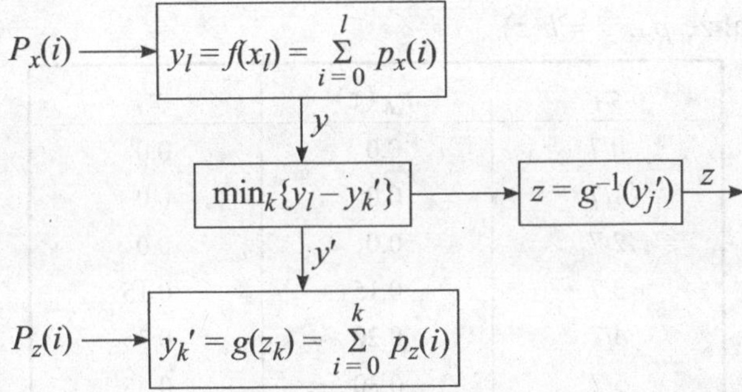

- **Step 1 :** Find histogram of input image $p_x(i)$, and find histogram equalization mapping:

$$F_x(j) = \sum_{i=0}^{j} p_x(i)$$

- **Step 2 :** Specify the desired histogram $p_z(i)$, and find histogram equalization mapping:

$$F_z(j) = \sum_{i=0}^{j} p_z(i)$$

- **Step 3 :** Build lookup table:
  For each gray level l, find $F_x(l)$ and then find a j level so that $F_x(j)$ best matches :

$$|F_x(l) - F_z(j)| = \min_k |F_x(l) - F_z(k)|$$

  setup a lookup entry lookup $[l] = j$.

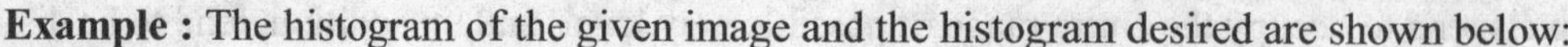

Example : The histogram of the given image and the histogram desired are shown below:

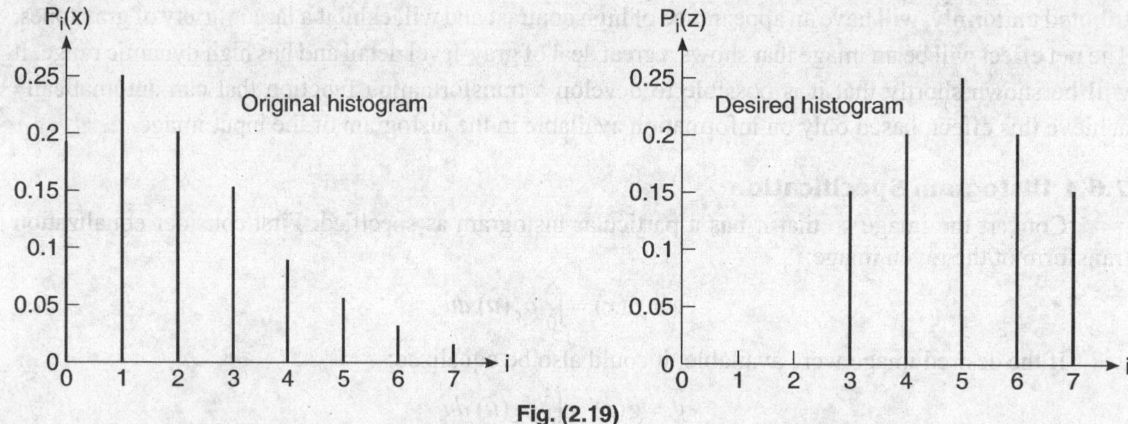

Fig. (2.19)

- **Step 1 :** Equalize p_x, $y = g(x)$.

x_i	y_i	n_j	$p_j(y)$
x_0	$y_1 = 1/7$	790	0.19
x_1	$y_1 = 3/7$	1023	0.25
x_2	$y_1 = 5/7$	850	0.21
x_3, x_4	$y_1 = 6/7$	985	0.24
x_5, x_6, x_7	$y_1 = 7/7$	448	0.11

- **Step 2 :** Equalize p_z, $y' = h(z)$.

z_i	$p_k(z)$	y_j'
0/7	0.0	0.0
1/7	0.0	0.0
2/7	0.0	0.0
3/7	0.15	0.15
4/7	0.20	0.35
5/7	0.30	0.65
6/7	0.20	0.85
7/7	0.15	1.0

- **Step 3 :** Obtain overal mapping, $x \to y \to y' \to z$

x	y	y'	z
x_0	$y_1 = 1/7 = 0.14$	$y_3' = 0.15$	z_3
x_1	$y_1 = 3/7 = 0.43$	$y_4' = 0.35$	z_4
x_2	$y_1 = 5/7 = 0.71$	$y_5' = 0.65$	z_5
x_3, x_4	$y_1 = 6/7 = 0.86$	$y_6' = 0.85$	z_6
x_5, x_6, x_7	$y_1 = 7/7 = 1.0$	$y_7' = 1.0$	z_7

This is the histogram of the resulting image:

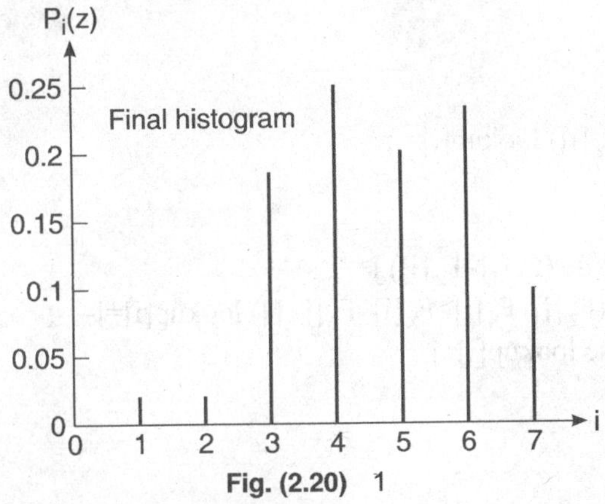

Fig. (2.20) 1

In the following example, the desired histogram is a triangle with linear increase in the lower half of the the gray level range, and linear decrease in the upper half. Again the cumulative histogram shows indeed the density histogram is such a triangle.

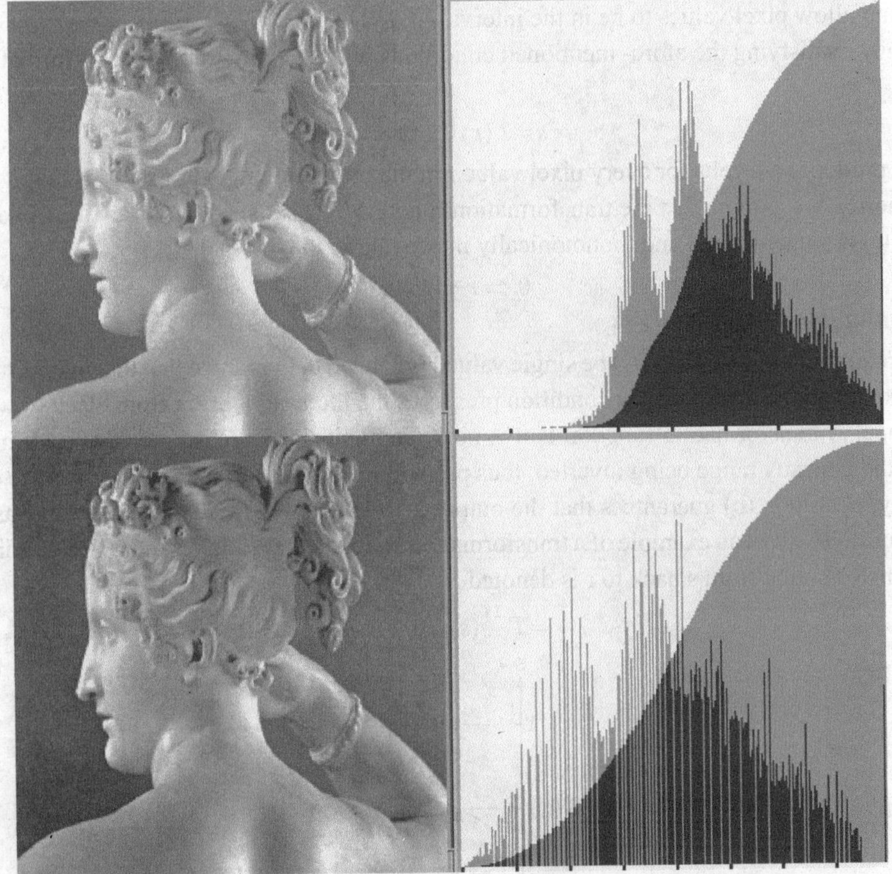

Fig. (2.21)

Programming issues :

```
j=0
for (i=0; i<256; i++)
    {
        if (Fx [i]≤Fz [j]) lookup[i]=j;
        else
        {
            while (Fx [i]>Fz [i]) j++;
            if (Fz [j]–Fx [i]>Fx [i]–Fz [j–1]) lookup[i]=j– –;
            else lookup[i]=j;
        }
    }
```

2.6.2 Histogram Equalization

Consider for a moment continuous functions, and let the variable r represent the gray levels of the image to be enhanced. In the initial part of our discussion we assume that r has been normalized to the interval [0, 1], with r=0 representing black and r=1 representing white. Later, we consider a discrete formulation and allow pixel values to be in the interval [0, L-1].

For any r satisfying the afore- mentioned conditions, we focus attention on transformations of the form

$$s = T(r)\, 0 \Leftarrow r \Leftarrow 1 \qquad \text{...(2.4)}$$

That produces a level s for every pixel value r in the original image. For reasons that will become obvious shortly, we assume that the transformation function T(r) satisfies the following conditions:

(a) T(r) is single-valued and monotonically increasing in the interval

$$0 \Leftarrow r \Leftarrow 1; \text{ and}$$

(b) $0 \Leftarrow T(r) \Leftarrow 1$ for $0 \Leftarrow r \Leftarrow 1$.

The requirement in (a) that T(r) be single valued is needed to guarantee that the inverse transformation will exist, and the monotonicity condition preserves the increasing order from black to white in the output image. A transformation function that is not monotonically increasing could result in at least a section of the intensity range being inverted, thus producing some inverted gray levels in the output image. Finally, condition (b) guarantees that the output gray levels will be in the same range as the input levels. Figure 2.16 gives an example of a transformation function that satisfies these two conditions. The inverse transformation from s back to r is denoted

$$r = T^{-1}(s) \quad 0 \le s \le 1 \qquad \text{...(2.5)}$$

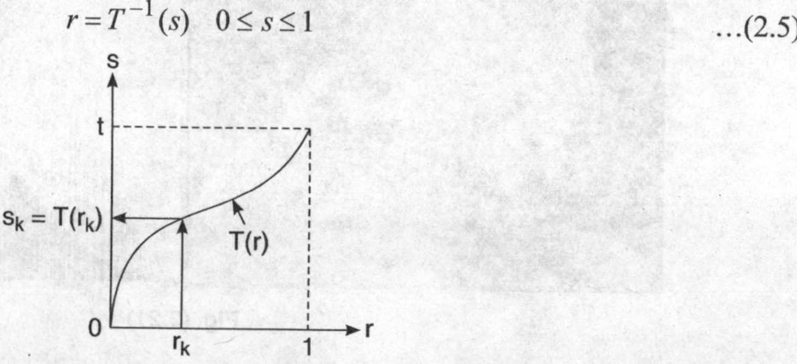

Fig. (2.22) A gray-level transformation function that is both single valued and monotonically increasing.

The objective of histogram equalization is to transfer the gray levels so that the histogram of the resulting image is equalized to be a constant:

$$h[i] = \text{constant}, \quad \text{for all } i$$

The purposes:

- To equally use all available gray levels;
- For further histogram specification.

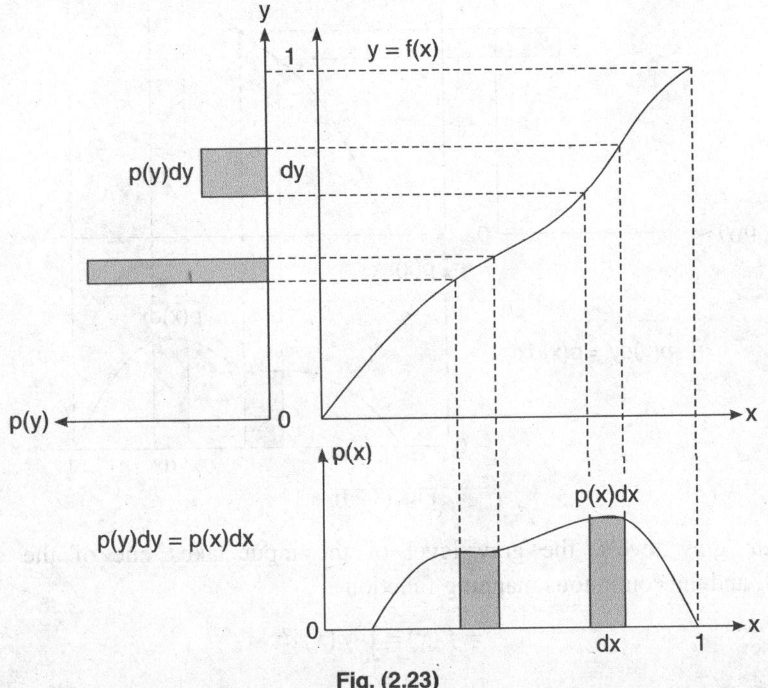

Fig. (2.23)

This figure shows that for any given mapping function $y = f(x)$ between the input and output images, the following holds:

$$p(y)\,dy = p(x)\,dx$$

i.e., the number of pixels mapped from x to y is unchanged.

To equalize the histogram of the output image, we let be a constant. In particular, if the gray levels are assumed to be in the ranges between 0 and 1 $(0 \le x \le 1, 0 \le y \le 1)$, then $p(y) = 1$. Then we have:

$$dy = p(x)\,dx \quad \text{or} \quad \frac{dy}{dx} = p(x)$$

i.e., the mapping function for histogram equalization is:

$$y = \int_0^x p(u)\,du = F(x) - F(0) = F(x)$$

where

$$F(x) = \int_0^x p(u)\,du, \quad F(0) = 0$$

is the cumulative probability distribution of the input image, which monotonically increases. Intuitively, histogram equalization is realized by the following:

- If $p(x)$ is high, $F(x)$ has a steep slope, dy will be wide, causing $p(y)$ to be low to keep $p(y)\,dy = p(x)\,dx$;

- If $p(x)$ is low, $F(x)$ has a shallow slope, dy will be narrow, causing $p(y)$ to be high.

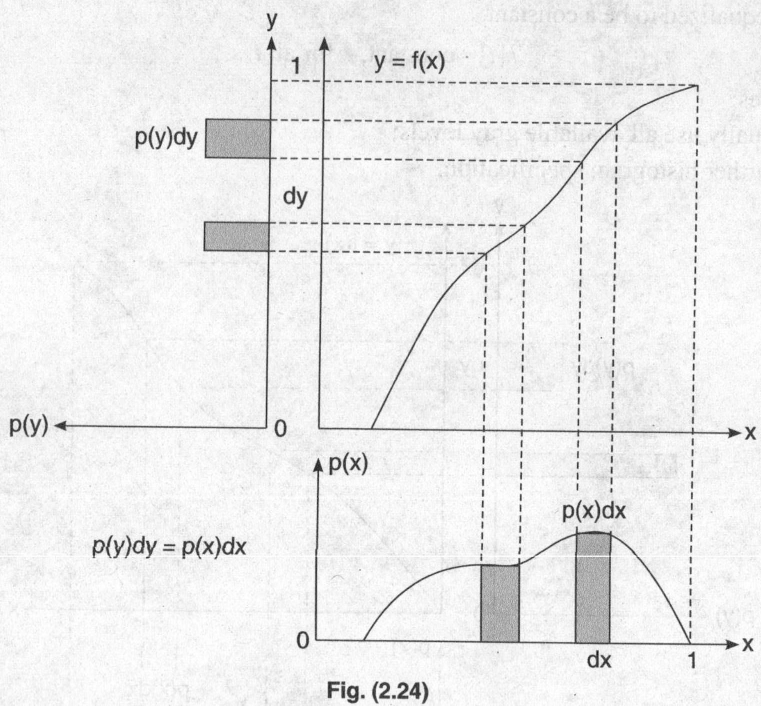

Fig. (2.24)

For discrete gray levels, the gray level of the input takes one of the discrete values: $x \in \{0, 1, \ldots, L-1\}$ and the continuous mapping function

$$y = f(x) = \int_0^x p(x)\, dx$$

becoems discrete:

$$y' = f(x) = \sum_{i=0}^{x} P_i$$

where p_i is the probability for the gray level of any given pixel to be i $(0 \le i \le L-1)$:

$$P_i = \frac{n_i}{\sum_{i=0}^{L-1} n_i} = \frac{n_i}{N} \quad \text{and} \quad \sum_{i=0}^{L-1} P_i = 1$$

The resulting function y' is in the range $0 \le y' \le 1$ and it needs to be converted to the gray levels $0 \le y \le L-1$ by one of the two following ways:

1. $y = [y'(L-1) + 0.5]$
2. $y = \left[\frac{y' - y_{\min}'}{1 - y_{\min}'}(L-1) + 0.5\right]$

where is the floor, or the integer part of a real number , and adding is for proper rounding. Note that while both conversions map to the highest gray level , the second conversion also maps to 0 to stretch the gray levels of the output image to occupy the entire dynamic range $0 \le y \le L-1$.

Example : Assume the images have $64 \times 64 = 4096$ pixels in 8 gray levels. The following table shows the equalization process corresponding to the two conversion methods above:

x_i	n_i	$P_i = n_i/N$	$y' = F_i$	y_j^1	P_j^1	F_j^1	y_j^2	P_j^2	F_j^2
0/7	790	0.19	0.19	1/7	0.19	0.19	0/7	0.19	0.19
1/7	1023	0.25	0.44	3/7	0.25	0.44	2/7	0.25	0.44
2/7	850	0.21	0.65	5/7	0.21	0.65	4/7	0.21	0.65
3/7	656	0.16	0.81	6/7			5/7	0.16	0.81
4/7	329	0.08	0.89	6/7	0.24	0.89	6/7	0.08	0.89
5/7	245	0.06	0.95	7/7			7/7		
6/7	122	0.03	0.98	7/7			7/7		
7/7	81	0.02	1.00	7/7	0.11	1.00	7/7	0.11	1.00

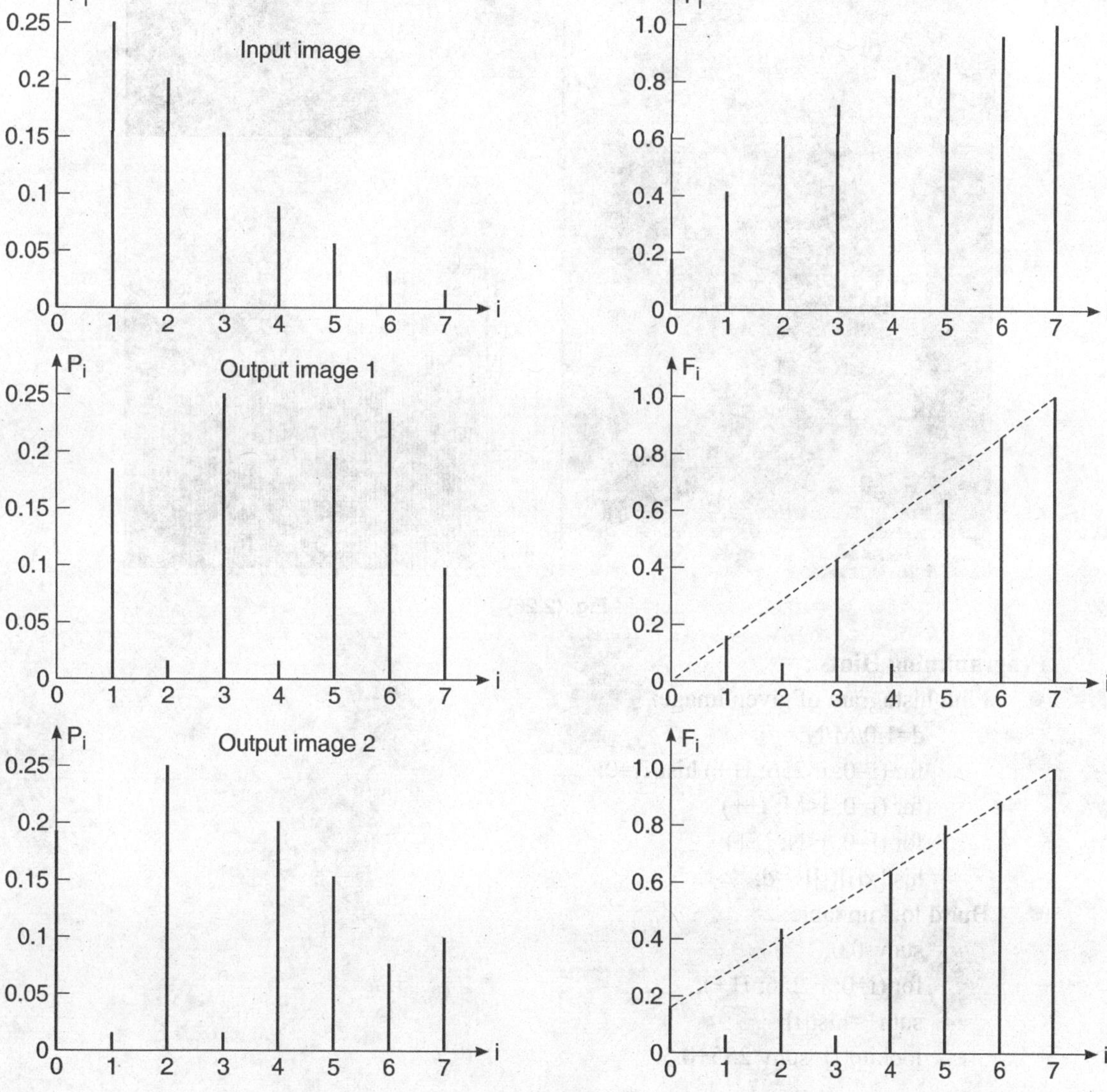

Fig. (2.25)

In the following example, the histogram of a given image is equalized. Although the resulting histogram may not look constant, but the cumulative histogram is a exact linear ramp indicating that the density histogram is indeed equalized. The density histogram is not guaranteed to be a constant because the pixels of the same gray level cannot be separated to satisfy a constant distribution.

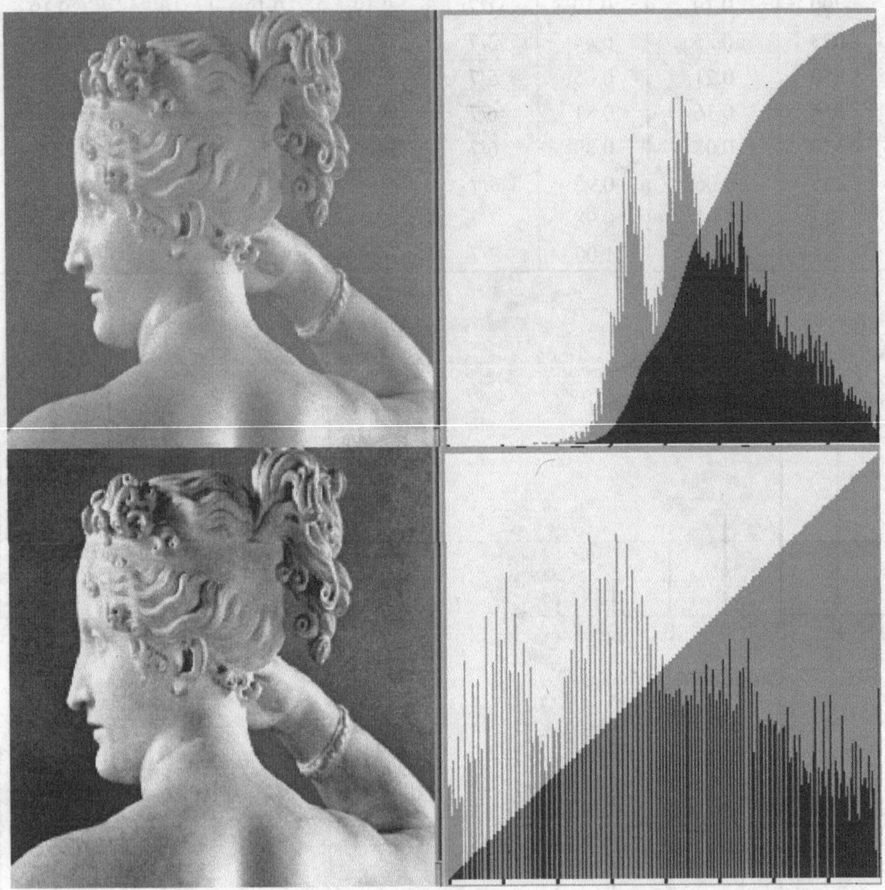

Fig. (2.26)

Programming Hints :

- Find histogram of given image:

```
d=1.0/M/N;
for (i=0; i<256; i++) hist[i]=0:
for (i=0; i<M; i++)
for (j=0; j<N; j++)
hist[x[i][j]]+=d;
```

- Build lookup table:

```
sum=0.0;
for (i=0; i<256; i++);
sum+=hist[i];
lookup[i]=sum*255+0.5;
```

- Image Mapping:

```
for (i=0; i<M; i++)
for (j=0; j<N; j++)
y[i][j]=lookup[x[i][j]];
```

2.7 LOCAL ENHANCEMENT

The histogram processing methods discussed in the previous two sections are global, in the sense that pixels are modified by a transformation function based on the gray-level content of an entire image. Although this global approach is suitable for overall enhancement, there are cases in which it is necessary to enhance details over small areas in an image. The number of pixels in these areas may have negligible influence on the computation of a global transformation whose shape does not necessarily guarantee the desired local enhancement.

The solution is to devise transformation functions based on the gray-level distribution or other properties in the neighborhood of every pixel in the image. The local histogram processing is used for the sake of clarity and continuity.

The histogram processing techniques previously described are easily adaptable to local enhancement. The procedure is to define a square or rectangular neighborhood and move the center of this area from pixel to pixel. At each location, the histogram of the points in the neighborhood is computed and either a histogram equalization or histogram specification transformation function is obtained. This function is finally used to map the gray level of the pixel centered in the neighborhood. The center of the neighborhood region is then moved to an adjacent pixel location and the procedure is repeated. Since only one new row or column of the neighborhood changes during a pixel-to-pixel translation of the region, updating the histogram obtained in the previous location with the new data introduced at each motion step is possible. This approach has obvious advantages over repeatedly computing the histogram over all pixels in the neighborhood region each time the region is moved one pixel location. Another approach used some times to reduce computation is to utilize non overlapping regions, but this method usually produces an undesirable checkerboard effect.

Figure 2.17(a) shows an image that has been slightly blurred to reduce its noise content, Figure 2.17(b) shows the result of global histogram equalization. As is often the case when this technique is applied to smooth, noisy areas, Fig. 2.17(b) shows considerable enhancement of the noise, with a slight increase in contrast. Note that no new structural details were brought out by this method. However, local histogram equalization using a 7*7 neighborhood revealed the presence of small squares inside the larger dark squares. The small squares were too close in gray level to the larger ones, and their sizes were

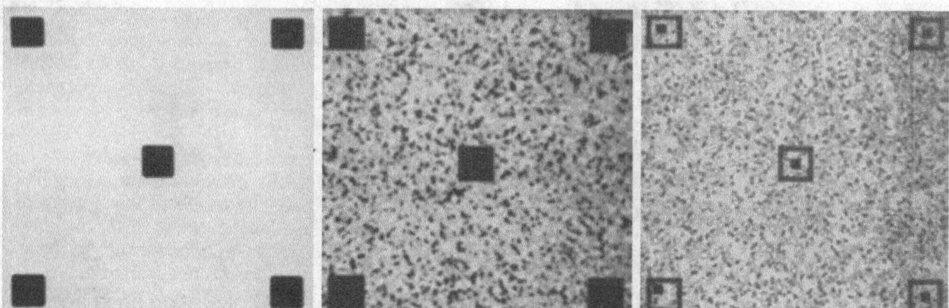

Fig. (2.27) (a) Original image (b) Result of global histogram equalization (c) Result of local histogram equalization using a 7 * 7 neighbourhood about each pixel.

too small to influence global histogram equalization significantly. Note also the finer noise texture in Fig. 2.17(c), a result of local processing using relatively small neighborhoods.

■ 2.8 ENHANCEMENT USING ARITHMETIC/LOGIC OPERATIONS

Arithmetic/logic operations involving images are performed on a pixel-by-pixel basis between two or more images (this excludes the logic operation NOT, which is performed on a single image). As an example, subtraction of two images results in a new image whose pixel at coordinates (x, y) is the difference between the pixels in that same location in the two images being subtracted. Depending on the hardware and/or software being used, the actual mechanics of implementing arithmetic/logic operations can be done sequentially, one pixel at a time, or in parallel, where all operations are performed simultaneously.

Logic operations similarly operate on a pixel-by-pixel basis†. We need only be concerned with the ability to implement the AND, OR, and NOT logic operators because these three operators are functionally complete. In other words, any other logic operator can be implemented by using only these three basic functions. When dealing with logic operations on gray-scale images, pixel values are processed as strings of binary numbers. For example, performing the NOT operation on a black, 8-bit pixel (a string of eight 0's) produces a white pixel (a string of eight 1's). Intermediate values are processed the same way, changing all 1's to 0's and vice versa. Thus, the NOT logic operator performs the same function as the negative transformation of Eq. (2.1). The AND and OR operations are used for masking; that is, for selecting sub-images in an image, as illustrated in Fig. 2.18. In the AND and OR image masks, light represents a binary 1 and dark represents a binary 0. Masking sometimes is referred to as region of interest (ROI) processing. In terms of enhancement, masking is used primarily to isolate an area for processing.

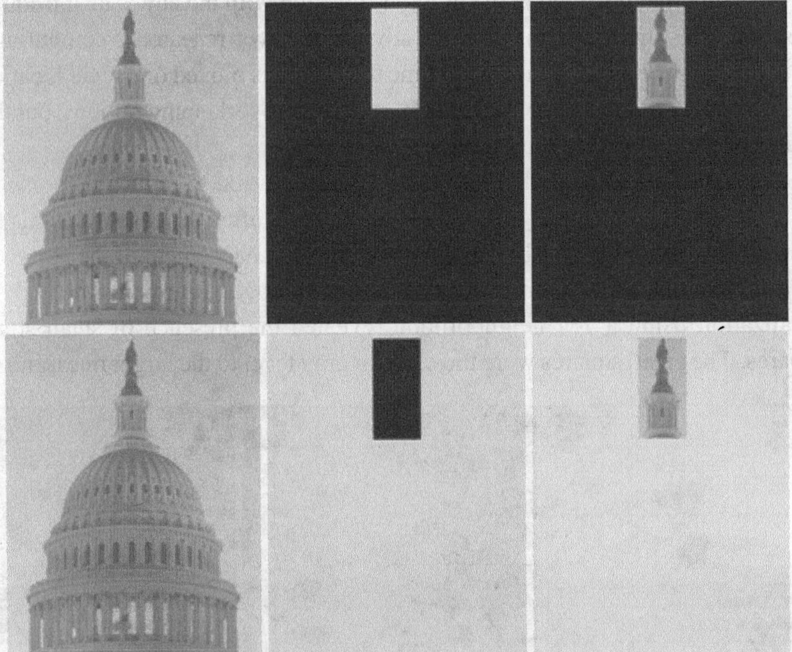

Fig. (2.28) (a) Original image, (b) AND image mask, (c) Result of the AND operation on images (a) and (b), (d) Original image, (e) OR image mask, (f) Result of operation OR on images (d) and (e).

This is done to highlight that area and differentiate it from the rest of the image. Logic operations also are used frequently in conjunction with morphological operations. Of the four arithmetic operations, subtraction and addition (in that order) are the most useful for image enhancement. We consider division of two images simply as multiplication of one image by the reciprocal of the other. Aside from the obvious operation of multiplying an image by a constant to increase its average gray level, image multiplication finds use in enhancement primarily as a masking operation that is more general than the logical masks discussed in the previous paragraph. In other words, multiplication of one image by another can be used to implement gray-level, rather than binary, masks.

2.9 IMAGE SUBTRACTION

The difference between two images f(x, y) and h(x, y), expressed as

$$g(x, y) = f(x, y) - h(x, y) \qquad \ldots(2.6)$$

is obtained by computing the difference between all pairs of corresponding pixels from f and h. The key usefulness of subtraction is the enhancement of differences between images. We illustrate this concept by the higher-order bit planes of an image carry a significant amount of visually relevant detail, while the lower planes contribute more to fine (often imperceptible) detail. Figure 2.19 (a) shows the fractal image used earlier to illustrate the concept of bit planes. Figure 2.19(b) shows the result of discarding (setting to zero) the four least significant bit planes of the original image. The images are nearly identical visually, with the exception of a very slight drop in overall contrast due to less variability of the gray level values in the image of Fig. 2.19(b).The pixel-by-pixel difference between these two images is shown in Fig.

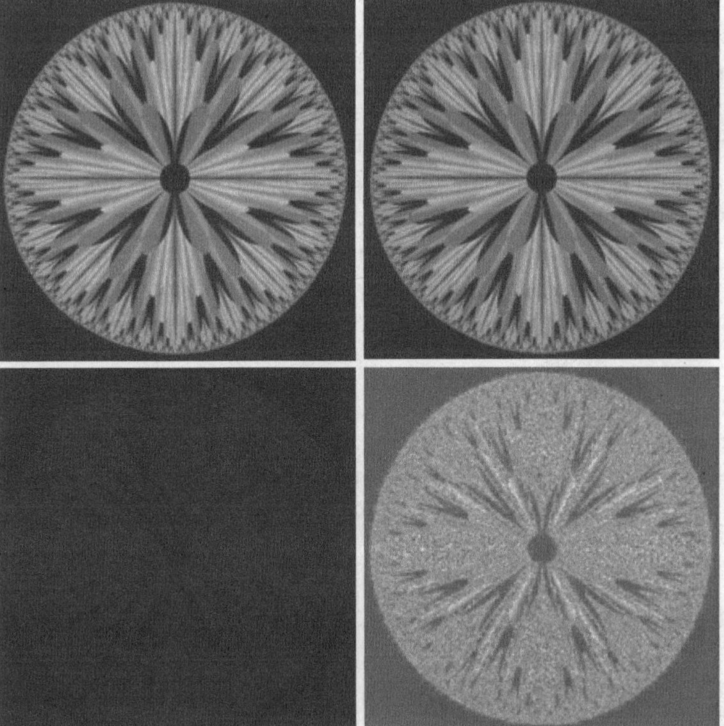

Fig. (2.29) (a) Original fractal image, (b) Result of setting the four lower-order bit planes to zero, (c) Difference between (a) and (b), (d) Histogram equalized difference image.

2.19(c).The differences in pixel values are so small that the difference image appears nearly black when displayed on an 8-bit display. In order to bring out more detail, we can perform a contrast stretching transformation. We chose histogram equalization, but an appropriate power-law transformation would have done the job also .The result is shown in Fig.2.19d).This is a very useful image for evaluating the effect of setting to zero the lower-order planes.

Eample : Use of image subtraction in mask mode radiography.

One of the most commercially successful and beneficial uses of image subtraction is in the area of medical imaging called mask mode radiography. In this case h(x, y), the mask, is an X-ray image of a region of a patient's body captured by an intensified TV camera (instead of traditional X-ray film) located opposite an X-ray source. The procedure consists of injecting a contrast medium into the patient's bloodstream, taking a series of images of the same anatomical region as h(x, y), and subtracting this mask from the series of incoming images after injection of the contrast medium. The net effect of subtracting the mask from each sample in the incoming stream of TV images is that the areas that are different between f(x, y) and h(x, y) appear in the output image as enhanced detail. Because images can be captured at TV rates, this procedure in essence gives a movie showing how the contrast medium propagates through the various arteries in the area being observed.

Figure 2.20(a) shows an X-ray image of the top of a patient's head prior to injection of an iodine medium into the bloodstream. The camera yielding this image was positioned above the patient's head, looking down. As a reference point, the bright spot in the lower one-third of the image is the core of the spinal column. Figure 2.20(b) shows the difference between the mask (Fig. 2.20a) and an image taken some time after the medium was introduced into the bloodstream. The bright arterial paths carrying the medium are unmistakably enhanced in Fig. 2.20(b).These arteries appear quite bright because they are not subtracted out (that is, they are not part of the mask image).The overall background is much darker than that in Fig. 2.20(a) because differences between areas of little change yield low values, which in turn appear as dark shades of gray in the difference image. Note, for instance, that the spinal cord, which is bright in Fig. 2.20(a), appears quite dark in Fig. 2.20(b) as a result of subtraction.

A few comments on implementation are an order before we leave this section. In practice, most images are displayed using 8 bits (even 24-bit color images consists of three separate 8-bit channels). Thus, we expect image values not to be outside the range from 0 to 255.The values in a difference image can range from a minimum of –255 to a maximum of 255, so some sort of scaling is required to display the re-

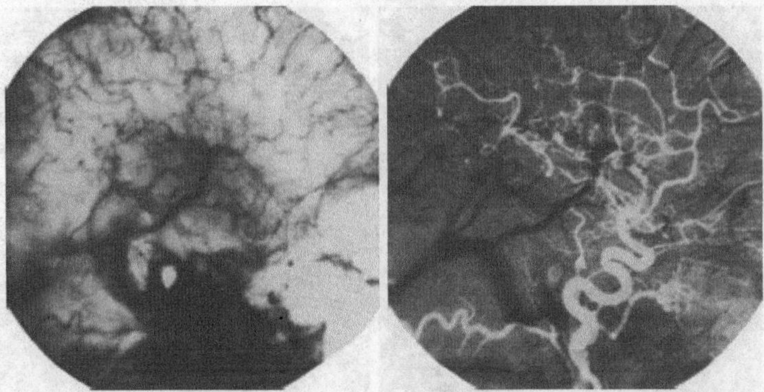

Fig. (2.30) Enhancement by image subtraction (a) Mask image, (b) An image (taken after injection of a contrast medium into the bloodstream) with mask subtracted out.

sults. There are two principal ways to scale a difference image. One method is to add 255 to every pixel and then divide by 2. It is not guaranteed that the values will cover the entire 8-bit range from 0 to 255, but all pixel values definitely will be within this range. This method is fast and simple to implement, but it has the limitations that the full range of the display may not be utilized and, potentially more serious, the truncation inherent in the division by 2 will generally cause loss in accuracy.

If more accuracy and full coverage of the 8-bit range are desired, then we can resort to another approach. First, the value of the minimum difference is obtained and its negative added to all the pixels in the difference image (this will create a modified difference image whose minimum values is 0). Then, all the pixels in the image are scaled to the interval [0, 255] by multiplying each pixel by the quantity 255_Max, where Max is the maximum pixel value in the modified difference image.

It is evident that this approach is considerably more complex and difficult to implement. Before leaving this section we note also that change detection via image subtraction finds another major application in the area of segmentation, which is the topic of Chapter 10. Basically, segmentation techniques attempt to subdivide an image into regions based on a specified criterion. Image subtraction for segmentation is used when the criterion is "changes." For instance, in tracking (segmenting) moving vehicles in a sequence of images, subtraction is used to remove all stationary components in an image. What is left should be the moving elements in the image, plus noise.

2.10 IMAGE AVERAGING

Consider a noisy image g(x, y) formed by the addition of noise h(x, y) to an original image f(x, y); that is,

$$g(x, y) = f(x, y) + g(x, y) \qquad \text{...(2.7)}$$

where the assumption is that at every pair of coordinates (x, y) the noise is uncorrelated† and has zero average value. The objective of the following procedure is to reduce the noise content by adding a set of noisy images, {gi(x, y)}.

If the noise satisfies the constraints just stated, it can be shown that if an is formed by averaging K different noisy images,

$$\bar{g}(x, y) = \frac{1}{K}\sum_{i=1}^{K} g_i\,(x, y) \qquad \text{...(2.8)}$$

then it follows that

$$E\{\bar{g}(x, y)\} = f(x, y) \qquad \text{...(2.9)}$$

and

$$\sigma^2_{\bar{g}(x, y)} = \frac{1}{K}\sigma^2_{g(x, y)} \qquad \text{...(2.10)}$$

where is the expected value of and and are the variances of , all at coordinates (x, y). The standard deviation at any point in the average image is

$$\sigma_{\bar{g}(x, y)} = \frac{1}{\sqrt{K}}(r_{g(x, y)}) \qquad \text{...(2.11)}$$

As K increases, Eqs. (2.10) and (2.11) indicate that the variability (noise) of the pixel values at each location (x, y) decreases. Because = f(x, y), this means that approaches f(x, y) as the number of noisy images used in the averaging process increases. In practice, the images gi(x, y) must be registered (aligned) in order to avoid the introduction of blurring and other artifacts in the output image.

Example : Noise reduction by image averaging.

An important application of image averaging is in the field of astronomy, where imaging with very low light levels is routine, causing sensor noise frequently to render single images virtually useless for analysis. Figure 2.21(a) shows an image of a galaxy pair called NGC 3314, taken by NASA's Hubble Space Telescope with a wide field planetary camera. NGC 3314 lies about 140 million light-years from Earth, in the direction of the southern-hemisphere constellation Hydra. The bright stars forming a pin-wheel shape near the center of the front galaxy have formed recently from interstellar gas and dust.

Figure 2.21(b) shows the same image, but corrupted by uncorrelated Gaussian noise with zero mean and a standard deviation of 64 gray levels. This image is useless for all practical purposes. Figures 2.21(c) through (f) show the results of averaging 8, 16, 64, and 128 images, respectively. We see that the result obtained with K=128 is reasonably close to the original in visual appearance. We can get a better appreciation from Fig. 2.22 for how reduction in the visual appearance of noise takes place as a function of increasing K. This figure shows the difference images between the original [Fig.2.21 (a)] and each of

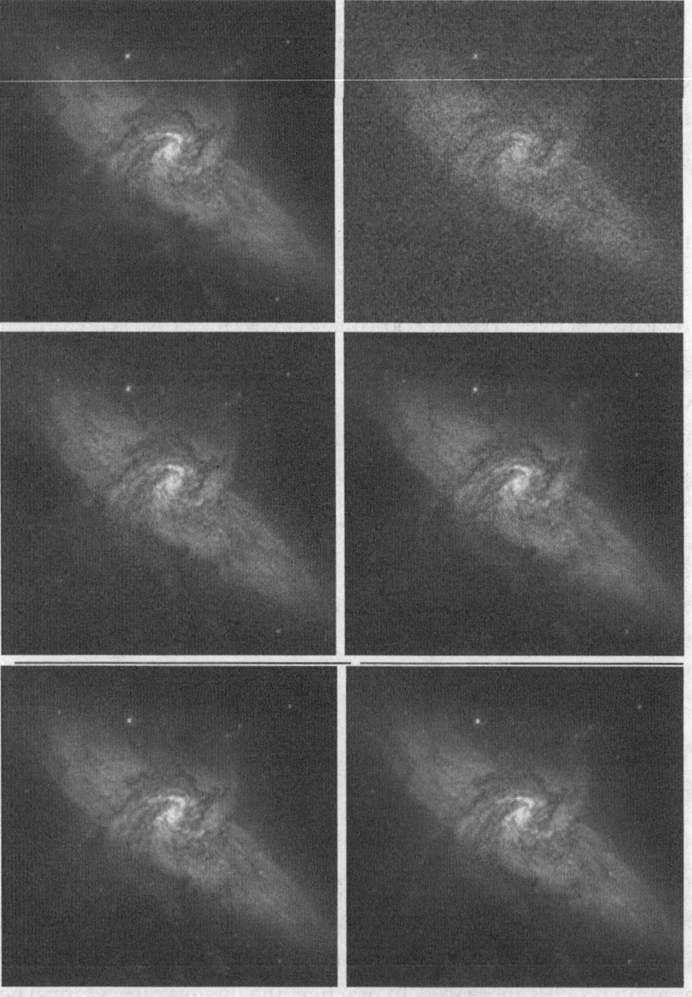

Fig. (2.31) (a) Image of Galaxy Pair NGC 3314, (b) Image corrupted by additive Gaussian noise with zero mean and a standard deviation of 64 gray levels, (c)-(f) Results of averaging K = 8, 16, 64 and 128 noisy images.

the averaged images in Figs. 2.21(c) through (f).The histograms corresponding to the difference images are also shown in the figure. As usual, the vertical scale in the histograms represents number of pixels and is in the range C0, 2.6*104 D.

The horizontal scale represents gray level and is in the range [0, 255].Notice in the histograms that the mean and standard deviation of the difference images decrease as K increases. This is as expected because, according to Eqs. (2.8) and (2.9), the average image should approach the original as K increases. We can also see the effect of a decreasing mean in the difference images on the left column of Fig. 2.22, which become darker as the K increases.

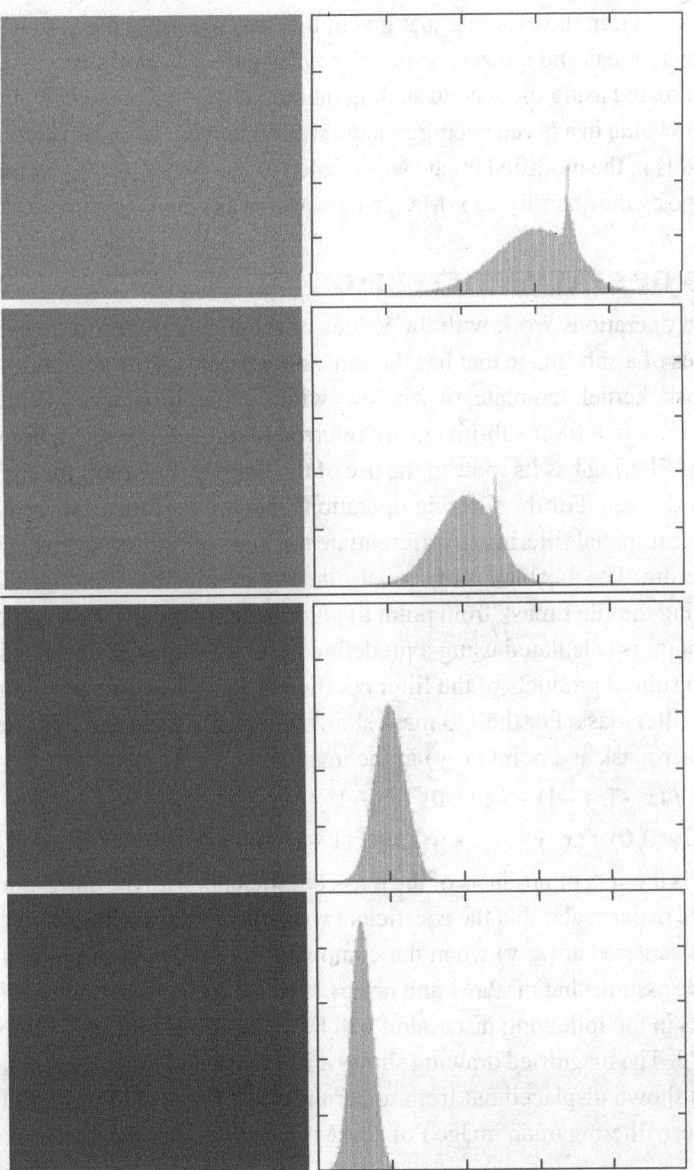

Fig. (2.32) (a) From top to bottom : Difference images between fig. (2.31a) and the four images in figs. (2.31c) through f, respectively, (b) Corresponding histograms.

Addition is the discrete formulation of continuous integration. In astronomical observations, a process equivalent to the method just described is to use the integrating capabilities of CCD or similar sensors for noise reduction by observing the same scene over long periods of time. The net effect, however, is analogous to the procedure just discussed. Cooling the sensor further reduces its noise level.

As in the case of image subtraction, adding two or more 8-bit images requires special care when it comes to displaying the result on an 8-bit display. The values in the sum of K, 8-bit images can range from 0 to 255*K. Scaling back to 8 bits in this case consists simply of dividing the result by K. Naturally, some accuracy will be lost in the process, but this is unavoidable if the display has to be limited to 8 bits.

It is possible in some implementations of image averaging to have negative values when noise is added to an image. In fact, in the example just given, this was precisely the case because Gaussian random variables with zero mean and nonzero variance have negative as well as positive values. The images in the example were scaled using the second scaling method discussed at the end of the previous section. That is, the minimum value in a given average image was obtained and its negative was added to the image. Then all the pixels in the modified image were scaled to the range [0, 255] by multiplying each pixel in the modified image by the quantity 255_Max, where Max was the maximum pixel value in that image.

2.11 BASICS OF SPATIAL FILTERING

Some neighborhood operations work with the values of the image pixels in the neighborhood and the corresponding values of a sub-image that has the same dimensions as the neighborhood. The sub-image is called a filter, mask, kernel, template, or window, with the first three terms being the most prevalent terminology. The values in a filter sub-image are referred to as coefficients, rather than pixels.

The concept of filtering has its roots in the use of the Fourier transform for signal processing in the so-called frequency domain. For the filtering operations that are performed directly on the pixels of an image. We use the term spatial filtering to differentiate this type of process from the more traditional frequency domain filtering. The mechanics of spatial filtering are illustrated in Fig. 2.23.The process consists simply of moving the filter mask from point to point in an image. At each point (x, y), the response of the filter at that point is calculated using a predefined relationship. For linear spatial filtering, the response is given by a sum of products of the filter coefficients and the corresponding image pixels in the area spanned by the filter mask. For the 3*3 mask shown in Fig. 2.23, the result (or response), R, of linear filtering with the filter mask at a point (x, y) in the image is

$$R = w(-1,-1)\, f(x-1,\ y-1) + w(-1,0)\, f(x-1,\ y) + \\ w(0,0)\, f(x,\ y) + \ldots + w(1,0)\, f(x+1,\ y) + w(1,1)\, f(x+1,\ y+1)$$

Which we see is the sum of products of the mask coefficients with the corresponding pixels directly under the mask. Note in particular that the coefficient w(0, 0) coincides with image value f(x, y), indicating that the mask is centered at (x, y) when the computation of the sum of products takes place. For a mask of size m*n, we assume that m=2a+1 and n=2b+1, where a and b are nonnegative integers. All this says is that our focus in the following discussion will be on masks of odd sizes, with the smallest meaningful size being 3*3. The magnified drawing shows a 3*3 mask and the image section directly under it; the image section is shown displaced out from under the mask for ease of readability.

In general, linear filtering of an image f of size M*N with a filter mask of size m*n is given by the expression:

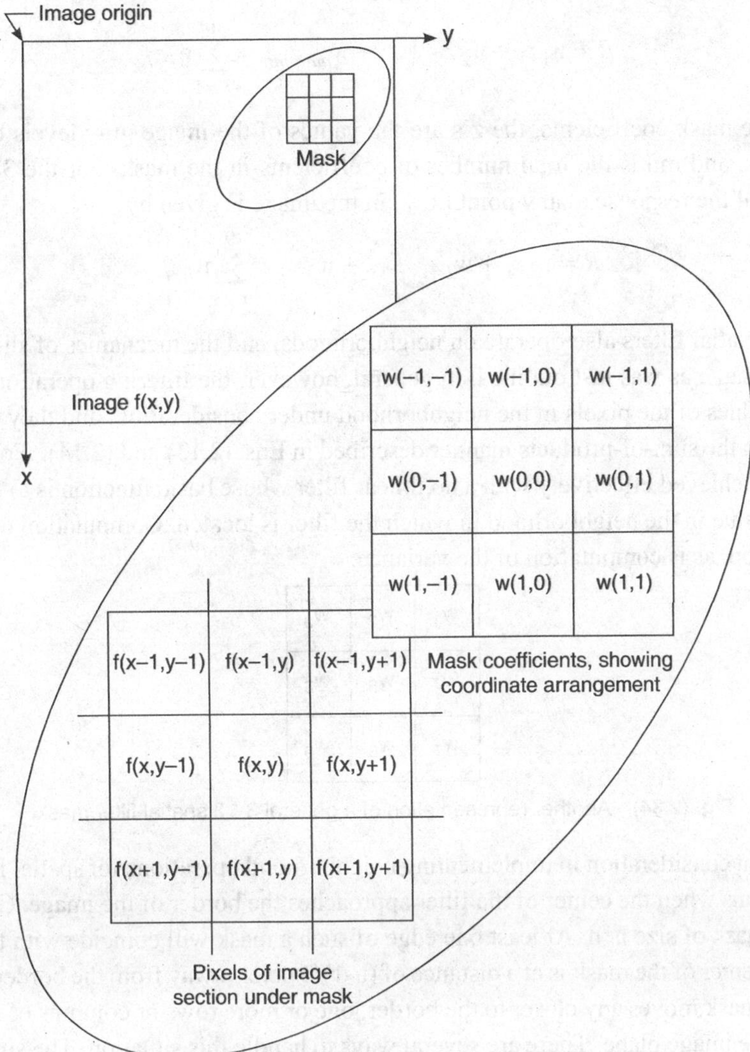

Fig. (2.33) The mechanics of spatial filtering.

$$g(x, y) = \sum_{s=-a}^{a} \sum_{i=-a}^{a} w(s, t)\, f(x+s, y+t) \qquad \ldots(2.12)$$

where, from the previous paragraph, a= (m-1)/2 and b=(n-1)/2. To generate a complete filtered image this equation must be applied for x=0, 1, 2, p , M-1 and y=0, 1, 2, p , N-1. In this way, we are assured that the mask processes all pixels in the image. It is easily verified when m=n=3that this expression reduces to the example given in the previous paragraph. The process of linear filtering given in Eq. (2.12) is similar to a frequency domain concept called convolution. For this reason, linear spatial filtering often is referred to as "convolving a mask with an image." Similarly, filter masks are sometimes called convolution masks. The term convolution kernel also is in common use. When interest lies on the response, R, of an m*n mask at any point (x, y), and not on the mechanics of implementing mask convolution, it is common practice to simplify the notation by using the following expression:

$$R = w_1 z_1 + w_2 z_2 + \ldots + w_{mn} z_{mn} = \sum_{i=1}^{mn} w_i z_i \qquad \ldots(2.13)$$

where the w's are mask coefficients, the z's are the values of the image gray levels corresponding to those coefficients, and mn is the total number of coefficients in the mask. For the 3*3 general mask shown in Fig. 2.24 the response at any point (x, y) in the image is given by

$$R = w_1 z_1 + w_2 z_2 + \ldots + w_9 z_9 = \sum_{i=1}^{9} w_i z_i \qquad \ldots(2.14)$$

Nonlinear spatial filters also operate on neighborhoods, and the mechanics of sliding a mask past an image are the same as was just outlined. In general, however, the filtering operation is based conditionally on the values of the pixels in the neighborhood under consideration, and they do not explicitly use coefficients in the sum-of-products manner described in Eqs. (2.13) and (2.14). For example, noise reduction can be achieved effectively with a nonlinear filter whose basic function is to compute the median gray-level value in the neighborhood in which the filter is located. Computation of the median is a nonlinear operation, as is computation of the variance.

w_1	w_2	w_3
w_4	w_5	w_6
w_7	w_8	w_9

Fig. (2.34) Another representation of a general 3 * 3 spatial filter mask.

An important consideration in implementing neighborhood operations for spatial filtering is the issue of what happens when the center of the filter approaches the border of the image. Consider for simplicity a square mask of size n*n. At least one edge of such a mask will coincide with the border of the image when the center of the mask is at a distance of (n-1)/2 pixels away from the border of the image. If the center of the mask moves any closer to the border, one or more rows or columns of the mask will be located outside the image plane. There are several ways to handle this situation. The simplest is to limit the excursions of the center of the mask to be at a distance no less than (n-1)/2 pixels from the border. The resulting filtered image will be smaller than the original, but all the pixels in the filtered imaged will have been processed with the full mask.

If the result is required to be the same size as the original, then the approach typically employed is to filter all pixels only with the section of the mask that is fully contained in the image. With this approach, there will be bands of pixels near the border that will have been processed with a partial filter mask. Other approaches include "padding" the image by adding rows and columns of 0's (or other constant gray level), or padding by replicating rows or columns. The padding is then stripped off at the end of the process. This keeps the size of the filtered image the same as the original, but the values of the padding will have an effect near the edges that becomes more prevalent as the size of the mask increases. The only way to obtain a perfectly filtered result is to accept a somewhat smaller filtered image by limiting the excursions of the center of the filter mask to a distance no less than (n-1)/2 pixels from the border of the original image.

2.12 SMOOTHING SPATIAL FILTERS

Smoothing filters are used for blurring and for noise reduction. Blurring is used in preprocessing steps, such as removal of small details from an image prior to (large) object extraction, and bridging of small gaps in lines or curves. Noise reduction can be accomplished by blurring with a linear filter and also by nonlinear filtering.

2.12.1 Smoothing Linear Filters

The output (response) of a smoothing, linear spatial filter is simply the average of the pixels contained in the neighborhood of the filter mask. These filters sometimes are called averaging filters. They also are referred to a low pass filters.

The idea behind smoothing filters is straightforward. By replacing the value of every pixel in an image by the average of the gray levels in the neighborhood defined by the filter mask, this process results in an image with reduced "sharp" transitions in gray levels. Because random noise typically consists of sharp transitions in gray levels, the most obvious application of smoothing is noise reduction. However, edges (which almost always are desirable features of an image) also are characterized by sharp transitions in gray levels, so averaging filters have the undesirable side effect that they blur edges. Another application of this type of process includes the smoothing of false contours that result from using an insufficient number of gray levels.

A major use of averaging filters is in the reduction of "irrelevant" detail in an image. By "irrelevant" we mean pixel regions that are small with respect to the size of the filter mask. Figure 2.25 shows two 3*3 smoothing filters. Use of the first filter yields the standard average of the pixels under the mask. This can best be seen by substituting the coefficients of the mask into Eq. (2.14):

$$R = \frac{1}{9}\sum_{i=1}^{9} z_i$$

Which is the average of the gray levels of the pixels in the 3*3 neighborhood defined by the mask. Note that, instead of being 1/9, the coefficients of the filter are all 1's.The idea here is that it is computationally more efficient to have coefficients valued 1. At the end of the filtering process the entire image is divided by 9.An m*n mask would have a normalizing constant equal to 1/mn. A spatial averaging filter in which all coefficients are equal is sometimes called a box filter.

The second mask shown in Fig. 2.25 is a little more interesting. This mask yields a so-called weighted average, terminology used to indicate that pixels are multiplied by different coefficients, thus giving more importance (weight) to some pixels at the expense of others. In the mask shown in Fig. 2.25(b) the pixel at the center of the mask is multiplied by a higher value than any other, thus giving this pixel more importance in the calculation of the average.

The other pixels are inversely weighted as a function of their distance from the center of the mask. The diagonal terms are further away from the center than the orthogonal neighbors and are weighed less than these immediate neighbors of the center pixel. The basic strategy behind weighing the center point the highest and then reducing the value of the coefficients as a function of increasing distance from the origin is simply an attempt to reduce blurring in the smoothing process. We could have picked other weights to accomplish the same general objective.

However, the sum of all the coefficients in the mask of Fig. 2.25(b) is equal to 16, an attractive feature for computer implementation because it has an integer power of 2. In practice, it is difficult in gen-

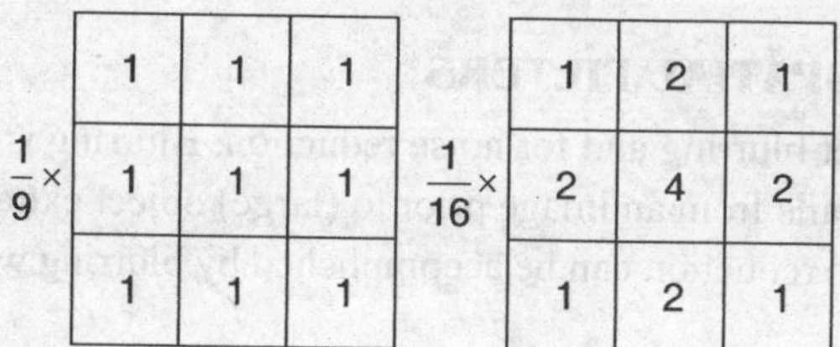

Fig. (2.35) Two 3 * 3 smoothing (averaging) filter masks.

eral to see differences between images smoothed by using either of the masks in Fig. 2.25, or similar arrangements, because the area these masks span at any one location in an image is so small.

The constant multiplier in front of each mask is equal to the sum of the values of its coefficients, as is required to compute an average.

With reference to Eq. (2.7), the general implementation for filtering an M*N image with a weighted averaging filter of size m*n (m and n odd) is given by the expression:

$$g(x, y) = \frac{\sum_{s=-a}^{a} \sum_{i=-b}^{b} w(s, t)\, f(x+s, y+t)}{\sum_{s=-a}^{a} \sum_{i=-b}^{b} w(s, t)} \qquad \ldots(2.15)$$

The parameters in this equation are as defined in Eq. (2.7). As before, it is understood that the complete filtered image is obtained by applying Eq. (1) for x=0, 1, 2, p , M-1 and y=0, 1, 2, p , N-1. The denominator in Eq. (2.7) is simply the sum of the mask coefficients and, therefore, it is a constant that needs to be computed only once. Typically, this scale factor is applied to all the pixels of the output image after the filtering process is completed.

2.12.2 Order-Statistics Filters

Order-statistics filters are nonlinear spatial filters whose response is based on ordering (ranking) the pixels contained in the image area encompassed by the filter, and then replacing the value of the center pixel with the value determined by the ranking result. The best-known example in this category is the median filter, which, as its name implies, replaces the value of a pixel by the median of the gray levels in the neighborhood of that pixel (the original value of the pixel is included in the computation of the median).

Median filters are quite popular because, for certain types of random noise, they provide excellent noise-reduction capabilities, with considerably less blurring than linear smoothing filters of similar size. Median filters are particularly effective in the presence of impulse noise, also called salt-and-pepper noise because of its appearance as white and black dots superimposed on an image. The median, j, of a set of values is such that half the values in the set are less than or equal to j, and half are greater than or equal to j. In order to perform median filtering at a point in an image, we first sort the values of the pixel in question and its neighbors, determine their median, and assign this value to that pixel. For example, in a 3*3 neighborhood the median is the 5th largest value, in a 5*5 neighborhood the 13th largest value, and so on. When several values in a neighborhood are the same, all equal values are grouped. For example, suppose that a 3*3 neighborhood has values (10, 20, 20, 20, 15, 20, 20, 25, 100). These values are sorted as (10, 15, 20, 20, 20, 20, 20, 25, 100), which results in a median of 20. Thus, the principal function of median filters is to force points with distinct gray levels to be more like their neighbors. In fact, isolated clusters of pixels that are light or dark with respect to their neighbors, and whose area is less than n2/2 (one-half the filter area), are eliminated by an n*n median filter. In this case "eliminated" means forced to the median intensity of the neighbors. Larger clusters are affected considerably less.

Although the median filter is by far the most useful order-statistics filter in image processing, it is by no means the only one. The median represents the 50th percentile of a ranked set of numbers, but the reader will recall from basic statistics that ranking lends itself to many other possibilities. For example, using the 100th percentile results in the so-called max filter, which is useful in finding the brightest points in an image. The response of a 3*3 max filter is given by R=max{zk (k=1, 2,3———, 9)}.The 0th percentile filter is the min filter, used for the opposite purpose.

■ 2.13 SHARPENING SPATIAL FILTERS

The principal objective of sharpening is to highlight fine detail in an image or to enhance detail that has been blurred, either in error or as a natural effect of a particular method of image acquisition. Uses of image sharpening vary and include applications ranging from electronic printing and medical imaging to industrial inspection and autonomous guidance in military systems.

The image blurring could be accomplished in the spatial domain by pixel averaging in a neighborhood. Since averaging is analogous to integration, it is logical to conclude that sharpening could be accomplished by spatial differentiation. This, in fact, is the case, and the discussion deals with various ways of defining and implementing operators for sharpening by digital differentiation. Fundamentally, the strength of the response of a derivative operator is proportional to the degree of discontinuity of the image at the point at which the operator is applied. Thus, image differentiation enhances edges and other discontinuities (such as noise) and deemphasizes areas with slowly varying gray-level values.

2.13.1 Foundation

In the two sections that follow, we consider in some detail sharpening filters that are based on first- and second-order derivatives, respectively. Before proceeding with that discussion, however, we stop to look at some of the fundamental properties of these derivatives in a digital context. To simplify the explanation, we focus attention on one-dimensional derivatives. In particular, we are interested in the behavior of these derivatives in areas of constant gray level (flat segments), at the onset and end of discontinuities (step and ramp discontinuities), and along gray-level ramps. These types of discontinuities can be used to model noise points, lines, and edges in an image. The behavior of derivatives during transitions into and out of these image features also is of interest.

The derivatives of a digital function are defined in terms of differences. There are various ways to define these differences. However, we require that any definition we use for a first derivative

(1) Must be zero in flat segments (areas of constant gray-level values).
(2) Must be nonzero at the onset of a gray-level step or ramp.
(3) Must be nonzero along ramps.

Similarly, any definitions of a second derivative have following properties:

(1) Must be zero in flat areas.
(2) Must be nonzero at the onset and end of a gray-level step or ramp.
(3) Must be zero along ramps of constant slope.

Since we are dealing with digital quantities whose values are finite, the maximum possible gray-level change also is finite, and the shortest distance over which that change can occur is between adjacent pixels.

A basic definition of the first-order derivative of a one-dimensional function f(x) is the difference

$$\frac{\partial f}{\partial x} = f(x+1) - f(x)$$

We used a partial derivative here in order to keep the notation the same as when we consider an image function of two variables, f(x, y), at which time we will be dealing with partial derivatives along the two spatial axes. Use of a partial derivative in the present discussion does not affect in any way the nature of what we are trying to accomplish.

Similarly, we define a second-order derivative as the difference

$$\frac{\partial^2 f}{\partial x^2} = f(x+1) + f(x-1) - 2f(x)$$

It is easily verified that these two definitions satisfy the conditions stated previously regarding derivatives of the first and second order. To see this, and also to highlight the fundamental similarities and differences between first- and second- order derivatives in the context of image processing, consider the example shown in Fig. 2.26.

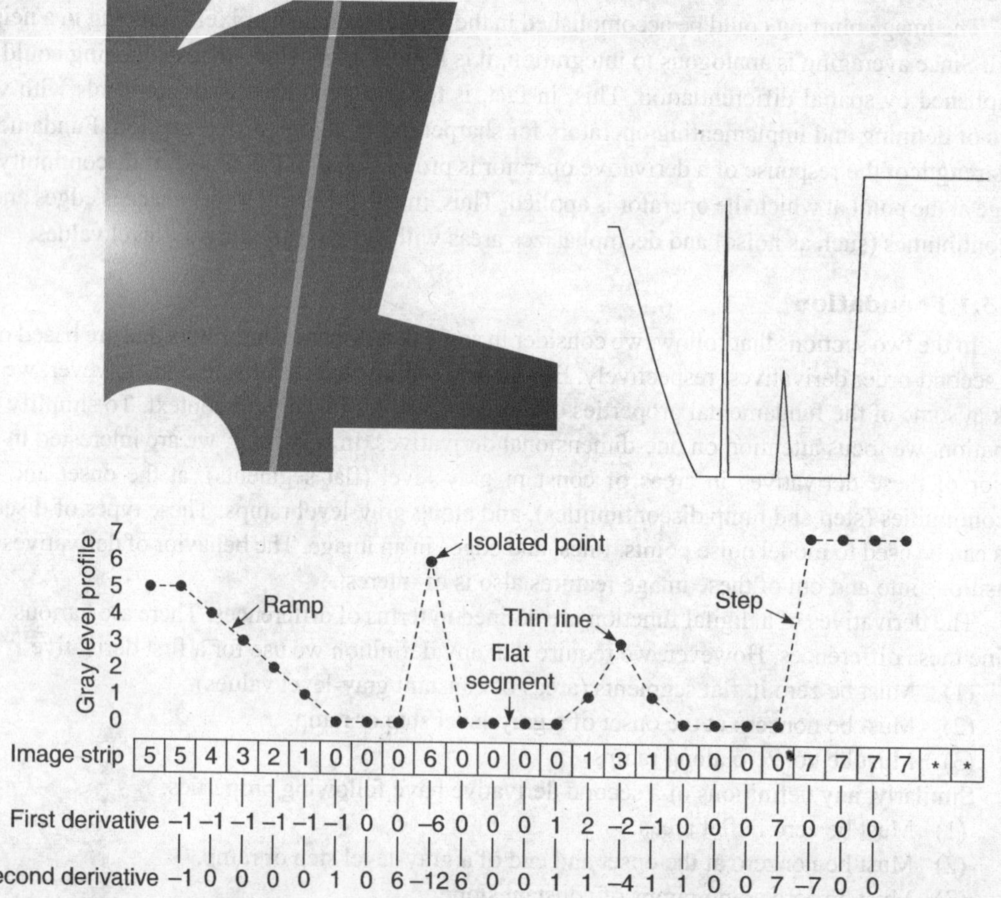

Fig. (2.36) (a) A simple image, (b) 1-D horizontal gray level profile along the center of the image and including the isolated noise point, (c) Simplified profile (the points are joined by dashed lines to simplify interpretation).

Figure 2.26(a) shows a simple image that contains various solid objects, a line, and a single noise point. Figure 2.26(b) shows a horizontal gray-level profile (scan line) of the image along the center and including the noise point. This profile is the one-dimensional function we will use for illustrations regarding this figure. Figure 2.26(c) shows a simplification of the profile, with just enough numbers to make it possible for us to analyze how the first- and second-order derivatives behave as they encounter a noise point, a line, and then the edge of an object. In our simplified diagram the transition in the ramp spans four pixels, the noise point is a single pixel, the line is three pixels thick, and the transition into the gray-level step takes place between adjacent pixels. The number of gray levels was simplified to only eight levels.

Let us consider the properties of the first and second derivatives as we traverse the profile from left to right. First, we note that the first-order derivative is nonzero along the entire ramp, while the second-order derivative is nonzero only at the onset and end of the ramp. Because edges in an image resemble this type of transition, we conclude that first-order derivatives produce "thick" edges and second-order derivatives, much finer ones. Next we encounter the isolated noise point. Here, the response at and around the point is much stronger for the second- than for the first-order derivative. Of course, this is not unexpected.

A second-order derivative is much more aggressive than a first-order derivative in enhancing sharp changes. Thus, we can expect a second-order derivative to enhance fine detail (including noise) much more than a first-order derivative. The thin line is a fine detail, and we see essentially the same difference between the two derivatives. If the maximum gray level of the line had been the same as the isolated point, the response of the second derivative would have been stronger for the latter.

Finally, in this case, the response of the two derivatives is the same at the gray-level step (in most cases when the transition into a step is not from zero, the second derivative will be weaker).We also note that the second derivative has a transition from positive back to negative. In an image, this shows as a thin double line. This "double-edge" effect is an issue, where we use derivatives for edge detection. It is of interest also to note that if the gray level of the thin line had been the same as the step, the response of the second derivative would have been stronger for the line than for the step.

In summary, comparing the response between first- and second-order derivatives, we arrive at the following conclusions.

(1) First-order derivatives generally produce thicker edges in an image.

(2) Second-order derivatives have a stronger response to fine detail, such as thin lines and isolated points.

(3) First order derivatives generally have a stronger response to a gray-level step. (4) Second- order derivatives produce a double response at step changes in gray level. We also note of second-order derivatives that, for similar changes in gray-level values in an image, their response is stronger to a line than to a step, and to a point than to a line.

In most applications, the second derivative is better suited than the first derivative for image enhancement because of the ability of the former to enhance fine detail. For this, and for reasons of simpler implementation and extensions, we will focus attention initially on uses of the second derivative for enhancement. Although the principle of use of first derivatives in image processing is for edge extraction, they do have important uses in image enhancement. In fact, we show in that they can be used in conjunction with the second derivative to obtain some impressive enhancement results.

2.13.2 Use of Second Derivatives for Enhancement–The Laplacian

The use of two-dimensional, second order derivatives for image enhancement is basically consists of defining a discrete formulation of the second-order derivative and then constructing a filter mask based on that formulation. We are interested in isotropic filters, whose response is independent of the direction of the discontinuities in the image to which the filter is applied. In other words, isotropic filters are rotation invariant; in the sense that rotating the image and then applying the filter gives the same result as applying the filter to the image first and then rotating the result.

Development of the Method

It can be shown that the simplest isotropic derivative operator is the Laplacian, which, for a function (image) f(x, y) of two variables, is defined as

$$\nabla^2 f = \frac{\partial^2 f}{\partial x^2} + \frac{\partial^2 f}{\partial y^2} \qquad \text{...(2.16)}$$

Because derivatives of any order are linear operations, the Laplacian is a linear operator. In order to be useful for digital image processing, this equation needs to be expressed in discrete form. There are several ways to define a digital Laplacian using neighborhoods. Whatever the definition, however, it has to satisfy the properties of a second derivative. The definition of the digital second derivative given in that section is one of the most used. Taking into account that we now have two variables.

We use the following notation for the partial second-order derivative in the x-direction:

$$\frac{\partial^2 f}{\partial^2 x^2} = f(x+1, y) + f(x-1, y) - 2f(x, y) \qquad \text{...(2.17)}$$

and, similarly in the y-direction, as

$$\frac{\partial^2 f}{\partial^2 y^2} = f(x, y+1) + f(x, y-1) - 2f(x, y) \qquad \text{...(2.18)}$$

The digital implementation of the two-dimensional Laplacian in Eq. (2.13-1) is Obtained by summing these two components:

$$\nabla^2 f = [f(x+1, y) + f(x-1, y) + f(x, y+1) + f(x, y-1) - 4f(x, y)] \qquad \text{...(2.19)}$$

This equation can be implemented using the mask shown in Fig. 2.27(a), which gives an isotropic result for rotations in increments of 90°. The mechanics of implementation are given in Eq. (2.16) and for the linear smoothing filters. We simply are using different coefficients here. The diagonal directions can be incorporated in the definition of the digital Laplacian by adding two more terms to Eq. (2.19), one for each of the two diagonal directions. The form of each new term is the same as either Eq. (2.17) or (2.18), but the coordinates are along the diagonals. Since each diagonal term also contains a –2f(x, y) term, the total subtracted from the difference terms now would be –8f(x, y). The mask used to implement this new definition is shown in Fig. 2.27(b). This mask yields isotropic results for increments of 45°. The other two masks shown in Fig. 2.27 also are used frequently in practice. They are based on a definition of the Laplacian that is the negative of the one we used here. As such, they yield equivalent results, but the difference in sign must be kept in mind when combining (by addition or subtraction) a Laplacian- filtered image with another image.

0	1	0	1	1	1
1	–4	1	1	–8	1
0	1	0	1	1	1

0	–1	0	–1	–1	–1
–1	–4	1	–1	8	–1
0	–1	0	–1	–1	–1

Fig. (2.37) (a) Filter mask used to implement the digital Laplacian, as defined in eq. (2.13-4), (b) Mask used to implement an extension of this equation that includes the diagonal neighbours, (c) and (d) Two other implementations of the Laplacian.

Because the Laplacian is a derivative operator, its use highlights gray-level discontinuities in an image and deemphasizes regions with slowly varying gray levels. This will tend to produce images that have grayish edge lines and other discontinuities, all superimposed on a dark, featureless background. Background features can be "recovered" while still preserving the sharpening effect of the Laplacian operation simply by adding the original and Laplacian images. As noted in the previous paragraph, it is important to keep in mind which definition of the Laplacian is used. If the definition used has a negative center coefficient, then we subtract, rather than add, the Laplacian image to obtain a sharpened result. Thus, the basic way in which we use the Laplacian for image enhancement is as follows:

$$g(x, y) = \begin{cases} f(x, y) - \nabla^2 f(x, y) & \text{if the center coefficient of the Laplacian mask is negative} \\ f(x, y) + \nabla^2 f(x, y) & \text{if the center coefficient of the Laplacian mask is positive} \end{cases} \quad \text{...(2.20)}$$

SUMMARY

- The principal objective of enhancement is to process an image so that the result is more suitable than the original image for a specific application. The word specific is important, because it establishes at the outset that the techniques discussed in this chapter are very much problem oriented.
- The term spatial domain refers to the image plane itself, and approaches in this category are based on direct manipulation of pixels in an image.
- Frequency domain processing techniques are based on modifying the Fourier transform of an image. Enhancement techniques based on various combinations of methods from these two categories are not unusual.
- Image enhancement is the improvement of digital image quality (wanted e.g. for visual inspection or for machine analysis), without knowledge about the source of degradation. If the source of degradation is known, one calls the process image restoration. Both are iconical processes, viz. input and outputs are images.
- The value of a pixel with coordinates (x, y) in the enhanced image is the result of performing some operation on the pixels in the neighbourhood of (x, y) in the input image, F. Neighbourhoods can be any shape, but usually they are rectangular.

- The study of image enhancement techniques begins by discussing gray-level transformation functions. These are among the simplest of all image enhancements techniques. The values of pixels, before and after processing, will be denoted by r and s, respectively.
- The negative of an image with gray levels in the range [0, L-1] is obtained by using the negative transformation.
- The principal advantage of piecewise linear functions over the types of functions we have discussed thus far is that the form of piecewise functions can be arbitrarily complex. In fact, as we will see shortly, a practical implementation of some important transformations can be formulated only as piecewise functions. The principal disadvantage of piecewise functions is that their specification requires considerably more user input.
- One of the simplest piecewise linear functions is a contrast-stretching transformation. Low-contrast images can result from poor illumination, lack of dynamic range in the imaging sensor, or even wrong setting of a lens aperture during image acquisition. The idea behind contrast stretching is to increase the dynamic range of the gray levels in the image being processed.
- Highlighting a specific range of gray levels in an image often is desired. Applications include enhancing features such as masses of water in satellite imagery and enhancing flaws in X-ray images.
- Instead of highlighting gray-level ranges, highlighting the contribution made to total image appearance by specific bits might be desired. Suppose that each pixel in an image is represented by 8 bits.
- The histogram of a digital image with gray levels in the range [0, L-1] is a discrete function h(rk)= nk, where rk is the kth gray level and nk is the number of pixels in the image having gray level rk.
- Histograms are the basis for numerous spatial domain processing techniques. Histogram manipulation can be used effectively for image enhancement. In addition to providing useful image statistics.
- Some neighborhood operations work with the values of the image pixels in the neighborhood and the corresponding values of a sub-image that has the same dimensions as the neighborhood.
- The sub-image is called a filter, mask, kernel, template, or window, with the first three terms being the most prevalent terminology. The values in a filter sub-image are referred to as coefficients, rather than pixels.
- Smoothing filters are used for blurring and for noise reduction. Blurring is used in preprocessing steps, such as removal of small details from an image prior to (large) object extraction, and bridging of small gaps in lines or curves. Noise reduction can be accomplished by blurring with a linear filter and also by nonlinear filtering.
- The principal objective of sharpening is to highlight fine detail in an image or to enhance detail that has been blurred, either in error or as a natural effect of a particular method of image acquisition.
- Uses of image sharpening vary and include applications ranging from electronic printing and medical imaging to industrial inspection and autonomous guidance in military systems.

- Order-statistics filters are nonlinear spatial filters whose response is based on ordering (ranking) the pixels contained in the image area encompassed by the filter, and then replacing the value of the center pixel with the value determined by the ranking result.
- The use of two-dimensional, second order derivatives for image enhancement is basically consists of defining a discrete formulation of the second-order derivative and then constructing a filter mask based on that formulation. We are interested in isotropic filters, whose response is independent of the direction of the discontinuities in the image to which the filter is applied.

Review Questions

1. Exponentials of the form with a positive constant, are useful for constructing smooth gray-level transformation functions. Start with this basic function and construct transformation functions having the general shapes shown in the following figures. The constants shown are input parameters, and your proposed Transformations must include them in their specification. (For simplicity in your answers, L0 is not a required parameter in the third curve.)

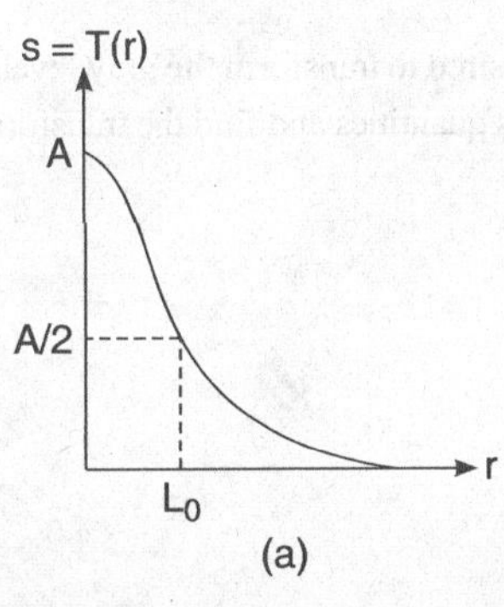

(a)

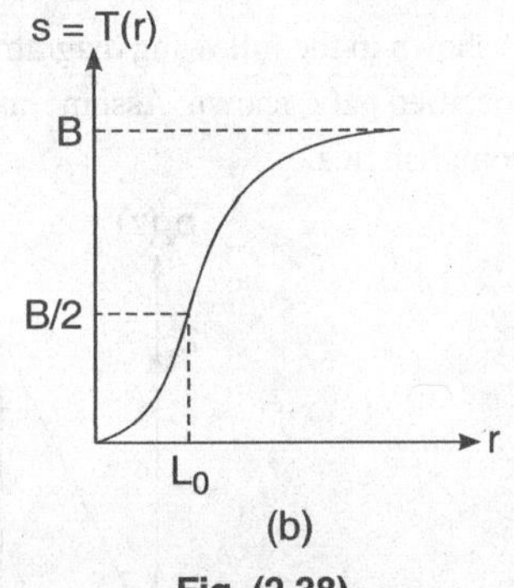

(b)

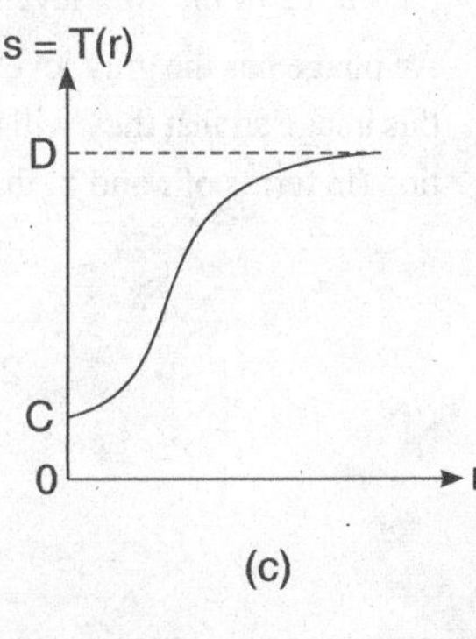

(c)

Fig. (2.38)

2. (a) Give a continuous function for implementing the contrast stretching transformation shown in Fig. 2.2(a). In addition tom, your function must include a parameter, E, for controlling the slope of the function as it transitions from low to high gray-level values. Your function should be normalized so that its minimum and maximum values are 0 and 1, respectively.

   (b) Sketch a family of transformations as a function of parameter E, for a fixed value m=L_2, where L is the number of gray levels in the image.

   (c) What is the smallest value of s that will make your function effectively perform? As the function in Fig. 2.2(b)? In other words, your function does not have to be dentical to Fig. 2.2(b). It just has to yield the same result of producing a binary image. Assume that you are working with 8-bit images, and let m=128.Also, let C be the smallest positive number representable in the computer you are using.

3. Propose a set of gray-level-slicing transformations capable of producing all the individual bit planes of an 8-bit monochrome image. (For example, a transformation function with the property T(r)=0 for r in the range [0, 127], and T(r)=255 for r in the range [128, 255] produces an image of the 7th bit plane in an 8-bit image.)

4. (a) What effect would setting to zero the lower-order bit planes have on the histogram of an image in general?

   (b) What would be the effect on the histogram if we set to zero the higher order bit planes instead?

5. Explain why the discrete histogram equalization technique does not, in general, yield a flat histogram.

6. Suppose that a digital image is subjected to histogram equalization. Show that a second pass of histogram equalization will produce exactly the same result as the first pass.

7. In some applications it is useful to model the histogram of input images as Gaussian probability density functions of the form

$$p_x(r) = \frac{1}{\sqrt{2\pi r}} e^{-(x-m)^2/2\pi^2}$$

where m and s are the mean and standard deviation of the Gaussian PDF. The approach is to let m and s be measures of average gray level and contrast of a given image. What is the transformation function you would use for histogram equalization?

8. Assuming continuous values, show by example that it is possible to have a case in which the transformation function given in Eq. (3.3-4) satisfies Conditions (a) and (b) in Section 3.3.1, but its inverse may fail to be single valued.

9. (a) Show that the discrete transformation function given in Eq. (3.3-8) for histogram equalization satisfies conditions (a) and (b) in Section 3.3.1.

(b) Show by example that this does not hold in general for the inverse discrete transformation function given in Eq. (3.3-9).

(c) Show that the inverse discrete transformation in Eq. (3.3-9) satisfies Conditions (a) and (b) in Section 3.3.1 if none of the gray levels rk, k=0, 1, p ,L-1, are missing.

10. An image has the gray level PDF pr(r) shown in the following diagram. It is desired to transform the gray levels of this image so that they will have the specified pz(z) shown. Assume continuous quantities and find the transformation (in terms of r and z) that will accomplish this.

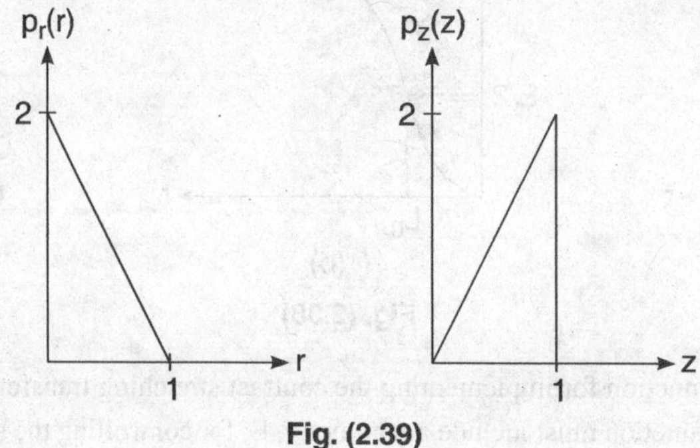

Fig. (2.39)

11. Propose a method for updating the local histogram for use in the local enhancement technique.

12. Two images, f(x, y) and g(x, y), have histograms hf and hg. Give the conditions under which you can determine the histograms of

(a) f(x, y)+g(x, y) (b) f(x, y)-g(x, y) (c) f(x, y)*g(x, y) (d) f(x, y) , g(x, y)

in terms of hf and hg. Explain how to obtain the histogram in each case.

13. Consider two 8-bit images whose gray levels span the full range from 0 to 255.

(a) Discuss the limiting effect of repeatedly subtracting image (b) from image (a).

(b) Would reversing the order of the images yield a different result?

Image subtraction is used often in industrial applications for detecting missing components in product assembly. The approach is to store a "golden" image that corresponds to a correct assembly; this image is then subtracted from incoming images of the same product. Ideally, the differences would be zero if the new products are assembled correctly. Difference images for products with missing components would be nonzero in the area where they differ from the golden image. What conditions do you think have to be met in practice for this method to work?

14. In an industrial application, X-ray imaging is to be used to inspect the inside of certain composite castings. The objective is to look for voids in the castings, which typically appear as small blobs in the image. However, due to properties in of the casting material and X-ray energy used, high noise content often makes inspection difficult, so the decision is made to use image averaging to reduce the noise and thus improve visible contrast. In computing the average, it is important to keep the number of images as small as possible to reduce the time the parts have to remain stationary during imaging. After numerous experiments, it is concluded that decreasing the noise variance by a factor of 10 is sufficient. If the imaging device can produce 30 frames. how long would the castings have to remain stationary during imaging to achieve the desired decrease in variance? Assume that the noise is uncorrelated and has zero mean.

15. The implementation of linear spatial filters requires moving the center of a mask throughout an image and, at each location, computing the sum of products of the mask coefficients with the corresponding pixels at that location (see Section 3.5). In the case of lowpass filtering, all coefficients are 1, allowing use of a so-called box-filter or moving-average algorithm, which consists of updating only the part of the computation that changes from one location to the next.

(a) Formulate such an algorithm for an n*n filter, showing the nature of the computations involved and the scanning sequence used for moving the mask around the image.

(b) The ratio of the number of computations performed by a brute-force implementation to the number of computations performed by the box-filter algorithm is called the computational advantage. Obtain the computational advantage in this case and plot it as a function of n for n>1.The 1_n2 scaling factor is common to both approaches, so you need not consider it in obtaining the computational advantage. Assume that the image has an outer border of zeros that is thick enough to allow you to ignore border effects in your analysis.

16. Discuss the limiting effect of repeatedly applying a 3*3 low pass spatial filter to a digital image.You may ignore border effects.

17. (a) It was stated in Section 3.6.2 that isolated clusters of dark or light (with respect to the background) pixels whose area is less than one-half the area of a median filter are eliminated (forced to the median value of the neighbors) by the filter. Assume a filter of size n*n, with n odd, and explain why this is so.

(b) Consider an image having various sets of pixel clusters. Assume that all points in a cluster are lighter or darker than the background (but not both simultaneously in the same cluster), and that the area of each cluster is less than or equal to n2_2. In terms of n, under what condition would one or more of these clusters cease to be isolated in the sense described in part (a)?

18. (a) Develop a procedure for computing the median of an n*n neighborhood.

(b) Propose a technique for updating the median as the center of the neighborhood is moved from pixel to pixel.

19. (a) In a character recognition application, text pages are reduced to binary form using a thresholding transformation function of the form shown in Fig. 3.2(b). This is followed by a procedure that thins the characters until they become strings of binary 1's on a background of 0's. Due to noise, the binarization and thinning processes result in broken strings of characters with gaps ranging from 1 to 3 pixels. One way to "repair" the gaps is to run an averaging mask over the binary image to blur it, and thus create bridges of nonzero pixels between gaps. Give the (odd) size of the smallest averaging mask capable of performing this task.

(b) After bridging the gaps, it is desired to threshold the image in order to convert it back to binary form.For your answer in (a), what is the minimum value of the threshold required to accomplish this, without causing the segments to break up again?

20. The three images shown were blurred using square averaging masks of sizes n=23, 25, and 45, respectively.The vertical bars on the left lower part of (a) and (c) are blurred, but a clear separation exists between them. However, the bars have merged in image (b), in spite of the fact that the mask that produced this image is significantly smaller than the mask that produced image (c). Explain this.

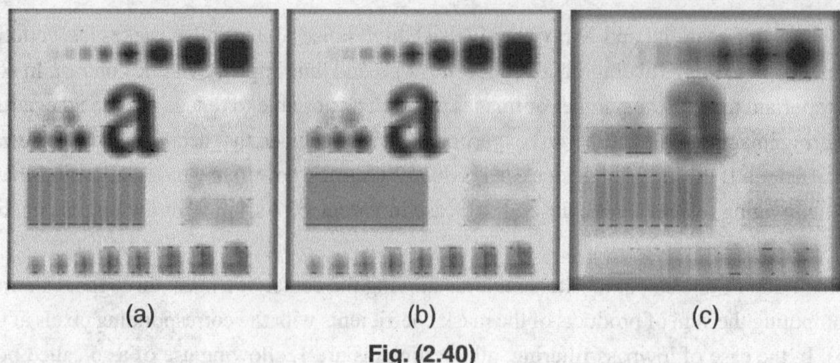

(a) (b) (c)

Fig. (2.40)

21. Consider an application such as the one shown in Fig. 3.36, in which it is desired to eliminate objects smaller than those enclosed in a square of size q*q pixels. Suppose that we want to reduce the average gray level of those objects to one-tenth of their original average gray level. In this way, those objects will be closer to the gray level of the background and they can then be eliminated by thresholding. Give the (odd) size of the smallest averaging mask that will accomplish the desired reduction in average gray level in only one pass of the mask over the image.

22. In a given application an averaging mask is applied to input images to reduce noise, and then a Laplacian mask is applied to enhance small details. Would the result be the same if the order of these operations were reversed?

3

IMAGE ENHANCEMENT IN FREQUENCY DOMAIN

3.1 FREQUENCY DOMAIN

Frequency domain is a term used to describe the analysis of mathematical functions or signals with respect to frequency. Speaking non-technically, a time domain graph shows how a signal changes over time, whereas a frequency domain graph shows how much of the signal lies within each given frequency band over a range of frequencies. A frequency domain representation can also include information on the phase shift that must be applied to each sinusoid in order to be able to recombine the frequency components to recover the original time signal.

The frequency domain relates to the Fourier transform or Fourier series by decomposing a function into an infinite or finite number of frequencies. This is based on the concept of Fourier series that any waveform can be expressed as a sum of sinusoids (sometimes infinitely many.).A spectrum analyzer is the tool commonly used to visualize real-world signals in the frequency domain.

3.1.1 Magnitude and Phase

In using the Laplace, Z-, or Fourier transforms, the frequency spectrum is complex and describes the frequency magnitude and phase. In many applications, phase information is not important. By discarding the phase information it is possible to simplify the information in a frequency domain representation to generate a frequency spectrum or spectral density. A spectrum analyzer is a device that displays the spectrum.

The power spectral density is a frequency-domain description that can be applied to a large class of signals that are neither periodic nor square-integrable; to have a power spectral density a signal needs only to be the output of a wide-sense stationary random process.

3.1.2 Partial Frequency-domain Example

Due to popular simplifications of the hearing process and titles such as Plomp's "The Ear as a Frequency Analyzer," the inner ear is often thought of as converting time-domain sound waveforms to frequency-domain spectra. The frequency domain is not actually a very accurate or useful model for hearing, but a time/frequency space or time/place space can be a useful description.

3.1.3 Concepts and the Frequency Domain

A signal can be viewed from two different standpoints:

1. The frequency domain 2. The time domain

In astronomy the frequency domain is perhaps the most familiar, because a spectrometer, e.g. a prism or a diffraction grating, splits light into its component color or frequencies and permits us to record its spectral content. This is like the trace on a spectrum analyzer, where the horizontal deflection is the frequency variable and the vertical deflection is the signals amplitude at that frequency.

In the lab we are also familiar with the time domain. This is like the trace on an oscilloscope where the vertical deflection is the signals amplitude, and the horizontal deflection is the time variable. Any signal can be fully described in either of these domains. We can go between the two by using a tool called the Fourier transform.

3.1.4 Why the Frequency Domain?

Depending on what we want to do with the signal, one domain tends to be more useful than the other, so rather than getting tied up in mathematics with a time domain signal we might convert it to the frequency domain where the mathematics are simpler.

3.1.5 Applications

The Fourier transform has many applications, in fact any field of physical science that uses sinusoidal signals, such as engineering, physics, applied mathematics, and chemistry, will make use of Fourier series and Fourier transforms. It would be impossible to give examples of all the areas where the Fourier transform is involved, but here are some examples from physics, engineering, and signal processing.

- Communications
- Astronomy
- Geology
- Optics

3.1.6 Fourier Series

The Fourier series is only briefly covered here as a backdrop to the Fourier Transform and the Discrete Fourier Transform. It is not covered in any depth as I assume that you have already encountered the Fourier series before. If there are enough requests this section can be expanded to give a FULL breakdown of the Fourier Transform.

To solve many engineering problems, we need to know the response of a Linear Time Invariant system to some input signal. If the input signal can be broken up into simple signals and we know how the system responds to these simple signals, then we can predict how the system will behave to our input.

Therefore anything that can break a signal down into its constituent parts would be very useful. One such tool is the Fourier series. With the exception of some mathematical curiosities, any periodic signal of period T can be expanded into a trigonometric series of sine and cosine functions, as long as it obeys the following conditions:

1. f(t) has finite number of maxima and minima within T
2. f(t) has finite number of discontinuities within T, and
3. It is necessary that you are able to calculate area nunder the graph.

These three conditions mean that you are able to calculate the area under the graph. If (1) is not true then the signal power goes to infinity and it is not absolutely integratable. If (2) is not true then once again it is not absolutely integratable, and (3) is simply reafirming conditions (1) and (2).

3.2 FOURIER TRANSFORM

The Fourier transform is simply a method of expressing a function (which is a point in some infinite dimensional vector space of functions) in terms of the sum of its projections onto a set of basis functions. Since an image is only defined on a closed and bounded domain (the image window), we can assume that the image is defined as being zero outside this window. In other words, we can assume that the image function is integrable over the real line.

In mathematics, the Fourier transform is a certain linear operator that maps functions to other functions. Loosely speaking, the Fourier transform decomposes a function into a continuous spectrum of its frequency components, and the inverse transform synthesizes a function from its spectrum of frequency components. A useful analogy is the relationship between a series of pure notes (the frequency components) and a musical chord (the function itself). In mathematical physics, the Fourier transform of a signal x(t) can be thought of as that signal in the "frequency domain." This is similar to the basic idea of the various other Fourier transforms including the Fourier series of a periodic function.

Definitions : There are several common conventions for defining the Fourier transform of a complex-valued Lebesgue integrable function, In communications and signal processing, for instance, it is often the function:

$$X(f)=\int_{-\infty}^{\infty} x(t)\, e^{-i2\pi ft}\, dt, \text{ for every real number } f.$$

When the independent variable represents time (with SI unit of seconds), the transform variable represents ordinary frequency (in hertz). The complex-valued function, is said to represent in the frequency domain. I.e., if is a continuous function, then it can be reconstructed from by the inverse transform:

$$x(t)=\int_{-\infty}^{\infty} X(f)\, e^{i2\pi ft}\, df, \text{ for every real number } t.$$

Other notations for $X(f)$ are: $\hat{x}(f)$ and $F\{x\}(f)$.

The interpretation of is aided by expressing it in polar coordinate form:

$X(f)=A(f)\,e^{i\phi(f)}$ where:

$A(f)=|X(f)|$, the amplitude

$\phi(f)=\angle X(f)$, the phase.

Then the inverse transform can be written:

$$x(t)=\int_{-\infty}^{\infty} A(f)\, e^{i(2\pi\, ft+\phi(f))}\, df,$$

which is a recombination of all the frequency components of Each component is a complex sinusoid of the form ei2?ft whose amplitude is A(f) and whose initial phase angle (at t = 0) is ?(f).

In mathematics, the Fourier transform is commonly written in terms of angular frequency: $\omega=2\pi f$, whose units are radians per second.

The substitution $f=\dfrac{\omega}{2\pi}$ into the formulas above produces this convention:

$$X(\omega)=\int_{-\infty}^{\infty} x(t)\, e^{-i\omega t}\, dt$$

$$x(t)=\frac{1}{2\pi}\int_{-\infty}^{\infty} X(\omega)\, e^{i\omega t}\, d\omega$$

which is also a bilateral Laplace transform evaluated at s = iω.

The 2π factor can be split evenly between the Fourier transform and the inverse, which leads to another popular convention:

$$X(\omega)=\frac{1}{\sqrt{2\pi}}\int_{-\infty}^{\infty}x(t)\,e^{-i\omega t}\,dt$$

$$x(t)=\frac{1}{\sqrt{2\pi}}\int_{-\infty}^{\infty}X(\omega)\,e^{i\omega t}\,d\omega$$

This convention and the X(f) convention are unitary transforms. Variations of all three conventions can be created by conjugating the complex-exponential kernel of both the forward and the reverse transform. The signs must be opposites. Other than that, the choice is (again) a matter of convention.

Summary of popular forms of the Fourier transform :

Angular frequency ω (rad/s)	Unit ary	$X_1(\omega)\overset{\text{def}}{=}\frac{1}{\sqrt{2\pi}}\int_{-\infty}^{\infty}x(t)\,e^{-i\omega t}\,dt=\frac{1}{\sqrt{2\pi}}X_2(\omega)=x(t)$ $=\frac{1}{\sqrt{2\pi}}\int_{-\infty}^{\infty}X_1(\omega)\,e^{-i\omega t}\,d\omega$
	Non-unit ary	$X_2(\omega)\overset{\text{def}}{=}\int_{-\infty}^{\infty}x(t)\,e^{-i\omega t}\,dt=\sqrt{2\pi}\,X_1(\omega)=X_3$ $x(t)=\frac{1}{2\pi}\int_{-\infty}^{\infty}X_2(\omega)\,e^{i\omega t}\,d\omega$
Ordinary frequency f (hertz)	Unit ary	$X_3(\omega)\overset{\text{def}}{=}\int_{-\infty}^{\infty}x(t)\,e^{-i2\pi ft}\,dt=\sqrt{2\pi}\,X_1(2\pi f)=x(t)$ $=\int_{-\infty}^{\infty}X_3(f)\,e^{i2\pi ft}\,df$

Generalization

There are several ways to define the Fourier transform pair. The "forward" and "inverse" transforms are always defined so that the operation of both transforms in either order on a function will return the original function. In other words, the composition of the transform pair is defined to be the identity transformation. Using two arbitrary real constants a and b, the most general definition of the forward 1-dimensional Fourier transform is given by

$$X(\omega)=\sqrt{\frac{|b|}{(2\pi)^{1-a}}}\int_{-\infty}^{+\infty}x(t)\,c^{-ib\omega t}\,dt$$

and the inverse is given by

$$x(t)=\sqrt{\frac{|b|}{(2\pi)^{1+a}}}\int_{-\infty}^{+\infty}X(\omega)\,e^{ib\omega t}\,d\omega$$

Note : The transform definitions are symmetric;

They can be reversed by simply changing the signs of a and b.

The convention adopted in this topic is $(a, b) = (0, 1)$. The choice of a and b is usually chosen so that it is geared towards the context in which the transform pairs are being used. The non-unitary convention above is $(a, b) = (1, 1)$. Another very common definition is $(a, b) = (0, 2\pi)$ which is often used in signal processing applications. In this case, the angular frequency ω becomes ordinary frequency f. If f (or ω) and t carry units, then their product must be dimensionless. For example, t may be in units of time, specifically seconds, and f (or ω) would be in hertz (or radian/s).

Properties

All the results are derived for the following definition (normalization) of the Fourier transform:

$$F(\omega) = F\{f(t)\} = \frac{1}{\sqrt{2\pi}} \int_{-\infty}^{\infty} f(t)\, e^{-\omega t}\, dt$$

The other properties of the continuous Fourier transform. are discussed in "Table of important Fourier transforms".

Completeness

We define the Fourier transform on the set of compactly-supported complex-valued functions of R and then extend it by continuity to the Hilbert space of square-integrable functions with the usual inner-product. Then $F: L^2(R) \to L^2(R)$ is a unitary operator. That is $F^* = F^{-1}$ and the transform preserves inner-products (see Parseval's theorem, also described below). Note that, F^* refers to adjoint of the Fourier Transform operator.

Moreover we can check that,

$$F^2 = J, F^3 = F^* = F^{-1} \text{ and } F^4 = I$$

where is the Time-Reversal operator defined as,

$$\|J\{f\}(t) - f(-t)\|_2 = 0$$

and I is the Identity operator defined as,

$$\|I\{f\}(t) - f(t)\|_2 = 0$$

Extensions

The Fourier transform can also be extended to the space of integrable functions defined on R^n

$$F : L^1(R^n) \to C(R^n)$$

where,

$$L^1(R^n) = \{f : R^n \to C \mid \int_{R^n} |f(x)|\, dx < \infty\}$$

and $C(R^n)$ is the space of continuous functions on R^n.

In this case the definition usually appears as

$$F\{f\}(\omega) \stackrel{\text{def}}{=} \left(\frac{1}{\sqrt{2\pi}}\right)^n \int_{R^n} f(x)\, e^{-i\omega . x}\, dx$$

where $\omega . R^n$ and $\omega . x$ is the inner product of the two vectors ω and x.

This can be used to define the continuous Fourier transform for compactly supported smooth functions, which are dense in $L^2(R^n)$. The Plancherel theorem then allows us to extend the definition of the Fourier transform to functions on $L^2(R^n)$ (even those not compactly supported) by continuity arguments..

The Plancherel theorem and Parseval's theorem

If $f(t)$ and $g(t)$ are square-integrable and $F(\omega)$ and $G(\omega)$ are their Fourier transforms, then we have Parseval's theorem:

$$\int_{R^n} f(t)\, g(t)\, dt = \int_{R^n} F(\omega)\, G(\omega)\, d\omega$$

where the bar denotes complex conjugation. Therefore, the Fourier transformation yields an isometric automorphism of the Hilbert space $L^2(R^n)$.

The Plancherel theorem, a special case of Parseval's theorem, states that

$$\int_{R^n} |f(t)|^2 \, dt = \int_{R^n} |F(\omega)|^2 \, d\omega$$

This theorem is usually interpreted as asserting the unitary property of the Fourier transform.

Localization Property

As a rule of thumb: the more concentrated $f(t)$ is, the more spread out is $F(\omega)$. In particular, if we "squeeze" a function in t, it spreads out in ? and vice-versa; and we cannot arbitrarily concentrate both the function and its Fourier transform.

Therefore a function which equals its Fourier transform strikes a precise balance between being concentrated and being spread out. It is easy in theory to construct examples of such functions (called self-dual functions) because the Fourier transform has order 4 (that is, iterating it four times on a function returns the original function). The sum of the four iterated Fourier transforms of any function will be self-dual. There are also some explicit examples of self-dual functions, the most important being constant multiples of the Gaussian functions

$$f(t) = \exp\left(\frac{-t^2}{2}\right).$$

This function is related to Gaussian distributions, and in fact, is an eigen function of the Fourier transform operators. Again, it is worth stressing that the mere fact that the Gaussian is self-dual does not make it in any way special: many self-dual functions exist.

The trade-off between the compaction of a function and its Fourier transform can be formalized in the form of a Fourier Uncertainty Principle. Suppose $f(t)$ and $F(\omega)$ are a Fourier transform pair for a finite-energy (i.e. square-integrable) function. Without loss of generality, we assume that $f(t)$ is normalized:

$$\int_{-\infty}^{\infty} |f(t)|^2 \, dt = 1$$

It follows from Parseval's theorem that $F(\omega)$ is also normalized.

Define the expected location of a particle (with probability density $|f(t)^2|$) as

$$u_f \stackrel{\text{def}}{=} \int_{-\infty}^{\infty} t|f(t)|^2 \, dt$$

and the expectation value of the momentum of the particle (with probability density $|f(\omega)|^2$) as

$$\xi_F \stackrel{\text{def}}{=} \int_{-\infty}^{\infty} \omega|F(\omega)|^2 \, d\omega$$

Also define the variances around the above-defined average values as

$$\sigma_f^2 \stackrel{\text{def}}{=} \int_{-\infty}^{\infty} (t - u_f)^2 \, |f(t)|^2 \, dt$$

and

$$\sigma_F^2 \stackrel{\text{def}}{=} \int_{-\infty}^{\infty} (\omega - \xi_F)^2 \, |F(\omega)|^2 \, d\omega$$

Then it can be shown that

$$\sigma_f^2 \, \sigma_F^2 \geq \frac{1}{4}.$$

The equality is achieved for the Gaussian function listed above, which shows that the Gaussian function is maximally concentrated in "time-frequency".

The most famous practical application of this property is found in quantum mechanics. Following from the axioms of quantum mechanics, the momentum and position wave functions are Fourier transform pairs to within a factor of $h/2\pi$ and are normalized to unity. The above expression then becomes a statement of the Heisenberg uncertainty principle.

The Fourier transform also translates between smoothness and decay. If $f(t)$ is several times differentiable, then $F(\omega)$ decays rapidly towards zero for $\omega \to \pm\infty$.

Analysis of Differential Equations

Fourier transforms, and the closely related Laplace transforms are widely used in solving differential equations. The Fourier transform is compatible with differentiation in the following sense: if $f(t)$ is a differentiable function with Fourier transform $F(\omega)$, then the Fourier transform of its derivative is given by $i\omega F(\omega)$. This can be used to transform differential equations into algebraic equations. Note that this technique only applies to problems whose domain is the whole set of real numbers. By extending the Fourier transform to functions of several variables (as outlined below), partial differential equations with domain R^n can also be translated into algebraic equations.

Convolution Theorem

The Fourier transform translates between convolution and multiplication of functions. If $f(t)$ and $h(t)$ are integrable functions with Fourier transforms $F(\omega)$ and $H(\omega)$ respectively, and if the convolution of f and h exists and is absolutely integrable, then the Fourier transform of the convolution is given by the product of the Fourier transforms $F(\omega)\,H(\omega)$ (possibly multiplied by a constant factor depending on the Fourier normalization convention).

In the current normalization convention, this means that if

$$g(t) = \{f * h\}(t) = \int_{-\infty}^{\infty} f(s)\,h(t-s)\,ds$$

where * denotes the convolution operation; then

$$G(\omega) = \sqrt{2\pi}\,.\,F(\omega)\,H(\omega).$$

The above formulas hold true for functions defined on both one- and multi-dimension real space. In linear time invariant (LTI) system theory, it is common to interpret $h(t)$ as the impulse response of an LTI system with input $f(t)$ and output $g(t)$, since substituting the unit impulse for $f(t)$ yields $g(t) = h(t)$. In this case, $H(\omega)$ represents the frequency response of the system.

Conversely, if $f(t)$ can be decomposed as the product of two other functions $p(t)$ and $q(t)$ such that their product $p(t)q(t)$ is integrable, then the Fourier transform of this product is given by the convolution of the respective Fourier transforms $P(\omega)$ and $Q(\omega)$, again with a constant scaling factor.

In the current normalization convention, this means that if $f(t) = p(t)\,q(t)$ then:

$$F(\omega) = \frac{1}{\sqrt{2\pi}}(P(\omega) * Q(\omega)) = \frac{1}{\sqrt{2\pi}}\int_{-\infty}^{\infty} P(\alpha)\,Q(\omega-\alpha)\,d\alpha$$

Cross-correlation Theorem

In an analogous manner, it can be shown that if $g(t)$ is the cross-correlation of $f(t)$ and $h(t)$:

$$g(t) = (f * h)(t) = \int_{-\infty}^{\infty} f(s)\,h(t+s)\,ds$$

then the Fourier transform of $g(t)$ is:

$$G(\omega) = \sqrt{2\pi}\,F(\omega)\,H(\omega)$$

where capital letters are again used to denote the Fourier transform.

Tempered Distributions

The most general and useful context for studying the continuous Fourier transform is given by the tempered distributions; these include all the integrable functions mentioned above and have the added advantage that the Fourier transform of any tempered distribution is again a tempered distribution and the rule for the inverse of the Fourier transform is universally valid. Furthermore, the useful Dirac delta is a tempered distribution but not a function; its Fourier transform is a constant function (whose specific value depends upon the form of the Fourier transform used). Distributions can be differentiated and the above mentioned compatibility of the Fourier transform with differentiation and convolution remains true for tempered distributions.

Table of Important Fourier Transforms

The following table records some important Fourier transforms. G and H denote Fourier transforms of $g(t)$ and $h(t)$, respectively. g and h may be integrable functions or tempered distributions. Note that the two most common unitary conventions are included.

Functional Relationships

	Signal	Fourier Unitary, Frequency	Transform Fourier Angular Unitary, Frequency	Transform Ordinary Remarks
	$g(t)$	$G(\omega) \stackrel{\text{def}}{=} \frac{1}{\sqrt{2\pi}} \int_{-\infty}^{\infty} g(t)\, e^{-i\omega t}$	$G(f) \stackrel{\text{def}}{=} \int_{-\infty}^{\infty} g(t)\, e^{-i2\pi f t}\, dt$	
1	$a\,.\,g(t) + b\,.\,h(t)$	$a\,.\,G(\omega) + b\,.\,H(\omega)$	$a\,.\,G(f) + b\,.\,H(f)$	Linearity
2	$g(t-a)$	$e^{-ia\omega}\; G(\omega)$	$e^{-2\pi a f}\; G(f)$	Shift in time domain
3	$e^{-iat}\; g(t)$	$G(\omega - a)$	$G\left(f - \frac{a}{2\pi}\right)$	Shift in frequency domain, dual of 2
4	$g(at)$	$\frac{1}{\lvert a\rvert} G\left(\frac{\omega}{a}\right)$	$\frac{1}{\lvert a\rvert} G\left(\frac{f}{a}\right)$	If $\lvert a\rvert$ is large, then $g(at)$ is concentrated around 0 and $\frac{1}{\lvert a\rvert} G\left(\frac{\omega}{a}\right)$ spreads out and flattens. It is interesting to consider the limit of this as $\lvert a\rvert$ tends to infinity - the delta function
5	$G(t)$	$g(-\omega)$	$g(-f)$	Duality property of the Fourier transform. Results from swapping "dummy" variables of t and ω.
6	$\frac{d^n g(t)}{dt^n}$	$(i\omega)^n G(\omega)$	$(i2\pi f)^n\; G(f)$	Generalized derivative property of the Fourier transform
7	$t^n g(t)$	$i^n \frac{d^n G(\omega)}{d\omega^n}$	$\left(\frac{1}{2\pi}\right)^n \frac{d^n G(f)}{df^n}$	This is the dual of 6

8	$(g * h)(t)$	$\sqrt{2\pi}\, G(\omega)\, H(\omega)$	$G(f)\, H(f)$	$g * h$ denotes the convolution of g and h – this rule is the convolution theorem
9	$g(t)\, h(t)$	$\dfrac{(G * H)(\omega)}{\sqrt{2\pi}}$	$(G * H)(f)$	This is the dual of 8
Square-integrable Functions				
10	$\text{rect}(at)$	$\dfrac{1}{\sqrt{2\pi a^2}} . \text{sinc}\left(\dfrac{\omega}{2\pi a}\right)$	$\dfrac{1}{\|a\|} . \text{sinc}\left(\dfrac{f}{a}\right)$	The rectangular pulse and the normalized sinc function
11	$\text{sinc}(at)$	$\dfrac{1}{2\pi a^2} . \text{rect}\left(\dfrac{\omega}{2\pi a}\right)$	$\dfrac{1}{\|a\|} . \text{rect}\left(\dfrac{f}{a}\right)$	Dual of rule 10. The rectangular function is an idealized low-pass filter, and the sinc function is the non-causal impulse response of such a filter.
12	$\text{sinc}^2(at)$	$\dfrac{1}{2\pi a^2} . \text{tri}\left(\dfrac{\omega}{2\pi a}\right)$	$\dfrac{1}{\|a\|} . \text{tri}\left(\dfrac{f}{a}\right)$	tri is the triangular function
13	$\text{tri}(at)$	$\dfrac{1}{\sqrt{2\pi a^2}} . \text{sinc}^2\left(\dfrac{\omega}{2\pi a}\right)$	$\dfrac{1}{\|a\|} . \text{sinc}^2\left(\dfrac{f}{a}\right)$	Dual of rule 12.
14	$e^{-\alpha t^2}$	$\dfrac{1}{\sqrt{2\alpha}} . \dfrac{e^{-\omega^2}}{4\alpha}$	$\sqrt{\dfrac{\pi}{\alpha}} . e^{-\frac{(\pi f)^2}{\alpha}}$	Shows that the Gaussian function exp $(-at^2)$ is its own Fourier transform. For this to be integrable we must have $\text{Re}(\alpha) > 0$
15	$e^{-iat^2} = e^{-\alpha t^2}$	$\dfrac{1}{\sqrt{2a}} . e^{-i\left(\frac{\omega^2}{4a} - \frac{\pi}{4}\right)}$	$\dfrac{\sqrt{\pi}}{a} . e^{-i\left(\frac{\pi^2 f^2}{a} - \frac{\pi}{4}\right)}$	Common in optics
16	$\cos(at^2)$	$\dfrac{1}{\sqrt{2a}} \cos\left(\dfrac{\omega^2}{4a} - \dfrac{\pi}{4}\right)$	$\sqrt{\dfrac{\pi}{a}} \cos\left(\dfrac{\pi^2 f^2}{a} - \dfrac{\pi}{4}\right)$	
17	$\sin(at^2)$	$\dfrac{-1}{\sqrt{2a}} \sin\left(\dfrac{\omega^2}{4a} - \dfrac{\pi}{4}\right)$	$-\sqrt{\dfrac{\pi}{a}} \sin\left(\dfrac{\pi^2 f^2}{a} - \dfrac{\pi}{4}\right)$	
18	$e^{-a\|t\|}$	$\sqrt{\dfrac{2}{\pi}} . \dfrac{a}{a^2 + \omega^2}$	$\dfrac{2a}{a^2 + 4\pi^2 f^2}$	$a > 0$
19	$\dfrac{1}{\sqrt{\|t\|}}$	$\dfrac{1}{\sqrt{\|\omega\|}}$	$\dfrac{1}{\sqrt{\|f\|}}$	The transform is the function itself
20	$J_0(t)$	$\sqrt{\dfrac{2}{\pi}} . \dfrac{\text{rec}\left(\dfrac{\omega}{2}\right)}{\sqrt{1 - \omega^2}}$	$\dfrac{2 . \text{rec}(\pi f)}{\sqrt{1 - 4\pi^2 f^2}}$	$J_0(t)$ is the Bessel function of first kind of order 0.

21	$J_n(t)$	$\sqrt{\frac{2}{\pi}}\frac{(-i)^n T_n(\omega)\,\text{rect}\left(\frac{\omega}{2}\right)}{\sqrt{1-\omega^2}}$	$\frac{2(-i)^n T_n(2\pi f)\,\text{rect}(\pi f)}{\sqrt{1-4\pi^2 f^2}}$	It's the generalization of the previous transform; $T_n(t)$ is the Chebyshev polynomial of the first kind.
22	$\frac{J_n(t)}{t}$	$\sqrt{\frac{2}{\pi}}\frac{i}{n}(-i)^n . U_{n-1}(\omega) . \sqrt{1-\omega^2}\ \text{rect}\left(\frac{\omega}{2}\right)$	$\frac{2i}{n}(-i)^n . U_{n-1}(2\pi f) . \sqrt{1-4\pi^2 f^2}\ \text{rect}(\pi f)$	$U_n(t)$ is the Chebyshev polynomial of the second kind
23	sech(at)	$\frac{1}{a}\sqrt{\frac{\pi}{2}}\ \text{sech}\left(\frac{\pi}{2a}\omega\right)$	$\frac{\pi}{a}\ \text{sech}\left(\frac{\pi^2}{a}f\right)$	Hyperbolic secant is its own Fourier transform
Distributions				
24	1	$\sqrt{2\pi}\,.\,\delta(\omega)$	$\delta(f)$	$\delta(\omega)$ denotes the Dirac delta distribution. This rule shows why the Dirac delta is important; it shows up as the Fourier transform of a constant function
25	$\delta(t)$	$\frac{1}{\sqrt{2\pi}}$	1	Dual of rule 23
26	e^{iat}	$\sqrt{2\pi}\,.\,\delta(\omega-a)$	$\delta\left(f-\frac{a}{2\pi}\right)$	This follows from and 3 and 24.
27	cos(at)	$\sqrt{2\pi}\,\frac{\delta(\omega-a)+\delta(\omega+a)}{2}$	$\frac{\delta\left(f-\frac{a}{2\pi}\right)+\delta\left(f+\frac{a}{2\pi}\right)}{2}$	Follows from rules 1 and 25 using Euler's formula : $\cos(at) = (e^{iat} + e^{-iat})/2$
28	sin(at)	$i\sqrt{2\pi}\,\frac{\delta(\omega+a)-\delta(\omega-a)}{2}$	$i\,\frac{\delta\left(f+\frac{a}{2\pi}\right)-\delta\left(f-\frac{a}{2\pi}\right)}{2}$	Also from 1 and 25
29	t^n	$i^n\sqrt{2\pi}\,\delta^{(n)}(\omega)$	$\left(\frac{i}{2\pi}\right)^n\delta^{(n)}(f)$	Here, n is a natural number. $\delta^n(\omega)$ is the nth distribution derivative of the Dirac delta. This rule follows from rules 7 and 24. Combining this rule with 1, we can transform all polynomials.
30	$\frac{1}{t}$	$-i\sqrt{\frac{\pi}{2}}\ \text{sgn}(\omega)$	$-i\pi\,.\,\text{sgn}(f)$	Here sgn(ω) is the sign function; note that this is consistent with rules 7 and 24.
31	$\frac{1}{t^n}$	$-i\sqrt{\frac{\pi}{2}}\,.\,\frac{(-i\omega)^{n-1}}{(n-1)!}\ \text{sgn}(\omega)$	$-i\pi\,\frac{(-i2\pi f)^{n-1}}{(n-1)!}\ \text{sgn}(f)$	Generalization of the rule 29

32	$\text{sgn}(t)$	$\sqrt{\frac{2}{\pi}} \cdot \frac{1}{i\omega}$	$\frac{1}{i\pi f}$	The dual of rule 29
33	$u(t)$	$\sqrt{\frac{\pi}{2}}\left(\frac{1}{i\pi\omega} + \delta(\omega)\right)$	$\frac{1}{2}\left(\frac{1}{i\pi f} + \delta(f)\right)$	Here $u(t)$ is the Heaviside unit step function; this follows from rules 1 and 31.
34	$e^{-at}u(t)$	$\frac{1}{\sqrt{2\pi}\,(a + i\omega)}$	$\frac{1}{a + i2\pi f}$	$u(t)$ is the Heaviside unit step function and $a > 0$
35	$\sum_{n=-\infty}^{\infty} \delta\left(t - n\frac{\sqrt{2\pi}}{T}\right)$	$\sum_{k=-\infty}^{\infty} \delta\left(\omega - k\frac{2\pi}{T}\right)$	$\frac{1}{T}\sum_{k=-\infty}^{\infty} \delta\left(f - \frac{k}{T}\right)$	The Dirac comb– helpful for explaining or understanding the transition from continuous to discrete time

Fourier Transform Properties

Notation : $f(t) \overset{F}{\Longleftrightarrow} F(\omega)$ denotes that $f(t)$ and $F(\omega)$ are a Fourier transform pair.

Linearity $\quad af_1(t) + bf_2(t) \overset{F}{\Longleftrightarrow} aF_1(\omega) + bF_2(\omega)$

Convolution $\quad f_1(t) * f_2(t) \overset{F}{\Longleftrightarrow} F_1(\omega)F_2(\omega)$

Conjugation $\quad \overline{f(t)} \overset{F}{\Longleftrightarrow} \overline{F(-\omega)}$

Scaling $\quad f(at) \overset{F}{\Longleftrightarrow} \frac{1}{|a|} F\left(\frac{\omega}{a}\right), a \in R, a \neq 0$

Time reversal $\quad f(-t) \overset{F}{\Longleftrightarrow} F(-\omega)$

Time shift $\quad f(t - t_0) \overset{F}{\Longleftrightarrow} e^{-i\omega t_0} F(\omega)$

Modulation (multiplication by complex exponential)

$$f(t) \,.\, e^{i\omega_0 t} \overset{F}{\Longleftrightarrow} F(\omega - \omega_0), \omega \in R,$$

Multiplication by $\sin \omega_0 t$

$$f(t) \sin \omega_0 t \overset{F}{\Longleftrightarrow} \frac{i}{2}[F(\omega + \omega_0) - F(\omega - \omega_0)]$$

Multiplication by $\cos \omega_0 t$

$$f(t) \cos \omega_0 t \overset{F}{\Longleftrightarrow} \frac{1}{2}[F(\omega + \omega_0) + F(\omega - \omega_0)]$$

Integration $\quad \int_{-\infty}^{t} f(u)\, du \overset{F}{\Longleftrightarrow} \frac{1}{i\omega} F(\omega) + \pi F(0)\,\delta(\omega)$

Parseval's theorem $\quad \int_R f(t) \,.\, \overline{g(t)}\, dt = \int_R F(\omega) \,.\, \overline{G(\omega)}\, d\omega$

3.3 SHORT-TIME FOURIER TRANSFORM

The short-time Fourier transform (STFT), or alternatively short-term Fourier transform, is a Fourier-related transform used to determine the sinusoidal frequency and phase content of local sections of a signal as it changes over time.

Simply described, in the continuous-time case, the function to be transformed is multiplied by a window function which is nonzero for only a short period of time. The Fourier transform (a one-dimensional function) of the resulting signal is taken as the window is slid along the time axis, resulting in a two-dimensional representation of the signal. Mathematically, this is written as:

$$\text{STFT}\{x(\ )\} \equiv X(\tau, \omega) = \int_{-\infty}^{\infty} x(t)\, w(t-\tau)\, e^{-j\omega t}\, dt$$

where $w(t)$ is the window function, commonly a Hann window or gaussian "hill" centered around zero, and $x(t)$ is the signal to be transformed. $X(\tau, \omega)$ is essentially the Fourier Transform of $x(t)\, w(t-\tau)$, a complex function representing the phase and magnitude of the signal over time and frequency. Often phase unwrapping is employed along either or both the time axis, τ and frequency axis, ?, to suppress any jump discontinuity of the phase result of the STFT. The time index ? is normally considered to be "slow" time and usually not expressed in as high resolution as time t.

In the discrete time case, the data to be transformed could be broken up into chunks or frames (which usually overlap each other). Each chunk is Fourier transformed, and the complex result is added to a matrix, which records magnitude and phase for each point in time and frequency. This can be expressed as:

$$\text{STFT}\{x[\ ]\} \equiv X(m, \omega) = \sum_{n=-\infty}^{\infty} x[n]\, w[n-m]\, e^{-j\omega n}$$

likewise, with signal $x[n]$ and window $w[n]$. In this case, m is discrete and ω is continuous, but in most typical applications the STFT is performed on a computer using the Fast Fourier Transform, so both variables are discrete and quantized. Again, the discrete-time index m is normally considered to be "slow" time and usually not expressed in as high resolution as time n.The magnitude squared of the STFT yields the spectrogram of the function:

$$\text{spectrogram}\{x(\ )\} \equiv |X(\tau, \omega)|^2$$

Inverse STFT

The STFT is invertible, that is, the original signal can be recovered from the transform by the Inverse STFT.

Continuous-time STFT

Given the width and definition of the window function $w(t)$, we initially require the height of the window function to be scaled so that

$$\int_{-\infty}^{\infty} w(\tau)\, d\tau = 1$$

It easily follows that

$$\int_{-\infty}^{\infty} \omega(t-\tau)\, d\tau = 1\, \forall\, t$$

and
$$x(t) = r(t) \int_{-\infty}^{\infty} w(t-\tau)\, d\tau = \int_{-\infty}^{\infty} x(t)\, w(t-\tau)\, d\tau$$

The continuous Fourier Transform is

$$X(\omega) = \int_{-\infty}^{\infty} x(t)\, e^{-j\omega t}\, dt$$

Substituting $x(t)$ from above:

$$X(\omega) = \int_{-\infty}^{\infty} \left[\int_{-\infty}^{\infty} x(t)\, w(t-\tau)\, d\tau \right] e^{-j\omega t}\, dt$$

$$= \int_{-\infty}^{\infty} \int_{-\infty}^{\infty} x(t)\, wt - \tau(\, e^{-j\omega t}\, d\tau\, dt$$

Swapping order of integration:

$$X(\omega) = \int_{-\infty}^{\infty} \int_{-\infty}^{\infty} x(t)\, w(t-\tau)\, e^{-j\omega t}\, dt\, d\tau$$

$$= \int_{-\infty}^{\infty} \left[\int_{-\infty}^{\infty} x(t)\, w(t-\tau)\, e^{-j\omega t}\, dt \right] d\tau$$

$$= \int_{-\infty}^{\infty} X(\tau, \omega)\, d\tau$$

So the Fourier Transform can be seen as a sort of phase coherent sum of all of the STFTs of $x(t)$. Since the inverse Fourier transform is

$$x(t) = \frac{1}{2\pi} \int_{-\infty}^{\infty} X(\omega)\, e^{+j\omega t}\, d\omega$$

then $x(t)$ can be recovered from $X(\tau, \omega)$ as

$$x(t) = \frac{1}{2\pi} \int_{-\infty}^{\infty} \int_{-\infty}^{\infty} X(\tau, \omega)\, e^{+j\omega t}\, d\tau\, d\omega$$

or

$$x(t) = \int_{-\infty}^{\infty} \left[\frac{1}{2\pi} \int_{-\infty}^{\infty} X(\tau, \omega)\, e^{+j\omega t}\, d\omega \right] d\tau$$

It can be seen, comparing to above that windowed "grain" or "wavelet" of $x(t)$ is

$$x(t)\, w(t-\tau) = \frac{1}{2\pi} \int_{-\infty}^{\infty} X(\tau, \omega)\, e^{+j\omega t}\, d\omega$$

The inverse Fourier transform of $X(\tau, \omega)$ for τ fixed.

Discrete-time STFT

One of the downfalls of the STFT is that it has a fixed resolution. The width of the windowing function relates to the how the signal is represented — it determines whether there is good frequency resolution (frequency components close together can be separated) or good time resolution (the time at which frequencies change). A wide window gives better frequency resolution but poor time resolution. A narrower window (said to be compactly supported) gives good time resolution but poor frequency resolution. These are called narrowband and wideband transforms, respectively.

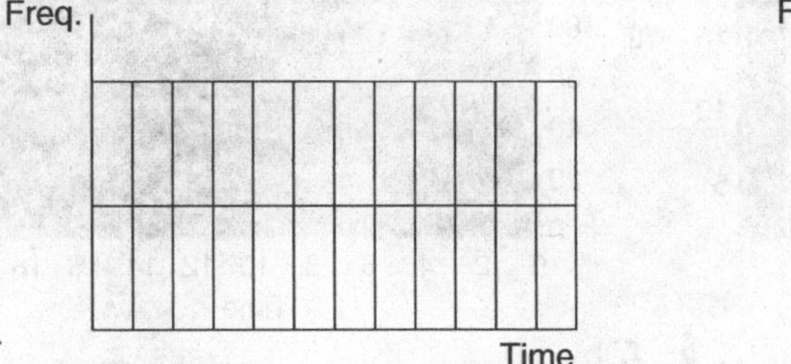

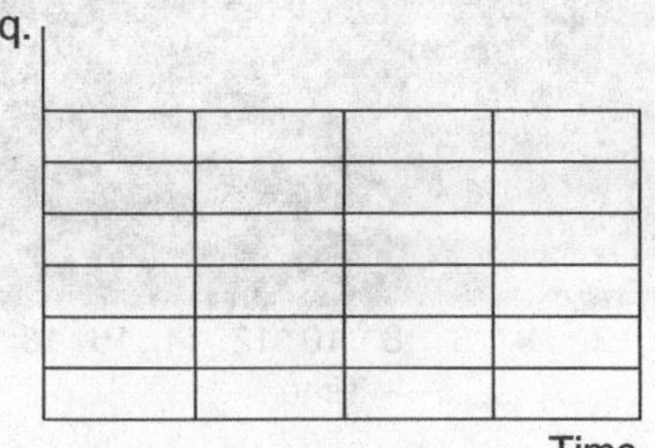

Fig. (3.1)

Comparison of STFT resolution. Left has better time resolution, and right has better frequency resolution. This is one of the reasons for the creation of the wavelet transform (or multiresolution analysis in general), which can give good time resolution for high-frequency events, and good frequency resolution for low-frequency events, which is the type of analysis best suited for many real signals.

This property is related to the Heisenberg uncertainty principle, but it is not a direct relationship. The product of the standard deviation in time and frequency is limited. The boundary of the uncertainty principle (best simultaneous resolution of both) is reached with a Gaussian window function.

Example : Using the following sample signal $x(t)$ that is composed of a set of 4 sinusoidal waveforms joined together in sequence. Each waveform is only composed of one of four frequencies (10, 25, 50, 100 Hz). The definition of $x(t)$ is:

$$x(t) = \cos(2\pi 10t) \text{ for } 0 \le t < 0.1s$$
$$x(t) = \cos(2\pi 25t) \text{ for } 0.1s \le t < 0.2s$$
$$x(t) = \cos(2\pi 50t) \text{ for } 0.2s \le t < 0.3s$$
$$x(t) = \cos(2\pi 100t) \text{ for } 0.3s \le t < 0.4s$$

The following spectrograms were produced:

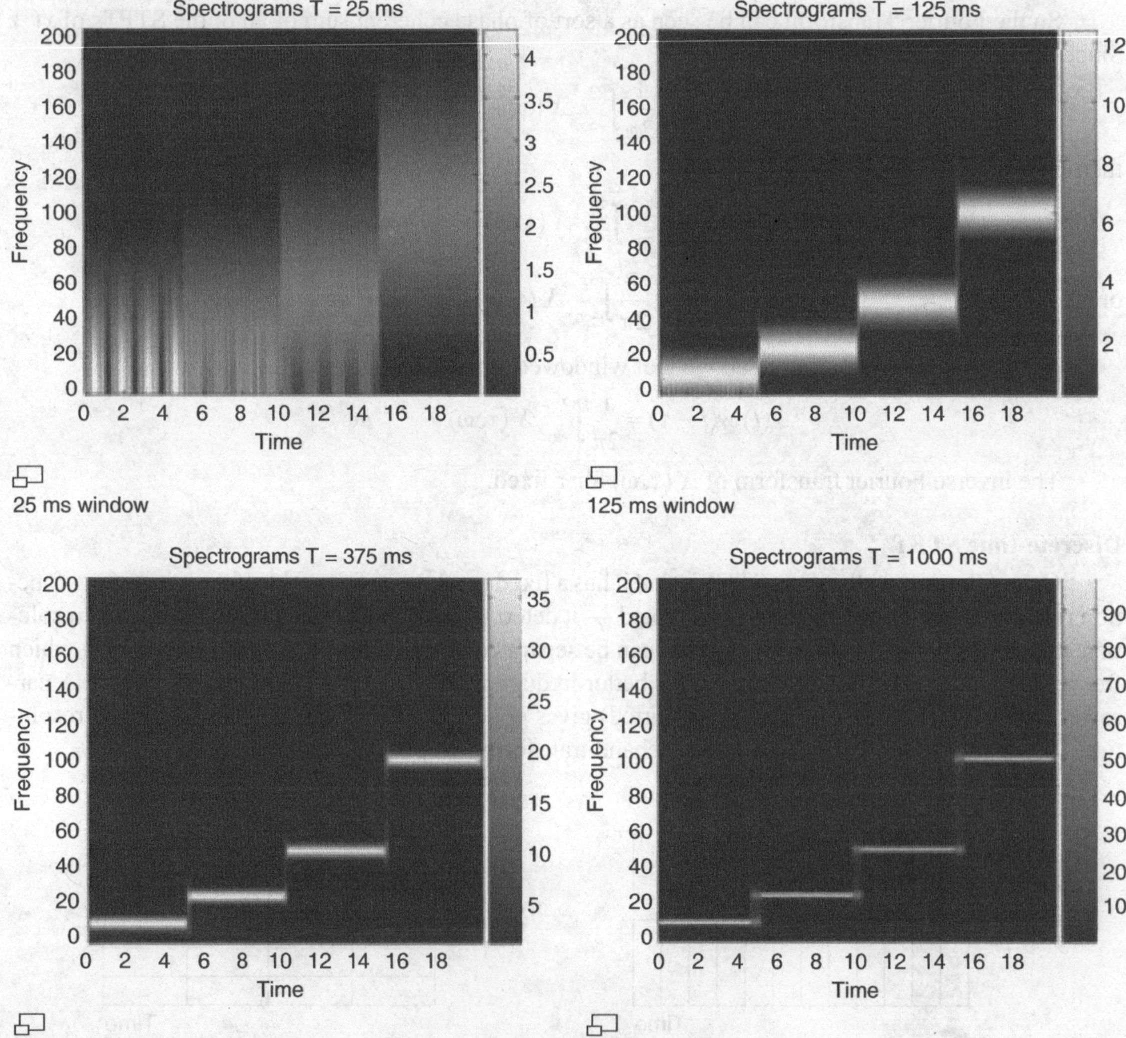

Fig. (3.2)

The 25 ms window allows us to identify a precise time at which the signals change but the precise frequencies are difficult to identify. At the other end of the scale, the 1000 ms window allows the frequencies to be precisely seen but the time between frequency changes is blurred.

Explanation : It can also be explained with reference to the sampling and Nyquist frequency. Take a window of N samples from an arbitrary real-valued signal at sampling rate f_s. Taking the Fourier transform produces N coefficients. Of these coefficients only the first $N/2$ are useful (the others are just a mirror image as this is a real valued signal). These $N/2$ coefficients represent the frequencies 0 to $f_s/2$ (Nyquist), meaning that two consecutive coefficients are spaced apart by

$$\frac{f_s/2}{(N/2)-1\,\text{Hz}}$$

For large N this approximates to $\frac{f_s}{N}$.

To increase the frequency resolution of the window the frequency spacing of the coefficients needs to be reduced. There are only two variables, but decreasing f_s (and keeping N constant) will cause the window size to increase — since there are now fewer samples per unit time. The other alternative is to increase N, but this again causes the window size to increase. So any attempt to increase the frequency resolution causes a larger window size and therefore a reduction in time resolution — and vice-versa.

Application : STFTs as well as standard Fourier transforms and other tools are frequently used to analyze music. The image shows frequency on the horizontal axis, with the lowest frequencies at left, and the highest at the right. The height of each bar (augmented by color) represents the amplitude of the

Fig. (3.3) A STFT being used to analyze a song across time.

frequencies within that band. The depth dimension represents time, where each new bar was a separate distinct transform. Audio engineers use this kind of visual to gain information about an audio sample, for example, to locate the frequencies of specific noises (especially when used with greater frequency resolution) or to find frequencies which may be more or less resonant in the space where the signal was recorded. This information can be used for equalization or tuning other audio effects.

3.4 FRACTIONAL FOURIER TRANSFORMS

In mathematics, in the area of harmonic analysis, the fractional Fourier transform (FRFT) is a linear transformation generalizing the Fourier transform. It can be thought of as the Fourier transform to the nth power where n need not be an integer — thus, it can transform a function to an intermediate domain between time and frequency. Its applications range from filter design and signal analysis to phase retrieval and pattern recognition.

The FRFT can be used to define fractional convolution, correlation, and other operations, and can also be further generalized into the linear canonical transformation (LCT). An early definition of the FRFT was given by Namias (1980), but it was not widely recognized until it was independently reinvented around 1993 by several groups of researchers (Almeida, 1994).

A completely different meaning for "fractional Fourier transform" was introduced by Bailey and Swartztrauber (1991) as essentially another name for a z-transform, and in particular for the case that corresponds to a discrete Fourier transform shifted by a fractional amount in frequency space (multiplying the input by a linear chirp) and evaluating at a fractional set of frequency points (e.g. considering only a small portion of the spectrum). (Such transforms can be evaluated efficiently by Bluestein's FFT algorithm.) This terminology has fallen out of use in most of the technical literature, however, in preference to the FRFT. The remainder of this article describes the FRFT.

Definition : If the continuous Fourier transform of a function $f(t)$ is denoted by $F(f)$, then $F^2(f) = F(F(f))$, and in general $F^{(n+1)}(f) = F(F^n(f))$; similarly, $F^{-n}(F)$ denotes the nth power of the inverse transform $F^{-1}(F)$ of $F(\omega)$. The FRFT further extends this definition to handle non-integer powers $n = 2a/\pi$ for any real α, denoted by $F_\alpha(f)$ and having the properties:

$$F_\alpha(f) = F^{2\alpha/\pi}(f)$$

when $n = 2a/\pi$ is an integer, and:

$$F_{\alpha+\beta}(f) = F_\alpha(F_\beta(f)) = F_\beta(F_\alpha(f))$$

More specifically, $F_\alpha(f)$ is given by the equation:

$$F_\alpha(f)(\omega) = \sqrt{\frac{1 - i\cot(\alpha)}{2\pi}}\, e^{i\cos(\alpha)\,\omega^2/2} \int_{-\infty}^{\infty} e^{-i\,\mathrm{cse}(\alpha)\,\omega t + i\cot(\alpha)\, t^2/2} f(t)\, dt$$

Note that, for $a = \pi/2$, this becomes precisely the definition of the continuous Fourier transform, and for $a = -\pi/2$ it is the definition of the inverse continuous Fourier transform.

If α is an integer multiple of π, then the cotangent and cosecant functions above diverge. However, this can be handled by taking the limit, and leads to a Dirac delta function in the integrand. More easily, since $F^2(f) = f(-t)$, $F_\alpha(f)$ must be simply $f(t)$ or $f(-t)$ for α an even or odd multiple of π, respectively. There also exist related fractional generalizations of similar transforms such as the discrete Fourier transform.

■ 3.5 DISCRETE FOURIER TRANSFORM (DFT)

In mathematics, the discrete Fourier transform (DFT), occasionally called the finite Fourier transform, is a transform for Fourier analysis of finite-domain discrete-time signals. It is widely employed in signal processing and related fields to analyze the frequencies contained in a sampled signal, to solve partial differential equations, and to perform other operations such as convolutions. The DFT can be computed efficiently in practice using a fast Fourier transform (FFT) algorithm.

Since FFT algorithms are so commonly employed to compute the DFT, the two terms are often used interchangeably in colloquial settings, although there is a clear distinction: "DFT" refers to a mathematical transformation, regardless of how it is computed, while "FFT" refers to any one of several efficient algorithms for the DFT. This distinction is further blurred, however, by the synonym "finite Fourier transform" for the DFT, which apparently predates the term "fast Fourier transform" (Cooley et al., 1969) but has the same initialism.

Definition : The sequence of N complex numbers $x_0, \ldots, x_{N-1}$ is transformed into the sequence of N complex numbers $X_0, \ldots, X_{N-1}$ by the DFT according to the formula:

$$X_k = \sum_{n=0}^{N-1} x_n \, e^{-\frac{2\pi i}{N} kn} \qquad k = 0, \ldots, N-1$$

where e is the base of the natural logarithm, i is the imaginary unit ($i^2 = -1$), and π is pi. The transform is sometimes denoted by the symbol F, as in $X = F\{x\}$ or $F(x)$ or Fx.

The inverse discrete Fourier transform (IDFT) is given by

$$x_n = \frac{1}{N} \sum_{k=0}^{N-1} X_k \, e^{\frac{2\pi i}{N} kn} \qquad n = 0, \ldots, N-1$$

Note that the normalization factor multiplying the DFT and IDFT (here 1 and 1/N) and the signs of the exponents are merely conventions, and differ in some treatments. The only requirements of these conventions are that the DFT and IDFT have opposite-sign exponents and that the product of their normalization factors be 1/N. A normalization of for both the DFT and IDFT makes the transforms unitary, which has some theoretical advantages, but it is often more practical in numerical computation to perform the scaling all at once as above (and a unit scaling can be convenient in other ways).

(The convention of a negative sign in the exponent is often convenient because it means that Xk is the amplitude of a "positive frequency" 2?k / N. Equivalently, the DFT is often thought of as a matched filter: when looking for a frequency of +1, one correlates the incoming signal with a frequency of ?1.)

Properties :

Completeness : The discrete Fourier transform is an invertible, linear transformation

$$F : C^N \to C^N$$

with C denoting the set of complex numbers. In other words, for any N > 0, an N-dimensional complex vector has a DFT and an IDFT which are in turn N-dimensional complex vectors.

Orthogonality : The vectors $e^{\frac{2\pi i}{N} kn}$ form an orthogonal basis over the set of N-dimensional complex vectors:

$$\sum_{n=0}^{N-1} \left(e^{\frac{2\pi i}{N} kn}\right)\left(e^{-\frac{2\pi i}{N} k'n}\right) = N\,\delta_{kk'}$$

where $\delta_{kk'}$ is the Kronecker delta. This orthogonality condition can be used to derive the formula for the IDFT from the definition of the DFT.

The Plancherel theorem and Parseval's theorem

If X_k and Y_k are the DFTs of x_n and y_n respectively then we have the Plancherel theorem:

$$\sum_{n=0}^{N-1} x_n \, y_n^* = \frac{1}{N} \sum_{k=0}^{N-1} X_k \, Y_k^*$$

where the star denotes complex conjugation. Parseval's theorem is a special case of the Plancherel theorem and states:

$$\sum_{n=0}^{N-1} |x_n|^2 = \frac{1}{N} \sum_{k=0}^{N-1} |X_k|^2$$

Periodicity : If the expression that defines the DFT is evaluated for all integers k instead of just for , then the resulting infinite sequence is a periodic extension of the DFT, periodic with period N.

The periodicity can be shown directly from the definition:

$$X_{k+N} = \sum_{n=0}^{N-1} x_n e^{-\frac{2\pi i}{N}(k+N)n} = \sum_{n=0}^{N-1} x_n e^{-\frac{2\pi i}{N}kn} e^{-2\pi i n} = \sum_{n=0}^{N-1} x_n e^{-\frac{2\pi i}{N}kn} = X_k$$

where we have used the fact that $e^{-2\pi i} = 1$. In the same way it can be shown that the IDFT formula leads to a periodic extension.

The Shift Theorem

Multiplying x_n by a linear phase $e^{\frac{2\pi i}{N}nm}$ for some integer m corresponds to a circular shift of the output X_k; X_k is replaced by X_{k-m}, where the subscript is interpreted modulo N (i.e. periodically). Similarly, a circular shift of the input x_n corresponds to multiplying the output X_k by a linear phase. Mathematically, if $\{x_n\}$ represents the vector x then

if $$F(\{x_n\})_k = X_k$$

then $$F(\{x_n e^{\frac{2\pi i}{N}nm}\})_k = X_{k-m}$$

and $$F(\{x_{n-m}\})_k = X_k e^{-\frac{2\pi i}{N}km}$$

Circular convolution theorem and cross-correlation theorem

The cyclic or circular convolution $x * y$ of the two vectors $x = x_k$ and $y = y_n$ is the vector $x * y$ with components

$$(x * y)_n = \sum_{m=0}^{N-1} x_m y_{n-m} \qquad n = 0, \ldots, N-1$$

where we continue y cyclically so that

$$y_{-m} = y_{N-m} \qquad m = 0, \ldots, N-1$$

The discrete Fourier transform turns cyclic convolutions into component-wise multiplication. That is, if

$$z_n = (x * y)_n$$

then $$Z_k = X_k Y_k \qquad k = 0, \ldots, N-1$$

where capital letters (X, Y, Z) represent the DFTs of sequences represented by small letters (x, y, z). Note that if a different normalization convention is adopted for the DFT (e.g., the unitary normalization), then there will in general be a constant factor multiplying the above relation.

The direct evaluation of the convolution summation, above, would require $O(N^2)$ operations, but the DFT (via an FFT) provides an $O(N \log N)$ method to compute the same thing. Conversely, convolutions can be used to efficiently compute DFTs via Rader's FFT algorithm and Bluestein's FFT algorithm.

In an analogous manner, it can be shown that if z_n is the cross-correlation of x_n and y_n:

$$z_n = (x * y)_n = \sum_{m=0}^{N-1} x_m^* \, y_{m+n}$$

where the sum is again cyclic in m, then the discrete Fourier transform of zn is:

$$Z_k = X_k^* \, Y_k$$

where capital letters are again used to signify the discrete Fourier transform.

Trigonometric interpolation polynomial

The trigonometric interpolation polynomial

$$p(t) = \frac{X_0}{N} + \frac{X_1}{N} e^{it} + \ldots + \frac{X_{N/2}}{N} \cos(Nt/2) + \frac{X_{N/2+1}}{N} e^{(-N/2+1)it} + \ldots + \frac{X_{N-1}}{N} e^{-it}$$

for N even,

$$p(t) = \frac{X_0}{N} + \frac{X_1}{N} e^{it} + \ldots + \frac{X_{[N/2]}}{N} e^{[N/2]it} + \frac{X_{[N/2]+1}}{N} e^{-[N/2]it} + \ldots + \frac{X_{N-1}}{N} e^{-it}$$

for N odd,

where the coefficients X_k / N are given by the DFT of x_n above, satisfies the interpolation property $p(2\pi n/N) = x_n$ for $n = 0, \ldots, N-1$.

For even N, notice that the Nyquist component $\frac{X_{N/2}}{N} \cos(Nt/2)$ is handled specially.

This interpolation is not unique: aliasing implies that one could add N to any of the complex-sinusoid frequencies (e.g. changing e^{-it} to $e^{i(N-1)t}$) without changing the interpolation property, but giving different values in between the x_n points. The choice above, however, is typical because it has two useful properties. First, it consists of sinusoids whose frequencies have the smallest possible magnitudes, and therefore minimizes the mean-square slope $\int |p^i(t)|^2 \, dt$ of the interpolating function. Second, if the xn are real numbers, then $p(t)$ is real as well.

In contrast, the most obvious trigonometric interpolation polynomial is the one in which the frequencies range from 0 to N ? 1 (instead of roughly ? N / 2 to + N / 2 as above), similar to the inverse DFT formula. This interpolation does not minimize the slope, and is not generally real-valued for real xn; its use is a common mistake.

The Unitary DFT

Another way of looking at the DFT is to note that in the above discussion, the DFT can be expressed as a Vandermonde matrix:

$$F = \begin{bmatrix} \omega_N^{0.0} & \omega_N^{0.0} & \cdots & \omega_N^{0.(N-1)} \\ \omega_N^{1.0} & \omega_N^{1.1} & \cdots & \omega_N^{1.(N-1)} \\ \vdots & \vdots & & \vdots \\ \omega_N^{(N-1).0} & \omega_N^{(N-1).1} & \cdots & \omega_N^{[(N-1)(N-1)} \end{bmatrix}$$

where $$\omega_N = e^{-2\pi i/N}$$

is a primitive *N*th root of unity. The inverse transform is then given by the inverse of the above matrix:

$$F^{-1} = \frac{1}{N} F^{+}$$

With unitary normalization constants $1/\sqrt{N}$, the DFT becomes a unitary transformation, defined by a unitary matrix:

$$U = F/\sqrt{N}$$

$$U^{-1} = U^{+}$$

$$|\det(U)| = 1$$

where det() is the determinant function. The determinant is the product of the eigenvalues, and therefore (see below) is always or . In a real vector space, a unitary transformation can be thought of as simply a rigid rotation of the coordinate system, and all of the properties of a rigid rotation can be found in the unitary DFT.

The orthogonality of the DFT is now expressed as an orthonormality condition (which arises in many areas of mathematics as described in root of unity):

$$\sum_{m=0}^{N-1} U_{km} U^{+}_{mn} = \delta_{kn}$$

If *X* is defined as the unitary DFT of the vector *X* then

$$X_k = \sum_{n=0}^{N-1} U_{kn} x_n$$

and the Plancherel theorem is expressed as:

$$\sum_{n=0}^{N-1} x_n y_n^* = \sum_{k=0}^{N-1} X_k Y_k^*$$

If we view the DFT as just a coordinate transformation which simply specifies the components of a vector in a new coordinate system, then the above is just the statement that the dot product of two vectors is preserved under a unitary DFT transformation. For the special case $x = y$, this implies that the length of a vector is preserved as well—this is just Parseval's theorem:

$$\sum_{n=0}^{N-1} |x_n|^2 = \sum_{k=0}^{N-1} |X_k|^2$$

Expressing the inverse DFT in terms of the DFT : A useful property of the DFT is that the inverse DFT can be easily expressed in terms of the (forward) DFT, via several well-known "tricks". (For example, in computations, it is often convenient to only implement a fast Fourier transform corresponding to one transform direction and then to get the other transform direction from the first.)

First, we can compute the inverse DFT by reversing the inputs:

$$F^{-1}(\{x_n\}) = F(\{x_{N-n}\})/N$$

(As usual, the subscripts are interpreted modulo *N*; thus, for $n = 0$, we have $x_{N-0} = x_0$).

Second, one can also conjugate the inputs and outputs:

$$F^{-1}(x) = F(x^*)^*/N$$

Third, a variant of this conjugation trick, which is sometimes preferable because it requires no modification of the data values, involves swapping real and imaginary parts (which can be done on a computer simply by modifying pointers). Define swap(xn) as xn with its real and imaginary parts swapped—that is, if xn = a + bi then swap(xn) is b + ai. Equivalently, swap(xn) equals . Then

$$F^{-1}(x) = \text{swap}\,(F(\text{swap}(x)))/N$$

That is, the inverse transform is the same as the forward transform with the real and imaginary parts swapped for both input and output, up to a normalization, The conjugation trick can also be used to define a new transform, closely related to the DFT, that is involutary—that is, which is its own inverse. In particular, is clearly its own inverse: . A closely related involutary transformation (by a factor of (1+i) /?2) is , since the (1 + i) factors in cancel the 2. For real inputs , the real part of is none other than the discrete Hartley transform, which is also involutary.

Eigenvalues and Eigenvectors

The eigenvalues of the DFT matrix are simple and well-known, whereas the eigenvectors are complicated, not unique, and are the subject of ongoing research.

Consider the unitary form defined above for the DFT of length N, where $U_{m,n} = \omega_N^{mn}/\sqrt{N} = \exp(-2\pi imn/N)/\sqrt{N}$. This matrix satisfies the equation:

$$U^4 + 1$$

This can be seen from the inverse properties above: operating twice gives the original data in reverse order, so operating four times gives back the original data and is thus the identity matrix. This means that the eigenvalues ? satisfy a characteristic equation:

$$\lambda^4 = 1$$

Therefore, the eigenvalues of are the fourth roots of unity: ? is +1, ?1, +i, or ?i.

Since there are only four distinct eigenvalues for this matrix, they have some multiplicity. The multiplicity gives the number of linearly independent eigenvectors corresponding to each eigenvalue. (Note that there are *N* independent eigenvectors; the matrix is not defective.)

The problem of their multiplicity was solved by McClellan and Parks (1972), although it was later shown to have been equivalent to a problem solved by Gauss (Dickinson and Steiglitz, 1982). The multiplicity depends on the value of *N* modulo 4, and is given by the following table:

Size *N*	**$\lambda = +1$**	**$\lambda = -1$**	**$\lambda = +1$**	**$\lambda = -1$**
$4m$	$m+1$	m	m	$m-1$
$4m+1$	$m+1$	m	m	m
$4m+2$	$m+1$	$m+1$	m	m
$4m+3$	$m+1$	$m+1$	$m+1$	m

Multiplicities of the eigenvalues ? of the unitary DFT matrix U as a function of the transform size N (in terms of an integer m).

Unfortunately, no simple analytical formula for the eigenvectors is known. Moreover, the eigenvectors are not unique because any linear combination of eigenvectors for the same eigenvalue is also an eigenvector for that eigenvalue. Various researchers have proposed different choices of eigenvectors, selected to satisfy useful properties like orthogonality and to have "simple" forms (e.g.,

McClellan and Parks, 1972; Dickinson and Steiglitz, 1982; Grünbaum, 1982; Atakishiyev and Wolf, 1997; Candan et al., 2000; Hanna et al., 2004).

The choice of eigenvectors of the DFT matrix has become important in recent years in order to define a discrete analogue of the fractional Fourier transform—the DFT matrix can be taken to fractional powers by exponentiating the eigenvalues (e.g., Rubio and Santhanam, 2005). For the continuous Fourier transform, the natural orthogonal eigenfunctions are the Hermite functions, so various discrete analogues of these have been employed as the eigenvectors of the DFT, such as the Kravchuk polynomials .The "best" choice of eigenvectors to define a fractional discrete Fourier transform remains an open question, however.

The Real-input DFT

If $x_0, \ldots, x_{N-1}$ are real numbers, as they often are in practical applications, then the DFT obeys the symmetry:

$$X_k = X^*_{N-k}$$

where the star denotes complex conjugation and the subscripts are interpreted modulo N.

Therefore, the DFT output for real inputs is half redundant, and one obtains the complete information by only looking at roughly half of the outputs $X_0, \ldots, X_{N-1}$. In this case, the "DC" element X0 is purely real, and for even N the "Nyquist" element XN / 2 is also real, so there are exactly N non-redundant real numbers in the first half + Nyquist element of the complex output X.

Using Euler's formula, the interpolating trigonometric polynomial can then be interpreted as a sum of sine and cosine functions.

Generalized/shifted DFT

It is possible to shift the transform sampling in time and/or frequency domain by some real shifts a and b, respectively. This is sometimes known as a generalized DFT (or GDFT), also called the shifted DFT or offset DFT, and has analogous properties to the ordinary DFT:

$$X_k = \sum_{n=0}^{N-1} x_n \, e^{-\frac{2\pi i}{N}(k+b)(n+a)} \qquad k = 0, \ldots, N-1$$

Most often, shifts of 1 / 2 (half a sample) are used. While the ordinary DFT corresponds to a periodic signal in both time and frequency domains, a = 1 / 2 produces a signal that is anti-periodic in frequency domain (Xk + N = ? Xk) and vice-versa for b = 1 / 2. Thus, the specific case of a = b = 1 / 2 is known as an odd-time odd-frequency discrete Fourier transform (or O2 DFT). Such shifted transforms are most often used for symmetric data, to represent different boundary symmetries, and for real-symmetric data they correspond to different forms of the discrete cosine and sine transforms.

Another interesting choice is a = b = ? (N ? 1) / 2, which is called the centered DFT (or CDFT). The centered DFT has the useful property that, when N is a multiple of four, all four of its eigenvalues have equal multiplicities.

The discrete Fourier transform can be viewed as a special case of the z-transform, evaluated on the unit circle in the complex plane; more general z-transforms correspond to complex shifts a and b above.

Multidimensional DFT

The ordinary DFT computes the transform of a "one-dimensional" dataset: a sequence (or array) xn that is a function of one discrete variable n. More generally, one can define the multidimensional DFT of a multidimensional array that is a function of d discrete variables for in :

$$X_{k_1, k_2, \ldots, k_d} = \sum_{n_1=0}^{N_1-1} \left(\omega_{N_1}^{k_1 n_1} \sum_{n_2=0}^{N_2-1} \left(\omega_{N_2}^{k_2 n_2} \cdots \sum_{n_d=0}^{N_d-1} \omega_{N_d}^{k_d n_d} \cdot x_{n_1, n_2, \ldots, n_d} \right) \cdots \right)$$

where as above and the d output indices run from . This is more compactly expressed in vector notation, where we define and as d-dimensional vectors of indices from 0 to , which we define as :

$$N - 1 = (N_1 - 1, N_2 - 1, \ldots, N_d - 1)$$

$$x_n = \frac{1}{\prod_{l=1}^{d} N_l} \sum_{k=0}^{N-1} e^{2\pi i n.(k/N)} X_k$$

where the division is defined as to be performed element-wise, and the sum denotes the set of nested summations above.

The inverse of the multi-dimensional DFT is, analogous to the one-dimensional case, given by:

$$x_n = \frac{1}{\prod_{l=1}^{d} N_l} \sum_{k=0}^{N-1} e^{2\pi i n.(k/N)} X_k$$

The multidimensional DFT has a simple interpretation. Just as the one-dimensional DFT expresses the input xn as a superposition of sinusoids, the multidimensional DFT expresses the input as a superposition of plane waves, or sinusoids oscillating along the direction in space and having amplitude . Such a decomposition is of great importance for everything from digital image processing (d = 2) to solving partial differential equations in three dimensions (d = 3) by breaking the solution up into plane waves.

Computationally, the multidimensional DFT is simply the composition of a sequence of one-dimensional DFTs along each dimension. For example, in the two-dimensional case one can first compute the N1 independent DFTs of the rows (i.e., along n2) to form a new array , and then compute the N2 independent DFTs of y along the columns (along n1) to form the final result . Or, one can transform the columns and then the rows—the order is immaterial because the nested summations above commute.

Because of this, given a way to compute a one-dimensional DFT (e.g. an ordinary one-dimensional FFT algorithm), one immediately has a way to efficiently compute the multidimensional DFT. This is known as a row-column algorithm, although there are also intrinsically multidimensional FFT algorithms.

Applications : The DFT has seen wide usage across a large number of fields; we only sketch a few examples below (see also the references at the end). All applications of the DFT depend crucially on the availability of a fast algorithm to compute discrete Fourier transforms and their inverses, a fast Fourier transform.

Spectral analysis : When the DFT is used for spectral analysis, the sequence usually represents a finite set of uniformly-spaced time-samples of some signal , where t represents time. The conversion from continuous time to samples (discrete-time) changes the underlying Fourier transform of x(t) into a discrete-time Fourier transform (DTFT), which generally entails a type of distortion called aliasing. Choice of an appropriate sample-rate is the key to minimizing that distortion. Similarly, the conversion from a very long (or infinite) sequence to a manageable size entails a type of distortion called leakage, which is manifested as a loss of detail (aka resolution) in the DTFT.

Choice of an appropriate sub-sequence length is the primary key to minimizing that effect. When the available data (and time to process it) is more than the amount needed to attain the desired frequency resolution, a standard technique is to perform multiple DFTs, for example to create a spectrogram. If the desired result is a power spectrum and noise or randomness is present in the data, averaging the magnitude components of the multiple DFTs is a useful procedure to reduce the variance of the spectrum (also called a periodogram in this context); two examples of such techniques are the Welch method and the Bartlett method.

A final source of distortion (or perhaps illusion) is the DFT itself, because it is just a discrete sampling of the DTFT, which is a function of a continuous frequency domain. That can be mitigated by increasing the resolution of the DFT. The procedure is sometimes referred to as zero-padding, which is a particular implementation used in conjunction with the fast Fourier transform (FFT) algorithm. The inefficiency of performing multiplications and additions with zero-valued "samples" is more than offset by the inherent efficiency of the FFT. leakage imposes a limit on the inherent resolution of the DTFT. So there is a practical limit to the benefit that can be obtained from a fine-grained DFT.

Data Compression

The field of digital signal processing relies heavily on operations in the frequency domain (i.e. on the Fourier transform). For example, several lossy image and sound compression methods employ the discrete Fourier transform: the signal is cut into short segments, each is transformed, and then the Fourier coefficients of high frequencies, which are assumed to be unnoticeable, are discarded. The decompressor computes the inverse transform based on this reduced number of Fourier coefficients. (Compression applications often use a specialized form of the DFT, the discrete cosine transform or sometimes the modified discrete cosine transform).

Partial Differential Equations

Discrete Fourier transforms are often used to solve partial differential equations, where again the DFT is used as an approximation for the Fourier series (which is recovered in the limit of infinite N). The advantage of this approach is that it expands the signal in complex exponentials einx, which are eigenfunctions of differentiation: d/dx einx = in einx. Thus, in the Fourier representation, differentiation is simple—we just multiply by i n. A linear differential equation with constant coefficients is transformed into an easily solvable algebraic equation. One then uses the inverse DFT to transform the result back into the ordinary spatial representation. Such an approach is called a spectral method.

Multiplication of large integers : The fastest known algorithms for the multiplication of large integers or polynomials are based on the discrete Fourier transform: the sequences of digits or coefficients are interpreted as vectors whose convolution needs to be computed; in order to do this, they are first Fourier-transformed, then multiplied component-wise, then transformed back.

Outline of DFT polynomial multiplication algorithm : Suppose we wish to compute the polynomial product $c(x) = a(x) \cdot b(x)$. The ordinary product expression for the coefficients of c involves a linear (acyclic) convolution, where indices do not "wrap around." This can be rewritten as a cyclic convolution by taking the coefficient vectors for a(x) and b(x) with constant term first, then appending zeros so that the resultant coefficient vectors a and b have dimension $d > \deg(a(x)) + \deg(b(x))$. Then,

$$c = a + b$$

where c is the vector of coefficients for c(x), and the convolution operator is defined so

$$c_n = \sum_{m=0}^{d-1} a_m \, b_{n-m \bmod d} \qquad n = 0, 1, \ldots, d-1$$

But convolution becomes multiplication under the DFT:

$$F(c) = F(a)\,F(b)$$

Here the vector product is taken elementwise. Thus the coefficients of the product polynomial c(x) are just the terms 0, ..., deg(a(x)) + deg(b(x)) of the coefficient vector

$$c = F^{-1}(F(a)\,F(b))$$

With a Fast Fourier transform, the resulting algorithm takes O (N log N) arithmetic operations. Due to its simplicity and speed, the Cooley-Tukey FFT algorithm, which is limited to composite sizes, is often chosen for the transform operation. In this case, d should be chosen as the smallest integer greater than the sum of the input polynomial degrees that is factorizable into small prime factors (e.g. 2, 3, and 5, depending upon the FFT implementation).

Some discrete Fourier transform pairs :

Some DFT pairs :

$x_n = \frac{1}{N} \sum_{k=0}^{N-1} X_k . e^{i2\pi kn/N}$	$X_k = \sum_{n=0}^{N-1} x_n . e^{-i2\pi kn/N}$	**Note :** Shift theorem
$x_n . e^{i2\pi nl/N}$	X_{k-l}	Real DFT
x_{n-l}	$X_k . e^{-i2\pi kl/N}$	
$x_n \in R$	$X_k = X_{N-k}^{*}$	
a^n	$\frac{1-a^N}{1-a . e^{-i2\pi k/N}}$	
$\binom{N-1}{n}$	$(1+e^{-i2\pi k/N})^{N-1}$	

Derivation as Fourier Series

The DFT can be derived as a truncation of the Fourier series of a periodic sequence of impulses.

■ 3.6 BASIS OF FILTERING IN FREQUENCY DOMAIN

Frequency filters process an image in the frequency domain. The image is Fourier transformed, multiplied with the filter function and then re-transformed into the spatial domain. Attenuating high frequencies results in a smoother image in the spatial domain, attenuating low frequencies enhances the edges.

All frequency filters can also be implemented in the spatial domain and, if there exists a simple kernel for the desired filter effect, it is computationally less expensive to perform the filtering in the spatial domain. Frequency filtering is more appropriate if no straightforward kernel can be found in the spatial domain, and may also be more efficient.

How It Works

Frequency filtering is based on the Fourier Transform. (For the following discussion we assume some knowledge about the Fourier Transform, therefore it is advantageous if you have already read the corresponding worksheet.) The operator usually takes an image and a filter function in the Fourier domain. This image is then multiplied with the filter function in a pixel-by-pixel fashion:

$$G(k, l) = F(k, l)\, H(k, l)$$

where F (k, l) is the input image in the Fourier domain, H (k,l) the filter function and G(k,l) is the filtered image. To obtain the resulting image in the spatial domain, G (k, l) has to be re-transformed using the inverse Fourier Transform.

Since the multiplication in the Fourier space is identical to convolution in the spatial domain, all frequency filters can in theory be implemented as a spatial filter. However, in practice, the Fourier domain filter function can only be approximated by the filtering kernel in spatial domain.

The form of the filter function determines the effects of the operator. There are basically three different kinds of filters: low pass, high pass and band pass filters. A low-pass filter attenuates high frequencies and retains low frequencies unchanged. The result in the spatial domain is equivalent to that of a smoothing filter; as the blocked high frequencies correspond to sharp intensity changes, i.e. to the fine-scale details and noise in the spatial domain image.

A high pass filter, on the other hand, yields edge enhancement or edge detection in the spatial domain, because edges contain many high frequencies. Areas of rather constant gray level consist of mainly low frequencies and are therefore suppressed.

A band pass attenuates very low and very high frequencies, but retains a middle range band of frequencies. Band pass filtering can be used to enhance edges (suppressing low frequencies) while reducing the noise at the same time (attenuating high frequencies).

The most simple low pass filter is the ideal low pass. It suppresses all frequencies higher than the cut-off frequency D_0 and leaves smaller frequencies unchanged:

$$H(k, l) = \begin{cases} 1 \text{ if } \sqrt{k^2 + l^2} < D_0 \\ 0 \text{ if } \sqrt{k^2 + l^2} > D_0 \end{cases}$$

In most implementations, D_0 is given as a fraction of the highest frequency represented in the Fourier domain image. The drawback of this filter function is a ringing effect that occurs along the edges of the filtered spatial domain image. This phenomenon is illustrated in Figure 1, which shows the shape of the one-dimensional filter in both the frequency and spatial domains for two different values of D_0.

We obtain the shape of the two-dimensional filter by rotating these functions about the y-axis. As mentioned earlier, multiplication in the Fourier domain corresponds to a convolution in the spatial domain. Due to the multiple peaks of the ideal filter in the spatial domain, the filtered image produces ringing along intensity edges in the spatial domain.

Better results can be achieved with a Gaussian shaped filter function. The advantage is that the Gaussian has the same shape in the spatial and Fourier domains and therefore does not incur the ringing effect in the spatial domain of the filtered image. A commonly used discrete approximation to the Gaussian is the Butter worth filter. Applying this filter in the frequency domain shows a similar result to the Gaussian smoothing in the spatial domain. One difference is that the computational cost of the spatial filter increases with the standard deviation (i.e. with the size of the filter kernel), whereas the costs for a frequency filter are independent of the filter function.

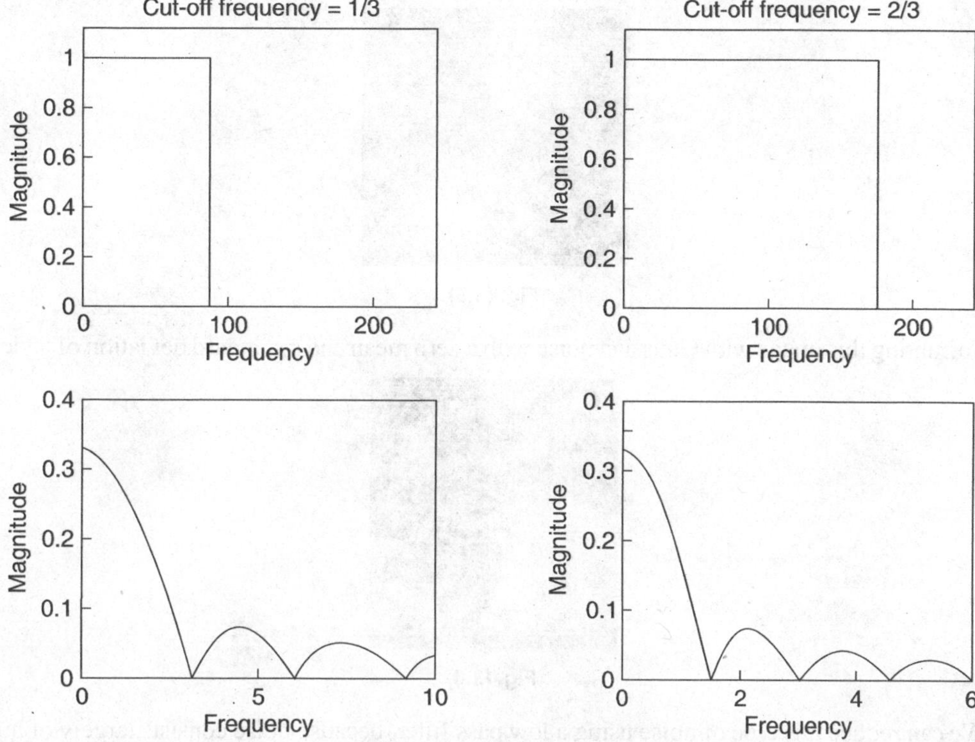

Fig. (3.4) Ideal low pass in frequency and spatial domain.

Hence, the spatial Gaussian filter is more appropriate for narrow low pass filters, while the Butter worth filter is a better implementation for wide low pass filters.

The same principles apply to high pass filters. We obtain a high pass filter function by inverting the corresponding low pass filter, e.g. an ideal high pass filter blocks all frequencies smaller than and leaves the others unchanged.

Band pass filters are a combination of both low pass and high pass filters. They attenuate all frequencies smaller than a frequency and higher than a frequency , while the frequencies between the two cut-offs remain in the resulting output image. We obtain the filter function of a band pass by multiplying the filter functions of a low pass and of a high pass in the frequency domain, where the cut-off frequency of the low pass is higher than that of the high pass.

Instead of using one of the standard filter functions, we can also create our own filter mask, thus enhancing or suppressing only certain frequencies. In this way we could, for example, remove periodic patterns with a certain direction in the resulting spatial domain image.

Guidelines for Use

Frequency domain filters are most commonly used as low pass filters. We will demonstrate this performance with

Fig. (3.5)

Corrupting this image with Gaussian noise with a zero mean and a standard deviation of 8 yields

Fig. (3.6)

We can reduce this type of noise using a low pass filter, because noise consists largely of high frequencies, which are attenuated by a low pass filter.

The image is the result of applying an ideal low pass filter to the noisy image with the cut-off frequency being . Although we managed to reduce the high frequency noise, this image is of no practical

Fig. (3.7)

use. We lost too many of the fine-scale details and the image exhibits strong ringing due to the shape of the ideal low pass filter.

Applying the same filter with a cut-off frequency of 0.5 yields

Fig. (3.8)

Since this filter keeps a greater number of frequencies, more details remain in the output image. The image is less blurred, but also contains more noise. The ringing is less severe, but still exists.

Better results can be achieved with Butter worth filter. We obtain with a cut-off frequency of . This image doesn't show any visible ringing and only little noise. However, it also lost some image information, i.e. the edges are blurred and the image contains less details than the original.

Fig. (3.9)

In order to retain more details, we increase the cut-off frequency to 0.5, as can be seen in

Fig. (3.10)

This image is less blurred, but also contains a reasonable amount of noise. In general, when using a low pass filter to reduce the high frequency noise, we have to compromise some desirable high frequency information if we want to smooth away significant amounts of noise.

The ringing effect originating from the shape of the ideal low pass can be better illustrated using

Fig. (3.11)

the following artificial image. The image is a binary image of a rectangle. Filtering this image with an ideal low pass filter (cut-off frequency) yields

Fig. (3.12)

The ringing is already recognizable in this image but is much more obvious in which is obtained af-

Fig. (3.13)

ter a histogram equalization. The effect gets even worse if we block more of the frequencies contained in the input image. In order to obtain

Fig. (3.14)

We used a cut-off frequency of . Apart from the (desired) smoothing the image also contains a severe ringing which clearly visible even without histogram equalization. We can also see that the cut-off frequency directly corresponds to the frequency of the ringing, i.e. as we double the cut-off frequency, we double the distance between two rings. The image

Fig. (3.15)

Has been filtered with Butter worth filter using a cut-off frequency of . In contrast to the above examples, this image doesn't exhibit any ringing.

We will illustrate the effects of high pass frequency filtering using as well. As a result of attenuating (or blocking) the low frequencies, areas of constant intensity in the input image are zero in the output

Fig. (3.16)

of the high pass filter. Areas of a strong intensity gradient, containing the high frequencies, have positive and negative intensity values in the filter output. In order to display the image on the screen, an offset is added to the output in the spatial domain and the image intensities are scaled. This results in a middle gray value for low frequency areas and dark and light values for the edges. The image

Fig. (3.17)

Shows the output of Butter worth high pass with the cut-off frequency being 0.5. An alternative way to display the filter output is to take the absolute value of the filtered spatial domain image. If we apply this method to the clown image (and threshold the result with 13) we obtain

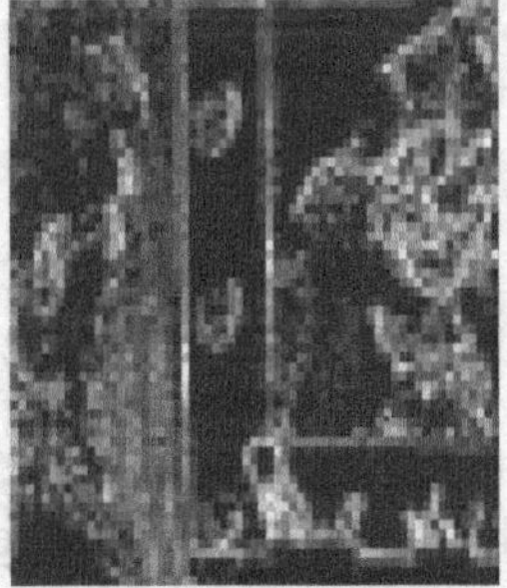

Fig. (3.18)

This image may be compared with

Fig. (3.19)

Which is an edge image produced by the Sobel operator and, thus, shows the absolute value of the edge magnitude. We can see that the Sobel operator detects the edges better than the high pass filter. In general, spatial filters are more commonly used for edge detection while frequency filters are more often used for high frequency emphasis. Here, the filter doesn't totally block low frequencies, but magnifies high frequencies relative to low frequencies. This technique is used in the printing industries to crispen image edges.

Frequency filters are quite useful when processing parts of an image, which can be associated with certain frequencies. For example, in each part of the house is made of stripes of a different frequency and

Fig. (3.20)

orientation. The corresponding Fourier Transform (after histogram equalization can be seen in

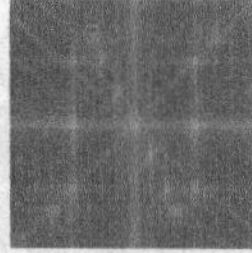

Fig. (3.21)

We can see the main peaks in the image corresponding to the periodic patterns in the spatial domain image which now can be accessed separately. For example, we can smooth the vertical stripes (i.e. those components which make up the wall in the spatial domain image) by multiplying the Fourier image with the frequency mask

Fig. (3.22)

The effect is that all frequencies within the black rectangle are set to zero, the others remain unchanged. Applying the inverse Fourier Transform and normalizing the resulting image yields in the spa-

Fig. (3.23)

tial domain. Although the image shows some regular patterns in the formerly constant background, the vertical stripes are almost totally removed whereas the other patterns remained mostly unchanged.

We can also use frequency filtering to achieve the opposite effect, i.e. finding all features in the image with certain characteristics in the frequency domain. For example, if we want to keep the vertical stripes (i.e. the wall) in the above image, we can use as a mask. To perform the frequency filtering we

Fig. (3.24)

transform both the image of the house and the mask into the Fourier domain where we multiply the two images with the effect that the frequencies occurring in the mask remain in the output while the others are set to zero. Re-transforming the output into the spatial domain and normalizing it yields

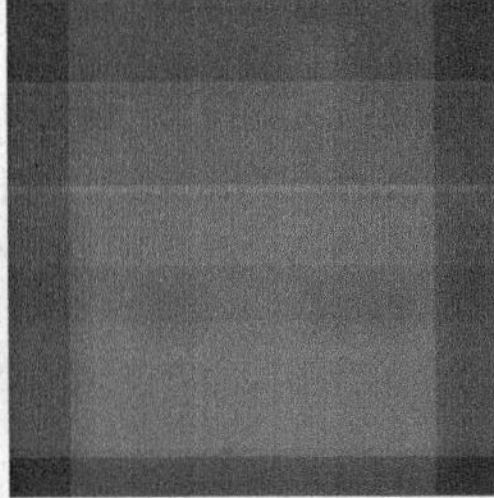

Fig. (3.25)

In this image, the dominant pattern is the one defined by the mask. The pixel values are the highest at places which were composed of this vertical pattern in the input image and are zero in most of the background areas. It is now possible to identify the desired area by applying a threshold, as can be seen in

Fig. (3.26)

To understand this process we should keep in mind that a multiplication in the Fourier domain is identical to a convolution in the spatial domain.

Frequency filters are also commonly used in image reconstruction. Here, the aim is to remove the effects of a non-ideal imaging system by multiplying the image in the Fourier space with an appropriate function. The easiest method, called inverse filtering, is to divide the image in the Fourier space with the optical transfer function (OTF). We illustrate this technique, also known as deconvolution, using

Fig. (3.27)

We simulate a non-ideal OTF by multiplying the Fourier Transform of the image with the Fourier Transform of a Gaussian image with a standard deviation of 5. Re-transforming the result into the spatial domain yields the blurred image

Fig. (3.28)

We can now reconstruct the original image using inverse filtering by taking the Fourier Transform of the blurred image and dividing it by the Fourier Transform of the Gaussian kernel, which was used to initially blur the image. The reconstructed image is shown in

Fig. (3.29)

Although we obtain, in the above case, exactly the original image, this method has two major problems. First, it is very sensitive to noise. If we, for example, add 0.1% spike noise to the blurred image, we obtain

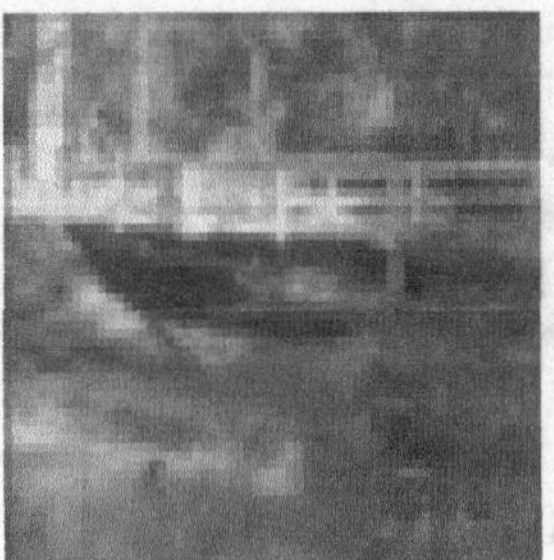

Fig. (3.30)

Inverse filtering the image (as described above) using this image in order to de-blur yields the low contrast result

Fig. (3.31)

(Note that doing contrast enhancement to emphasize the original image features can produce an image very similar to the original, except for a loss of fine details). The situation can be slightly improved if we ignore all values of the Fourier space division in which the divisor (i.e. the value of the OTF) is below a certain threshold. The effect of using a threshold of 3 can be seen in

Fig. (3.32)

However, if we increase the threshold we have to discard more of the Fourier values and therefore lose more image information. Hence, we will be less successful in reconstructing the original image.

The second problem with this image restoration method is that we need to know the OTF which corrupted the image in the first place. If we, for example, blur the image by convolving it with the Gaussian image in the spatial domain, we obtain

Fig. (3.33)

Although this should theoretically be the same image as obtained from the multiplication in the Fourier Space, we obtain small differences due to quantization errors and effects around the border of an image when convolving it in spatial domain. Reconstructing the original image by dividing the blurred image in the Fourier space with the Fourier Transform of the Gaussian yields

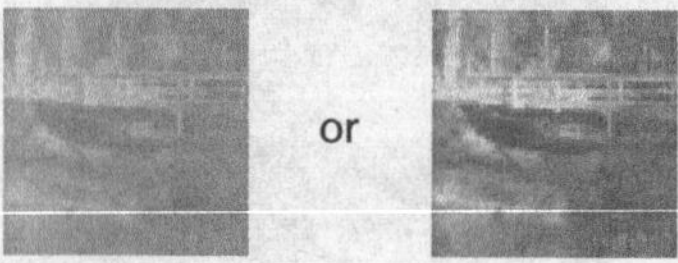

Fig. (3.34)

if we use a minimum OTF threshold of 5.

We face a similar problem if we want to deconvolve a real blurred image like

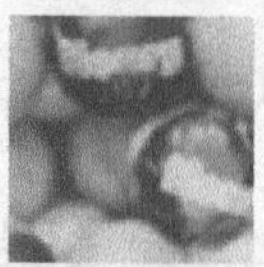

Fig. (3.35)

Since we do not know the transfer function which caused the blurring, we have to estimate it. The images are the results of estimating the OTF with a Gaussian image with a standard deviation of 3 and 10,

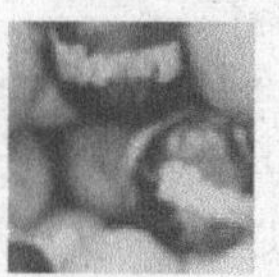

and

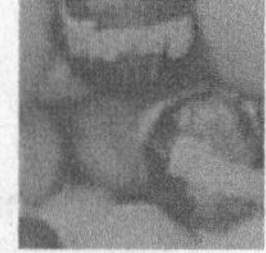

Fig. (3.36) **Fig. (3.37)**

respectively and applying an inverse filtering with a minimum OTF threshold of 10. We can see that the image improved only very little, if at all.

Due to the above problems, in most practical cases more sophisticated reconstruction methods are used. For example, Wiener filtering and Maximum Entropy filtering are two techniques that are based on the same principle as inverse filtering, but produce better results on real world images.

Finally, frequency filtering can also be used for pattern matching. For example, we might want to

Fig. (3.38)

find all locations in which are occupied by a certain letter, say X. To do this, we need an image of an isolated X which can act as a mask, in this case

Fig. (3.39)

To perform the pattern matching, we transform both image and mask into the Fourier space and multiply them. We apply the inverse Fourier Transform to the resulting Fourier image and scale the out-

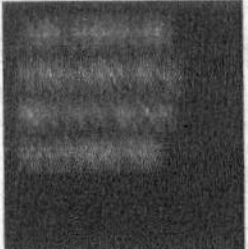

Fig. (3.40)

put to obtain in the spatial domain. This image is (theoretically) identical to the result of convolving image and mask in the spatial domain. Hence, the image shows high values at locations in the image which match the mask well. However, apart from the X, these are also other letters like the R and the K which match well. In fact, if we threshold the image at 255, as can be seen in we have two locations indicating an X, one of them being incorrect.

Fig. (3.41)

Since we multiplied the two complex Fourier images, we also changed the phase of the original text image. This results in a constant shift between the position of the letter in the original and its response in the processed image. The example shows that this straightforward method runs into problems if we want to distinguish between similar patterns or if the mask and the corresponding pattern in the data differ slightly. Another problem includes the fact that this operation is neither rotation- nor scale-invariant. (Note that we also run into these problems if we implement the operation as a simple convolution in the spatial domain.) The size of the pattern determines whether it is better to perform the matching in the spatial or frequency domain. In our case (the letter was approximately 10×20 pixels); it is substantially faster to do the matching in the frequency domain.

The above method might be modified in the following way: instead of multiplying the Fourier Transforms of the image and the mask as a first step, we threshold the Fourier image of the mask to identify the most important frequencies which make up the letter X in the spatial domain. For example, scaling the Fourier magnitude of the above mask to 255 and thresholding it at a value of 10 yields all the frequencies with at least 4% of the peak magnitude, as can be seen in

Fig. (3.42)

Now, we multiply this modified mask with the Fourier image of the text, thus retaining only frequencies which also appear in the letter X. Inverse Fourier Transforming this image yields

Fig. (3.43)

We can see that the X is the letter which preserved its shape the best and also has higher intensity values. Thresholding this image yields which correctly identifies the position of the X.

Fig. (3.44)

Interactive Experimentation : You can interactively experiment with this operator by clicking here.

Exercises

1. Apply median, mean and Gaussian smoothing to

Fig. (3.45)

and compare the results with the images obtained via lowpass filtering.

2. Add `salt and pepper' noise to

Fig. (3.46)

and then enhance the resulting image using a low pass filter. Which method would be more suitable and why?

3. Remove single parts from

Fig. (3.47)

(e.g. a window, the roof or the wall) by creating an appropriate mask and multiplying it with the Fourier Transform of the image

■ 3.7 FREQUENCY DOMAIN METHODS OF IMAGES FILTERING

Image enhancement in the frequency domain is straightforward. We simply compute the Fourier transform of the image to be enhanced, multiply the result by a filter (rather than convolve in the spatial domain), and take the inverse transform to produce the enhanced image.

The idea of blurring an image by reducing its high frequency components or sharpening an image by increasing the magnitude of its high frequency components is intuitively easy to understand. However, computationally, it is often more efficient to implement these operations as convolutions by small spatial filters in the spatial domain. Understanding frequency domain concepts is important, and leads to enhancement techniques that might not have been thought of by restricting attention to the spatial domain.

Filtering in the frequency domain is a common image and signal processing technique. It can smooth, sharpen, de-blur, and restore some images.

There are three basic steps to frequency domain filtering:

1. The image must be transformed from the spatial domain into the frequency domain using the Fast Fourier transform.
2. The resulting complex image must be multiplied by a filter (that usually has only real values).
3. The filtered image must be transformed back to the spatial domain.

These steps can be implemented in IDL using the Fast Fourier transform function FFT. A -1 argument to the FFT function indicates a transformation from the spatial to the frequency domain, and a 1 indicates the reverse transformation. The general form of the command is written like this, where image is either a vector or a two-dimensional image and filter is a vector or two-dimensional array designed to filter out certain frequencies in the image:

```
filtered_image = FFT(FFT(image, –1) * filter, 1)
```

3.7.1 Building Image Filters

IDL makes it easy to build many types of image filters with its array-oriented operators and functions. Many common filters take advantage of what is called a frequency image or Euclidean distance map. An Euclidean distance map for a two-dimensional image is an array of the same size as the image. Each pixel in the distance map is given a value that is equal to its distance from the nearest corner of the two-dimensional array. The DIST command in IDL is used to create the Euclidean distance map or frequency image. For example, to see a surface representation of a simple distance map, type:

```
SURFACE, DIST(40)
```

A common type of filter to use in frequency domain filtering is a Butterworth frequency filter. The general form of a low-pass Butterworth frequency filter is given by this equation:

filter = 1 / [1 + C(R/Ro)^2n]

Here the constant C is set equal to 1.0 or 0.414 (the value defines the magnitude of the filter at the point where R=Ro as either 50% or 1/Sqrt(2)), R is the frequency image, Ro is the nominal filter cutoff frequency (represented as a pixel width in practice), and n is the order of the filter and is usually 1.

A high-pass Butterworth frequency filter is given by this equation:

filter = 1 / [1 + C(Ro/R)^2n]

To see how frequency domain filtering works, open the image file convec.dat, which is among the files Research Systems provides with its demonstation directories. Your code will look something like this.

```
file = FILEPATH('convec.dat', SUBDIR='training')
OPENR, lun, file, /GET_LUN
convec = BYTARR(248,248)
READU, lun, convec
FREE_LUN, lun
```

Open a large window, load a color table, and display the unprocessed image in the upper left-hand corner, like this:

```
WINDOW, 0, XSIZE=248*2, YSIZE=248*2
LOADCT, 13
TV, convec, 0
```

3.7.2 Transforming the Image into the Frequency Domain

The first step in frequency domain filtering is to transform the image from the spacial domain into the frequency domain with the FFT function, like this:

```
freqDomainImage = FFT(convec, -1)
```

In general, the low frequency terms usually represent the general shape of the image and the high frequency terms are needed to sharpen the edges and provide fine detail. Looking at the frequency domain image is not usually instructive, but it is sometimes useful to observe the power spectrum of the frequency domain image.

The power spectrum is a plot of the magnitude of the various components of the frequency domain image. Different frequencies are represented at different distances from the origin (usually represented as the center of the image) and different directions from the origin represent different orientations of features in the original image. The power at each location shows how much of that frequency and orientation is present in the image. The power spectrum is particularly useful for isolating periodic structures or noise in the image. The power spectrum magnitude is usually represented on a log scale, since power can vary dramatically from one frequency to the next.

To see the power spectrum of this image next to the image, type:

```
power = SHIFT(ALOG(ABS(freqDomainImage)), 124, 124)
power = power - Min(power)
power = power * (255.0/Max(power))
TV, power, 1
```

You can see from the power spectrum that this image has lots of periodic structure at increasing frequencies. (Your display screen should look similar to the illustration below.) The next step will filter out the higher frequencies.

3.7.3 Appling the Frequency Domain Filter

The next step in the frequency domain filtering of an image is to apply a filter to the frequency domain image. Here you are going to construct a Butterworth low-pass frequency filter. This will filter out the high image frequencies that give detail to the image, and will result in an image smoothing operation. Construct the filter by typing:

```
filter = 1.0 / ( 1.0d + (DIST(248)/15.0)^2 )
```

Notice that the cutoff frequency width is 15 pixels here. You will be eliminating about half of the higher frequencies that you see in the power spectrum in the illustration below. These frequencies are normally those that provide detail in an image.

To apply the filter, back transform the image from the frequency domain to the spacial domain, and display the filtered image, type:

```
filtered = FFT(freqDomainImage * filter, 1)
TV, filtered, 2
```

Your display screen should look similar to the illustration below. The original image is on the left. The power spectrum of the original image is shown in the middle. Notice that there is a lot of periodic

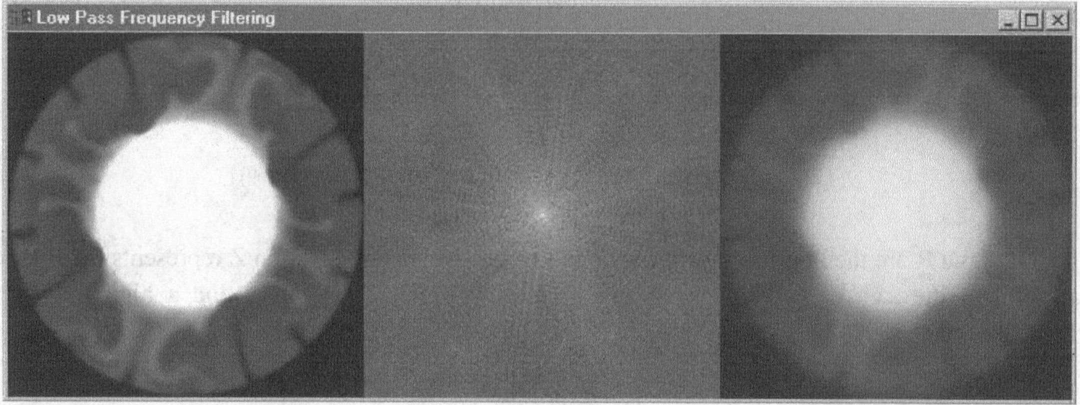

Fig. (3.48)

structure in this image. The filtered image is shown on the right. A low pass filter tends to blur or smooth the image, since it is the high frequency components that give the image detail.

3.8 FILTERING

Low pass filtering involves the elimination of the high frequency components in the image. It results in blurring of the image (and thus a reduction in sharp transitions associated with noise). An ideal low pass filter would retain all the low frequency components, and eliminate all the high frequency components. However, ideal filters suffer from two problems: blurring and ringing. These problems are caused by the shape of the associated spatial domain filter, which has a large number of undulations. Smoother transitions in the frequency domain filter, such as the Butter worth filter, achieve much better results.

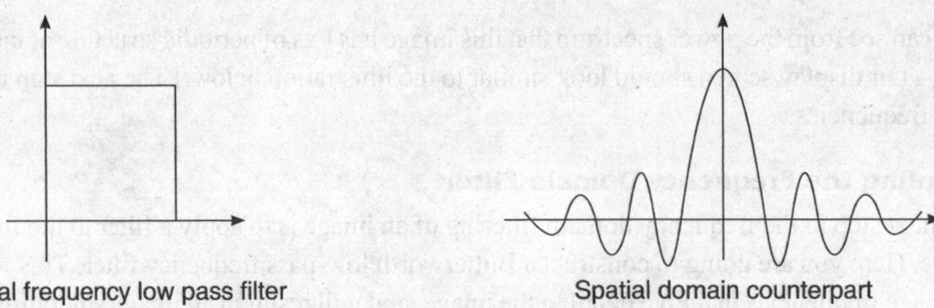

Fig. (3.49) Transfer function for an ideal low pass filer.

3.8.1 Homomorphic Filtering

Images normally consist of light reflected from objects. The basic nature of the image F(x,y) may be characterized by two components: (1) the amount of source light incident on the scene being viewed, and (2) the amount of light reflected by the objects in the scene. These portions of light are called the illumination and reflectance components, and are denoted i(x,y) and r(x,y) respectively. The functions i and r combine multiplicatively to give the image function F:

$$F(x, y) = i(x, y)\, r(x, y)$$

where and $0 < r(x,y) < 1$. We cannot easily use the above product to operate separately on the frequency components of illumination and reflection because the Fourier transform of the product of two functions is not separable; that is

$$F(F(x, y)) \neq F(i(x, y))\, F(r(x, y))$$

Suppose, however, that we define

$$x(x, y) = \ln F(x, y) = \ln i(x, y) + \ln r(x, y)$$

Then

$$F(z(x, y)) = F(\ln F(x, y)) = F(ln\, i(x, y)) + F(\ln r(x, y))$$

or

$$Z(\omega, \nu) = I(\omega, \nu) + R(\omega, \nu)$$

where Z, I and R are the Fourier transforms of and respectively. The function Z represents the Fourier transform of the sum of two images: a low frequency illumination image and a high frequency reflectance image.

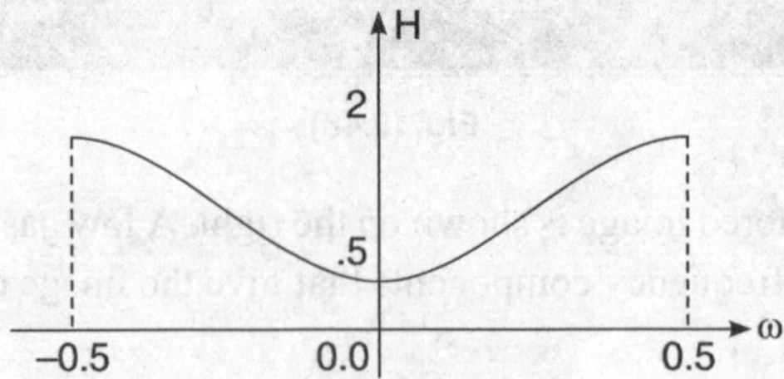

Fig. (3.50) Transfer function for homomorphic filtering.

If we now apply a filter with a transfer function that suppresses low frequency components and enhances high frequency components, then we can suppress the illumination component and enhance the reflectance component. Thus

$$S(\omega, \nu) = H(\omega, \nu)\, Z(\omega, nu) = H(\omega, \nu)\, I(\omega, \nu) + H(\omega, \nu)\, R(\omega, \nu)$$

where S is the Fourier transform of the result. In the spatial domain

$$s(x, y) = F^{-1}(S(\omega, v)) = F^{-1}(H(\omega, nu)\, I(\omega, v)) + F^{-1}(H(\omega, v)\, R(\omega, v))$$

By letting

$$i'(x, y) = F^{-1}(H(\omega, v)\, I(\omega, v))$$

and

$$r'(x, y) = F^{-1}(H(\omega, v)\, R(\omega, v))$$

we get

$$s(x, y) = i'(x, y) + r'(x, y)$$

Finally, as z was obtained by taking the logarithm of the original image F, the inverse yields the desired enhanced image : that is

$$\hat{F}(x, y) = \exp[s(x, y)] = \exp[i'(x, y)] \exp[r'(x, y)] = i_0(x, y)\, r_0(x, y)$$

Thus, the process of homomorphic filtering can be summarized by the following diagram:

f(x, y) ---> In ---> FFT ---> H ---> FFT^{-1} ---> exp ---> g(x, y)

Fig. (3.51) The process of homomorphic filtering.

3.8.2 Low-pass Filter

A low-pass filter is a filter that passes low frequencies but attenuates (or reduces) frequencies higher than the cutoff frequency. The actual amount of attenuation for each frequency varies from filter to filter. It is sometimes called a high-cut filter, or treble cut filter when used in audio applications.

A high-pass filter is the opposite, and a bandpass filter is a combination of a high-pass and a low-pass. The concept of a low-pass filter exists in many different forms, including electronic circuits (like a hiss filter used in audio), digital algorithms for smoothing sets of data, acoustic barriers, blurring of images, and so on. Low-pass filters play the same role in signal processing that moving averages do in some other fields, such as finance; both tools provide a smoother form of a signal which removes the short-term oscillations, leaving only the long-term trend.

Examples of Low-pass Filters

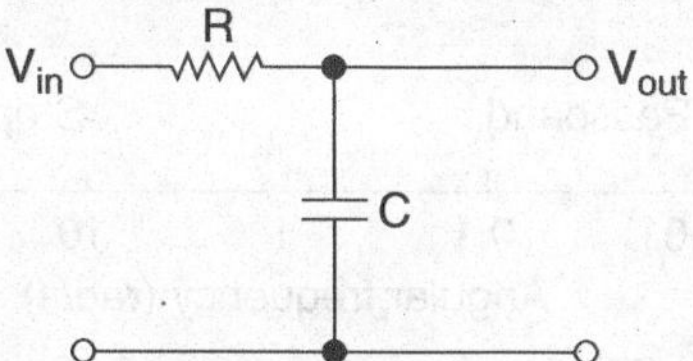

Fig. (3.52) A low-pass electronic filter realized by an RC circuit.

A fairly stiff barrier reflects more higher frequencies, and so acts as a low-pass filter for transmitting sound waves. When music is playing in another room, the low notes are easily heard, while the high notes are largely filtered out. Similarly, very loud music played in one car is heard as a low throbbing by occupants of other cars, because the closed vehicles (and air gap) function as a very low-pass filter, attenuating all of the treble. Electronic low-pass filters are used to drive subwoofers and other types of loudspeakers, to block high pitches that they can't efficiently broadcast. Radio transmitters use low pass filters to block harmonic emissions which might cause interference with other communications. An integrator is another example of a low-pass filter. DSL splitters use low-pass and high-pass filters to separate DSL and POTS signals sharing the same pair of wires. Low-pass filters also play a significant role in the sculpting of sound for electronic music as created by analogue synthesizers.

3.8.3 Ideal and Real Filters

An ideal low-pass filter completely eliminates all frequencies above the cut-off frequency while passing those below unchanged. The transition region present in practical filters does not exist. An ideal low pass filter can be realized mathematically (theoretically) by multiplying a signal by the rectangular function in the frequency domain or, equivalently, convolution with a sinc function in the time domain.

However, this filter is not realizable for practical, real signals because the sinc function extends to infinity. The filter would therefore need to predict the future and have infinite knowledge of the past in order to perform the convolution. It is effectively realizable for pre-recorded digital signals (by padding the ends of the signal with zeros to the point that the error after filtering is less than the quantization error), or perfectly cyclic signals that repeat for infinity.

Real filters for real-time applications approximate the ideal filter by delaying the signal for a small period of time, allowing them to "see" a little bit into the future. This is manifested as phase shift. Greater accuracy in approximation requires a longer delay.

The Nyquist–Shannon sampling theorem describes how to use a perfect low-pass filter (equivalent to the Whittaker–Shannon interpolation formula) to reconstruct a continuous signal from a sampled digital signal. Real digital-to-analog converters use real filter approximations.

3.8.4 Electronic Low-pass Filters

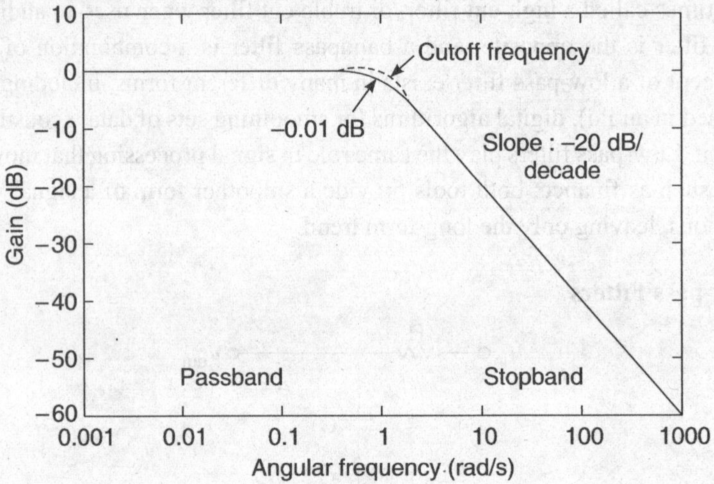

Fig. (3.53) The frequency response of a first-order filter.

There are a great many different types of filter circuits, with different responses to changing frequency. The frequency response of a filter is generally represented using a Bode plot.

- A first-order filter, for example, will reduce the signal amplitude by half (about –6 dB) every time the frequency doubles (goes up one octave). The magnitude Bode plot for a first-order filter looks like a horizontal line below the cutoff frequency, and a diagonal line above the cutoff frequency. There is also a "knee curve" at the boundary between the two, which smoothly transitions between the two straight line regions.
- A second-order filter does a better job of attenuating higher frequencies. The Bode plot for this type of filter resembles that of a first-order filter, except that it falls off more quickly. For example, a second-order Butterworth filter will reduce the signal amplitude to one fourth its

original level every time the frequency doubles (–12 dB per octave). Other second-order filters may roll off at different rates initially depending on their Q factor, but approach the same final rate of –12 dB per octave.

- Third- and higher-order filters are defined similarly. In general, the final rate of rolloff for an n-order filter is 6n dB per octave.

On any Butterworth filter, if one extends the horizontal line to the right and the diagonal line to the upper-left (the asymptotes of the function), they will intersect at exactly the "cutoff frequency". The frequency response at the cutoff frequency in a first-order filter is –3 dB below the horizontal line. The various types of filters — Butterworth filter, Chebyshev filter, Bessel filter, etc. — all have different-looking "knee curves". Many second-order filters are designed to have "peaking" or resonance, causing their frequency response at the cutoff frequency to be above the horizontal line. See electronic filter for other types.

The meanings of 'low' and 'high' — that is, the cutoff frequency — depend on the characteristics of the filter. The term "low-pass filter" merely refers to the shape of the filter's response; a high-pass filter could be built that cuts off at a lower frequency than any low-pass filter – it is their responses that set them apart. Electronic circuits can be devised for any desired frequency range, right up through microwave frequencies (above 1000 MHz) and higher.

Passive Electronic Realization

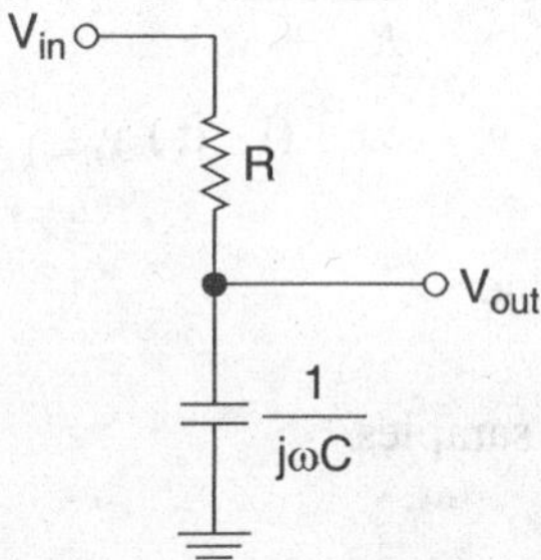

Fig. (3.54) A passive low-pass filter showing impedances of the components.

One simple electrical circuit that will serve as a low-pass filter consists of a resistor in series with a load, and a capacitor in parallel with the load. The capacitor exhibits reactance, and blocks low-frequency signals, causing them to go through the load instead. At higher frequencies the reactance drops, and the capacitor effectively functions as a short circuit. The combination of resistance and capacitance gives you the time constant of the filter ? = RC (represented by the Greek letter tau). The break frequency, also called the turnover frequency or cutoff frequency (in hertz), is determined by the time constant:

$$f_c = \frac{1}{2\pi\tau} = \frac{1}{2\pi RC}$$

or equivalently (in radians per second):

$$\omega_c = \frac{1}{\tau} = \frac{1}{RC}$$

One way to understand this circuit is to focus on the time the capacitor takes to charge. It takes time to charge or discharge the capacitor through that resistor:

- At low frequencies, there is plenty of time for the capacitor to charge up to practically the same voltage as the input voltage.
- At high frequencies, the capacitor only has time to charge up a small amount before the input switches direction. The output goes up and down only a small fraction of the amount the input goes up and down. At double the frequency, there's only time for it to charge up half the amount.

Another way to understand this circuit is with the idea of reactance at a particular frequency:

- Since DC cannot flow through the capacitor, DC input must "flow out" the path marked Vout (analogous to removing the capacitor).
- Since AC flows very well through the capacitor — almost as well as it flows through solid wire — AC input "flows out" through the capacitor, effectively short circuiting to ground (analogous to replacing the capacitor with just a wire).

It should be noted that the capacitor is not an "on/off" object (like the block or pass fluidic explanation above). The capacitor will variably act between these two extremes. It is the Bode plot and frequency response that show this variability.

Passive Digital Realization

A model of a simple digital implementation of a low-pass RC filter is:

$$\alpha = \frac{\Delta t}{RC + \Delta t}$$

$$y_n = \alpha x + (1 - \alpha)\, y_{n-1}$$

where, y_n is the current output value
y_{n-1} is the previous output value
x input value
Δt is the time interval between samples
RC is the time constant

Active Electronic Realization

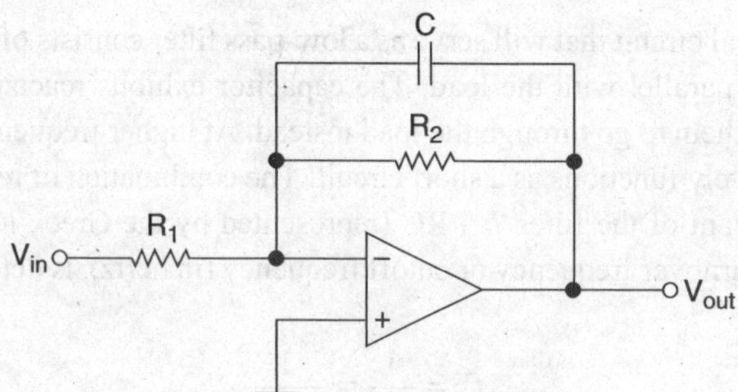

Fig. (3.55) An active low-pass filter.

Another type of electrical circuit is an active low-pass filter.

In this example, the cutoff frequency (in hertz) is defined as:

$$f_c = \frac{1}{2\pi R_C}$$

or equivalently (in radians per second):

$$\omega_c = \frac{1}{R_2 C}$$

The gain in the passband is $-\frac{R_2}{R_1}$, and the stopband drops off at ?6 dB per octave, as it is a first-order filter.Many times, a simple gain or attenuation amplifier is turned into a lowpass filter by adding the capacitor C. This decreases the frequency response at high frequencies and helps to avoid oscillation in the amplifier. For example, an audio amplifier can be made into a lowpass filter with cutoff frequency 100 kHz to reduce gain at frequencies which would otherwise oscillate. Since the audio band (what we can hear) only goes up to 20 kHz or so, the frequencies of interest fall entirely in the passband, and the amplifier behaves the same way as far as audio is concerned.

Laplace Notation

Continuous-time filters can also be described in terms of the Laplace transform of their impulse response in a way that allows all of the characteristics of the filter to be easily analyzed by considering the pattern of poles and zeros of the Laplace transform in the complex plane (in discrete time, one can similarly consider the Z-transform of the impulse response).

A first-order low-pass filter can be described in Laplace notation as

$$\frac{\text{Output}}{\text{Input}} = \frac{1}{1 + s\tau}$$

3.8.5 Digital Filter

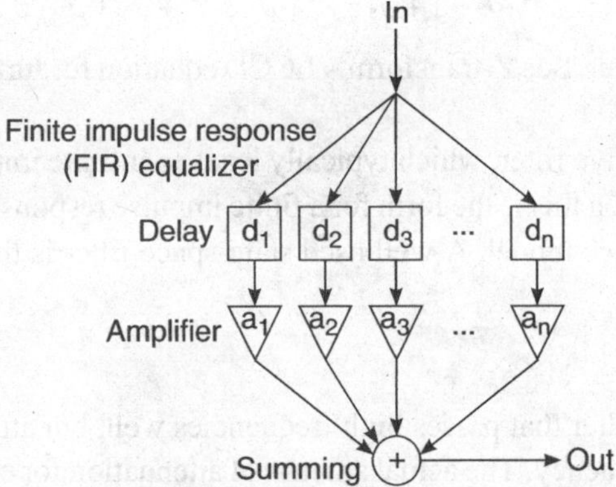

Fig. (3.56) An FIR filter.

In electronics, a digital filter is any electronic filter that works by performing digital mathematical operations on an intermediate form of a signal. This is in contrast to older analog filters which work entirely in the analog realm and must rely on physical networks of electronic components (such as resistors, capacitors, transistors, etc.) to achieve the desired filtering effect.

Digital filters can achieve virtually any filtering effect that can be expressed as a mathematical function or algorithm. The two primary limitations of digital filters are their speed (the filter can't operate any faster than the computer at the heart of the filter), and their cost. However as the cost of integrated circuits has continued to drop over time, digital filters have become increasingly commonplace and are now an essential element of many everyday objects such as radios, cellphones, and stereo receivers.

Digital Filter Advantages

Digital filters can easily realize performance characteristics far beyond what are practically implementable with analog filters. It is not particularly difficult, for example, to create a 1000 Hz low-pass filter which can achieve near-perfect transmission of a 999 Hz input while entirely blocking a 1001 Hz signal. Practical analog filters cannot discriminate between such closely spaced signals.

Also, for complex multi-stage filtering operations, digital filters have the potential to attain much better signal-to-noise ratios than analog filters. This is because whereas at each intermediate stage the analog filter adds more noise to the signal, the digital filter performs noiseless mathematical operations at each intermediate step in the transform. The primary source of noise in a digital filter is to be found in the initial analog-to-digital conversion (ADC) step, where in addition to any circuit noise introduced, the signal is subject to an unavoidable quantization error which is due to the finite resolution of the digital representation of the signal.

Note also that frequency components exceeding half the sampling rate of the filter (cf. Nyquist sampling theorem) will be confounded (or aliased) by the filter. Thus an anti-aliasing filter is usually placed ahead of the ADC circuitry to prevent these high-frequency components from aliasing.

Types of Digital Filters

Many digital filters are based on the Fast Fourier transform, a mathematical algorithm that quickly extracts the frequency spectrum of a signal, allowing the spectrum to be manipulated (such as to create pass-band filters) before converting the modified spectrum back into a time-series signal.

Another form of a typical linear digital filter, expressed as a transform in the Z-domain, is

$$H(z)=\frac{B(z)}{A(z)}=\frac{b_0+b_1z^{-1}+b_2z^{-2}+\ldots+b_Nz^{-N}}{1+a_1z^{-1}+a_2z^{-2}+\ldots+a_Mz^{-M}}$$

where M is the order of the filter. See Z-transform's LCCD equation for further discussion of this transfer function.

This form is for a recursive filter, which typically leads to infinite impulse response behaviour, but if the denominator is unity, then this is the form for a finite impulse response filter.Another form of a digital filter is that of a state-space model. A well used state-space filter is the Kalman filter published by Rudolf Kalman in 1960.

3.8.6 High-pass Filter

A high-pass filter is a filter that passes high frequencies well, but attenuates (or reduces) frequencies lower than the cutoff frequency. The actual amount of attenuation for each frequency varies from filter to filter. It is sometimes called a low-cut filter; the terms bass-cut filter or rumble filter are also used in audio applications. A high-pass filter is the opposite of a low-pass filter, and a bandpass filter is a combination of a high-pass and a low-pass.

It is useful as a filter to block any unwanted low frequency components of a complex signal while passing the higher frequencies. Of course, the meanings of 'low' and 'high' frequencies are relative to the cutoff frequency chosen by the filter designer.

Implementation

The simplest electronic high-pass filter consists of a capacitor in series with the signal path in conjunction with a resistor in parallel with the signal path. The resistance times the capacitance (R×C) is the

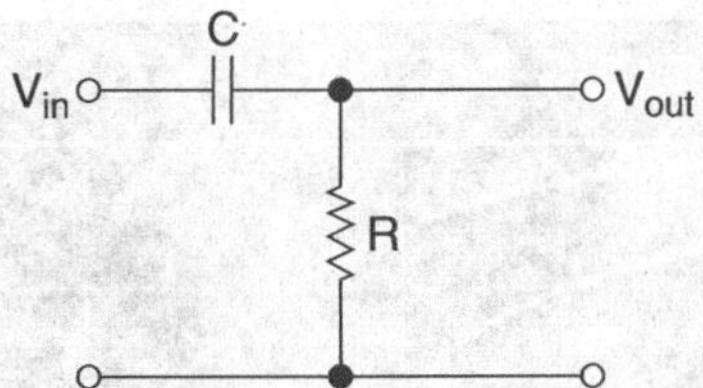

Fig. (3.57) A passive, analog, first-order high-pass filter, realized by an RC circuit.

time constant (?); it is inversely proportional to the cutoff frequency, at which the output power is half the input (?3 dB):

$$f = \frac{1}{2\pi\tau} = \frac{1}{2\pi RC}$$

where f is in hertz, ? is in seconds, R is in ohms, and C is in farads.

Applications : Such a filter could be used to direct high frequencies to a tweeter speaker while blocking bass signals which could interfere with or damage the speaker. A low-pass filter, using a coil instead of a capacitor, could simultaneously be used to direct low frequencies to the woofer. See audio crossover. High-pass and low-pass filters are also used in digital image processing to perform transformations in the spatial frequency domain.

Most high-pass filters have zero gain (-inf dB) at DC. Such a high-pass filter with very low cutoff frequency can be used to block DC from a signal that is undesired in that signal (and pass nearly everything else). These are sometimes called DC blocking filters.

3.8.7 Gaussian Filters

The Gaussian Filter is the filter type that results in the most gradual pass band roll-off and the lowest group delay. The step response of the Gaussian filter NEVER overshoots the steady state value. As the name states, the Gaussian Filter is derived from the same basic equations used to derive the Gaussian Distribution. The significant characteristic of the Gaussian Filter is that the step response contains no overshoot at all.

Filter Solutions normalizes the Gaussian filter such that the prototype high frequency attenuation matches the Butterworth filter. The pass band attenuation of the Gaussian filter increases with the order of the filter when this normalization is applied. However, Filter Solutions allows the user the option of selecting the desired pass band attenuation in dB's. 3dB attenuation is a popular choice for some.

Gaussian Transitional Filters

It is occasionally desirable to transition from a Gaussian frequency response to a stepper roll off response at a user defined attenuation point.. Filter Solutions provides 3, 6, 9, 12, and 15 dB Transitional Filters. Pass band attenuation is always set to 3.01 dB for Gaussian Transitional filters.

Below are examples of Gaussian and Gaussian Transitional low pass frequency response and Gaussian low pass step response

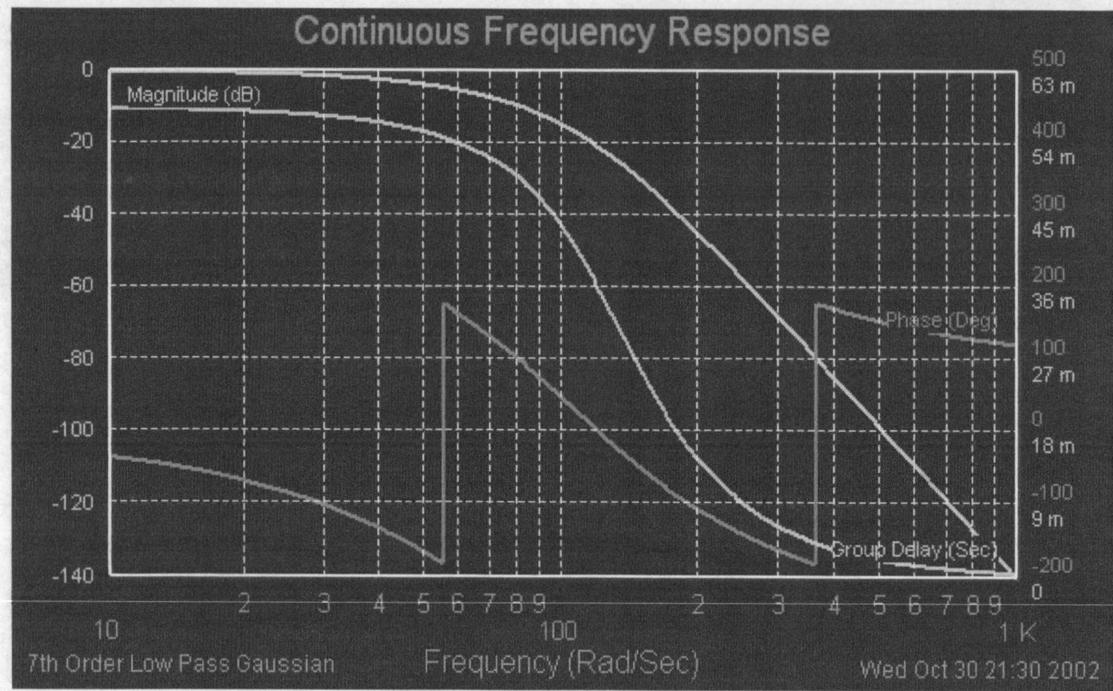

Fig. (3.58a) Gaussian low pass filter, 100 Hz pass band frequency.

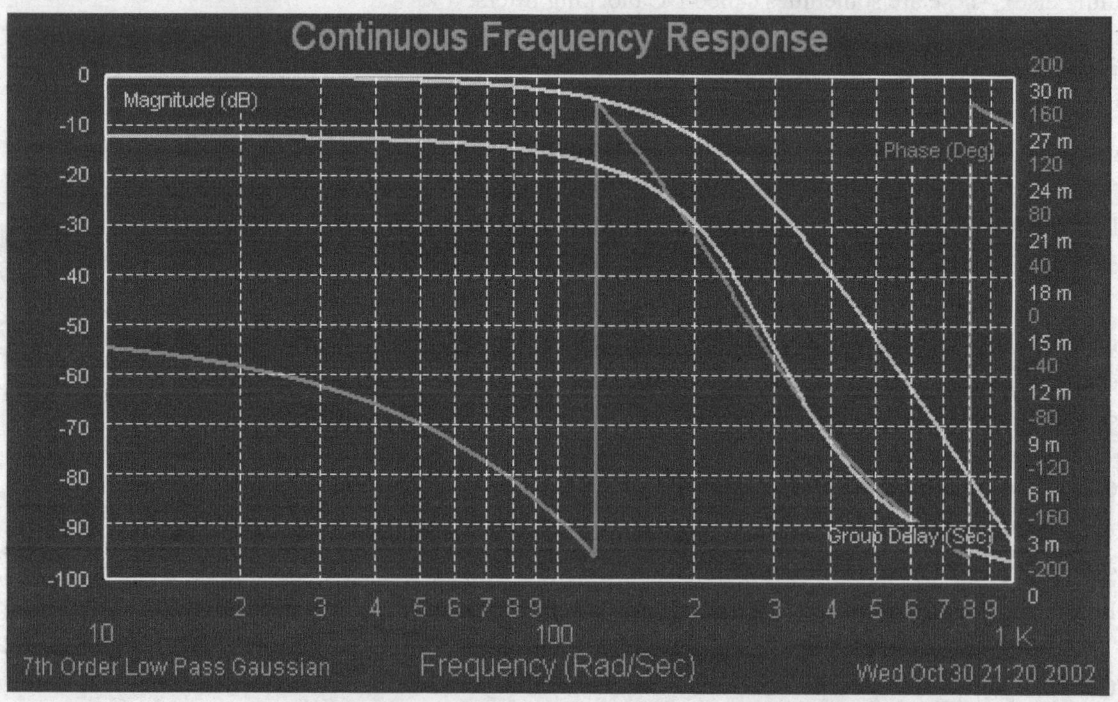

Fig. (3.58b) Gaussian with –3.01 dB pass band attenuation.

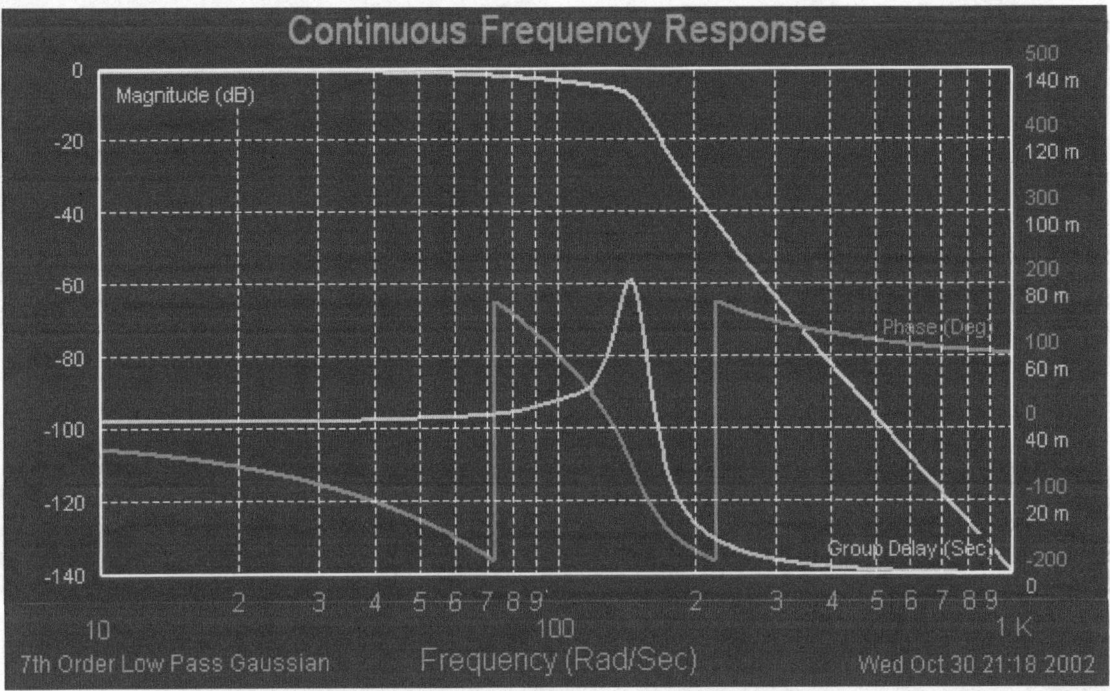

Fig. (3.59a) Gaussian with 6 dB transition.

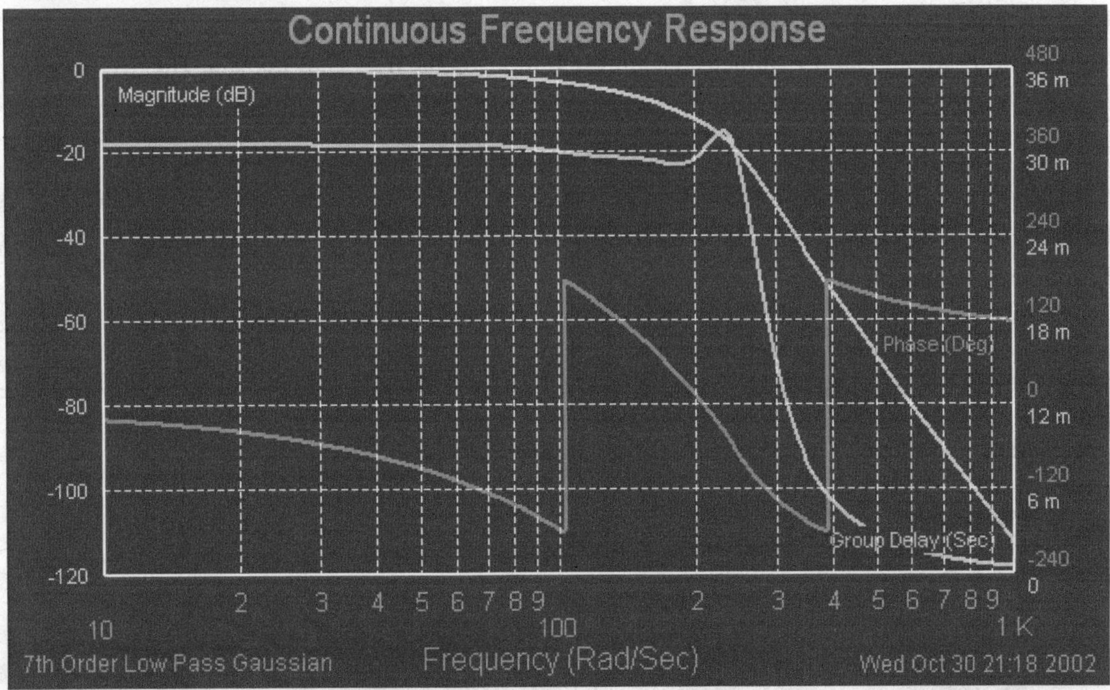

Fig. (3.59b) Gaussian with 15 dB transition.

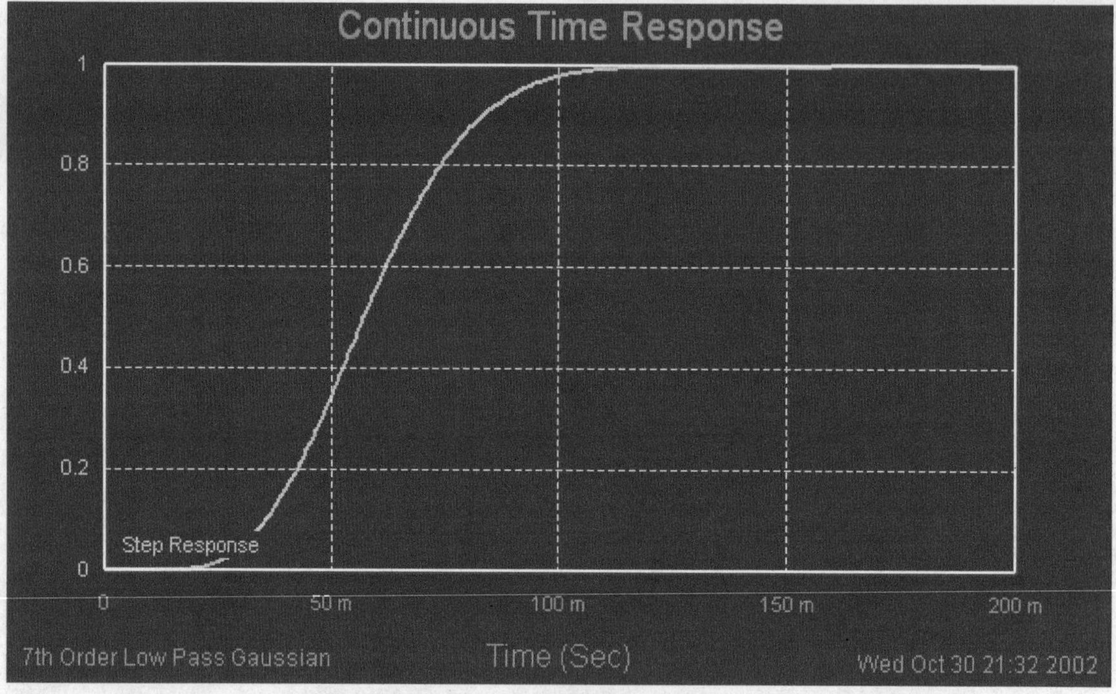

Fig. (3.60) Gaussian step response.

■ 3.9 IMAGE FILTERING IN THE FREQUENCY DOMAIN

The following will discuss two dimensional image filtering in the frequency domain. The reason for doing the filtering in the frequency domain is generally because it is computationally faster to perform two 2D Fourier transforms and a filter multiply than to perform a convolution in the image (spatial) domain. This is particularly so as the filter size increases.

In what follows it is assumed that the reader is familiar with the Discrete Fourier Transform, its properties, and the transforms of commonly used functions (delta, noise, rectangular pulse, step, etc).

Example 1 : General

The following example will apply "ideal" low, high, and band pass filters to a 2 dimensional rectangular pulse with low level added noise. For each step in the process two representations will be given, the image and a surface rendering. Seeing both together can often give different clues as to what is going on.

The original signal is a rectangular pulse with added noise.

Fig. (3.61)

The fourier transform of the rectangular pulse is the two dimensional equivalent of the sync function, the fourier transform of white noise is a constant.

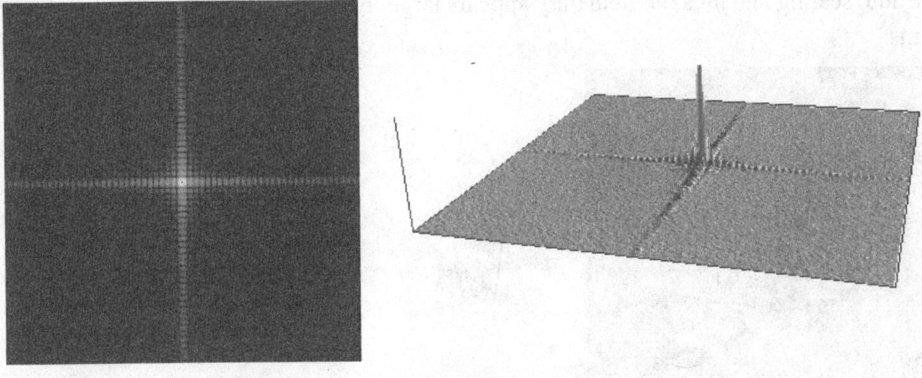

Fig. (3.62)

Applying a low pass filter in the frequency domain means zeroing all frequency components above a cutoff frequency. This is similar to what one would do in a 1 dimensional case except now the ideal filter is a cylindrical "can" instead of a rectangular pulse.

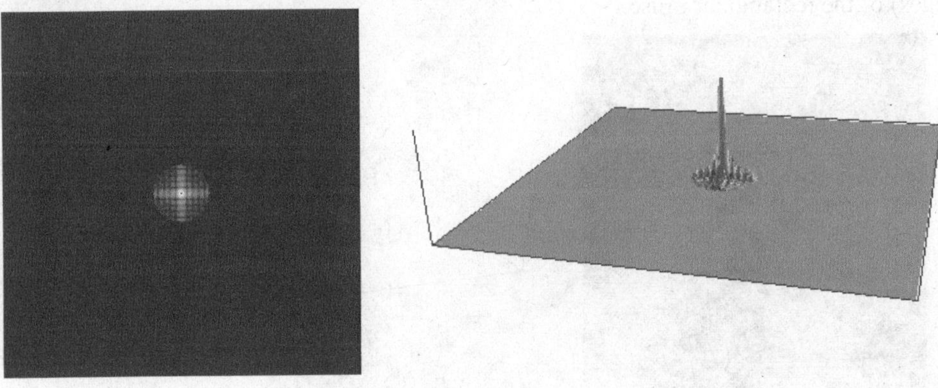

Fig. (3.63)

The result transformed back into the spatial domain. As expected the high frequency components have been removed. The rectangular pulse is "rounded" since high frequency components were required for the transition.

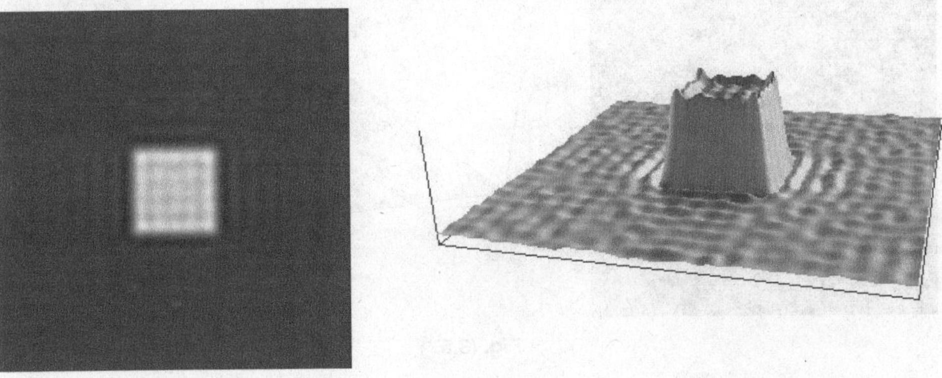

Fig. (3.64)

Applying a high pass filter frequency domain is the opposite to the low pass filter, that is, all the frequencies below some cutoff radius are removed. Note the apparently higher noise levels are false, the graphs are auto scaling and thus the field only appears larger because of the removal of the low frequency components.

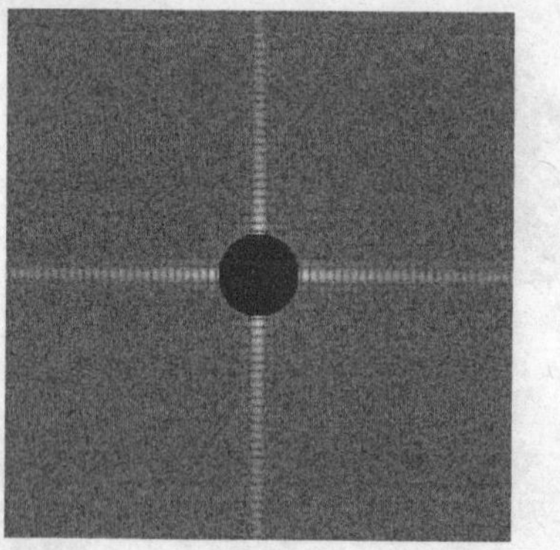

Fig. (3.65)

Transformed back into the spatial domain shows that the noise field is retained as well as the transitions (edges) of the rectangular pulse.

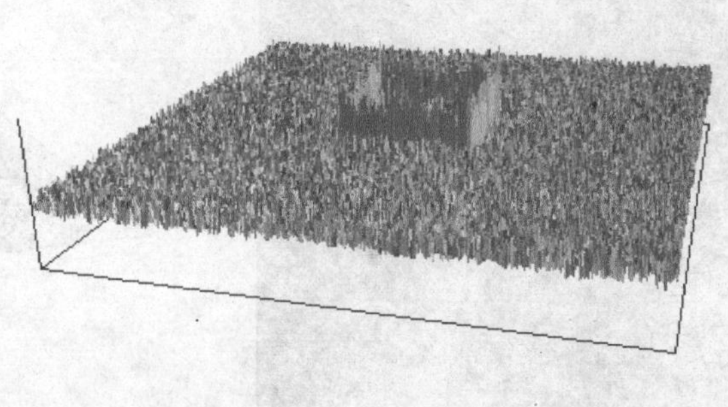

Fig. (3.66)

Applying a band pass filter, frequency domain.

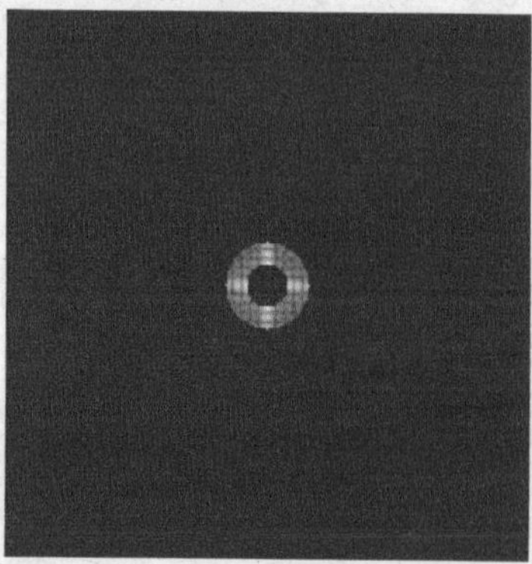
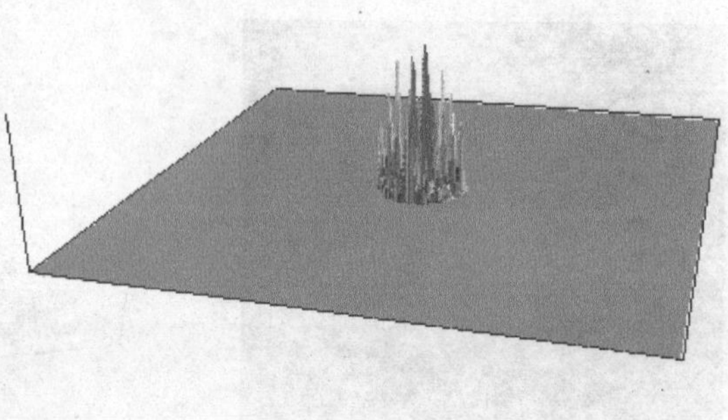

Fig. (3.67)

Transformed back into the spatial domain

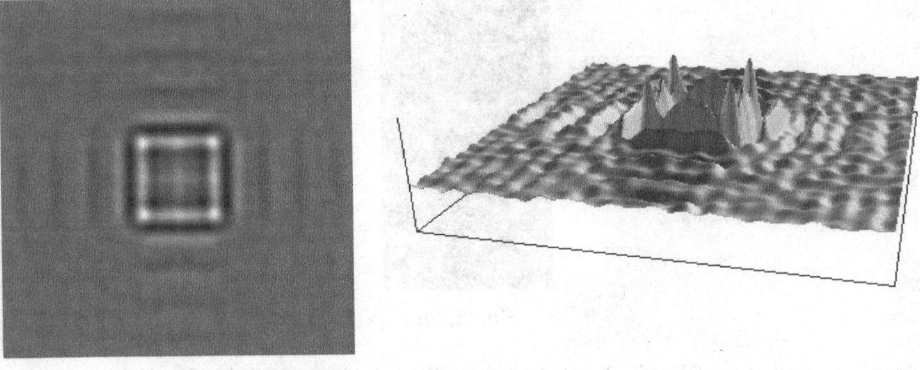

Fig. (3.68)

Sketch showing how the 4 quadrants returned from the 2D Fourier transform are rearranged so as to position the DC component in the middle of the image. A very clear understanding of the position of DC, the Nyquist frequency, and positive/negative frequencies is necessary to get this translation correct.

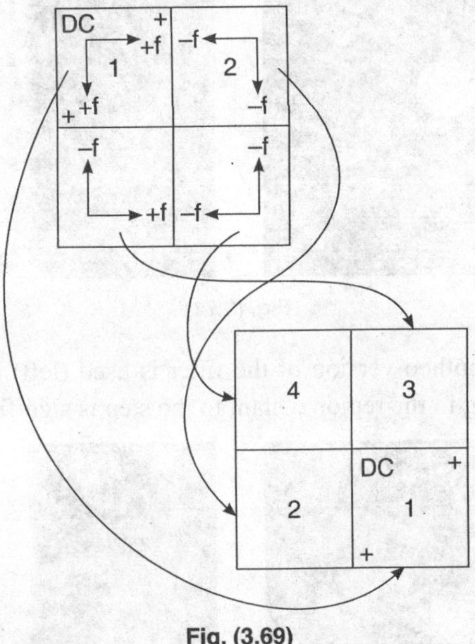

Fig. (3.69)

Example 2 : Smooth Low Pass Filters

As with time series filtering, using ideal rectangular filters can result in unwanted ringing. In two dimensions instead of using a radial rectangular filter (a can) one can smooth the transition between the stop and pass band. This is often done using Hanning or Hamming windows which are rectangular windows smoothed by cosine functions.

In the following example two low pass filters will be applied to the step function shown below. One filter will have a sharp transition as used in example 1, the other filter will have a more gradual transition between the stop and pass band. (Actually this is two steps, the other occurs where the right hand edge wraps to the left hand edge.)

Fig. (3.70)

The "can" type low pass filter is shown below on the left along with the filtered step function on the right.

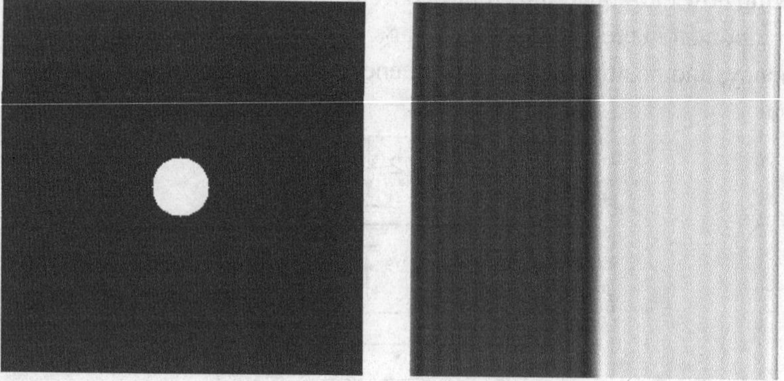

Fig. (3.71)

In this next image a smoothed version of the filter is used (left) and the filtered result is again shown no the right. The ringing in the region distant to the step is significantly reduced.

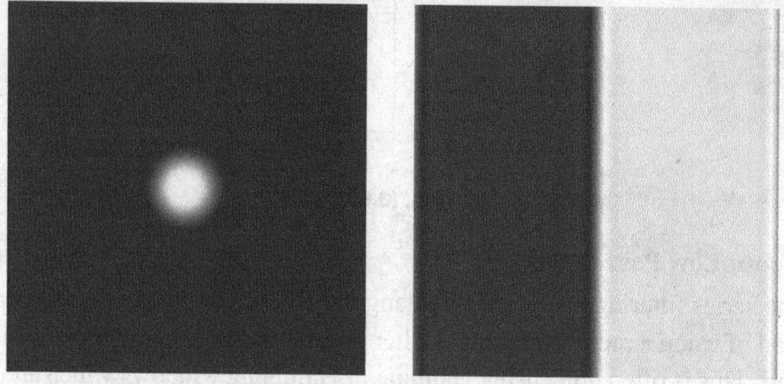

Fig. (3.72)

Example 3 : Smooth High Pass Filter

In a less artificial example of using smooth filters, consider a high pass filtering of the following photograph.

Fig. (3.73)

The following uses the sharp high pass filter from example 1 shown on the left and the resulting filtered image is on the right.

Fig. (3.74)

The following uses a smooth version of the same high pass filter (left) and the filtered image is shown on the right. The ringing is greatly reduced, see the large regions of constant (low frequency) content such as the path or the door.

Fig. (3.75)

4

IMAGE RESTORATION

Image restoration concerns the removal or reduction of degradations which have occurred during the acquisition of the image. Such degradations may include noise, which are errors in the pixel values, or optical effects such as out of focus blurring, or blurring due to camera motion. We shall see that some restoration techniques can be performed very successfully using neighbourhood operations, while others require the use of frequency domain processes. Image restoration remains one of the most important areas of image processing.

The purpose of image restoration is to "compensate for" or "undo" defects which degrade an image. Degradation comes in many forms such as motion blur, noise, and camera misfocus. In cases like motion blur, it is possible to come up with a very good estimate of the actual blurring function and "undo" the blur to restore the original image. In cases where the image is corrupted by noise, the best we may hope to do is to compensate for the degradation it caused. In this project, we will introduce and implement several of the methods used in the image processing world to restore images.

Degradation Model

The block diagram for our general degradation model is

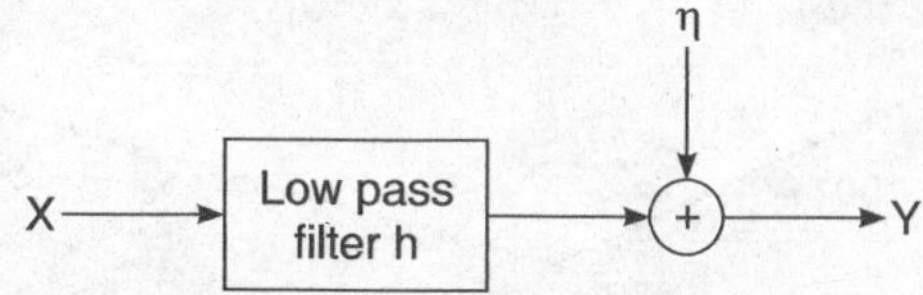

Fig. (4.1) Degradation model.

where g is the corrupted image obtained by passing the original image f through a low pass filter (blurring function) b and adding noise to it. We present four different ways of restoring the image.

Inverse Filtering

In this method we look at an image assuming a known blurring function. We will see that restoration is good when noise is not present and not so good when noise is present.

If we know of or can create a good model of the blurring function that corrupted an image, the quickest and easiest way to restore that is by inverse filtering. Unfortunately, since the inverse filter is a form of high pass filer, inverse filtering responds very badly to any noise that is present in the image because noise tends to be high frequency. In this section, we explore two methods of inverse filtering - a thresholding method and an iterative method.

Method 1 : Thresholding :

We can model a blurred image by

$$g(n_1, n_2) = f(n_1, n_2) * b(n_1, n_2)$$

where f is the original image, b is some kind of a low pass filter and g is our blurred image. So to get back the original image, we would just have to convolve our blurred function with some kind of a high pass filter

$$f(n_1, n_2) = g(n_1, n_2) * h(n_1, n_2)$$

But how do we find h? If we take the DFT of b so that B=DFT2 (b), we would get something that looks like this

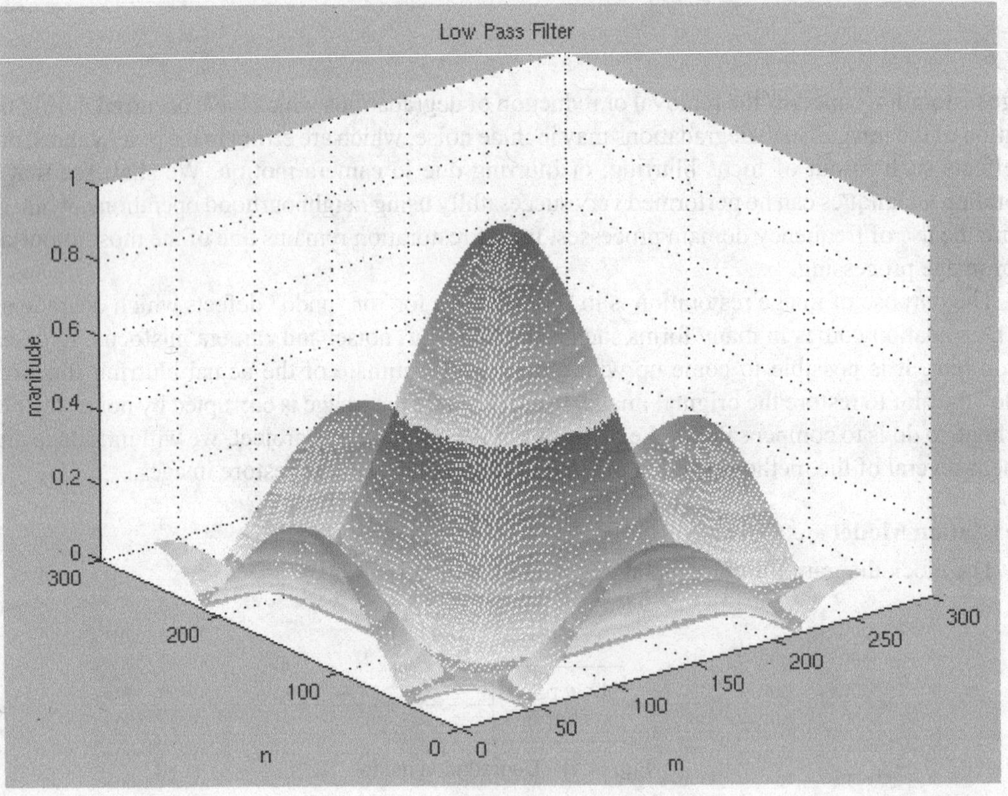

Fig. (4.2)

In the ideal case, we would just invert all the elements of B to get a high pass filter. However, notice that a lot of the elements in B have values either at zero or very close to it. Inverting these elements would give us either infinities or some extremely high values. In order to avoid these values, we will need to set some sort of a threshold on the inverted element. So instead of making a full inverse out of B, we can an "almost" full inverse by

$$H(\omega_1, \omega_2) = \begin{cases} \dfrac{1}{B(\omega_1, \omega_2)} & \text{if } \dfrac{1}{B(\omega_1, \omega_2)} < \gamma \\ \gamma & \text{else} \end{cases}$$

So the higher we set, the closer H is to the full inverse filter.

Implementation and Results

Since Matlab does not deal well with infinity, we had to threshold B before we took the inverse. So we did the following:

$$B(\omega_1, \omega_2) = \begin{cases} B(\omega_1, \omega_2) & \text{if } B(\omega_1, \omega_2) > n \\ n & \text{else} \end{cases}$$

where n is essentially and is set arbitrarily close to zero for noiseless cases. The following images shows our results for n=0.0001.

Fig. (4.3)

We see that the image is almost exactly like the original. The MSE is 2.5847. Because an inverse filter is a high pass filter, it does not perform well in the presence of noise. There is a definite tradeoff between de-blurring and de-noising. In the following image, the blurred image is corrupted by AWGN with variance 10. n=0.2.

Fig. (4.4)

The MSE for the restored image is 1964.5. We can see that the sharpness of the edges improved but we also have a lot of noise specs in the image. We can get rid of more specs (thereby getting a smoother image) by increasing n. In general, the more noise we have in the image, the higher we set n. The higher the n, the less high pass the filter is, which means that it amplifies noise less. It also means, however, that the edges will not be as sharp as they could be.

MATLAB CODE :

```
N=256;
n=.2;
f=freadbin('lenna.256',N,N);
figure(1)
imagesc(f)
colormap(gray)
b=ones(4,4)/4^2;
F=fft2(f);
B=fft2(b,N,N);
G=F.*B;
g=ifft2(G)+10*randn(N,N);
G=fft2(g);
figure(2)
imagesc(abs(ifft2(G)))
colormap(gray)
BF=find(abs(B)<n);
%B(BF)=max(max(B))/1.5;
B(BF)=n;
```

```
H=ones(N,N)./B;
I=G.*H;
im=abs(ifft2(I));
figure(3)
imagesc(im)
colormap(gray)
```

Method 2 : Iterative Procedure :

The idea behind the iterative procedure is to make some initial guess of f based on g and to update that guess after every iteration. The procedure is

$$\hat{f}_0(n_1, n_2) = \lambda g(n_1, n_2)$$

$$\hat{f}_{k+1}(n_1, n_2) = \hat{f}_k(n_1, n_2) + \lambda(g(n_1, n_2) - \hat{f}_k(n_1, n_2) * b(n_1, n_2))$$

where is an initial guess based on g. If our is a good guess, eventually convolved with b will be close to g. When that happens the second term in the equation will disappear and and will converge. is our convergence factor and it lets us determine how fast and converge.

If we take both of the above equations to the frequency domain, we get

$$\hat{F}_0 = \lambda G(\omega_1, \omega_2)$$

$$\hat{F}_{k+1}(\omega_1, \omega_2) = \hat{F}_k(\omega_1, \omega_2) + \lambda(G(\omega_1, \omega_2) - \hat{F}_k(\omega_1, \omega_2)\, B(\omega_1, \omega_2))$$

Solving for recursively, we get

$$\hat{F}_k(\omega_1, \omega_2) = \lambda G(\omega_1, \omega_2)[1 + (1 - \lambda B(\omega_1, \omega_2)) + \ldots + (1 - \lambda B(\omega_1, \omega_2))^k]$$

$$= \frac{G(\omega_1, \omega_2)}{B(\omega_1, \omega_2)}[1 - (1 - \lambda B(\omega_1, \omega_2))^{k+1}]$$

So if goes to zero as k goes to infinity, we would get the result as obtained by the inverse filter. In general, this method will not give the exact same results as inverse filtering, but can be less sensitive to noise in some cases.

Implementation and Results

The first thing we have to do is pick a . must satisfy the following

$$|1 - \lambda B(\omega_1, \omega_2)| < 1$$

and thus will be a positive integer in the range of 0 to 1. The bigger is, the faster and will converge. However, picking too large a may also make and diverge instead of converge. Imagine that we're walking along a path and the end of the path is a cliff. is the size of of the steps we take. We want to go to the edge of the path as fast as possible without falling off. Taking large steps will ensure that we will get there fast but we'd probably first. Taking small will ensure that we get there without falling off but it could take an infinite amount of time. So the compromise would be to take big steps at the start and decrease our step size as we get close to our destination.

The following is the noiseless image after 150 iterations. starts off at 0.1 and decreases by 10% every 25 iterations.

Fig. (4.5)

The MSE is 364.6897. The image is sharper than the blurred image although the MSE is high. But the image restored using the direct inverse filter is much better. The following is the blurred image corrupted with AWGN with a variance of 10. The number of iterations is 150.

Fig. (4.6)

The MSE for the restored image is 1247.3. We see the same noise specs as we had seen with the inverse filter. But the image is in general better than the the noisy image restored using the inverse filtering method and has a lower MSE. So we can conclude that the direct inverse filtering method is better for a noiseless case and the iterative method is better when noise is present.

MATLAB CODE:

```
N=256;
lambda=0.1;
f=freadbin('lenna.256',N,N);
figure(1)
imagesc(f)
colormap(gray)
F=fft2(f);
b=ones(4,4)/16;
B=fft2(b,N,N);
G=F.*B;
%g=ifft2(G)+10*randn(N,N);
%G=fft2(g);
figure(2)
imagesc(abs(ifft2(G)))
colormap(gray)
K=lambda*G;
for l=1:1500,
if mod(l,25)==0
lambda=lambda/5;
end
A=G-K.*B;
K=K+lambda*A;
if mod(l,50)==0
1
```

```
sum(sum(A))
figure(3)
imagesc(abs(ifft2(K)))
colormap(gray)
pause
end
end
```

Wiener Filtering

This method provides us with the optimal trade-off between de-noising and inverse filtering. We will see that the result is in general better than with straight inverse filtering. The inverse filtering is a restoration technique for deconvolution, i.e., when the image is blurred by a known low pass filter, it is possible to recover the image by inverse filtering or generalized inverse filtering. However, inverse filtering is very sensitive to additive noise. The approach of reducing one degradation at a time allows us to develop a restoration algorithm for each type of degradation and simply combine them. The Wiener filtering executes an optimal tradeoff between inverse filtering and noise smoothing. It removes the additive noise and inverts the blurring simultaneously.

The Wiener filtering is optimal in terms of the mean square error. In other words, it minimizes the overall mean square error in the process of inverse filtering and noise smoothing. The Wiener filtering is a linear estimation of the original image. The approach is based on a stochastic framework. The orthogonality principle implies that the Wiener filter in Fourier domain can be expressed as follows:

$$W(f_1, f_2) = \frac{H^*(f_1, f_2)\, S_{xx}(f_1, f_2)}{|H(f_1, f_2)|^2\, S_{xx}(f_1, f_2) + S_{\eta\eta}(f_1, f_2)}$$

where are respectively power spectra of the original image and the additive noise, and is the blurring filter. It is easy to see that the Wiener filter has two separate part, an inverse filtering part and a noise smoothing part. It not only performs the deconvolution by inverse filtering (high pass filtering) but also removes the noise with a compression operation (low pass filtering).

Implementation

To implement the Wiener filter in practice we have to estimate the power spectra of the original image and the additive noise. For white additive noise the power spectrum is equal to the variance of the noise. To estimate the power spectrum of the original image many methods can be used. A direct estimate is the periodogram estimate of the power spectrum computed from the observation:

$$S_{yy}^{per} = \frac{1}{N^2}\,[Y(k, l)\, Y(k, l)^*]$$

where Y(k,l) is the DFT of the observation. The advantage of the estimate is that it can be implemented very easily without worrying about the singularity of the inverse filtering. Another estimate which leads to a cascade implementation of the inverse filtering and the noise smoothing is

$$S_{xx} = \frac{S_{yy} - S_{\eta\eta}}{|H|^2}$$

which is a straightforward result of the fact: The power spectrum can be estimated directly from the observation using the periodogram estimate. This estimate results in a cascade implementation of inverse filtering and noise smoothing:

$$W = \frac{1}{H} \frac{S_{yy}^{per} - S_{\eta\eta}}{S_{yy}^{per}}$$

The disadvantage of this implementation is that when the inverse filter is singular, we have to use the generalized inverse filtering. People also suggest the power spectrum of the original image can be estimated based on a model such as the model.

Experimental Result

To illustrate the Wiener filtering in image restoration we use the standard 256x256 Lena test image. We blur the image with the low pass filter

$$H = \frac{1}{16}\begin{bmatrix} 1 & 1 & 1 & 1 \\ 1 & 1 & 1 & 1 \\ 1 & 1 & 1 & 1 \\ 1 & 1 & 1 & 1 \end{bmatrix}$$

Then put into the blurred image the additive white Gaussian noise of variance 100. The Wiener filtering is applied to the image with a cascade implementation of the noise smoothing and inverse filtering. The images are listed as follows together with the PSNRs and MSEs. Notice that the restored image is improved in terms of the visual performance, but the MSEs don't indicate this, the reason of which is that MSE is not a good metric for deconvolution.

Standard Lena image
PSNR = infinity,
MSE = zero

Blurred Lena image
PSNR = 23.2993,
MSE = 304.1938

Restored Lena image
PSNR = 19.1447,
MSE = 791.7906

Fig. (4.7) Test image Lena and blurred image Lena.

Matlab Programs :

inverseFilter.m

```
function ex = inverseFilter(y,h,gamma);
%
% ex = inverseFilter(y,h,gamma);
%
% Generalized inverse filtering using threshold gamma:
%
%  inv_g(H) = gamma*abs(fft(h))/fft(h), if abs(fft(h)) <= 1/gamma
%  inv_g(H) = inv(H),                   otherwise
```

```
%
% Reference: Lim's book
% Created: Tue May 4 16:22:57 CDT 1999, Huipin Zhang

N = size(y,1);
Yf = fft2(y);
Hf = fft2(h,N,N);

% handle singular case (zero case)
sHf = Hf.*(abs(Hf)>0)+1/gamma*(abs(Hf)==0);
iHf = 1./sHf;

%lengthzero = length(abs(Hf)==0)
% invert Hf using threshold gamma
iHf = iHf.*(abs(Hf)*gamma>1)+gamma*abs(sHf).*iHf.*
                                          (abs(sHf)*gamma<=1);
ex = real(ifft2(iHf.*Yf));

return
```

wienerFilter.m

```
function ex = wienerFilter(y,h,sigma,gamma,alpha);
%
% ex = wienerFilter(y,h,sigma,gamma,alpha);
%
% Generalized Wiener filter using parameter alpha. When
% alpha = 1, it is the Wiener filter. It is also called
% Regularized inverse filter.
%
% Reference: Richb's paper
% Created: Tue May 4 16:24:06 CDT 1999, Huipin Zhang

N = size(y,1);
Yf = fft2(y);
Hf = fft2(h,N,N);
Pyf = abs(Yf).^2/N^2;

% direct implementation of the regularized inverse filter,
% when alpha = 1, it is the Wiener filter
% Gf = conj(Hf).*Pxf./(abs(Hf.^2).*Pxf+alpha*sigma^2);
%
% Since we don't know Pxf, the following
% handle singular case (zero case)
sHf = Hf.*(abs(Hf)>0)+1/gamma*(abs(Hf)==0);
iHf = 1./sHf;
iHf = iHf.*(abs(Hf)*gamma>1)+gamma*abs(sHf).*iHf.*(abs(sHf)*
                                                    gamma<=1);
```

```
Pyf = Pyf.*(Pyf>sigma^2)+sigma^2*(Pyf<=sigma^2);
Gf = iHf.*(Pyf-sigma^2)./(Pyf-(1-alpha)*sigma^2);

% max(max(abs(Gf).^2)) % should be equal to gamma^2
% Restorated image without denoising
eXf = Gf.*Yf;
ex = real(ifft2(eXf));

return
```

wienerDriver.m

```
clear;clf;

% Input and display the binary image
N = 256;
x = readbin('lenna.256',N,N);
figure(1)
imshow(x,gray(256))

% Blur the image, corrupt the image using WGN and display it
% h is the blurring filter, and sigma is the noise std
h = ones(4,4)/16;
sigma = 10;

Xf = fft2(x);
Hf = fft2(h,N,N);
y = real(ifft2(Hf.*Xf))+sigma*randn(N,N); % circular convolution
%y = filter2(h,x)+sigma*randn(N,N);      % linear convolution
figure(2)
imshow(y,gray(256))

% restoration using generalized inverse filtering
gamma = 2;
eix = inverseFilter(y,h,gamma);
figure(3)
imshow(eix,gray(256))

% restoration using generalized Wiener filtering
gamma = 1;
alpha = 1;
ewx = wienerFilter(y,h,sigma,gamma,alpha);
figure(4)
imshow(ewx,gray(256))

PSNR = [psnr(y,x) psnr(eix,x) psnr(ewx,x)]
return
```

Wavelet-based Image Restoration

Although the Wiener filtering is the optimal tradeoff of inverse filtering and noise smoothing, in the case when the blurring filter is singular, the Wiener filtering actually amplify the noise. This suggests that a denoising step is needed to remove the amplified noise. Wavelet-based denoising scheme, a successful approach introduced recently by Donoho, provides a natural technique for this purpose. Therefore, the image restoration contains two separate steps: Fourier-domain inverse filtering and wavelet-domain image denoising. The diagram is shown as follows.:

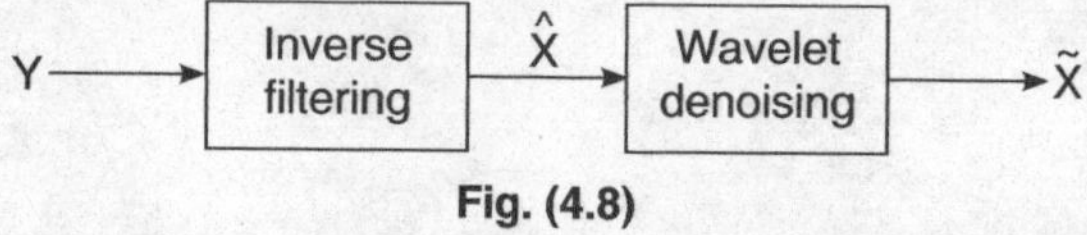

Fig. (4.8)

Donoho's approach for image restoration improves the performance; however, in the case when the blurring function is not invertible, the algorithm is not applicable. Furthermore, since the two steps are separate, there is no control over the overall performance of the restoration. Recently, R. Neelamani et al. proposed a wavelet-based deconvolution technique for ill-conditioned systems. The idea is simple: employ both Fourier-domain Wiener-like and wavelet-domain regularization. The regularized inverse filter is introduced by modifying the Wiener filter with a new-introduced parameter:

$$G_{\alpha} = \frac{S_{xx}}{|H + S_{xx}| + \alpha S_{\eta\eta}}$$

The parameter can be optimally selected to minimize the overall mean-square error. The diagram of the algorithm is displayed as follows.

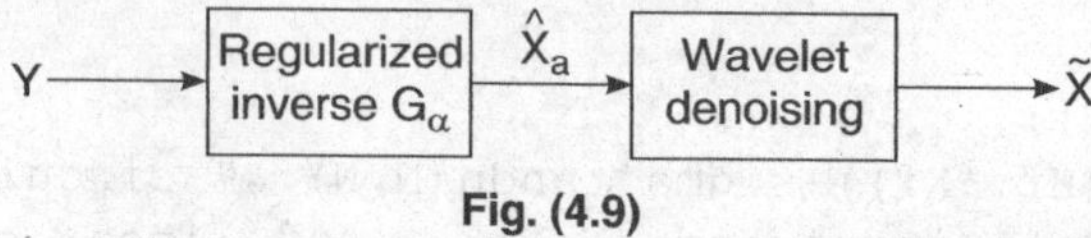

Fig. (4.9)

The implementation of the regularized inverse filter involves the estimation of the power spectrum of the original image in the spatial domain. Since wavelet transforms have good decorrelation property, the wavelet coefficients of the image can be better modeled in a stochastic model, and the power spectrum can be better estimated. This inspires a new approach: changing the order of the regularized inverse filtering and the wavelet transform. See the following digram :

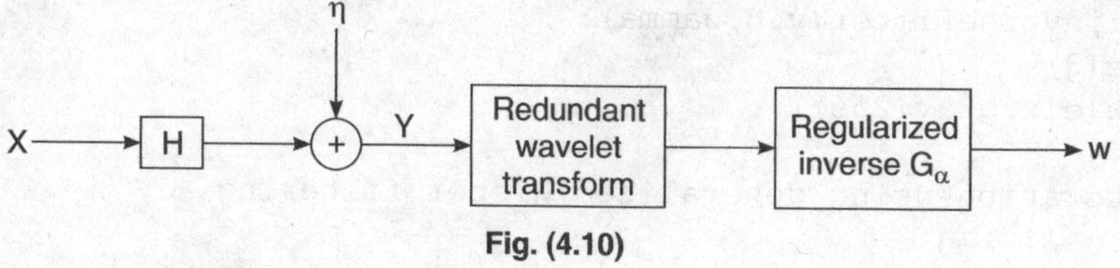

Fig. (4.10)

This way the both inverse filtering and noise smoothing can be performed in wavelet domain. Specifically, the power spectrum of the image in a same sub band can be estimated under the assumption that the wavelet coefficients are independent. Therefore, the power spectrum is just the variance of the wavelet coefficients. We note that the exchange of the order of inverse filtering and wavelet transform is valid only when un decimated wavelet transform is used and the blurring function is separable. Therefore, for interpretation we can exchange the order of the blurring operation and the wavelet transform, which

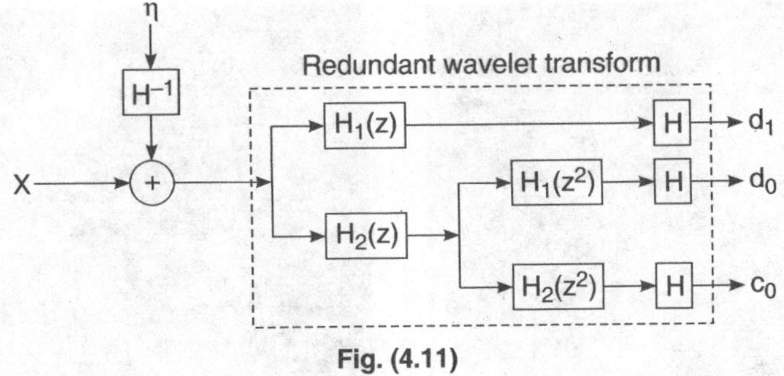

Fig. (4.11)

means that the inverse filtering cancels the blurring in the wavelet domain. So, wavelet thresholding results in a reasonable estimate. The above explanation can be visualized using the figure 4.12.

Simulation

As usual we corrupted the standard 256x256 lena test image by convolving wit the simple 4x4 square blurring filter

$$H = \frac{1}{16}\begin{bmatrix} 1 & 1 & 1 & 1 \\ 1 & 1 & 1 & 1 \\ 1 & 1 & 1 & 1 \\ 1 & 1 & 1 & 1 \end{bmatrix}$$

and adding zero-mean white Gaussian noise of variance 100. The three introduced wavelet-based image restoration algorithms are applied to the corrupted image, and the results are reported in the following table. According to the visual performance and the mean square error, the algorithms improve the restoration performance. However, the denoising step uses wavelet thresholding to remove the noise, the images are blurred a little bit again, although the MSE is improved.

Blurred Lena image
PSNR = 23.2993, MSE = 304.1938

Restored Lena image (Donoho)
PSNR = 16.8552, MSE = 1341.4

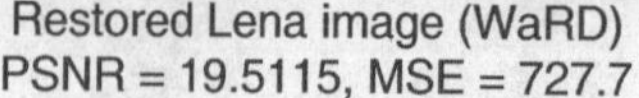

Restored Lena image (WaRD)
PSNR = 19.5115, MSE = 727.7

Restored Lena image (Subband)
PSNR = 20.1223, MSE = 632.2

Fig. (4.12) *Test image Lena and blurred image Lena.*

Matlab Programs :

subbandFilter.m

```
function ex = subbandFilter(y,h,LO_R,level,sigma,gamma,alpha);
%
% ex = subbandFilter(y,h,LO_R,level,sigma,gamma,alpha);
%
% Regularized inverse filtering for each subband (with different)
% regularized parameter alpha) followed by wavelet thresholding
% to remove the noise.
%
% Ref: Richb's paper and Donoho's wavelet shrinkage scheme
% Created: Tue May 4 16:39:27 CDT 1999, Huipin Zhang

N = size(y,1);
[yl,yh] = mrdwt(y,LO_R,level);
gamma0 = 0.5;
alpha0 = 1;
eyl = wienerFilter(yl,h,sigma,gamma0,alpha0);

eyh = [];
for j = 1:level*3
  alp = alpha/2^round((j+1)/3-1);
  eyh = [eyh wienerFilter(yh(:,(j-1)*N+1:j*N),h,sigma,gamma,alp)];
end
ex = mirdwt(eyl,eyh,LO_R,level);

for k = 1:level
  cx(k) = corrbound(LO_R,k,0);
```

```
end
thres = sqrt(2*log(N)*(1+cx))*sigma*gamma/3;

eyh = eyh.*(abs(eyh) > kron(thres,ones(N,3*N)));
ex = mirdwt(eyl,eyh,LO_R,level);

return

waveletDriver.m

clear;clf;

% Input and display the binary image
N = 256;
x = readbin('lenna.256',N,N);
figure(1)
imshow(x,gray(256))

% Blur the image, corrupt the image using WGN and display it
% h is the blurring filter, and sigma is the noise std
h= ones(4,4)/16;
sigma = 10;

Xf = fft2(x);
Hf = fft2(h,N,N);
y = real(ifft2(Hf.*Xf))+sigma*randn(N,N); % circular convolution
%y = filter2(h,x)+sigma*randn(N,N);      % linear convolution

figure(2)
imshow(y,gray(256))

% restoration using generalized inverse filtering
gamma = 2;
eix = inverseFilter(y,h,gamma);
figure(3)
imshow(eix,gray(256))

% restoration using generalized Wiener filtering
gamma = 1;
alpha = 1;
ewx = wienerFilter(y,h,sigma,gamma,alpha);
figure(4)
imshow(ewx,gray(256))

% Wavelet denoising using Daubechies tap 8 wavelet transform
level = 6;
[LO_D,HI_D,LO_R,HI_R] = wfilters('db4');

[yl,yh] = mrdwt(ewx,LO_R,level);
```

```
for k = 1:level
  cx(k) = corrbound(LO_R,k,0);
end
thres = sqrt(2*log(N)*(1+cx))*sigma*gamma/3;

eyh = yh.*(abs(yh) > kron(thres,ones(N,3*N)));
ee = mirdwt(yl,eyh,LO_R,level);
figure(5)
imshow(ee,gray(256))

gamma = 1;
alpha = 1;
esx = subbandFilter(y,h,LO_R,level,sigma,gamma,alpha);
figure(6)
imshow(esx,[])

[psnr(y,x) psnr(eix,x) psnr(ewx,x) psnr(ee,x) psnr(esx,x)]
return
```

Blind Deconvolution

In this method, we assume nothing about the image. We do not have any information about the blurring function or on the additive noise. We will see that restoring an image when we know nothing about it is very hard.

To this point, we have studied restoration techniques assuming that we knew the blurring function h . Actually, we have also assumed that we knew the image spectral density Suu and Spectral noise Snn as well. This section will focus on some techniques for estimating h based on our degraded image. For comparison, we will demonstrate how the MSE between our restored image and the original image changes depending on whether or not we know h, Suu, or Snn.

Two restoration filters will be the basis for our procedures. The first is the Wiener Filter, which exhibits the optimal tradeoff (in the MSE sense) between inverse filtering and noise smoothing. The second filter tries to restore the power spectrum of the degraded image, and is known as Power Spectrum Equalization.

We use as our degradation model the standard idea that our input image is blurred through convolution with a low pass LSI filter (h) and then Gaussian Noise is added to the result. Moreover, because Power Spectrum Equalization (PSE) works best assuming h is phaseless, so we generate our h to have zero phase. This is not too unrealistic because common degradations such as camera misfocus, uniform motion (linear phase), and atmospheric turbulence can all be modelled with zero phase filters. Note also that because we used a different filter for our degradation model than for Inverse Filtering and Wavelet Denoising, the MSEs of our restored images for this section should not be compared to those from the previous sections. Let's begin by recalling the Wiener filter:

$$G = \frac{H^* S_{yy}}{|H|^2 S_{yy} + S_{\eta\eta}}$$

where H is the Fourier Transform of h, and Suu and Snn are defined as above. The following example shows lenna.256 degraded with our phaseless filter and AGN with variance 80. Suu is estimated as the magnitude squared of the Fourier Transform of the input image.

Fig. (4.13)

The above images were generated using wien.m. Much of the blockiness is due to the compression we used on the gifs to store the images. This will be true for all the images in this section. The important things to note are the excellent reduction of MSE, and the improved definition in the boa of the restored image. In general, the blurriness of the degraded image has been removed.

Next we will examine the effectiveness of Power Spectrum Equalization. The equation is as follows:

$$G = \left[\frac{S_{yy}}{|H|^2 S_{uu} + S_{\eta\eta}} \right]^{1/2}$$

Note the similarity to Wiener Filtering, but we only use the magnitude of H. The following example demonstrates restoration using the same specs as for the Wiener Filter above.

Fig. (4.14)

The above images were generated using pse.m. We have again removed a great deal of the blur, but our restoration is not as good as with Wiener Filtering. In general, Wiener filtering is the optimal restoration technique, and this should be remembered later on.

Next we will perform the same restoration using estimated spectral noise. For this we will assume that the noise is white and therefore has a flat (constant) spectral density. Experimentation showed us that overestimating the noise was better than underestimating the noise. This is due to the high pass characteristic of inverse filtering during restoration. When in doubt, suppress the inverse filter. The degraded images below where generated the same way as before, but Snn was estimated as 100.

Lenna restored using wiener filtering

Mean squared error = 252.6

Lenna restored using PSE

Mean squared error = 1.3932e + 05

Fig. (4.15)

The above images were generated using wien2.m and pse2.m, respectively. Clearly, Power Spectrum Equalization is not very robust. A precise representation of the noise is required. This is because PSE does not use inverse filtering, so the noise estimation is doubly important. The code was checked thoroughly, and the only difference between this restoration and the one above was the estimation of Snn.

Our final preliminary investigation was to see what happens when we know h and Snn but not Suu. We estimated the image spectral density as the magnitude squared of the Fourier Transform of the degraded image (rather than of the original image, as before). The degradation was the same as before.

Lenna restored using wiener filtering

Mean squared error = 132.4

Lenna restored using PSE

Mean squared error = 371.9

Fig. (4.16)

The above images were generated using wien3.m and pse3.m, respectively. Again, we see that the Wiener filter has a lower MSE than the PSE filter. Also, for the Wiener Filter, our MSE isn't much worse than when we estimate Suu from the original image. For the PSE, our MSE has actually improved! We attribute this to the fact that our estimation of Suu isn't exact in either case. So generally, using the degraded image to estimate Suu won't hurt us with either restoration filter. The biggest unknown that hurts us so far is Snn for the PSE filter.

Blind Deconvolution

Many different methods were attempted to restore our image when we don't explicitly know h. Most of them had very little success. The reasons will be explained as we explain the general approach we used. The methods for estimating h are known as Blind Deconvolution because our inverse filtering (deconvolution) is being performed without knowledge of our blurring function. The methods we used were all homomorphic ideas.

In general, our degradation is modeled as a convolution plus noise. In the frequency domain, convolution becomes multiplication. If we ignore the additive noise, we can take the log of the multiplication and get addition. Thus, the log of the FT of our degraded image DI is equal to the log of the FT of the original image OI plus the log of the Transfer Function H. Now that we have addition, we can use statistical estimation to estimate H and thus solve for OI.

The problem with this method is that in practice we can't ignore the noise. Therefore, we need ways to estimate the log of the multiplication of OI and H plus the Noise Spectrum. The first approach we had success with came from the Jain text. It uses the following estimate for H.

$$\log|H| = \frac{1}{M}\sum_{k=1}^{M}[\log|V_k| - \log|U_k|]$$

Uk and Vk are obtained by breaking the input image (u) and degraded image (v) into M smaller blocks and computing their Fourier Transforms. H is then used with Snn and Suu to compute the Wiener Filter. Notice that this method only computes Magnitude of H, so its best for phaseless LSI filters. This necessitated our filter design of a phaseless h. The following pictures show the Magnitude Plots of the actual and estimated transfer functions. Our image degration model is the same as always, and we calculated H using the above equation with M = 16. This broke down the images into 64x64 pixel blocks.

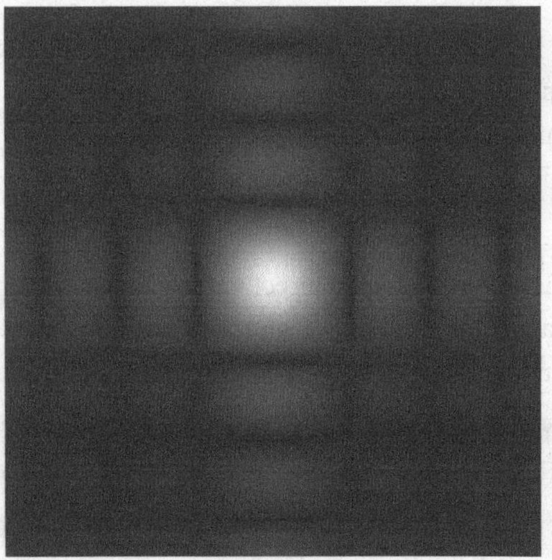

Magnitude plot of blurring filter

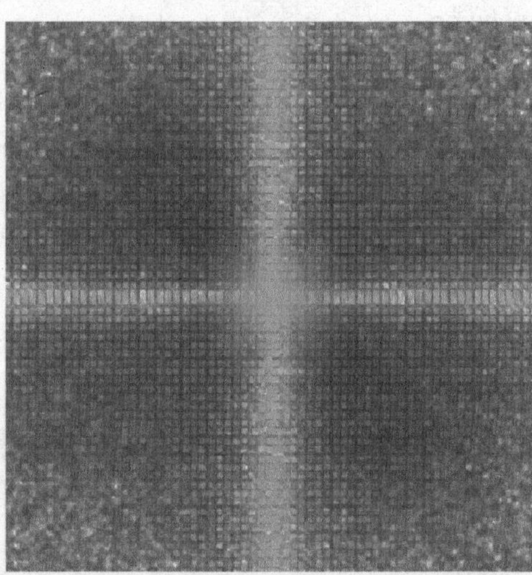

Magnitude plot of estimated blurring filter

Fig. (4.17)

Note that we capture the form of the degradation filter, but we have a lot more noise. Surprisingly, our restoration MSE isn't too bad, depicted below. Both the above and below images were created using jain.m with noise variance 80. Also, since we are restoring using Wiener Filtering, we estimate Snn and Suu for restoration.

Lenna after blurring plus noise

Mean squared error = 1.0660e + 05

Lenna restored using jain approach

Mean squared error = 283.1

Fig. (4.18)

We see that our MSE has gone from 256 with unknown Snn to 283 with all three Wiener Filter componenents (h, Suu, * Snn). We can see that some of the blurring has been reduced in our restored image. Lines can be seen in the band around the hat and the boa is a bit clearer. However, even though our MSE isn't too bad, this is clearly the worst image restoration thus far with respect to visual aspects. Most of the restoration was magnitude restoration. But this was by far our greatest success at blind deconvolution.

Our second approach came from the Lim text. It was proposed by Stockham. The homomorphic idea of taking the log in the frequency domain is again present, as is the notion of breaking up the picture into M sub-blocks. The equation estimates the denominator of the PSE filter as follows:

$$|H|^2 \; S_{uu} + S_{\eta\eta} \, U_v = \alpha \prod_{i=1}^{M} |S_{yy}|$$

where C is Euler's constant (0.57221...). Note that H is never calculated directly. Instead, we use this estimation to choose our PSE filter and restore our image. Our attempt at restoration with this method is shown below. Again, variance is 80, but Suu and Snn are assumed known. Recall that if Snn is not explicitly known, then our PSE restoration fails.

Lenna after blurring plus noise

Mean squared error = 1.0656e + 05

Lenna restored using stockham approach

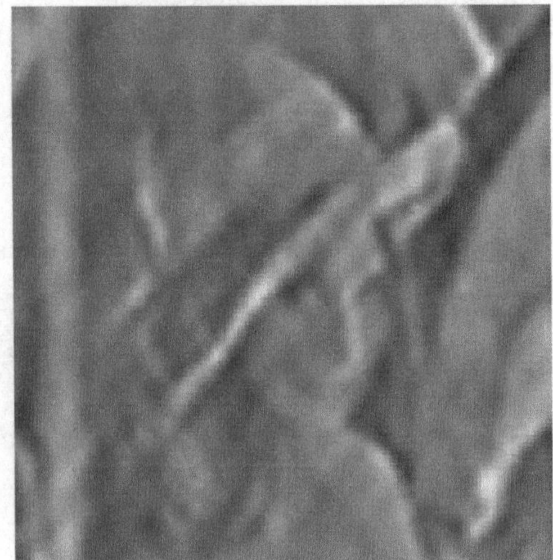

Mean squared error = 7.4031e + 07

Fig. (4.19)

The above images were generated using stockham.m. Clearly, our restoration has further degraded our image. This was seen earlier when we attempted PSE restoration without knowledge of Snn. In this case, we are trying to estimate the entire denominator, not just Snn. Our restoration suffers greatly.

We conclude that Power Spectrum Equalization is just a poor restoration choice in general. It fails for unknown Snn and for our attempt at unknown h. The lack of inverse filtering makes the denominator extremely important in restoration, so no estimation will be very robust. Supposedly, there are cases where PSE is preferable to Wiener Filtering, but our models do not fit them.

There are direct methods for blind deconvolution as well, but we attempted only indirect methods, because they are less ad hoc. An example of a direct method for blind deconvolution is to model lines normal to a suspected edge in the degraded image as the integral of h, and use this measurement for deconvolution. Another indirect method we tried was to assume there was no additive noise in the system. Thus, if our average blurring function goes to zero over many images, we can estimate our original frequency information as the geometric mean of the degraded images. However, geometric means are extremely vulnerable to noise, and much iteration was required for our approximations to hold. In general, we did not get good results for this method. You can view our code baran.m and try to improve it.

```
% Project 2
% Andy Doran
%
% function baran(name,xdim,M,No)
%
% name  = 'input image' (as in 'lenna.256')
% xdim  = x dimension of input image (usually 256 or 512)
% M     = Number of Images to average over.
% No    = Variance of the noise in the filter
%
% This function takes an input image and runs it through a LSI
                                                          filter
% M times, generating M degraded images. We assume we know the
                                                         average
```

```
% transfer function of the filter H.The degraded images are taken to
% the Fourier domain and geometrically averaged, then multiplied by
                                                                   the
% average H.Our LSI filter H is generated differently each time with
% zero mean Gaussian noise added each time to the filter components.
% This method comes Elec539 class notes).
%
% The average blurring filter is calculated as h = zeros(4);

function baran(name,xdim,M,No)

% Load and Plot image
pict = freadbin(name,xdim,xdim);

figure(1)
clf
colormap(gray);
imagesc(pict);
txt = [num2str(name) ' before degradation'];
title(txt)
axis square
axis off

% Create LSI degradation model
blur = 4;
h = zeros(blur);

% Initialize degraded frequency spectra
DEG = ones(xdim);

% Initialize average logarithm transfer function
HM = zeros(xdim);
hm = zeros(4);

% Create Gaussian noise, mean = 0, variance comes from input (No)
% To insure ergodicity, make sure each noise filter index has zero
% mean over all the input images.
% To insure zero mean noise, subtract out the mean each time.

h1 = sqrt(No)*randn(1,M);
h1 = h1 - mean(h1);
h2 = sqrt(No)*randn(1,M);
h2 = h2 - mean(h2);
h3 = sqrt(No)*randn(1,M);
h3 = h3 - mean(h3);
h4 = sqrt(No)*randn(1,M);
h4 = h4 - mean(h4);
h5 = sqrt(No)*randn(1,M);
h5 = h5 - mean(h5);
```

```
h6 = sqrt(No)*randn(1,M);
h6 = h6 - mean(h6);
h7 = sqrt(No)*randn(1,M);
h7 = h7 - mean(h7);
h8 = sqrt(No)*randn(1,M);
h8 = h8 - mean(h8);
h9 = sqrt(No)*randn(1,M);
h9 = h9 - mean(h9);
h10 = sqrt(No)*randn(1,M);
h10 = h10 - mean(h10);
h11 = sqrt(No)*randn(1,M);
h11 = h11 - mean(h11);
h12 = sqrt(No)*randn(1,M);
h12 = h12 - mean(h12);
h13 = sqrt(No)*randn(1,M);
h13 = h13 - mean(h13);
h14 = sqrt(No)*randn(1,M);
h14 = h14 - mean(h14);
h15 = sqrt(No)*randn(1,M);
h15 = h15 - mean(h15);
h16 = sqrt(No)*randn(1,M);
h16 = h16 - mean(h16);

% Create degraded images and get geometric mean of Fourier
                                                          Magnitudes
for i = 1:M
  hd = h + [h1(i) h2(i) h3(i) h4(i);h5(i) h6(i) h7(i) h8(i);h9(i)
                            h10(i) h11(i) h12(i);h13(i) h14(i) h15(i)
                                                                h16(i)];
  HM = HM + (abs(fft2(hd,xdim,xdim)));
  hm = hm + hd;
  % Run image through LSI Filter with additive noise set to 0
  dpict = distimag(pict,hd,0);
  DPICT = fft2(dpict);
  DEG = DEG.*abs(DPICT.^(1/M));    % Get geometric mean of degraded
                                                            spectrum
end

% Plot restored image spectra
figure(1)
clf
imagesc(fftshift(abs(DEG)));
colormap(gray);
txt = ['Frequency Spectra of Restored Image'];
title(txt)
axis square
axis off

% Calculate Transfer function of average LSI filter
```

```
H = fft2(h,xdim,xdim);

% Restore Image
scale = exp((-H)/M);
index = find(scale == 1);
length(index)
RPICT = scale.*DEG;
rpict = ifft2(DEG);

% Plot restored image
figure(3)
clf
imagesc(abs(rpict));
colormap(gray);
txt = [num2str(name) ' restored using Homomorphic Restoration'];
title(txt)
axis square
axis off

% Calculate MSE of restored image
error = abs(rpict) - pict;
sqerr = sum(sum(error.^2));
RMSE = sqerr/(xdim^2)

% Calculate a degraded image to test
noise = sqrt(No)*randn(blur);
hd = h + noise
dpict = distimag(pict,hd,0);

% Plot abs(fft(h)) to see type of filter we have
H = fft2(hd,xdim,xdim);

figure(4)
clf
colormap(gray);
imagesc(fftshift(abs(H)));
txt = ['Magnitude of blurring filter'];
title(txt)
axis square
axis off

% Plot degraded image
figure(2)
clf
colormap(gray);
imagesc(dpict);
txt = [num2str(name) ' degraded with 4x4 averaging Filter with
                                                          Noise'];
title(txt)
```

```
axis square
axis off

% Plot magnitude of original image
PICT = fft2(pict);
figure(5)
clf
imagesc(fftshift(abs(PICT)));
colormap(gray);
txt = ['Frequency Spectra of Original Image'];
title(txt)
axis square
axis off
% Calculate MSE of degraded image
error = dpict - pict;
sqerr = sum(sum(error.^2));
DMSE = sqerr/(xdim^2)
```

The Imaging Model

The image degradation process can be modeled by the following equation;

$$g = Hf + \omega \qquad ...(1)$$

where, H represents a convolution matrix that models the blurring that many imaging systems introduce. For example, camera defocus, motion blur, imperfections of the lenses all can be modeled by H. The vectors g, f, and w represent the observed, the original and the noise images. More specifically, w is a random vector that models the random errors in the observed data. These errors can be due to the electronics used (thermal and shot noise) the recording medium (film grain) or the imaging process (photon noise).

Problems : Obtaining f from Eq. (1) is not a straight forward task since in most cases of interest the matrix H is ill-posed. Mathematically this means that certain eigenvalues of this matrix are close to zero, which makes the inversion process very unstable. For practical purposes this implies that the inverse or the pseudo-inverse solutions.

$$H^{-1}g \text{ and } f_2 = (H^{\tau}H)^{-1}H^{\tau}g \qquad ...(1)$$

amplify the noise and provide useless results. This fact is demonstrated in what follows.

Solution : Regularization is one way to avoid the problems due to the ill-posed nature of H. According to regularization instead of minimizing || g – Hf ||2 in order to find f one minimizes:

$$||g - Hf||^2 + \wedge||QF||^2 \qquad ...(3)$$

The additional term ||Qf||2 is called regularization term and can be viewed as capturing the properties of the desired solution. In other words, the first term in Eq. (3) stirs the solution f to be "close" to the observed data g while the second term enforces "prior knowledge" to the solution. The prior knowledge that is used is that the image is locally smooth. In most cases Q represents the convolution with a high-pass filter. Thus the term ||Qf||2 can be viewed as the high-pass energy of the restored image. The parameter ë is called regularization parameter and controls the closeness to the data vs. the prior knowledge of the solution. Finding f based on Eq. (3) gives

$$f_g = (H^{\tau}H + \wedge Q^{\tau}Q)^{-1}H^{\tau}g \qquad ...(4)$$

Finding the proper value for the parameter ë is an important problem. In the demo that follows one can choose different values of ë and observe the effect to the restored image. A large value of ë results in a smoother image and is necessary if the noise variance is high or H is highly ill-conditioned. On the other hand a large ë blurs out the image details. So one has to decide between smoothness and detail in the solution.

Blind Image Restoration

In many practical cases of interest H is not known. For example when taking the photograph of a moving object when the shutter speed and the speed of the object are unknowns. In this case we are faced with the very difficult problem of "blind" image restoration. In such cases we have to utilize prior knowledge in order to somehow recover simultaneously BOTH f and H. There are many different ways to incorporate prior knowledge about the image f and the degradation H in the problem. One of them is using deterministic constraints in the form of CONVEX SETS.

Example of Blind Deconvolution

Fig. (4.20)

This is an example of the application of blind de convolution in an image degraded by UNKNOWN blur. Notice the plates of the car in this image are not readable.

Fig. (4.21) Restored image obtained by 50 iterations of the algorithm.

Other Examples of Recovering Information Hidden in Images

Fig. (4.22a) Degraded image by film-grain noise.

Fig. (4.22b) Restored by adaptive window median filter.

Fig. (4.22c) Area of interest.

Image Restoration

In many applications (e.g., satellite imaging, medical imaging, astronomical imaging, poor-quality family portraits) the imaging system introduces a slight distortion. Often images are slightly blurred and image restoration aims at *deblurring* the image.

The blurring can usually be modeled as an LSI system with a given PSF $h[m, n]$.

$$h[m, n] \xleftrightarrow{FT} H(u, v)$$

Fourier transform (FT) relationship between the two functions.

The observed image is

$$g[m, n] = h[m, n] * f[m, n] \quad \ldots(1)$$

$$G(u, v) = H(u, v)\, F(u, v) \quad \ldots(2)$$

$$F(u, v) = G(u, v)\, H(u, v) \quad \ldots(3)$$

Example 1 : Image Blurring

Above we showed the equations for representing the common model for blurring an image. In Figure 4.23 we have an original image and a PSF function that we wish to apply to the image in order to model a basic blurred image.

Fig. (4.23)

Once we apply the PSF to the original image, we receive our blurred image that is shown in Figure 4.24:

Fig. (4.24)

Frequency Domain Analysis

Example 1 looks at the original images in its typical form; however, it is often useful to look at our images and PSF in the frequency domain. In Figure 4.3, we take another look at the image blurring example above and look at how the images and results would appear in the frequency domain if we applied the fourier transforms.

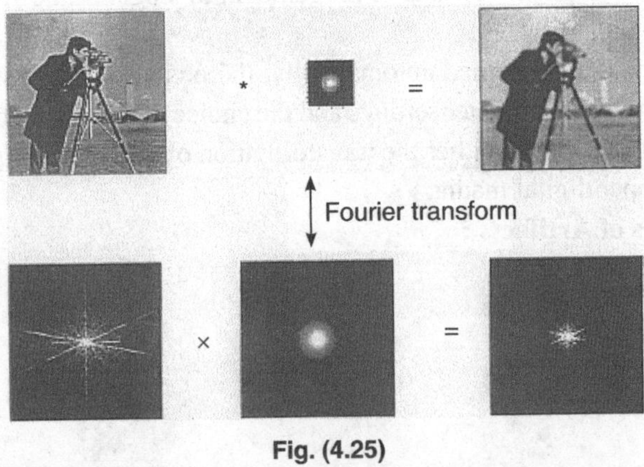

Fig. (4.25)

■ 4.1 THE DIGITAL FILM RESTORATION PROCESS

The restoration process starts with the conversion of each frame to a digital image with a high-resolution film scanner. The size of a digital color image is up to 45 MBytes per frame.

The next phase includes the detection of cuts and scratches parallel to the direction of film transport, which are the first defects to be removed. In each shot or scene a reference frame is automatically chosen for the brightness.

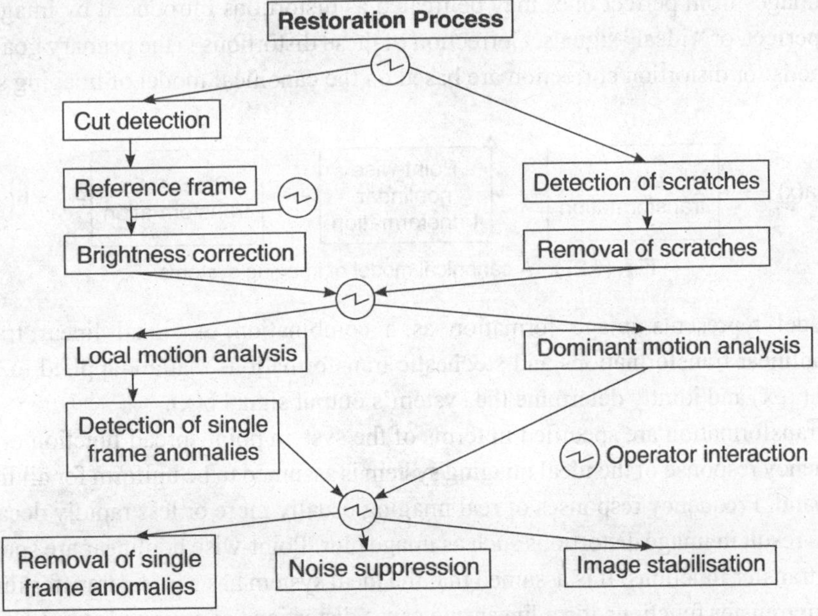

Fig. (4.26) Digital film restoration process.

The digital film restoration system LIMELIGHT was developed by Joanneum Research (Graz) and has been successfully applied to restoring parts of the Austrian film 'Opernball'. The split-screen image shows the heavily distorted original on the left half and the restored frame on the right. Furthermore a motion analysis (local and dominant) is performed to enable the detection of single frame anomalies by motion compensated frame differencing as well as camera movement necessary for detecting image vibrations. The final restoration phase consists of the removal of single frame artifacts, of noise suppression and image stabilization.

While all these steps are performed automatically, there is also the possibility for an operator to make changes if necessary. The parameter settings and the choice of reference frames can be modified on operator request. The last step can be either the transformation of the image sequences back to celluloid film or the storage on proper digital media.

Removable Classes of Artifacts :

- Dust and mud
- Image vibrations
- Mould
- Scratches
- Flicker
- Missing frames
- Color variations
- Noise

■ 4.2 MATHEMATICAL MODELS OF IMAGING SYSTEMS

Imaging systems always have certain technical limitations in their design and implementations and generate images that are not as perfect as they would be if there were no implementation limitations. Deviations of real images from perfect ones may be treated as distortions introduced by imaging systems to hypothetical perfect, or " ideal" signals. Correction of these distortions is the primary goal of image processing. Methods for distortion correction are based on the canonical model of imaging systems shown in Fig. 4.27.

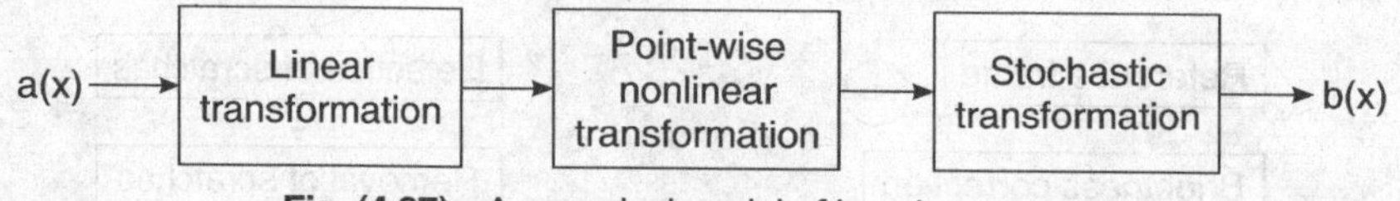

Fig. (4.27) A canonical model of imaging systems.

The model represents image formation as a combination of signal linear transformations, point-wise nonlinear transformations and stochastic transformations that are applied to a hypothetical perfect signal (a x) and jointly determine the system's output signal b(x).

Linear transformation are specified in terms of the system point spread function or frequency response. Frequency response of the ideal imaging system is assumed to be uniform for all frequencies in a certain base band. Frequency responses of real imaging usually more or less rapidly decay on high frequencies. This result in image distortions such as image blur. Point-wise nonlinear are specified in terms of the system transfer functions. It is assumed that the ideal system has a linear transfer function. Deviations of system transfer functions form linear one cause distortions of gray scale nonlinear distortions.

Stochastic transformations model signal random distortions and cause random interferences, or noise in output images. Stochastic transformations are specified by statistical noise models:

The processing goal is estimating the perfect signal a(x) given distorted signal b(x) produced by the system. This problem is frequently referred to as the inverse problem. Signal transformations that are applied to system's output signals {b(x)} to produce an estimate a^(x) of the "ideal" signal are called signal recovery or, in application to image processing, image restoration. Similar problem is image reconstruction. This term is usually refers to image formation in transform domain imaging such as tomography and holography. If the system does not introduce any random distortions and system's parameters such as point spread function and transfer function are known, the inverse problem has a trivial solution: signal b(x) has to be subjected to transformations inverse to those introduced by the system. However, one can not, in general, neglect random or similar uncontrolled distortions such as round-off errors in digital processing. In reality, applying inverse transformation may result in artifacts that may even be useless. To solving the inverse problem in such cases, the statistical approach that explicitly accounts for signal random distortions appears to be the most appropriate.

Generally, signal recovery, image restoration and reconstruction is indivisible procedure that should account for and correct all distortions. However, in practice this process is divided into separate steps carried out in the order inverse to that distortion factors have in the model.

■ 4.3 IMAGE RESTORATION AS INVERSE CONVOLUTION OF THE WHOLE IMAGE

- Most image restoration methods are based on convolution applied globally to the whole image.
- Degradation causes:
  — Defects of optical lenses,
  — No linearity of the electro-optical sensor,
  — Graininess of the film material,
  — Relative motion between an object and camera
  — Wrong focus,
  — Atmospheric turbulence in remote sensing or astronomy, etc.
- The objective of image restoration is to reconstruct the original image from its degraded version.
- Image restoration techniques - two groups:
- Deterministic methods - applicable to images with little noise and a known degradation function.
  — The original image is obtained from the degraded one by a transformation inverse to the degradation.
- Stochastic techniques - the best restoration is sought according to some stochastic criterion, e.g., a least squares method.
  — In some cases the degradation transformation must be estimated first.
- It is advantageous to know the degradation function explicitly.
- The better this knowledge is, the better are the results of the restoration.
- There are three typical degradations with a simple function:
  — Relative constant speed movement of the object with respect to the camera,

— wrong lens focus,

— and atmospheric turbulence.

- In most practical cases, there is insufficient knowledge about the degradation, and it must be estimated and modeled.
- **Methods :**

  — A priori knowledge about degradation - either known in advance or obtained before restoration.

  — If it is clear in advance that the image was degraded by relative motion of an object with respect to the sensor then the modeling only determines the speed and direction of the motion.
- An example of parameters obtained before restoration is an attempt to estimate parameters of a capturing device such as a TV camera or digitizer.
- A posteriori knowledge is obtained by analyzing the degraded image.
- A typical example is to find some interest points in the image (e.g. corners, straight lines) and guess how they looked before degradation.
- Another possibility is to use spectral characteristics of the regions in the image that are relatively homogeneous.
- A degraded image g can arise from the original image f by a process which can be expressed as :

$$g(i, j) = s\left(\int \int_{(a, b) \in 0} f(a, b)\, h(a, b, i, j)\, da\, db\right) + v(i, j)$$

where s is some nonlinear function and nu describes the noise.

- The degradation is very often simplified by

  — neglecting the nonlinearity

  — assuming that the function h is invariant with respect to position in the image.
- Degradation can be then expressed as convolution

$$g(i, j) = (f * h)\,(i, j) + v(i, j)$$

- If the degradation is given by equation (4.78) and the noise is not significant then image restoration equates to inverse convolution (also called deconvolution).
- If noise is not negligible then the inverse convolution is solved as an overdetermined system of linear equations.

Degradations that are easy to restore :

- Some degradations can be easily expressed mathematically (convolution) and also restored simply in images.
- The Fourier transform H of the convolution function is used.

Relative motion of the camera and object :

- Assume an image is acquired with a camera with a mechanical shutter.
- Relative motion of the camera and the photographed object during the shutter open time T causes smoothing of the object in the image.
- Suppose V is the constant speed in the direction of the x axis; the Fourier transform H(u,v) of the degradation caused in time T is given by

$$H(u, v) = \frac{\sin(\pi VTu)}{\pi Vu}$$

Wrong lens focus :

- Image smoothing caused by imperfect focus of a thin lens can be described by the following function

$$H(u, v) = \frac{J_1(ar)}{ar}$$

where J_1 is the Bessel function of the first order, r^2 = u^2 + v^2, and a is the displacement.

Atmospheric turbulence :

- needs to be restored in remote sensing and astronomy
- caused by temperature non-homogeneity in the atmosphere that deviates passing light rays.
- The mathematical model

$$H(u, v) = e^{-c(u^2 + v^2)^{5/6}}$$

where c is a constant that depends on the type of turbulence which is usually found experimentally.

The power 5/6 is sometimes replaced by 1.

4.4 THE IMAGE RESTORATION PROBLEM

- Common sources of blurring and noise
- The point-spread function (PSF) model of blurring
- Noise models

4.4.1 Common Sources of Blurring and Noise

Blurring is present in any imaging system which uses electromagnetic radiation (for example, visible light and X-rays). Diffraction limits the resolution of an imaging device to features on the order of the illuminating wavelength. Scattering of light between the target object and imaging system (for example, by the atmosphere) introduces additional blurring. Lenses and mirrors cause blurring because they have limited spatial extent and optical imperfections. Discretization results in yet more blurring because devices such as CCDs average illumination over regions rather than sampling it at discrete points.

Noise is similarly omnipresent: any imaging device must use a finite exposure (or integration) time, which introduces stochastic noise from the random arrival of photons. Optical imperfections and instrumentation noise (for example, thermal noise in CCD devices) result in more noise. Sampling causes noise due to aliasing of high-frequency signal components, and digitization produces quantization errors. Further noise can be introduced by communication errors and compression.

Blurring and noise processes can be accurately approximated by mathematical models. The next sections review some common models for blurring and noise.

4.4.2 The Point-Spread Function (PSF) Model of Blurring

Most blurring processes can be approximated by convolution integrals, also known as Fredholm integral equations of the first kind. The blurring is characterized by a Point-Spread Function (PSF) or impulse response. The PSF is the output of the imaging system for an input point source. All the blurring processes considered in this thesis are linear and have a spatially invariant PSF.

For discrete image processing, the convolution integral is replaced by a sum. The blurry image x(n,m) is obtained from the original image s(n,m) by this convolution:

$$x(n, m) = \sum_{a=-\infty}^{+\infty} \sum_{b=-\infty}^{+\infty} s(n+a, m+b)\, h(-a, -b) \qquad \ldots(1)$$

The function h(n,m) is the discrete Point Spread Function for the imaging system. Also of interest is the Discrete Fourier Transform (DFT) representation of the point-spread function, given by

$$H(u, v) = \sum_{n=0}^{N-1} \sum_{m=0}^{M-1} h(n, m)\, e^{-2\pi j\,(un/N + um/M)} \qquad \ldots(2)$$

for $u = [-N/2]+1, \ldots, [N/2]$ and $v = [-M/2]+1, \ldots, [M/2]$. $H(u, v)$ gives a set of coefficients for plane waves of various frequencies and orientations. These plane waves, called spatial frequency components, reconstruct the PSF exactly when multiplied by the coefficients H(u,v) and summed. The function H(u,v) is referred to as the transfer function, or system frequency response. By examining |H(u,v)|, one can quickly determine which spatial frequency components are passed or attenuated by the imaging system.

As an example, consider this 3x3 mask which can be used to model small amounts of blurring

$$\frac{1}{15}\begin{bmatrix} 1 & 2 & 1 \\ 2 & 3 & 2 \\ 1 & 2 & 1 \end{bmatrix} \qquad \ldots(3)$$

The DFT of this mask is:

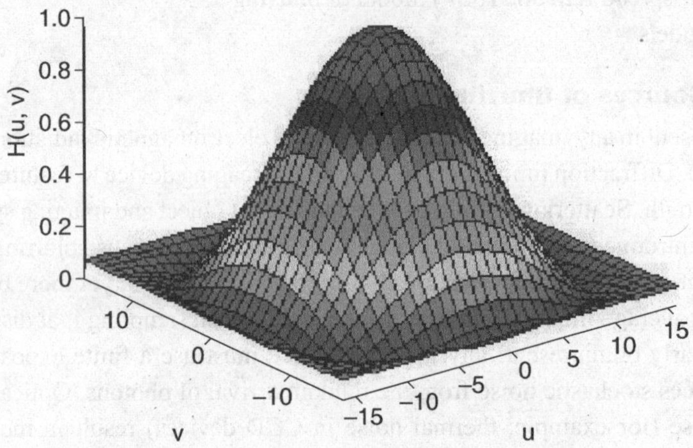

Fig. (4.28) $|H(u, v)|$ for a 3×3 blurring mask, with $N = M = 33$.

$$H(u, v) = \frac{1}{15}\left[3 + 4\cos\left(\frac{2\pi u}{N}\right) + 4\cos\left(\frac{2\pi v}{M}\right) + 4\cos\left(\frac{2\pi u}{N}\right)\cos\left(\frac{2\pi v}{M}\right)\right] \qquad \ldots(4)$$

Figure 4.5 shows a plot of |H(u,v)|. Near , the transfer function has . This indicates that low-frequency components are passed. Near the perimeter of the plot, , meaning that high frequency components are blocked.

4.4.3 Noise models

Noise in imaging systems is usually either additive or multiplicative. The basic noise is additive noise which is zero-mean and white. White noise is spatially uncorrelated: the noise for each pixel is independent and identically distributed (iid). Common noise models are:

Gaussian noise provides a good model of noise in many imaging systems. Its probability density function (pdf) is:

$$p_n(n) = \frac{1}{\sqrt{\pi\sigma^2}} e^{-n^2/\sigma^2} \quad \text{...(5)}$$

The Gaussian distribution has an important property: to estimate the mean of a stationary Gaussian random variable, one can't do any better than the linear average. This makes Gaussian noise a worst-case scenario for nonlinear image restoration filters, in the sense that the improvement over linear filters is least for Gaussian noise. To improve on linear filtering results, nonlinear filters can exploit only the non-Gaussianity of the signal distribution.

Laplacian noise (also called biexponential) which has this pdf:

$$p_n(n) = \frac{1}{\sqrt{2}\sigma} e^{-\sqrt{2}|n|/\sigma} \quad \text{...(6)}$$

Nonlinear estimators can provide a much more accurate estimate of the mean of a stationary Laplacian random variable than the linear average.

Uniform noise is not often encountered in real-world imaging systems, but provides a useful comparison with Gaussian noise. The linear average is a comparatively poor estimator for the mean of a uniform distribution. This implies that nonlinear filters should be better at removing uniform noise than Gaussian noise. The Uniform pdf is given by:

$$p_n(n) = \begin{cases} \dfrac{1}{\sigma\, 2\sqrt{3}} & \text{for } |n| \le \sigma\sqrt{3} \\ 0 & \text{else} \end{cases} \quad \text{...(7)}$$

Figure 4.29 illustrates these PDFs for zero-mean, unit variance noise.

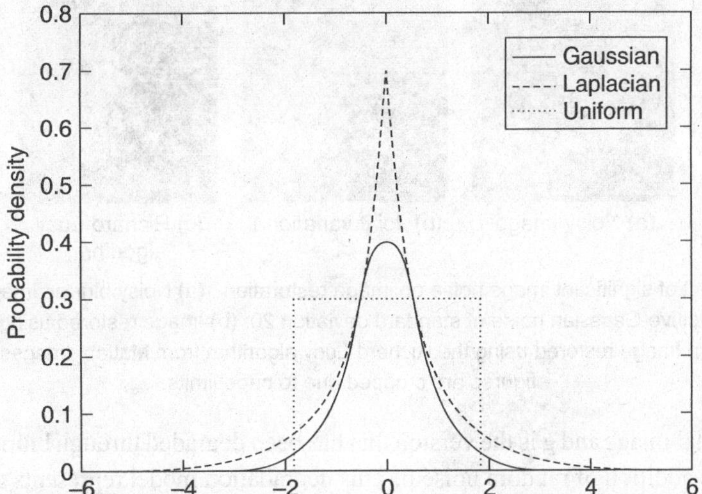

Fig. (4.29) Probability density functions of the Gaussian, Laplacian and uniform distributions.

Due to limitations of computational and storage capacity, it is practically always impossible to take into account all the available knowledge about minor details which possibly have some impact on the observation. It is then reasonable to ignore the details and model only their net effect, which manifests itself in minor fluctuations not predictable from the things included in the model. These fluctuations are called noise.

For real valued parameters, the standard choice of noise model is the Gaussian distribution. The central limit theorem states, roughly, that if a very large number of very small independent fluctuations are summed linearly, then the distribution of the resulting total fluctuation will be Gaussian. In reality, neither the requirement of all the fluctuations being small nor the linearity of summation are perfectly met, but Gaussian noise models are used anyway because they are mathematically very convenient.

4.5 IMAGE RESTORATION IN THE PRESENCE OF NOISE

The task of deblurring, a form of image restoration, is to recover an image from its blurred version. Whereas most existing methods assume a small amount of additive noise, image restoration under significant additive noise remains an interesting research problem. We describe two techniques to improve the noise handling characteristics of a recently proposed variational framework for semi-blind image deblurring that is based on joint segmentation and deblurring. One technique uses a structure tensor as a robust edge-indicating function. The other uses non-local image averaging to suppress noise.

The task of deblurring, a form of image restoration, is to obtain the original, sharp version of a blurred image. There exist many applications for image restoration, including astronomical imaging, medical imaging, law enforcement, and digital media restoration. The problem has attracted strong research interest and will continue to do so, not only because it has many applications but also because it has a simple mathematical formulation yet it is a classical inverse problem for which good solutions are not easily obtained. The simple equation for expressing image blurring/degradation is as follows:

$$g = f * h + n$$

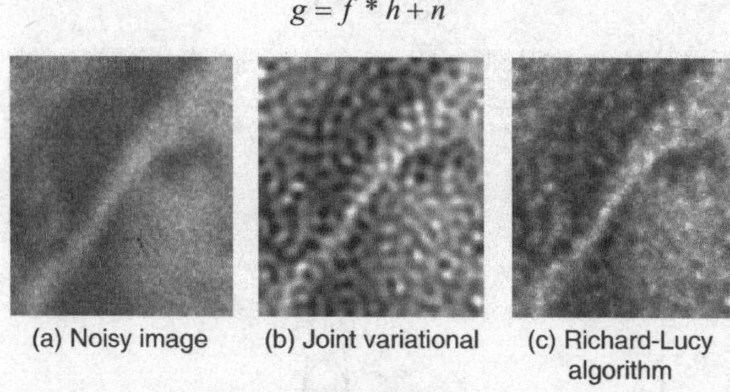

(a) Noisy image (b) Joint variational (c) Richard-Lucy algorithm

Fig. (4.30) The effect of significant image noise on image restoration : (a) Noisy blurred image with imae intensity in [0, 255] and additive Gaussian noise of standard deviation 20; (b) Image restored using a joint variational framework [5]; (c) Image restored using the Richard-Lucy algorithm from Matlab. Images in this and other figures are cropped due to page limits.

where f is the original image and g is the version that has been degraded through blurring (convolution *) by kernel h and the addition of random noise n. This degradation model represents a linear relationship between f and g; hence, the problem of recovering f from g is called linear image restoration. Often the blur kernel is assumed to be space-invariant. If we lack prior knowledge of the blur kernel h, we have the more difficult blind (linear) image restoration problem which h also needs to be estimated.

4.6 SPATIAL FILTERING

A spatial filter is an optical device which uses the principles of Fourier optics to alter the structure of a beam of coherent light or other electromagnetic radiation. Spatial filtering is commonly used to "clean up" the output of lasers, removing aberrations in the beam due to imperfect, dirty, or damaged optics, or due to variations in the laser gain medium itself. This can be used to produce a laser beam containing only a single transverse mode of the laser's optical resonator.

In spatial filtering, a lens is used to focus the beam. Because of diffraction, a beam that is not a perfect plane wave will not focus to a single spot, but rather will produce a pattern of light and dark regions in the focal plane. For example, an imperfect beam might form a bright spot surrounded by a series of concentric rings, as shown in the figure to the right. It can be shown that this two-dimensional pattern is the two-dimensional Fourier transform of the initial beam's transverse intensity distribution. In this context, the focal plane is often called the transform plane. Light in the very center of the transform pattern corresponds to a perfect, wide plane wave. Other light corresponds to "structure" in the beam, with light further from the central spot corresponding to structure with higher spatial frequency. A pattern with very fine details will produce light very far from the transform plane's central spot. In the example above, the large central spot and rings of light surrounding it are due to the structure resulting when the beam passed through a circular aperture. The spot is enlarged because the beam is limited by the aperture to a finite size, and the rings relate to the sharp edges of the beam created by the edges of the aperture. This pattern is called an Airy pattern, after its discoverer George Airy.

By altering the distribution of light in the transform plane and using another lens to reform the collimated beam, the structure of the beam can be altered. The most common way of doing this is to place an aperture in the beam that allows the desired light to pass, while blocking light that corresponds to undesired structure in the beam. In particular, a small circular aperture or "pinhole" that passes only the central bright spot can remove nearly all fine structure from the beam, producing a smooth transverse intensity profile, which may be almost a perfect Gaussian beam. With good optics and a very small pinhole, one could even approximate a plane wave.

In practice, the diameter of the aperture is chosen based on the focal length of the lens, the diameter and quality of the input beam, and its wavelength (longer wavelengths require larger apertures). If the hole is too small, the beam quality is greatly improved but the power is greatly reduced. If the hole is too large, the beam quality may not be improved as much as desired.

The size of aperture that can be used also depends on the size and quality of the optics. To use a very small pinhole, one must use a focusing lens with a low f-number, and ideally the lens should not add significant aberrations to the beam. The design of such a lens becomes increasingly more difficult as the f-number decreases. In practice, the most commonly used configuration is to use a microscope objective lens for focusing the beam, and an aperture made by punching a small, precise, hole in a piece of thick metal foil. Such assemblies are available commercially.

Definition : "Spatial filtering" is a term used to describe the methods that are used to compute spatial density estimates for events that have been observed at individual locations.

The term describes a set of tools for displaying functions estimated from these data points that are distributed in two-dimensional space.

- Spatial filtering is a form of data smoothing designed to give us a clearer view of the general, unencumbered by details which do not answer our questions of interest.
- Spatial filtering is a non-parametric analysis method which belongs within the field of exploratory spatial analysis which relies, to a large degree, on graphical methods of analysis.

Purpose : Spatial filters are used when we have no a priori curve to fit to a data series. Instead, we rely on nearby, adjacent, values to estimate the value at a given point. Filters take out variability in a data set while retaining the local features of data. By varying the size of the filter, features in the data that vary at different spatial scales can be differentially removed. Spatial filtering is useful as an exploratory technique for identifying areas that are homogeneous or areas that have larger or smaller values than generally occurs. The graph of the spatial filtering process is generally a "map" which is a concise representation of the phenomena studied.

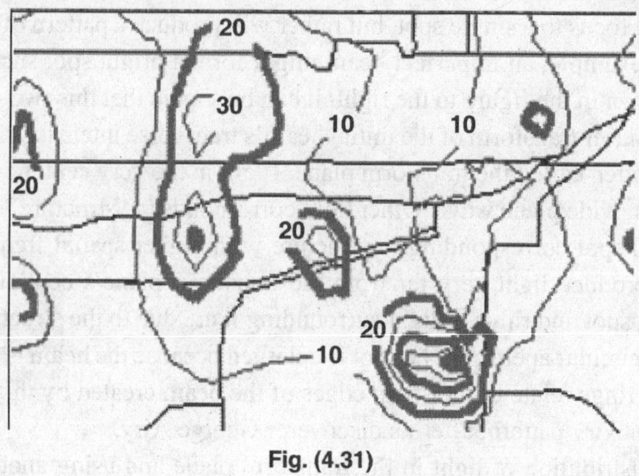

Fig. (4.31)

Why Filter?

Any presentation of the spatial distribution of the density of health events in a population is a model of the data. Features of the distribution are to be explained. The density distribution is the fundamental entity to which the events observed relate. Our concept of disease risk is expressed in terms of expected density. Therefore, the spatial density distribution is not just a convenient presentational device. It is the fundamental entity of interest to us. Results of spatial filtering are useful for identifying possible models of the data or for analyzing how well a given model fits the observed data.

■ 4.7 MEAN FILTERS

The mean filter is a simple sliding-window spatial filter that replaces the center value in the window with the average (mean) of all the pixel values in the window. The window, or kernel, is usually square but can be any shape. An example of mean filtering of a single 3x3 window of values is shown below in figure 4.32.

Unfiltered values		
5	3	6
2	1	9
8	4	7

Fig. (4.32) Mean filters.

$$5 + 3 + 6 + 2 + 1 + 9 + 8 + 4 + 7 = 45$$

$$45/9 = 5$$

Mean filtered		
*	*	*
*	5	*
*	*	*

Fig. (4.33) Center value (previously 1) is replaced by the mean of all nine values.

Mean filtering is a simple, intuitive and easy to implement method of *smoothing* images, *i.e.* reducing the amount of intensity variation between one pixel and the next. It is often used to reduce noise in images.

How It Works

The idea of mean filtering is simply to replace each pixel value in an image with the mean ('average') value of its neighbors, including itself. This has the effect of eliminating pixel values, which are unrepresentative of their surroundings. Mean filtering is usually thought of as a convolution filter. Like other convolutions it is based around a kernel, which represents the shape and size of the neighborhood to be sampled when calculating the mean. Often a 3×3 square kernel is used, as shown in Figure 4.34, although larger kernels (*e.g.* 5×5 squares) can be used for more severe smoothing. (Note that a small kernel can be applied more than once in order to produce a similar - but not identical - effect as a single pass with a large kernel.)

1/9	1/9	1/9
1/9	1/9	1/9
1/9	1/9	1/9

Fig. (4.34) 3 × 3 averaging kernel of ten used in mean filtering.

Computing the straightforward convolution of an image with this kernel carries out the mean filtering process.

4.7.1 Arithmetic Mean Filter

This is the simplest of the mean filters. Let Sxv represent the set of coordinates in a rectangular sub image window of size m X n, centered at point (x, y).The arithmetic mean filtering process computes the average value of the corrupted image g(x, y) in the area defined by Sxy. The value of the restored image at any point (x, y) is simply the arithmetic mean computed using the pixels in the region defined by S. In other words

$$\hat{f}(x, y) = \frac{1}{mn} \sum_{(s,t) \in S_\sigma} g(s, t)$$

This operation can be implemented using a convolution mask in which ail coefficients have value 1/mn. As discussed in Section 3.6.1, a mean filter simply smoothes local variations in an image. Noise is reduced as a result of blurring.

4.7.2 Geometric Mean Filter

An image restored using a geometric mean filter is given by the expression

$$\hat{f}(x, y) = \left[\prod_{(s,t) \in S_{xy}} g(s, t) \right]^{1/mn}$$

Here, each restored pixel is given by the product of the pixels in the sub image window, raised to the power 1/mn. A geometric mean filter achieves smoothing comparable to the arithmetic mean filter, but it tends to lose less image detail in the process.

4.7.3 Harmonic Mean Filter

The harmonic mean filtering operation is given by the expression

$$\hat{f}(x, y) = \frac{mn}{\sum_{(s,t) \in S_{xy}} \frac{1}{g(s, t)}}$$

The harmonic mean filter works well for salt noise, but fails for pepper noise. It does well also with other types of noise tike Gaussian noise.

4.7.4 Contra Harmonic Mean Filter

The contra harmonic mean filtering operation yields a restored image based on the expression

$$\hat{f}(x, y) = \frac{\sum_{(s,t) \in S_{xy}} g(s, t)^{Q+1}}{\sum_{(s,t) \in S_{xy}} g(s, t)^{Q}}$$

where Q is called the order of the filter. This filter is well suited for reducing or virtually eliminating the effects of salt-and-pepper noise. For positive values of Q, the filter eliminates pepper noise. For negative values of Q it eliminates salt noise. It cannot do both simultaneously. Note that the contra harmonic filter reduces to the arithmetic mean filter if Q = 0, and to the harmonic mean filter if Q = - 1.

■ 4.8 ORDER-STATISTICS FILTERS

Order-statistics filters are spatial filters whose response is based on ordering (ranking) the pixels contained in the image area encompassed by the filter. The response of the filter at any point is determined by the ranking result.

4.8.1 Median Filter

The best-known order-statistics filter is the median filter, which, as its name implies, replaces the value of a pixel by the median of the gray levels in the neighborhood of that pixel:

$$\hat{f}(x, y) = \underset{(s,t) \in S_{xy}}{\text{median}} \{g(s, t)\}$$

The original value of the pixel is included in the computation of the median. Median filters are quite popular because, for certain types of random noise, they provide excellent noise-reduction capabilities, with considerably less blurring than linear smoothing filters of similar size. Median filters are particularly effective in the presence of both bipolar and unipolar impulse noise.

The median filter is also a sliding-window spatial filter, but it replaces the center value in the window with the median of all the pixel values in the window. As for the mean filter, the kernel is usually square but can be any shape. An example of median filtering of a single 3x3 window of values is shown below.

Unfiltered values		
6	2	0
3	97	4
19	3	10

Fig. (4.35) Median filter.

In Order : 0, 2, 3, 3, 4, 6, 10, 15, 97

Median filtered		
*	*	*
*	4	*
*	*	*

Fig. (4.36) Center value (previously 97) is replaced by the median of all nine values (4).

Note that for the first (top) example, the median filter would also return a value of 5, since the ordered values are 1, 2, 3, 4, 5, 6, 7, 8, 9. For the second (bottom) example, though, the mean filter returns the value 16 since the sum of the nine values in the window is 144 and 144 / 9 = 16. This illustrates one of the celebrated features of the median filter: its ability to remove 'impulse' noise (outlying values, either high or low). The median filter is also widely claimed to be 'edge-preserving' since it theoretically preserves step edges without blurring. However, in the presence of noise it does blur edges in images slightly.

The median filter is normally used to reduce noise in an image, somewhat like the mean filter. However, it often does a better job than the mean filter of preserving useful detail in the image.

How It Works

Like the mean filter, the median filter considers each pixel in the image in turn and looks at its nearby neighbors to decide whether or not it is representative of its surroundings. Instead of simply replacing the pixel value with the *mean* of neighboring pixel values, it replaces it with the *median* of those values. The median is calculated by first sorting all the pixel values from the surrounding neighborhood into numerical order and then replacing the pixel being considered with the middle pixel value. (If the neighborhood under consideration contains an even number of pixels, the average of the two middle pixel values is used.) Figure 4.37 illustrates an example calculation.

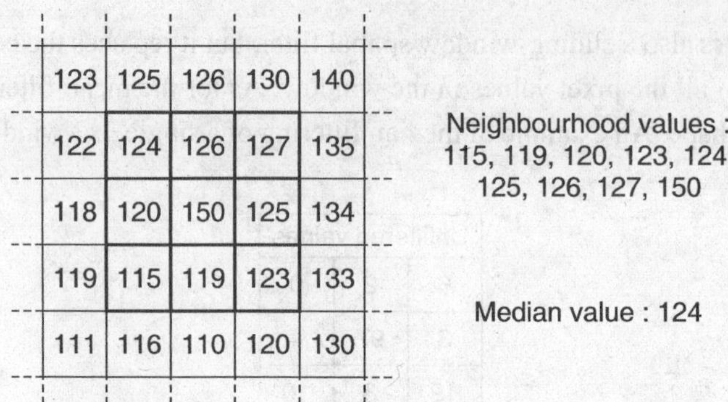

Fig. (4.37) Calculating the median value of a pixel neighbourhood. As can be seen the central pixel value of 150 is rather unrepresentative of the surrounding pixels and is replaced with the median value : 124. A 3×3 square neighbourhood is used here .... large4r neighbourhoods will produce more severe smoothing.

4.8.2 Max and Min Filters

Although the median filter is by far the order-statistics filter most used in image processing. It is by no means the only one. The median represents the 50th percentile of a ranked set of numbers, but the reader will recall from basic statistics that ranking lends itself to many other possibilities. For example, using the 100th percentile results in the so-called max filter given by:

$$\hat{f}(x, y) = \max_{(s,t) \in S_{xy}} \{g(s, t)\}$$

This filter is useful for finding the brightest points in an image. Also, because pep-per noise has very low values, it is reduced by this filter as a result of the max selection process in the subimage area S. The 0th percentile filter is the Min filter.

$$\hat{f}(x, y) = \min_{(s,t) \in S_{xy}} \{g(s, t)\}$$

■ 4.9 REMOVING SHOT NOISE FROM FACE IMAGE

The median filter is very good at removing shot noise (but not perfect). We will compare it with the mean filter, and look for artifacts of smoothing. If you are using a vanilla version of Image J from the website, you need to add the drawing tools. Alternatively, use Process / Noise / Salt and Pepper to add some black & white dots to the image, then try the median filter (radius 1.0)

These first steps to demonstrate the median filter are from the NIH Image manual.

- With File / Open, load Sample Images / Filter Samples / Face.tiff
  — (PC: You might have to move the image a bit to the right to uncover the tool.)
- Click on the zoom (magnifying glass) tool . Then click once on the image. A zoom factor of x2 will clearly show what is going on. (PC: Scion 1.61 - you might have to enlarge the window by mousing the lower right corner, to view the entire image.)
- Control-click with the magnifying glass to zoom down.
- Double click on the spray can tool. (if you use the spraycan macro, the tool looks like this)
  — Set the spray can diameter to 250 pixels. (It is set already to 50, which works fine. To set the width, double-click on the tool.)
  — You do not need to change the diameter - it is already sufficiently large.

- Click on the black bar [white/black] in the LUT window to set the drawing color to black. This bar is not available in ImageJ. To set the drawing color to black, click on the color picker (eye dropper tool), then click on a black area of the image.
- Holding the mouse down, move the spray can tool over the image spattering black pixels on it.
  - — If you don't spray too much, so that all (or most of) the black pixels are isolated, then the median filter will completely remove them.

Here is a piece of the image

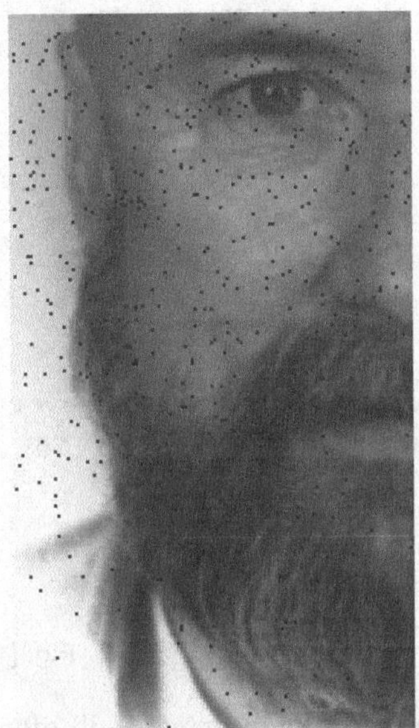

Fig. (4.38)

- Click on the white bar [white/black] and spray again. Again, use the color picker to set the drawing color to white.

Your can spray with any gray level and the filter will still work.

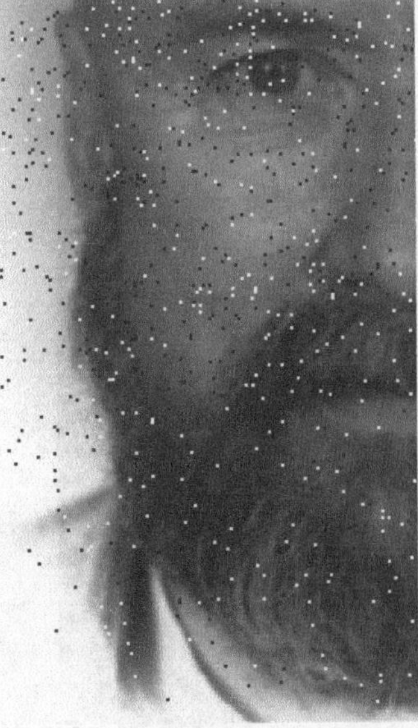

Fig. (4.39)

- Duplicate the image with the File -> Duplicate menu. Use Image / Duplicate.
- Apply the median filter to one of the images.
  - — Process -> Rank Filters ... menu, click the Median (reduce noise) filter, use 1 iteration.
  - — Process / Noise / Despeckle or Process / Filters / Median (radius = 1 is the same as despeckle).

Most of the noise spots should be removed - the noise pixels are too close together in any small area, some noise pixels may remain.

The filtered image looks almost the same as the original, if both are not zoomed. The zoomed image shows a slight degree of smoothing e.g. the gray hairs in the heard loose detail.

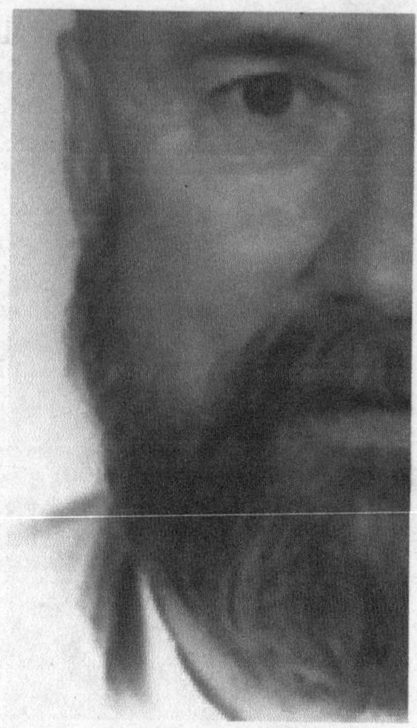

Fig. (4.40)

Image processing on filtered images will often enhance artifacts. Note the difference below between the sharpened median filtered image and the sharpened origina.

- Try the Sharpen filter. Process -> Sharpen menu.

Sharpened median filtered image

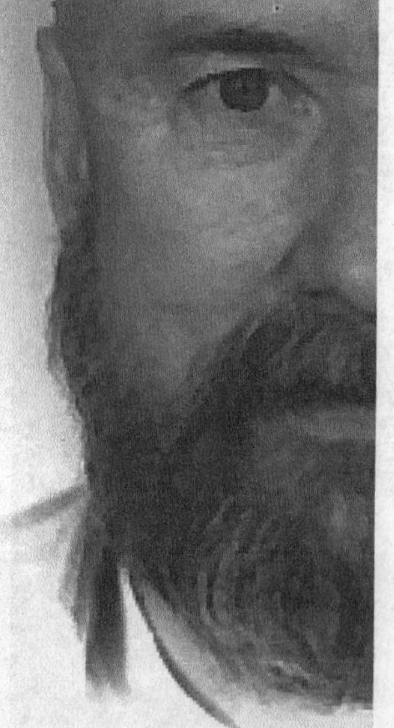

Shapened original

Fig. (4.41)

The median filter is distinctly better at removing shot noise than is the mean filter. This 3x3 mean filter (using the Smooth menu with the option key held down) replaces a pixel in the center of a 3x3 pixel square with the average value of all of the pixels within the square. The median filter replaces the center pixel with the median value.

- Mean filter the copy of the noisy image using the Process -> Smooth menu with the option key held down.

If the option key is not held down, less smoothing is done - the image is less blurry, but the noise pixels are very prominent.

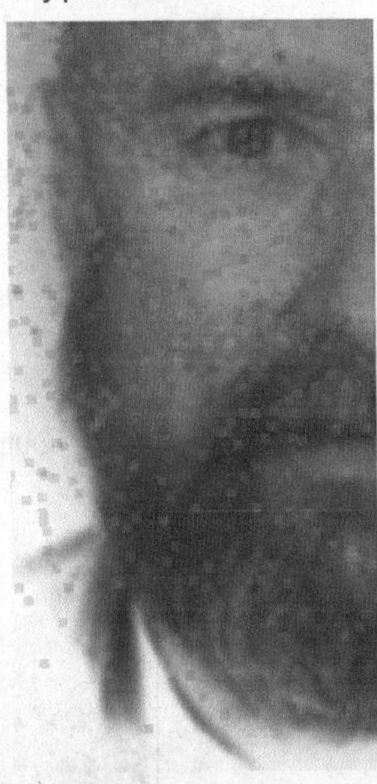

This is the image to the left, sharpened with the process → sharpen menu, option key not held down.

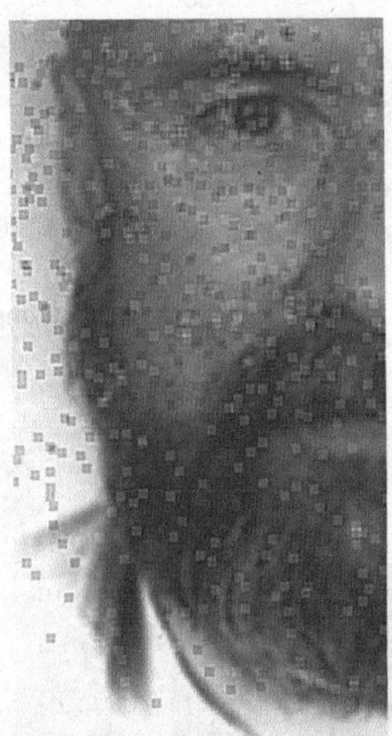

Fig. (4.42)

Note that the Smooth and Sharpen operations are not inverses of each other - one undoes the other almost - but not completely.

■ 4.10 FREQUENCY DOMAIN FILTERING

Filtering is an operation on an acoustic signal that changes the shape of the spectrum of the signal. A filter is a device (or a computer program) which applies such a change to a signal. Examples of filters are the bass/treble controls on your stereo which attenuate the higher or lower frequency ranges in the music signal. Each filter has a characteristic spectral shape which describes which parts of the original signal will be attenuated and which will be left alone. An example for a low pass filter might be as shown in Figure 4.43.

The effect of applying a filter to a signal is to modify the shape of the signal's spectrum. In the frequency domain the effect of applying a filter to a signal is to *multiply* the spectrum of the signal by that of the filter. (Note that we multiply the raw spectra and not the dB spectra — since dB spectra are logarithms they should be added to achieve the same effect since log(a*b) = log(a)+log(b).) The result is a spectrum that combines the features of those of the input signal and the filter. An example is shown in

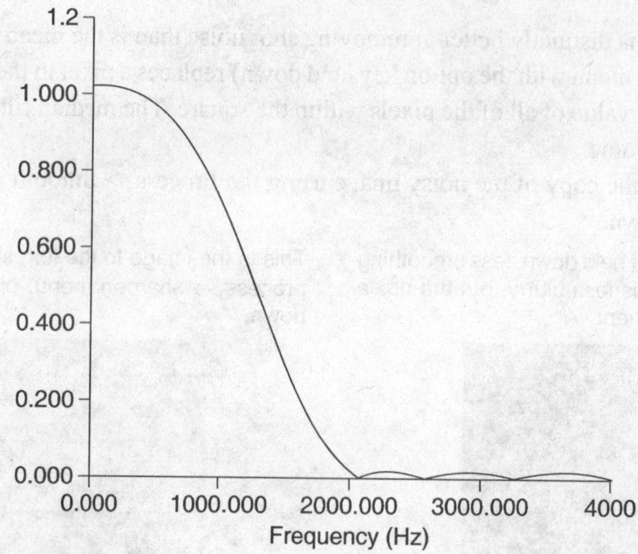

Fig. (4.43) An example of the spectral shape for a low pass filter.

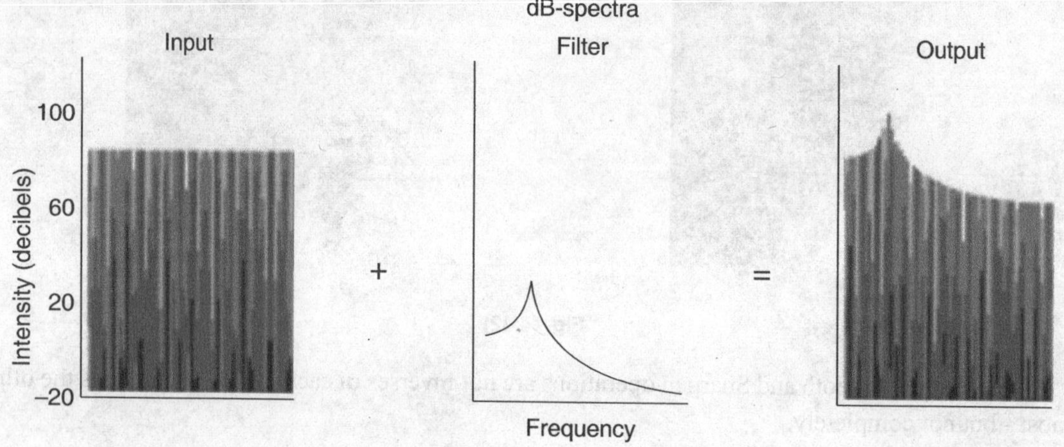

Fig. (4.44) Applying a filter in the frequency domain.

Figure 4.44 of a simple impulse train input signal (which has a `flat' spectrum) filtered through a band pass filter; the output signal shows the characteristics of both spectra.

Having applied a filter by combining the spectra, a new filtered signal can be derived by performing an inverse Fourier transform on the new spectrum. The question arises as to how we can find the spectrum of a filter, or indeed how a filter is represented digitally. A digital filter can be characterized by an acoustic signal called an *impulse response* — literally this is the result of passing an impulse (a 1 followed by lots of zeros) through the filter. The spectrum of a filter can be derived by taking the spectrum of its impulse response.

Filters are an incredibly important topic in the study of speech acoustics. As we will see, the vocal tract acts as a filter which changes the spectral characteristics of the acoustic source generated by the glottis or by frication. Understanding the nature of filters and the separability of the source and filter are fundamental to the study of speech acoustics and form the basis of much of speech technology research.

■ 4.11 BAND-PASS FILTERS

A band-pass filter is a device that passes frequencies within a certain range and rejects (attenuates) frequencies outside that range. An example of an analogue electronic band-pass filter is an RLC circuit (a resistor–inductor–capacitor circuit). These filters can also be created by combining a low-pass filter with a high-pass filter.

Band pass is an adjective that describes a type of filter or filtering process; it is frequently confused with pass band, which refers to the actual portion of affected spectrum. The two words are both compound words that follow the English rules of formation: the primary meaning is the latter part of the compound, while the modifier is the first part. Hence, one may correctly say 'A dual band pass filter has two pass bands'.

An ideal band pass filter would have a completely flat passband (e.g. with no gain/attenuation throughout) and would completely attenuate all frequencies outside the passband. Additionally, the transition out of the passband would be instantaneous in frequency. In practice, no band pass filter is ideal. The filter does not attenuate all frequencies outside the desired frequency range completely; in particular, there is a region just outside the intended passband where frequencies are attenuated, but not rejected. This is known as the filter roll-off, and it is usually expressed in dB of attenuation per octave or decade of frequency. Generally, the design of a filter seeks to make the roll-off as narrow as possible, thus allowing the filter to perform as close as possible to its intended design. Often, this is achieved at the expense of pass-band or stop-band ripple.

The bandwidth of the filter is simply the difference between the upper and lower cutoff frequencies. The shape factor is the ratio of bandwidths measured using two different attenuation values to determine the cutoff frequency, e.g., a shape factor of 2:1 at 30/3 dB means the bandwidth measured between frequencies at 30 dB attenuation is twice that measured between frequencies at 3 dB attenuation.

Outside of electronics and signal processing, one example of the use of band-pass filters is in the atmospheric sciences. It is common to band-pass filter recent meteorological data with a period range of, for example, 3 to 10 days, so that only cyclones remain as fluctuations in the data fields. In neuroscience, visual cortical simple cells were first shown by David Hubel and Torsten Wiesel to have response properties that resemble Gabor filters, which are band-pass.

There are applications where a particular band, or spread, or frequencies need to be filtered from a wider range of mixed signals. Filter circuits can be designed to accomplish this task by combining the properties of low-pass and high-pass into a single filter. The result is called a band-pass filter. Creating a band pass filter from a low-pass and high-pass filter can be illustrated using block diagrams, in figure 4.45.

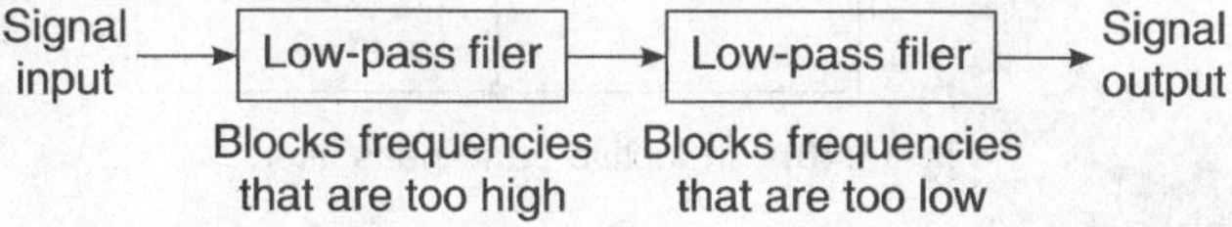

Fig. (4.45) System level block diagram of a band-pass filter.

What emerges from the series combination of these two filter circuits is a circuit that will only allow passage of those frequencies that are neither too high nor too low. Using real components, here is what a typical schematic might look like Figure below. The response of the band-pass filter is shown in figure 4.47.

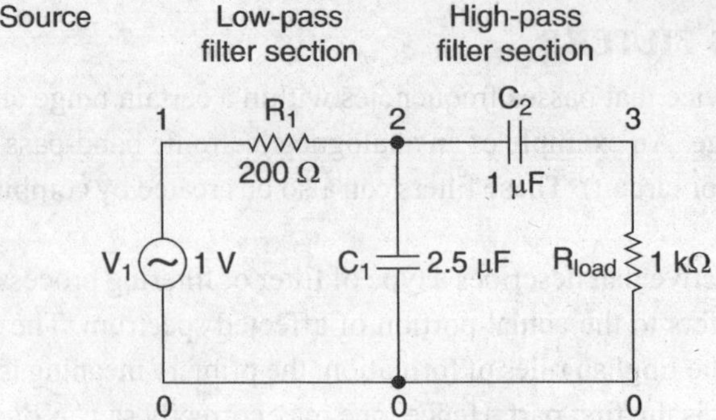

Fig. (4.46) Capacitive band-pass filter.

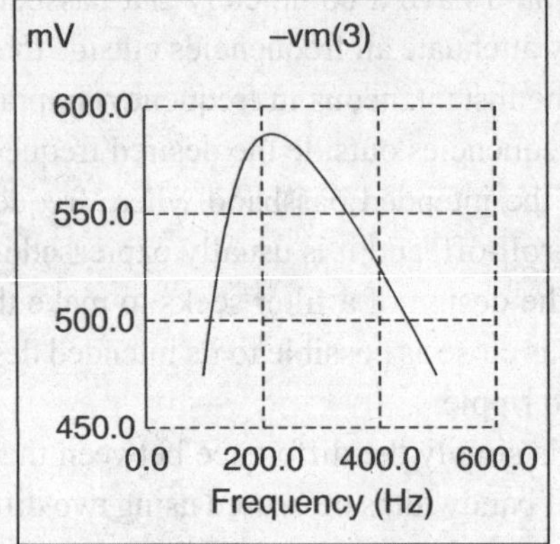

Fig. (4.47) The response of a capacitive band pass filter peaks within a narrow frequency range.

Band-pass filters can also be constructed using inductors, but as mentioned before, the reactive "purity" of capacitors gives them a design advantage. If we were to design a band pass filter using inductors, it might look something like, shown in figure 4.48.

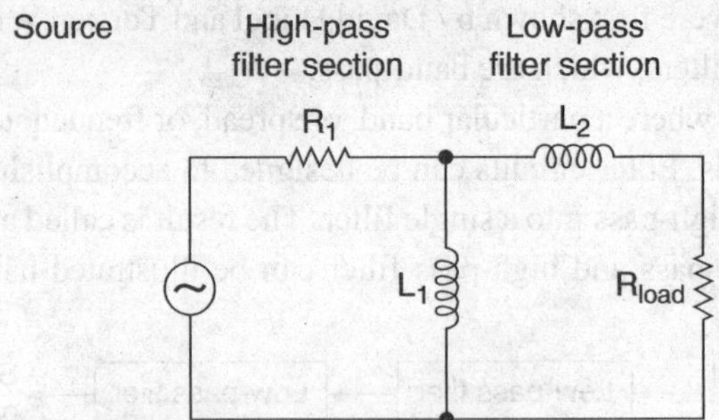

Fig. (4.48) Inductive band-pass filter.

The fact that the high-pass section comes "first" in this design instead of the low-pass section makes no difference in its overall operation. It will still filter out all frequencies too high or too low. While the general idea of combining low-pass and high-pass filters together to make a band pass filter is sound, it is not without certain limitations. Because this type of band-pass filter works by relying on either section to block unwanted frequencies, it can be difficult to design such a filter to allow unhindered passage within the desired frequency range.

Both the low-pass and high-pass sections will always be blocking signals to some extent, and their combined effort makes for an attenuated (reduced amplitude) signal at best, even at the peak of the "pass-band" frequency range. Notice the curve peak on the previous SPICE analysis: the load voltage of this filter never rises above 0.59 volts, although the source voltage is a full volt. This signal attenuation becomes more pronounced if the filter is designed to be more selective (steeper curve, narrower band of passable frequencies). There are other methods to achieve band-pass operation without sacrificing signal strength within the pass-band.

- A band-pass filter works to screen out frequencies that are too low or too high, giving easy passage only to frequencies within a certain range.
- Band-pass filters can be made by stacking a low-pass filter on the end of a high-pass filter, or vice versa.
- "Attenuate" means to reduce or diminish in amplitude. When you turn down the volume control on your stereo, you are "attenuating" the signal being sent to the speakers.

4.12 MINIMUM MEAN-SQUARE ERROR RESTORATION

The process of image acquisition frequently leads (inadvertently) to image degradation. Due to mechanical problems, out-of-focus blur, motion, inappropriate illumination, and noise the quality of the digitized image can be inferior to the original. The goal of enhancement is— starting from a recorded image c [m, n]—to produce the most visually pleasing image â [m, n]. The goal of restoration is—starting from a recorded image c [m, n]—to produce the best possible estimate â [m, n] of the original image a [m, n]. The goal of enhancement is beauty; the goal of restoration is truth.

The measure of success in restoration is usually an error measure between the original a [m, n] and the estimate â [m, n]: E{â [m,n], a[m,n]}. No mathematical error function is known that corresponds to human perceptual assessment of error. The mean-square error function is commonly used because:

1. It is easy to compute;
2. It is differentiable implying that a minimum can be sought;
3. It corresponds to "signal energy" in the total error, and;
4. It has nice properties vis à vis Parseval's theorem, eqs. (22) and (23).

The mean-square error is defined by:

$$E\{\hat{a}, a\} = \frac{1}{MN} \sum_{m=0}^{M-1} \sum_{n=0}^{N-1} |\hat{a}[m, n] - a[m, n]|^2$$

In some techniques an error measure will not be necessary; in others it will be essential for evaluation and comparative purposes.

Unsharp Masking

A well-known technique from photography to improve the visual quality of an image is to enhance the edges of the image. The technique is called unsharp masking. Edge enhancement means first isolating the edges in an image, amplifying them, and then adding them back into the image. Examination of Figure 4.48 shows that the Laplacian is a mechanism for isolating the gray level edges. This leads immediately to the technique:

$$\hat{a}[m, n] = a[m, n] - (k * \nabla^2 a[m, n])$$

The term k is the amplifying term and k > 0. The effect of this technique is shown in Figure 4.19. The Laplacian used to produce Figure 4.49 is given by eq. (120) and the amplification term k = 1.

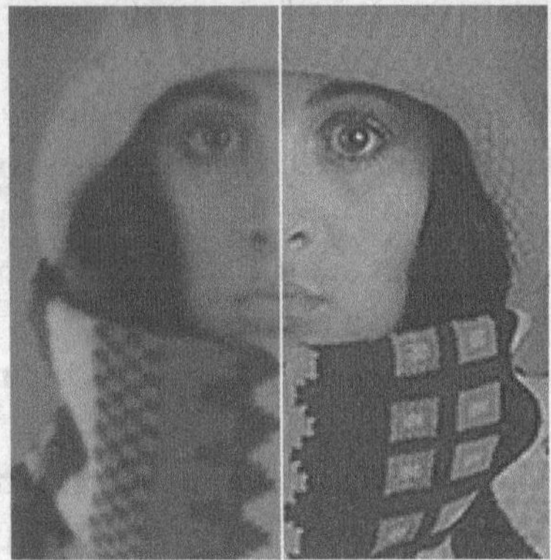

Original ↑↑ Laplacian-enhanced

Fig. (4.49) Edge enhanced compared to original.

Noise Suppression

The techniques available to suppress noise can be divided into those techniques that are based on temporal information and those that are based on spatial information. By temporal information we mean that a sequence of images {ap [m,n] | p=1,2,...,P} are available that contain exactly the same objects and that differ only in the sense of independent noise realizations. If this is the case and if the noise is additive, then simple averaging of the sequence:

Temporal Averaging

$$\hat{a}[m, n] = \frac{1}{P} \sum_{p=1}^{F} a_p [m, n]$$

Will produce a result where the mean value of each pixel will be unchanged. For each pixel, however, the standard deviation will decrease from to . If temporal averaging is not possible, then spatial averaging can be used to decrease the noise. This generally occurs, however, at a cost to image sharpness. Four obvious choices for spatial averaging are Gaussian filtering, median filtering, Kuwahara filtering, and morphological smoothing.

Within the class of linear filters, the optimal filter for restoration in the presence of noise is given by the Wiener filter. The word "optimal" is used here in the sense of minimum mean-square error (mse). Because the square root operation is monotonic increasing, the optimal filter also minimizes the root mean-square error (rms). The Wiener filter is characterized in the Fourier domain and for additive noise that is independent of the signal it is given by:

$$H_w(u, v) = \frac{S_{aa}(u, v)}{S_{aa}(u, v) - S_{nn}(u, v)}$$

where Saa(u,v) is the power spectral density of an ensemble of random images {a[m,n]} and Snn(u,v) is the power spectral density of the random noise. If we have a single image then Saa(u,v) = |A(u,v)|2. In practice it is unlikely that the power spectral density of the uncontaminated image will be available. Because many images have a similar power spectral density that can be modeled, used as an estimate of Saa(u,v).

A comparison of the five different techniques described above is shown in Figure 4.19. The Wiener filter was constructed directly from eq. because the image spectrum and the noise spectrum were known. The parameters for the other filters were determined choosing that value (either or window size) that led to the minimum rms.

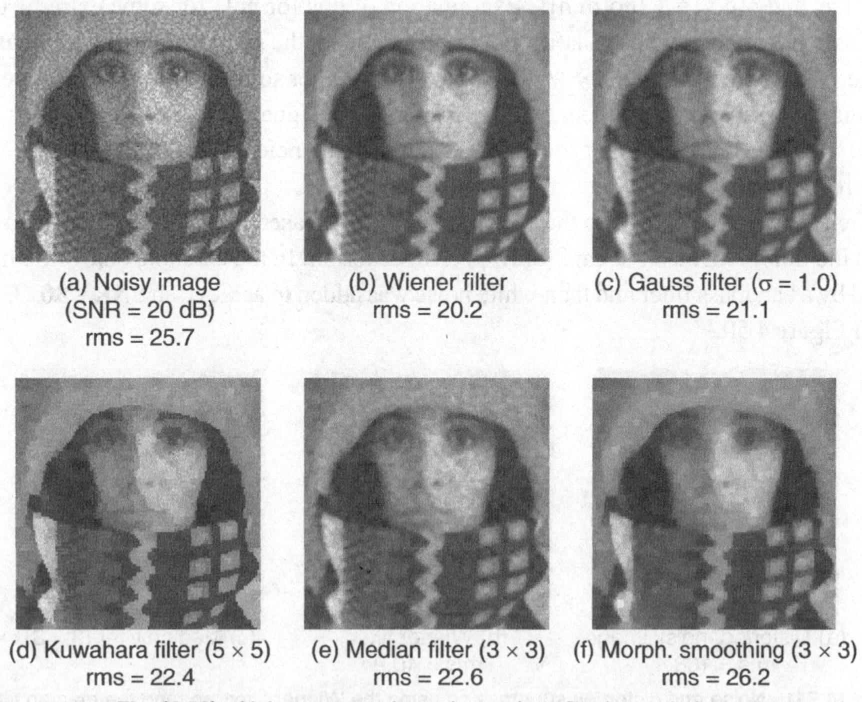

Fig. (4.50) Noise suppression using various filtering techniques.

The root mean-square errors (rms) associated with the various filters are shown in Figure 4.50. For this specific comparison, the Wiener filter generates a lower error than any of the other procedures that are examined here. The two linear procedures, Wiener filtering and Gaussian filtering, performed slightly better than the three non-linear alternatives.

Distortion Suppression

The model presented above—an image distorted solely by noise—is not, in general, sophisticated enough to describe the true nature of distortion in a digital image. A more realistic model includes not only the noise but also a model for the distortion induced by lenses, finite apertures, possible motion of the camera and/or an object, and so forth. One frequently used model is of an image a[m,n] distorted by a linear, shift-invariant system ho[m,n] (such as a lens) and then contaminated by noise [m,n]. Various aspects of ho[m,n] and [m,n] have been discussed in earlier sections. The most common combination of these is the additive model:

$$c[m, n] = (a[m, n] \otimes h_0[m, n]) + \kappa[m, n]$$

The restoration procedure that is based on linear filtering coupled to a minimum mean-square error criterion again produces a Wiener filter:

$$H_w(u, v) = \frac{H_0^*(u, v)\, S_{aa}(u, v)}{|H_0(u, v)|^2\, S_{aa}(u, v) + S_{an}(u, v)}$$

$$= \frac{H_0^*(u, v)}{|H_0(u, v)|^2 + (S_{aa}(u, v)/S_{an}(u, v))}$$

Once again Saa(u,v) is the power spectral density of an image, Snn(u,v) is the power spectral density of the noise, and o(u,v) = F{ho[m,n]}. Examination of this formula for some extreme cases can be useful. For those frequencies where Saa(u,v) > Snn(u,v), where the signal spectrum dominates the noise spectrum, the Wiener filter is given by 1/o(u,v), the inverse filter solution. For those frequencies where Saa(u,v) < Snn(u,v), where the noise spectrum dominates the signal spectrum, the Wiener filter is proportional to o*(u,v), the matched filter solution. For those frequencies where o(u,v) = 0, the Wiener filter W(u,v) = 0 preventing overflow.

The Wiener filter is a solution to the restoration problem based upon the hypothesized use of a linear filter and the minimum mean-square (or rms) error criterion. In the example below the image a[m,n] was distorted by a bandpass filter and then white noise was added to achieve an SNR = 30 dB. The results are shown in Figure 4.50.

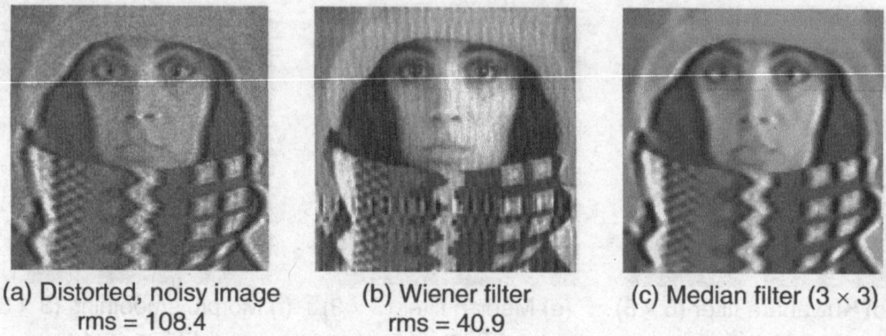

(a) Distorted, noisy image rms = 108.4 (b) Wiener filter rms = 40.9 (c) Median filter (3 x 3)

Fig. (4.51) Noise and distortion suppression using the Wiener filter, eq. and the median filter.

The rms after Wiener filtering but before contrast stretching was 108.4; after contrast stretching with eq. (77) the final result as shown in Figure 4.51b has a mean-square error of 27.8. Using a 3 x 3 median filter as shown in Figure 4.50c leads to a rms error of 40.9 before contrast stretching and 35.1 after contrast stretching. Although the Wiener filter gives the minimum rms error over the set of all linear filters, the non-linear median filter gives a lower rms error. The operation contrast stretching is itself a non-linear operation. The "visual quality" of the median filtering result is comparable to the Wiener filtering result. This is due in part to periodic artifacts introduced by the linear filter which are visible in Figure 4.51b.

■ SUMMARY

- In many applications (e.g., satellite imaging, medical imaging, astronomical imaging, poor-quality family portraits) the imaging system introduces a slight distortion. Often images are slightly blurred and image restoration aims at *deblurring* the image.
- The restoration process starts with the conversion of each frame to a digital image with a high-resolution film scanner. The size of a digital color image is up to 45 MBytes per frame.
- Blurring is present in any imaging system which uses electromagnetic radiation (for example, visible light and X-rays). Diffraction limits the resolution of an imaging device to features on the order of the illuminating wavelength.

- Most blurring processes can be approximated by convolution integrals, also known as Fredholm integral equations of the first kind. The blurring is characterized by a Point-Spread Function (PSF) or impulse response.
- Noise in imaging systems is usually either additive or multiplicative. The basic noise is additive noise which is zero-mean and white. White noise is spatially uncorrelated: the noise for each pixel is independent and identically distributed (iid)
- The task of deblurring, a form of image restoration, is to recover an image from its blurred version. Whereas most existing methods assume a small amount of additive noise, image restoration under significant additive noise remains an interesting research problem.
- "Spatial filtering" is a term used to describe the methods that are used to compute spatial density estimates for events that have been observed at individual locations.
- The term describes a set of tools for displaying functions estimated from these data points that are distributed in two-dimensional space.
- Spatial filtering is a form of data smoothing designed to give us a clearer view of the general, unencumbered by details which do not answer our questions of interest.
- Spatial filtering is a non-parametric analysis method which belongs within the field of exploratory spatial analysis which relies, to a large degree, on graphical methods of analysis.
- The mean filter is a simple sliding-window spatial filter that replaces the center value in the window with the average (mean) of all the pixel values in the window. The window, or kernel, is usually square but can be any shape.
- Order-statistics filters are spatial filters whose response is based on ordering (ranking) the pixels contained in the image area encompassed by the filter. The response of the filter at any point is determined by the ranking result.
- In the median filter considers each pixel in the image in turn and looks at its nearby neighbors to decide whether or not it is representative of its surroundings. Instead of simply replacing the pixel value with the *mean* of neighboring pixel values, it replaces it with the *median* of those values.
- Filtering is an operation on an acoustic signal that changes the shape of the spectrum of the signal. A filter is a device (or a computer program) which applies such a change to a signal.
- Examples of filters are the bass/treble controls on your stereo which attenuate the higher or lower frequency ranges in the music signal. Each filter has a characteristic spectral shape which describes which parts of the original signal will be attenuated and which will be left alone.
- A band-pass filter is a device that passes frequencies within a certain range and rejects (attenuates) frequencies outside that range. An example of an analogue electronic band-pass filter is an RLC circuit (a resistor–inductor–capacitor circuit). These filters can also be created by combining a low-pass filter with a high-pass filter.
- Band pass is an adjective that describes a type of filter or filtering process; it is frequently confused with pass band, which refers to the actual portion of affected spectrum. The two words are both compound words that follow the English rules of formation: the primary meaning is the latter part of the compound, while the modifier is the first part. Hence, one may correctly say 'A dual band pass filter has two pass bands'.
- The process of image acquisition frequently leads (inadvertently) to image degradation. Due to mechanical problems, out-of-focus blur, motion, inappropriate illumination, and noise the quality of the digitized image can be inferior to the original.

Review Questions

1. Discuss the Imaging model.
2. Explain the BLIND IMAGE RESTORATION with example.
3. Explain Digital Film Restoration Process.
4. What are the image restoration problem and write short notes on the following:
   - Common sources of blurring and noise.
   - The point-spread function (PSF) model of blurring
   - Noise models
5. Explain the Image Restoration In the Presence Of Noise.
6. Discuss the procedures of removing Shot noise from Face Image.
7. Explain the Minimum Mean-square Error Restoration.
8. Write short notes on the following
   - Mean filter.
   - Median filter.
   - Band pass filter.
   - Spatial Filtering.
9. Describe the canonic model of imaging systems
10. Formulate the image restoration problem and explain why it is usually implemented as a multi-stage process
11. What is transform domain scalar filtering?
12. Formulate the principle of MSE optimal filtering
13. Derive optimal scalar Wiener filters for image denoising
14. Derive optimal scalar Wiener filters for image deblurring and show its relation to inverse filtering
15. Explain what is empirical Wiener filter and give examples of implementations of the empirical Wiener filter.
16. When Wiener filtering can be efficiently used for image restoration and when it fails?
17. What is image sensor aperture correction and how can it be implemented?

5

COLOR IMAGE PROCESSING

Introduction

From an abstract point of view, an image can be considered as a function F, where F(x, y) gives the value of the pixel at position (x, y). For black and white images, F(x, y) will be a single value representing the gray level of the point; for color images, F(x, y) will be a tuple representing a color in a color system.

Usually x and y are integer numbers, but this is not necessarily so. If x, y are integers, F is a discrete function, if x, y are real numbers then F is a continuous function. Since an image stored in a computer is always a discrete matrix of pixels, how can we think of it as a continuous area? The answer is by interpolation.

Consider the following slice of an image:

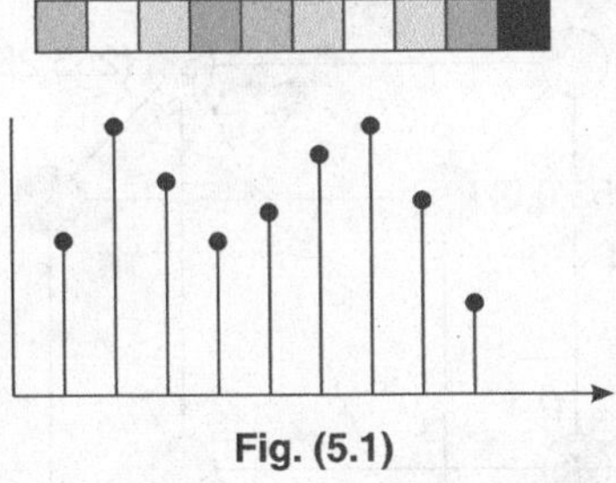

Fig. (5.1)

We can think of the known values (the black dots) as points in a continuous curve, and try to reconstruct the curve with an interpolation method, be it linear, quadratic, cubic, etc:

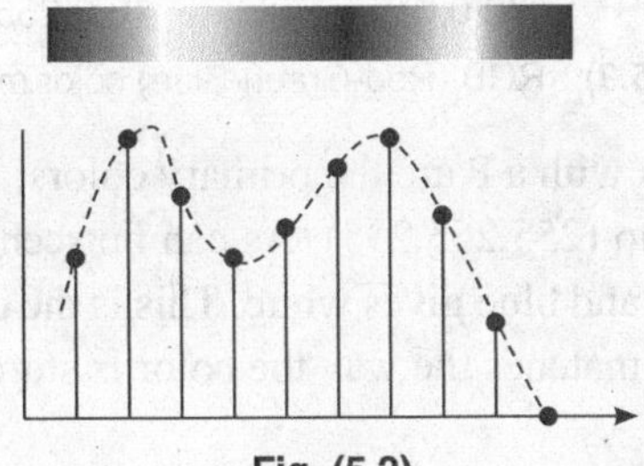

Fig. (5.2)

5.1 COLOR FUNDAMENTALS

For human beings, colour provides one of the most important descriptors of the world around us. The human visual system is particularly attuned to two things: edges, and colour. We have mentioned that the human visual system is not particularly good at recognizing subtle changes in grey values. In this section we shall investigate colour briefly, and then some methods of processing colour images.

What is colour?

Colour study consists of

1. The physical properties of light which give rise to colour,
2. The nature of the human eye and the ways in which it detects colour,
3. The nature of the human vision centre in the brain, and the ways in which messages from the eye are perceived as colour.

5.2 COLOR MODEL

A color model is a method to specify colors with respect to some reference framework. The color models can be grouped in additive color models and subtractive color models. In an additive color model, any combination of two or more colors results in a color with higher luminance than the original colors. An example of how an additive color model work is the cathodic ray tube found in TVs and computer monitors; a white point results from the combination of red, green and blue points. In a subtractive color model, any combination of two colors gives a color with lower luminance. An example of a subtractive color model working can be found in mixing watercolor; the resulting color becomes darker and darker, and ideally it will finally becomes black, although it will not due to the characteristics of the pigments.

The most commonly used color models are RGB, CYM and HSI. We will examine each of them.

5.2.1 RGB (Red-Green-Blue) Color Model

The RGB color model has three basic primary (basic) colors: red, green, and blue. All other colors are obtained by combining them. This model can be thought as a cube, where 3 non-adjacent and perpendicular corners are R, G and B, like in the following figure 5.3:

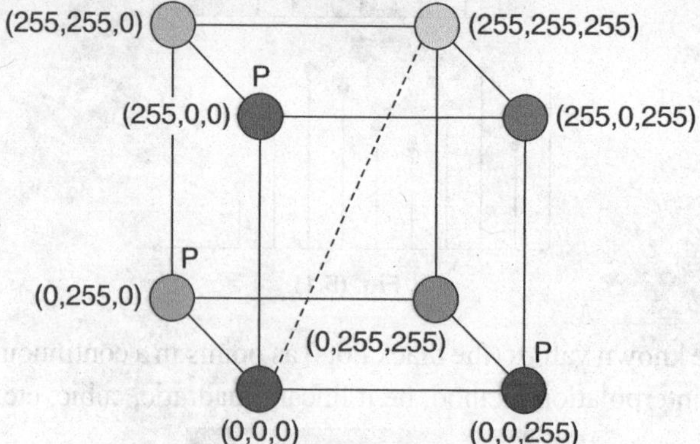

Fig. (5.3) RGB (Red-Green-Blue) color model.

RGB Color Space. The colors with a P are the primary colors. The dashed line indicates where to find the grays, going from (0,0,0) to (255,255,255). As can be seen, RGB is an additive color model, since the combination of green, red and blue gives white. This is the color model that is most commonly used in computer graphics, since it matches the way the color is stored in video memory.

5.2.2 CYM (Cyan-Yellow-Magenta) Color Model

CYM is the substractive counterpart of RGB. If you look at the RGB color model, you will notice that if you take out the primary colors and the white and black (which are not colors), you get the CYM triple. RGB and CYM are complementary; what is a secondary color in RGB is a primary color in CYM.

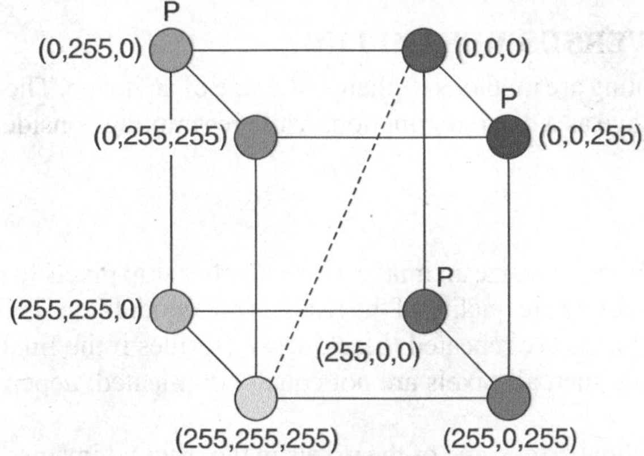

Fig. (5.4) CYM (Cyan-Yellow-Magenta) color model.

Due to this, transforming from RGB to CYM and back is very simple:

$$\begin{bmatrix} C \\ Y \\ M \end{bmatrix} = \begin{bmatrix} 255 - R \\ 255 - G \\ 255 - B \end{bmatrix}$$

This color model is used in the printing industry with a variation known as CYMK (Cyan-Magenta-Yellow-Black). This is due to the fact that is very difficult (and expensive) to obtain a pure black combining cyan, yellow and magenta pigments, so a black pigment is added.

5.2.3 SI (Hue-Saturation-Intensity) Color Model

The HSI Color Model was designed having in mind the way graphic designers and artists think of colors. Artists use terms like saturation (the "pureness"of a color), hue (the color in itself) and intensity (the brightness of the color). This is exactly what the HSI Color Model Represents. The Color Space is strange, since it is not orthogonal; it looks like this:

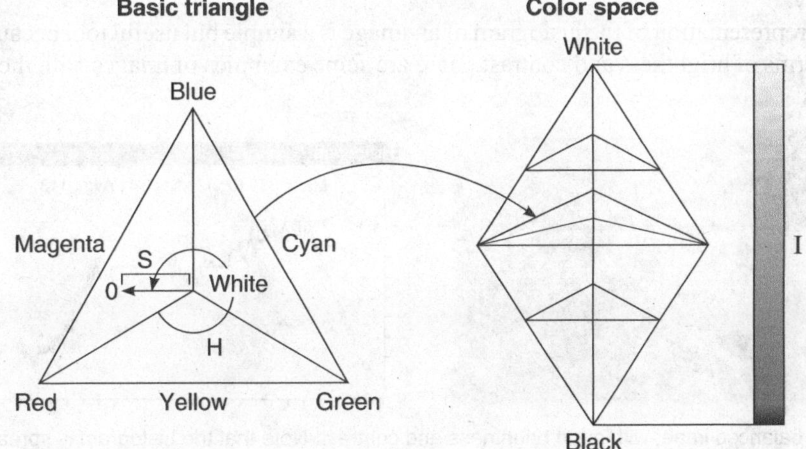

Fig. (5.5) SI (Hue-Saturation-Intensity) color model.

In this color space, like in the others, a color is a vector. H (Hue) is the angle of the vector over the basic triangle, starting from Red (o degrees). S (Saturation) is the proportional size of the module of the projection of the vector over the basic triangle; and I (Intensity) is the distance from the end of the vector to the basic triangle.

5.3 RESCALING VERSUS RESAMPLING

Both rescaling and resampling are methods to change the size of an image. The difference consists in that rescaling considers the image as a discrete function, while resampling considers it as a continuous function.

Rescaling

This is the fastest method to resize an image, since it either skip pixels to reduce the image or duplicate pixels to stretch it. However the quality of the result is not good. If the final size of the image > original size, then some of the pixels are repeated (blockiness). Besides if the final size of the image is not a multiple of the original size, then all pixels are not equally duplicated, depending on the proportion final_size/original_size.

If the final size < original size, some of the pixels in the original image are skipped. Besides, if the final size is not a sub multiple of the original size, the image may look distorted because not all of the skipped pixels were equally distant. Pixels are skipped every original_size//final_size pixels.

Resampling

In resampling, if final size > original size, new pixels are created by interpolating and scaling the continuous function F that represents the image. New Image(x', y')=F(x, y), where x'=x.k1 and y'=y.k2 (k1 and k2 are the proportionality factors in x and y between the new and old image). The new image may look blurry, but resampling does not create artificial blocks like rescaling.

If the final size < original size, the pixels in the new image are created like in the case of stretching the image. However, in this case there will be more than one pixel in the original image that can be mapped to the same pixel in the new image. Those values of F that fall in the same position in the new image are averaged to create the pixel in the new image.

Histogram and Histogram Functions

A histogram is a function that, for a gray level g in an image, returns the proportion of pixels in the image with a gray level of g. In a color image, the color components can be converted to gray or manipulated separately.

A visual representation of the histogram of an image is a simple but useful tool because it describes the image in terms of brightness and contrast. Here are some examples of images with their corresponding histograms:

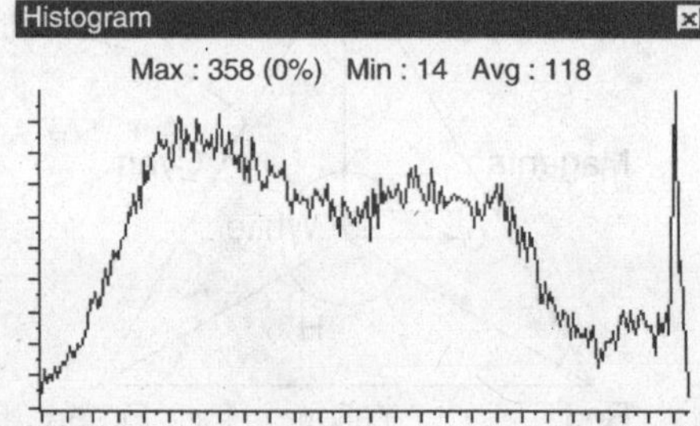

Fig. (5.6a) A balanced imae, with good brightness and contrast. Note that the histogram is spread and more or less balanced across all gray levels. This is a characteristic of these kinds of images.

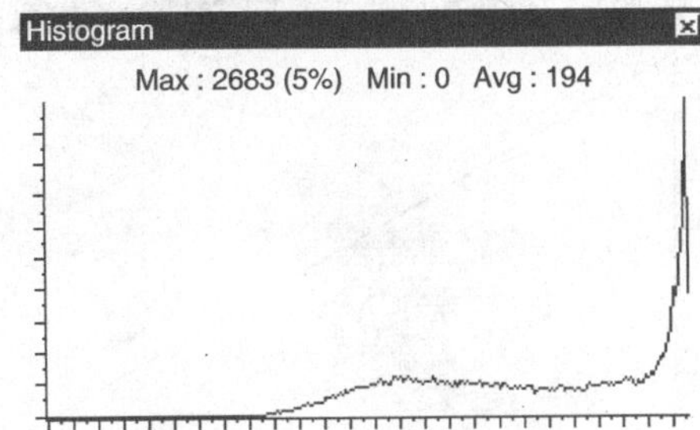

Fig. (5.6b) The same image after enhancing brightness. Note that the histogram is skewed to the high values, which indicates too much brightness, and that is concentrated in a small set of values, which indicates low contrast.

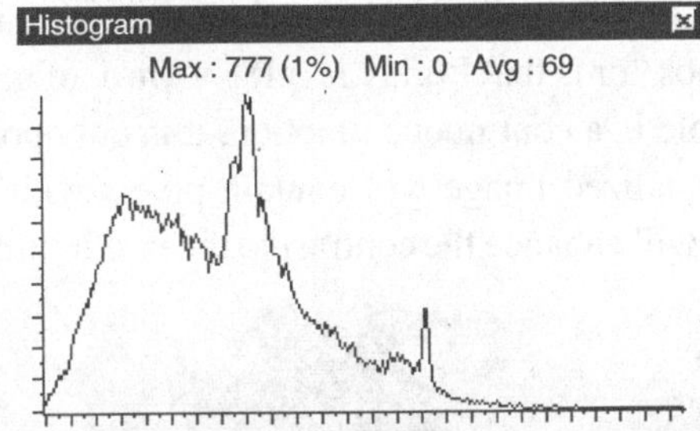

Fig. (5.6c) The same image, now after diminishing brightness. Note that the histogram is skewed to the low values, which indicates the image is too dark, and that is concentrated in a small set of values, which indicates low contrast.

The histogram can be manipulated by Stretching and contracting the histogram: By defining a function that maps bright levels in the old image to the desired bright level desired in the new image it is possible to enhance or contract the histogram.

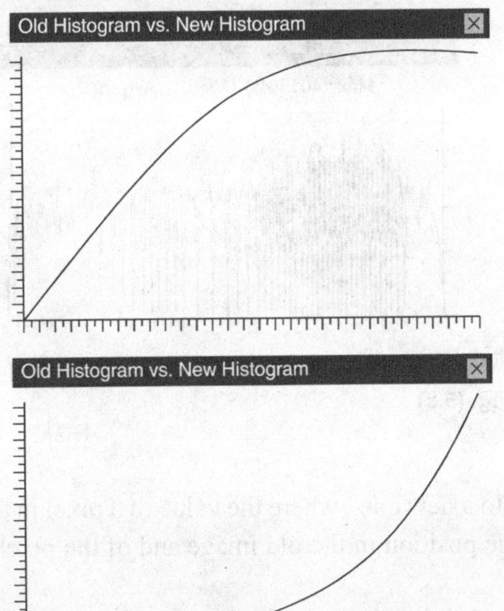

A function like this will stretch the histogram...

...While a function like this will contract the histogram...

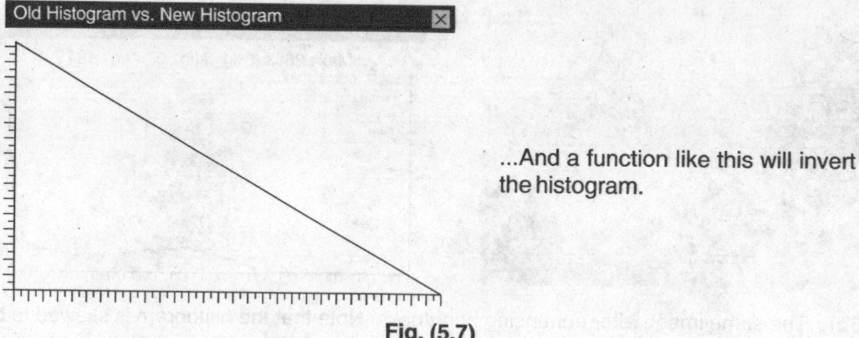

Fig. (5.7)

Histogram Equalization

Histogram Equalization is a technique to obtain an uniform distribution of gray levels in an image. What we look for is that P(gray level) ~ 1/(nro. of gray levels), for all gray levels. While this is theoretically possible in a continuous function, it is only possible to approximate in a discrete function (an image). An equalized image will contain pixels with almost all gray levels, including black and white. Equalizing will enhance the contrast to the maximum; the appealing of the result depends on the image.

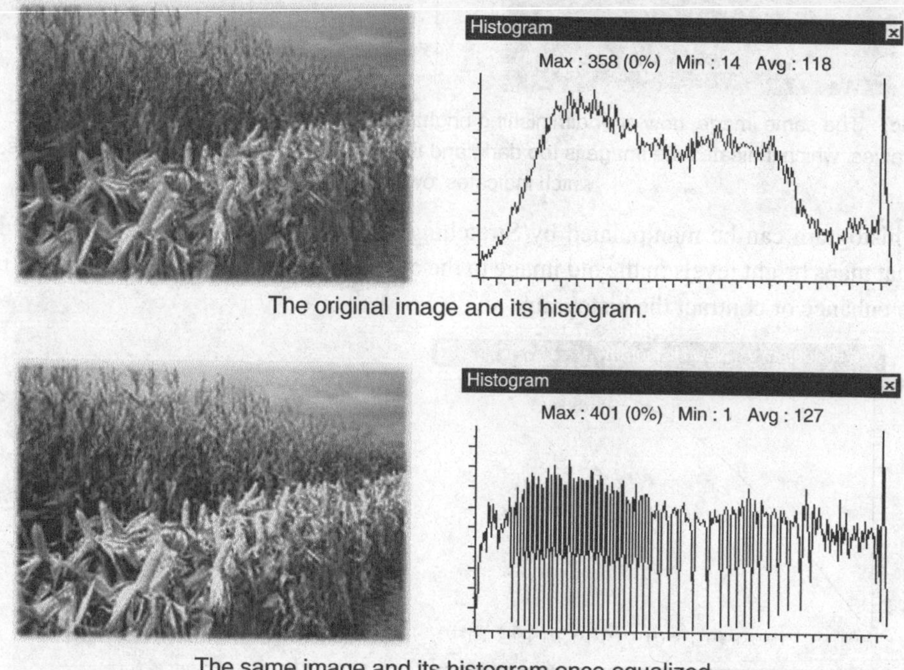

Fig. (5.8)

Spatial Filters

A spatial filter is a function from an image to a new one , where the value of a pixel in the new image depends on the value of the pixel in the same position in the old image and of the pixels around it (what is called the neighborhood of a pixel).

A pixel and its neighbours are combined multiplying the by a set of coefficients called the mask. A mask is usually a square array of odd size, like this is the averaging filter, that smoothes (blurs) the image by averaging the sum of a pixel and its neighbours. Note that the coefficients are chosen so that the value of a pixels in not changed in a constant image.

1/9	1/9	1/9
1/9	**1/9**	1/9
1/9	1/9	1/9

Similarly, we have a sharpening mask

–1/9	–1/9	–1/9
–1/9	**w**	–1/9
–1/9	–1/9	–1/9

where **w** = 9A-1, for A>=1.

The effect of this mask is to enhance the edges while keeping the details of the original image. The constant A determines the proportion between the edges and the original image:

- if A=1 the result if a high-pass filter (only edges are visible)
- if A>1 then part of the original image is added to the edges.

Where all those values come from?

From the discussion about JPEG compression in past classes we know that any signal, be a sound or an image, can be considered not only in the spatial domain (the x,y coordinates) but also in the frequency domain, as the combination of different frequencies; that is what the DCT or the DFT do. When we talk about images, we usually do in spatial terms, but we can also think of it in frequency terms. High frequencies in an image correspond to edges, so if we want to cut the edges of an image, we can use either a filter in the spatial domain or in the frequency domain.

In the spatial domain, the filter

–1/9	–1/9	–1/9
–1/9	**8**	–1/9
–1/9	–1/9	–1/9

makes smooth transitions to become almost uniform, and highlights sudden changes in values (the edges). Note that if we get an uniform image, then the result of applying this mask is a pixel with a value of 0, which is right, since we are looking for edges.

A mask that remarks the edges and almost deletes the rest of the image is called a high-band pass filter, because in the frequency domain it blocks the low frequencies, leaving the high ones that contain most of the information related to edges.

The problem with this mask is that smooth surfaces dissapear from the image. We would like to have a filter that highlights the edges while keeping details of the original image. To do that, note that

High-pass filter = Original - low-pass filter

where a low-pass filter may be the averaging filter we saw above. Now we can define

sharp = A . Original – lowpass = (A – 1) . Original + Original – lowpass
= (A – 1) . Original + highpass (A is a constant of proportionality between the image and the filer)

and here we have the reason for w in the sharpen mask, and where the constant A comes from.

The Median Filter

The Median filter replaces a pixel value by the mean value of the set made of the pixel and its neighbors within a certain radius. The effect of the median filter is to eliminate sudden changes when the surrounding area is more or less uniform, and because of that is used to remove noise in scanned or transmitted images. The Median filter removes detail from the image like the averaging filter, but instead of blurring the image the result is that the image becomes progressively more uniform in color areas.

Fig. (5.9) Here the original image, and the result after a median and a sharpen filter is shown. Note that the color areas are more uniform, specially in the leaves behind the corns.

Finding Edges

There are many times when, as part of an algorithm or as an objective in itself, we need to find the edges of an image in a certain direction. An example of this need is the emboss filter, found in many image processing packages like Photoshop or Paint Shop Pro. Emboss creates a light and shadow version of the image, where the edges appear as if they were basreliefs, and they were illuminated from a side.

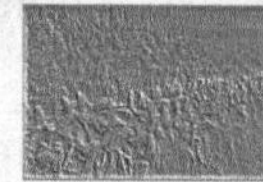

Fig. (5.10)

This is the crop field of the previous examples, once processed with the emboss filter. Illumination comes from the upper right corner.

But first, what is an edge? We can say that an edge is a change in the pixel values beyond a threshold in a certain direction. This idea of measuring the change rate in a certain direction looks quite similar to the idea of a derivative, and this is in fact how many edge detecting filters are implemented: by looking for high values in the magnitude of gradient or the derivative of the function in a certain direction. But calculating the gradient or general derivative of an image is too costly, so we look for approximations.

The masks

1	1	1
0	0	0
–1	–1	–1

and

–1	0	1
–1	0	1
–1	0	1

detects edges in the vertical and horizontal directions, respectively. These masks are called Prewitt operators, and there are other masks designed to detect other type of edges, or to work with masks of even size. Nevertheless all of them work with the idea of approximating the derivative.

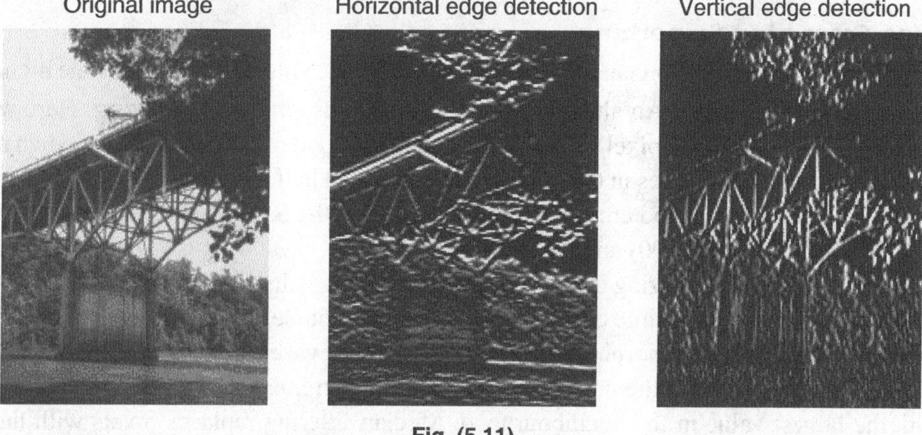

Fig. (5.11)

An example of the effect of the Prewitt operators. Note the difference in the edges highlighted by each filter.

■ 5.4 IMAGE SMOOTHING

The aim of image smoothing is to diminish the effects of camera noise, spurious pixel values, missing pixel values etc. There are many different techniques for image smoothing; we will consider neighborhood averaging and edge-preserving smoothing.

5.4.1 Neighbourhood Averaging

Each point in the smoothed image, is obtained from the average pixel value in a neighbourhood of (x, y) in the input image.

For example, if we use a neighbourhood around each pixel we would use the mask

1/9	1/9	1/9
1/9	1/9	1/9
1/9	1/9	1/9

Each pixel value is multiplied by , summed, and then the result placed in the output image. This mask is successively moved across the image until every pixel has been covered. That is, the image is *convolved* with this smoothing mask (also known as a spatial filter or kernel).

However, one usually expects the value of a pixel to be more closely related to the values of pixels close to it than to those further away. This is because most points in an image are spatially coherent with their neighbours; indeed it is generally only at edge or feature points where this hypothesis is not valid. Accordingly it is usual to weight the pixels near the centre of the mask more strongly than those at the edge. Some common weighting functions include the rectangular weighting function above (which just takes the average over the window), a triangular weighting function, or a Gaussian.

In practice one doesn't notice much difference between different weighting functions, although Gaussian smoothing is the most commonly used. Gaussian smoothing has the attribute that the frequency components of the image are modified in a smooth manner. Smoothing reduces or attenuates the higher frequencies in the image. Mask shapes other than the Gaussian can do odd things to the frequency spectrum, but as far as the appearance of the image is concerned we usually don't notice much.

5.4.2 Edge Preserving Smoothing

Neighbourhood averaging or Gaussian smoothing will tend to blur edges because the high frequencies in the image are attenuated. An alternative approach is to use ***median filtering***. Here we set the grey level to be the median of the pixel values in the neighbourhood of that pixel. The median m of a set of values is such that half the values in the set are less than m and half are greater. For example, suppose the pixel values in a neighbourhood are (10, 20, 20, 15, 20, 20, 20, 25, 100). If we sort the values we get (10, 15, 20, 20, |20|, 20, 20, 25, 100) and the median here is 20.

The outcome of median filtering is that pixels with outlying values are forced to become more like their neighbours, but at the same time edges are preserved. Of course, median filters are non-linear.

Median filtering is in fact a morphological operation. When we erode an image, pixel values are replaced with the smallest value in the neighbourhood. Dilating an image corresponds to replacing pixel values with the largest value in the neighbourhood. Median filtering replaces pixels with the median value in the neighbourhood. It is the rank of the value of the pixel used in the neighbourhood that determines the type of morphological operation.

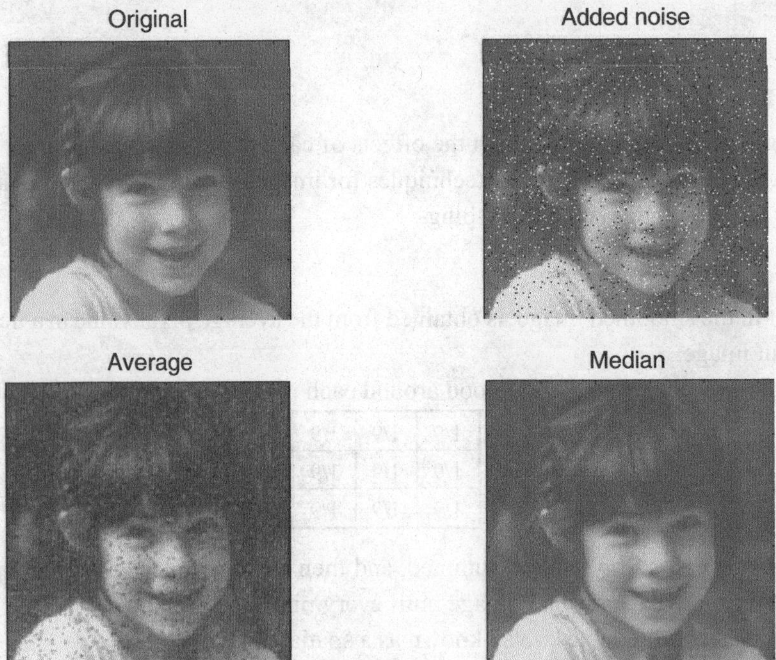

Fig. (5.12) Image of Genevieve; with salt and pepper noise : the result of averaging; and the result of median filtering.

■ 5.5 IMAGE SHARPENING

The main aim in image sharpening is to highlight fine detail in the image, or to enhance detail that has been blurred (perhaps due to noise or other effects, such as motion). With image sharpening, we want to enhance the high-frequency components; this implies a spatial filter shape that has a high positive component at the centre (see figure 5.5 below).

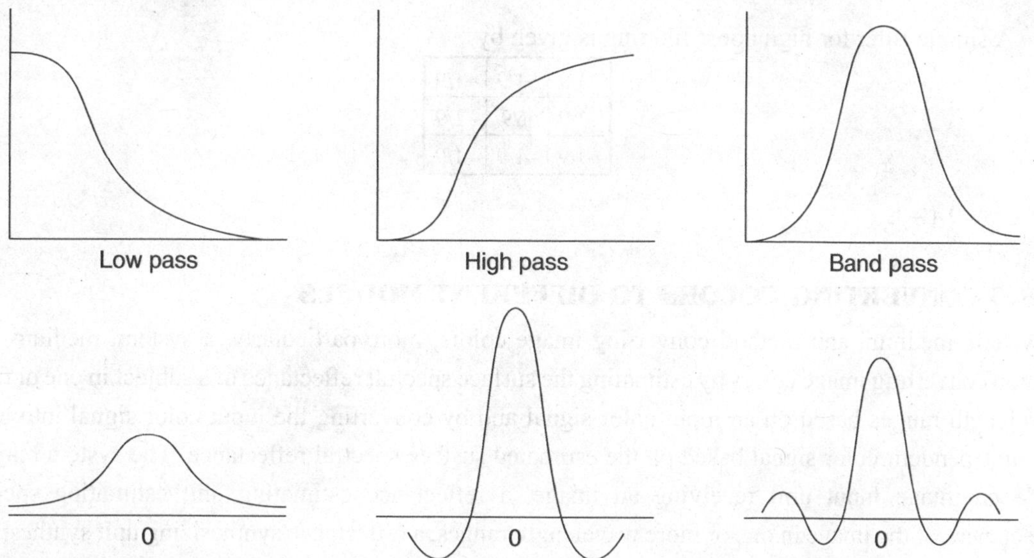

Fig. (5.13) Frequency domain filters (top) and their corresponding spatial domain counterparts (bottom).

A simple spatial filter that achieves image sharpening is given by

–1/9	–1/9	–1/9
–1/9	8/9	–1/9
–1/9	–1/9	–1/9

Since the sum of all the weights is zero, the resulting signal will have a zero DC value (that is, the average signal value, or the coefficient of the zero frequency term in the Fourier expansion). For display purposes, we might want to add an offset to keep the result in the range.

High Boost Filtering

We can think of high pass filtering in terms of subtracting a low pass image from the original image, that is,

$$\text{High pass} = \text{Original} - \text{Low pass}$$

However, in many cases where a high pass image is required, we also want to retain some of the low frequency components to aid in the interpretation of the image. Thus, if we multiply the original image by an amplification factor A before subtracting the low pass image, we will get a high boost or high frequency emphasis filter. Thus,

$$\begin{aligned}\text{High boos} &= A \,.\, \text{Original} - \text{Low pass}\\ &= (A - 1) \,.\, \text{Original} + \text{Original} - \text{Low pass}\\ &= (A - 1) \,.\, \text{Original} + \text{High pass}\end{aligned}$$

Now, if A = 1 we have a simple high pass filter. When A > 1 part of the original image is retained in the output.

A simple filter for high boost filtering is given by

–1/9	–1/9	–1/9
–1/9	ω/9	–1/9
–1/9	–1/9	–1/9

where $\omega = 9A - 1$.

■ 5.6 CONVERTING COLORS TO DIFFERENT MODELS

A system, medium, and method converting image colors, more particularly, a system, medium, and method converting image colors by estimating the surface spectral reflectance of a subject in one or more wavelength ranges based on an input color signal and by converting the input color signal into a device-independent color signal based on the estimated surface spectral reflectance. The system may include an image input unit receiving an image, a reflectance estimating unit estimating spectral reflectances of the image in one or more wavelength ranges, a reflectance synthesizing unit synthesizing the estimated spectral reflectances into one spectral reflectance, and a color converting unit converting the color of the image on the basis of the synthesized spectral reflectance.

■ 5.7 COLOR TRANSFORMATION

Transforming graphics shapes from one state to another but did you ever think about transforming colors? Why would you want to transform an image's colors? Suppose you want to provide gray scale effects, or need to reduce or increase the contrast, brightness, or redness of an image. That's when a color matrix is needed.

The color of each pixel of a GDI+ image or bitmap is represented by a 32-bit number where 8-bits are used for each of the red, green, blue, and alpha components. Each of the four components is a number from 0 to 255. For red, green, and blue components, 0 represents no intensity and 255 represents full intensity. For the alpha component, 0 represents fully transparent and 255 represents fully opaque. A color vector includes four items, i.e., (R, G, B, A). The minimum values for this vector are (0, 0, 0, 0) and the maximum values for this vector are (255, 255, 255, 255). These values are used in a color matrix to represent the intensity and opacity of color components. For example, the color vector with the minimum values is (0, 0, 0, 0) and the color vector with maximum values is (1, 1, 1, 1).

In color transformation, we apply a color matrix on a color vector. This can be done by multiplying a 4 x 4 matrix. However a 4 x 4 matrix supports only linear transformations such as rotation, and scaling. To perform non-linear transformations such as translation, you need to use a 5 x 5 matrix. The element of the fifth row and the fifth column of the matrix must be 1 and all of the other entries in the five columns must be 0.

The elements of the matrix are identified using a zero-based index. Thus the first element of the matrix is M [0][0] and the last element of a 5 x 5 matrix is M[4][4]. A 5x5 identity matrix is shown in Figure 10-19. In this matrix, the elements M [0] [0], M [1] [1], M [2] [2] and M [3] [3] represent the red, blue, green, and alpha factors respectively. The element M [4][4] means nothing and it must always be 1.

$$\begin{bmatrix} 1 & 0 & 0 & 0 & 0 \\ 0 & 1 & 0 & 0 & 0 \\ 0 & 0 & 1 & 0 & 0 \\ 0 & 0 & 0 & 1 & 0 \\ 0 & 0 & 0 & 0 & 1 \end{bmatrix}$$

Fig. (5.14) Identity matrix.

Now suppose you want to double the intensity of the red component of a color: simply set M [0] [0] = 2. For example, the matrix shown in Figure 10-20 doubles the intensity of the red component, decreases the intensity of the green component by half, triples the intensity of the blue component, and decreases the opacity of the color by half (semi-transparent).

$$\begin{bmatrix} 2 & 0 & 0 & 0 & 0 \\ 0 & 0.5 & 0 & 0 & 0 \\ 0 & 0 & 3 & 0 & 0 \\ 0 & 0 & 0 & 0.5 & 0 \\ 0 & 0 & 0 & 0 & 1 \end{bmatrix}$$

Fig. (5.15) A matrix with different intensities.

In the above matrix, we multiplied the intensity values. You can also add by using other matrix elements. For example, the matrix shown in Figure 10-21 will double the intensity of red component and add 0.2 to each of the red, green, and blue component intensities:

$$\begin{bmatrix} 2 & 0 & 0 & 0 & 0 \\ 0 & 1 & 0 & 0 & 0 \\ 0 & 0 & 1 & 0 & 0 \\ 0 & 0 & 0 & 1 & 0 \\ 0.2 & 0.2 & 0.2 & 0 & 1 \end{bmatrix}$$

Fig. (5.16) A color matrix with multiplication and addition.

The Color Matrix Class

This class defines a matrix of colors. The Color Matrix class is not very different from the Matrix class. The Matrix class is used in general transformation to transform graphics shapes and images, while the Color Matrix class is specifically designed to transform colors. Before we see practical use of the color transformation, we will discuss the Color Matrix class, its properties and methods.

The Color Matrix class constructor takes an array, which contains the values of matrix items. The Item property of this class represents a cell of the matrix and can be used to get and set cell values. Besides the Item property, the Color Matrix class provides 25 MatrixXY properties, which represent items of the matrix at row (X+1) and column (Y+1). MatrixXY properties can be used to get and set an item's value. Listing 10-15 creates a ColorMatrix object with item(4,4) set to 0.5 (half opacity). After that it sets the value of item (3, 4) to 0.8 and item (1, 1) to 0.3.

```
float[][] ptsArray ={ new float[] {1, 0, 0, 0, 0},
new float[] {0, 1, 0, 0, 0},
new float[] {0, 0, 1, 0, 0},
new float[] {0, 0, 0, 0.5f, 0},
```

```
new float[] {0, 0, 0, 0, 1}};
ColorMatrix clrMatrix = new ColorMatrix(ptsArray);
if( clrMatrix.Matrix34 <= 0.5)
{
clrMatrix.Matrix34 = 0.8f;
clrMatrix.Matrix11 = 0.3f;
}
```

Listing 10-15. Creating a Color Matrix object

Now let's apply color matrices transform colors.

Matrix Operations in Image Processing

Re-coloring, the process of changing image colors is a good example of color transformation. Re-coloring includes changing colors, intensity, contrast, and brightness of an image. It all can be done using the Image Attribute class and its methods.

The ColorMatrix can be applied on an Image using the SetColorMatrix method of the ImageAttribute class. The ImageAttribute object is used as a parameter when you call DrawImage.

Translating Colors

Translating colors increases or decreases color intensities by a set amount (not by multiplying them). Each color component (red, green, and blue) has 255 different intensity levels ranging from 0 to 255. For example, assume the current intensity level for the red component of a color is 100. Changing its intensity level to 150 would imply translating by 50.

In a color matrix representation, the intensity varies from 0 to 1. The last row's first four elements of a color matrix represent the translation of red, green, blue, and alpha components of a color, per Figure 10-21. Hence adding a value to these elements will transform a color. For example, t1, t2, t3, and t4 values in the following color matrix represent the red, green, blue and alpha component translations:

Color Matrix = {1, 0, 0, 0, 0},{0, 1, 0, 0, 0},{0, 0, 1, 0, 0},{0, 0, 0, 1, 0},{t1, t2, t3, t4, 1}};

Listing 10-16 uses a ColorMatrix to translate colors. We change the current intensity of the red component to 0.90. First we create a Graphics object using the CreateGraphics method and create a Bitmap object from a file. After that we create an array of ColorMatrix elements and create a ColorMatrix from this array. Then we create an ImageAttributes object and set the color matrix using SetColorMatrix, which takes the ColorMatrix object as its first parameter. After all that we draw two images. The first image has no effects, while the second image shows the result of our color matrix transformation. Finally, we dispose the objects.

```
private void TranslationMenu_Click(object sender,System.EventArgs e)
{
// Create a Graphics object
Graphics g = this.CreateGraphics();
g.Clear(this.BackColor);
// Create a Bitmap
Bitmap curBitmap = new Bitmap("roses.jpg");
// ColorMatrix elements
float[][] ptsArray =
{
```

```
new float[] {1, 0, 0, 0, 0},
new float[] {0, 1, 0, 0, 0},
new float[] {0, 0, 1, 0, 0},
new float[] {0, 0, 0, 1, 0},new float[] {.90f, .0f, .0f, .0f, 1}
};
// Create a ColorMatrix
ColorMatrix clrMatrix = new ColorMatrix(ptsArray);
// Create ImageAttributes
ImageAttributes imgAttribs = new ImageAttributes();
// Set color matrix
imgAttribs.SetColorMatrix(clrMatrix,
ColorMatrixFlag.Default,
ColorAdjustType.Default);
// Draw image with no affects
g.DrawImage(curBitmap, 0, 0, 200, 200);
// Draw image with ImageAttributes
g.DrawImage(curBitmap,
new Rectangle(205, 0, 200, 200),
0, 0, curBitmap.Width, curBitmap.Height,
GraphicsUnit.Pixel, imgAttribs) ;
// Dispose
curBitmap.Dispose();
g.Dispose();
}
```

Listing 10-16. Translating colors using ColorMatrix.

Listing 10-16 generates Figure 10-22. The original image is on the left, while on the right we have the results of our color translation. If you change the values of other components (red, blue, and alpha) in the last row of the ColorMatrix, you'll see different results.

Fig. (5.17) Translating colors.

Scaling Colors

Scaling color involves multiplying a color component value by a scaling factor. For example, the t1, t2, t3, and t4 values in the following color matrix represent the red, green, blue and alpha components. If you change the value of M[2][2] to 0.5, the transformation operation will multiply the green component by 0.5, cutting its intensity by half.

Color Matrix

```
{t1, 0, 0, 0, 0},
{0, t2, 0, 0, 0},
{0, 0, t3, 0, 0},
{0, 0, 0, t4, 0},
{0, 0, 0, 0, 1}};
```

Listing 10-17 uses the ColorMatrix to scale image colors.

```
private void ScalingMenu_Click(object sender,System.EventArgs e)
{
// Create a Graphics
Graphics g = this.CreateGraphics();
g.Clear(this.BackColor);
// Create a Bitmap
Bitmap curBitmap = new Bitmap("roses.jpg");
// ColorMatrix elements
float[][] ptsArray =
{
new float[] {1, 0, 0, 0, 0},
new float[] {0, 0.8f, 0, 0, 0},
new float[] {0, 0, 0.5f, 0, 0},
new float[] {0, 0, 0, 0.5f, 0},
new float[] {0, 0, 0, 0, 1}
};
// Create a ColorMatrix
ColorMatrix clrMatrix = new ColorMatrix(ptsArray);
// Create ImageAttributes
ImageAttributes imgAttribs = new ImageAttributes();
// Set color matrix
imgAttribs.SetColorMatrix(clrMatrix,
ColorMatrixFlag.Default,
ColorAdjustType.Default);
// Draw an image with no affects
g.DrawImage(curBitmap, 0, 0, 200, 200);
// Draw Image with image attributes
g.DrawImage(curBitmap,
new Rectangle(205, 0, 200, 200),
0, 0, curBitmap.Width, curBitmap.Height,
GraphicsUnit.Pixel, imgAttribs) ;
// Dispose
curBitmap.Dispose();
g.Dispose();
}
```

Listing 10-17. Scaling Colors

Output from Listing 10-18 is shown in Figure 10-23. The original image is on the left, and on the right is the image after color scaling. If you change the values of t1, t2, t3, and t4, you will see different results.

Fig. (5.18) Scaling image colors using color matrix.

Shearing Colors

Earlier in this chapter, we saw image shearing. It can be thought of as anchoring one corner of a rectangular region and stretching the opposite corner horizontally, vertically or in both directions. Shearing colors is basically the same process, but shearing color components rather than the image itself.

Color shearing increases or decreases a color component by an amount proportional to another color component. For example, consider the transformation where the red component is increased by one half the value of the blue component. Under such a transformation, the color (0.2, 0.5, 1) would become (0.7, 0.5, 1). The new red component is 0.2 + (1/2)(1) = 0.7. The following ColorMatrix is used to shear image colors.

```
float[][] ptsArray = {
new float[] {1, 0, 0, 0, 0},
new float[] {0, 1, 0, 0, 0},
new float[] {.50f, 0, 1, 0, 0},
new float[] {0, 0, 0, 1, 0},
new float[] {0, 0, 0, 0, 1}};
ColorMatrix clrMatrix = new ColorMatrix(ptsArray);
```

Now if you substitute this color matrix in Listing 10-17, the output will look like Figure 5-19.

Fig. (5.19) Shearing colors.

Rotating Colors

Color; in GDI+ have four components: red, green, blue, and alpha. Rotating all four components in a four dimension space is hard to visualize. However it can be visualized in a three dimensional space. To do this, we drop the alpha component from the color structure and assume that there are only three colors: red, green, and blue as shown in Figure 5-20. The three colors, red, green, and blue are perpendicular to each other, so the angle between any two primary colors is 90 degrees.

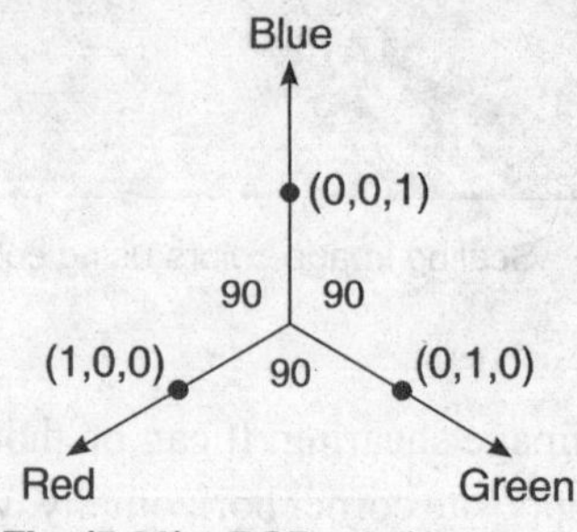

Fig. (5.20) RGB rotation space.

Let's say the red, green, and blue colors are represented by points (1, 0, 0), (0, 1, 0), and (0, 0, 1) respectively. If you rotate a color with green component 1, and red and blue component 0 each by 90 degrees, the new value of the color would have red component 1, and green and blue component 0 each. If you rotate less than 90 degrees, the location would be in between green and red.

Figure 5-21 shows how to initialize a color matrix to perform rotations about each of the three components: red, green, blue.

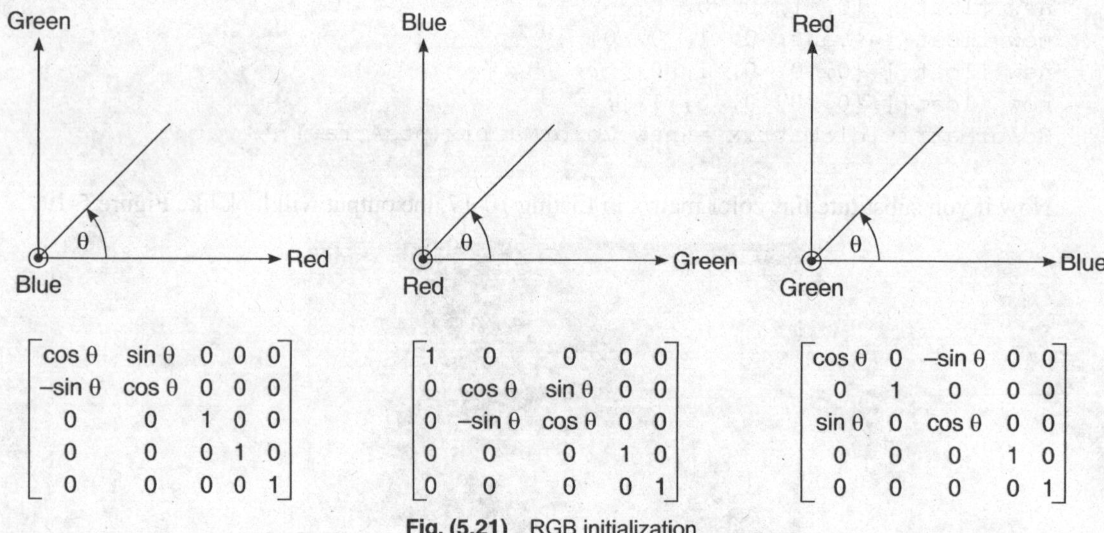

Fig. (5.21) RGB initialization.

Listing 10-18 rotates the colors by 45 degrees from the red component.

```
private void RotationMenu_Click(object sender, System.EventArgs e)
{
float degrees = 45.0f;
double r = degrees*System.Math.PI/180;
// Create a Graphics object
Graphics g = this.CreateGraphics();
g.Clear(this.BackColor);
// Create a Bitmap from a file
Bitmap curBitmap = new Bitmap("roses.jpg");
// ColorMatrix elements
float[][] ptsArray =
{
new float[] {(float)System.Math.Cos(r),
(float)System.Math.Sin(r),0, 0, 0},
new float[] {(float)-System.Math.Sin(r),
(float)-System.Math.Cos(r),
0, 0, 0},
new float[] {.50f, 0, 1, 0, 0},
new float[] {0, 0, 0, 1, 0},
new float[] {0, 0, 0, 0, 1}
};
/ Create a ColorMatrix
ColorMatrix clrMatrix = new ColorMatrix(ptsArray);
// Create ImageAttributes
ImageAttributes imgAttribs = new ImageAttributes();
// Set ColorMatrix to ImageAttributes
imgAttribs.SetColorMatrix(clrMatrix,
ColorMatrixFlag.Default,
ColorAdjustType.Default);
// Draw image with no affects
g.DrawImage(curBitmap, 0, 0, 200, 200);
// Draw image with ImageAttributes
g.DrawImage(curBitmap,
new Rectangle(205, 0, 200, 200),
0, 0, curBitmap.Width, curBitmap.Height,
GraphicsUnit.Pixel, imgAttribs) ;
// Dispose
curBitmap.Dispose();
g.Dispose();
}
```

Listing 10-18. Color Rotation

Figure 5-22 slows output from Listing 10-18. On the left is the original image, and on the right is the image after color rotation.

Fig. (5.22) Rotating colors.

5.8 COLOR SEGMENTATION

To find a colored dot in its search window, we first determine the pixel that has the smallest RGB-distance to the color of the dot's model. We assume that this pixel belongs to the dot and try to segment the remaining pixels from the background by analyzing a quadratic window with a side length of about twice the dot's diameter that is centered at the selected pixel. We use two methods for color segmentation. The first method that is illustrated in Figure 2 works in HSI color space. Since we are looking for colorful dots, we apply a saturation mask and an intensity mask to the window. Only pixels that are saturated and neither too bright nor too dark are analyzed further. The final segmentation decision is done using the hue distance to the model's color. Working in HSI space has the advantage that the method is quite insensitive against changes in intensity. However, it can only be applied to saturated dots. If the model dot

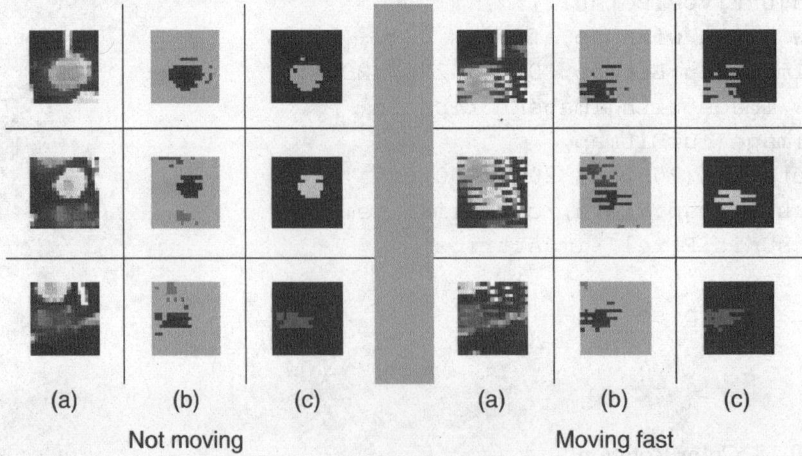

Fig. (5.23) Segmentation of colored dots in HSI space. Shown are (a) the original images, (b) the saturation/intensity masks, (c) and the segmented pixels, that have been selected using the hue distance to the model.

is not saturated or the HSI segmentation fails, we try to segment the dot in RGB color space. This backup method is needed, since some teams might use unsaturated markers, and also since saturated markers may appear as unsaturated dots when viewed in shadow or hot spots. Here, we use only the RGB-distance between the pixels color and the color of the model. All pixels of similar color are segmented as belonging to the dot.

Aquality measure is computed for the dot from the similarity to its model. If the size and the color are similar to the model, then the quality is high. The dot's position is updated if its quality is high enough and the dot is part of a valid robot, or if it is the ball. We estimate the position of the dot with sub-pixel resolution as the average location of the segmented pixels. If the quality is good, the size and average color of the dot are adapted slowly, as long as they do not deviate significantly from the initial model.

The segmentation does not explicitly take the shape of the dot into account. If enforces compact dots by searching many pixels in a small quadratic window.

■ SUMMARY

- From an abstract point of view, an image can be considered as a function F, where F(x, y) gives the value of the pixel at position (x, y). For black and white images, F(x, y) will be a single value representing the gray level of the point; for color images, F(x, y) will be a tuple representing a color in a color system.
- A color model is a method to specify colors with respect to some reference framework. The color models can be grouped in additive color models and subtractive color models.
- In an additive color model, any combination of two or more colors results in a color with higher luminance than the original colors. An example of how an additive color model work is the cathodic ray tube found in TVs and computer monitors; a white point results from the combination of red, green and blue points.
- In a subtractive color model, any combination of two colors gives a color with lower luminance. An example of a subtractive color model working can be found in mixing watercolor; the resulting color becomes darker and darker, and ideally it will finally becomes black, although it will not due to the characteristics of the pigments.
- This is the fastest method to resize an image, since it either skip pixels to reduce the image or duplicate pixels to stretch it. However the quality of the result is not good. If the final size of the image > original size, then some of the pixels are repeated (blockiness).
- In resampling, if final size > original size, new pixels are created by interpolating and scaling the continuous function F that represents the image. New Image(x', y')=F(x, y), where x'=x.k1 and y'=y.k2 (k1 and k2 are the proportionality factors in x and y between the new and old image). The new image may look blurry, but resampling does not create artificial blocks like rescaling.
- A histogram is a function that, for a gray level g in an image, returns the proportion of pixels in the image with a gray level of g. In a color image, the color components can be converted to gray or manipulated separately.
- A visual representation of the histogram of an image is a simple but useful tool because it describes the image in terms of brightness and contrast.

- The aim of image smoothing is to diminish the effects of camera noise, spurious pixel values, missing pixel values etc.
- The main aim in image sharpening is to highlight fine detail in the image, or to enhance detail that has been blurred (perhaps due to noise or other effects, such as motion). With image sharpening, we want to enhance the high-frequency components; this implies a spatial filter shape that has a high positive component at the centre.

Review Questions

1. Explain the Color Fundamentals.
2. Discuss the Color Models.
3. Discuss the Converting Colors to different models.
4. Write short on the following:
   - ColorTransformation
   - Smoothing
   - Sharpening
   - Color Segmentation.

6

MORPHOLOGICAL IMAGE PROCESSING

The identification of objects within an image can be a very difficult task. One way to simplify the problem is to change the grayscale image into a binary image, in which each pixel is restricted to a value of either 0 or 1. The techniques used on these binary images go by such names as: blob analysis, connectivity analysis, and morphological image processing (from the Greek word morph?, meaning shape or form). The foundation of morphological processing is in the mathematically rigorous field of set theory; however, this level of sophistication is seldom needed. Most morphological algorithms are simple logic operations and very ad hoc.

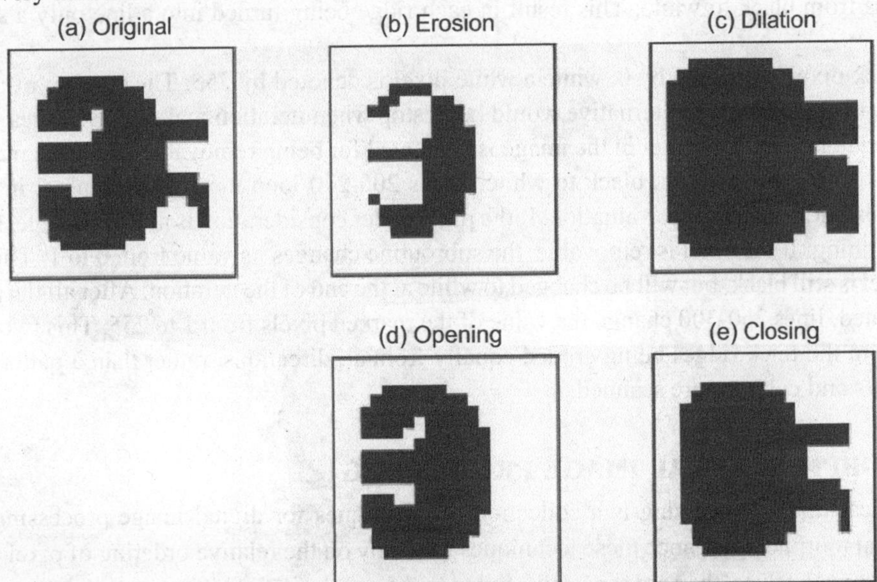

Fig. (6.1) Morphological operations : Four basic morphological operations are used in the processing of binary images : *erosion, dilation, opening,* and *closing*. Figure (a) shows an example binary image. Figures (b) to (e) show the result of applying these operations to the image in (a).

In other words, each application requires a custom solution developed by trial-and-error. This is usually more of an art than a science. A bag of tricks is used rather than standard algorithms and formal mathematical properties. Here are some examples.

Figure 6.1a shows an example binary image. This might represent an enemy tank in an infrared image, an asteroid in a space photograph, or a suspected tumor in a medical x-ray. Each pixel in the background is displayed as white, while each pixel in the object is displayed as black. Frequently, binary images are formed by thresholding a grayscale image; pixels with a value greater than a threshold are set to 1, while pixels with a value below the threshold are set to 0. It is common for the grayscale image to be processed with linear techniques before the thresholding. For instance, illumination flattening can often improve the quality of the initial binary image.

Figures (b) and (c) show how the image is changed by the two most common morphological operations, erosion and dilation. In erosion, every object pixel that is touching a background pixel is changed into a background pixel. In dilation, every background pixel that is touching an object pixel is changed into an object pixel. Erosion makes the objects smaller, and can break a single object into multiple objects. Dilation makes the objects larger, and can merge multiple objects into one.

As shown in (d), opening is defined as erosion followed by dilation. Figure (e) shows the opposite operation of closing, defined as dilation followed by erosion. As illustrated by these examples, opening removes small islands and thin filaments of object pixels. Likewise, closing removes islands and thin filaments of background pixels. These techniques are useful for handling noisy images where some pixels have the wrong binary value. For instance, it might be known that an object cannot contain a "hole", or that the object's border must be smooth.

Figure 6.1 shows an example of morphological processing. Figure (a) is the binary image of a fingerprint. Algorithms have been developed to analyze these patterns, allowing individual fingerprints to be matched with those in a database. A common step in these algorithms is shown in (b), an operation called skeletonization. This simplifies the image by removing redundant pixels; that is, changing appropriate pixels from black to white. This result in each ridge being turned into a line only a single pixel wide.

A black pixel is denoted by 0, while a white pixel is denoted by 255. The number of iterations is chosen by trial and error. An alternative would be to stop when iteration makes no changes.

During iteration, each pixel in the image is evaluated for being removable; the pixel meets a set of criteria for being changed from black to white. Lines 200-240 loop through each pixel in the image, while the subroutine makes the evaluation. If the pixel under consideration is not removable, the subroutine does nothing. If the pixel is removable, the subroutine changes its value from 0 to 1. This indicates that the pixel is still black, but will be changed to white at the end of the iteration. After all the pixels have been evaluated, lines 260-300 change the value of the marked pixels from 1 to 255. This two-stage process results in the thick ridges being eroded equally from all directions, rather than a pattern based on how the rows and columns are scanned.

■ 6.1 MORPHOLOGICAL IMAGE PROCESSING

Morphological image processing is a collection of techniques for digital image processing based on mathematical morphology. Since these techniques rely only on the relative ordering of pixel values, not on their numerical values, they are especially suited to the processing of binary images and grayscale images whose light transfer function is not known.

Mathematical morphology (MM) is a theoretical model for digital images built upon lattice theory and topology. It is the foundation of morphological image processing, which is based on shift-invariant (translation invariant) operators based principally on Minkowski addition.

Mathematical morphology was originally developed for binary images, viewed as subsets of the integer grid Z2 (or Zd, for any dimension d), and was later extended to grayscale images and multi-band images.

Basic Operators

- Erosion of object A by the structural element B is defined by:

$$A \ominus B = \{z | (B)_z \subset A\}$$

- Dilation of object A by the structural (and symmetrical) element B is defined by:

$$A \oplus B = \{z | (B)_z \cap A \neq \varnothing$$

- The Opening of A by B is obtained by the erosion of A by B, followed by dilation of the resulting structure by B:

$$A \circ B = (A \ominus B) \oplus B$$

- The Closing of A by B is obtained by the dilation of A by B, followed by erosion of the resulting structure by B:

$$A \bullet B = (A \oplus B) \ominus B$$

Some morphological operations are:

- Erosion
- Dilation
- Opening
- Closing
- Shrinking
- Thinning
- Thickening
- Skeletonization
- Pruning
- Distance transform

By combining these operators one can obtain algorithms for many image processing tasks, such as feature detection, image segmentation, image sharpening, image filtering, and granulometry.

6.1.1 Erosion (Morphology)

Erosion is one of two fundamental operations in Morphological image processing from which all other morphological operations are based. The operation is a subset of set theory, where each pixel in an image is considered to be a member of a set of pixel, rather that the usual interpretation of an image being a strict function of two dimensions.

Definition :

Erosion : Let A denote a binary image and B denote a structuring element. Then the erosion of A by B is given by:

The concept of erosion can also be extended to greyscale images. See, for example, Gonzalez (2002).

Example : Suppose A is a 13 * 13 matrix and B is a 5 * 1 matrix:

```
0 0 0 0 0 0 0 0 0 0 0 0 0
0 0 0 0 0 0 0 0 0 0 0 0 0
0 0 0 0 0 0 0 0 0 0 0 0 0
0 0 0 0 0 0 0 0 0 0 0 0 0
0 0 0 1 1 1 1 1 1 1 0 0 0      1
0 0 0 1 1 1 1 1 1 1 0 0 0      1
0 0 0 1 1 1 1 1 1 1 0 0 0      1
0 0 0 1 1 1 1 1 1 1 0 0 0      1
0 0 0 1 1 1 1 1 1 1 0 0 0      1
0 0 0 0 0 0 0 0 0 0 0 0 0
0 0 0 0 0 0 0 0 0 0 0 0 0
0 0 0 0 0 0 0 0 0 0 0 0 0
0 0 0 0 0 0 0 0 0 0 0 0 0
```

Assuming that the origin B is at its center, for each pixel in A superimpose the origin of B, if B is completely contained by A the pixel is retained, else deleted.

The Erosion of A by B is given by

```
0 0 0 0 0 0 0 0 0 0 0 0 0
0 0 0 0 0 0 0 0 0 0 0 0 0
0 0 0 0 0 0 0 0 0 0 0 0 0
0 0 0 0 0 0 0 0 0 0 0 0 0
0 0 0 0 0 0 0 0 0 0 0 0 0
0 0 0 0 0 0 0 0 0 0 0 0 0
0 0 0 1 1 1 1 1 1 1 0 0 0
0 0 0 0 0 0 0 0 0 0 0 0 0
0 0 0 0 0 0 0 0 0 0 0 0 0
0 0 0 0 0 0 0 0 0 0 0 0 0
0 0 0 0 0 0 0 0 0 0 0 0 0
0 0 0 0 0 0 0 0 0 0 0 0 0
0 0 0 0 0 0 0 0 0 0 0 0 0
```

This means that only when B is completely contained inside A that the pixels values are retained, else it gets deleted or in other words it gets eroded.

6.1.2 Minkowski Addition (Dilation)

In geometry, the Minkowski sum of two sets A and B in Euclidean space is the result of adding every element of A to every element of B, i.e. the set

$$A + B = \{a + b \mid a \in A, b \in B\}$$

For example, if we have two 2-simplices (triangles), with points represented by

$$A = \{(1, 0), (0, 1), (0, ?1)\}$$

and $$B = \{(0, 0), (1, 1), (1, ?1)\},$$

then the Minkowski sum is

$$A + B = \{(1, 0), (2, 1), (2, ?1), (0,1), (1, 2), (1, 0), (0, ?1), (1, 0), (1, ?2)\},$$

which looks like a hexagon, with three 'repeated' points at (1,0).

This defines a binary operation called Minkowski addition, named after Hermann Minkowski. It occurs in a basic step in proving Minkowski's theorem, in the form

$$C + C = 2C$$

for a convex symmetric set containing 0, where the left-hand side is the Minkowski sum and the right-hand side the enlargement by a factor of 2.

This operation is sometimes called (somewhat inappropriately) the convolution of the two sets. The actual convolution of the indicator functions of the set will be a function with the same support as the Minkowski sum.

Minkowski addition is also called the binary dilation of A by B.

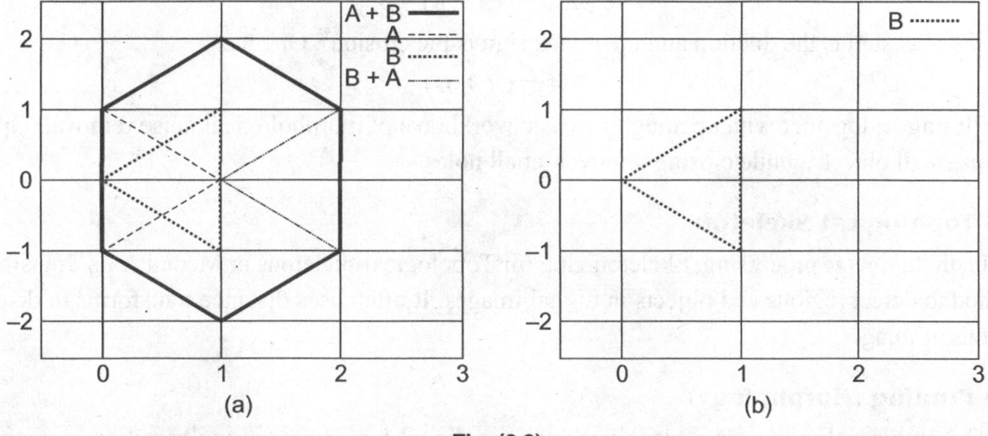

Fig. (6.2)

6.1.3 Opening (Morphology)

In computer vision and image processing, opening is, together with closing, a basic workhorse of morphological noise removal. Opening removes small objects, while closing removes small holes. These techniques can also be used to find specific shapes in an image. Opening can be used to find things into which a specific structuring element can fit (edges, corners, ...).

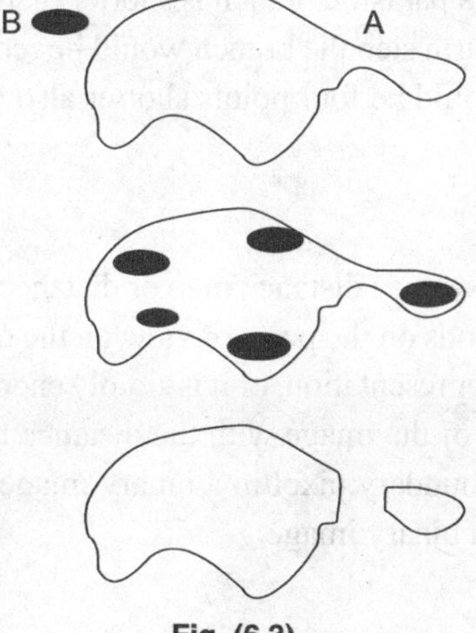

Fig. (6.3)

The Opening (morphology) is the Dilation (morphology) of the Erosion (morphology) of the set A. B is the structuring element.

One can think of B sweeping around the inside of the boundary of A, so that it does not extend beyond the boundary, and shaping the A boundary around the boundary of the element.

$$O(A, B) = (A - B) + B$$

where + is the Minkowski addition.

$$O(A, B) \subset A$$

6.1.4 Closing (Morphology)

In image processing, the closing of a 2-dimensional set (image) A by another set B is the erosion of the dilation of that set,

$$C(A, B) = (A + B) - B$$

(here, the plus sign is the dilation and the minus sign is the erosion). One has

$$A \subset C(A, B)$$

Closing is, together with opening, the basic workhorse of morphological noise removal. Opening removes small objects, while closing removes small holes.

6.1.5 Topological Skeleton

In digital image processing, Skeletonizing (or Topological skeletons or Medial Axis Transform) is a method to detect regions and objects in digital images. It often uses distance transforms to detect the skeletons of images.

6.1.6 Pruning (Morphology)

The pruning algorithm is a technique used for digital image processing based on mathematical morphology. It is used as a complement to the skeleton and thinning algorithms to remove unwanted parasitic components.

The process in itself will remove all branches shorter than a given number of points, for character recognition for example on skeletons of the letters. The pruning algorithm starts at the end points and recursively removes a given number N of points from each found branch. After this step it will apply dilatation on the new end points with a (2N+1)(2N+1) structuring element of 1's and will intersect the result with the original image. If suppose a parasitic branch is shorter than four points and we try to remove all the branches that short, after the fourth step the branch would be removed and no end point would be remaining there. A normal branch would be four points shorter also but after the second step it would go back to it's original size.

6.1.7 Distance Transform

A distance transform, also known as distance map or distance field, is a representation of a digital image. The choice of the term depends on the point of view on the object in question: whether the initial image is transformed into another representation, or it is simply endowed with an additional map or field.

The map supplies each pixel of the image with the distance to the nearest obstacle pixel. A most common type obstacle pixel is a boundary pixel in a binary image. See the image for an example of a chessboard distance transform on a binary image.

0	0	0	0	0	0	0
0	1	1	1	1	1	0
0	1	1	1	1	1	0
0	1	1	1	1	1	0
0	1	1	1	1	1	0
0	1	1	1	1	1	0
0	0	0	0	0	0	0

Binary image

0	0	0	0	0	0	0
0	1	1	1	1	1	0
0	1	2	2	2	1	0
0	1	2	3	2	1	0
0	1	2	2	2	1	0
0	1	1	1	1	1	0
0	0	0	0	0	0	0

Distance transformation

Fig. (6.4) A distance transformation

Usually the transform/map is qualified with the chosen metric. For example, one may speak of Manhattan distance transform, if the underlying metric is Manhattan distance. Common metrics are:

- Euclidean distance
- Taxicab geometry, also known as City block distance or Manhattan distance.
- Chessboard distance

Among applications are digital image processing (e.g., blurring effects, skeletonizing), motion planning in robotics, and even pathfinding.

6.2 FEATURE EXTRACTION

In pattern recognition and in image processing, Feature extraction is a special form of dimensionality reduction. Feature extraction involves simplifying the amount of resources required to describe a large set of data accurately. When performing analysis of complex data one of the major problems stems from the number of variables involved. Analysis with a large number of variables generally requires a large amount of memory and computation power or a classification algorithm which overfits the training sample and generalizes poorly to new samples. Feature extraction is a general term for methods of constructing combinations of the variables to get around these problems while still describing the data with sufficient accuracy.

Best results are achieved when an expert constructs a set of application-dependent features. Nevertheless, if no such expert knowledge is available general dimensionality reduction techniques may help. These include:

- Principal components analysis
- Semidefinite embedding
- Multifactor dimensionality reduction
- Nonlinear dimensionality reduction
- Isomap
- Kernel PCA
- Latent semantic analysis
- Partial least squares

It can be used in the area of image processing which involves using algorithms to detect and isolate various desired portions or shapes (features) of a digitized image or video stream. It is particularly important in the area of Optical Character Recognition.

6.3 SEGMENTATION (IMAGE PROCESSING)

In computer vision, segmentation refers to the process of partitioning a digital image into multiple regions (sets of pixels). The goal of segmentation is to simplify and/or change the representation of an image into something that is more meaningful and easier to analyze. Image segmentation is typically used to locate objects and boundaries (lines, curves, etc.) in images.

The result of image segmentation is a set of regions that collectively cover the entire image, or a set of contours extracted from the image. Each of the pixels in a region are similar with respect to some characteristic or computed property, such as color, intensity, or texture. Adjacent regions are significantly different with respect to the same characteristic(s).

Some of the practical applications of image segmentation are:

- Medical Imaging
  - Locate tumors and other pathologies
  - Measure tissue volumes
  - Computer-guided surgery
  - Diagnosis
  - Treatment planning
  - Study of anatomical structure
- Locate objects in satellite images (roads, forests, etc.)
- Face recognition
- Automatic traffic controlling systems
- Machine vision

Several general-purpose algorithms and techniques have been developed for image segmentation. Since there is no general solution to the image segmentation problem, these techniques often have to be combined with domain knowledge in order to effectively solve an image segmentation problem for a problem domain.

6.4 CLUSTERING METHODS

K-Means Clustering is an iterative technique that is used to partition an image into K clusters. The basic algorithm is:

1. Pick K cluster centers, either randomly or based on some heuristic
2. Assign each pixel in the image to the cluster that minimizes the variance between the pixel and the cluster center
3. Re-compute the cluster centers by averaging all of the pixels in the cluster
4. Repeat steps 2 and 3 until convergence is attained (e.g. no pixels change clusters)

In this case, variance is the squared or absolute difference between a pixel and a cluster center. The difference is typically based on pixel color, intensity, texture, and location, or a weighted combination of these factors. K can be selected manually, randomly, or by a heuristic. This algorithm is guaranteed to converge, but it may not return the optimal solution. The quality of the solution depends on the initial set of clusters and the value of K.

6.4.1 Histogram-Based Methods

Histogram-based methods are very efficient when compared to other image segmentation methods because they typically require only one pass through the pixels. In this technique, a histogram is computed from all of the pixels in the image, and the peaks and valleys in the histogram are used to locate the clusters in the image.Color or intensity can be used as the measure.

A refinement of this technique is to recursively apply the histogram-seeking method to clusters in the image in order to divide them into smaller clusters. This is repeated with smaller and smaller clusters until no more clusters are formed.

One disadvantage of the histogram-seeking method is that it may be difficult to identify significant peaks and valleys in the image. This may affect the quality and usefulness of the final solution.

6.4.2 Region-Growing Methods

In the region-growing technique, a region is started with a single pixel. Adjacent pixels are recursively examined and added to the region if they are sufficiently similar to the region. If a pixel is too dissimilar to the current region, it is used to start a new region.

One variant of this technique, proposed by Haralick and Shapiro (1985),is based on pixel intensities. The mean and scatter of the region and the intensity of the candidate pixel is used to compute a test statistic. If the test statistic is sufficiently small, the pixel is added to the region, and the region's mean and scatter are recomputed. Otherwise, the pixel is rejected, and is used to form a new region.

6.4.3 Graph Partitioning Methods

The "normalized cuts" method was first proposed by Shi and Malik in 1997. In this method, the image being segmented is modelled as a weighted undirected graph. Each pixel is a node in the graph, and an edge is formed between every pair of pixels. The weight of an edge is a measure of the similarity between the pixels. The image is partitioned into disjoint sets (segments) by removing the edges connecting the segments. The optimal partitioning of the graph is the one that minimizes the weights of the edges that were removed (the "cut"). Shi's algorithm seeks to minimize the "normalized cut", which is the ratio of the "cut" to all of the edges in the set.

6.4.4 Model based Segmentation

By inner forces (ideal: circle) and forces which are computed from the image data, which pull the model towards the object boundary.

Statistical Models: If the object to be segmented is known beforehand, a statistical model can be used to serve as a template.

6.4.5 Multi-scale Segmentation

Image segmentations are computed at multiple scales in scale-space and sometimes propagated from coarse to fine scales; see scale-space segmentation. Segmentation criteria can be arbitrarily complex and may take into account global as well as local criteria. A common requirement is that each region must be connected in some sense.

6.4.6 Semi-automatic Segmentation

In this kind of segmentation, the user outlines the region of interest with the mouse clicks and algorithms are applied so that the path that best fits the edge of the image is shown. Techniques like Livewire or Intelligent Scissors are used in this kind of segmentation.

6.4.7 Neural Networks Segmentation

That kind of segmentation relays on processing small areas of an image by the neural network or a set of neural networks. After such processing the decision-taking mechanism marks the areas of an image accordingly to the category recognized by the neural network.

6.5 EXTRACTION OF CONNECTED COMPONENTS

In image processing, a connected components algorithm finds regions of connected pixels, which have the same value. For example, the image below contains 4 components: there are 2 red components, one blue component, and the white, background component. The label image to the right colors each pixel according to the ID of its blob, identifying blob membership. The goal of connected components is to compute this label image.

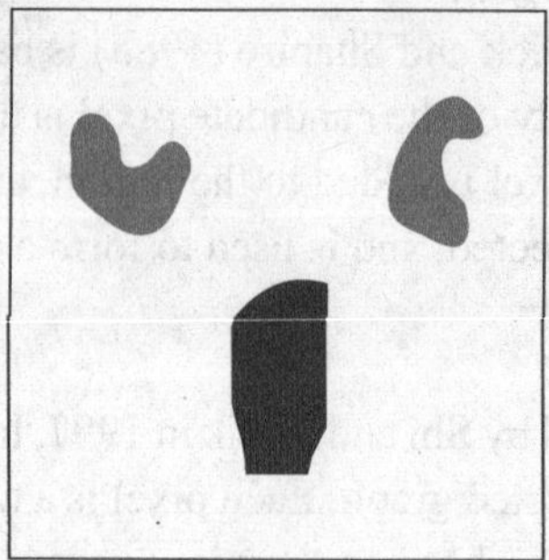
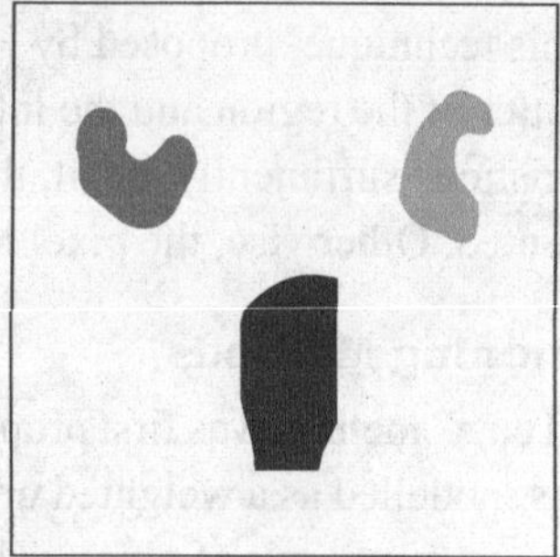

Fig. (6.5)

To find connected components, one could start a flood-fill (like the paint bucket in a painting program) at every pixel. This runs an expensive process for every pixel. In fact, calling a recursive function for each pixel is bad because recursion doesn't take advantage of the compiler's loop optimizations. In addition, recursive methods typically touch the image in an incoherent way, producing lots of cache faults.

To maintain cache locality, it is best to process the image one image line at a time or two lines at a time. The code makes one forward two-line-at-a-time pass through the image, building up a data structure, and does an additional pass through this data structure to get the final labeling. The data structure is a union-find data structure that keeps track of the equivalence between connected components. Its running time is approximately O(N), where N is the number of pixels.

The Algorithm

For each pixel on the line, this implementation first checks to see if the pixel to the left has the same pixel value. If so, we know for sure that we're in the same blob, and the current pixel is so labeled. If the pixel at the top has the same value as the pixel to the left but not the same blob ID, we know at once that the pixels to the left and to the top are in the same region and that these regions should be merged. If a pixel is found with left and top neighbor having different pixel values, a new blob id is created and assigned to this pixel.

The algorithm continues this way, creating new blobs and merging them whenever they are discovered to be the same. The key to a fast algorithm, however, is how this merging is done. This algorithm uses the union-find data structure, which provides excellent performance for keeping track of equivalence. Union-find essentially stores labels, which correspond to the same blob in a tree, making it easy to remember the equivalence of two labels.

Examples : The following images show the result of running the algorithm on a screen dump. The left image is the original image. The right one is the label image.

```
al: "/public_html/connected>
al: "/public_html/connected> pkio (KProtocol I

mmand not found.
 snapple. You will live longer.
al: "/public_html/connected> xv
as/u/rahimi/public_html/connected/
–k connected
```

```
al: "/public_html/connected>
al: "/public_html/connected> pkio (KProtocol I

mmand not found.
 snapple. You will live longer.
al: "/public_html/connected> xv
as/u/rahimi/public_html/connected/
–k connected
```

Fig. (6.6)

Notice that letter that are not touching are correctly segmented with differentiate IDs.

Here's another example run on a hand-drawn image:

Fig. (6.1)

Using : There are only two functions that you need to worry about when using this algorithm. It is implemented in C++ and the class Connected Components exports all the functionality.

First, create a Connected Components by calling the constructor. Specify a soft maximum number of labels you expect in the image. This number is used to allocate some arrays which are resized while the algorithm runs, so don't worry about an exact value.

Then call Connected Components: connected(). The signature of this function is:

```
template<class Tin, class Tlabel, class Comparator, class Boolean>
int ConnectedComponents::connected(const Tin * img, Tlabel * out, int width, int height,
                                   Comparator, Boolean K8_connectivity)
```

img and out are arrays pointing to the grayscale image an the resulting label image respectively. Width and height are the dimensions of both of these images. The pitch of both images must be 0. The algorithm doesn't depend on this, but I used the simplest image format possible to avoid requiring a specific image class. Comparator is an STL compare object. It is an object which defines operator () to take two Tin's and returns true if these values are equivalent. The example code in the library uses STL's equal function object, but you can use anything you like. The final argument specifies whether the algorithm looks at all

8 neighbors of a pixel or just 4 neighbors (sideways and up-down). It is a template argument, but you can pass a bool if you like. I pass a constant template, which i describe in Compile Time Flags.

Here is an example of how you would use this class:

```
//using a bool
Connected Components cc(30);
cc.connected(img, out_uc, width, height,
              std::equal_to<unsigned char>(),
              false);
//using a template constant
ConnectedComponents cc(30);
cc.connected(img, out, width, height,
              std::equal_to<unsigned char>(),
              constant<bool, true>);
```

■ 6.6 CONVEX HULL

In mathematics, the convex hull or convex envelope for a set of points X in a real vector space V is the minimal convex set containing X.

The convex hull of a set of points is the smallest convex set that includes the points. For a two dimensional finite set the convex hull is a convex polygon. This applet lets you get a feel for the way the convex hull depends on the points. You can move a point by dragging it with the mouse, add a new one by clicking the mouse, and delete one by holding down the Shift key while clicking on it.

Intuitive Picture

For planar objects, i.e., lying in the plane, the convex hull may be easily visualized by imagining an elastic band stretched open to encompass the given object; when released, it will assume the shape of the required convex hull.

It may seem natural to generalise this picture to higher dimensions by imagining the objects enveloped in a sort of idealised unpressurised elastic membrane or balloon under tension. However, the equilibrium (minimum-energy) surface in this case may not be the convex hull — parts of the resulting surface may have negative curvature, like a saddle surface. For the case of points in 3-dimensional space, if a rigid wire is first placed between each pair of points, then the balloon will spring back under tension to take the form of the convex hull of the points.

Existence of the Convex Hull

To show that the convex hull of a set X in a real vector space V exists, notice that X is contained in at least one convex set (the whole space V, for example), and any intersection of convex sets containing X is also a convex set containing X. It is then clear that the convex hull is the intersection of all convex sets containing X. This can be be used as an alternative definition of the convex hull.

More directly, the convex hull of X can be described constructively as the set of convex combinations of points from X: that is, the set of points of the form , where n is an arbitrary natural number, the numbers tj are non-negative and sum to 1, and the points xj are in X. It is simple to check that this set satisfies either of the two definitions above. So the convex hull Hconvex(X) of set X is:

$$H_{\text{convex}}(X) = \left\{ \sum_{i=1}^{k} \alpha_i x_i \,\middle|\, x_i \in X, \alpha_i \in R, \alpha_i \geq 0 \sum_{i=1}^{k} \alpha_k = 1, k = 1, 2, \ldots \right\}$$

In fact, if X is a subset of an N-dimensional vector space, sums of up to N+1 points are sufficient in the definition above. This is equivalent to saying that the convex hull of X is the union of all simplexes with at most N+1 vertices from X. This is known as Carathéodory's theorem.

The convex hull is defined for any kind of objects made up of points in a vector space, which may have any number of dimensions. The convex hull of finite sets of points and other geometrical objects in a two-dimensional plane or three-dimensional space are special cases of practical importance.

Computation of Convex Hulls

In computational geometry, numerous algorithms are proposed for computing the convex hull of a finite set of points, with various computational complexities.

Computing the convex hull means that a non-ambiguous and efficient representation of the required convex shape is constructed. The complexity of the corresponding algorithms is usually estimated in terms of n, the number of input points, and h, the number of points on the convex hull.

Relations to other Geometric Structures

The Delaunay triangulation of a point set and its dual, the Voronoi Diagram, are mathematically related to convex hulls: the *Delaunay triangulation of a point set in* Rn can be viewed as the projection of a convex hull in Rn+1 .

The orthogonal convex hull of a point set is the intersection of all orthogonally convex supersets of the point set, where an orthogonally convex set is defined to intersect each axis-parallel line in a connected subset. Orthogonal convex hulls have properties similar to those of convex hulls, and can be constructed by algorithms with similar time bounds as those for convex hulls.

Applications : The problem of finding convex hulls finds its practical applications in pattern recognition, image processing, statistics and GIS. It also serves as a tool, a building block for a number of other computational-geometric algorithms. For example, consider the problem of finding the diameter of a set of points, which is the pair of points a maximum distance apart. The diameter will always be the distance between two points on the convex hull. The O(n log n). algorithm for computing diameter proceeds by first constructing the convex hull, then for each hull vertex finding which other hull vertex is farthest away from it. This so-called "rotating-calipers" method can be used to move efficiently from one hull vertex to another.

What is the convex hull of a set of points? This can be answered two ways:

- Formally: It is the smallest convex set containing the points.
- Informally: It is a rubber band wrapped around the "outside" points.

In the example below, the convex hull of the blue points is the black line that contains them.

Try moving the points around, to see how the hull changes. To gain some insight, try the following:

- Move a point which is a vertex of the hull
- Choose a point inside the hull, and move it outside.
- Rearrange the points to get a convex hull with as few edges as possible. What is the minimum possible number of edges?

How do we compute the convex hull of a set of points? There are many ways. Here are a few:

- Graham's scan
- Jarvis' march (gift-wrapping).
- Quick hull

6.6.1 Graham's Scan

Given a set of points on the plane, Graham's scan computes their convex hull. The algorithm works in three phases:

1. Find an extreme point. This point will be the pivot, is guaranteed to be on the hull, and is chosen to be the point with largest y coordinate.
2. Sort the points in order of increasing angle about the pivot. We end up with a star-shaped polygon (one in which one special point, in this case the pivot, can "see" the whole polygon).
3. Build the hull, by marching around the star-shaped poly, adding edges when we make a left turn, and back-tracking when we make a right turn.

6.6.2 Jarvis' March

This is perhaps the most simple-minded algorithm for the convex hull, and yet in some cases it can be very fast. The basic idea is as follows:

- Start at some extreme point, which is guaranteed to be on the hull.
- At each step, test each of the points, and find the one, which makes the largest right-hand turn. That point has to be the next one on the hull.

Because this process marches around the hull in counter-clockwise order, like a ribbon wrapping itself around the points, this algorithm also called the "gift-wrapping" algorithm.

6.6.3 Quick-Hull

Here's an algorithm that deserves its name. It's a fast way to compute the convex hull of a set of points on the plane. It shares a few similarities with its namesake, quick-sort:

- It is recursive.
- Each recursive step partitions data into several groups.

The partitioning step does all the work. The basic idea is as follows:

1. We are given a some points, and line segment AB which we know is a chord of the convex hull (IE, it's endpoints are known to be on the convex hull). A good chord to start the algorithm goes from the leftmost to the rightmost point in the set.
2. Among the given points, find the one which is farthest from AB. Let's call this point C.
3. The points inside the triangle ABC cannot be on the hull. Put them in set s0.
4. Put the points which lie outside edge AC in set s1, and points outside edge BC in set s2.

Once the partitioning is done, we recursively invoke quick-hull on sets s1 and s2. The algorithm works fast on random sets of points because step 3 of the partition typically discards a large fraction of the points.

6.7 THINNING & THICKENING

Thinning is a term used in agricultural sciences to mean the removal of some plants, or parts of plants, to make room for the growth of others.

Thickening is a morphological operation that is used to grow selected regions of foreground pixels in binary images, somewhat like dilation or closing. It has several applications, including determining the approximate convex hull of a shape, and determining the skeleton by zone of influence. Thickening is normally only applied to binary images, and it produces another binary image as output. The thickening operation is related to the hit-and-miss transform, and so it is helpful to have an understanding of that operator before reading on.

How It Works

Like other morphological operators, the behavior of the thickening operation is determined by a structuring element. The binary structuring elements used for thickening are of the extended type described under the hit-and-miss transform (i.e. they can contain both ones and zeros).

The thickening operation is related to the hit-and-miss transform and can be expressed quite simply in terms of it. The thickening of an image I by a structuring element J is:

$$\text{thicken } (I, J) = I \cup \text{hit and miss } (I, J)$$

Thus the thickened image consists of the original image plus any additional foreground pixels switched on by the hit-and-miss transform.

In everyday terms, the thickening operation is calculated by translating the origin of the structuring element to each possible pixel position in the image, and at each such position comparing it with the underlying image pixels. If the foreground and background pixels in the structuring element exactly match foreground and background pixels in the image, then the image pixel underneath the origin of the structuring element is set to foreground (one). Otherwise it is left unchanged. Note that the structuring element must always have a zero or a blank at its origin if it is to have any effect.

The choice of structuring element determines under what situations a background pixel will be set to foreground, and hence it determines the application for the thickening operation. We have described the effects of a single pass of a thickening operation over the image. In fact, the operator is normally applied repeatedly until it causes no further changes to the image (i.e. until convergence). Alternatively, in some applications, the operations may only be applied for a limited number of iterations.

Thickening is the dual of thinning, i.e. thinning the foreground is equivalent to thickening the background. In fact, in most cases thickening is performed by thinning the background.

Guidelines for Use

We will illustrate thickening with two applications, determining the convex hull, and finding the skeleton by zone of influence or SKIZ.

The convex hull of a binary shape can be visualized quite easily by imagining stretching an elastic band around the shape. The elastic band will follow the convex contours of the shape, but will `bridge' the concave contours. The resulting shape will have no concavities and contains the original shape. Where an image contains multiple disconnected shapes, the convex hull algorithm will determine the convex hull of each shape, but will not connect disconnected shapes, unless their convex hulls happen to overlap (e.g. two interlocked `U'-shapes).

1	1	
1	0	
1		0

	1	1
	0	1
0		1

Fig. (6.8) Structuring elements for determining the convex hull using thickening. During each iteration of the thickening, each element should be used in turn, and then in each of their 90° rotations, giving 8 effective structuring elements in total. The thickening is continued until no further changes occur, at which point the convex hull is complete.

An approximate convex hull can be computed using thickening with the structuring elements shown in Figure 1. The convex hull computed using this method is actually a `45° convex hull' approximation, in which the boundaries of the convex hull must have orientations that are multiples of 45°. Note that this computation can be very slow.

The image

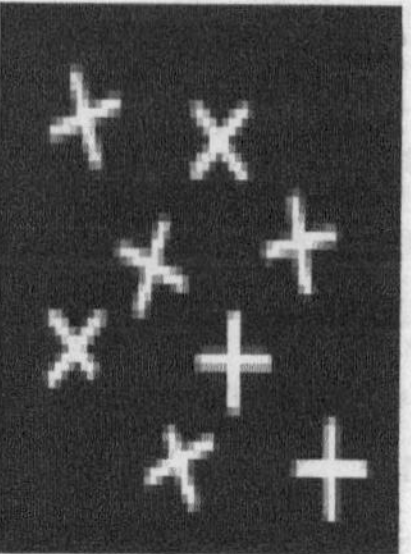

Fig. (6.9)

is an image containing a number of cross-shaped binary objects.

Applying the 45° convex hull algorithm described above results in

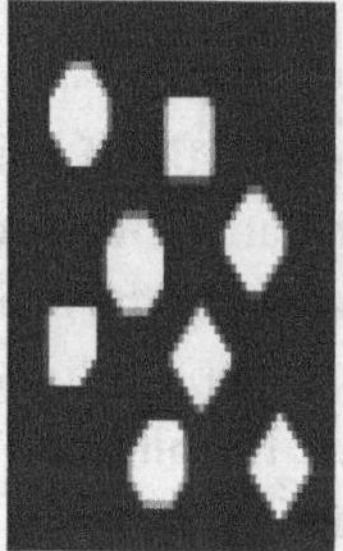

Fig. (6.10)

This process took a considerable amount of time — over 100 thickening passes with each of the eight structuring elements!

Another application of thickening is to determine the skeleton by zone of influence, or SKIZ. The SKIZ is a skeletal structure that divides an image into regions, each of which contains just one of the distinct objects in the image. The boundaries are drawn such that all points within a particular boundary are closer to the binary object contained within that boundary than to any other. As with normal skeletons, various possible distance metrics can be used. The SKIZ is also sometimes called the Voronoi diagram.

0	0	0
	0	
1	1	1

1(a)

	0	
1	0	0
1	1	

1(b)

1		
1	0	1
1	1	1

2(a)

		1
1	0	1
1	1	1

2(b)

Fig. (6.11) Structuring elements used in determining the SKIZ. 1(a) and 1(b) are used to perform the skeletonization of the background. Note that these elements are juust the duals of the corresponding skeletonization by thinning elements. On each thickening iteration, each element is used in turn, and in each of its 90° rotations. Thickening is continued until convergence. When this is finished, structuring elements 2(a) and 2(b) are used in similar fashion to prune the skeleton until convergence and leave behind the SKIZ.

One method of calculating the SKIZ is to first determine the skeleton of the background, and then prune this until convergence to remove all branches except those forming closed loops, or those intersecting the image boundary. Both of these concepts are described (applied to foreground objects) under thinning. Since thickening is the dual of thinning, we can accomplish the same thing using thickening. The structuring elements used in the two processes are shown in Figure 2.

We illustrate the SKIZ using the same starting image as for the convex hull.

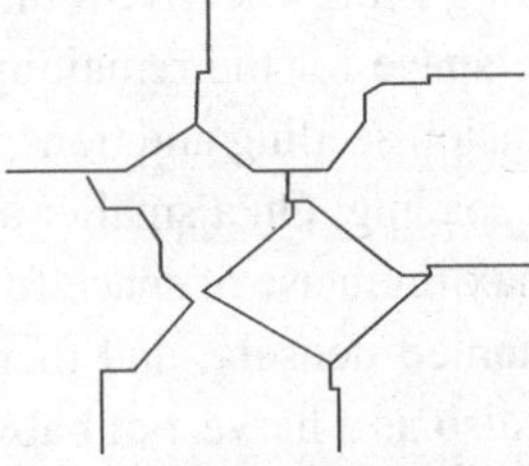

Fig. (6.12)

shows the image after the skeleton of the background has been found.

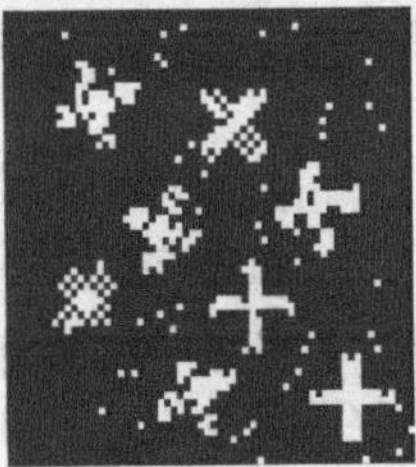

Fig. (6.13)

is the same image after pruning until convergence. This is the SKIZ of the original image.

Since the SKIZ considers each foreground pixel as an object to which it assigns a zone of influence, it is rather sensitive to noise. If we, for example, add some 'salt noise' to the above image, we obtain

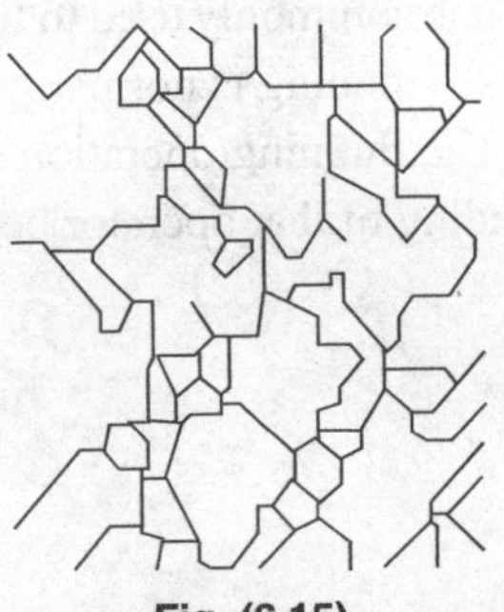

Fig. (6.14)

The SKIZ of that image is given by

Fig. (6.15)

Now, we not only have a zone of influence for each of the crosses, but also for each of the noise points. Since thickening is the dual to thinning, it can be applied for the same range of tasks as thinning. Which operator is used depends on the polarity of the image, i.e. if the object is represented in black and the background is white, the thickening operator thins the object.

Forestry

Thinning in forestry is the selective removal of trees, primarily undertaken to improve the growth rate or health of the remaining trees. This may be done to make the stand more profitable in an upcoming final felling. Overcrowded trees are under competitive stress from their neighbors. Thinning may be done to increase the resistance of the stand to environmental stress such as drought, insect infestation or extreme temperature. A thinning in which the trees removed have little or no economic value is called a pre-commercial thinning. Ecological Thinning is a variant of this being trialled for use in forest conservation in Australia.

Agriculture

In agriculture and gardening, thinning is the selective removal of flowers, fruits, shoots, and seedlings or young plants to allow adequate space for the remaining organs/plants to grow efficiently. In large-scale farming, techniques like precision seeding and transplanting can eliminate the need for thinning by starting plants at their optimum spacing. On a smaller scale, such as a home vegetable garden, thinning can be used as a way to make maximum use of space for certain crops. For example, beets, carrots, green onions and others can be planted densely, and then thinned to make room for continued growth of the plants left in the soil, and also as a harvest of baby vegetables (beet greens, baby carrots, baby onions).

Digital Geometry

In digital geometry, thinning is the transformation of a digital image into a simplified, but topologically equivalent image.

Thickening

In cooking, thickening is the process of increasing the viscosity of a liquid either by reduction, or by the addition of a thickening agent, typically containing starch. Desserts are often thickened with sago, tapioca, gelatin or a gelatine substitute such as agar. Soups, sauces and stews are more often thickened with a starchy product like cornstarch, arrowroot or wheat flour, or a fat and flour mixture such as roux or beurre manié. More rarely, savoury dishes may be thickened with blood.

Thinning is a morphological operation that is used to remove selected foreground pixels from binary images, somewhat like erosion or opening. It can be used for several applications, but is particularly useful for skeletonization. In this mode it is commonly used to tidy up the output of edge detectors by reducing all lines to single pixel thickness. Thinning is normally only applied to binary images, and produces another binary image as output. The thinning operation is related to the hit-and-miss transform, and so it is helpful to have an understanding of that operator before reading on.

How It Works

Like other morphological operators, the behavior of the thinning operation is determined by a structuring element. The binary structuring elements used for thinning are of the extended type described under the hit-and-miss transform (i.e. they can contain both ones and zeros).

The thinning operation is related to the hit-and-miss transform and can be expressed quite simply in terms of it. The thinning of an image I by a structuring element J is:

$$\text{thin}\,(I, J) = I - \text{hit and miss}\,(I, J)$$

where the subtraction is a logical subtraction defined by $X - Y = X \cap \text{NOT}\, Y$.

In everyday terms, the thinning operation is calculated by translating the origin of the structuring element to each possible pixel position in the image, and at each such position comparing it with the underlying image pixels. If the foreground and background pixels in the structuring element exactly match foreground and background pixels in the image, then the image pixel underneath the origin of the structuring element is set to background (zero). Otherwise it is left unchanged. Note that the structuring element must always have a one or a blank at its origin if it is to have any effect. The choice of structuring element determines under what situations a foreground pixel will be set to background, and hence it determines the application for the thinning operation.

We have described the effects of a single pass of a thinning operation over the image. In fact, the operator is normally applied repeatedly until it causes no further changes to the image (i.e. until convergence). Alternatively, in some applications, e.g. pruning, the operations may only be applied for a limited number of iterations. Thinning is the dual of thickening, i.e. thickening the foreground is equivalent to thinning the background.

Guidelines for Use

One of the most common uses of thinning is to reduce the threshold output of an edge detector such as the Sobel operator, to lines of a single pixel thickness, while preserving the full length of those lines (i.e. pixels at the extreme ends of lines should not be affected). A simple algorithm for doing this is the following:

Consider all pixels on the boundaries of foreground regions (i.e. foreground points that have at least one background neighbor). Delete any such point that has more than one foreground neighbor, as long as doing so does not locally disconnect (i.e. split into two) the region containing that pixel. Iterate until convergence. This procedure erodes away the boundaries of foreground objects as much as possible, but does not affect pixels at the ends of lines. This effect can be achieved using morphological thinning by iterating until convergence with the structuring elements shown in Figure 1, and all their 90° rotations ($4\times2 = 8$ structuring elements in total).

In fact what we are doing here is determining the octagonal skeleton of a binary shape — the set of points that lie at the centers of octagons that fit entirely inside the shape, and which touch the boundary of the shape at at least two points. See the section on skeletonization for more details on skeletons and on other ways of computing it. Note that this skeletonization method is guaranteed to produce a connected skeleton.

0	0	0
	1	
1	1	1

	0	0
1	1	0
	1	

Fig. (6.16) Structuring elements for skeletonization by morphological thinning. At each iteration, the image is first thinned by the left hand structuring element and then by the right hand one, and then with the remaining six 90° rotations of the two elements. The process is repeated by cyclic fashion until none of the thinning produces any further change. As usual, the origin of the structuring element is at the center.

Figure 2 shows the result of this thinning operation on a simple binary image.

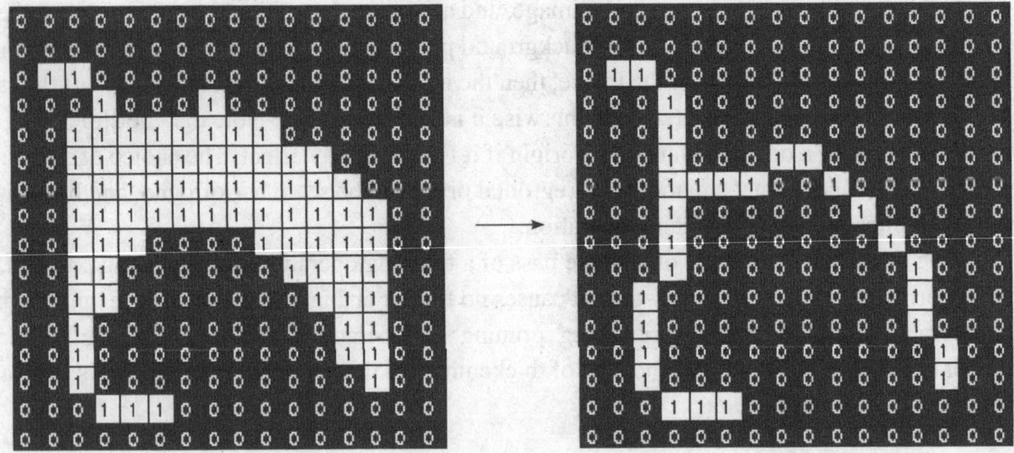

Fig. (6.17) Example skeletonization by morphological thinning of a simple binary shape, using the above structuring elements. Note that the resulting skeleton is connected.

Note that skeletons produced by this method often contain undesirable short spurs produced by small irregularities in the boundary of the original object. These spurs can be removed by a process called pruning, which is in fact just another sort of thinning. The structuring element for this operation is shown in Figure 3, along with some other common structuring elements.

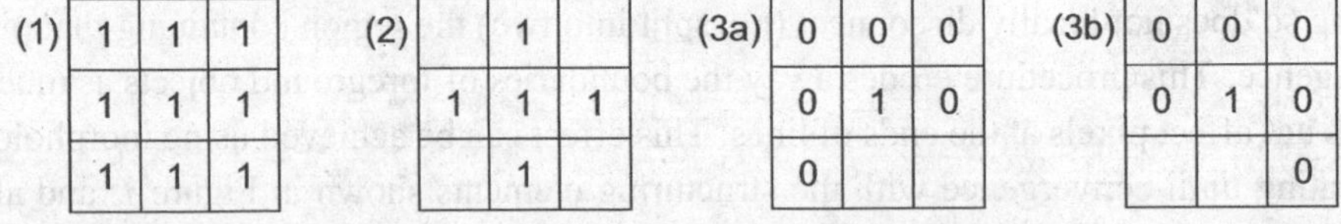

Fig. (6.18) Some applications of thinning (1) simply finds the boundary of a binary object, *i.e.*, it deletes any foreground point sthat don't have at least one neighbouring background point. Note that the detected boundary is 4-connected. (2) does the same thing but produces an 8-connected boundary. (3a) and (3b) are used for pruning. At each thinning iteration, each element must be used in each of its four 90° rotations. Pruning is normally carried out for only a limited convergence will actually remove all pixels except those that form closed loops.

Note that many implementations of thinning have a particular structuring element `hardwired' into them (usually the skeletonization structuring elements), and so the user does not need to be concerned about selecting one.

The image

Fig. (6.19)

is the result of applying the Sobel operator to

Fig. (6.20)

Note that the detected boundaries of the object are several pixels thick. We first threshold the image at a gray level value of 60 producing

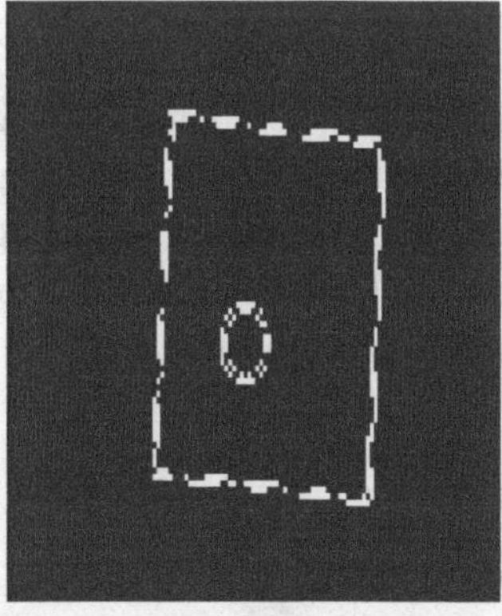

Fig. (6.21)

in order to obtain a binary image.

Then, iterating the thinning algorithm until convergence, we get

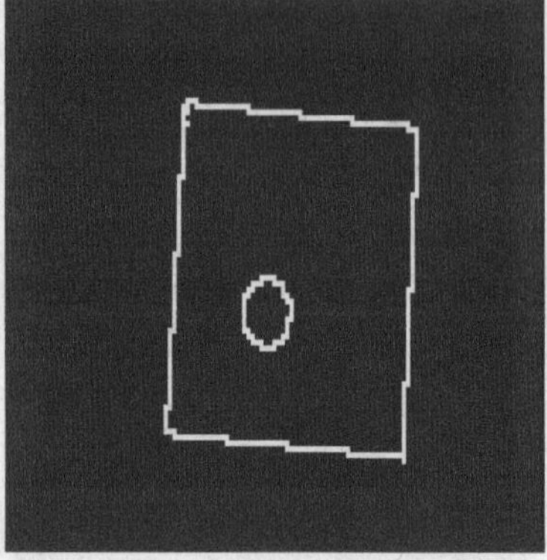

Fig. (6.22)

The detected lines have all been reduced to a single pixel width. Note however that there are still one or two `spurs' present, which can be removed using pruning.

The image

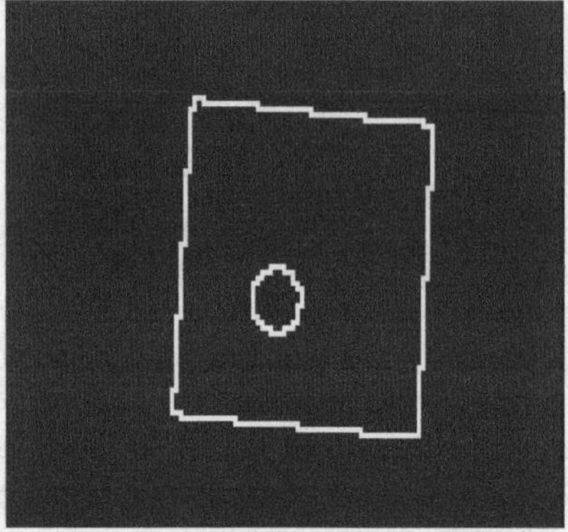

Fig. (6.23)

is the result of pruning (using thinning) for five iterations. The spurs are now almost entirely gone.

Thinning is often used in combination with other morphological operators tp extract a simple representation of regions. A common example is the automated recognition of hand-written characters. In this case, morphological operators are used as pre-processing to obtain the shapes of the characters which then can be used for the recognition. We illustrate a simple example using

Fig. (6.24)

Which shows a Japanese character. Note that this and the following images were zoomed by a factor of 4 for a better display. Hence, a 4×4 pixel square here corresponds to 1 pixel during the processing. Since we want to work on binary images, we start off by thresholding the image at a value of 180, obtaining

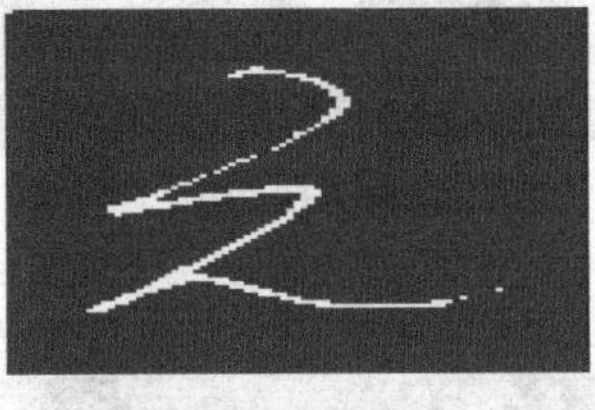

Fig. (6.25)

A simple way to obtain the skeleton of the character is to thin the image with the structuring elements shown in Figure 4 until convergence. The result is shown in

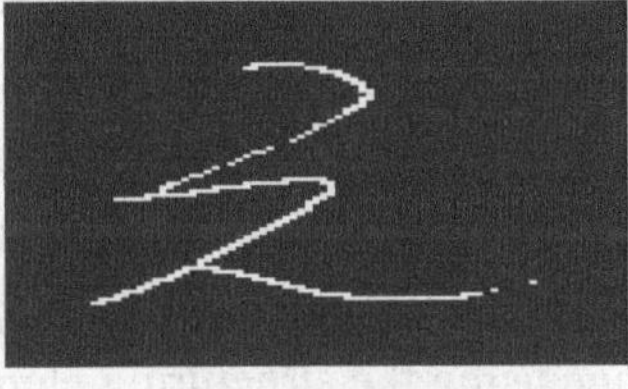

Fig. (6.26)

The character is now reduced to a single pixel-wide line. However, the line is broken at some locations, which might cause problems during the recognition process. To improve the situation we can first dilate the image to connect the lines before thinning it. Dilating the image twice with a 3×3 square structuring element yields

Fig. (6.27)

then the result of the thinning is

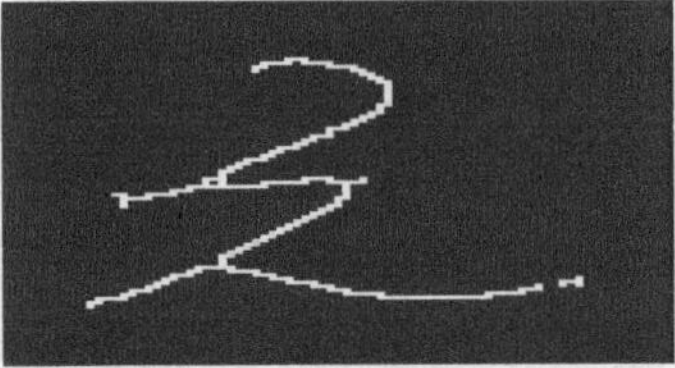

Fig. (6.28)

The corresponding images for three dilations are

Fig. (6.29)

and

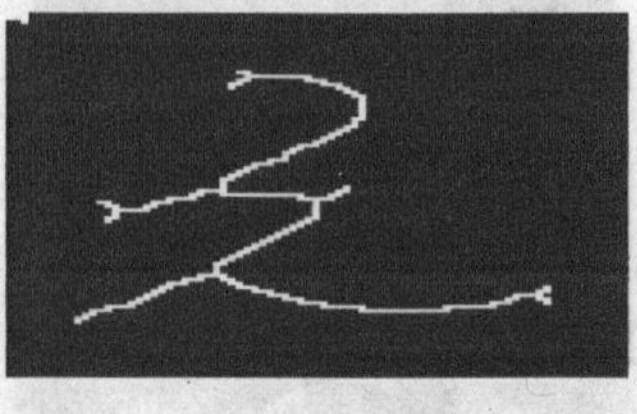

Fig. (6.30)

Although the line is now connected the process also had negative effects on the skeleton: we obtain spurs on the end points of the lines and the skeleton changes its shape at high curvature locations. We try to prune the spurs by thinning the image using the structuring elements shown in Figure 4.

(1)

1	1	1
	1	
0	0	0

(2)

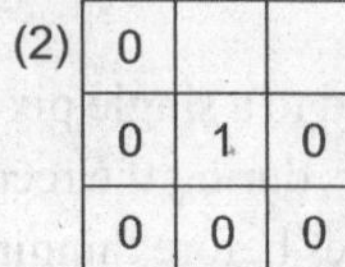

0		
0	1	0
0	0	0

Fig. (6.31) Shows the structuring elements used in the character recognition example. (1) show the structuring element used in combination with thinning to obtain the skeleton. (2) were used in combination with thinning to prune the skeleton and with the hit-and-miss operator to find the end points of the skeleton. Each structuring element was used in each of its 45° rotations.

Pruning the image which was obtained after 2 dilations and thinning yields,

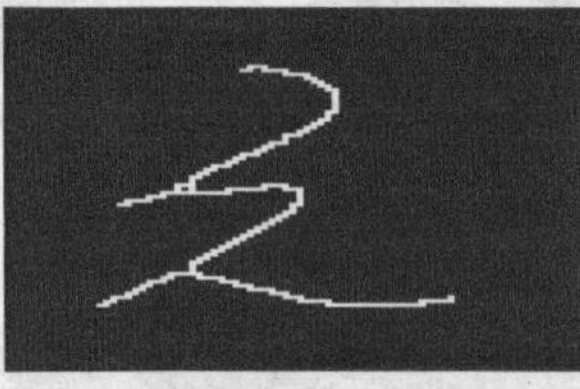

Fig. (6.32)

using two iterations for each orientation of the structuring element. For the example obtained after 3 dilations we get

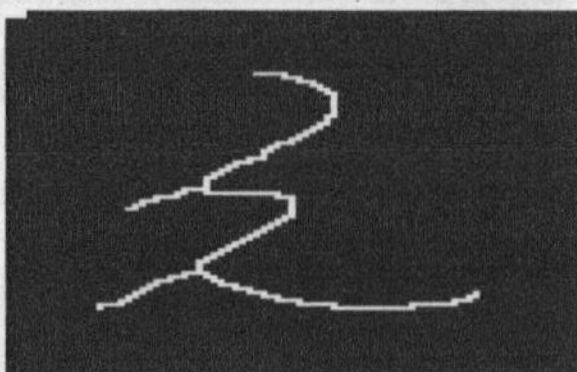

Fig. (6.33)

Using 4 iterations of pruning. The spurs have now disappeared, however, the pruning has also suppressed pixels at the end of correct lines. If we want to restore these parts of the image, we can combine the dilation operator with a logical AND operator. First, we need to know the end points of the skeleton so that we know where to start the dilation. We find these by applying a hit-and-miss operator using the structuring element shown in Figure 4. The end points of the latter of the two pruned, images are shown in

Fig. (6.34)

Now, we dilate this image using a 3×3 structuring element. ANDing it with the thinned, but not pruned image prevents the dilation from spreading out in all direction, hence it limits the dilation along the original character. This process is known as conditional dilation. After repeating this procedure 5 times, we obtain

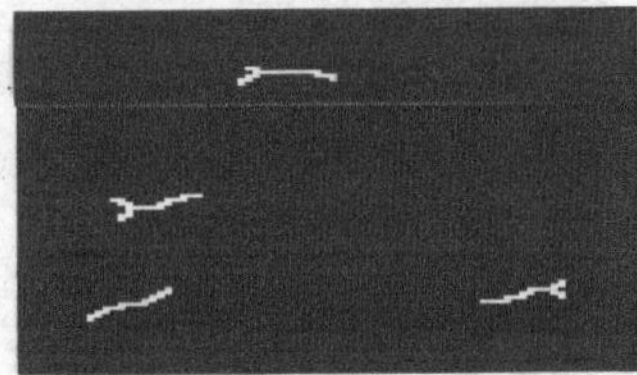

Fig. (6.35)

Although one of the parasitic branches has disappeared, the ones appearing close to the end of the lines remain.

Our final step is to OR this image with the pruning output thus obtaining

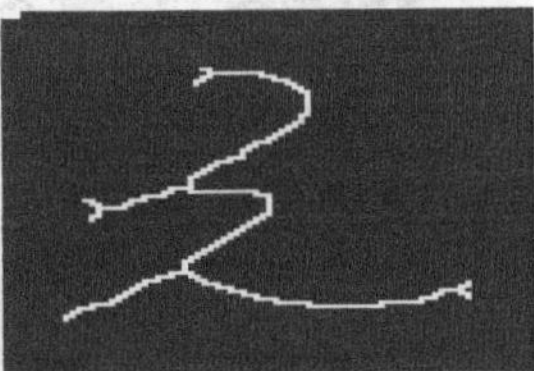

Fig. (6.36)

This simple example illustrates that we can successfully apply a variety of morphological operators to obtain information about the shape of a character. However, in a real world application, more sophisticated algorithms and structuring elements would be necessary to get good results.

Thinning more complicated images often produces less spectacular results.

For instance

Fig. (6.37)

is the output from the Sobel operator applied to

Fig. (6.38)

The image

Fig. (6.39)

is the same image threshold at a gray level value of 200.
and

Fig. (6.40)

is the effect of skeletonization by thinning. The result is a lot less clear than before. Compare this with the results obtained using the Canny operator.

■ SUMMARY

- The identification of objects within an image can be a very difficult task. One way to simplify the problem is to change the grayscale image into a binary image, in which each pixel is restricted to a value of either 0 or 1.
- Morphological image processing is a collection of techniques for digital image processing based on mathematical morphology. Since these techniques rely only on the relative ordering of pixel values, not on their numerical values, they are especially suited to the processing of binary images and grayscale images whose light transfer function is not known.
- Mathematical morphology (MM) is a theoretical model for digital images built upon lattice theory and topology. It is the foundation of morphological image processing, which is based on shift-invariant (translation invariant) operators based principally on Minkowski addition.
- Erosion is one of two fundamental operations in Morphological image processing from which all other morphological operations are based. The operation is a subset of set theory, where each pixel in an image is considered to be a member of a set of pixel, rather that the usual interpretation of an image being a strict function of two dimensions.
- In computer vision and image processing, opening is, together with closing, a basic workhorse of morphological noise removal. Opening removes small objects, while closing removes small holes. These techniques can also be used to find specific shapes in an image.
- The pruning algorithm is a technique used for digital image processing based on mathematical morphology. It is used as a complement to the skeleton and thinning algorithms to remove unwanted parasitic components.
- A distance transform, also known as distance map or distance field, is a representation of a digital image. The choice of the term depends on the point of view on the object in question: whether the initial image is transformed into another representation, or it is simply endowed with an additional map or field.
- Feature extraction involves simplifying the amount of resources required to describe a large set of data accurately. When performing analysis of complex data one of the major problems stems from the number of variables involved.
- Analysis with a large number of variables generally requires a large amount of memory and computation power or a classification algorithm which overfits the training sample and generalizes poorly to new samples.
- Feature extraction is a general term for methods of constructing combinations of the variables to get around these problems while still describing the data with sufficient accuracy.
- Segmentation refers to the process of partitioning a digital image into multiple regions (sets of pixels). The goal of segmentation is to simplify and/or change the representation of an image into something that is more meaningful and easier to analyze. Image segmentation is typically used to locate objects and boundaries (lines, curves, etc.) in images.
- The result of image segmentation is a set of regions that collectively cover the entire image, or a set of contours extracted from the image. Each of the pixels in a region are similar with respect to some characteristic or computed property, such as color, intensity, or texture. Adjacent regions are significantly different with respect to the same characteristic(s).

- K-Means Clustering is an iterative technique that is used to partition an image into K clusters.
- In image processing, a connected components algorithm finds regions of connected pixels, which have the same value. For example, the image below contains 4 components: there are 2 red components, one blue component, and the white, background component. The label image to the right colors each pixel according to the ID of its blob, identifying blob membership. The goal of connected components is to compute this label image.
- In mathematics, the convex hull or convex envelope for a set of points X in a real vector space V is the minimal convex set containing X.
- The convex hull of a set of points is the smallest convex set that includes the points. For a two dimensional finite set the convex hull is a convex polygon.
- Thinning is a term used in agricultural sciences to mean the removal of some plants, or parts of plants, to make room for the growth of others.
- Thickening is a morphological operation that is used to grow selected regions of foreground pixels in binary images, somewhat like dilation or closing.
- Thickening is the process of increasing the viscosity of a liquid either by reduction, or by the addition of a thickening agent, typically containing starch.

Review Questions

1. What is the difference of a thinned line obtained from the slightly different skeleton structuring elements in Figure 1 and Figure 4?
2. The conditional dilation in the character recognition example `followed' the original character not only towards the initial end of the line but also backwards. Hence it also might restore unwanted spurs which were located in this direction. Can you think of a way to avoid that using a second condition?
3. Can you think of any situation in the character recognition example, in which the pruning structuring element shown in Figure 4 might cause problems?
4. Find the boundaries of

Fig. (6.41)

using morphological edge detection. First threshold the image, then apply thinning using the structuring element shown in Figure 3. Compare the result with

Fig. (6.42)

which was obtain using the Sobel operator and morphological post-processing.

5. Compare and contrast the effect of the Canny operator with the combined effect of Sobel operator plus thinning and pruning.
6. If an edge detector has produced long lines in its output that are approximately x pixels thick, what is the longest length spurious spur (prune) that you could expect to see after thinning to a single pixel thickness? Test your estimate out on some real images.
7. Hence, approximately how many iterations of pruning should be applied to remove spurious spurs from lines that were thinned down from a thickness of x pixels?
8. Write short notes on the following
   - Boundary Extraction
   - Region Filling
   - Extraction of Connected Components
   - Convex Hull
   - Thinning
   - Thickening

7

REGISTRATION

Image registration is the process of establishing point-by-point correspondence between two images of a scene. This process is needed in various computer vision applications, such as stereo depth perception, motion analysis, change detection, object localization, object recognition, and image fusion.

Image registration is the process of overlaying two or more images of the same scene taken at different times, from different viewpoints, and/or by different sensors. It geometrically aligns two images—the reference and sensed images. The present differences between images are introduced due to different imaging conditions. Image registration is a crucial step in all image analysis tasks in which the final information is gained from the combination of various data sources like in image fusion, change detection, and multi channel image restoration. Typically, registration is required in remote sensing (multi spectral classification, environmental monitoring, change detection, image mosaicing, weather forecasting, creating super-resolution images, integrating information into geographic information systems (GIS)), in medicine (combining computer tomography (CT) and NMR data to obtain more complete information about the patient, monitoring tumor growth, treatment verification, comparison of the patient's data with anatomical atlases), in cartography (map updating), and in computer vision (target localization, automatic quality control), to name a few.

During the last decades, image acquisition devices have undergone rapid development and growing amount and diversity of obtained images invoked the research on automatic image registration. A comprehensive survey of image registration methods was published in 1992 by Brown.

The Image Registration tool is used to bring images into alignment, for example:

- When multiple scans are performed on the same subject, but the image planes are not in the same locations on every scan (intra-subject registration). The multiple scans may be performed at different times on the same medical scanning device, or they may be collected using a different modality (e.g. MRI, CT, SPECT, PET).
- When you have scans of the same type performed on different subjects (inter-subject registration). You may want to register one of your scans to an atlas, or register several scans to create an atlas.

You can choose the type and number of degrees of freedom to meet the demands of your problem. The degrees of freedom allow different types of image distortion allowed to obtain a good match.

The Image Registration tool works by calculating a "cost function" that reaches a maximum or minimum as images are brought into alignment. The alignment is adjusted iteratively until the best value of the cost function is found.

There is also a version of the Registration Tool that is specifically "tuned" for time-series registration where the image to be registered are from a single subject, and where the images are already in a fairly close alignment. This situation is often encountered in functional imaging, where a series of images is collected an there is very little patient motion between the images. Use of the Time Series Registration tool allows much quicker registration of such data.

■ 7.1 IMAGE REGISTRATION METHODOLOGY

Image registration, as it was mentioned above, is widely used in remote sensing, medical imaging, computer vision etc. In general, its applications can be divided into four main groups according to the manner of the image acquisition:

Different viewpoints (multi view analysis) : Images of the same scene are acquired from different viewpoints. The aim is to gain larger a 2D view or a 3D representation of the scanned scene.

Examples of applications:

- Remote sensing—mosaicing of images of the surveyed area.
- Computer vision—shape recovery (shape from stereo).

Different times (multitemporal analysis) : Images of the same scene are acquired at different times, often on regular basis, and possibly under different conditions. The aim is to find and evaluate changes in the scene which appeared between the consecutive images acquisitions.

Examples of applications:

- Remote sensing—monitoring of global land usage, landscape planning.
- Computer vision—automatic change detection for security monitoring, motion tracking.
- Medical imaging—monitoring of the healing therapy, monitoring of the tumor evolution.

Different sensors (multimodal analysis) : Images of the same scene are acquired by different sensors. The aim is to integrate the information obtained from different source streams to gain more complex and detailed scene representation.

Examples of applications:

- Remote sensing—fusion of information from sensors with different characteristics like panchromatic images, offering better spatial resolution, color/multispectral images with better spectral resolution, or radar images independent of cloud cover and solar illumination.
- Medical imaging—combination of sensors recording the anatomical body structure like magnetic resonance image (MRI), ultrasound or CT with sensors monitoring functional and metabolic body activities like positron emission tomography (PET), single photon emission computed tomography (SPECT) or magnetic resonance spectroscopy (MRS). Results can be applied, for instance, in radiotherapy and nuclear medicine.

Scene to model registration : Images of a scene and a model of the scene are registered. The model can be a computer representation of the scene, for instance maps or digital elevation models (DEM) in GIS, another scene with similar content (another patient), 'average' specimen, etc. The aim is to localize the acquired image in the scene/model and/or to compare them.

Examples of applications:

- Remote sensing—registration of aerial or satellite data into maps or other GIS layers.
- Computer vision—target template matching with real-time images, automatic quality inspection.
- Medical imaging— comparison of the patient's image with digital anatomical atlases, specimen classification.

Due to the diversity of images to be registered and due to various types of degradations it is impossible to design a universal method applicable to all registration tasks. Every method should take into account not only the assumed type of geometric deformation between the images but also radiometric deformations and noise corruption, required registration accuracy and application-dependent data characteristics.

The registration methods consists of the following four steps:

Feature detection : Salient and distinctive objects (closed-boundary regions, edges, contours, line intersections, corners, etc.) are manually or, preferably, automatically detected. For further processing, these features can be represented by their point representatives (centers of gravity, line endings, distinctive points), which are called control points (CPs) in the literature.

Feature matching : In this step, the correspondence between the features detected in the sensed image and those detected in the reference image is established. Various feature descriptors and similarity measures along with spatial relationships among the features are used for that purpose.

Transform model estimation : The type and parameters of the so-called mapping functions, aligning the sensed image with the reference image, are estimated. The parameters of the mapping functions are computed by means of the established feature correspondence.

Image resampling and transformation : The sensed image is transformed by means of the mapping functions. Image values in non-integer coordinates are computed by the appropriate interpolation technique.

The implementation of each registration step has its typical problems. First, we have to decide what kind of features is appropriate for the given task. The features should be distinctive objects, which are frequently spread over the images and which are easily detectable. Usually, the physical interpretability of the features is demanded. The detected feature sets in the reference and sensed images must have enough common elements, even in situations when the images do not cover exactly the same scene or when there are object occlusions or other unexpected changes. The detection methods should have good localization accuracy and should not be sensitive to the assumed image degradation. In an ideal case, the algorithm should be able to detect the same features in all projections of the scene regardless of the particular image deformation.

■ 7.2 IMAGE REGISTRATION ALGORITHMS

In computer vision, sets of data acquired by sampling the same scene or object at different times, or from different perspectives, will be in different coordinate systems. Image registration is the process of transforming the different sets of data into one coordinate system. Registration is necessary in order to be able to compare or integrate the data obtained from different measurements.

Medical imaging registration (e.g. for data of the same patient taken at different points in time) often additionally involves elastic (or non rigid) registration to cope with elastic deformations of the body parts imaged. Non rigid registration of medical images can also be used to register a patient's data to an anatomical atlas, such as the Talairach atlas for neuro imaging.

Image registration algorithms fall within two realms of classification:

- Area based methods.
- Feature based methods.

The original image is often referred to as the reference image and the image to be mapped onto the reference image is referred to as the target image. For area based image registration methods, the algorithm looks at the structure of the image via correlation metrics, Fourier properties and other means of structural analysis. However, most feature based methods, instead of looking at the overall structure of images, fine tunes its mapping to the correlation of image features: lines, curves, points, line intersections, boundaries, etc.

Transformation Model

Image registration algorithms can also be classified according to the transformation model used to relate the reference image space with the target image space. The first broad category of transformation models includes linear transformations, which are a combination of translation, rotation, global scaling, shear and perspective components. Linear transformations are global in nature, thus not being able to model local deformations. Usually, perspective components are not needed for registration, so that in this case the linear transformation is an affine one.

The second category includes 'elastic' or 'nonrigid' transformations. These transformations allow local warping of image features, thus providing support for local deformations. Nonrigid transformation approaches include polynomial wrapping, interpolation of smooth basis functions (thin-plate splines and wavelets), and physical continuum models (viscous fluid models and large deformation diffeomorphisms).

Search-based vs Direct Methods

Image registration methods can also be classified in terms of the type of search that is needed to compute the transformation between the two image domains. In search-based methods the effect of different image deformations is evaluated and compared. In direct methods, such as the Lucas Kanade method and phase-based methods, an estimate of the image deformation is computed from local image statistics and is then used for updating the estimated image deformation between the two domains.

Image Nature

Another useful classification is between single-modality and multi-modality registration algorithms. Single-modality registration algorithms are those intended to register images of the same modality (i.e. acquired using the same kind of imaging device), while multi-modality registration algorithms are those intended to register images acquired using different imaging devices.

There are several examples of multi-modality registration algorithms in the medical imaging field. Examples include registration of brain CT/MRI images or whole body PET/CT images for tumor localization, registration of contrast-enhanced CT images against non-contrast-enhanced CT images for segmentation of specific parts of the anatomy and registration of ultrasound and CT images for prostate localization in radiotherapy.

Other Classifications

Further ways of classifying an algorithm consist of the amount of data it is optimized to handle, the algorithm's application, and the central theory the algorithm is based around. Image registration has applications in remote sensing (cartography updating), medical imaging (change detection, tumor monitoring), and computer vision. Due to the vast applications to which image registration can be applied, it's impossible to develop a general algorithm optimized for all uses.

Image similarity-based methods : Image similarity-based methods are broadly used in medical imaging. A basic image similarity-based method consists of a transformation model, which is applied to reference image coordinates to locate their corresponding coordinates in the target image space, an image similarity metric, which quantifies the degree of correspondence between features in both image spaces achieved by a given transformation, and an optimization algorithm, which tries to maximize image similarity by changing the transformation parameters.

The choice of an image similarity measure depends on the nature of the images to be registered. Common examples of image similarity measures include Cross-correlation, Mutual information, Mean-square difference and Ratio Image Uniformity. Mutual information and its variant, Normalized Mutual Information, are the most popular image similarity measures for registration of multimodality images. Cross-correlation, Mean-square difference and Ratio Image Uniformity are commonly used for registration of images of the same modality.

■ 7.3 GEOMETRIC TRANSFORMATION OF IMAGES USING SPLINE-INTERPOLATION

To perform geometric transforms on discrete images such as a rotation or zooming we need to first fit the discrete data to a continuous function. This can be done using splines. B-splines can be used to interpolate and form the continuous image from the discrete samples.

Here we illustrate the use of splines in two-dimensions for transforming discrete images. When we apply a transformation (such as rotation or zooming) it becomes necessary to know the image intensity at a location in between the sample points. This is an interpolation problem and splines come in handy.

Application of collocation to transformation of deformed maps : Transformation of deformed maps into an existing coordinate system has been designed. Coordinate transformation is frequent task namely when a GIS is created from several spatial databases of different resolution and precision. For such purposes, content of a digital map has to be transformed to some reference coordinate system. Parameters of such transformation are estimated by means of control points, i.e. points with known coordinates of two or more associated coordinate systems.

The main problem is to design appropriate transformation equations that consider systematic local deformation of maps (e.g. paper shrinkage of an original map). To solve this problem properly, special transformation model was designed. This model is based on assumption that local deformations of a map are random. This assumption is statistically tested during the transformation procedure with the aid of measured coordinates of control points. Two kinds of random variables are therefore considered: measurement errors of coordinates and corrections of local deformations. The most adequate method for estimation of transformation parameters and prediction of resulting coordinates of a common transformed point seems to be method of collocation.

7.3.1 Plane-to-Plane Transformation

In many imaging systems, detected images are subject to geometric distortion introduced by perspective irregularities wherein the position of the camera(s) with respect to the scene alters the apparent dimensions of the scene geometry. Applying an affine transformation to a uniformly distorted image can correct for a range of perspective distortions by transforming the measurements from the ideal coordinates to those actually used. (For example, this is useful in satellite imaging where geometrically correct ground maps are desired.)

An affine transformation is an important class of linear 2-D geometric transformations which maps variables (*e.g.* pixel intensity values located at position in an input image) into new variables (*e.g.* in an output image) by applying a linear combination of translation, rotation, scaling and/or shearing (*i.e.* non-uniform scaling in some directions) operations.

How It Works

In order to introduce the utility of the affine transformation, consider the image

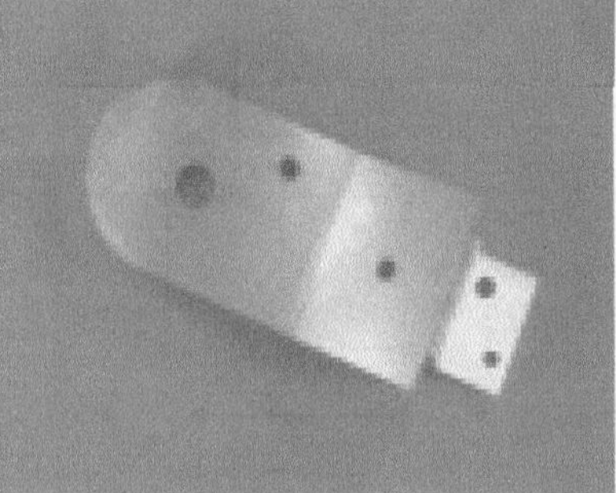

Fig. (7.1)

wherein a machine part is shown lying in a fronto-parallel plane. The circular hole of the part is imaged as a circle, and the parallelism and perpendicularity of lines in the real world are preserved in the image plane. We might construct a model of this part using these primitives; however, such a description would be of little use in identifying the part from

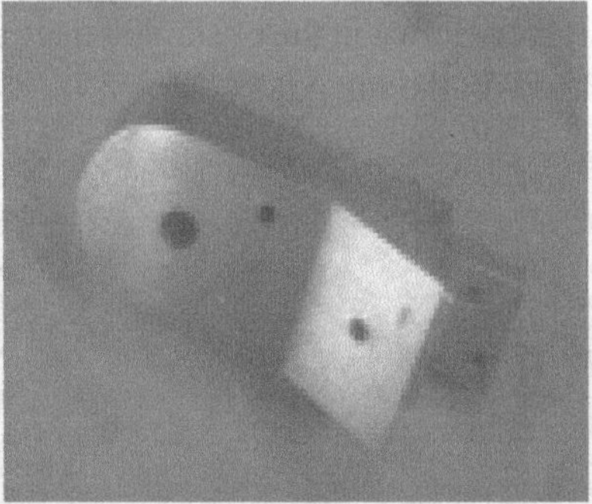

Fig. (7.2)

Here the circle is imaged as an ellipse, and orthogonal world lines are not imaged as orthogonal lines.

This problem of perspective can be overcome if we construct a shape description, which is *invariant* to perspective projection. Many interesting tasks within model based computer vision can be accomplished without recourse to Euclidean shape descriptions (*i.e.* those requiring absolute distances, angles and areas) and, instead, employ descriptions involving *relative* measurements (*i.e.* those which depend only upon the configuration's intrinsic geometric relations). These relative measurements can be determined directly from images. Figure 7.1 shows a hierarchy of planar transformations which are important to computer vision.

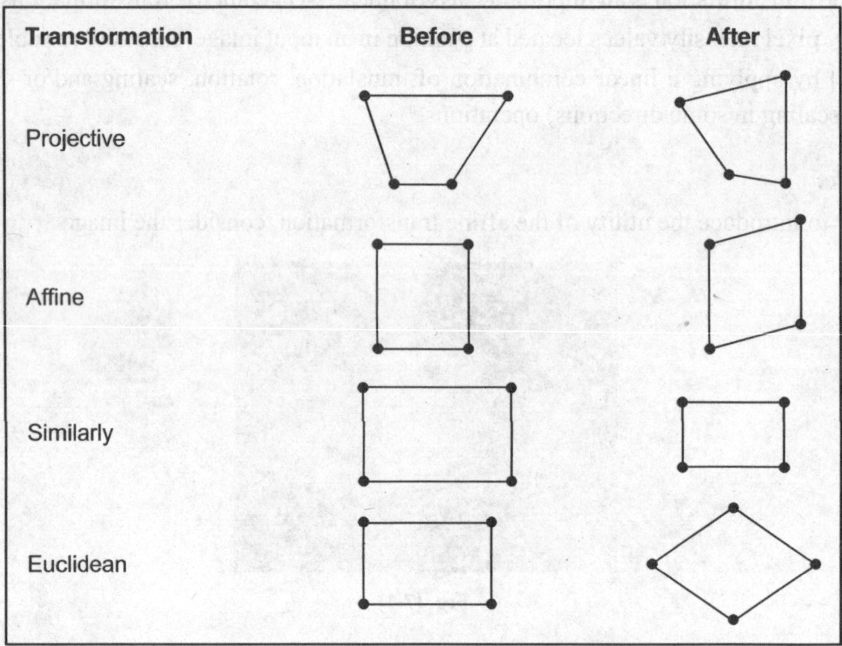

Fig. (7.3) Hierarchy of plane-to-plane transformation from Euclidean (where only rorations and translations are allowed) to projective (where a square can be transformed into any more general quadrilateral where no 3 points are collinear). Note that transformations lower in the table inherit the invariants of those above, but because they possess their own groups of definitive axioms as well, the converse is not true.

The transformation of the part face shown in the example image above is approximated by a planar *affine* transformation. (Compare this with the image

Fig. (7.4)

where the distance to the part is not large compared with its depth and, therefore, parallel object lines begin to converge. Because the scaling varies with depth in this way, a description to the level of *projective* transformation is required.) An affine transformation is equivalent to the composed effects of translation, rotation, isotropic scaling and shear.

The general affine transformation is commonly written in homogeneous coordinates as shown below:

$$\begin{vmatrix} x_2 \\ y_2 \end{vmatrix} = A \times \begin{vmatrix} x_1 \\ y_1 \end{vmatrix} + B$$

By defining only the B matrix, this transformation can carry out pure translation:

$$A = \begin{vmatrix} 1 & 0 \\ 0 & 1 \end{vmatrix}, B = \begin{vmatrix} b_1 \\ b_2 \end{vmatrix}$$

Pure rotation uses the A matrix and is defined as (for positive angles being clockwise rotations):

$$A = \begin{vmatrix} \cos(\theta) & -\sin(\theta) \\ \sin(\theta) & \cos(\theta) \end{vmatrix}, B = \begin{vmatrix} 0 \\ 0 \end{vmatrix}$$

Here, we are working in image coordinates, so the y axis goes downward. Rotation formula can be defined for when the y axis goes upward.

Similarly, pure scaling is:

$$A = \begin{vmatrix} a_{11} & 0 \\ 0 & a_{22} \end{vmatrix}, B = \begin{vmatrix} 0 \\ 0 \end{vmatrix}$$

(Note that several different affine transformations are often combined to produce a resultant transformation. The order in which the transformations occur is significant since a translation followed by a rotation is not necessarily equivalent to the converse.)

Since the general affine transformation is defined by 6 constants, it is possible to define this transformation by specifying the new output image locations of any three input image coordinate pairs.

Guidelines for Use : Most implementations of the affine operator allow the user to define a transformation by specifying to where 3 (or less) coordinate pairs from the input image re-map in the output image . (It is often the case, as with the implementation used here, that the user is restricted to re-mapping *corner coordinates* of the input image to *arbitrary* new coordinates in the output image.) Once the transformation has been defined in this way, the re-mapping proceeds by calculating, for each output pixel location , the corresponding input coordinates . If that input point is outside of the image, then the output pixel is set to the background value. Otherwise, the value of (i) the input pixel itself, (ii) the neighbor nearest to the desired pixel position, or (iii) a bilinear interpolation of the neighboring four pixels is used.

We will illustrate the operation of the affine transformation by applying a series of special-case transformations (*e.g.* pure translation, pure rotation and pure scaling) and then some more general transformations involving combinations of these.

Starting with the 256×256 binary artificial image

Fig. (7.5)

we can apply a translation using the affine operator in order to obtain the image

Fig. (7.6)

In order to perform this pure translation, we define a transformation by re-mapping a single point (*e.g.* the input image lower-left corner) to a new position at.

A pure rotation requires re-mapping the position of two corners to new positions. If we specify that the lower-left corner moves to and the lower-right corner moves to , we obtain

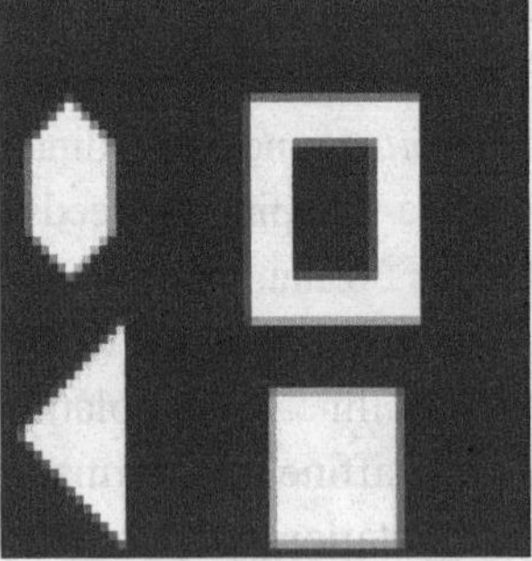

Fig. (7.7)

Similarly, reflection can be achieved by swapping the coordinates of two opposite corners, as shown in

Fig. (7.8)

Scaling can also be applied by re-mapping just two corners. For example, we can send the lower-left corner to , while pinning the upper-right corner down at , and thereby uniformly shrink the size of the image subject by a quarter, as shown in

Fig. (7.9)

Note that here we have also translated the image. Re-mapping any 2 points can introduce a combination of translation, rotation and scaling.

A general affine transformation is specified by re-mapping 3 points. If we re-map the input image so as to move the lower-left corner up to along the 45 degree oblique axis, move the upper-right corner down by the same amount along this axis, and pin the lower-right corner in place, we obtain an image which shows some shearing effects

Fig. (7.10)

Notice how parallel lines remain parallel, but perpendicular corners are distorted.

Affine transformations are most commonly applied in the case where we have a detected image which has undergone some type of distortion. The geometrically correct version of the input image can be obtained from the affine transformation by re-sampling the input image such that the information (or intensity) at each point is mapped to the correct position in a corresponding output image.

One of the more interesting applications of this technique is in remote sensing. However, because most images are transformed before they are made available to the image processing community, we will demonstrate the affine transformation with the terrestrial image.

Fig. (7.11)

which is a contrast-stretched (cutoff fraction = 0.9) version of

Fig. (7.10)

We might want to transform this image so as to map the door frame back into a rectangle. We can do this by defining a transformation based on a re-mapping of the (i) upper-right corner to a position 30%

Fig. (7.13)

lower along the y-axis, (ii) the lower-right corner to a position 10% lower along the x-axis, and (iii) pinning down the upper-left corner. The result is shown in figure 7.14.

Notice that we have defined a transformation, which works well for objects at the depth of the door frame, but nearby objects have been distorted because the affine plane transformation cannot account for distortions at widely varying depths.

It is common for imagery to contain a number of perspective distortions. For example, the original image

Fig. (7.14)

shows both affine and projective type distortions due to the proximity of the camera with respect to the subject. After affine transformation, we obtain figure 7.15.

Fig. (7.15)

Notice that the front face of the captain's house now has truly perpendicular angles where the vertical and horizontal members meet. However, the far background features have been distorted in the process and, furthermore, it was not possible to correct for the perspective distortion which makes the bow appear much larger than the hull.

7.3.2 Mapping

After the feature correspondence has been established the mapping function is constructed. It should transform the sensed image to overlay it over the reference one. The correspondence of the CPs from the sensed and reference images together with the fact that the corresponding CP pairs should be as close as possible after the sensed image transformation are employed in the mapping function design.

The task to be solved consists of choosing the type of the mapping function and its parameter estimation. The type of the mapping function should correspond to the assumed geometric deformation of the sensed image, to the method of image acquisition (e.g. scanner dependent distortions and errors) and to the required accuracy of the registration.

Fig. (7.16) Examples of various mapping functions : similarity transform (top left), affine transform (top right), perspective projection (bottom left), and elastic transform (bottom right).

In special situations when the geometric deformation is partially known, e.g. when there exists a model for the distortion caused by the acquisition device and/or the scene geometry, the pre-correction based on the inverse of the deformation can be performed the satellite orbit and the scanning geometry of the sensor.

Models of mapping functions can be divided into two broad categories according to the amount of image data they use as their support. Global models use all CPs for estimating one set of the mapping function parameters valid for the entire image. On the other hand, the local mapping functions treat the image as a composition of patches and the function parameters depend on the location of their support in the image. It leads to the tessellation of the image, usually a triangulation, and to the defining of parameters of the mapping function for each patch separately.

From another point of view, mapping functions can be categorized according to the accuracy of overlaying of the CPs used for computation of the parameters. Interpolating functions map the sensed image CPs on the reference image CPs exactly, whereas approximating functions try to find the best trade-off between the accuracy of the final mapping and other requirements imposed on the character of the mapping function. Since the CP coordinates are usually supposed not to be precise, the approximation model is more common.

■ 7.4 REGISTERING TWO IMAGES MANUALLY

This procedure will warp an image to match a reference image, using manually-obtained landmark points.

1. Identify a number of points that are landmarks visible in both images. In the example above, 6 protein spots were selected and labeled 1 to 6. The greater number of points that are selected, the more complicated the warping that can be done.
2. Click the ``Image no.'' settings to ensure the desired image numbers are shown.
3. Click on ``Obtain landmarks'' for the reference image and click on each spot. Press Space when finished. Keep a mental note of the order in which the points were clicked.
4. Repeat for the unknown image, making sure to click on the point in the second image that corresponds to a point in the first image.
5. Click ``Edit landmarks'' if desired to check the selected coordinates and edit if necessary.
6. If the unknown image needs to be rotated, click ``Rotate image''. This should be done before any warping. The landmark points will also be rotated, so that the same landmarks can be used for warping.
7. Click ``Calculate vector map''. This will create a new image illustrating the vector map using a color-coding scheme.
8. Click on the image to be unknown to select it.
9. Click ``Warp image'' to perform the warping alignment using the vector map.
10. (optional) Select ``Config..Configure..Main cursor'' and change the cursor to ``multiple crosshairs''. The corresponding spots will now be indicated by crosshair cursors on both images.

Notes :

1. If the image is both rotated and warped, rotation should be performed first. Better results are occasionally obtained if new control points are obtained after rotating.
2. Only one point is needed to rotate or warp an image. If a single point is used, the rotation or translation will be constant over the entire image. More points allow correction for more complicated twists and warps.
3. Don't click ``Correlate points'' when using manually-selected control points. Manually selected points are already correlated.
4. Rotation and warping are done independently for greater flexibility. If the image is known not to be rotated, you can click on ``Warp image'' to warp without rotating (and vice versa).
5. The control points are automatically moved to new locations after rotation and warping.
6. Avoid selecting control points for rotation near the exact center of the image, since the image is rotated around the center point. This might cause excessive twisting near the center of the image.

2D Gel Analysis

Although image registration will work with any type of image, it has been optimized for automatically aligning 2D protein gels. Aligning and measuring the hundreds of spots on a typical 2D gel can be tedious and time-consuming. Here is a procedure for performing densitometry on two 2D gels rapidly.

Part 1 : Obtaining Spot Coordinates :

1. Open the ``reference'' image. This should be the best 2D gel available, showing as many spots as possible.
2. Clean up the 2D gel image to eliminate streaks, edges, molecular weight markers, labels, borders, dirt, etc. The algorithm can match spots correctly if as few as half the points correspond to actual spots, but matching will be more accurate if no noise is present.
3. Filter the image (using ``Force background to fixed value'' or ``Remove low frequencies'' if necessary to ensure that the background is constant.
4. If some of the spots are faint, make them darker by increasing the contrast or by drawing/painting on the spot. This will not affect the results, as the spot signals are ignored at this step. (Don't save the modified image, however. The original image will be needed for densitometry).
5. Using the ``draw'' function; draw white lines on the image to separate any spots that are overlapping.
6. If the `unknown' gel is rotated with respect to the reference gel, better results will be obtained if you rotate it manually before starting. This can be done in Image Registration or by clicking ``Image...Rotate''.
7. Click ``Grain/Pattern counting''
8. Perform Grain Counting on both images, using appropriate threshold and minimum size values so that all the spots are counted.
9. Click ``Save Grain Results'' to write the spot locations to disk.
10. Make a backup copy of the grain counting data. This will be used during densitometry.
11. Save a copy of the modified, marked image for future reference. (Don't overwrite the original image).
12. Repeat for the other ``unknown'' images.

Part 2 : Generating Spot List :

1. Click ``Image.Image registration''.
2. Read the data points for reference image. This is a list of all the spots that were found, obtained from Grain Counting in part 1.
3. Repeat for unknown image.
4. Save match table - if something goes wrong or you wish to reanalyze, you can just click on ``Read match table'' (optional).
5. Create a landmarks file by taking a subset of the most salient points from the reference and `unknown' data. (See below for format). These can either be a list of manually aligned spots, or an uncorrelated list of the most significant spots. The landmarks file should be a list of at least 6 of the most reproducible spots on each image, or at least 6 aligned spots.
6. Read the landmarks file. If the landmarks file is a list of manually obtained landmarks, proceed to step 8.
7. Correlate points - If the landmarks file is a list of the most significant spots, but the correspondence between the spots is unknown, they must be correlated before generating a vector map. The image will attempt to calculate the correspondence using pattern-matching. The spots from the unknown image will be reordered so that the best statistical matching is shown. As the number of landmark spots increases, the difficulty in determining which unknown spot

corresponds to which reference spot increases by n. Thus, best results are obtained if the total number of landmarks to be determined from each image is kept below 100.

8. Calculate vector map - uses landmark spots from the previous steps to create a mapping of the `unknown' image onto the reference image.
9. The calculated shifts will be shown on a new image, with changes in red indicating horizontal shifts and changes in blue indicating vertical shifts. Thus, the color code would be:
   - o Green = large left shift
   - o Red = large right shift
   - o Yellow = large up shift
   - o Blue = large down shift

   Mixed vertical and horizontal shifts are indicated by intermediate colors. The landmark points and their vectors are superimposed on the map.
10. Referring to the displayed vector map, click ``Edit matching table'' and edit the match table to remove any incorrect links (see figure below). The vector map should be a smooth gradient of colors. All the displayed vectors should be roughly parallel to the vectors nearby. Any points containing two or more vectors should be inspected and the incorrect link removed in the editor. Any vectors wildly different from their neighbors should be inspected and removed if necessary.
11. Recalculate vector map and repeat the previous step until an accurate and reasonable vector map is obtained.
12. Once the correct matching has been obtained, click ``Save'' in the matching table editor to save the matches. This file can also be reloaded later if desired.
13. Create unwarped spot list - Changes the x,y coordinates of the data points from the unknown image to match the reference image. (Note that this does not warp the image.)
14. In the Spot List Editor, click `Save' to save the corrected spot coordinates for part 3.
15. The spot list can be used to create a composite image displaying the spots lined up in a rectangular array.

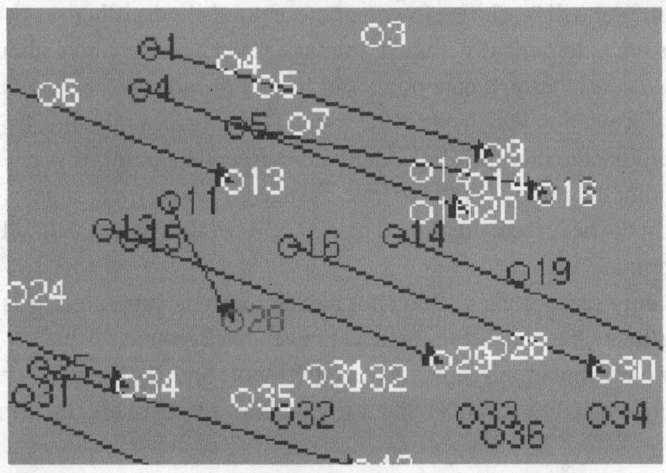

Fig. (7.17)

Part of a vector map showing an incorrect link that should be removed. The vectors point from landmark points on the unknown image to landmark points on the reference image. The numbers are user-specified point labels; black labels are from the unknown image, and white labels are from the reference image. In this example, the data files were created by grain/spot counting, so the labels are all numbers. The link from 11 to 28 is incorrect because it has a markedly different size and angle than its neighbors. The ``28'' is also shown in red because its coordinates were found in the landmarks file but not the data file. The link from 5 to 16 may also be incorrect.

Part 3 : Measuring the Signals in each Spot :

1. Reload the original, unmodified image.
2. Click on ``Spot densitometry''
3. Set pixel calibration, maximum signal, calibration factor, and background value or automatic background as desired.
4. Select data source:
   1. Spot list from image registration (kept in memory)
   2. Disk file in `spot list' format (see below for details)
5. Click `Accept'. The image will automatically perform densitometry on each spot and create a list.
6. Click ``Save'' on the editor box to save the results.

Notes :

- The data points should be loaded before creating the vector map from the landmark points in order to estimate the correct size to make the vector map. Otherwise, the vector map may be too small. If this happens, load the data points and click ``Calculate vector map'' again.
- The distance metric used in creating the vector map is appropriate for images of objects that have undergone elastic deformation or some equivalent shape change, such as 2D polyacrylamide gels being warped by temperature gradients. Some other types of images may require a different method for calculating the vector map. Contact author for assistance.
- Deleting links: If the numbers of points in the two data sets are unequal, some of the data points in one set will be closest to two or more points in the other set. Although most of these extra links are automatically pruned, tnimage is very conservative about pruning links. This means that occasionally, a data point will have 2 or more vectors pointing to it. It is usually obvious by inspection which one is incorrect. Deleting the entire line from the match table editor will remove the incorrect link and the incorrect data point. If you wish to keep the incorrect data point but remove only the link, change the x and y coordinates of its matching point to zeros. On the next recalculation, the point will still be plotted, but will be listed as an ``Unmatched point''.
- Currently only rectangular region spot densitometry is supported. It is recommended to set `Auto bkg/fuzzy k means' if there is an uneven background.
- The editor has a maximum capacity of 10,000 spots and 384K characters. These limits can be increased by changing RPOINTS and EDITSIZE, respectively, in xmtnimage.h and recompiling.

File formats for landmark and data point lists : The data points are stored in plain text files in the same format as the grain counting files produced by the image. The five-line grain counting header is optional, and is ignored if present. Lines starting with a # are ignored. Data points are stored one per line as shown below, in the order: label tab x-coordinate tab y-coordinate tab value. The label can be any string, but cannot contain white space. The x and y coordinates are distances in pixels from the upper left corner of the image. The data points do not have to be in any particular sequence.

All lines containing non-data must start with a #.

File format for single sets of data points : There are two data files: one for the reference image, containing the coordinates and labels of all the known spots, and one for the unknown image, containing all the data points to be remapped. The first 9 columns of each file are used. Columns are separated by white space. If a column is empty, values are set to 0. Columns cannot be skipped. A complete table is shown below. The columns for minx, miny, maxx, and maxy are used for densitometry. If the minx, miny, maxx, and maxy columns are omitted, the image asks for a spot size. Enter the width in pixels for the spots. In this case, all the spots will be assumed to be the same size.

Example data file with 5 columns :

```
# Size analysis of /home/tjnelson/data/30a/30a38a-filtered5.tif
# Largest signal    2793
# Most frequent size 23 (count=7)
# Largest object    457
# Label     x pos   y pos   Size   Signal
# All the above lines are ignored
calcineurin       566   149   149    422
trypsin           618   176   325   1018
S6_kinase         575   194    86    139
36                698   209   373   1015
49                694   238   413   1468
```

Example data file with 9 columns The additional columns are produced by tnimage's grain counting and are essential if the results are to be used for densitometry (The minima and maxima are the bounding box of the spot). Any calibration data is included in columns 10-12.

```
# Obj.  x pos  y pos  Size   Signal  Min.x  Min.y  Max.x  Max.y
1  158    6      18.02  20.10   155    5      162    12
2  152    13     5.12   5.4     151    12     156    15
3  262    18     11     11.5    260    17     265    23
```

In the above example, spot ``1'' is centered at (158, 6), and fits in a bounding box between (155,5) and (162, 12).

File format for 2 sets of data points (a.k.a. match table) (Created by ``Save match table'') These files contain the two original data sets. If you clicked ``correlate points'', the Unknown data set will be permuted so that identified corresponding points are on the same line. Any unmatched data points are listed at the end.

```
#Ref Ref.x Ref.y Unk Unk.x Unk.y xmin1 ymin1 xmax1 ymax1 xmin2
1  158  6     1  158  6     155  5     162  12   155
2  152  13    2  152  13    151  12    156  15   151
3  262  18    3  262  18    260  17    265  23   260
4  276  18    4  276  18    275  17    278  21   275
5  238  22    5  238  22    234  21    243  30   234
```

#Unmatched reference points

11 272 133 None 0 0 259 132 297 158 0

Unmatched unknown points

None 0 0 3 1170 101 0 0 0 0 1167

(continued)

ymin2	xmax2	ymax2	Score
5	162	12	20
12	156	15	5
17	265	23	11
17	278	21	3
21	243	30	35
0	0	0	0
100	1178	114	0

Unwarped Spot list and Warped spot list - contains spot name, spot x, spot y, xmin, ymin, xmax, and ymax of each spot after remapping (Created by ``Create warped spot list'' or ``Create unwarped spot list''). This format is the same as the original data files with the addition of an extra column for Identity. This means files of both types can also be used for spot densitometry. The unwarped spot list shows the spots in their original locations, along with their identification. This would be the appropriate file to create if you did not warp the image. The warped spot list shows the spots in their new locations after warping. This would be the appropriate file if you warped the image.

Unwarped spot list

#Label	orig.x	orig.y	Size	Signal	xmin	ymin	xmax	ymax	Identity
1	398	97	374	1103	395	96	402	103	9
spot_21	1905	117	32	39	1888	98	1905	117	cytochrome_C
spot_22	1509	153	70	112	1491	134	1509	153	actin
25	1817	157	123	177	1802	139	1817	157	protein-44
27	679	185	133	269	659	165	679	185	1234

This means spot ``spot_21'' is centered at (1905, 117), is bounded by a rectangle from (1888, 98) to (1905, 117), and was calculated to be the same as the cytochrome_C spot in the reference image.

Landmark list containing corresponding points and locations This file shows the label and x and y coordinates of each known landmark and of its counterpart in the unknown image. The file has to be created manually from the data point files. If the point correspondences are unknown, clicking ``Correlate points'' will rearrange the right 3 columns to put matching points on the same line.

#ref	ref x	ref y	unk	unk x	unk y
20	494	145	40	461	116
28	503	185	49	468	152
29	486	189	53	452	163
46	430	227	65	376	196
42	462	221	67	418	198
49	694	238	68	653	200

In the above example, spot ``20'' on the reference image is centered at (494, 145), and corresponds to spot ``40'', which is centered at (461, 116) on the unknown image.

■ 7.5 STEREO IMAGING

Stereo imaging is the audio jargon term used for that aspect of sound recording and reproduction concerning spatial locations of the performers, both laterally and in depth. An image is 'good' if the performers can be effortlessly located; 'bad' if there is no hope of doing so. A well-made stereo recording, properly reproduced, can provide good imaging within the front quadrant; a well-made Ambisonic recording, properly reproduced, can offer good imaging all around the listener and even including height information.

For many listeners, good imaging adds markedly to the pleasure of reproduced music. One may speculate that this is due to the evolutionary importance to humans of knowing where sounds are coming from, and that imaging may therefore be more important than some purely esthetic considerations in satisfying the listener. Listeners do exist who have difficulty paying attention to the musical content of a recording if the imaging is not good.

The quality of the imaging arriving at the listener's ear depends on numerous factors, of which the most important is the original "miking", that is, the choice and arrangement of the recording microphones (where "choice" refers here not to the brands chosen, but to the size and shape of the microphone diaphragms, and "arrangement" refers to microphone placement and orientation relative to other microphones). This is partly because miking simply affects imaging more than any other factor, and because, if the miking spoils the imaging, nothing later in the chain can recover it.

If miking is done well, then quality of imaging can be used to evaluate components in the record/playback chain (remembering that once the imaging is destroyed, it cannot be recovered). It is worth noting that only a handful of recordings are miked for optimal imaging, and what usually passes for stereo, while being two-channel recording, is not true stereo because the imaging information is incoherent.

Imaging is usually thought of in the context of recording with two or more channels, though single-channel recording may convey depth information convincingly, and at least one expert thinks it can convey information about lateral placement, also.

Let us consider a simplified approach to the mathematics of the problem in order to aid understanding of the tasks involved. We will consider a set up using two cameras in *stereo*. — other methods that involve stereo are similar. Let's consider a simplified optical set up:

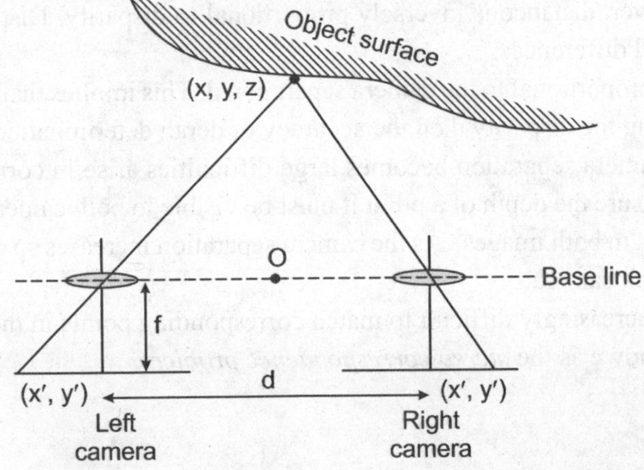

Fig. (7.18) A simplified stereo imaging system.

Fig. 7.3 shows :

- 2 cameras with their optical axes parallel and separated by a distance d.
- Lline connecting the camera lens centres is called the *baseline.*
- Let baseline be perpendicular to the line of sight of the cameras.
- Let the x axis of the three-dimensional world coordinate system be parallel to the baseline
- Let the origin O of this system be mid-way between the lens centres.

Consider a point (x,y,z), in three-dimensional world coordinates, on an object.

Let this point have image coordinates and in the left and right image planes of the respective cameras.

Let f be the focal length of both cameras, the perpendicular distance between the lens centre and the image plane. Then by similar triangles:

$$\frac{xt_l}{f} = \frac{x + d/2}{z} \quad \text{...(1)}$$

$$\frac{xf_r}{f} = \frac{x - d/2}{z} \quad \text{...(2)}$$

$$\frac{yf_l}{f} = \frac{yl_r}{f} = \frac{y}{z} \quad \text{...(3)}$$

Solving for (*x, y, z*) gives:

$$x = \frac{d(xf_l + xf_r)}{2(xf_l - xf_r)^r} \quad \text{...(4)}$$

$$y = \frac{d(yf_l + yf_r)}{2(yf_l - yf_r)^r} \quad \text{...(5)}$$

$$z = \frac{df}{xf_l - xf_r} \quad \text{...(6)}$$

The quantity which appears in each of the above equations is called the *disparity*.

There are several practical problems with this set up:

- Near objects accurately acurately but impossible for far away objects. Normally, d and f are fixed. However, distance is inversely proportional to disparity. Disparity can only be measured in pixel differences.
- Disparity is proportional to the camera separation d. This implies that if we have a fixed error in determining the disparity then the accuracy of depth determination will increase with d.

However as the camera separation becomes large difficulties arise in correlating the two camera images. In order to measure the depth of a point it must be visible to both cameras and we must also be able to identify this point in both images. As the camera separation increases so do the differences in the scene as recorded by each camera.

Thus it becomes increasingly difficult to match corresponding points in the images.

This problem is known as the *stereo correspondence problem*.

■ SUMMARY

- Image registration is the process of overlaying two or more images of the same scene taken at different times, from different viewpoints, and/or by different sensors. It geometrically aligns two images—the reference and sensed images. The present differences between images are introduced due to different imaging conditions.
- Image registration is a crucial step in all image analysis tasks in which the final information is gained from the combination of various data sources like in image fusion, change detection, and multichannel image restoration.
- Image registration, as it was mentioned above, is widely used in remote sensing, medical imaging, computer vision etc. In general, its applications can be divided into four main groups according to the manner of the image acquisition.
- Images of a scene and a model of the scene are registered. The model can be a computer representation of the scene, for instance maps or digital elevation models (DEM) in GIS, another scene with similar content (another patient), 'average' specimen, etc. The aim is to localize the acquired image in the scene/model and/or to compare them.
- Image registration is the process of transforming the different sets of data into one coordinate system. Registration is necessary in order to be able to compare or integrate the data obtained from different measurements.
- Image registration algorithms can also be classified according to the transformation model used to relate the reference image space with the target image space.
- To perform geometric transforms on discrete images such as a rotation or zooming we need to first fit the discrete data to a continuous function. This can be done using splines. B-splines can be used to interpolate and form the continuous image from the discrete samples.
- In many imaging systems, detected images are subject to geometric distortion introduced by perspective irregularities wherein the position of the camera(s) with respect to the scene alters the apparent dimensions of the scene geometry.
- Applying an affine transformation to a uniformly distorted image can correct for a range of perspective distortions by transforming the measurements from the ideal coordinates to those actually used.
- After the feature correspondence has been established the mapping function is constructed. It should transform the sensed image to overlay it over the reference one. The correspondence of the CPs from the sensed and reference images together with the fact that the corresponding CP pairs should be as close as possible after the sensed image transformation are employed in the mapping function design.
- Stereo imaging is the audio jargon term used for that aspect of sound recording and reproduction concerning spatial locations of the performers, both laterally and in depth. An image is 'good' if the performers can be effortlessly located; 'bad' if there is no hope of doing so.
- A well-made stereo recording, properly reproduced, can provide good imaging within the front quadrant; a well-made Ambisonic recording, properly reproduced, can offer good imaging all around the listener and even including height information.

Review Questions

1. Explain the image registration process.
2. Discuss the Geometric Transformation and write short notes on the following: Plane-to-Plane transformation & Mapping.
3. Explain the concepts of Stereo Imaging.
4. Explain the Algorithms to Establish Correspondence.
5. Explain the Algorithms to Recover Depth.

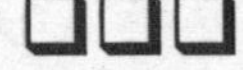

8

IMAGE SEGMENTATION

The term segmentation stands for division, into similar parts. So image segmentation refer to the process of partitioning a digital image into multiple segments. Segmentation subdivides an image into it's constitute regions or objects. The level to which the subdivision is carried depends on the problem being solved. That is, segmentation should stop when the objects of interests in an application have been isolated. Image segmentation algorithms generally are based on one of two basic properties of intensity values, discontinuity and similarity.

The segmentation of images has always been a key problem in computer vision. Up to the early 80ies bottom-up techniques like edge detection and split-and-merge algorithms were the primary focus of research. However, by that time people realized that "perfect segmentation " would not be possible without incorporation of higher level knowledge. Thus the focus shifted towards model based techniques like snakes and methods based on geometric models. These techniques generally give very satisfying segmentation results. However, on a number of reasons which have been underemphasized in the past, the bottom-up techniques are still necessary as a natural complement of the top-down approaches:

- If the model base consists of a great number of different models, say 10 000, we need effective strategies to choose, among all models in the database, those models which have a great chance of being a correct description of the image content. If we lack a-priori scene knowledge this can only be done by bottom-up analysis of the image itself.
- Many model based techniques are based on iterative improvement of an initial model configuration. Appropriate low-level information is needed to find an initial estimate of the model that ensures convergence.
- Often one and the same image may be analyzed using several different models depending on the task to be fulfilled. This is typically the case with content based retrieval in image databases. A primary segmentation could be stored as a common starting point for all those tasks.

These examples show that the full power of top-down methods can only be exploited if they are built upon a well defined bottom-up analysis. Its main goal is to divide an image into parts that have a strong correlation with objects or areas of the real world contained in the image.

In computer vision, segmentation refers to the process of partitioning a digital image into multiple regions (sets of pixels). The goal of segmentation is to simplify and/or change the representation of an image into something that is more meaningful and easier to analyze. Image segmentation is typically used to locate objects and boundaries (lines, curves, etc.) in images.

The result of image segmentation is a set of regions that collectively cover the entire image, or a set of contours extracted from the image. Each of the pixels in a region are similar with respect to some characteristic or computed property, such as color, intensity, or texture. Adjacent regions are significantly different with respect to the same characteristic(s).

Some of the practical applications of image segmentation are:

- Medical Imaging
  - — Locate tumors and other pathologies
  - — Measure tissue volumes
  - — Computer-guided surgery
  - — Diagnosis
  - — Treatment planning
  - — Study of anatomical structure
- Locate objects in satellite images (roads, forests, etc.)
- Face recognition
- Fingerprint recognition
- Automatic traffic controlling systems
- Machine vision

Several general-purpose algorithms and techniques have been developed for image segmentation. Since there is no general solution to the image segmentation problem, these techniques often have to be combined with domain knowledge in order to effectively solve an image segmentation problem for a problem domain.

Complete segmentation - set of disjoint regions uniquely corresponding with objects in the input image, Cooperation with higher processing levels which use specific knowledge of the problem domain is necessary.

Partial segmentation - regions do not correspond directly with image objects, Image is divided into separate regions that are homogeneous with respect to a chosen property such as brightness, color, reflectivity, texture, etc.

In a complex scene, a set of possibly overlapping homogeneous regions may result. The partially segmented image must then be subjected to further processing, and the final image segmentation may be found with the help of higher-level information.

■ 8.1 IMAGE SEGMENTATION

A central problem, called *segmentation*, is to distinguish objects from background. For intensity images (i.e., those represented by point-wise intensity levels) four popular approaches are: threshold techniques, edge-based methods, region-based techniques, and connectivity-preserving relaxation methods. Threshold techniques, which make decisions based on local pixel information, are effective when the intensity levels of the objects fall squarely outside the range of levels in the background. Because spatial information is ignored, however, blurred region boundaries can create havoc.

Edge-based methods center around contour detection: their weakness in connecting together broken contour lines make them, too, prone to failure in the presence of blurring.

A region-based method usually proceeds as follows: the image is partitioned into connected regions by grouping neighboring pixels of similar intensity levels. Adjacent regions are then merged under some criterion involving perhaps homogeneity or sharpness of region boundaries. Over stringent criteria create fragmentation; lenient ones overlook blurred boundaries and over merge. Hybrid techniques using a mix of the methods above are also popular.

A connectivity-preserving relaxation-based segmentation method, usually referred to as the *active contour model*, was proposed recently. The main idea is to start with some initial boundary shape represented in the form of spline curves, and iteratively modify it by applying various shrink/expansion operations according to some energy function. Although the energy-minimizing model is not new, coupling it with the maintenance of an ``elastic'' contour model gives it an interesting new twist. As usual with such methods, getting trapped into a local minimum is a risk against which one must guard; this is no easy task.

In contrast to the heuristic nature of these approaches, computational geometry suggests a more algorithmic tack. One would first formalize a mathematical criterion for the ``goodness'' of a given segmentation. This would allow us to formulate the segmentation problem as an optimization problem under certain geometric constraints.

The objective function that one would seek to optimize is the *interclass variance* that is used in discriminant analysis. Experimentation seems to suggest that this approach might be very promising. Formally, the criterion is described as follows. Imagine that an image is to be partitioned into two connected sets and. The average intensity levels of the sets are denoted by and, respectively. Then, the objective is to minimize the potential function.

Computational geometry provides several tools (for instance, hand probing, Monge matrix searching) that lead to efficient solutions for optimal segmentation, as long as one is only interested in separation of an object defined by monotone chains. Without such assumptions the problem is NP-hard, and efficient heuristics remain to be found.

Discriminant analysis has also been applied successfully to the problem of transforming an intensity image into a binary black white picture. This line of research relates directly to what has long been an active line of research in computational geometry, point clustering: Partition a set of points in into clusters so that some inter-cluster criterion is minimized.

■ 8.2 QUICK SEGMENTATION

Quick segmentation Uses a highly efficient segmentation algorithm to separate features, converting an image into a line drawing in which the lines depict outlines of objects in the image. Its purpose is to reduce the complexity of the image for pattern counting or further analysis. The algorithm is rapid but does not always give perfect segmentation.

The image to be segmented should be converted to grayscale and 8 bits/pixel for best results. If the segmentation appears incorrect, try one or more of the following:

- Select ``Color..Colorgrayscale'' to make sure tnimage is handling the image as grayscale. (Image may appear to be shades of gray and still be some other colortype).
- Invert the colors and segment the negative of the image. This often works if areas in the background were outlined.
- Try changing Maximum Signal from Black to White.
- Try changing Structuring element from N8 to N4.

- Change the brightness or contrast of the image.
- Filter the image to flatten the background using the following parameters:
  — Filter type: Remove low frequencies
  — Kernel: 1515
  — Kernel multiplier: 2
  — Amount of filtering: 100

The structuring element is the morphological kernel that determines how pixels are added or removed. Two structuring elements can be selected in tnimage:

- N4 consists of the 4 closest pixels, directly above, below, left, and right of each pixel.
- N8 consists of all 8 of the nearest neighbors to the pixel. N8 generally produces a smoother result, but takes longer.

This parameter is not used by watershed segmentation, which uses the ``Watershed kernel size'' parameter instead.

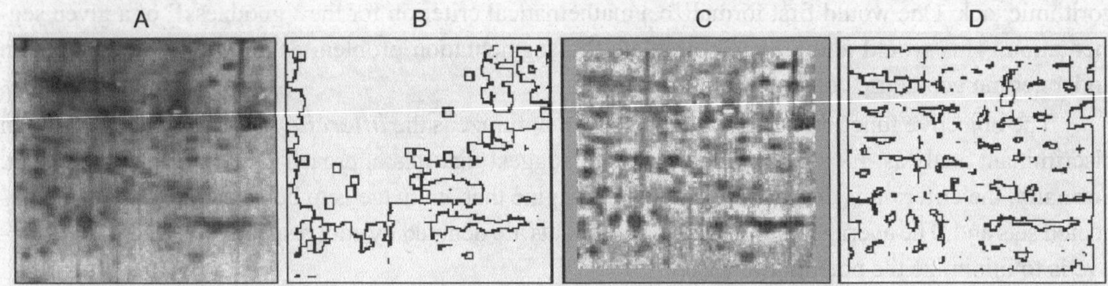

Fig. (8.1)

Quick segmentation of an image of a 2D protein gel.

A Original image

B Quick segmentation classifies much of upper left of image as a big feature.

C Same image filtered to remove low frequencies (kernel = 15x15, multiplier = 1).

D Quick segmentation of filtered image (threshold = 180).

Binary vs Graylevel - Binary filtering produces a solid white or black result, while graylevel filtering retains the original shades of gray. This is also not used by segmentation.

Maximum signal - If the features of interest in an image are black, this should be set to black. For grayscale erosion, switching the maximum signal is the same as switching from erosion to dilation.

Threshold - Determines the cutoff value for deciding whether a pixel is a feature or the background. A higher threshold causes more pixels to be considered features and produces more lines in the segmentation.

Watershed kernel - Used for watershed segmentation instead of structuring element. Determines distance from pixel to be considered as part of a neighborhood group. Large values will take a long time.

Notes :

1. For quick segmentation, a threshold that is too high or too low will produce an all-white image.
2. For watershed segmentation, excessive low-pass smoothing can result in no watersheds being found, while no smoothing can result in over-segmentation.

Contour Map Uses the quick segmentation algorithm to create a new image consisting of contours following areas of steepest gradient. The image should be low-pass filtered first to avoid drawing circles around small noise features. The number of contours is determined by the ``Contour sep'' setting. A larger value results in fewer lines but is faster. The actual number of contours also depends on the image. The product is still an image and does not contain vectorized data. Note that it is not a true iso-intensity contour map since the number of lines is determined by the gradient.

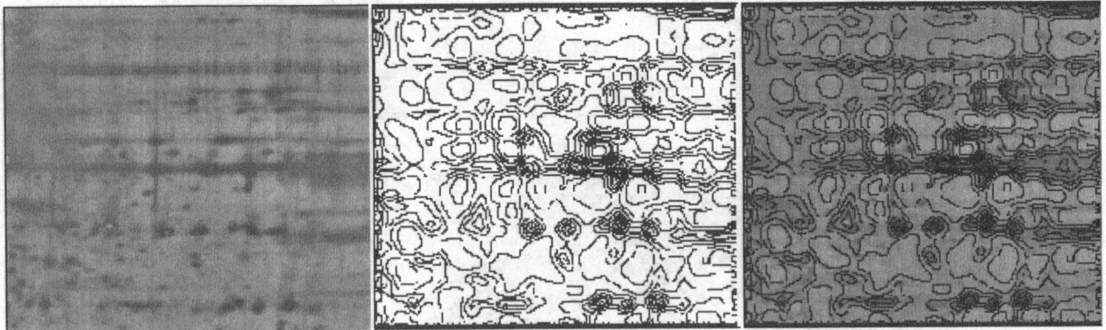

Fig. (8.2)

Contour map Image was low-pass filtered with a 99 kernel before creating the map using a spacing of 10. Left: Original, Center:Contours, Right: Contours superimposed on original image.

8.3 WATERSHED SEGMENTATION

Watershed segmentation finds pixels at the midpoints between features by treating the pixel values as topographic elevations. The areas between features become catchment basins which depict the influence zones in the image (see figure below). Images should be low-pass filtered first to avoid over-segmentation.

The output is a new image in which each catchment basin is given a different gray scale value. The actual watershed points are those points on the new image with a value of 0. These points can be selected by inverting and increasing the contrast, or by applying the formula

$$\text{if } (i>0)\ i=255$$

to the image. These edges form a tessellation of the image while the constant color regions indicate the catchment basins. If the gray scale of the image is inverted first, the result is that lines are drawn connecting the highest elevation routes through the features instead of around them, the resultant image is shown in figure 8.5.

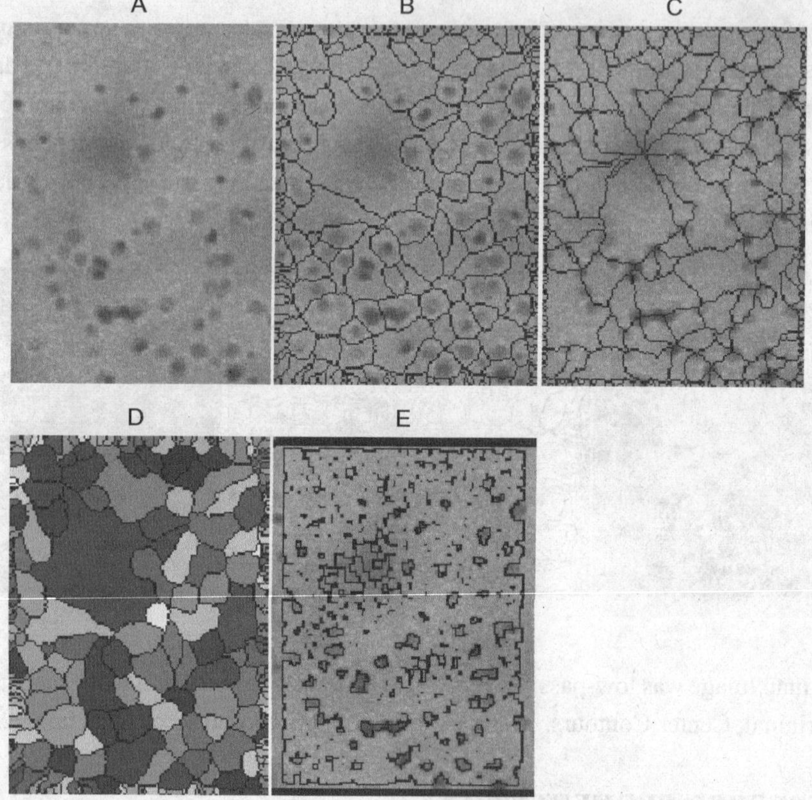

Fig. (8.5) Watershed segmentation of an emulsion autoradiagram.

A Original image

B Watershed segmentation superimposed on the image. The image was low-pass filtered twice using a 55 kernel before segmentation. The segmentation edges (i=0 points) were pasted over the original using the ``Mask..Add'' function.

C Watershed segmentation of grayscale-inverted image, created as in A except the image colors were inverted before segmentation. The watersheds now track the closest distance between the grains instead of the greatest distance between them.

D Actual watershed segmentation obtained in B, with a spectrum colormap added.

E Quick segmentation result superimposed on the same image in A for comparison.

Image was filtered once with a 15 × 15 low frequency removal filter, using a kernel multiplier of 2 before quick segmentation. Line around outside is an edge artifact caused by the filtering.

Simple segmentation problems :

- Contrasted objects on a uniform background.
- Simple assembly tasks, blood cells, printed characters, etc.
- Image data ambiguity.
- Information noise.

Totally correct and complete segmentation of complex scenes usually cannot be achieved in this processing phase. A reasonable aim is to use partial segmentation as an input to higher level processing.

■ 8.4 THRESHOLDING

8.4.1 Single Thresholding

A greyscale image is turned into a binary (black and white) image by first choosing a grey level T in the original image, and then tu rning every pixel black or white according to whether its grey value is greater than or less than T :

$$\text{A pixel becomes} \begin{cases} \text{white if its grey level is} > T \\ \text{black if its grey level is} \leq T \end{cases}$$

Thresholding is a vital part of image segmentation, where we wish to isolate objects from the background. It is also an important component of robot vision. Thresholding can be done very simply in MATLAB. Suppose we have an 8 bit image, stored as the variable X. Then the command

$$X > T$$

will perform the thresholding. We can view the result with imshow. For example, the command

```
r=imread('rice.tif');
imshow(r),figure,imshow(r>110)
```

will produce the image shown in figure 8.6. The resulting image can then be further processed to find the number, or average size of the grains.

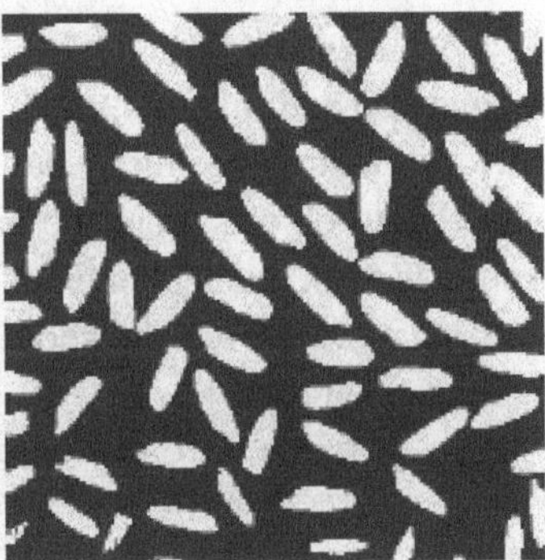

Fig. (8.6) Threshold image of rice grains.

To see how this works, recall that in MATLAB, an operation on a single number, when applied to a matrix, is interpreted as being applied simultaneously to all elements of the matrix. The command $X > T$ will thus return I (for true) for all those pixels for which they grey values are greater than T, and 0 (for false) for all those pixels for which the grey values are less than or equal to T. We thus end up with a matrix of 0's and 1's, which can be viewed as a binary image.

The rice image shown above has light grains on a dark background; an image with dark objects over light background may be treated the same :

```
b=imread('bacteria.tif');
imshow(b),figure,imshow(b>100)
```

will produce the images shown in figure 8.7.

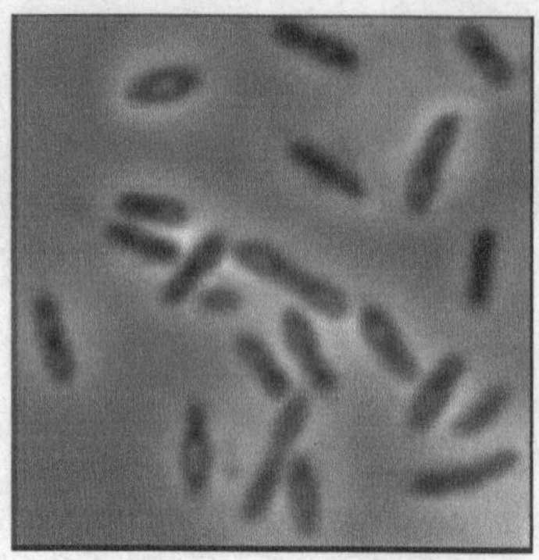
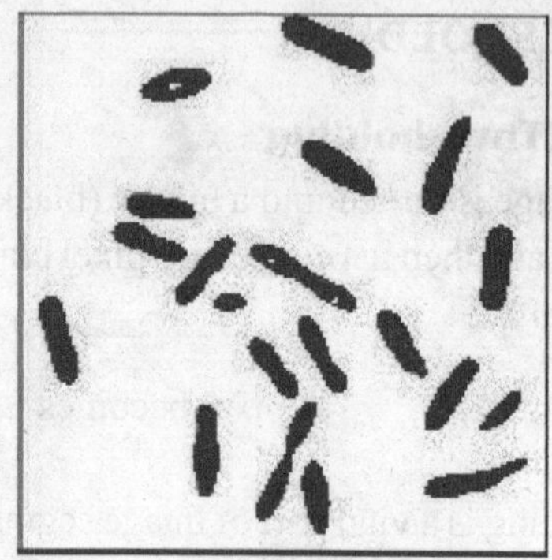

Fig. (8.7) Thresholded image of bacteria.

As well as the above method, MATLAB has the im2bw function, which thresholds an image *of any data type,* using the general syntax.

```
im2bw(image,level)
```

where level is a value between 0 and 1 (inclusive), indicatin the fraction of grey values to be turned white. This command will work on greyscale, coloured and indexed images of data type uint8, uint16 or double. For example, the thresholded rice and bacteria images above could be obtained using

```
im2bw(r,0.43);
im2bw(b,0.39);
```

The im2bw function automatically scales the value level to a grey value appropriate to the image type, and then performs a thresholding by our first method.

As well as isolating objects from the background, thresholding provides a very simple way of showing hidden aspects of an image. For example, the image paper.tif appears all white, as nearly all the grey values are very high. However, thresholding at a high level produces an image of far greater interest. We can use the commands.

```
p=imread('paper1.tif');
imshow(p),figure,imshow(p>241)
```

to provide the image shown in figure 8.8.

Fig. (8.8) The paper image and result after thresholding.

8.4.2 Double Thresholding

Here we choose two values T_1 and T_2 and apply a thresholding operation as :

$$\text{A pixel becomes} \begin{cases} \text{white if its grey level is between } T_1 \text{ and } T_2 \\ \text{black if its grey level is otherwise.} \end{cases}$$

We can implement this by a simple variation on the above method :

$$X > T_1 \text{ and } X < T_2$$

Since the ampersand acts as a logical "and", the result will only produce a one where both inequalities are satisfied. Consider the following sequence of commands, which start by producing an 8-bit grey version of the indexed image spine.tif:

```
[x,map]=imread('spine.tif');
s=uint8(256*ind2gray(x,map));
imshow(s),figure,imshow(s>115 & s<125)
```

The output is shown in figure 8.9. Note how double thresholding brings out subtle features of the spine which single thresholding would be unable to do. We can obtain similar results using im2bw:

```
imshow(im2bw(x,map,0.45)&~{}im2bw(x,map,0.5))}
```

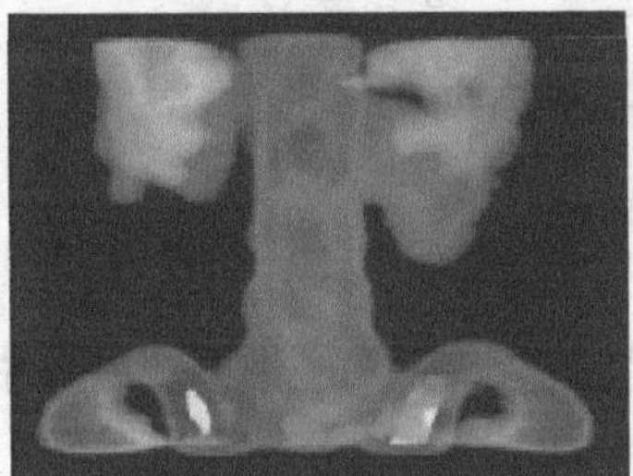
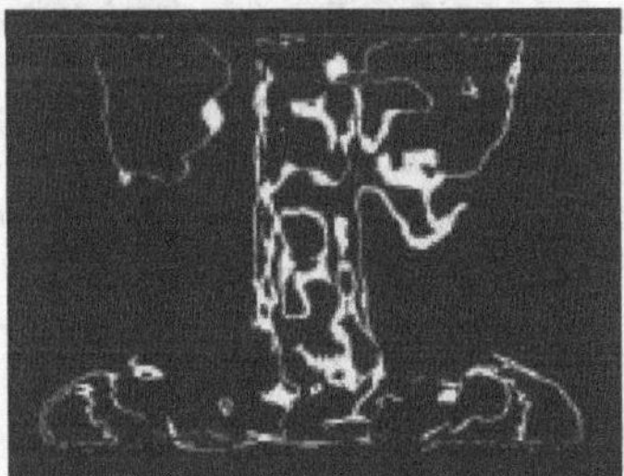

Fig. (8.9) The image spine.tif an the result after double thresholding.

but this is somewhat slower because of all the extra computation involved when dealing with an indexed image.

■ 8.5 APPLICATIONS OF THRESHOLDING

We have seen that thresholding can be useful in the following situations :

1. When we want to remove unnecessary detail from an image, to concentrate on essentials. Examples of this were given in the rice and bacteria images: by removing all grey level information, the rice and bacteria were reduced to binary blobs. But this information may be all we need to investigate sizes, shapes, or numbers of blobs.
2. To bring out hidden detail. This was illustrated with paper and spine images. In both, the detail was obscured because of the similarly of the grey levels involved.

But thresholding can be vital for other purposes. We list a few more :

3. When we want to remove a varying background from text or a drawing. We can simulate a varying background by taking the image text.tif and placing it on a random background. This can be easily implemented wi th some simple MATLAB commands :

```
r=rand(256)*128+127;
t=imread('text.tif');
tr=uint8(r,*double(not(t)));
imshow(tr)
```

The first command simply uses the rand function (which produces matrices of uniformly generated random numbers between 0.0 and 1.0), and scales the result so the random numbers are between 127 and 255. We then read in the text image, which shows white text on a dark background.

The third command does several things at once: not(t) reverses the text image so as to have black text on a white background; double changes the numeric type so that the matrix can be used with arithmetic operations; finally the result is multiplied into the random matrix, and the whole thing converted to uint8 for display. The result is shown on the left in figure 8.10.

Fig. (8.10) Text on a varying background, and thresholding.

If we threshold this image and display the r esult with

```
imshow(tr>100)
```

the result is shown on the right in figure 8.10, and the background has been completely removed.

■ 8.6 ADAPTIVE THRESHOLDING

Sometimes it is not possible to obtain a single threshold value which will isolate an object completely. This may happen if both the object and its background vary. For example, suppose we take the circles image and adjust it so that both the circles and the background vary in brightness across the image.

```
c=imread('circles.tif');
x=ones(256,1)*[1:256];
c2=double(c).*(x/2+50)+(1-double(c)).*x/2;
c3=uint(255*mat2gray(c2));
```

Figure 8.11 shows an attempt at thresholding, using graythresh.

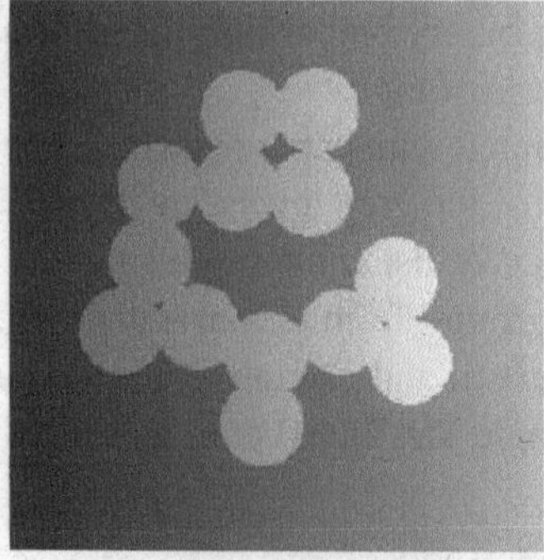

(a) Circles image : c3

(b) Thresholding attempt : ct

Fig. (8.11) An attempt at thresholding.

```
t=graythresh(c3)
t=0.4196
ct=im2bw(c3,t);
```

As you see, the result is not particularly good; not all of the object has been isolated from its background. Even if different thresholds are used, the results are similar. Figure 8.12 illustrates the reason why a single thr eshold cannot work. In this figure the image is being ashown as a function; the threshold is shown on the fight as a horizontal plane. It can be seen that no position of the plane can cut off the circles from the background.

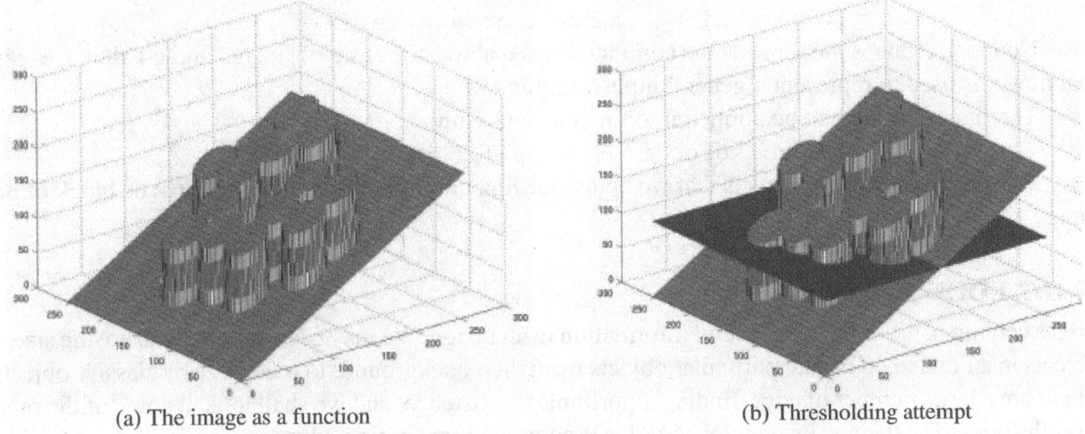

(a) The image as a function (b) Thresholding attempt

Fig. (8.12) All attempt at thresholding—functional version.

What can be done in a situationsituation like this is to cut the i mage into small pieces, and apply thresholding to each piece individually. Since in this particular example the brightness changes from left to right, we shall cut up the image into four pieces :

```
p1=c3(:, 1:64);
p2=c3(:, 65:128);
p3=c3(:, 129:192);
p4=c3(:, 193:256);
```

Figure 8.13(a) shows how the image is sliced up. Now we can threshold each piece:

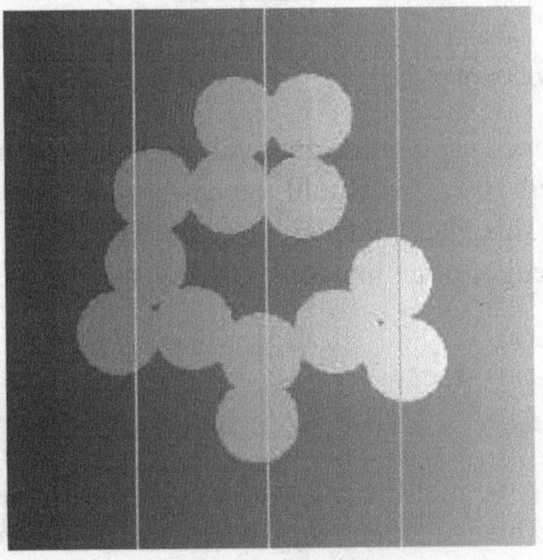

(a) Cutting up the image

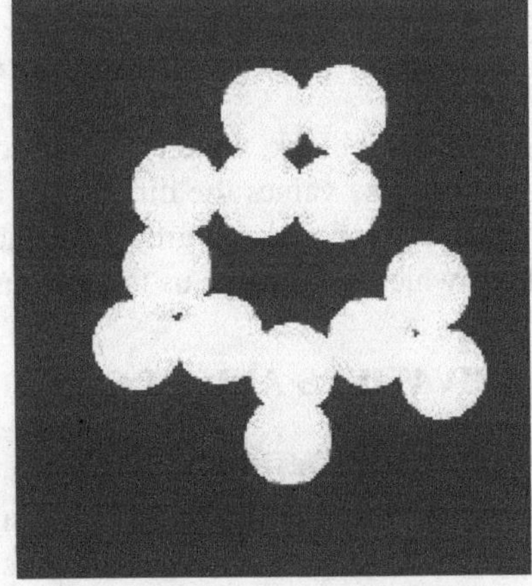

(b) Thresholding each part separately

Fig. (8.13) Adaptive thresholding.

```
g1=im2bw(p1,graythresh(p1));
g2=im2bw(p2,graythresh(p2));
g3=im2bw(p3,graythresh(p3));
g4=im2bw(p4,graythresh(p4));
```

and how display them as a single image :

```
imshow([g1 g2 g3 g4])
```

and the result is shown in figure 8.13(b). The above commands can be d one much more simply by using the command blkproc, which applies a particular function to each block of the image. We can define our function with

```
fun=inline('im2bw(x,graythresh(x))');
```

Notice that this is the same as the commands used above to create g1, g2, g3 and g4 above, except that now x is used to represent a general input variable.

The function can then be applied it to the image t3 with

```
t4=blkproc(t3,[256,64],fun);
```

What this command means is that we apply our function fun to each distinct 256 × 64 block of our image.

8.7 EDGE DETECTION

Edges contain some of the most useful information in an image. We may use edges to measure the size of objects in an image; to isolate particular objects from their background; to recognize or classify objects. There are a large number of edge-finding algorithms in existence, and we shall look at some of the more straightforward of them. The general MATLAB command for finding edges

```
edge(image, 'method', parameters...)
```

where the parameters available depend on the method used. In this chapter, we shall show how to create edge image using basic filtering methods, and discuss the MATLAB edge function.

An edge may be loosely defined as a local discontinuity in the pixel values which exceeds a given threshold. More informally, an edge is an observable difference in pixel values. For example, consider the two 4 blocks of pixels shown in figure 8.14.

51	52	53	59
54	52	53	62
50	52	53	68
55	52	53	55

50	53	155	160
51	53	160	170
52	53	167	190
51	53	162	155

Fig. (8.14) Blocks of pixels.

In the right hand block, there is a clear difference between the grey values in the second and third columns, and for these values the differences exceed 100. This would be easily discernible in an image—the human eye can pick out grey differences of this magnitude with relative ease. Our aim is to develop methods which will enable us to pick out the edges of an image.

8.8 DERIVATIVES AND EDGES

8.8.1 Fundamental Definitions

Consider the image in figure 8.15, and suppose we plot the gray values as we traverse the image from left to right. Two types of edges are illustrated here: a *ramp edge*, where the grey values change slowly, and a *step edge*, or an *ideal edge*, where the grey values change suddenly.

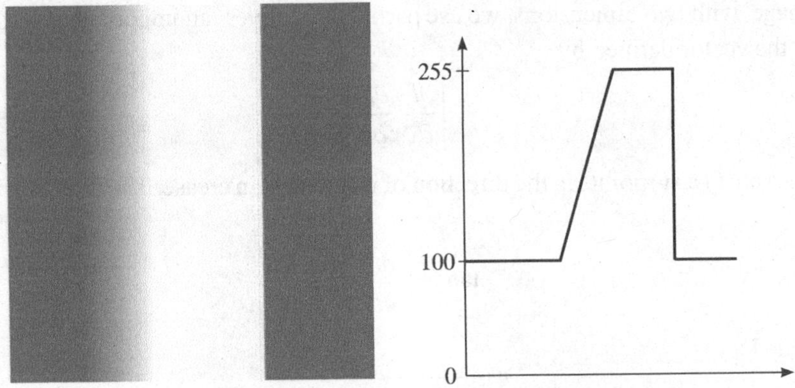

Fig. (8.15) Edges and their profiles.

Suppose the function which provides the profile in figure 8.15 is $f(x)$; then its derivative $f'(x)$ can be plotted; this is shown in figure 8.16. The derivative, as expected, returns zero for all constant sections

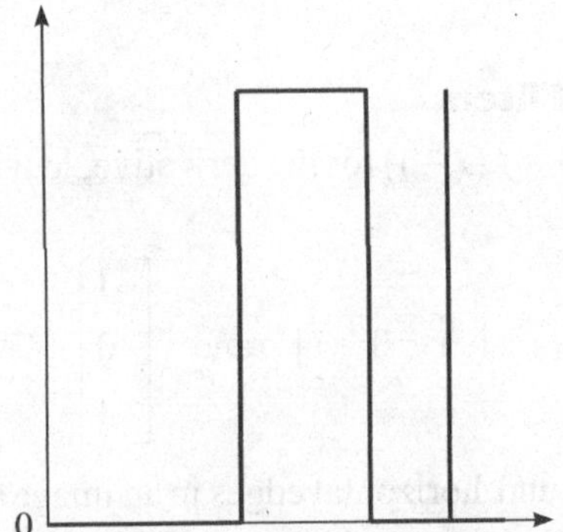

Fig. (8.16) The derivative of the edge profile.

of t he profile, and is non-zero (in this example) only in those parts of the image in which difference occur.

Many edge finding operators are based on differentiation; to apply the continuous derivative to a discrete image, first recall the definition of the derivative :

$$\frac{df}{dx} = \lim_{h \to 0} \frac{f(x+h) - f(x)}{h}$$

Since in an image, the smallest possible value of h is 1, being the difference between the index values of two adjacent pixels, a discrete version of the derivative expression is

$$f(x+1) - f(x).$$

Other expressions for the derivative are

$$\lim_{h \to 0} \frac{f(x) - f(x-h)}{h}, \lim_{h \to 0} \frac{f(x+h) - f(x-h)}{2h}$$

with discrete counterparts

$$f(x) - f(x-1), (f(x+1) - f(x-1))/2$$

For an image, with two dimensions, we use partial derivatives; an important expression is the *gradient,* which is the vector defined by

$$\left[\frac{\partial f}{\partial x} \ \frac{\partial f}{\partial y}\right]$$

which for a function $f(x, y)$ points in the direction of its greatest in crease. The direction of that increase is given by

$$\tan^{-1}\left(\frac{\partial f/\partial y}{\partial f/\partial x}\right).$$

and its magnitude by

$$\sqrt{\left(\frac{\partial f}{\partial x}\right)^2+\left(\frac{\partial f}{\partial f}\right)^2}$$

Most edge detection methods are concenred with finding the magnitude of the gradient, and then applying a threshold to the result.

8.8.2 Some Edge Detection Filters

Using the expression $f(x+1)-f(x-1)$ for the derivative, leaving the scaling factor out, produces horizontal and vertical filters:

$$[-1 \ \ 0 \ \ 1] \text{ and } \begin{bmatrix}-1\\0\\1\end{bmatrix}$$

These filters will find vertical and horizontal edges in an image and produce a reasonably bright result. However, the edges in the result can be a bit "jerky"; this can be overcome by smoothing the result in the opposite direction; by using the filters

$$\begin{bmatrix}1\\1\\1\end{bmatrix} \text{ and } [1 \ \ 1 \ \ 1]$$

Both filters can be applied at once, using the combined filter :

$$P_x=\begin{bmatrix}-1 & 0 & 1\\-1 & 0 & 1\\-1 & 0 & 1\end{bmatrix}$$

This filter, and its companion for finding horizontal edges :

$$P_y=\begin{bmatrix}-1 & -1 & -1\\0 & 0 & 0\\1 & 1 & 1\end{bmatrix}$$

are the *Prewitt* filters for edge detection.

If p_x and p_y are the grey values produced by applying P_x and P_y to an image, then the magnitude of the gradient is obtained with

$$\sqrt{p_x^2 + p_y^2}$$

In practice, however, its is more convenient to use either of

$$\max\{|p_x|, |p_y|\}$$

or

$$|p_x| + |p_y|$$

For example, let us take the image of the integrated circuit shown in figure 8.17, which can be read into MATLAB with

```
ic=imread('ic.tif');
```

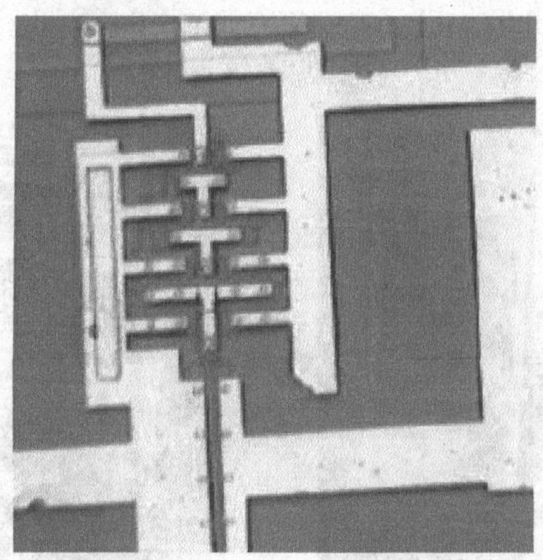

Fig. (8.17) An integrated circuit.

Applying each of P_x and P_y individually provides the results shown in figure 8.18. Figure 8.18(a) was produced with the following MATLAB commands :

```
px=[-1 0 1; -1 0 1; -1 0 1];
icx=filter2(px,ic);
figure,imshow(icx/255)
```

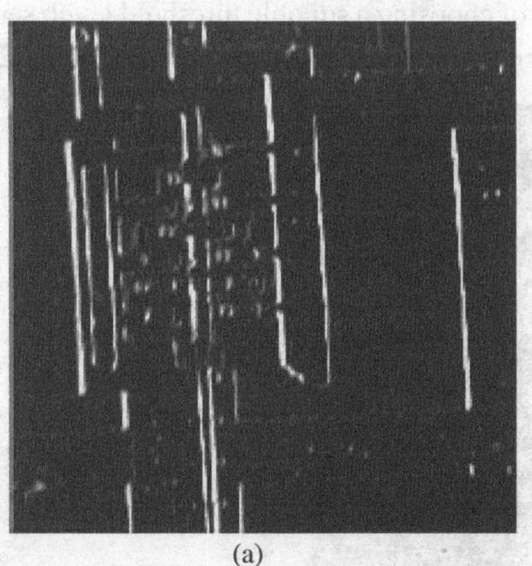

(a)

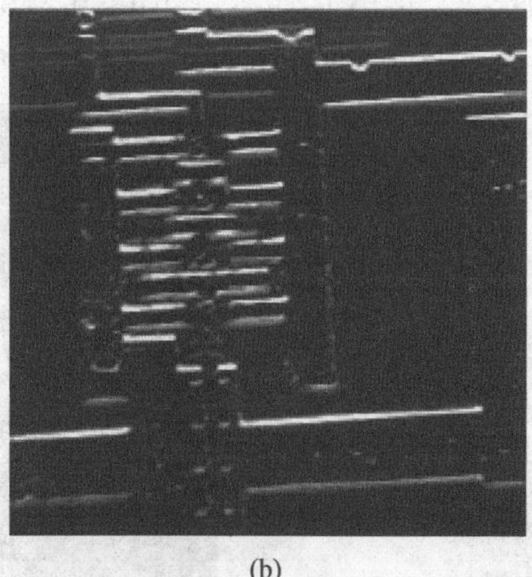

(b)

Fig. (8.18) The circuit after filtering with the Prewitt filters.

and figure 8.18(b) with

```
py=px;
icy=filter2(py,ic);
figure,imshow(icy/255)
```

Note that the filter P_x highlights vertical edges, and P_y horizontal edges. We can create a figure containing all the edges with :

```
edge_p=sqrt(icx.^2+ic.^2);
figure,imshow(edge_p/255)
```

and the result is shown in figure 8.18(a). This is a grey-scale image; a binary image containing edges only can be produced by thresholding. Figure 8.19(b) shows the result after the command

```
edge_t=im2bw(edge_p/255,0.3);
```

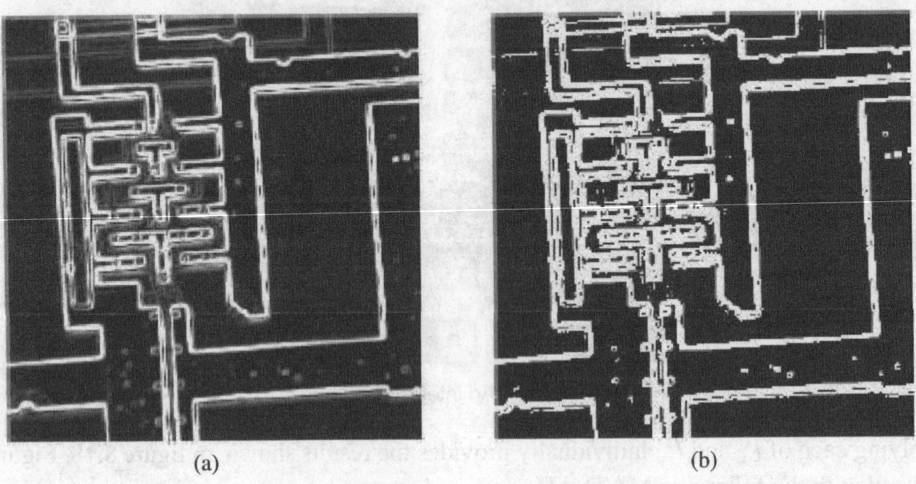

(a) (b)

Fig. (8.19) All t he edges of the circuit.

We can obtain edges by the Prewitt filter directly by using the command

```
edge_p=edge(ic.'prewitt');
```

and the edge function takes care of all the filtering, and of choosing a suitable threshold level; see its help text for more information. The result is shown in figure 8.20. Note that figures 8.19(b) and 8.20 seems

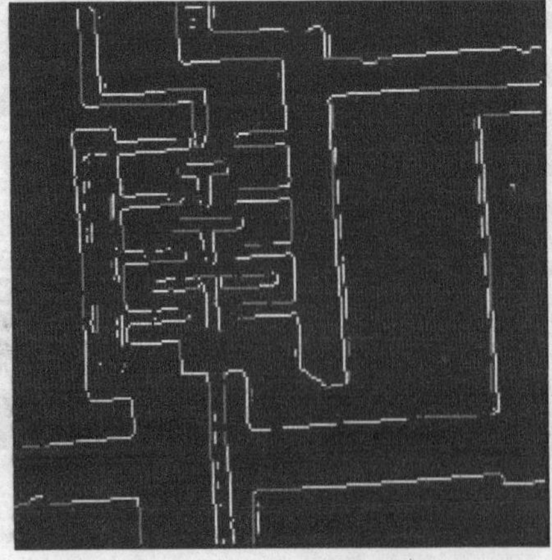

Fig. (8.20) The prewitt option of edge.

different to each other. This is because the edge function does some extra processing over and above taking the square root of the sum of the squares of the filters.

Slightly different edge finding filters are the *Roberts cross-gradient filters* :

$$\begin{bmatrix} 1 & 0 & 0 \\ 0 & -1 & 0 \\ 0 & 0 & 0 \end{bmatrix} \text{ and } \begin{bmatrix} 0 & 1 & 0 \\ -1 & 0 & 0 \\ 0 & 0 & 0 \end{bmatrix}$$

and the *Sobel filters;*

$$\begin{bmatrix} -1 & 0 & 1 \\ -2 & 0 & 2 \\ -1 & 0 & 1 \end{bmatrix} \text{ and } \begin{bmatrix} -1 & -2 & 1 \\ 0 & 0 & 0 \\ 1 & 2 & 1 \end{bmatrix}$$

The *Sobel filters* are similar to the Prewitt filters, in that they apply a smoothing filter in the opposite direction to the central difference filter. In the Sobel filters, the smoothing takes the form [1 2 1].

Which gives slightly more prominence to the central pixel. Figure 8.21 shows the respective results of the MATLAB commands

```
edge_r=edge(ic,'roberts')
figure,imshow(edge,r)
```

and

```
edge_s=edge(ic,'sobl');
figure,imshow(edge_s)
```

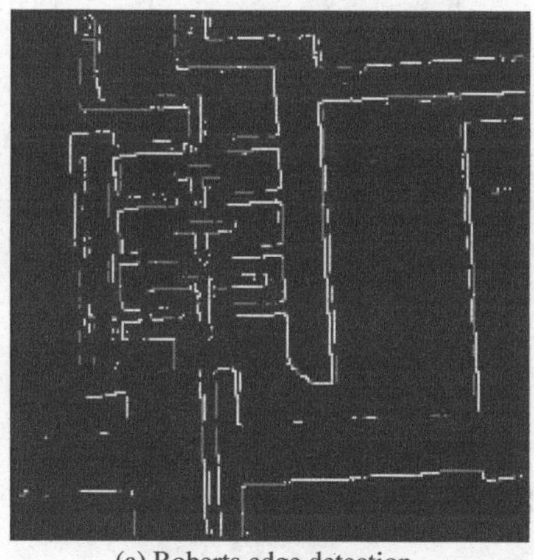
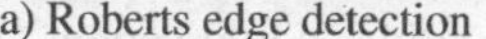

(a) Roberts edge detection

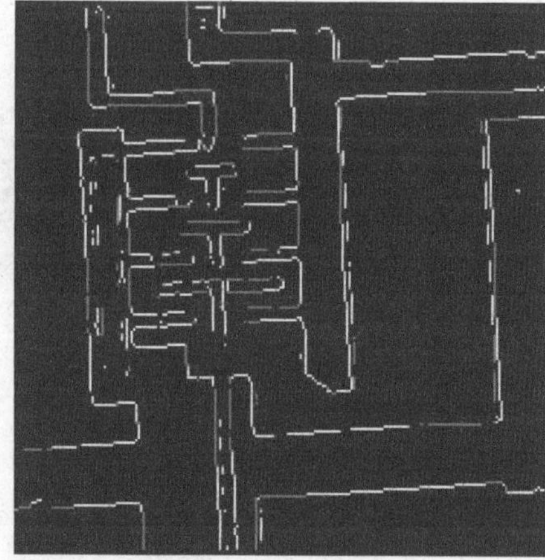

(b) Sobel edge detection

Fig. (8.21) Results of the Roberts and Sobel filters.

The appearance of each of these can be changed by specifying a threshold level. Of the three filters the Sobel filters are probably the best and they provide good edges, and they perform reasonably well in the presence of noise.

8.9 SECOND DERIVATIVES

8.9.1 The Laplacian

Another class of edge-detection method is obtained by considering the second derivatives. The sum of second derivative in both directions is called the *laplacian;* it is written as

$$\nabla^2 f = \frac{\partial^2 f}{\partial x^2} + \frac{\partial^2 f}{\partial y^2}$$

and it can be implemented by the filter

$$\begin{bmatrix} 0 & 1 & 0 \\ 1 & -4 & 1 \\ 0 & 1 & 0 \end{bmatrix}$$

This is known as a *discrete Laplacian.* The laplacian has the advantage over first derivative methods in that it is an *isotropic filter*. This means it is invariant under rotation. That is, if the laplacian is applied to an image, and the image then rotated, the same result would be obtained if the image were rotated first and the laplacian applied second. This would appear to make this class of filters ideal for edge detection. However, a major problem with all second derivative filters is that they are very sensitive to noise.

To see how the second derivative affects an edge, take the derivative of the pixel values as plotted in figure 8.15; the results are shown schematically in figure 8.22.

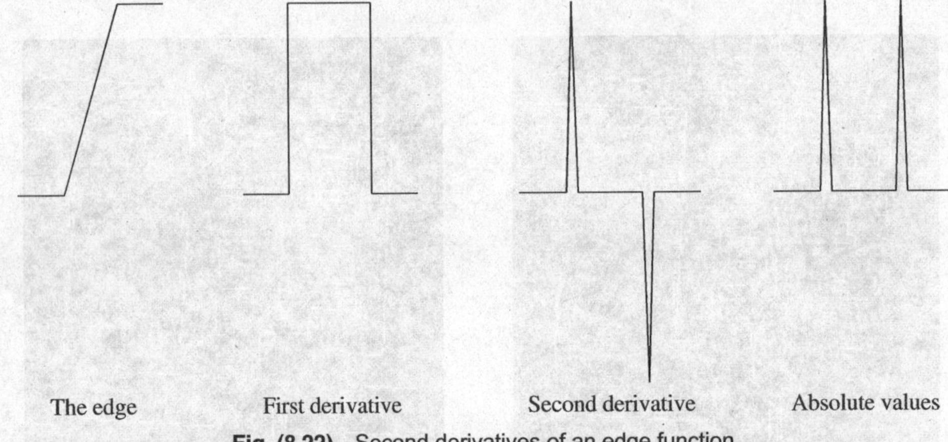

Fig. (8.22) Second derivatives of an edge function.

The Laplacian (after taking an absolute value, or squaring) gives double edges. To see an example, suppose we enter the MATLAB commands :

```
l=fspecial('laplacian',0);
ic_l=filter2(l,ic);
figure,imshow(mat2gray(ic_l))
```

the result of which is shown in figure 8.23.

Although the result is adequate, it is very messy when compared to the result of the Prewitt and Sobel methods discussed earlier. Other Laplacian masks can be used; some are :

$$\begin{bmatrix} 1 & 1 & 1 \\ 1 & -8 & 1 \\ 1 & 1 & 1 \end{bmatrix} \text{ and } \begin{bmatrix} -2 & 1 & -2 \\ 1 & 4 & 1 \\ -2 & 1 & -2 \end{bmatrix}$$

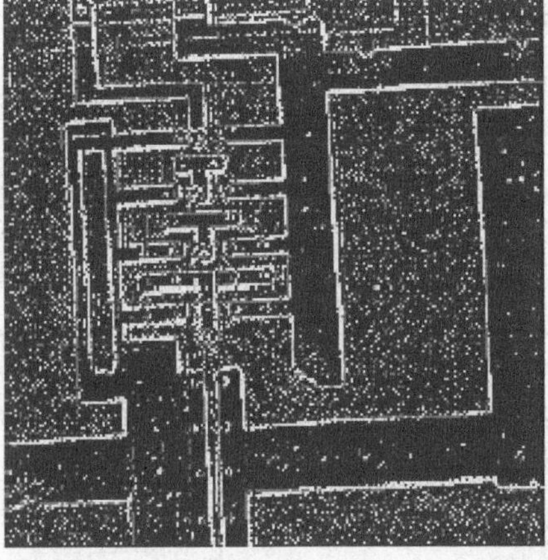

Fig. (8.23) Result after filtering with a discrete laplacian.

In MATLAB, Laplacians of all sorts can be generated us ing the fspecial function, in the form

```
fspecial('laplacian',ALPHA)
```

which produces the Laplacian

$$\frac{1}{\alpha+1}\begin{bmatrix} \alpha & 1-\alpha & \alpha \\ 1-\alpha & -4 & 1-\alpha \\ \alpha & 1-\alpha & \alpha \end{bmatrix}$$

If the parameter ALPHA (which is optional) is omitted, it is assumed to be 0.2. The value 0 gives Laplacian developed earlier.

8.9.2 Zero Crossings

A more appropriate use for the Laplacian is to find the *position* of edges by locating *zero crossings*. From figure 8.22, the position of the edge is given by the place where the value of the filter takes on a zero value. In general, these are places where the result of the filter changes sign. For example, consider the simple image given in figure 8.11(a) and the result after filtering with a Laplacian mask in figure 8.24(b).

We define the *zero crossings* in such a filtered image to be pixels which satisfy either of the following :

1. They have a negative grey value and are next to (by four-adjacency) a pixel whose grey value is positive.
2. They have a value of zero, and are between negative and positive valued pixels.

To give an indication of the way zero-crossings work, look at the edge plots and their second differences in figure 8.25.

50	50	50	50	50	50	50	50	50	50
50	50	50	50	50	50	50	50	50	50
50	50	200	200	200	200	200	200	50	50
50	50	200	200	200	200	200	200	50	50
50	50	200	200	200	200	200	200	50	50
50	50	200	200	200	200	200	200	50	50
50	50	50	50	200	200	200	200	50	50
50	50	50	50	200	200	200	200	50	50
50	50	50	50	50	50	50	50	50	50
50	50	50	50	50	50	50	50	50	50

(a) A simple image

−100	−50	−50	−50	−50	−50	−50	−50	−50	−100
−50	0	150	150	150	150	150	150	0	−50
−50	150	−300	−150	−150	−150	−150	−300	150	−50
−50	150	−150	0	0	0	0	−150	150	−50
−50	150	−150	0	0	0	0	−150	150	−50
−50	150	−300	−150	0	0	0	−150	150	−50
−50	0	150	300	−150	0	0	−150	150	−50
−50	0	0	150	−300	−150	−150	−300	150	−50
−50	0	0	0	150	150	150	150	0	−50
−100	−50	−50	−50	−50	−50	−50	−50	−50	−100

(b) After laplace filtering

Fig. (8.24) Locating zero crossings in an image.

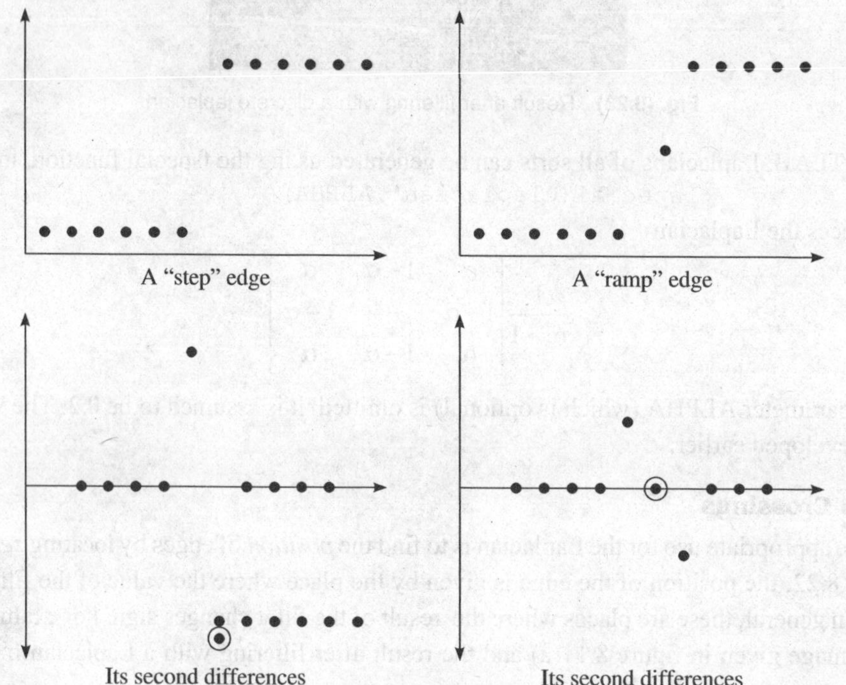

Fig. (8.25) Edges and second differences.

In each case the zero-crossing is circled. The important point is to note that across any edge there can be only *one* zero-crossing. Thus an image formed from zero-crossings has the potential to be very neat.

In figure 8.24(b) the zero crossings are shaded. We now have a further method of edge detection: take the zero-crossings after a laplace filtering. This is imple mented in MATLAB with the zerocross option of edge, which takes the zero crossings after filtering with a given filter :

```
l=fspecial('laplace',0);
icz=edge(ic,'zerocross',l);
imshow(icz)
```

The result is shown in figure 8.26(a). This is not in fact a very good result—far too many grey level changes have been interpreted as edges by this method. To eliminate them, we may first smooth the image with a Gaussian filter. This leads to the following sequences of steps for edge detection; the *Marr-Hildreth* method.

1. smooth the image with a Gaussian filter,
2. convolve the result with a laplacian,
3. find the zero crossings.

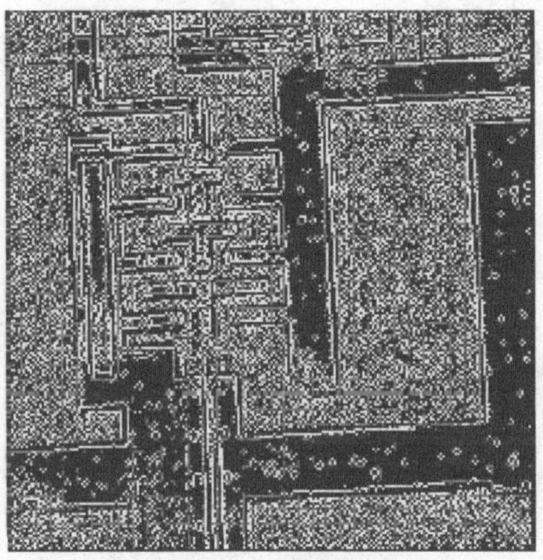

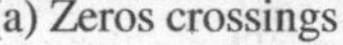

(a) Zeros crossings

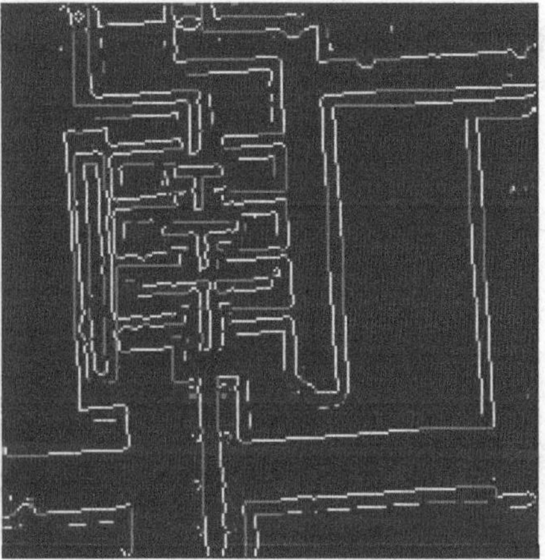

(b) Using an LoG filter first

Fig. (8.26) Edge detection using zero crossings.

This method was designed to provide a edge detection method to be as close as possible to biological vision. The first two steps can be combined into one, to produce a "Laplacian of Gaussian" or "LoG" filter. These filters can be created with the fspecial f unction. If no extra parameters are provided to the zerocross edge option, then the filter is chosen to be the LoG filter found by

```
fspecial('log',13,2)
```

This means that the following command :

```
edge(ic,'log');
```

produces exactly the same result as the commands :

```
log=fspecial('log',13,2);
edge(ic,'zerocross',log);
```

In fact the LoG and zerocross options implement the same edge finding method; the difference being that the zerocross option allows you to specify your own filter. The result after applying an LoG filter and finding its zero crossings is given in figure 8.26(b).

■ 8.10 THE HOUGH TRANSFORM

If the edge points found by the above edge detection methods are sparse, the resulting edge image may consist of individual points, rather than straight lines or curves. Thus in order to establish a boundary between the regions, it might be necessary to fit a line to those points. This can be a time consuming and computationally inefficient process, especially if there are many such edges points. One way of finding such boundary lines is by use of the "Hough transform".

The *Hough transform* is designed to find lines in images, but it can be easily varied to find other shapes. The idea is simple. Suppose (x, y) is a point in the image (which we shall assume to be binary). We can write $y = ax + b$, and consider all pairs (a, b) which satisfy this equation, and plot them into an "accumulator array". The (a, b) array is the "transform array".

For example, take $(x, y) = (1, 1)$. Since the equation relating a and b is

$$1 = a, 1 + b$$

we can write

$$b = -a + 1$$

Thus the line $b = -a + 1$ consists of all pairs of points relating to the single point (1, 1). This is shown in figure 8.27.

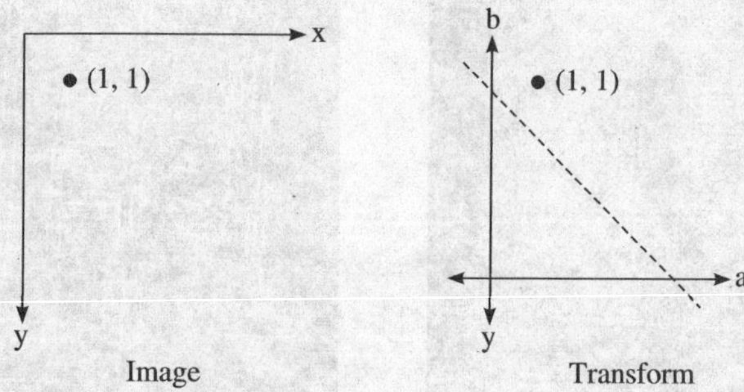

Fig. (8.27) A p oint in an image and its corresponding line in the transform.

Each point in the imageis mapped onto a line in the transform. The points in the transform corresponding to the greatest number of intersections correspond to the strongest line in the image.

For example, suppose we consider an image with five points : (1, 0), (1, 1), (2, 1), (4, 1) and (3, 2). Each of these points corresponds to a line as follows :

$$(1, 0) \rightarrow b = -a$$
$$(1, 1) \rightarrow b = -a + 1$$
$$(2, 1) \rightarrow b = -2a + 1$$
$$(4, 1) \rightarrow b = -4a + 1$$
$$(3, 2) \rightarrow b = -3a + 2$$

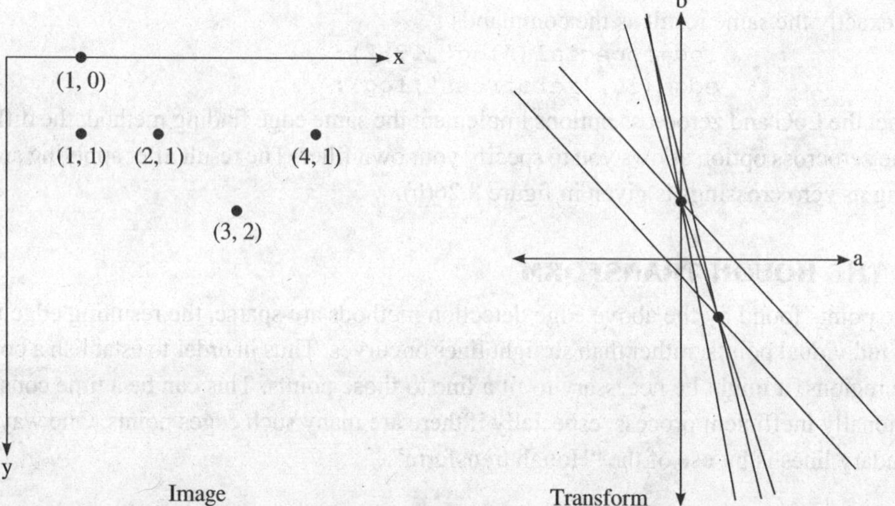

Fig. (8.28) An image and its corresponding lines in the transform.

Each of these lines appears in the transform as shown in figure 8.28.

The dots in the transform indicate places where there are maximum intersections of lines : at each dot three lines intersect. The coordinates of these dots are $(a, b) = (1, 0)$ and $(a, b) = (1, -1)$. These values correspond to the lines

$$y = 1.x + 0$$

and
$$y = 1.x + (-1)$$

or $y = x$ and $y = x - 1$. These lines are shown on the image in figure 8.29.

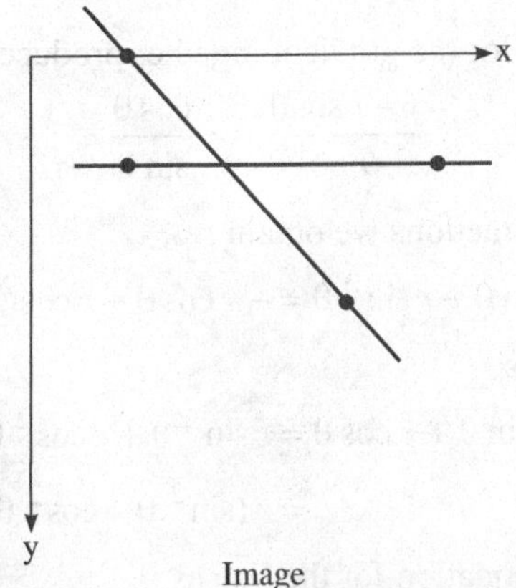

Fig. (8.29) Lines found by the Hough transform.

These are indeed the "strongest" lines in the image in that they contain the greatest number of points. There is a problem with this implementation of the Hough transform, and that is that it can't find vertical lines: we can't express a vertical line in the form $y = mx + c$, as m represents the gradient, and a vertical line has infinite gradient. We need another parameterization of lines.

Consider a general line, as shown in figure 8.30. Cleearly any line can be described in terms of the two parameters r and θ; r is the perpendicular distance from the line to the origin, and θ is the angle of the line's perpend icular to the x-axis. In this parameterization, vertical lines are simply those which have $\theta = 0$. If we allow r to have negative values, we can restrict θ to the range

$$-90 < \theta \leq 90$$

Fig. (8.30) A line and its parameters.

Given this parameterization, we need to be able to find the equation of the line. First note that the point (p, q) where the perpendicular to the line meets the line is $(p, q) = (r\cos\theta, r\sin\theta)$. Also note that the gradient of the perpendicular is $\tan\theta = \sin\theta/\cos\theta$. Now let (x, y) be any point on then line. The gradient of the line is

$$\frac{\text{rise}}{\text{run}} = \frac{y-q}{x-p} = \frac{y - r\sin\theta}{x - r\cos\theta}$$

But since the gradient of the line's perpendicular is $\tan\theta$, the gradient of the line itself must be

$$-\frac{1}{\tan\theta} = -\frac{\cos\theta}{\sin\theta}$$

Putting these two expressions for the gradient together produces :

$$\frac{y - r\sin\theta}{x - r\cos\theta} = -\frac{\cos\theta}{\sin\theta}$$

If we now multiply out these fractions we obtain :

$$y\sin\theta - r\sin^2\theta = -x\cos\theta + r\cos^2\theta$$

and this equation can be rewritten as

$$y\sin\theta + x\cos\theta = r\sin^2\theta + r\cos^2\theta$$

$$= r(\sin^2\theta + \cos^2\theta) = r$$

We finally have the required equation for the line as :

$$x\cos\theta + y\sin\theta = r$$

The Hough transform can then be implemented as follows : we start by choosing a discrete set of values of r and θ to use. For each pixel (x, y) in the image, we compute

$$x\cos\theta + y\sin\theta$$

for each value of θ, and place the result in the appropriate position in the (r, θ) array. At the end, the values of (r, θ) with the highest values in the array will correspond to strongest lines in the image.

An example will clarify this: consider the image shown in figure 8.31.

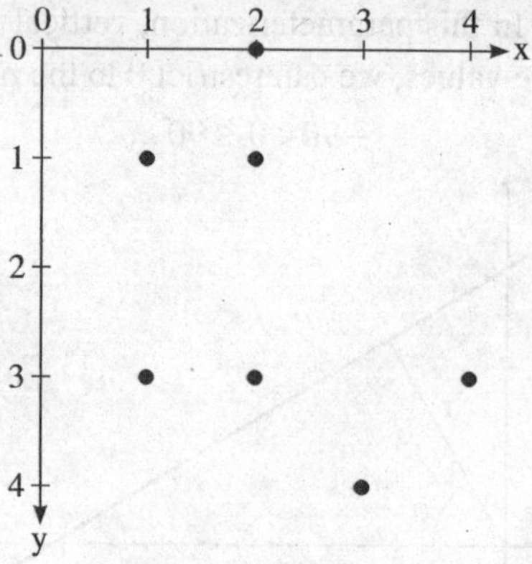

Fig. (8.31) A small image.

We shall discretize θ to use only the values

$$-45°, \quad 0°, \quad 45°, \quad 90°$$

We can start by making a table containing all values $x\cos\theta + y\sin\theta$ for each point, and for each value of θ.

(x, y)	$-45°$	$0°$	$45°$	$90°$
(2, 0)	1.4	2	1.4	0
(1, 1)	0	1	1.4	1
(2, 1)	0.7	2	2.1	1
(1, 3)	–1.4	1	2.8	3
(2, 3)	–0.7	2	3.5	3
(4, 3)	0.7	4	4.9	3
(3, 4)	–0.7	3	4.9	4

The accumulator array contains the number of times each value of (r, θ) appears in the above table :

	–1.4	–0.7	0	0.7	1	1.4	2	2.1	2.8	3	3.5	4	4.9
–45°	1	2	1	2		1							
0°					2		3			1		1	
45°						2		1	1		1		1
90°			1		2					3		2	

In practice this array will be very large and can be displayed as an image. In this example the two equal largest values occur at $(r, \theta) = (2, 0°)$ and $(r, \theta) = (3, 90°)$. The lines then are

$$x \cos 0 + y \sin 0 = 2$$

or

$$x = 2$$

and

$$x \cos 90 + y \sin 90 = 3$$

or

$$y = 3.$$

These lines are shown in figure 8.32.

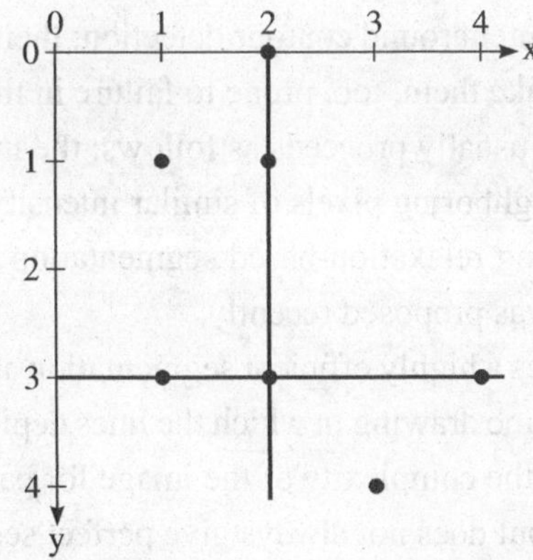

Fig. (8.32) Lines found by the Hough transform.

■ SUMMARY

- Segmentation subdivides an image into it's constitute regions or objects. The level to which the subdivision is carried depends on the problem being solved.
- Segmentation should stop when the objects of interests in an application have been isolated. Image segmentation algorithms generally are based on one of two basic properties of intensity values: discontinuity and similarity.
- The segmentation of images has always been a key problem in computer vision.

- Many model based techniques are based on iterative improvement of an initial model configuration. Appropriate low-level information is needed to find an initial estimate of the model that ensures convergence.
- In computer vision, segmentation refers to the process of partitioning a digital image into multiple regions (sets of pixels). The goal of segmentation is to simplify and/or change the representation of an image into something that is more meaningful and easier to analyze. Image segmentation is typically used to locate objects and boundaries (lines, curves, etc.) in images.
- The result of image segmentation is a set of regions that collectively cover the entire image, or a set of contours extracted from the image. Each of the pixels in a region are similar with respect to some characteristic or computed property, such as color, intensity, or texture. Adjacent regions are significantly different with respect to the same characteristic(s).
- Complete segmentation - set of disjoint regions uniquely corresponding with objects in the input image, Cooperation with higher processing levels which use specific knowledge of the problem domain is necessary.
- Partial segmentation - regions do not correspond directly with image objects, Image is divided into separate regions that are homogeneous with respect to a chosen property such as brightness, color, reflectivity, texture, etc.
- Threshold techniques, which make decisions based on local pixel information, are effective when the intensity levels of the objects fall squarely outside the range of levels in the background. Because spatial information is ignored, however, blurred region boundaries can create havoc.
- Edge-based methods center around contour detection: their weakness in connecting together broken contour lines make them, too, prone to failure in the presence of blurring.
- A region-based method usually proceeds as follows: the image is partitioned into connected regions by grouping neighboring pixels of similar intensity levels.
- A connectivity-preserving relaxation-based segmentation method, usually referred to as the *active contour model*, was proposed recently.
- Quick segmentation Uses a highly efficient segmentation algorithm to separate features, converting an image into a line drawing in which the lines depict outlines of objects in the image. Its purpose is to reduce the complexity of the image for pattern counting or further analysis. The algorithm is rapid but does not always give perfect segmentation.
- Threshold Determines the cutoff value for deciding whether a pixel is a feature or the background. A higher threshold causes more pixels to be considered features and produces more lines in the segmentation.
- Contour Map Uses the quick segmentation algorithm to create a new image consisting of contours following areas of steepest gradient.
- Watershed segmentation finds pixels at the midpoints between features by treating the pixel values as topographic elevations.

Review Questions

1. Suppose you thresholded an image at value t_1, and thresholded the result at value t_2. Describe the result if
   (a) $t_1 > t_2$ (b) $t_1 < t_2$
2. Create a simple image with

```
[x,y]=meshgrid(1:256,1:256);
z=sqrt((x-128).^2+(y-128).^2);
z2=1-mat2gray(z);
```

   Using im2bw, threshold z2 at different values and comment on the results. What happens to the amount of white as t he threshold value increases? Can you state and prove a general result?
3. Repeat the above question, but with the image cameraman.tif.
4. Can you can create a small image which produces an "X" shape when thresholded at one level and a cross shape "+" when thresholded at another level?
   If not, why not?
5. Superimpose the image text.tif onto the image cameraman.tif. You can do this with :

```
t=imread('text.tif');}
c=imread('cameraman.tif');}
m=uint8(double(c)+255*double(t));}
```

   Can you threshold this new image m to isolate the text?
6. Try the same problem as above, but define m as :

```
m=uint8(double(c).*double(~t));
```

7. Create a version of the circles image with

```
t=imread('circles.tif');
[x,y]=meshgrid(1:256,1:256);
t2=double(t).((x+y)/2+64)+x+y;
t3=uint8(255*mat2gray(t2));
```

   Attempt to threshold the i maget3 to obtain the circles alone, using adaptive thr esholding and the bl k pr oc function. What sized blocks produce the best result?
8. Enter the following matrix into MATLAB

201	195	203	203	199	200	204	190	198	203
201	204	209	197	210	202	205	195	202	199
205	198	46	60	53	37	50	51	194	205
208	203	54	50	51	50	55	48	193	194
200	193	50	56	42	53	55	49	196	211
200	198	203	49	51	60	51	205	207	198
205	196	202	53	52	34	46	202	199	193
199	202	194	47	51	55	48	191	190	197
194	206	198	212	195	196	204	204	199	200
201	189	203	200	191	196	207	203	193	204

   and use imfilter to apply each of the Roberts, Prewitt, Sobel, Laplacian and zero-crossing edge-finding methods to the image. In the case of applying two filters (such as with Roberts, Prewitt, or Sobel) apply each filter s eparately, and join the results.
   Apply thresholding it necessary to obtain a binary image sh ow ingonly the edges.
   Which method seems to produce the best results?

9. Open up the image cameraman.tif in MATLAB, and apply each of the following edge finding techniques in turn :
(a) Roberts
(b) Prewitt
(c) Sobel
(d) Laplacian
(e) Zero-crossings of a laplacian
(f) the Marr-Hildreth method
Which seems to you to provide the best looking result?

11. Repeat the above exercise but use the image tire.tif.

12. Obtain a grey scale flower image with

```
fl=imread('flowers.tif');
f=im2uint(rgb2gray(f1));
```

Now repeat question 3.

13. Pick a grey-scale image, and add some noise t o it; say with

```
c=imread('cameraman.tif');
c1=imnoise(c, 'salt & pepper',0.1);
c2=imnoise(c, 'gaussian',0,0.02);
```

Now apply the edge finding techniques t oeach of the "noisy" images c1 and c2.
Which technique seems to give
(a) the best results in the presence of noise?
(b) the worst results in the presence of noise?

14. Write the lines $y = x - 2$, $y = 1 - x/2$ i n(r, θ) form.

15. Use of Hough-transform to detect the strongest line inthe binary image shown below. Use the form $x \cos\theta + y \sin\theta = r$ with θ in steps of 45° from –45° to 90° and place the result in an accumulator array.

16. Repeat the above question with the images :

17. Find some more lines on the cameraman image, and plot them with houghline.

18. Read and d isp la ythe image alumgrns.tif.
(a) Where does it appear that the "strongest" lines will be?
(b) Using hough and houghline, plot the five strongest lines.

19. Experiment with the two routines by changing the initial edges detection of hough. Can you affect the lines found by the Hough transform?

9

FEATURE EXTRACTION

In computer vision and image processing the concept of feature is used to denote a piece of information which is relevant for solving the computational task related to a certain application. More specifically, features can refer to the result of a general neighborhood operation (feature extractor or feature detector) applied to the image, specific structures in the image itself, ranging from simple structures such as points or edges to more complex structures such as objects. Other examples of features are related to motion in image sequences, to shapes defined in terms of curves or boundaries between different image regions, or to properties of such a region. The feature concept is very general and the choice of features in a particular computer vision system may be highly dependent on the specific problem at hand.

■ 9.1 FEATURE EXTRACTION

When features are defined in terms of local neighborhood operations applied to an image, a procedure commonly referred to as feature extraction, one can distinguish between feature detection approaches that produce local decisions whether there is a feature of a given type at a given image point or not, and those who produce non-binary data as result. The distinction becomes relevant when the resulting detected features are relatively sparse. Although local decisions are made, the output from a feature detection step does not need to be a binary image. The result is often represented in terms sets of (connected or unconnected) coordinates of the image points where features have been detected, sometimes with sub pixel accuracy.

When feature extraction is done without local decision making, the result is often referred to as a feature image. Consequently, a feature image can be seen as an image in the sense that it is a function of the same spatial (or temporal) variables as the original image, but where the pixel values hold information about image features instead of intensity or color. This means that a feature image can be processed in a similar way as an ordinary image generated by an image sensor. Feature images are also often computed as integrated step in algorithms for feature detection.

9.2 FEATURE REPRESENTATION

A specific image feature, defined in terms of a specific structure in the image data, can often be represented in different ways. For example, an edge can be represented as a boolean variable in each image point that describes whether an edge is present at that point. Alternatively, we can instead use a representation which provides a certainty measure instead of a boolean statement of the edge's existence and combine this with information about the orientation of the edge. Similarly, the color of a specific region can either be represented in terms of the average color (three scalars) or a color histogram (three functions).

When a computer vision system or computer vision algorithm is designed the choice of feature representation can be a critical issue. In some cases, a higher level of detail in the description of a feature may be necessary for solving the problem, but this comes at the cost of having to deal with more data and more demanding processing. Below, some of the factors which are relevant for choosing a suitable representation are discussed.

9.2.1 Certainty or Confidence

Two examples of image features are local edge orientation and local velocity in an image sequence. In the case of orientation, the value of this feature may be more or less undefined if more than one edge are present in the corresponding neighborhood. Local velocity is undefined if the corresponding image region does not contain any spatial variation. As a consequence of this observation it may be relevant use a feature representation which includes a measure of certainty or confidence related to the statement about the feature value. Otherwise, it is a typical situation that the same descriptor is used to represent feature values of low certainty and feature values close to zero, with a resulting ambiguity in the interpretation of this descriptor. Depending on the application, such an ambiguity may or may not be acceptable.

In particular if a feature image will be used in subsequent processing, it may be a good idea to employ a feature representation which includes information about certainty or confidence. This enables a new feature descriptor to be computed from several descriptors, for example computed at the same image point but at different scales, or from different but neighboring points, in terms of a weighted average where the weights are derived from the corresponding certainties. In the simples case, the corresponding computation can be implemented as a low-pass filtering of the feature image. The resulting feature image will, in general, be more stable to noise.

9.2.2 Averageablity

In addition to having certainty measures included in the representation, the representation of the corresponding feature values may itself be suitable for an average operation or not. Most feature representations can be averaged in practice, but only in certain cases can the resulting descriptor be given a correct interpretation in terms of a feature value. Such representations are referred to as averageable.

For example, if the orientation of an edge is represented in terms of an angle, this representation must have a discontinuity where the angle wraps from its maximal value to its minimal value. Consequently, it can happen that two similar orientations are represented by angles which have a mean that does not lie close to either of the original angles and, hence, this representation is not averageable. There are other representations of edge orientation, such as the structure tensor, which are averageable.

Another example relates to motion, where in some cases only the normal velocity relative to some edge can be extracted. If two such features have been extracted and they can be assumed to refer to same true velocity, this velocity is not given as the average of the normal velocity vectors. Hence, normal velocity vectors are not averageable. Instead, there are other representations of motions, using matrices or tensors that give the true velocity in terms of an average operation of the normal velocity descriptors.

9.2.3 Feature Vectors and Feature Spaces

In some applications it is not sufficient to extract only one type of feature to obtain the relevant information from the image data. Instead two or more different features are extracted, resulting in two or more feature descriptors at each image point. A common practice is to organize the information provided by all these descriptors as the elements of one single vector, commonly referred to as a feature vector. The set of all possible feature vectors constitute a feature space.

A common example of feature vectors appears when each image point is to be classified as belonging to a specific class. Assuming that each image point has a corresponding feature vector based on a suitable set of features, meaning that each class is well separated in the corresponding feature space, the classification of each image point can be done using standard classification method. Another, and related example, occurs when neural network based processing is applied to images. The input data fed to the neural network is often given in terms of a feature vector from each image point, where the vector is constructed from several different features extracted from the image data. During a learning phase, the networks can itself find which combinations of different features those are useful for solving the problem at hand.

9.2.4 Multi-level Feature Processing

The extraction of feature are sometimes made over several processing steps. In computer vision and image processing the concept of feature detection refers to methods that aim at computing abstractions of image information and making local decisions at every image point whether there is an image feature of a given type at that point or not. The resulting features will be subsets of the image domain, often in the form of isolated points, continuous curves or connected regions.

9.3 TYPES OF IMAGE FEATURES

9.3.1 Edges

Edges are points where there is a boundary (or an edge) between two image regions. In general, an edge can be of almost arbitrary shape, and may include junctions. In practice, edges are usually defined as sets of points in the image which have a strong gradient magnitude. Furthermore, some common algorithms will then chain high gradient points together to form a more complete description of an edge. These algorithms may place some constraints on the shape of an edge. Locally, edges have a one dimensional structure.

9.3.2 Corners/Interest Points

The terms corners and interest points are used somewhat interchangeably and refer to point-like features in an image, which have a local two dimensional structure. The name "Corner" arose since early algorithms first performed edge detection, and then analysed the edges to find rapid changes in direction (corners). These algorithms were then developed so that explicit edge detection was no longer required, for instance by looking for high levels of curvature in the image gradient. It was then noticed that the so-called corners were also being detected on parts of the image which were not corners in the traditional sense (for instance a small bright spot on a dark background may be detected). These points are frequently known as interest points, but the term "corner" is used by tradition.

9.3.3 Blobs/Regions of Interest or Interest Points

Blobs provide a complementary description of image structures in terms of regions, as opposed to corners that are more point-like. Nevertheless, blob descriptors often contain a preferred point (a local maximum of an operator response or a center of gravity) which means that many blob detectors may also be regarded as interest point operators. Blob detectors can detect areas in an image which are too smooth to be detected by a corner detector.

Consider shrinking an image and then performing corner detection. The detector will respond to points which are sharp in the shrunk image, but may be smooth in the original image. It is at this point that the difference between a corner detector and a blob detector becomes somewhat vague. To a large extent, this distinction can be remedied by including an appropriate notion of scale. Nevertheless, due to their response properties to different types of image structures at different scales, the LoG and DoH blob detectors are also mentioned in the article on corner detection.

9.3.4 Ridges

For elongated objects, the notion of ridges is a natural tool. A ridge descriptor computed from a grey-level image can be seen as a generalization of the a medial axis. From a practical viewpoint, a ridge can be thought of as a one-dimensional curve that represents an axis of symmetry, and in addition has an attribute of local ridge width associated with each ridge point. Unfortunately, however, it is algorithmically harder to extract ridge features from general classes of grey-level images than edge-, corner- or blob features. Nevertheless, ridge descriptors are frequently used for road extraction in aerial images and for extracting blood vessels in medical images.

9.4 FEATURE DETECTORS

Common feature detectors and their classification are discussed in the following table.

Table 9.1 : Common feature detectors and their classifications.

Feature Detector	Edge	Corner	Blob
Canny	×		
Sobel	×		
Harris and Stephens/Plessey	×	×	
SUSAN	×	×	
Shi and Tomasi		×	
FAST		×	
Laplacian of Gaussian		×	×
Difference of Gaussian		×	×
Determinant of Hessian		×	×
MSER			×
Grey-level blobs			×

Once features have been detected, a local image patch around the feature can be extracted. This extraction may involve quite considerable amounts of image processing. The result is known as a feature descriptor or feature vector. Among the approaches that are used to feature description, one can mention N-jets and local histograms (see scale-invariant feature transform for one example of a local histogram descriptor). In addition to such attribute information, the feature detection step by itself may also provide complementary attributes, such as the edge orientation and gradient magnitude in edge detection and the polarity and the strength of the blob in blob detection.

Definition : In pattern recognition and in image processing, Feature extraction is a special form of dimensionality reduction. Feature extraction is the operation to extract various image features for identifying or interpreting meaningful physical objects from images.

Feature extraction involves simplifying the amount of resources required to describe a large set of data accurately. When performing analysis of complex data one of the major problems stems from the number of variables involved. Analysis with a large number of variables generally requires a large amount of memory and computation power or a classification algorithm which overfits the training sample and generalizes poorly to new samples. Feature extraction is a general term for methods of constructing combinations of the variables to get around these problems while still describing the data with sufficient accuracy.

Features are classified into three types :

- **Spectral features:** color, tone, ratio, spectral index etc. Principle components and normalized vegetation index are widely used.

  The first and second principle components computed from satellite multi-spectral scanner data such as Landsat TM will give "brightness" and "greenness" respectively.

  Normalized difference vegetation index (NDVI) is often used for vegetation classification.

$$NDVI = \frac{\text{Infrared} - \text{Red}}{\text{Infrared} + \text{Red}}$$

- **Geometric features:** edges, linearments etc.

  Spatial filtering of edge detection is commonly used to extract linear features such as roads, geological linearments, boundaries of agricultural fields etc.
- **Textural features:** pattern, homogeneity, spatial frequency, etc.

  Though many computer approaches have been tried, human pattern recognition is much better than the computer results.

Table 9.2 summarizes major operations of feature extraction.

Table 9.2 : Major Operations of Feature Extraction

Feature Type	Operation	Extracted Feature
Special features	Principal component analysis	• Color composition with PC1, PC2 and PC3 will give more colorful image output • PC1 brightness • PC2 greenness
	Normalized difference vegetation index (NDVI)	• High value corresponds to higher vegetation density • Forest, grassland bare soil and water are easily delineated by NDVI
Geometric features	Spatial filtering	• Edges are detected for identifying roads, lineaments, building etc.
	Stereo-matching	• 3D coordinates of terrain points are computed for DEM • 3D lines are identified from edges
Textural features	Statistical operations	• Homogeneous areas are recognized • Coarse patterns with peaks are detected
	Fourier transformation	• Repeated patterns and orientation are recognized

9.5 REPRESENTATION AND RECOGNITION

To recognize individual objects in a digital image, there are two problems that need to be solved:

- Given a collection of named objects, construct a computer representation or model of each object.
- Given a digitized sensor image (intensity or range data, for example), find either or all of the following:
  1. An identity or name,
  2. The location, and
  3. The orientation of each object in the scene.

An example occurs in the polyhedral world where the task is to match predicted and observed line labeling through a graph isomorphism or endomorphism search. We will consider this in more detail later, but will first concentrate on some of the common modeling schemes used in computer vision.

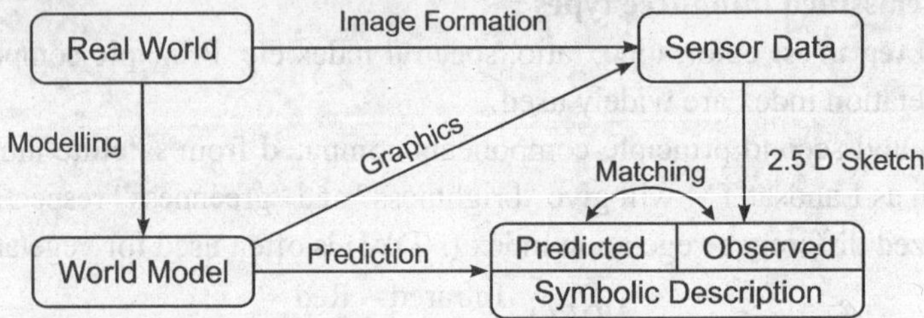

Fig. (9.1) From image capture of the real world to object recognition.

9.5.1 Topological Attributes

Shape representation and description :

- Defining the shape of an object can prove to be very difficult. Shape is usually represented verbally or in figures.
- There is no generally accepted methodology of shape description. Further, it is not known what in shape is important.
- Current approaches have both positive and negative attributes; computer graphics or mathematics use effective shape representations, which are unusable in shape recognition and vice versa.
- In spite of this, it is possible to find features common to most shape description approaches.
- Common shape description methods can be characterized from different points of view.
  - — Input representation form: Object description can be based on boundaries or on more complex knowledge of whole regions.
  - — Object reconstruction ability: That is, whether an object's shape can or cannot be reconstructed from the description.
  - — Incomplete shape recognition ability: That is, to what extent an object's shape can be recognized from the description if objects are occluded and only partial shape information is available.
  - — Local/global description character: Global descriptors can only be used if complete object data are available for analysis. Local descriptors describe local object properties using partial information about the objects. Thus, local descriptors can be used for description of occluded objects.

— Mathematical and heuristic techniques: A typical mathematical technique is shape description based on the Fourier transform. A representative heuristic method may be elongatedness.
— Statistical or syntactic object description.
— A robustness of description to translation, rotation, and scale transformations: Shape description properties in different resolutions.

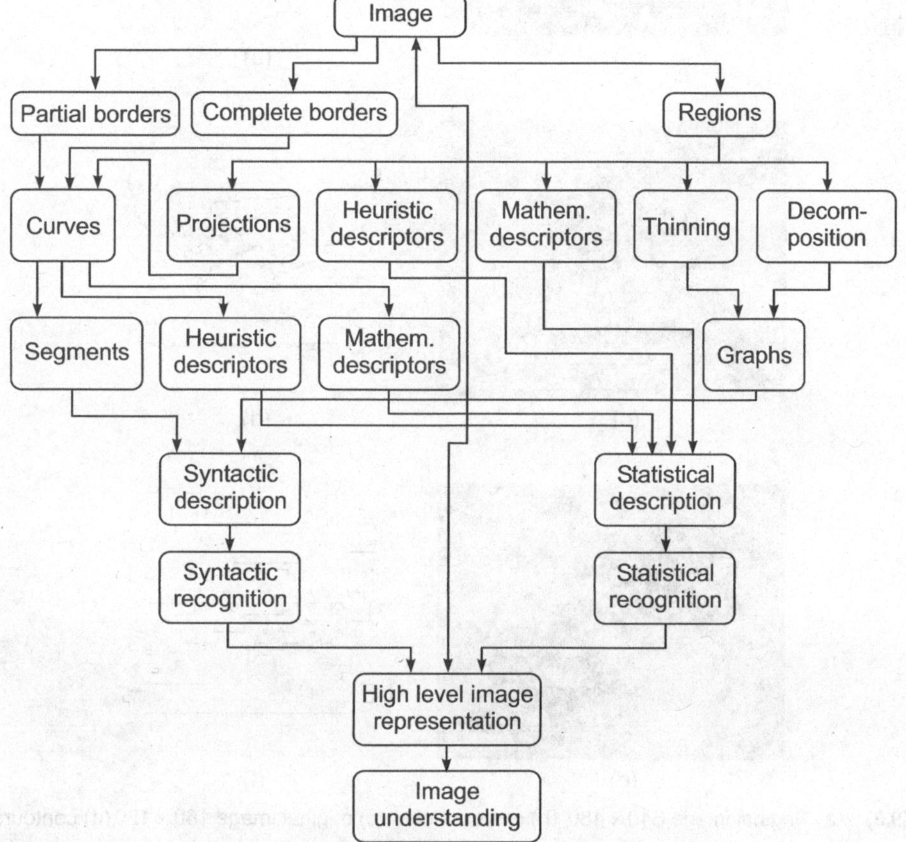

Fig. (9.2) Image analysis and understanding methods.

- Sensitivity to scale is even more serious if a shape description is derived, because shape may change substantially with image resolution.
- Therefore, shape has been studied in multiple resolutions which again causes difficulties with matching corresponding shape representations from different resolutions.
- Moreover, the conventional shape descriptions change discontinuously.
- A scale-space approach aims to obtain continuous shape descriptions if the resolution changes continuously.
- In many tasks, it is important to represent classes of shapes properly, e.g. shape classes of apples, oranges, pears, bananas, etc.
- The shape classes should represent the generic shapes of the objects belonging to the same classes well. Obviously, shape classes should emphasize shape differences among classes

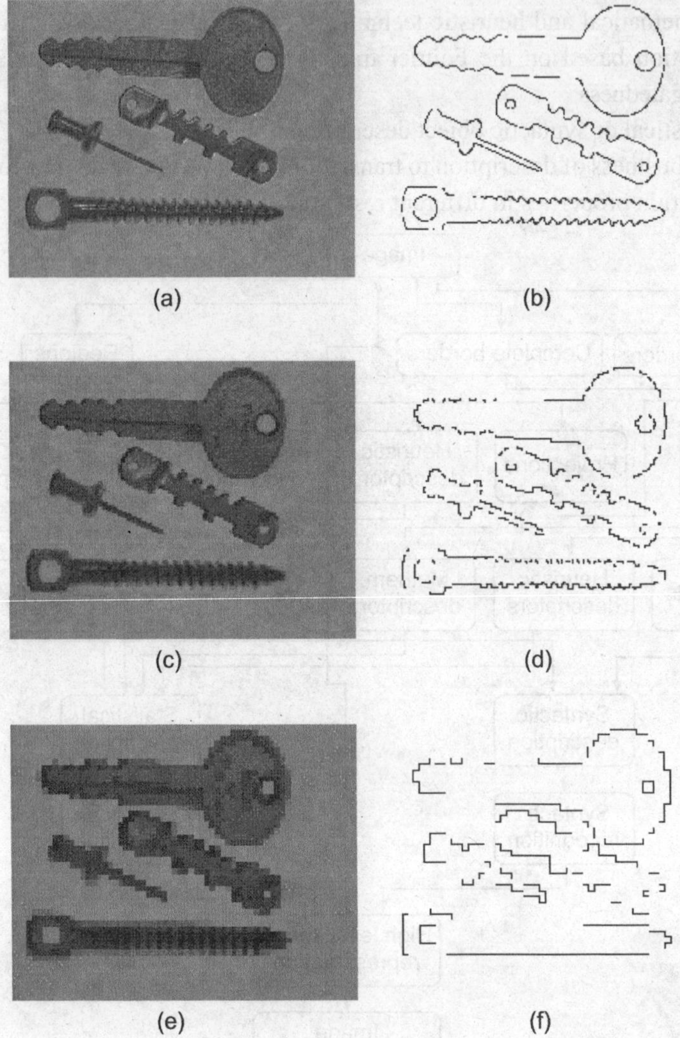

Fig. (9.3) (a) Original image 640 × 480, (b) contours of a, (c) original image 160 × 120 (d) contours of c, (e) original image 64 × 48, (f) contours of e.

while the influence of shape variations within classes should not be reflected in the class description.

- Despite the fact that we are dealing with two-dimensional shape and its description, our world is three-dimensional and the same objects, if seen from different angles (or changing position/orientation in space), may form very different 2D projections.
- The ideal case would be to have a universal shape descriptor capable of overcoming these changes — to design projection-invariant descriptors.
- Consider an object with planar faces and imagine how many very different 2D shapes may result from a given face if the position and 3D orientation of this simple object changes with respect to an observer. In some special cases, like circles which transform to ellipses, or planar polygons, projectively invariant features (invariants} can be found.

- Object occlusion is another hard problem in shape recognition. However, the situation is easier here (if pure occlusion is considered, not combined with orientation variations yielding changes in 2D projections as discussed above), since visible parts of objects may be used for description.
- Here, the shape descriptor choice must be based on its ability to describe local object properties — if the descriptor only gives a global object description, such a description is useless if only a part of an object is visible. If a local descriptor is applied, this information may be used to compare the visible part of the object to all objects which may appear in the image. Clearly, if object occlusion occurs, the local or global character of the shape descriptor must be considered first.

9.5.2 Geometric Attributes

The raw information available for each line segment is its orientation (angle with respect to the horizontal axis) and its length (see figure 9.1 (a). To illustrate how the Euclidean invariant pair wise feature attributes are computed, suppose that we denote the line segments indexed (ab) and (cd) by the vectors and respectively. The vectors are directed away from their point of intersection. The relative angle attribute is given by

$$\theta_{x_{ab},x_{cd}} = \arccos\left[\frac{x_{ab}\cdot x_{ce}}{|x_{ab}||x_{cd}|}\right]$$

From the relative angle we compute the directed relative angle. This is an extension to the attribute used by Evans et al. , that consists of giving the relative angle a positive sign if the direction of the angle from the baseline to its pair is clockwise and a negative sign if it is counter-clockwise. This allows us to extend the range of angles describing pairs of segments from [0,] to [,] and therefore, reduce indexation errors associated with angular ambiguities.

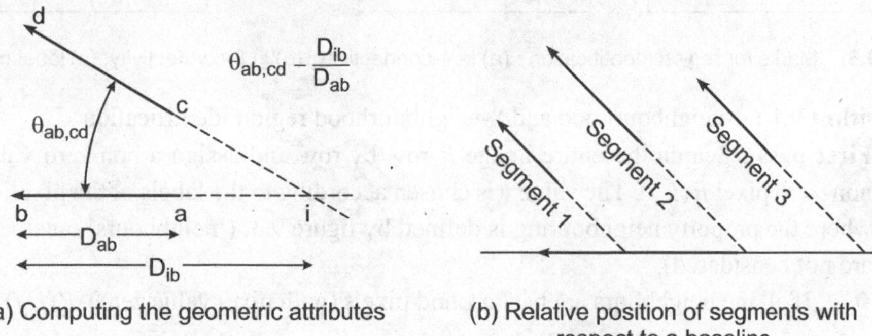

(a) Computing the geometric attributes

(b) Relative position of segments with respect to a baseline

Fig. (9.4) Geometry for shape representation.

In order to describe the relative position between a pair of segments and resolve the local shape ambiguities produced by the relative angle attribute we introduce a second attribute. This second attribute allows the representation to capture the structural information of the shape. Figure 9.1 (b) shows a configuration where the relative angle attribute alone does not allow unambiguous representation. In this figure, the segments labeled 1, 2 and 3 all have the same relative angle with respect to the base line. The configuration may be unambiguously defined if the relative angle attribute is coupled with a directed relative position attribute that uniquely defines the local structure.

The directed relative position is represented by the length ratio between the oriented baseline vector and the vector joining the end (b) of the baseline segment (ab) to the intersection of the segment pair (cd).

$$\theta_{x_{ab}, x_{cd}} = \frac{D_{ib}}{D_{ab}}$$

Both the directed relative angle and the directed relative position attributes are invariant to changes of scale, rotation and translation. This is an important advantage over the representation proposed by Evans et al. if the technique is to be used for shape retrieval from real world image data-bases where the size of objects or, more generally shapes, is not known in advance.

9.6 REGION IDENTIFICATION

- Region identification is necessary for region description. One of the many methods for region identification is to label each region (or each boundary) with a unique (integer) number; such identification is called labeling or coloring, also connected component labeling.
- Goal of segmentation was to achieve complete segmentation, now, the regions must be labeled.

$$R_b^G = \bigcup_{i=1, i \neq b}^{m} R_i$$

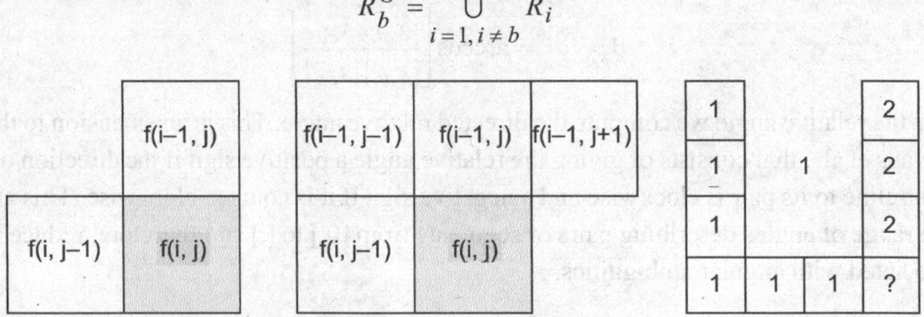

Fig. (9.5) Marks for region identification : (a) in 4-connectivity, (b) in 8-connectivity, (c) label collision.

Algorithm 9.1 : 4-neighbourhood and 8-neighbourhood region identification.

1. **First pass :** Search the entire image *R* row by row and assign a non-zero value *v* to each non-zero pixel $R(i, j)$. The value *v* is chosen according to the labels of the pixel's neighbours where the property neighbouring is defined by figure 9.3. ('neighbours' outside the image *R* are not considered),
   - If all the neighbours are background pixels (with pixel value zero), $R(i, j)$ is assigned a new (and as yet) unused label.
   - If there is just one neigbouring pixel with a non-zero label, assign this label to the pixel $R(i, j)$.
   - If there is more than one non-zero pixel among the neighbours, assign the label of any one to the labelled pixel. If the labels of any one to the labelled pixel. If the labels of any of the neighbours differ (label collision) store the label pair as being equivalent. Equivalence pairs awre stored in a separate data structure – an equivalence table.
2. **Second pass :** All of the region-pixel were labelled during the first pass but some regions have pixels with different labels (due to label collisions). The whole image is scanned again,

and pixels re-labelled using the equivalence table information (for example, with the lowest value in an equivalence class).

- Label collision is a very common occurrence — examples of image shapes experiencing this are U-shaped objects, mirrored E objects, etc.
- The equivalence table is a list of all label pairs present in an image; all equivalent labels are replaced by a unique label in the second step.
- The algorithm is basically the same in 4-connectivity and 8-connectivity, the only difference being in the neighborhood mask shape.

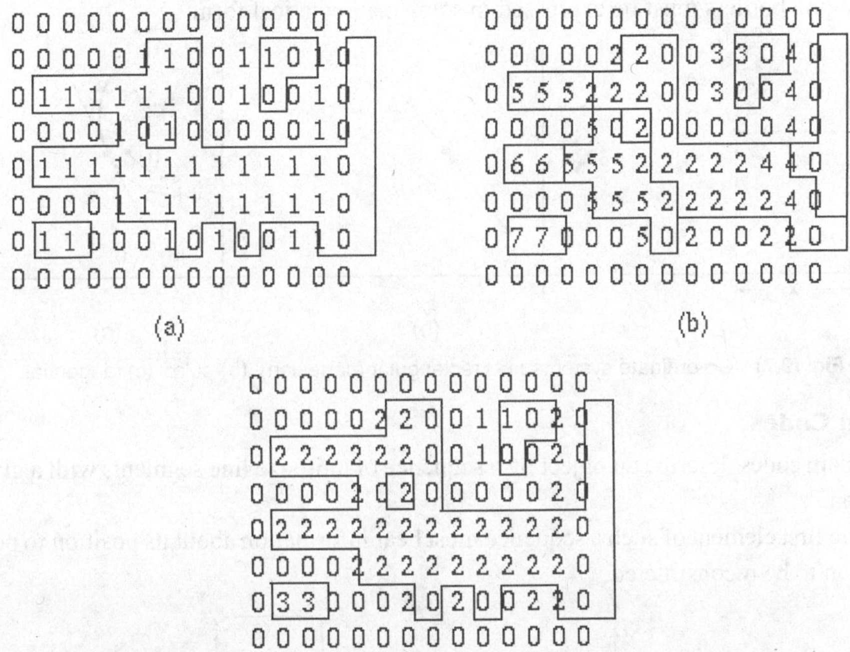

Fig. (9.6) Object identification in 8-connectivity : (a), (b), (c) algorithm steps. Equivalence table after step (b) :2-5, 5-6, 2-4.

Algorithm 9.2 : Region identification in run length encoded data.

1. **First pass :** Use a new label for each continuous run in the first image row that is not part of the background.
2. For the second and subsequent rows, compare positions of runs. If a run in a row does not neighbour (in the 4- or 8-sense) any run in the previous row, assign a new label. If a run neigbours precisely one run in the previous row, assign its label to the row run. If the new run neighbours more than one run in the previous row, a label collision has occurred. Collision information is stored in an equivalence table, and the new run is labelled using the label of any one of its neighbours.
3. **Second pass :** Search the image row by row and re-label the image according to the equivalence table information.

Algorithm 9.3 : Quadtree region identification.

1. **First pass :** Search quadtree nodes in a given order – *e.g.*, beginning from the root and in NW, NE, SW, SE directions. Whenever an unlabelled non-zero leaf node is entered, a new label is

assigned to it. Then search for neighbouring leaf nodes in the E and S directions (plus SE in 8-connectivity). If those leaves are non-zero and have not yet been labelled, assign the label of the node from which the search started. If the neighbouring leaf node has already been labelled, store the collision information in an equivalence table.

2. Repeat step (1) until the whole tree has been searched.
3. **Second pass :** Re-label the leaf nodes of the quadtree according to the equivalence table.

9.7 CONTOUR-BASED SHAPE REPRESENTATION AND DESCRIPTION

- Region borders must be expressed in some mathematical form.

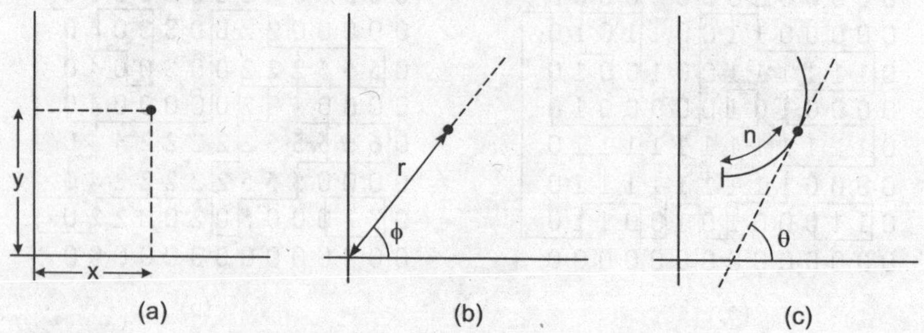

Fig. (9.7) Co-ordinate systems : (a) rectangular (cartesian), (b) polar, (c) tangential.

9.7.1 Chain Codes

- Chain codes describe an object by a sequence of unit-size line segments with a given orientation.
- The first element of such a sequence must bear information about its position to permit the region to be reconstructed.

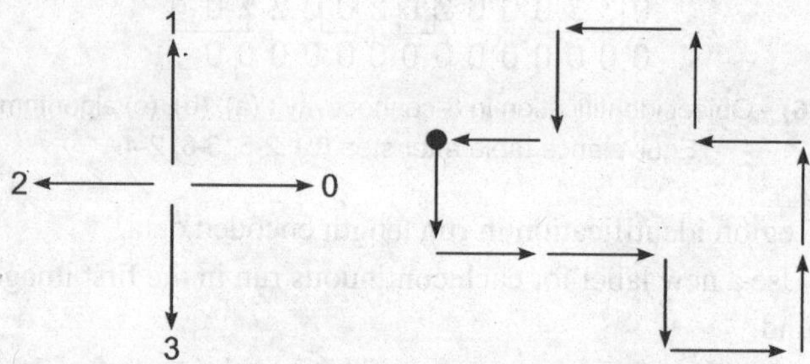

Fig. (9.8) Chain code in 4-connectivity, and its derivative. Code : 3, 0, 0, 3, 0, 1, 1, 2, 1, 2, 3, 2, derivative : 1, 0, 3, 1, 1, 0, 1, 3, 1, 1, 3, 1.

- If the chain code is used for matching it must be independent of the choice of the first border pixel in the sequence. One possibility for normalizing the chain code is to find the pixel in the border sequence which results in the minimum integer number if the description chain is interpreted as a base four number — that pixel is then used as the starting pixel.

  — A mod 4 or mod 8 difference is called a chain code derivative.

9.7.2 Other Contour-Based Shape Description Approaches

- Many other methods and approaches can be used to describe two-dimensional curves and contours.
- The Hough transform has excellent shape description abilities.
- Region-based shape description using statistical moments is covered below.
- Fractal approach to shape is gaining attention in image shape description.
- Mathematical morphology can be used for shape description, typically in connection with region skeleton construction.
- Neural networks can be used to recognize shapes in raw boundary representations directly. Contour sequences of noiseless reference shapes are used for training, and noisy data are used in later training stages to increase robustness; effective representations of closed planar shapes result.

9.7.3 Shape Invariants

- Shape invariants represent a very active current research area in machine vision.
- Importance of shape invariance has been known for a long time however it is somewhat novel approach in machine vision.
- Invariant theory is not new and many of its principles were introduced in the nineteenth century.
- Shape descriptors discussed so far depend on viewpoint, meaning that object recognition may often be impossible as a result of changed object or observer position.
- The role of shape description invariance is obvious — shape invariants represent properties of such geometric configurations which remain unchanged under an appropriate class of transforms.
- Machine vision is especially concerned with the class of projective transforms.

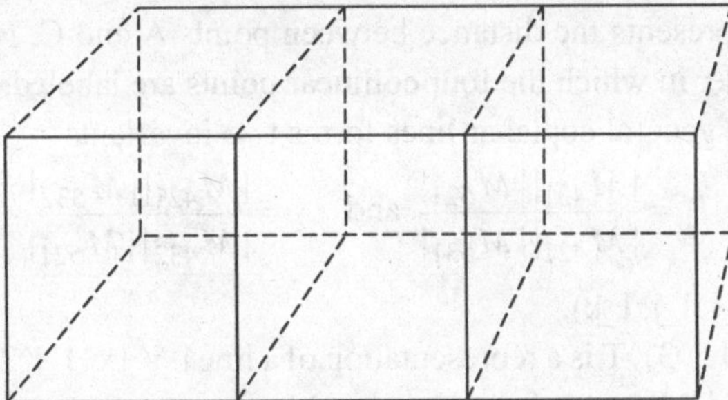

Fig. (9.9) Change of shape caused by a projective transform. The same rectangular cross-section is represented by different polygons in the image plane.

- Co linearity is the simplest example of a protectively invariant image feature. Any straight line is projected as a straight line under any projective transform.
- Similarly, the basic idea of the projection-invariant shape description is to find such shape features that are unaffected by the transform between the object and the image plane.

- A standard technique of projection-invariant description is to hypothesize the pose (position and orientation) of an object and transform this object into a specific co-ordinate system; then shape characteristics measured in this co-ordinate system yield an invariant description.
- However, the pose must be hypothesized for each object and each image which makes this approach difficult and unreliable.
- Application of invariant theory, where invariant descriptors can be computed directly from image data without the need for a particular co-ordinate system, represents another approach.
- Let corresponding entities in two different co-ordinate systems be distinguished by large and small letters. An invariant of a linear transformation may be defined as:
  — An invariant, I(P), of a geometric structure described by a parameter vector P, subject to a linear transformation T of the co-ordinates x=TX, is transformed according to I(p)=I(P)|T|^w.
  — Here I(p) is the function of the parameters after the linear transformation, and |T| is the determinant of the matrix T.
- In this definition, w is referred to as the weight of the invariant. If w=0, the invariants are called scalar invariants, which are considered below.
- Invariant descriptors are unaffected by object pose, by perspective projection, and by the intrinsic parameters of the camera.
- Several examples of invariants are now given.
- Cross ratio:
- The cross ratio represents a classic invariant of a projective line.
  — A straight line is always projected as a straight line. Any four collinear points A,B,C,D may be described by the cross-ratio invariant

$$I = \frac{(A-C)(B-D)}{(A-D)(B-C)}$$

- Where (A-C) represents the distance between points A and C. Note that the cross ratio depends on the order in which the four collinear points are labeled.
- A system of five general coplanar lines forms two invariants

$$I_1 = \frac{|M_{431}||M_{521}|}{|M_{421}||M_{531}|} \text{ and } I_2 = \frac{|M_{421}||M_{532}|}{|M_{432}||M_{521}|}$$

  where M_ijk=(l_i, l_j, l_k).
  l_i=(l_i^1,l_i^2,l_i^3)^T is a representation of a line l_i^1x+l_i^2y+l_i^3=0, where i is from interval [1,5], and |M| is the determinant of M.
  If the three lines forming the matrix M_ijk are concurrent, the matrix becomes singular and the invariant is undefined.
- A system of five coplanar points is dual to a system of five lines and the same two invariants are formed.
- These two functional invariants can also be formed as two cross ratios of two coplanar concurrent line quadruples.
- Note that even though combinations other than those given in Figure may be formed, only the two presented functionally independent invariants exist.

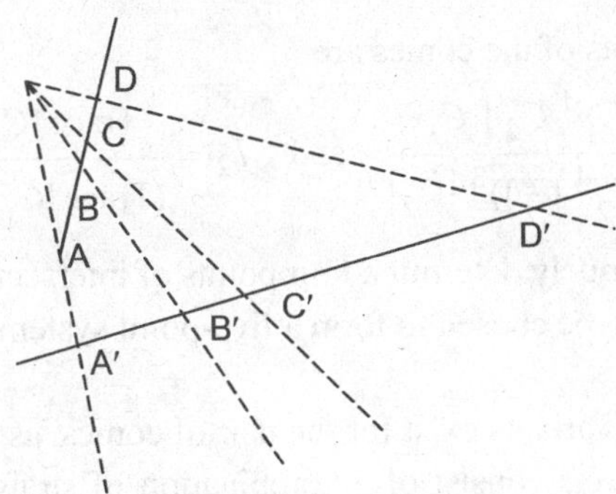

Fig. (9.10) Cross ratio; four collinear points form a projective invariant.

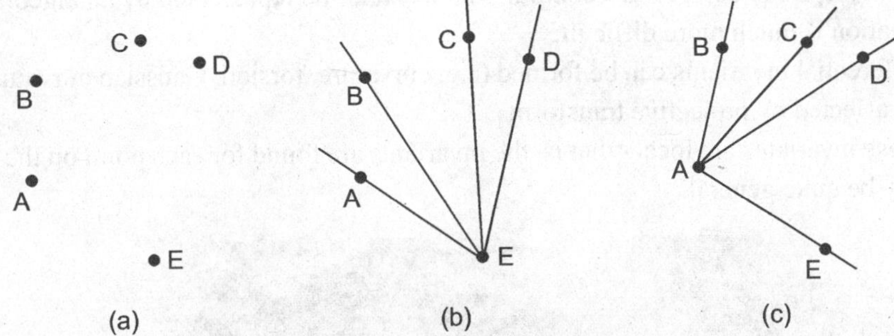

Fig. (9.11) Five coploanar points form two cross-ratio invariants : (a) coplanar points (b) five points form a system of four concurrent lines (c) the same five points form another system of four coplanar lines.

9.7.4 Plane Conics

A plane conic may be represented by an equation

$$ax^2 + bxy + cy^2 + dx + cy + f = 0$$

for x=(x,y,1)^T.

Then the conic may also be defined by a matrix C

$$x^T < x = 0$$

- For any conic represented by a matrix C, and any two coplanar lines not tangent to the conic, one invariant may be defined

$$I = \frac{(1_1^T\ C^{-1}\ 1_2)^2}{(1_1^T\ C^{-1}\ 1_1)\,(1_2^T\ C^{-1}\ 1_2)}$$

- The same invariant can be formed for a conic and two coplanar points.
- Two invariants can be determined for a pair of conics represented by their respective matrices C_1, C_2 normalized so that |C_i|=1

$$I_1 = \text{Trace}\,[C_1^{-1}\ C_2] \quad \text{and} \quad I_2 = \text{Trace}\,[C_2^{-1}\ C_1]$$

- For non-normalized conics, the invariants of associated quadratic forms are

$$I_1 = \text{Trace}\,[C_1^{-1}\ C_2]\left(\frac{|C_1|}{|C_2|}\right)^{1/3} \quad \text{and} \quad I_2 = \text{Trace}\,[C_2^{-1}\ C_1]\left(\frac{|C_2|}{|C_1|}\right)^{1/3}$$

- The two true invariants of the conics are

$$I_1 = \frac{\text{Trace}\,[C_1^{-1}\,C_2]|C_1|}{(\text{Trace}\,[C_2^{-1}\,C_1])^3\,|C_2|} \quad \text{and} \quad I_2 = \frac{\text{Trace}\,[C_2^{-1}\,C_1]|C_2|}{(\text{Trace}\,[C_1^{-1}\,C_2])^2\,|C_1|}$$

- Two plane conics uniquely determine four points of intersection, and any point that is not an intersection point may be chosen to form a five-point system together with the four intersection points.
  — Therefore, two invariants exist for the pair of conics, as for the five-point system.
- Many man-made objects consist of a combination of straight lines and conics, and these invariants may be used for their description.
- However, if the object has a contour which cannot be represented by an algebraic curve, the situation is much more difficult.
- Differential invariants can be formed (e.g. curvature, torsion, Gaussian curvature) which are not affected by projective transforms.
- These invariants are local - that is, the invariants are found for each point on the curve, which may be quite general.

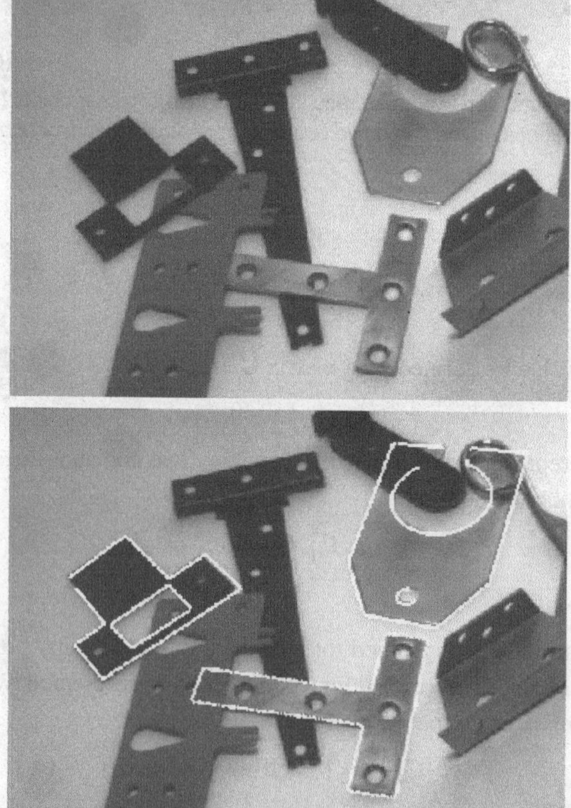

Fig. (9.12) Object recognition based on shape five coplanar (b) original image of overlapping objects taken form an arbitrary invariant (b) object recognition based on line and came invariants, courtesy D, Faraday, the university of Iowa; C. Rathwe, A. Zise, University of Coford, I. Mundy General, Electric Coporate and Meni , NY.

- Unfortunately, these invariants are extremely large and complex polynomials, requiring up to seventh derivatives of the curve, which makes them practically unusable due to image noise and acquisition errors, although noise-resistant local invariants are beginning to appear.
- However, if additional information is available, higher derivatives may be avoided.
- Stability of invariants is another crucial property, which affects their applicability. The robustness of invariants to image noise and errors introduced by image sensors is of prime importance, although not much is known about this.
- Different invariants have different stability and distinguishing powers.
- An example of recognition of man-made objects using invariant description of four coplanar lines, a conic and two lines, and a pair of coplanar conics is given.
- The recognition system is based on a model library containing over thirty object models - significantly more than that reported for other recognition systems.
- Moreover, the construction of the model library is extremely easy; no special measurements are needed, the object is digitized in a standard way and the protectively invariant description is stored as a model.
  - Further, there is no need for camera calibration. The recognition accuracy is 100% for occluded objects viewed from different viewpoints if the objects are not severely disrupted by shadows and specularities.

Region-based shape representation and description.

Simple scalar region descriptors :

- A large group of shape description techniques is represented by heuristic approaches, which yield acceptable results in description of simple shapes.
- Heuristic region descriptors:
  - Area,
  - Rectangularity,
  - Elongatedness,
  - Direction,
  - Compactness, etc.
- These descriptors cannot be used for region reconstruction and do not work for more complex shapes.
- Procedures based on region decomposition into smaller and simpler sub regions must be applied to describe more complicated regions, then sub regions can be described separately using heuristic approaches.
- Simple scalar region descriptors
- Area is given by the number of pixels of which the region consists.
- The real area of each pixel may be taken into consideration to get the real size of a region.
- If an image is represented as a rectangular raster, simple counting of region pixels will provide its area.
- If the image is represented by a quadtree, then:

Algorithm 9.4 : Calculating area in quadtrees

1. Set all region area variables to zero and determine the global quadtree depth H; for example, the global quadtree depth is $H = 8$ for a 256×256 image.

2. Search the tree in a systematic way. If a leaf node at a depth h has a non-zero label, proceed to step (3).
3. Compute:

$$\text{area[region\_label]} = \text{area[region\_label]} + 4^{(H-h)}$$

4. The region areas are stored in variables area [region_label].

- The region can also be represented by n polygon vertices

$$\text{area} = \frac{1}{2}\left|\sum_{k=0}^{n-1} (i_k\, j_{k+1} - i_{k+1}\, j_k)\right|$$

The sign of the sum represents the polygon orientation.

- If the region is represented by the (anti-clockwise) Freeman chain code the following algorithm provides the area.

Algorithm 9.5 : Region area calculation from Freeman 4-connectivity chain code representation.

1. Set the region area to zero. Assign the value of the starting point i co-ordinate to the variable vertical position.
2. For each element of the chain code (values 0, 1, 2, 3) do

```
switch(code){
     Case 0;
          area := area - vertical_position;
          break;
     Case 1;
          vertical_position := vertical_position + 1;
          break;
     Case 2;
          area := area + vertical_position;
          break;
     Case 3;
          vertical_position := vertical_position - 1;
          break;
}
```

3. If all boundary chain elements have been processed, the region area is stored in the variable area.

- Euler's number.
- (sometimes called Genus or the Euler-Poincare characteristic) describes a simple topologically invariant property of the object.
  — S is the number of contiguous parts of an object and N is the number of holes in the object (an object can consist of more than one region).

$$\vartheta = S - N$$

- Projections
  — Horizontal and vertical region projections

$$p_h(i) = \sum_j f(i, j), \;\; p_v(j) = \sum_i f(i, j)$$

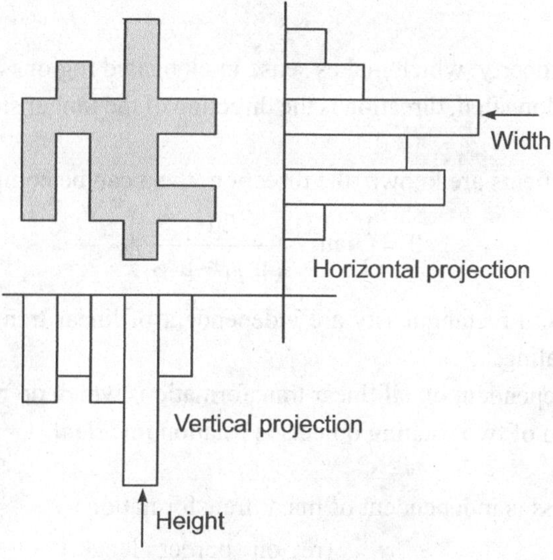

Fig. (9.13) Projections.

- Eccentricity
- The simplest is the ratio of major and minor axes of an object.
- Elongatedness
- A ratio between the length and width of the region-bounding rectangle.

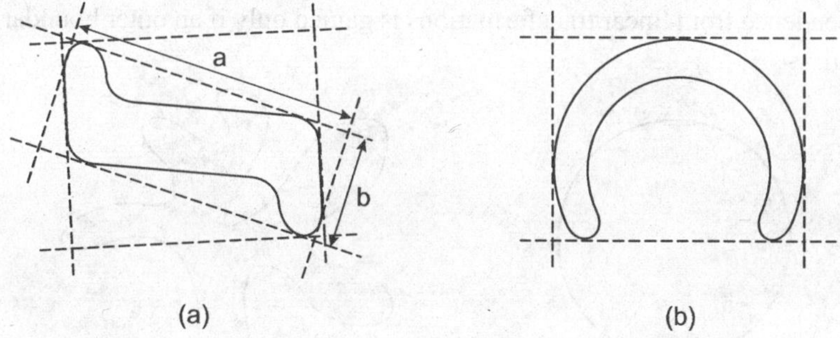

Fig. (9.14) Elongatedness : (a) Bounding rectangle gives acceptable results, (b) bounding rectangle cannot represent elongatedness.

- This criterion cannot succeed in curved regions, for which the evaluation of elongatedness must be based on maximum region thickness.
- Elongatedness can be evaluated as a ratio of the region area and the square of its thickness.
- The maximum region thickness (holes must be filled if present) can be determined as the number d of erosion steps that may be applied before the region totally disappears.

$$\text{elongatedness} = \frac{\text{area}}{(2-I)^2}$$

- Rectangularity
  — Let F_k be the ratio of region area and the area of a bounding rectangle, the rectangle having the direction k. The rectangle direction is turned in discrete steps as before, and rectangularity measured as a maximum of this ratio F_k

$$\text{rectangularity} = \max_k (F_k)$$

- Direction
- Direction is a property, which makes sense in elongated regions only.
- If the region is elongated, direction is the direction of the longer side of a minimum-bounding rectangle.
- If the shape moments are known, the direction \theta can be computed as

$$\vartheta = \frac{1}{2}\tan^{-1}\left(\frac{2\mu_{11}}{\mu_{20} - \mu_{02}}\right)$$

- Elongatedness and rectangularity are independent of linear transformations — translation, rotation, and scaling.
- Direction is independent on all linear transformations which do not include rotation.
- Mutual direction of two rotating objects is rotation invariant.
- Compactness
  — Compactness is independent of linear transformations

$$\text{compactness} = \frac{(\text{region\_ border\_ length})^2}{\text{area}}$$

- The most compact region in a Euclidean space is a circle.
- Compactness assumes values in the interval [1,infty) in digital images if the boundary is defined as an inner boundary, while using the outer boundary, compactness assumes values in the interval [16,infty).
- Independence from linear transformations is gained only if an outer boundary representation is used.

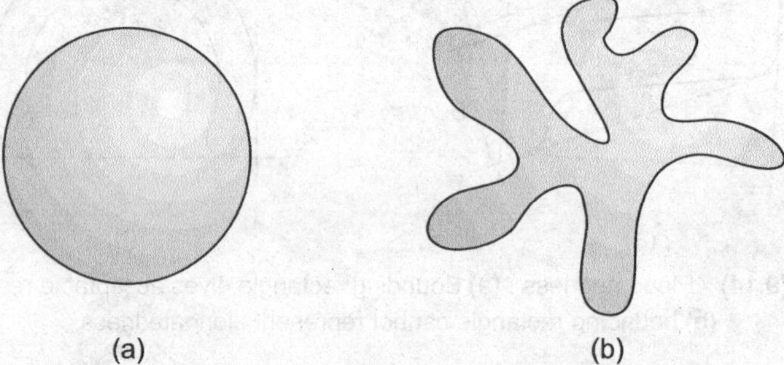

Fig. (9.15) Compactness (a) compact, (b) non-compact.

Moments :

- Region moment representations interpret a normalized gray level image function as a probability density of a 2D random variable.
- Properties of this random variable can be described using statistical characteristics - moments.
- Assuming that non-zero pixel values represent regions, moments can be used for binary or gray level region description.
- A moment of order (p+q) is dependent on scaling, translation, rotation, and even on gray level transformations and is given by

$$m_{pq} = \int_{-\infty}^{\infty}\int_{-\infty}^{\infty} x^p\, y^q\, f(x, y)\, dx\, dy$$

- In digitized images we evaluate sums

$$m_{pq} = \sum_{i=-\infty}^{\infty} \sum_{j=-\infty}^{\infty} i^p \, j^p \, f(i, j)$$

- Where x, y, i, j are the region point co-ordinates (pixel co-ordinates in digitized images).
- Translation invariance can be achieved if we use the central moments

$$\mu_{pq} = \int_{-\infty}^{\infty} \int_{-\infty}^{\infty} (x - x_c)^p \, (y - y_c)^q \, f(x, y) \, dx \, dy$$

- Or in digitized images

$$\mu_{pq} = \sum_{i=-\infty}^{\infty} \sum_{i=-\infty}^{\infty} (i - x_c)^p \, (j - y_c)^q \, f(i, j)$$

- Where x_c, y_c are the co-ordinates of the region's centroid

$$x_c = \frac{m_{0}}{m_{00}}$$

$$y_c = \frac{m_{01}}{m_{00}}$$

- In the binary case, m_00 represents the region area.
  — Scale invariant features can also be found in scaled central moments

$$\eta_{pq} = \frac{\mu'_{pq}}{(\mu'_{00})^{\gamma}}$$

$$\gamma = \frac{p+q}{2} + 1$$

$$\mu'_{pq} = \frac{\mu_{pq}}{\alpha^{(p+q+2)}}$$

and normalized unscaled central moments

$$\vartheta_{pq} = \frac{\mu_{pq}}{(\mu_{00})^{\gamma}}$$

- Rotation invariance can be achieved if the co-ordinate system is chosen such that mu_11 = 0.
- A less general form of invariance is given by seven rotation, translation, and scale invariant moment characteristics

$$\psi_1 = \vartheta_{20} + \vartheta_{02}$$

$$\psi_2 = (\vartheta_{20} - \vartheta_{02})^2 + 4\vartheta_{11}^2$$

$$\psi_3 = (\vartheta_{20} - 3\vartheta_{12})^2 + (3\vartheta_{21} - \vartheta_{03})^2$$

$$\psi_4 = (\vartheta_{20} + \vartheta_{12})^2 + (\vartheta_{21} + \vartheta_{03})^2$$

$$\psi_5 = (\vartheta_{20} - 3\vartheta_{12})(\vartheta_{30} - \vartheta_{12})[(\vartheta_{30} + \vartheta_{12})^2 - 3(\vartheta_{21} + \vartheta_{03})^2] + (3\vartheta_{21} - \vartheta_{03})(\vartheta_{21} + \vartheta_{03})[3(\vartheta_{30} + \vartheta_{12})^2 - (\vartheta_{21} + \vartheta_{03})^2]$$

$$\psi_6 = (\vartheta_{20} - \vartheta_{02})[(\vartheta_{30} + \vartheta_{12})^2 - (\vartheta_{21} + \vartheta_{03})^2] + 4\vartheta_{11}(\vartheta_{30} + \vartheta_{12})(\vartheta_{21} + \vartheta_{03})$$

$$\psi_7 = (3\vartheta_{21} - \vartheta_{03})(\vartheta_{30} + \vartheta_{12})[(\vartheta_{30} + \vartheta_{12})^2 - 3(\vartheta_{21} + \vartheta_{03})^2] - (\vartheta_{30} - 3\vartheta_{12})(\vartheta_{21} + \vartheta_{03})[3(\vartheta_{30} + \vartheta_{12})^2 - (\vartheta_{21} + \vartheta_{03})^2]$$

- While the seven moment characteristics presented above were shown to be useful, they are only invariant to translation, rotation, and scaling.
- A complete set of four affine moment invariants derived from second- and third-order moments is

$$I_1 = \frac{\mu_{20}\,\mu_{02} - \mu_{11}^2}{\mu_{00}^4}$$

$$I_2 = \frac{\mu_{30}^2\mu_{03}^2 - 6\mu_{30}\mu_{21}\mu_{12}\mu_{03} + 4\mu_{30}\mu_{13}^3 + 4\mu_{31}^3\mu_{03} - 3\mu_{21}^2\mu_{12}^2}{\mu_{00}^{10}}$$

$$I_3 = \frac{\mu_{20}(\mu_{21}\mu_{03} - \mu_{12}^2) - \mu_{11}(\mu_{30}\mu_{03} - \mu_{21}\mu_{12}) + \mu_{02}(\mu_{20}\mu_{12} - \mu_{21}^2)}{\mu_{00}^7}$$

$$I_4 = \frac{\begin{array}{c}(\mu_{20}^3\mu_{03}^2 - 6\mu_{20}^3\mu_{11}\mu_{13}\mu_{03} - 6\mu_{20}^2\mu_{02}\mu_{21}\mu_{03} + 9\mu_{20}^2\mu_{02}\mu_{12}^2 + 12\mu_{20}\mu_{11}^2\mu_{21}\mu_{03} + \\ 6\mu_{20}\mu_{11}\mu_{02}\mu_{30}\mu_{03} - 18\mu_{20}\mu_{11}\mu_{03}\mu_{21}\mu_{12} - 8\mu_{11}^3\mu_{30}\mu_{03} - 6\mu_{30}\mu_{02}^2\mu_{30}\mu_{12} + \\ 9\mu_{20}\mu_{02}^2\mu_{21}^2 + 12\mu_{11}^2\mu_{02}\mu_{30}\mu_{12} - 6\mu_{11}\mu_{02}^2\mu_{30}\mu_{21} + \mu_{02}^2\mu_{30}^2)\end{array}}{\mu_{00}^{11}}$$

- All moment characteristics are dependent on the linear gray level transformations of regions; to describe region shape properties, we work with binary image data (f(i,j)=1 in region pixels) and dependence on the linear gray level transform disappears.
- Moment characteristics can be used in shape description even if the region is represented by its boundary.
- A closed boundary is characterized by an ordered sequence z(i) that represents the Euclidean distance between the centroid and all N boundary pixels of the digitized shape.
- No extra processing is required for shapes having spiral or concave contours.
- Translation, rotation, and scale invariant one-dimensional normalized contour sequence moments can be estimated as

$$m_r = \frac{1}{N}\sum_{i=1}^{N} [x(i)]^r$$

$$\mu_r = \frac{1}{N}\sum_{i=1}^{N} [x(i) - m_1]^r$$

- The r-th normalized contour sequence moment and normalized central contour sequence moment are defined as

$$\overline{m}_r = \frac{m_r}{(\mu_2)^{r/2}} = \frac{\frac{1}{N}\sum_{i=1}^{N} [z(i)]^r}{\left[\frac{1}{N}\sum_{i=1}^{N} [z(i) - m_1]^2\right]^{r/2}}$$

$$\bar{\mu}_r = \frac{\mu_r}{(\mu_2)^{r/2}} = \frac{\frac{1}{N}\sum_{i=1}^{N}[z(i)-m_1]^r}{\left[\frac{1}{N}\sum_{i=1}^{N}[z(i)-m_1]^2\right]^{r/2}}$$

- Less noise-sensitive results can be obtained from the following shape descriptors

9.8 SIMPLE GEOMETRIC BORDER REPRESENTATION

- The following descriptors are mostly based on geometric properties of described regions. Because of the discrete character of digital images, all of them are sensitive to image resolution.
  — Boundary length

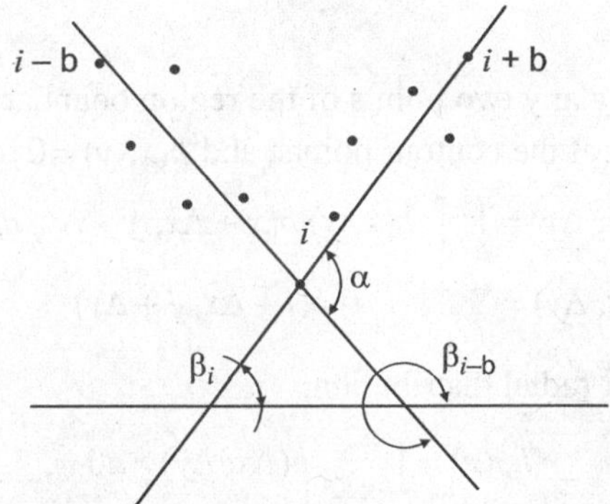

Fig. (9.16) Curvature.

  — Curvature
- Bending energy

$$BE = \frac{1}{L}\sum_{k=1}^{L} c^2(k)$$

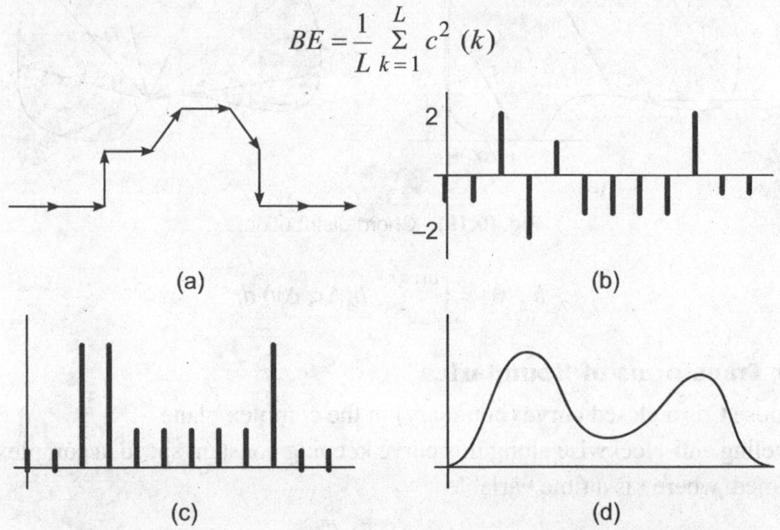

Fig. (9.17) Bending energy : (a) Chain code 0, 0, 2, 0, 1, 0, 7, 6, 0, 0, (b) curvature 0, 2, –2, 1, –1, –1, –1, 2, 0 (c) sum of squares gives the bending energy, (d) smoothed version.

- Signature

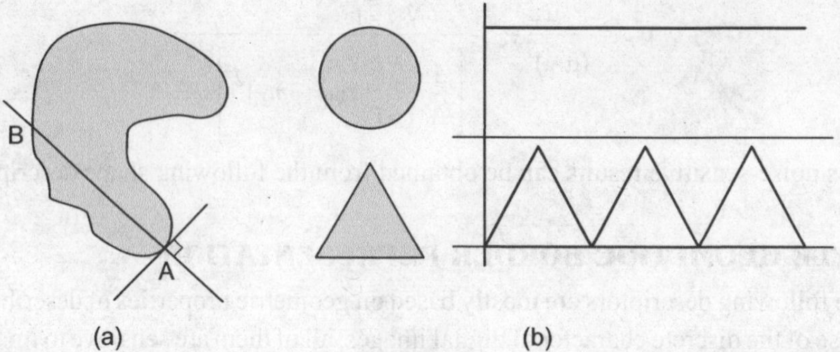

Fig. (9.18) Signature : (a) construction, (b) signatures for a circle and a triangle.

- Chord
- Chord is a line joining any two points of the region boundary is a chord.
- Let $b(x, y) = 1$ represent the contour points, and $b(x, y) = 0$ represent all other points.

$$h(\Delta x, \Delta y) = \int \int b(x, y)\, b(x + \Delta x, y + \Delta y)\, dx\, dy$$

$$h(\Delta x, \Delta y) = \sum_i \sum_j b(i, j)\, b(i + \Delta x, j + \Delta y)$$

- Rotation-independent radial distribution:

$$h_r(r) = \int_{-\pi/2}^{\pi/2} h(\Delta x, \Delta y)\, r\, d\theta$$

- The angular distribution h_a(theta) is independent of scale, while rotation causes a proportional offset

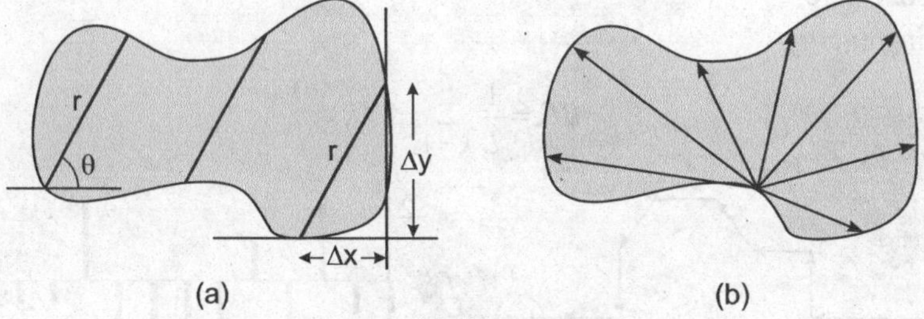

Fig. (9.19) Chord distribution.

$$h_\alpha(\theta) = \int_0^{\max(r)} h(\Delta x, \Delta y)\, dr$$

9.8.1 Fourier Transforms of Boundaries

- Suppose C is a closed curve (boundary) in the complex plane.
- Traveling anti-clockwise along this curve keeping constant speed, a complex function z(t) is obtained, where t is a time variable.

$$z(t) = \sum_n T_n e^{int}$$

- The coefficients T_n of the series are called the Fourier descriptors of the curve C. It is more useful to consider the curve distance s in comparison to time

$$t = 2\pi s/L$$

- Where L is the curve length. The Fourier descriptors T_n are given by

$$T_n = \frac{1}{L}\int_0^L z(s)\, e^{-i(2\pi/L)ns}\, ds$$

- The descriptors are influenced by the curve shape and by the initial point of the curve. Working with digital image data, boundary co-ordinates are discrete and the function z(s) is not continuous. Assume that z(k) is a discrete version of z(s), where 4-connectivity is used to get a constant sampling interval; the descriptors T_n can be computed from the discrete Fourier transform.

$$z(k) \leftarrow DFT \rightarrow T_n$$

- The Fourier descriptors can be invariant to translation and rotation if the co-ordinate system is appropriately chosen.

$$a_n = \frac{1}{L-1}\sum_{m=1}^{L-1} x_m\, e^{-i(2\pi/(L-1))\,nm}$$

$$b_n = \frac{1}{L-1}\sum_{m=1}^{L-1} y_m\, e^{-i(2\pi/(L-1))\,nm}$$

- The coefficients a_n, b_n are not invariant, but after the transform

$$r_n = (|a_n|^2 + |b_n|^2)^{1/2}$$

- r_n are translation and rotation invariant.
- To achieve a magnification invariance the descriptors w_n are used:

$$w_n = r_n / r_1$$

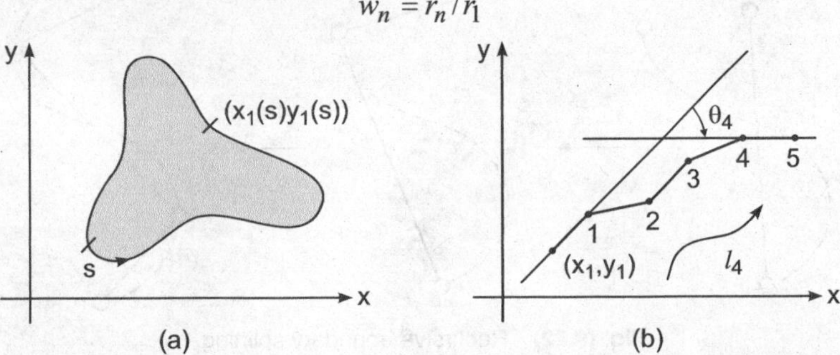

Fig. (9.20) Fourier description of boundaries : (a) descriptors T_n, (b) descriptors S_n.

- The first 10 — 15 descriptors w_n are found to be sufficient for character description.
- A closed boundary can be represented as a function of angle tangents versus the distance between the boundary points from which the angles were determined

$$a(l_k) = \psi_k + u_k$$

$$u_k = 2\pi\, l_k / L$$

- The descriptor set is then

$$S_n = \frac{1}{2\pi}\int_0^{2\pi} a(u)\, e^{-inu}\, du$$

- The high quality boundary shape representation obtained using only a few lower order coefficients is a favorable property common to Fourier descriptors.

9.8.2 Boundary Description Using Segment Sequences

- If the segment type is known for all segments, the boundary can be described as a chain of segment types, a code-word consisting of representatives of a type alphabet.
- A polygonal representation approximates a region by a polygon, the region being represented using its vertices. Polygonal representations are obtained as a result of a simple boundary segmentation.
- Another method for determining the boundary vertices is a tolerance interval approach based on setting a maximum allowed difference e.

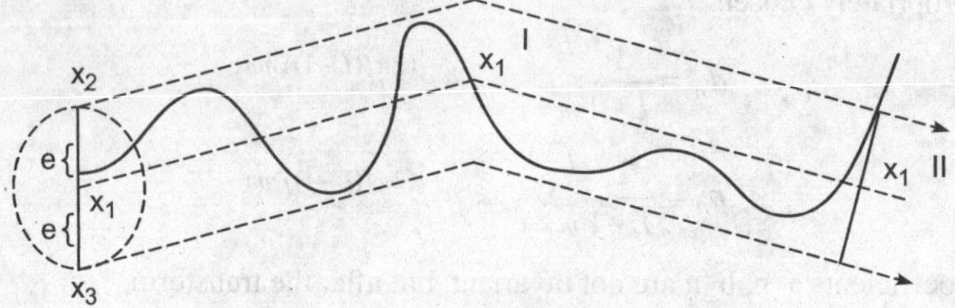

Fig. (9.21) Tolerance interval.

9.8.3 Recursive Boundary Splitting

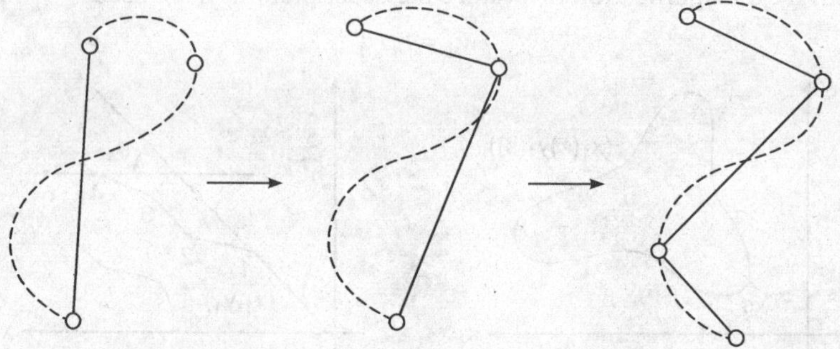

Fig. (9.22) Recursive boundary splitting.

- Boundary segmentation into segments of constant curvature or curve segmentation into circular arcs and straight lines is used.

— Segments are considered as primitives for syntactic shape recognition procedures.

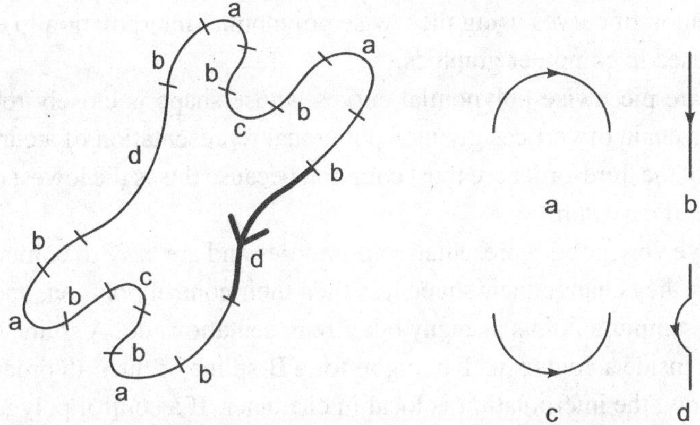

Fig. (9.23) Structural description of chromosomes by a chain of boundary segments, code word : d, b, a, b, c, b, a, b, d, b, a, b, c, b, a, b (adapted from [Fu 74]).

- Sensitivity of shape descriptors to scale is also important if a curve is to be divided into segments — a scale-space approach to curve segmentation.
- Only new segmentation points can appear at higher resolutions, and no existing segmentation points can disappear.
- Fine details of the curve disappear in pairs with increasing size of the Gaussian smoothing kernel, and two segmentation points always merge to form a closed contour showing that any segmentation point existing in coarse resolution must also exist in finer resolution.
- Moreover, the position of a segmentation point is most accurate in finest resolution and this position can be traced from coarse to fine resolution using the scale-space image.
- A multiscale curve description can be represented by an interval tree.

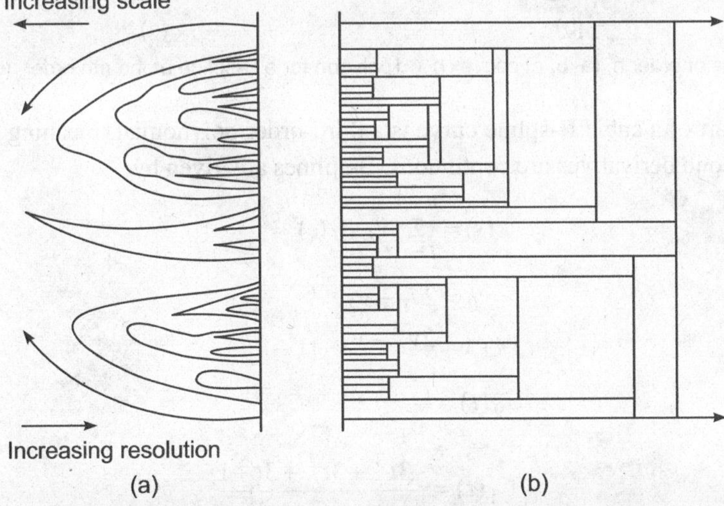

Fig. (9.24) Scale-space image : (a) Varying number and locations of curve segmentation points as a function of scale, (b) curve representation by an interval tree.

9.9 B-SPLINE REPRESENTATION

- Representation of curves using piecewise polynomial interpolation to obtain smooth curves is widely used in computer graphics.
- B-splines are piecewise polynomial curves whose shape is closely related to their control polygon - a chain of vertices giving a polygonal representation of a curve.
- B-splines of the third-order are most common because this is the lowest order, which includes the change of curvature.
- Splines have very good representation properties and are easy to compute:
  - — Firstly, they change their shape less then their control polygon, and do not oscillate between sampling points as many other representations do. A spline curve is always positioned inside a convex n+1-polygon for a B-spline of the n-th order.
  - — Secondly, the interpolation is local in character. If a control polygon vertex changes its position, a resulting change of the spline curve will occur only in a small neighborhood of that vertex.
  - — Thirdly, methods of matching region boundaries represented by splines to image data are based on a direct search of original image data.

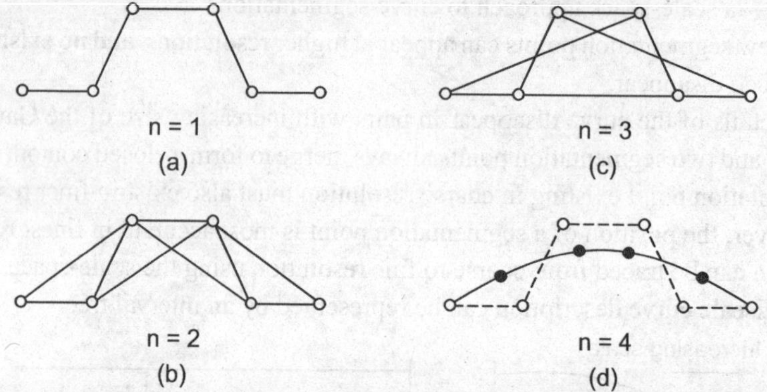

Fig. (9.25) Splines of order n, (a, b, c) convex $n + 1$-polygon for a B-spline of the nth order, (d) 3rd order spline.

- Each part of a cubic B-spline curve is a third-order polynomial, meaning that it and its first and second derivatives are continuous. B-splines are given by

$$x(s) = \sum_{i=0}^{n+1} v_i \, B_i(s)$$

$$v_0 = 2v_1 - v_2$$

$$v_{n+1} = 2v_n - v_{a-1}$$

$$C_0(t) = \frac{t^3}{6}$$

$$C_1(t) = \frac{-3t^3 + 3t^2 + 3t + 1}{6}$$

$$C_2(t) = \frac{3t_3 - 6t^2 + 4}{6}$$

$$C_3(t) = \frac{-t^3 + 3t^2 - 3t + 1}{6}$$

$$x(s) = C_{i=1,3}\,(s) v_{i-1} + C_{1,2}\,(s)\, v_i + C_{i+1,1}\,(s)\, v_{i+1} + C_{i+2,0}\,(s)\, v_{i+3}$$

$$C_{i,j}\,(s) = C_j\,(s-i) \qquad i = 0, \ldots, +1;\; j = 0, 1, 2, 3$$

$$x(s) = C_3\,(s-1)\, v_{i-1} + C_2(s-1)\, v_i + C_1(s-i)\, v_{i+1} + C_0\, v_{i+2}$$

Fig. (9.26) Splines of order n, (a, b, c) Convex $n+$ 1-polygon for a B-spline of the nth order, (d) 3rd order spline.

$$x(5) = C_3\,(0)\, v_4 + C_2\,(0)\, v_5 + C_1(0)\, v_e = \frac{1}{6} v_4 + \frac{4}{6} v_5 + \frac{1}{6} v_6$$

$$x(5) = C_3\,(0.7)\, v_6 + C_2\,(0.7)\, v_7 + C_1(0.7)\, v_s + C_0\,(0.7)\, v_s$$

9.10 CONVEX HULL

- A region R is convex if and only if for any two points x_1, x_2 from R, the whole line segment defined by its end-points x_1, x_2 is inside the region R.
- The convex hull of a region is the smallest convex region H which satisfies the condition R is a subset of H.
- The convex hull has some special properties in digital data which do not exist in the continuous case. For instance, concave parts can appear and disappear in digital data due to rotation, and therefore the convex hull is not rotation invariant in digital space.
- The convex hull can be used to describe region shape properties and can be used to build a tree structure of region concavity.

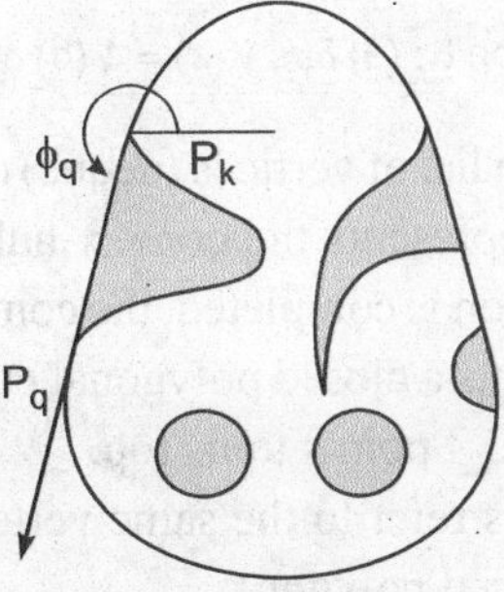

Fig. (9.27) Convex hull.

- A discrete convex hull can be defined by the following algorithm which may also be used for convex hull construction.
  - This algorithm has complexity O(n^2) and is presented here as an intuitive way of detecting the convex hull.

Algorithm 9.6 : Region convex hull construction.

1. Find all pixels of a region R with the minimum row co-ordinate; among them, find the pixel P_1 with the minimum column co-ordinate.
   Assign $P_k = P_1$, $v = (0, -1)$; the vector v represents the direction of the previous line segment of the convex hull.
2. Search the region bounday in an anti-clockwise direction (Algorithm ??) and compute the angle orientation ψ_n for every boundary point P_n which lies after the point P_1 (in the direction of boundary search – see)
3. Assign $v - P_k P_q, P_k = P_q$.
4. Repeat steps (2) and (3) until $P_k = P_1$.

- More efficient algorithms exist, especially if the object is defined by an ordered sequence of n vertices representing a polygonal boundary of the object.
- If the polygon P is a simple polygon (self-non-intersecting polygon) which is always the case in a polygonal representation of object borders, the convex hull may be found in linear time O(n).
- In the past two decades, many linear-time convex hull detection algorithms have been published, however more than half of them were later discovered to be incorrect with counter-examples published.
- The simplest correct convex hull algorithm was developed by Melkman and is now discussed further.
  - Let the polygon for which the convex hull is to be determined be a simple polygon P = v_1, v_2, ... v_n and let the vertices be processed in this order.
  - For any three vertices x,y,z in an ordered sequence, a directional function delta may be evaluated.

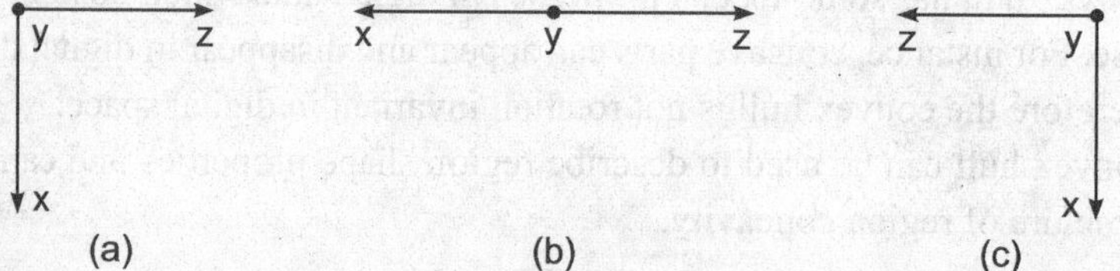

Fig. (9.28) Directional function δ : (a) δ(*x*, *y*, *z*) = 1, (b) δ(*x*, *y*, *z*) = 0, (c) δ(*x*, *y*, *z*) = – 1

- The main data structure H is a list of vertices (deque) of polygonal vertices already processed.
- The current contents of H represents the convex hull of the currently processed part of the polygon, and after the detection is completed, the convex hull is stored in this data structure.
- Therefore, H always represents a closed polygonal curve, H={d_b, ... ,d_t} where d_b points to the bottom of the list and d_t points to its top.
- Note that d_b and d_t always refer to the same vertex simultaneously representing the first and the last vertex of the closed polygon.

- Main ideas of the algorithm:
  - — The first three vertices A,B,C from the sequence P form a triangle (if not collinear) and this triangle represents a convex hull of the first three vertices.
  - — The next vertex D in the sequence is then tested for being located inside or outside the current convex hull.
  - — If D is located inside, the current convex hull does not change.

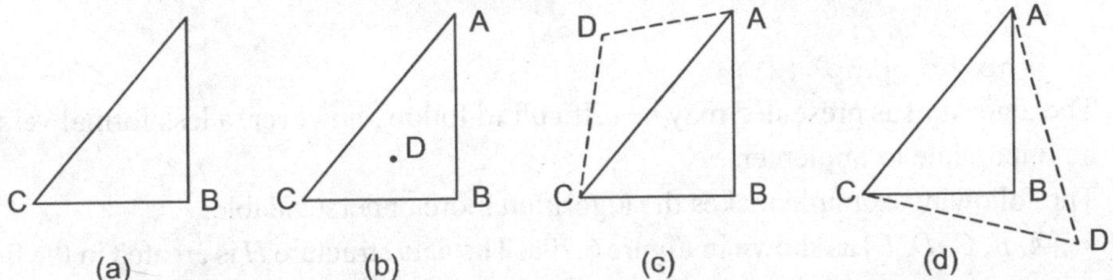

Fig. (9.29) Convex hull detection : (a) Fixed three vertices A, B, C form a triangle, (b) if the next vertex D is positioned inside the current convex hull ABC, current convex hull done not change, (c) if the next vertex D is outside of the current convex hull, it becames in new vertex of the new current convex hull ABCDA, (d) in this case, vertex B must be removed from the current convex hull and the new current convex hull is ADCA.

  - — If D is outside of the current convex hull, it must become a new convex hull vertex and based on the current convex hull shape, either none, one, or several vertices must be removed from the current convex hull.
  - — This process is repeated for all remaining vertices in the sequence P.
- The variable v refers to the input vertex under consideration, and the following operations are defined:

push v	:	$t := t + 1;\ d_1 \rightarrow v$
pop d_i	:	$t := t - 1$
insert v	:	$b := b - 1;\ d_1 \rightarrow v$
remove d_b	:	$b := b + 1;$
input v	:	next vertex is entered from sequence P, if P is empty, stop.

- The algorithm is then;

Algorithm 9.7 : Simple polygon convex hull detection.

1. Initialize;

```
t := - 1;
b := 0;
input v1; input v2; input v3;
if (δ(v1, v2, v3) > 0)
        {push v1; push v2;}
  else
        {push v2; push v1;}
push v3;
insert v3;
```

2. If the next vertex v is inside the current convex hull H, enter and check a new vertex; otherwise process steps (3) and (4);

```
input v;
while (δ(v, db, db + 1) ≥ 0 and δ(di - 1, di, v) ≥ 0)
        input v;
```

3. Rearrange vertices in H, top of the list

```
while (δ(d_{t-1}, d_t, v) ≤ 0)
        pop d_t'
push v;
```

4. Rearrange vertices in H, bottom of the list

```
while (δ(v, d_b, d_{b+1}) ≤ 0)
        remove d_t;
insert v;
go to step (2);
```

- The algorithm as presented may be difficult to follow, however, a less formal version would be impossible to implement.
- The following example makes the algorithm more understandable.

Let $P = \{A, B, C, D, E\}$ as shown in Figure 6.29a. The data structure H is created in the first step;

$t, b\ldots$		-1	0	1	2
H	$=$	C	A	B	C
		d_b			d_t

In the second step, vertex D is entered (Figure 6.29b);

$$\delta(D, d_b, d_{b+1}) = \delta(D, C, A) = 1 > 0$$

$$\delta(d_{t-1}, d_t, D) = \delta(B, C, D) = -1 < 0$$

Based on the values of the directional function δ, inthis case, no other vertex is entered during this step. Step (3) results in the following current convex hull H;

$$\delta(B, C, D) = -1 \rightarrow \text{pop } d_t \rightarrow$$

$t, b\ldots$		-1	0	1	2
H	$=$	C	A	B	C
		d_b		d_t	

$$\delta(A, B, D) = -1 \rightarrow \text{pop } d_t \rightarrow$$

$t, b\ldots$		-1	0	1	2
H	$=$	C	A	B	C
		d_b	d_t		

$$\delta(C, A, D) = -1 \rightarrow \text{push } D \rightarrow$$

$t, b\ldots$		-1	0	1	2
H	$=$	C	A	D	C
		d_b		d_t	

In step (4) – Figure 6.29c;

$$\delta(D, C, A) = 1 \rightarrow \text{insert } D \rightarrow$$

$t, b\ldots$		-2	-1	0	1	2
H	$=$	D	C	A	D	C
		d_b			d_t	

Go to step (2); vertex E is entered – Figure 6.29d;

$$\delta(E, D, C) = 1 > 0$$

$$\delta(A, D, E) = 1 > 0$$

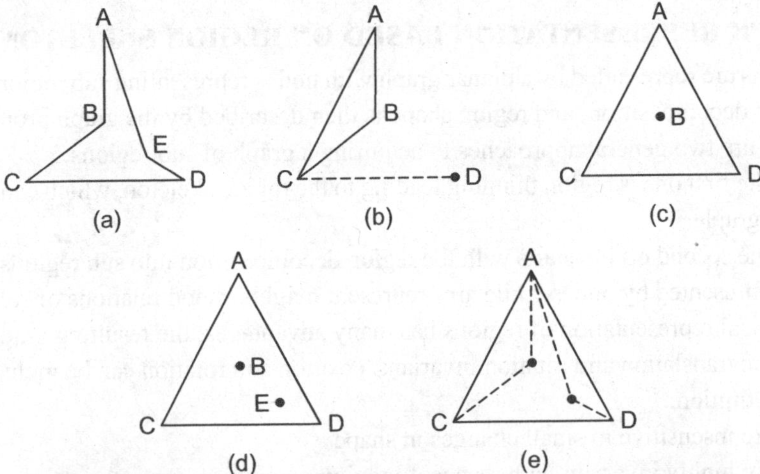

Fig. (9.30) Example of convex hull detection : (a) the processed region-polygon ABCDEA, (b) vertex D is entered and processed, c(vertex D becomes a new vertex of the current convex hull ADC, (d) vertex E is entered and processed, E does not becomes a new vertex of the current convex hull (e) the resulting convex hull DCAD.

- A new vertex should be entered from P, however there is no unprocessed vertex in the sequence P and the convex hull generating process stops.
- The resulting convex hull is defined by the sequence H={d_b, ... ,d_t}={D,C,A,D} which represents a polygon DCAD, always in the clockwise direction.
- A region concavity tree is generated recursively during the construction of a convex hull.
- A convex hull of the whole region is constructed first, and convex hulls of concave residua are found next.
- The resulting convex hulls of concave residua of the regions from previous steps are searched until no concave residuum exists.
- The resulting tree is a shape representation of the region.

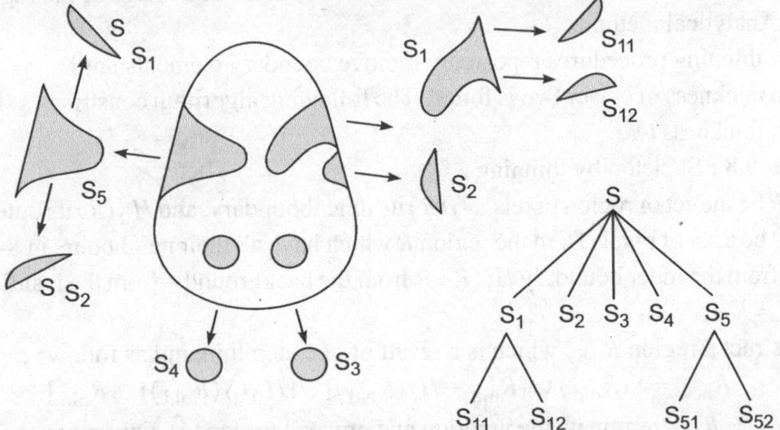

Fig. (9.31) Concavity tree construction : (a) Convex hull and concave residue, (b) concavity tree.

9.11 GRAPH REPRESENTATION BASED ON REGION SKELETON

- Objects are represented by a planar graph with nodes representing sub regions resulting from region decomposition, and region shape is then described by the graph properties.
- There are two general approaches to acquiring a graph of sub regions:
  — The first one is region thinning leading to the region skeleton, which can be described by a graph.
  — The second option starts with the region decomposition into sub regions, which are then represented by nodes while arcs represent neighborhood relations of sub regions.
- Graphical representation of regions has many advantages; the resulting graphs:
  — Are translation and rotation invariant; position and rotation can be included in the graph definition.
  — Are insensitive to small changes in shape
  — Are highly invariant with respect to region magnitude
  — Generate a representation which is understandable
  — Can easily be used to obtain the information-bearing features of the graph
  — Are suitable for syntactic recognition.
- Graph representation based on region skeleton
- This method corresponds significantly curving points of a region boundary to graph nodes.
- The main disadvantage of boundary-based description methods is that geometrically close points can be far away from one another when the boundary is described - graphical representation methods overcome this disadvantage.
- The region graph is based on the region skeleton, and the first step is the skeleton construction.
- There are four basic approaches to skeleton construction:
  — Thinning - iterative removal of region boundary pixels
  — Wave propagation from the boundary
  — Detection of local maxima in the distance-transformed image of the region
  — Analytical methods
- Most thinning procedures repeatedly remove boundary elements until a pixel set with maximum thickness of one or two is found. The following algorithm constructs a skeleton of maximum thickness two.

Algorithm 9.8 : Skeleton by thinning

1. Let R be the set of region pixels, $H_i(R)$ its inner boundary, and $H_0(R)$ its outer boundary. Let $S(R)$ be a set of pixels from the region R which have all their neighbours in 8-connectivity either from the inner boundary $H_i(R)$ or from the background – from the residium of R. Assign $R_{old} = R$.
2. Construct a region R_{new} which is a result of one-step thinning as follows :
$$R_{new} = S(R_{old}) \cup [R_{old} - H_i(R_{old})] \cup [H_0(S(R_{old})) \cap R_{old}]$$
3. If $R_{new} = R_{old}$, terminate the iteration and proceed to step (4). Otherwise assign $R_{old} = R_{new}$ and repeat step (2).
4. R_{new} is a set of skeleton pixels, the skeleton of the region R.

- Steps of this algorithm are illustrated in the next Figure.

- If there are skeleton segments which have a thickness of two, one extra step can be added to reduce those to a thickness of one, although care must be taken not to break the skeleton connectivity.

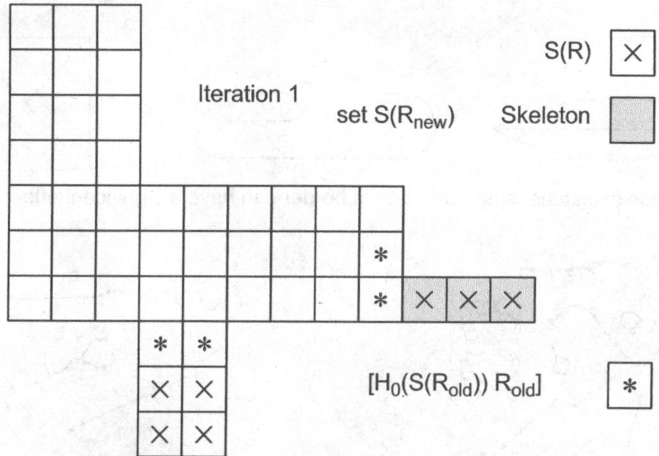

Fig. (9.32) Skeleton by thinning (algorithm 6.8).

- Thinning is generally a time-consuming process, although sometimes it is not necessary to look for a skeleton, and one side of a parallel boundary can be used for skeleton-like region representation.
- Mathematical morphology is a powerful tool used to find the region skeleton.
- Thinning procedures often use a medial axis transform to construct a region skeleton.
- Under the medial axis definition, the skeleton is the set of all region points, which have the same minimum distance from the region boundary for at least two separate boundary points.
- Such a skeleton can be constructed using a distance transform, which assigns a value to each region pixel representing its (minimum) distance from the region's boundary.
- The skeleton can be determined as a set of pixels whose distance from the region's border is locally maximal.
- Every skeleton element can be accompanied by information about its distance from the boundary — this gives the potential to reconstruct a region as an envelope curve of circles with center points at skeleton elements and radii corresponding to the stored distance values.
- Small changes in the boundary may cause serious changes in the skeleton.
- This sensitivity can be removed by first representing the region as a polygon, then constructing the skeleton.
- Boundary noise removal can be absorbed into the polygon construction.
- A multi-resolution approach to skeleton construction may also result in decreased sensitivity to boundary noise.
- Similarly, the approach using the Marr-Hildreth edge detector with varying smoothing parameter facilitates scale-based representation of the region's skeleton.

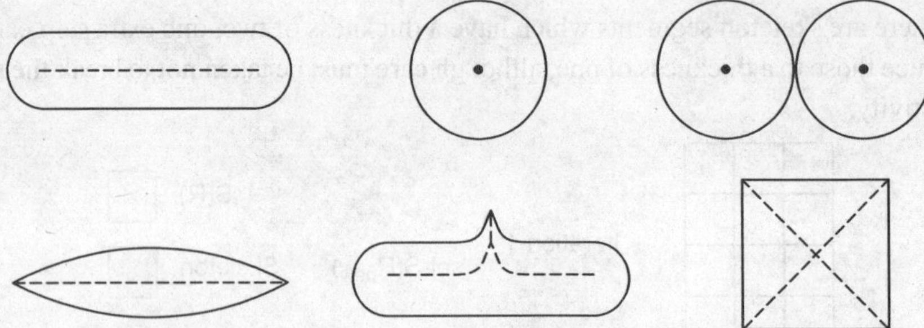

Fig. (9.33) Region skeletons; small changes in border can have a significant effect on the skeleton.

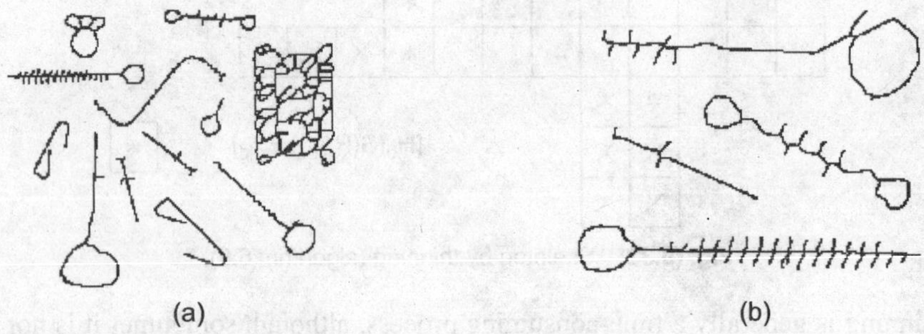

(a) (b)

Fig. (9.34) Region skeletons, see figures for original images; thickned for visibility.

- Skeleton construction algorithms do not result in graphs but the transformation from skeletons to graphs is relatively straightforward.
- Consider first the medial axis skeleton, and assume that a minimum radius circle has been drawn from each point of the skeleton, which has at least one point common with a region boundary.
- Let contact be each contiguous subset of the circle, which is common to the circle and to the boundary.
- If a circle drawn from its center A has one contact only, A is a skeleton end-point.
- If the point A has two contacts, it is a normal skeleton point.
- If A has three or more contacts, the point A is a skeleton node-point.

Algorithm 9.9 : Region graph construction from skeleton.

1. Assign a point description to all skeleton points – end-point, node-point, normal-point.
2. Let graph node-points be all end-points and node-points. Connect any two graph nodes by a graph edge if they are connected by a sequence of normal-points in the region ekeleton.

- It can be seen that boundary points of high curvature have the main influence on the graph.
- They are represented by graph nodes, and therefore influence the graph structure.
- If other than medial axis skeletons are used for graph construction, end-points can be defined as skeleton points having just one skeleton neighbor, normal-points as having two skeleton neighbors, and node-points as having at least three skeleton neighbors.
- It is no longer true that node-points are never neighbors and additional conditions must be used to decide when node-points should be represented as nodes in a graph and when they should not.

9.12 REGION DECOMPOSITION

- The decomposition approach is based on the idea that shape recognition is a hierarchical process.
- Shape primitives are defined at the lower level, primitives being the simplest elements, which form the region.
- A graph is constructed at the higher level - nodes result from primitives, arcs describe the mutual primitive relations.
- Convex sets of pixels are one example of simple shape primitives.

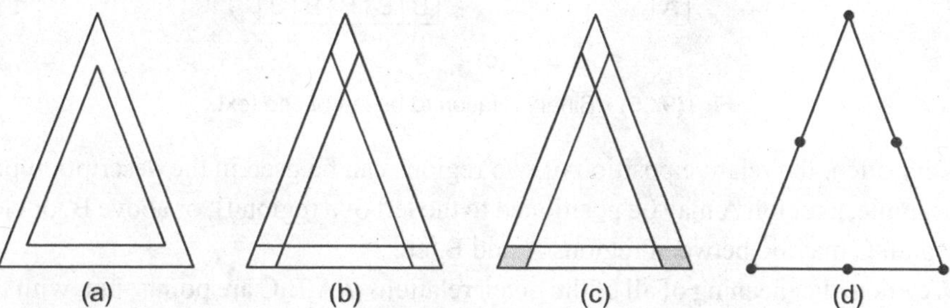

Fig. (9.35) Region decomposition : (a) region, (b) primary regions, (c) primary subregions and kernals, (d) decomposition graph.

- The solution to the decomposition problem consists of two main steps:
  - — The first step is to segment a region into simpler sub regions (primitives) and the second is the analysis of primitives.
  - — Primitives are simple enough to be successfully described using simple scalar shape properties.
  - — If sub regions are represented by polygons, graph nodes bear the following information;
    - Node type representing primary sub region or kernel.
    - Number of vertices of the sub region represented by the node.
    - Area of the sub region represented by the node.
    - Main axis direction of the sub region represented by the node.
    - Center of gravity of the sub region represented by the node.
  - — If a graph is derived using attributes 1-4, the final description is translation invariant.
  - — A graph derived from attributes 1-3 is translation and rotation invariant.
  - — Derivation using the first two attributes results in a description, which is size invariant in addition to possessing translation and rotation invariance.

9.12.1 Region Neighborhood Graphs

- Any time region decomposition into sub regions or image decomposition into regions is available, the region or image can be represented by a region neighborhood graph (the region adjacency graph being a special case).
- This graph represents every region as a graph node, and nodes of neighboring regions are connected by edges.
- A region neighborhood graph can be constructed from a quadtree image representation, from run-length encoded image data, etc.

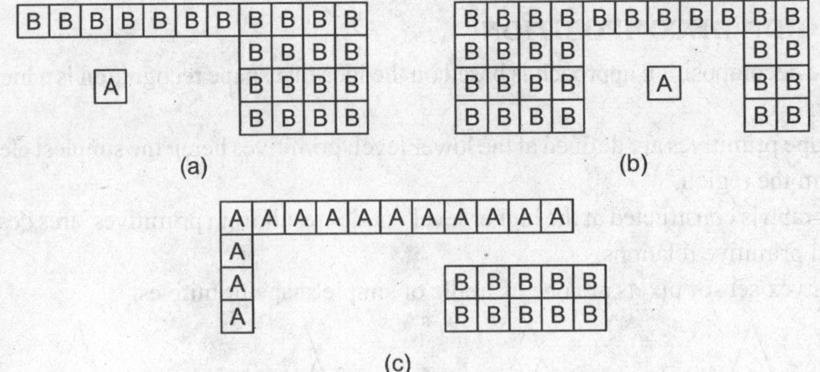

Fig. (9.36) Binary relation to be left of see text.

- Very often, the relative position of two regions can be used in the description process — for example, a region A may be positioned to the left of a region B, or above B, or close to B, or a region C may lie between regions A and B, etc.
- We know the meaning of all of the given relations if A,B,C are points, but, with the exception of the relation to be close, they can become ambiguous if A,B,C are regions.
- For instance, human observers are generally satisfied with the definition:
  — The center of gravity of A must be positioned to the left of the leftmost point of B and (logical AND) the rightmost pixel of A must be left of the rightmost pixel of B.

■ SUMMARY

- Write the underlined matter, are place matter at one dots. Means :
  (i) one place matter (ii) another place matter.

Review Questions

1. Define the term feature extraction. Discuss the feature representations in detail.
2. Differentiate topological attributes and geometric attributes.
3. Discuss the boundary based descriptions.
4. Discuss the region based descriptions of rote of relationship.
5. Write short notes on the following :
   (i) Feature detectors (ii) Region identification
   (iii) Convex hull (iv) Recursive boundary spiliting.

10

OBJECT RECOGNITION

Object recognition stands for the visual perception of familiar objects. The problem in object recognition is to determine which, if any, of a given set of objects appear in a given image or image sequence. Thus object recognition is a problem of *matching* models from a database with representations of those models extracted from the image luminance data. Early work involved the extraction of three-dimensional models from stereo data, but more recent work has concentrated on recognizing objects from geometric invariants extracted from the two-dimensional luminance data.

Of course, the *representation* of the object model is extremely important. Clearly, it is impossible to keep a database that has examples of every view of an object under every possible lighting condition. Thus, object views will be subject to certain transformations; certainly *perspective* transformations depending on the viewpoint, but also transformations related to the lighting conditions and other possible factors.

Two approaches have been developed to deal with the many possible transformations that an object may undergo in the imaging process:

- Determine the transformation in question and then try and undo its effects.
- Find measurements of the object that are *invariant* to these types of transformations.

There are two stages to any recognition system. The first is the *acquisition* stage, where a model library is constructed from certain descriptions of the objects. The second is *recognition*, where the system is presented with a perspective image and determines the location and identity of any library objects in the image.

Generally, the most reliable type of object information that is available from an image is *geometric* information. So object recognition systems draw upon a library of geometric models, containing information about the shape of known objects. Usually, recognition is considered successful if the geometric configuration of an object can be explained as a perspective projection of a geometric model of the object.

Model-based Recognition

All object recognition systems contain the following modules to some extent:

- Selection. What subset of the data corresponds to an object?
  This problem, also known as the *perceptual grouping* problem, aims to organise the features that come from a single object into a single set. The types of features considered might be edges, corners, lines, curves represented as splines, or regional features such as texture. The grouping is usually accomplished using cues such as proximity, parallelism, co linearity, and continuity in curvature.
- **Indexing.** Which object model corresponds to the data subset?
- **Correspondence.** Which individual model features correspond to each data feature?

Thus object recognition is a process of hypothesizing an object-to-model correspondence and then verifying that the hypothesis is correct. Generally an hypothesis is considered successful if the error between the projected model features and the corresponding image features is below some threshold, and a reasonable fraction of the object outline is covered by the image features.

For the two approaches mentioned above, that of estimating the transformation undergone in the imaging process has complexity , where is the number of models, i is the number of image features, m is the number of features per model, and k is the number of features needed to determine the object-image transformation. Typically, k is about 4.

The approach that uses transformation-invariant measurements of the object in the image for recognition has complexity O(ik), where k is the number of features required to form the indexing. In this case, recognition need not be proportional to the number of models in the library. This can be a considerable advantage when the number of models is large.

10.1 GEOMETRIC INVARIANTS

An invariant of a geometric configuration is a function of the configuration whose value is unchanged by a particular transformation. For example, the distance between two points is unchanged for a Euclidean transformation (translation or rotation).

There are a number of geometric invariants for perspective transformations. Here we will illustrate just one of them, the cross-ratio of four points on a line. Suppose we are given a configuration of four points on a line, as shown in Figure 10.1.

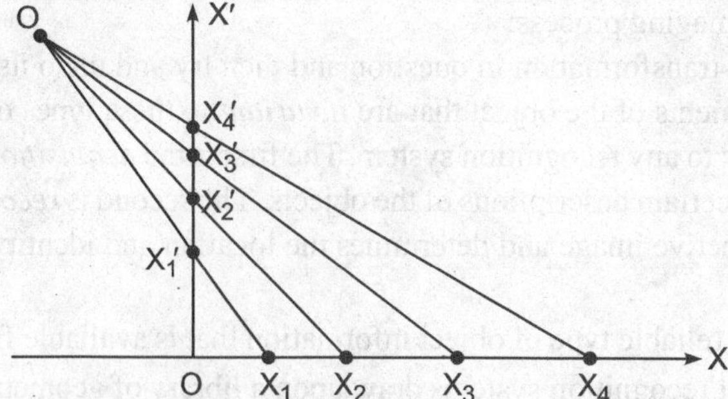

Fig. (10.1) A one-dimensional construction of perspective viewing. The optical center of the camera is O. Under perspective projection, the length and ratios of lengths, on a line are not invariant, but ratios of ratios are.

The ratio of ratios of lengths on the line, called the *cross-ratio*, is given by

$$I = \frac{(X_3' - X_1')(X_4' - X_2')}{(X_3' - X_2')(X_4' - X_1')}$$

where X_1', X_2', X_3' and X_4' represent the corresponding positions of each point along the line.

The perspective transformation between the lines X and X' is given by

$$\begin{pmatrix} X_i' \\ 1 \end{pmatrix} = k_i \begin{pmatrix} m_{11} & m_{12} \\ m_{21} & m_{22} \end{pmatrix} \begin{pmatrix} X_i \\ 1 \end{pmatrix}$$

Now to see why the cross-ratio of four points on a line is preserved under such a transformation we note that the distance $(X_i' - X_j')$ can be written as a determinant:

$$X_i' - X_j' = |S(X_i, X_j')| = \begin{vmatrix} X_i' & X_j' \\ 1 & 1 \end{vmatrix}$$

Under the projective transformation above, the matrix S(Xi', Xj') transforms as follows:

$$\begin{pmatrix} x_i' & X_j' \\ 1 & 1 \end{pmatrix} = \begin{pmatrix} m_{11} & m_{12} \\ m_{21} & m_{22} \end{pmatrix} \times \begin{pmatrix} k_i X_i & k_j X_j \\ k_i & k_j \end{pmatrix}$$

and taking the determinant of both sides gives

$$|S(X_i'.X_j')| = k_i k_j \, |M| . |S(X_i, X_j)|$$

Substituting this relation into the expression for the cross-ratio gives

$$\frac{(X_3' - X_1')(X_4' - X_2')}{(X_3' - X_2')(X_4' - X_1')} = \frac{|S(X_3', X_1')||S(X_4', X_2')|}{|S(X_3', X_2')||S(X_4', X_1')|}$$

$$= \frac{k_3 k_1 |M||S(X_3, X_1)| k_4 k_2 |M||S(X_4, X_2)|}{k_3 k_2 |M||S(X_3, X_2)| k_4 k_1 |M||S(X_4, X_1)|}$$

$$= \frac{(X_3 - X_1)(X_4 - X_2)}{(X_3 - X_2)(X_4 - X_1)}$$

In summary, the cross-ratio is an invariant of any sets of four collinear points in projective correspondence. It is unaffected by the relative position of the line or the position of the optical center, as shown in Figure 10.2.

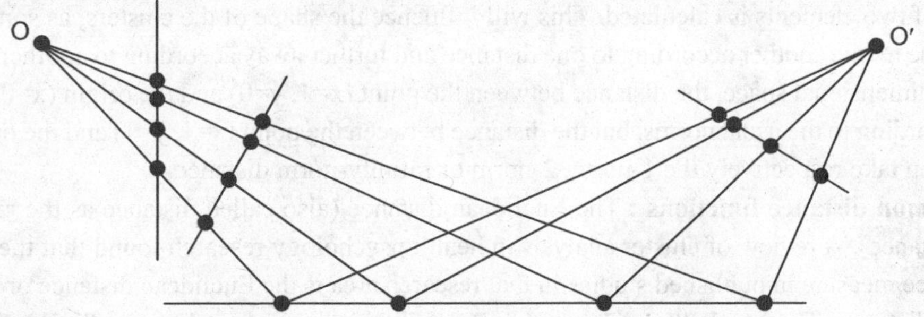

Fig. (10.2) The cross-ratio of very set of four collinear points shown in this figure has the same value.

Recognition using invariants : There are two stages to model-based recognition using invariants:

1. Model acquisition. Models of objects to be recognised are acquired directly from images. For planar objects, this involves computing their plane projective invariants. Their outline is also stored for the verification process.

2. Recognition. Invariants are computed for geometric invariants in the target image. If the invariant value corresponds to one in the model library, a recognition hypothesis is generated. This hypothesis is either confirmed or denied by verification: The model outline from the acquisition image is projected onto the target image. If the projected edges overlap image edges sufficiently then the hypothesis is verified.

■ 10.2 CLUSTERING

Clustering is the classification of objects into different groups, or more precisely, the partitioning of a data set into subsets (clusters), so that the data in each subset (ideally) share some common trait - often proximity according to some defined distance measure. Data clustering is a common technique for statistical data analysis, which is used in many fields, including machine learning, data mining, pattern recognition, image analysis and bioinformatics.

Types of Clustering

Data clustering algorithms can be hierarchical or partitional. Hierarchical algorithms find successive clusters using previously established clusters, whereas partitional algorithms determine all clusters at once. Hierarchical algorithms can be agglomerative ("bottom-up") or divisive ("top-down"). Agglomerative algorithms begin with each element as a separate cluster and merge them into successively larger clusters. Divisive algorithms begin with the whole set and proceed to divide it into successively smaller clusters.

Two-way clustering, co-clustering or bi-clustering are clustering methods where not only the objects are clustered but also the features of the objects, i.e., if the data is represented in a data matrix, the row and columns are clustered simultaneously.

Another important distinction is whether the clustering uses symmetric or asymmetric distances. A property of Euclidean space is that distances are symmetric (the distance from object A to B is the same as the distance from B to A).

Distance Measure

An important step in any clustering is to select a distance measure, which will determine how the similarity of two elements is calculated. This will influence the shape of the clusters, as some elements may be close to one another according to one distance and further away according to another. For example, in a 2-dimensional space, the distance between the point (x=1, y=0) and the origin (x=0, y=0) is always 1 according to the usual norms, but the distance between the point (x=1, y=1) and the origin can be 2, or 1 if you take respectively the 1-norm, 2-norm or infinity-norm distance.

Common distance functions : The Euclidean distance (also called distance as the crow flies or 2-norm distance). A review of cluster analysis in health psychology research found that the most common distance measure in published studies in that research area is the Euclidean distance or the squared Euclidean distance. The Manhattan distance (also called taxicab norm or 1-norm) the maximum norm the Mahalanobis distance corrects data for different scales and correlations in the variables the angle between two vectors can be used as a distance measure when clustering high dimensional data.

Hierarchical Clustering

Hierarchical clustering builds (agglomerative), or breaks up (divisive), a hierarchy of clusters. The traditional representation of this hierarchy is a tree (called a dendrogram), with individual elements at one end and a single cluster containing every element at the other. Agglomerative algorithms begin at the top of the tree, whereas divisive algorithms begin at the bottom. (In the figure, the arrows indicate an agglomerative clustering.)

Cutting the tree at a given height will give a clustering at a selected precision. In the following example, cutting after the second row will yield clusters {a} {b c} {d e} {f}. Cutting after the third row will yield clusters {a} {b c} {d e f}, which is a coarser clustering, with a smaller number of larger clusters.

Agglomerative hierarchical clustering : For example, suppose this data is to be clustered, and the euclidean distance is the distance metric.

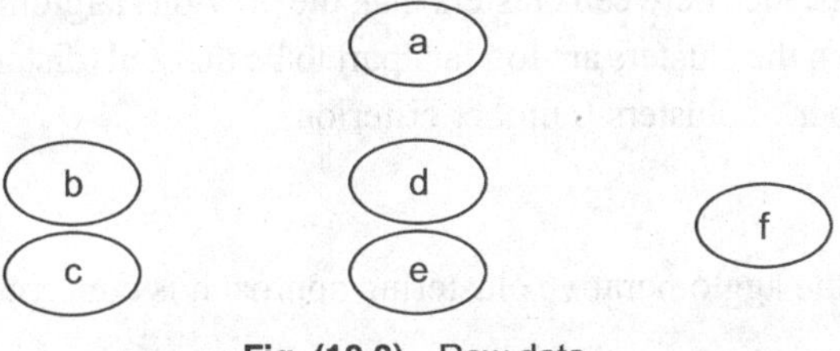

Fig. (10.3) Raw data.

The hierarchical clustering dendrogram would be as such.

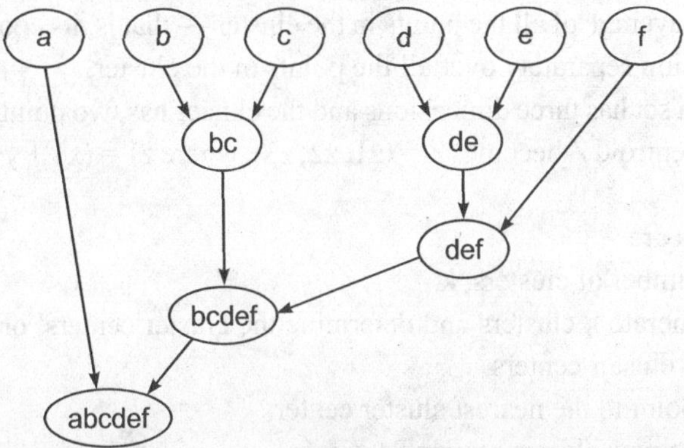

Fig. (10.4) Traditional representation.

This method builds the hierarchy from the individual elements by progressively merging clusters. In our example, we have six elements {a} {b} {c} {d} {e} and {f}. The first step is to determine which elements to merge in a cluster. Usually, we want to take the two closest elements, according to the chosen distance.

Optionally, one can also construct a distance matrix at this stage, where the number in the i-th row j-th column is the distance between the i-th and j-th elements. Then, as clustering progresses, rows and columns are merged as the clusters are merged and the distances updated. This is a common way to implement this type of clustering, and has the benefit of catching distances between clusters.

Suppose we have merged the two closest elements b and c, we now have the following clusters {a}, {b, c}, {d}, {e} and {f}, and want to merge them further. To do that, we need to take the distance between {a} and {b c}, and therefore define the distance between two clusters. Usually the distance between two clusters is one of the following:

The maximum distance between elements of each cluster (also called complete linkage clustering):

$$\max \{d(x, y) : x \in A,\ y \in B\}$$

The minimum distance between elements of each cluster (also called single linkage clustering):

$$\min \{d(x, y) : x \in A,\ y \in B\}$$

The mean distance between elements of each cluster (also called average linkage clustering):

$$\frac{1}{\text{card}(A)\,\text{card}(B)} \sum_{x \in A} \sum_{y \in B} d(x, y)$$

The sum of all intra-cluster variance and increase in variance for the cluster being merged.The probability that candidate clusters spawn from the same distribution function (V-linkage)Each agglomeration occurs at a greater distance between clusters than the previous agglomeration, and one can decide to stop clustering either when the clusters are too far apart to be merged (distance criterion) or when there is a sufficiently small number of clusters (number criterion).

Concept Clustering

Another variation of the agglomerative clustering approach is conceptual clustering.

K-means Clustering

The K-means algorithm assigns each point to the cluster whose center (also called centroid) is nearest. The center is the average of all the points in the cluster — that is, its coordinates are the arithmetic mean for each dimension separately over all the points in the cluster.

Example : The data set has three dimensions and the cluster has two points: X = (x1, x2, x3) and Y = (y1, y2, y3). Then the centroid Z becomes Z = (z1, z2, z3), where z1 = (x1 + y1)/2 and z2 = (x2 + y2)/2 and z3 = (x3 + y3)/2.

The algorithm steps are

- Choose the number of clusters, k.
- Randomly generate k clusters and determine the cluster centers, or directly generate k random points as cluster centers.
- Assign each point to the nearest cluster center.
- Recompute the new cluster centers.
- Repeat the two previous steps until some convergence criterion is met (usually that the assignment hasn't changed).

The main advantages of this algorithm are its simplicity and speed which allows it to run on large datasets. Its disadvantage is that it does not yield the same result with each run, since the resulting clusters depend on the initial random assignments. It minimizes intra-cluster variance, but does not ensure that the result has a global minimum of variance.

Fuzzy-c-Means Clustering

In fuzzy clustering, each point has a degree of belonging to clusters, as in fuzzy logic, rather than belonging completely to just one cluster. Thus, points on the edge of a cluster may be in the cluster to a lesser degree than points in the center of cluster. For each point x we have a coefficient giving the degree of being in the kth cluster uk(x). Usually, the sum of those coefficients is defined to be 1:

$$\forall x \quad \sum_{k=1}^{\text{num. clusters}} u_k(r) = 1$$

With fuzzy-c-means, the centroid of a cluster is the mean of all points, weighted by their degree of belonging to the cluster:

$$\text{center}_k = \frac{\sum_x {}_k (x)^m \, x}{\sum_x u_k (x)^m}$$

The degree of belonging is related to the inverse of the distance to the cluster

$$u_k(x) = \frac{1}{d(\text{center}_k, x)}$$

then the coefficients are normalized and fuzzyfied with a real parameter m > 1 so that their sum is 1. So

$$u_k(x) = \frac{1}{\sum_j \left(\frac{d(\text{center}_k, x)}{d(\text{center}_j, x)} \right)^{2/(m-1)}}$$

For m equal to 2, this is equivalent to normalizing the coefficient linearly to make their sum 1. When m is close to 1, then cluster center closest to the point is given much more weight than the others, and the algorithm is similar to k-means.

The fuzzy c-means algorithm is very similar to the k-means algorithm:

- Choose a number of clusters.
- Assign randomly to each point coefficients for being in the clusters.
- Repeat until the algorithm has converged (that is, the coefficients' change between two iterations is no more than $\in$, the given sensitivity threshold).
- Compute the centroid for each cluster, using the formula above.
- For each point, compute its coefficients of being in the clusters, using the formula above.

The algorithm minimizes intra-cluster variance as well, but has the same problems as k-means, the minimum is a local minimum, and the results depend on the initial choice of weights. The Expectation-maximization algorithm is a more statistically formalized method which includes some of these ideas: partial membership in classes. It has better convergence properties and is in general preferred to fuzzy-k-means.

QT Clustering Algorithm

QT (quality threshold) clustering is an alternative method of partitioning data, invented for gene clustering. It requires more computing power than k-means, but does not require specifying the number of clusters a priori, and always returns the same result when run several times. The algorithm is:

- The user chooses a maximum diameter for clusters.
- Build a candidate cluster for each point by including the closest point, the next closest, and so on, until the diameter of the cluster surpasses the threshold.
- Save the candidate cluster with the most points as the first true cluster, and remove all points in the cluster from further consideration.
- Recurse with the reduced set of points.
- The distance between a point and a group of points is computed using complete linkage, i.e. as the maximum distance from the point to any member of the group.

Graph-theoretic Methods

Formal concept analysis is a technique for generating clusters of objects and attributes, given a bipartite graph representing the relations between the objects and attributes. Other methods for generating overlapping clusters (a cover rather than a partition) are discussed by Jardine and Sibson (1968) and Cole and Wishart (1970).

Elbow Criterion

The elbow criterion is a common rule of thumb to determine what number of clusters should be chosen, for example for k-means and agglomerative hierarchical clustering. It should also be noted that the initial assignment of cluster seeds has bearing on the final model performance. Thus, it is appropriate to re-run the cluster analysis multiple times.

The elbow criterion says that you should choose a number of clusters so that adding another cluster doesn't add sufficient information. More precisely, if you graph the percentage of variance explained by the clusters against the number of clusters, the first clusters will add much information (explain a lot of variance), but at some point the marginal gain will drop, giving an angle in the graph (the elbow). This elbow can not always be unambiguously identified.

On the following graph, the elbow is indicated by the red circle. The number of clusters chosen should therefore be 4. Percent of variance explained or percent of total variance is the ratio of within-group variance to total variance.

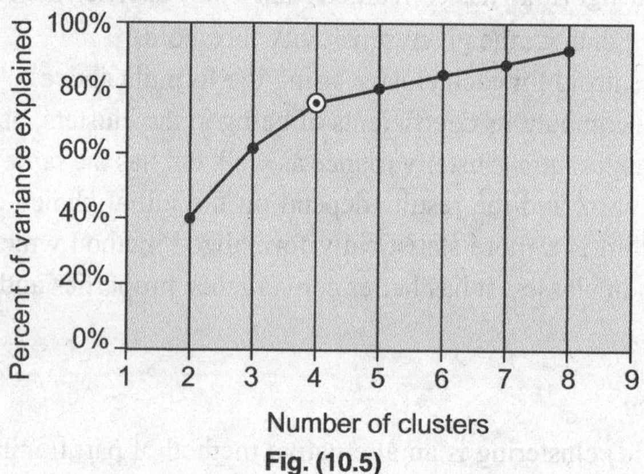

Fig. (10.5)

Spectral Clustering

Given a set of data points A, the similarity matrix may be defined as a matrix S where Sij represents a measure of the similarity between points . Spectral clustering techniques make use of the spectrum of the similarity matrix of the data to perform dimensionality reduction for clustering in fewer dimensions. One such technique is the Shi-Malik algorithm, commonly used for image segmentation. It partitions points into two sets (S_1, S_2) based on the eigenvector v corresponding to the second-smallest eigenvalue of the Laplacian matrix

$$L = I - D^{-1/2}\ SD^{-1/2}$$

of *S*, where *D* is the diagonal matrix

$$D_{ii} = \sum_j S_{ij}$$

This partitioning may be done in various ways, such as by taking the median m of the components in v, and placing all points whose component in v is greater than m in S1, and the rest in S2. The algorithm can be used for hierarchical clustering by repeatedly partitioning the subsets in this fashion. A related algorithm is the Meila-Shi algorithm, which takes the eigenvectors corresponding to the k largest eigenvalues of the matrix $P = SD - 1$ for some k, and then invokes another (e.g. k-means) to cluster points by their respective k components in these eigenvectors.

Applications :

Biology : In biology clustering has many applications In imaging, data clustering may take different form based on the data dimensionality. For example, the SOCR EM Mixture model segmentation activity and applet shows how to obtain point, region or volume classification using the online SOCR computational libraries.

In the fields of plant and animal ecology, clustering is used to describe and to make spatial and temporal comparisons of communities (assemblages) of organisms in heterogeneous environments; it is also used in plant systematic to generate artificial phylogenies or clusters of organisms (individuals) at the species, genus or higher level that share a number of attributes.

In computational biology and bioinformatics : In transcriptomics, clustering is used to build groups of genes with related expression patterns. Often such groups contain functionally related proteins, such as enzymes for a specific pathway, or genes that are co-regulated. High throughput experiments using expressed sequence tags (ESTs) or DNA micro arrays can be a powerful tool for genome annotation, a general aspect of genomics.

In sequence analysis, clustering is used to group homologous sequences into gene families. This is a very important concept in bioinformatics, and evolutionary biology in general. See evolution by gene duplication. In high-throughput genotyping platforms clustering algorithms are used to automatically assign genotypes.

Market research : Cluster analysis is widely used in market research when working with multivariate data from surveys and test panels. Market researchers use cluster analysis to partition the general population of consumers into market segments and to better understand the relationships between different groups of consumers/potential customers.

- Segmenting the market and determining target markets
- Product positioning.
- New product development
- Selecting test markets

Other applications :

- **Social network analysis:** In the study of social networks, clustering may be used to recognize communities within large groups of people.
- **Image segmentation:** Clustering can be used to divide a digital image into distinct regions for border detection or object recognition.
- **Data mining:** Many data mining applications involve partitioning data items into related subsets; the marketing applications discussed above represent some examples. Another common application is the division of documents, such as World Wide Web pages, into genres.
- **Slippy map optimization:** Flickr's map of photos and other map sites use clustering to reduce the number of markers on a map. This makes it both faster and reduces the amount of visual clutter.

Comparisons between data clustering : There have been several suggestions for a measure of similarity between two clustering. Such a measure can be used to compare how well different data clustering algorithms perform on a set of data. Many of these measures are derived from the matching matrix (aka confusion matrix), e.g., the Rand measure and the Fowlkes-Mallows Bk measures.

Marina Meila's Variation of Information metric is a more recent approach for comparing distance between clustering. It uses mutual information and entropy to approximate the distance between two clustering across the lattice of possible clusterings.

■ 10.3 PATTERN RECOGNITION

The essential problem of pattern recognition is to identify an object as belonging to a particular group. Assuming that the objects associated with a particular group share common attributes more so than with objects in other groups, the problem of assigning an unlabeled object to a group can be accomplished by determining the attributes of the object (i.e., the pattern) and identifying the group of which those attributes are most representative (i.e., the recognition). If information about the universe of all possible objects and the groups to which they can be assigned is known, then the identification problem is straightforward in that the attributes that best discriminate among groups and the mapping from attributes to groups can both be determined with certainty.

When the information about the identification problem is imperfect or incomplete, then the attributes and mapping to use must be inferred from example objects whose group membership is known. Given the goal of classifying objects based on their attributes, the functionality of an automated pattern recognition system can be divided into two basic tasks: the description task generates attributes of an object using feature extraction techniques, and the classification task assigns a group label to the object based on those attributes with a classifier. The description and classification tasks work together to determine the most accurate label for each unlabeled object analyzed by the pattern recognition system. This is accomplished with a training phase that configures the algorithms used in both the description and classification tasks based on a collection of objects whose labels are known—i.e., training set. During the training phase, a training set is analyzed to determine the attributes and mapping which assigns labels to the objects in the training set with the fewest errors. Once trained, a pattern recognition system assigns a classification to an unlabeled object by applying the mapping to the attributes of that object.

A measure of the effectiveness of a trained pattern recognition system can be computed by comparing the known labels with the labels assigned by the classification task to the training set: as the agreement between known and assigned labels increases, the accuracy of the pattern recognition system increases. Such a methodology for configuring and evaluating the description and classification tasks of a pattern recognition system is called supervised learning. If training set is not available, then unsupervised learning techniques can be used. The generality of the description and classification architecture in conjunction with the flexibility afforded by the training phase makes automated pattern recognition systems useful for solving a wide range of real world problems. The objects under analysis in real world pattern recognition systems typically are data sets containing attributes that were automatically collected and are representative of the physical or behavioral objects to be identified.

In electrocardiogram analysis, for example, a data set might contain the electrical activity recorded during one heartbeat by an electrode placed on a patient, and a collection of such data sets would constitute a description of a patient's cardiac behavior over a period of time. Given such a collection of data sets, the goal of a pattern recognition system for electrocardiogram analysis would be to classify each heartbeat (i.e., data set) as being indicative of normal or abnormal cardiac behavior, thereby assisting the physician in diagnosing the condition of a patient's heart. Other real world applications of automated pattern recognition include the following:

- Industrial Applications
- Character recognition
- Process control
- Signature analysis
- Speech analysis
- Medical Applications
- Electroencephalogram analysis
- Genetic studies
- Government Applications
- Smog detection and measurement
- Traffic analysis and control
- Fingerprint matching
- Military Applications
- Sonar detection and classification
- Automatic target recognitio

Automated Pattern Recognition Systems

The ability of living organisms to solve identification problems is rooted in their perceptual and cognitive abilities to collect and analyze information from the environment. The field of pattern recognition focuses on mechanizing these abilities with the goal of automating the identification process. In contrast to biological systems, automated pattern recognition systems use algorithms to process data collected either electronically (via monitors or sensors) or transcribed by a human, resulting in an identification of the group of which the data are most representative. Figure 10.6 illustrates the parallel between living organisms and automated pattern recognition systems.

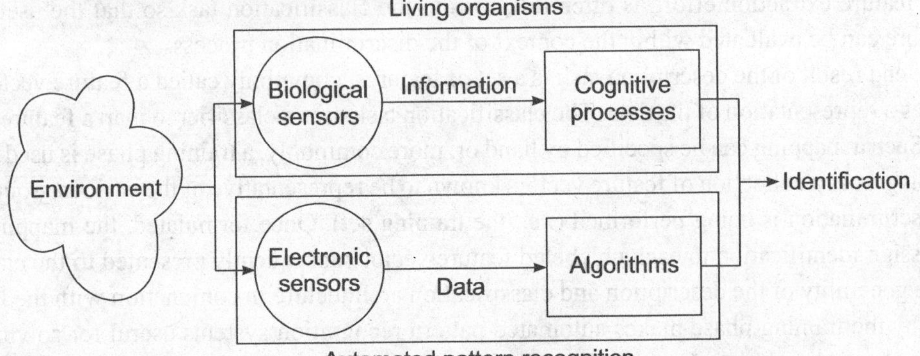

Fig. (10.6) The identification problem as solved by living organisms and automated pattern recognition systems. Automated pattern recognition systems deploy electronic sensors and implement algorithms which approximate the f unc tion ingof the perceptual and cognitive abilities of living organisms.

The algorithms used by pattern recognition systems are commonly divided into two tasks, as shown in Figure 10.7. The description task transforms data collected from the environment into fea-

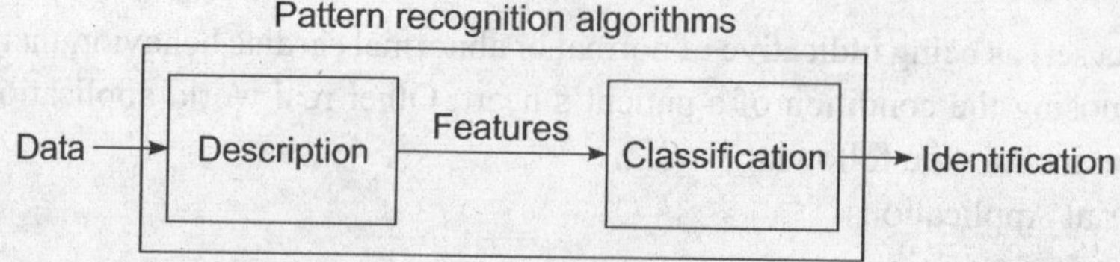

Fig. (10.7) The two separate tasks commonly used to divide the algorithms within automated pattern recognition systems. The description task transforms data collected from the environment into features. The classification task arrives at an identification based on the features provided by the description task.

tures—i.e., any value that can be derived from and is representative of the data—which are used in the classification task to arrive at identification. The description task can involve several different, but interrelated, activities:

- Preprocessing is sometimes necessary to modify the data either to correct deficiencies in the data due to limitations of the sensor, or to prepare the data for subsequent activities later in the description task or in the classification task.
- Feature extraction is the process of generating features to be used in the classification task. Elementary features are explicitly present in the data and can be passed directly to the classification task. Higher order features are derived from elementary features and are generated by performing manipulations and/or transformations on the data.
- Feature selection reduces the number of features provided to the classification task. Those features which are likely to assist in discrimination are picked out and allowed to be used in the classification task. Features which are not selected are discarded; higher order features which are determined to be unnecessary for classification can be eliminated from the feature extraction process.

Of these three activities, feature extraction is most critical because the particular features made available for discrimination directly influence the effectiveness of the classification task: features which truly discriminate among groups will assist in identification, while the lack of such features can impede the classification task from arriving at an accurate identification. Feature selection, while useful to minimize the feature extraction effort, is often relegated to the classification task so that the usefulness of each feature can be evaluated within the context of the discrimination process.

The end result of the description task is a set of features, commonly called a feature vector, which constitutes a representation of the data. The classification task uses a classifier to map a feature vector to a group. Such a mapping can be specified by hand or, more commonly, a training phase is used to induce the mapping from a collection of feature vectors known to be representative of the various groups among which discrimination is being performed (i.e., the training set). Once formulated, the mapping can be used to assign identification to each unlabeled feature vector subsequently presented to the classifier.

The generality of the description and classification architecture in conjunction with the flexibility afforded by the training phase makes automated pattern recognition systems useful for solving a wide range of real world problems. Various algorithms can be used for the description and classification tasks to implement a pattern recognition system that is appropriate for a particular domain and application. Different combinations of algorithms have proven to be effective, resulting in two basic approaches to implementing pattern recognition systems.

10.4 TYPES OF PATTERN RECOGNITION

There are two fundamental approaches to implementing a pattern recognition system: statistical and structural. Each approach employs different techniques within the description and classification tasks which constitute a pattern recognition system. Statistical pattern recognition draws from established concepts in statistical decision theory to discriminate among data from different groups based upon quantitative features of the data. The quantitative nature of statistical pattern recognition, however, makes it difficult to discriminate among groups based on the morphological (i.e., shape based or structural) sub patterns and their interrelationships embedded within the data. This limitation provided the impetus for the development of a structural approach to pattern recognition.

Structural pattern recognition, sometimes referred to as syntactic pattern recognition due to its origins in formal language theory, relies on syntactic grammars to discriminate among data from different groups based upon the morphological interrelationships (or interconnections) present within the data. Structural pattern recognition systems have proven to be effective for data which contain an inherent, identifiable organization such as image data (which is organized by location within a visual rendering) and time series data (which is organized by time). The usefulness of structural pattern recognition systems, however, is limited as a consequence of fundamental complications associated with the implementation of the description and classification tasks.

10.4.1 Statistical Pattern Recognition

Statistical classification is a statistical procedure in which individual items are placed into groups based on quantitative information on one or more characteristics inherent in the items (referred to as traits, variables, characters, etc) and based on a training set of previously labeled items.

Formally, the problem can be stated as follows: given training data produce a classifier which maps an object to its classification label . For example, if the problem is filtering spam, then is some representation of an email and y is either "Spam" or "Non-Spam". Statistical classification algorithms are typically used in pattern recognition systems.

Statistical pattern recognition draws from established concepts in statistical decision theory to discriminate among data from different groups based upon quantitative features of the data. There are a wide variety of statistical techniques that can be used within the description task for feature extraction, ranging from simple descriptive statistics to complex transformations. Examples of statistical feature extraction techniques include mean and standard deviation computations, frequency count summarizations, KarhunenLo eve transformations, Fourier transformations, wavelet transformations, and Hough transformations.

The quantitative features extracted from each object for statistical pattern recognition are organized into a fixed length feature vector where the meaning associated with each feature is determined by its position within the vector (i.e., the first feature describes a particular characteristic of the data, the second feature describes another characteristic, and so on). The collection of feature vectors generated by the description task are passed to the classification task.

Statistical techniques used as classifiers within the classification task include those based on similarity (e.g., template matching, k-nearest neighbor), probability (e.g., Bayes rule), boundaries (e.g., decision trees, neural networks), and clustering (e.g., k-means, hierarchical). The quantitative nature of statistical pattern recognition makes it difficult to discriminate among groups based on the morphological (i.e., shape based or structural) sub patterns and their interrelationships embedded within the data.

This limitation provided the impetus for the development of a structural approach to pattern recognition that is supported by psychological evidence pertaining to the functioning of human perception and cognition.

Object recognition in humans has been demonstrated to involve mental representations of explicit, structure oriented characteristics of objects, and human classification decisions have been shown to be made on the basis of the degree of similarity between the extracted features and those of a prototype developed for each group. For instance, Biederman proposed the recognition by components theory to explain the process of pattern recognition in humans:

(1) The object is segmented into separate regions according to edges defined by differences in surface characteristics (e.g., luminance, texture, and color).

(2) Each segmented region is approximated by a simple geometric shape.

(3) The object is identified based upon the similarity in composition between the geometric representation of the object and the central tendency of each group.

This theorized functioning of human perception and cognition serves as the foundation for the structural approach to pattern recognition. Structural pattern recognition, sometimes referred to as syntactic pattern recognition due to its origins in formal language theory, relies on syntactic grammars to discriminate among data from different groups based upon the morphological interrelationships (or interconnections) present within the data. Structural features, often referred to as primitives, represent the sub patterns (or building blocks) and the relationships among them which constitute the data. The semantics associated with each feature are determined by the coding scheme (i.e., the selection of morphologies) used to identify primitives in the data. Feature vectors generated by structural pattern recognition systems contain a variable number of features (one for each primitive extracted from the data) in order to accommodate the presence of superfluous structures which have no impact on classification. Since the interrelationships among the extracted primitives must also be encoded, the feature vector must either include additional features describing the relationships among primitives or take an alternate form, such as a relational graph, that can be parsed by a syntactic grammar.

The emphasis on relationships within data makes a structural approach to pattern recognition most sensible for data which contain an inherent, identifiable organization such as image data (which is organized by location within a visual rendering) and time series data (which is organized by time); data composed of independent samples of quantitative measurements, such as the Fisher iris data, lack ordering and require a statistical approach. Methodologies used to extract structural features from image data such as morphological image processing techniques result in primitives such as edges, curves, and regions; feature extraction techniques for time series data include chain codes, piecewise linear regression, and curve fitting which are used to generate primitives that encode sequential, time ordered relationships.

The classification task arrives at an identification using parsing: the extracted structural features are identified as being representative of a particular group if they can be successfully parsed by a syntactic grammar. When discriminating among more than two groups, a syntactic grammar is necessary for each group and the classifier must be extended with an adjudication scheme so as to resolve multiple successful parsings. Figure 10.8 demonstrates how both approaches can be applied to the same identification problem. The goal is to differentiate between the square and the triangle. A statistical approach extracts quantitative features such as the number of horizontal, vertical, and diagonal segments which are then passed to a decision theoretic classifier.

Statistical		Structural
Number of segments : 4 Number of horizontal segments : 2 Number of vertical segments : 2 Number of diagonal segments : 0	(square)	horizontal ↙ ↘ vertical vertical ↘ ↙ horizontal
Number of segments : 3 Number of horizontal segments : 1 Number of vertical segments : 0 Number of diagonal segments : 2	(triangle)	vertical ↔ vertical ↘ ↙ horizontal

Fig. (10.8) The statistical and structural approaches to pattern recognition applied to a common identification problem. The goal is to discriminate between the square and the triangle. A statistical approach extracts quantitative features which are assembled into feature vectors for classification with a decision theoretic classifier. A structural approach extracts morphological features and their interrelationships, encoding them in relational graphs; classification is performed by parsing the relational graphs with syntactic grammars.

A structural approach extracts morphological features and their interrelationships within each figure. Using a straight line segment as the elemental morphology, a relational graph is generated and classified by determining the syntactic grammar that can successfully parse the relational graph. In this example, both the statistical and structural approaches would be able to accurately distinguish between the two geometries. In more complex data, however, discriminability is directly influenced by the particular approach employed for pattern recognition because the features extracted represent different characteristics of the data.

Table 10.1 A summary of the differences between statistical and structural approaches to pattern recognition. Due to their divergent theoretical foundations, the two approaches focus on different data characteristics and employ distinctive techniques to implement both the description and classification tasks.

	Statistical	Structural
Foundation	Statistical decision theory	Human perception and cognition
Description	1. Quantitative features 2. Fixed number of features 3. Ignores feature relationships 4. Semantics from feature position	1. Morphological primitives 2. Variable number of primitives 3. Captures primitive relationships 4. Semantics from primitive encoding
Classification	Statistical classifiers	Parsing with syntactic grammars

A summary of the differences between statistical and structural approaches to pattern recognition is shown in Table 10.1. The essential dissimilarities are twofold:

(1) The description generated by the statistical approach is quantitative, while the structural approach produces a description composed of sub patterns or building blocks.

(2) The statistical approach discriminates based upon numeric differences among features from different groups, while grammars are used by the structural approach to define a "language" encompassing the acceptable configurations of primitives for each group. Hybrid systems can combine the two approaches as a way to compensate for the drawbacks of each approach, while conserving the advantages of each.

As a single level system, structural features can be used with either a statistical or structural classifier. Statistical features cannot be used with a structural classifier because they lack relational information, however statistical information can be associated with structural primitives and used to resolve ambiguities during classification (e.g., as when parsing with attributed grammars) or embedded directly in the classifier itself (e.g., as when parsing with stochastic grammars). Hybrid systems can also combine the two approaches into a multilevel system using a parallel or a hierarchical arrangement.

10.4.2 Syntactic Pattern Recognition

Syntactic pattern recognition or structural pattern recognition is a form of pattern recognition, where items are presented pattern structures which can take into account more complex interrelationships between features than simple numerical feature vectors used in statistical classification.

Syntactic pattern recognition can be used (instead of statistical pattern recognition) if there is clear structure in the patterns. One way to present such structure is strings of a formal language. In this case differences in the structures of the classes are encoded as different grammars. An example of this would be diagnosis of the heart with ECG measurements. ECG waveforms can be approximated with diagonal and vertical line segments. If normal and unhealthy waveforms can be described as formal grammars, measured ECG signal can be classified as healthy or unhealthy by first describing it in term of the basic line segments and then trying to parse the descriptions according to the grammars.Another example is tessellation of tiling patterns.

Another way to represent relations are graphs, where nodes are connected if corresponding subpatterns are related. An item can be labeled as belonging to a class if its graph representation is isomorphic with prototype graphs of the class. Typically, patterns are constructed from simpler subpatterns in a hierarchical fashion. This helps in dividing the recognition task into easier subtask of first identifying subpatterns and only then the actual patterns. Structural methods provide description of items, which may useful on its own right. For example, syntactic pattern recognition can be used to find out what object are present in an image.

10.4.2.1 Description

There is no general solution for extracting structural features from data. Pattern recognition texts give scant attention to the topic of primitive selection, most often describing the process as being domain and application specific. For example, Friedman addresses the issue by saying, "The selection of primitives by which the patterns of interest are going to be described depends upon the type of data and the associated application." Nadler seems to support this position when he states, "...features are generally designed by hand, using the experience, intuition, and/or cleverness of the designer."

The lack of a general approach for extracting primitives puts designers of structural pattern recognition systems in an awkward position: feature extractors are necessary to identify primitives in the data, and yet there is no established methodology for deciding which primitives to extract. The result is that feature extractors for structural pattern recognition systems are developed to extract either the simplest and most generic primitives possible, or the domain and application specific primitives that best support the subsequent classification task. Some structural pattern recognition systems justify the use of a particular set of feature extractors by claiming that the same set had been used successfully by a previous system developed for a similar application within the same domain; such claims simply shift the burden of feature extractor development onto previously implemented systems.

Neither of these two philosophies for developing feature extractors for structural pattern recognition is optimal. Simplistic primitives are domain independent, but capture a minimum of structural information and postpone deeper interpretation until the classification step. At the other extreme, domain and application specific primitives can be developed with the assistance of a domain expert, but obtaining and formalizing knowledge from a domain expert, called knowledge acquisition, can be problematic.

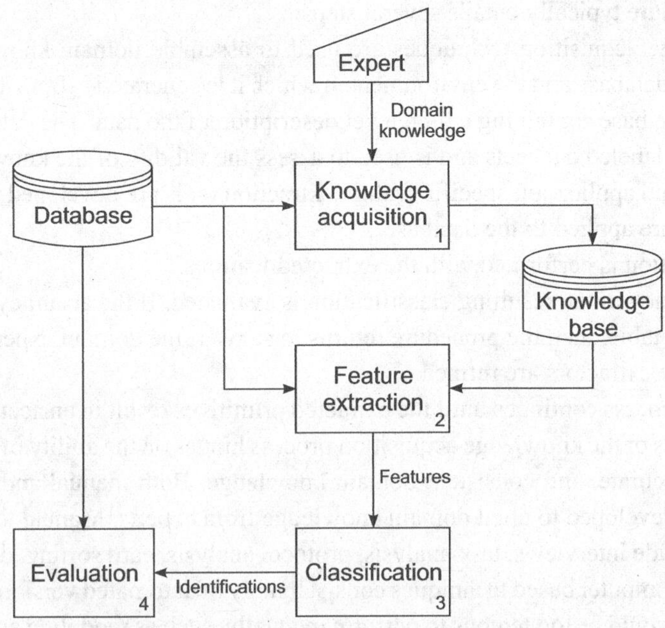

Fig. (10.9) The process of knowledge acquisition for developing domain and application specific feature extractors for structural pattern recognition.

Referring to the numbered activities in the figure 10.9, the procedure typically entails several steps:

(1) Knowledge acquisition techniques are used to assemble domain knowledge from an expert to produce a knowledge base containing a high level description of the data. The database contains a collection of labeled data sets and is used to assess the validity of the knowledge base.

(2) Domain and application specific feature extraction tools are developed using the knowledge base and are applied to the database.

(3) Classification is performed with the extracted features.

(4) The accuracy of the resulting classification is evaluated. The process iterates until an accurate and robust classification is achieved.

Table 10.2 A summary of the effectiveness of four knowledge acquisition techniques applied within three different domains to elicit knowledge from experts regarding features useful for classification. For each combination of technique and domain, the average coverage of knowledge elicited from multiple experts is reported.

Domain	Knowledge Acquisition Technique			
	Structured Interview	Protocol Analysis	Laddred Grid	Card Sort
Flint Artifacts [16]	33%	11%	33%	33%
Glacier Attributes [15]	33%	16%	35%	23%
Igneous Rocks [14]	28%	8%	28%	30%

The process of knowledge acquisition for developing domain and application specific. Feature extractors for structural pattern recognition is shown in Figure 10.8. Referring to the numbered activities in the figure, the procedure typically entails several steps:

(1) Knowledge acquisition techniques are used to assemble domain knowledge—information about the database and the environment in which it is generated—from an expert to produce a knowledge base containing a high level description of the data. The database contains a collection of labeled data sets and is used to assess the validity of the knowledge base.

(2) Domain and application specific feature extraction tools are developed using the knowledge base and are applied to the database.

(3) Classification is performed with the extracted features.

(4) The accuracy of the resulting classification is evaluated. If the accuracy of the classification is unacceptable, then the procedure returns to step #1, the domain expert is reconsulted, and the feature extractors are refined.

This iterative process continues until the extracted primitives result in an accurate and robust classification. The success of the knowledge acquisition process hinges on the ability of the domain expert to provide complete, accurate, and consistent domain knowledge. Both manual and computer based approaches have been developed to elicit domain knowledge from experts. Manual techniques for knowledge acquisition include interviews, task analysis, protocol analysis, card sorting, decision analysis, and graph construction, computer based techniques consist mainly of automated versions of manual methods and approaches that would be too tedious to perform manually, such as modeling and simulation. Applications of these techniques are most often reported in the literature as case studies, leaving effectiveness a matter of anecdote rather than experimental evaluation.

One study, however, has been undertaken to compare rigorously the effectiveness of four knowledge acquisition techniques: structured interview (a designed and ordered set of domain specific questions is answered by the expert), protocol analysis (the expert "thinks aloud" while classifying domain objects), laddered grid (a conceptual graph representing the relationships among domain elements is developed by the expert), and card sort (the expert repeatedly sorts domain objects or cards representing domain elements and describes the rationale behind each unique sorting).

Table 10.2 summarizes the effectiveness of each of these knowledge acquisition techniques when used to extract features for classification. Within a domain, each technique was used to elicit knowledge from multiple experts, coverage was computed for each expert (i.e., the percentage of knowledge elicited as compared to a complete knowledge base), and the average coverage for each technique was reported as a measure of its effectiveness. As shown in Table 10.2, the overall coverage of elicited knowledge was poor, where the most effective techniques achieved a coverage between 25 and 35 percent (pair wise combinations of these techniques were able to achieve a coverage between 35 and 45 percent). These findings are echoed in a survey of around seventy case studies describing the development of industrial expert systems: almost half reported problems with the quality of knowledge elicited from the expert. This phenomenon, dubbed the knowledge acquisition bottleneck, was identified twenty years ago and is still being cited as a major flaw in techniques used for knowledge acquisition.

Using knowledge acquisition techniques to obtain domain knowledge from an expert has two major drawbacks:

(1) It is a time consuming process.
(2) The resulting knowledge base is likely to be incomplete. Developing domain and application specific feature extractors, therefore, can be burdensome and will not necessarily produce a robust set of features for classification. As a result, the effort needed to implement the description task for a new domain and application can act as a barrier to using structural approaches to pattern recognition.

10.4.2.2 Classification

The classifier for a structural pattern recognition system is composed of a set of syntactic grammars, one for each group among which discrimination is being performed, and a parser. The identification generated by the classifier is the group whose associated syntactic grammar successfully parses the primitives extracted from the data. An adjudication scheme is necessary to resolve the situation where there is more than one successful parse.

The main difficulty in developing the classifier for a structural pattern recognition system lies in constructing the syntactic grammars. Since the grammars embody the precise criteria which differentiate among the groups, they are by their very nature domain and application specific. Complicating matters is the lack of a general solution for extracting structural features from data, causing the primitives used within the grammars to vary among domains, identification problems, and pattern recognition systems. Grammar inference techniques can be used to construct automatically a grammar from examples, but these methods can fail in the most general cases such as when the grammar for a group is context free.

Existing structural pattern recognition systems are typically applied to domains where the grammars required for discrimination can be constructed by hand. For example, structural pattern recognition systems developed for electrocardiogram diagnosis routinely use hand tooled grammars because the domain knowledge is extensive, the primitives are distinct, and the relationships among the primitives are well defined. This approach, however, quickly becomes tedious, unmanageable, and error prone as the complexities of the domain and identification problem increase. Moreover, specification of grammars by hand is impractical for domains that are complex, and infeasible for domains that are poorly understood.

10.4.2.3. Applications to Time Series Data

Identification problems involving time series (or waveform) data constitute a subset of pattern recognition applications that is of particular interest because of the large number of domains that involve such data. Both statistical and structural approaches can be used for pattern recognition of time series data: standard statistical techniques have been established for discriminant analysis of time series data, and structural techniques have been shown to be effective in a variety of domains involving time series data. Structural approaches are particularly appropriate in domains where domain experts classify time series data sets based on the arrangement of morphological events evident in the waveform—e.g., speech recognition, electrocardiogram diagnosis, seismic activity identification, radar signal detection, and process control.

Structural approaches for pattern recognition in time series data are typically employed within well explored domains where the necessary domain knowledge is readily available to guide the implementation of the description and classification tasks. In electrocardiogram diagnosis, for example, the types of morphologies that occur within the waveform and their implications with respect to cardiac behavior are clearly understood. Consequently, the existing body of knowledge within the domain of electrocardiography can serve as a solid foundation for constructing a domain specific structural pattern recognition system for electrocardiogram diagnosis. Most domains involving time series data, however, are not nearly as well understood as is electrocardiography.

To implement a structural pattern recognition system for poorly understood domains, knowledge acquisition techniques must be used to assemble the required domain knowledge. To avoid the burden of knowledge acquisition and to enable structural approaches to be applied to unexplored domains where knowledge acquisition techniques would generate an inadequate knowledge base, a domain independent approach to structural pattern recognition is necessary.

10.4.2.4 Domain Independent Structural Pattern Recognition

A domain independent structural pattern recognition system is one that is capable of acting as a "black box" to extract primitives and perform classification without the need for domain knowledge. Such a system would automatically describe and classify data, thereby eliminating the overhead associated with traditional approaches to structural pattern recognition. A domain independent structural pattern recognition system for time series data must incorporate techniques for the description and classification tasks that are not dependent on domain knowledge—i.e., generalized description and generalized classification. Since syntactic grammars are inherently tied to the domain and application, a sensible approach to generalized classification for time series data is a statistical classifier that performs discrimination based on structural features extracted from the data.

Generalized description can be implemented using a foundation of generally useful morphological features that are effective regardless of the domain. The field of signal processing offers a suggestion for morphological features that can provide the foundation for generalized description of time series data. Six fundamental types of modulation commonly used in signal processing systems—constant, straight, exponential, sinusoidal, triangular, and rectangular—entail morphologies deliberately introduced into a continuous medium with the intent of conveying information regardless of the domain or application.

Moreover, these six modulation types subsume the small set of domain independent. Morphological features commonly extracted by structural pattern recognition systems—straight lines, parabolas, and peaks. A suite of feature extractors which identify morphological features based on these six modulation types, therefore, would constitute a first pass at implementing generalized feature extraction to support domain independent structural pattern recognition in time series data.

10.5 GENERALIZED FEATURE EXTRACTION

The six morphology types suggested by the field of signal processing—constant, straight, exponential, sinusoidal, triangular, and rectangular—serve as the foundation for a set of feature extractors, called structure detectors, for generalized feature extraction in time series data. Each structure detector fits a unique function to a time series data set that embodies the morphology type and contains free parameters. A structure detector extracts an instance of its associated morphology type by instantiating values for the free parameters so as to minimize the difference between the raw data and the function; the extracted structure is defined by the function once the free parameters have been fixed. There are six structure detectors, one for each of the six morphology types.

The structure detector associated with the rectangular modulation type, however, was generalized to extract instances of trapezoidal modulation so as to increase its descriptive power. Each structure detector approximates an entire time series with a single structure. Since the values of the free parameters are set so as to minimize the difference between the raw data and the function, the extracted structure must balance the effects of the disparate sub regions of the time series by following the general, global trend of the data. Local trends can be captured via the piecewise application of the structure detectors: applying a structure detector to contiguous sub regions of a time series such that the union of the sub regions is the entire time series and the intersection of the sub regions is empty.

The application of a structure detector in such a piecewise manner results in an approximation of a time series composed of a sequence of extracted substructures such that each sub region is represented by the same function but with different values instantiated onto the free parameters within each sub region. The local trend in a time series can be better represented by allowing the structure detector used to approximate each sub region to vary among the sub regions: the structure detector that most minimizes the difference between the function and the data within a sub region is selected to represent the sub region, regardless of the structure detectors used to represent the other sub regions. The piecewise application of these six structure detectors provides the foundation for generalized feature extraction in time series data.

10.5.1 Structure Detector Evaluation

The relative effectiveness of the structure detectors can be evaluated by comparing the classification accuracies achieved when using the various structure detectors for feature extraction. Additionally, established techniques for extracting features from time series data can serve as a benchmark: If the classification accuracy achieved with features generated by the structure detectors is at least as high as the accuracies achieved with the other techniques, then it can be concluded that the structure detectors capture characteristics of time series data suitable for classification at least as well as commonly used methods. Since the structure detectors subsume general purpose feature extractors for structural pattern recognition in time series data (e.g., chain codes, curve fitting), the comparable feature extractors must be drawn from those techniques commonly used for statistical pattern recognition: the identity transformation (i.e., the extracted features are the raw data itself), the Fourier transformation, and the wavelet transformation.

An experiment to evaluate the effectiveness of the structure detectors under a range of conditions incorporates several factors: feature extraction method, training set size, composition of training set, and data preprocessing technique. Each experimental factor is allowed to vary over a range of values in order to fully explore the performance of the various feature extractors. For each combination of experimental factors, the experiment proceeds by randomly selecting a training set from the collection of data sets under analysis, configuring the feature extractor with the randomly selected training set, extracting the attributes from each data set using the trained feature extractor, and classifying the entire collection of data sets based on the extracted features.

Two different domains serve as a source of time series data for the experiment, namely semiconductor fabrication and electrocardiography. The data sets for each domain were inspected by appropriate domain experts, and a label of normal or abnormal was assigned to each data set. The labels assigned by the domain experts are considered to be completely accurate—i.e., the "ground truth." The classification accuracy achieved by the classifier can be summarized with a pair of percentages: the percent of data sets known to be normal that are classified as normal, and the percent of data sets known to be abnormal that are classified as abnormal.

To compensate for the random selection involved in assembling the training set, twenty experimental iterations are performed for each combination of experimental factors and the mean and standard deviation of the percentage pairs over the twenty iterations are computed. Therefore, the overall classification accuracy for each combination of experimental factors is represented by two pairs of values: the mean and standard deviation of the percent of known normal data sets classified as normal, and the mean and standard deviation of the percent of known abnormal data sets classified as abnormal.

The mean classification accuracies achieved by the structure detectors are generally as good as or better than those achieved by the statistical feature extraction methods. Rarely did any of the structure detectors perform poorer overall than the statistical feature extraction methods. The ability of the structure detectors to achieve classification accuracies comparable to the baseline statistical methods demonstrates that the suite of structure detectors effectively performs generalized feature extraction for structural pattern recognition in time series data.

■ 10.6 GRAPH MATCHING

Graph matching is the process of comparing two graphs by establishing a correspondence between their nodes and edges that reflect (to an extent depending on the kind of matching) the structure of the involved graphs. Conceptually, the simplest form of graph matching is graph isomorphism, where an exact structural correspondence is sought: there must be a bijective mapping between the nodes of the two graphs that preserves the edges of both graphs. Because of its strict requirements, isomorphism is not very used in Pattern Recognition applications, where it is customary that the graphs representing different instances of a same pattern have some structural differences due to noise or occlusions or to other causes.

A slightly weaker form of matching is sub graph isomorphism that requires the existence of an isomorphism between one of the graphs and a sub graph of the other. In other words, one of the graphs may have extra nodes and extra edges linking these new nodes to the rest. Sub graph isomorphism is often confused with monomorphism which is a little more relaxed matching. In monomorphism extra edges in the larger graph are allowed also between nodes that do have a correspondent in the smaller graph.

In sub graph isomorphism, instead, one of the ends of the extra edges must be an extra node. In other words, while isomorphism and sub graph isomorphism impose a two way constraint on the edges of the graphs, monomorphism imposes a one-way constraint. Sub graph isomorphism and monomorphism have been widely used in Pattern Recognition for comparing the graph representing an object to a model graph, or prototype, in order to describe the object to a class. A more robust form of graph matching is based on the computation of the Maximum Common Sub graph (MCS) that is the largest sub graph of one of the two graphs that is isomorphic to a sub graph of the other. This kind of matching allows both graphs to have extra nodes and edges, but is also significantly more expensive from a computational viewpoint. It has been demonstrated that the MCS problem is equivalent to the determination of the maximum clique (i.e. fully connected sub graph) in a so-called association graph, encoding the possible mappings between the nodes of the two graphs being matched.

Many authors formulate the graph matching algorithm in terms of clique detection. A generalization of MCS is Weighted Graph Matching (WGM), where the edges of the graphs have a weight, and the goal is to find the common sub graph with the largest total weight. In order to accommodate for significant variations of the graphs due to noise or occlusions, many authors have proposed error-correcting versions of the above matching kinds, where some more or less general error model takes into account the deformations, usually attributing them a cost, used to compute a similarity measure. Strongly related to error correcting matching is the definition of a graph edit distance, that measures the similarity of two graphs by computing the minimum-cost set of edit operations needed to transform one of the graphs into the other.

All the matching types outlined above are significantly expensive in the general case: no polynomial algorithms are known, not even for the simple graph isomorphism, except for special kinds of graphs (e.g. trees). For this reason, a large number of inexact, or suboptimal, matching algorithms have been proposed. Suboptimal algorithms provide no guarantee to find the optimal solution for the desired kind of matching, but usually run in polynomial time. Among the techniques used for exact graph matching the most commonly used is tree search (e.g. the A* algorithm), where the algorithms differ in the heuristics used to prune the search tree. Suboptimal graph matching involves a significantly wider choice. A (far from being exhaustive) list includes: soft computing methods (neural networks, genetic algorithms), relaxation methods, techniques based on continuous optimization, method based on Eigen values/eigenvectors of the adjacency matrix, dynamic programming. Some of the inexact techniques reduce the problem to bipartite graph matching. This latter is not a matching between two graphs, but between two sets of nodes, with a graph structure used to represent constraints on the matching.

Bipartite graph matching is considerably simpler, and can be solved in polynomial time. Finally, we can cite here the problem of elastic graph matching, that despite of its name is not a form of graph matching, and that is widely used in some applications of pattern recognition. In the elastic graph matching problem the mapping between the two graphs (the object being recognized and the model graph) is already known. What is searched for is a deformation of the geometric attributes associated with nodes and edges of the model that will make the model as similar as possible to the object. The amount of the deformation is used as a similarity measure for comparing the object with the model. Also elastic graph matching, because of its complexity, is dealt with suboptimal methods.

10.6.1 Application Taxonomy

In the last decades several applications of graph-based techniques in pattern recognition and image processing have been reported in the literature. At least six application areas in which graph matching techniques have been successfully employed can be individuated:

- 2D and 3D image analysis and processing;
- Document processing;
- Biometric identification;
- Image databases;
- Video analysis.
- Biological and biomedical applications.

In the field of 2D image analysis and processing, pattern recognition was considered in while in an application in the field of visual inspection was presented. As regards 3D applications, in the problem of automatic navigation was addressed, while in and in the 3D object recognition and the 3D object reconstruction are considered, respectively. While the above mentioned 2D applications use quite different matching techniques (tree isomorphism, error correcting sub graph isomorphism with a similarity measure, inexact graph matching with a neural approach, weighted bipartite matching , the 3D applications use only two different matching techniques: a maximal clique search on the association graph or an error and correcting sub graph isomorphism algorithm.

Graph matching have been used in document processing applications such as OCR, handwritten recognition, string recognition, symbol and graphics recognition. In the fields of OCR and handwritten recognition. While in an elastic graph matching is used in the recognition phase, other use inexact graph matching for addressing the high variability of handwritten characters. They use different inexact matching techniques: a Hopfield network is proposed in while a tree search is performed in and a bipartite weighted matching is used in. Within the OCR field, in an error-correcting matching algorithm based on tree search is used.

Graph based techniques have been widely used within the context of biometric applications. In the areas of face authentication and face recognition, the face identification process is carried out by elastic graph matching algorithms. Among the other applications dealing with face images, makes use of graph matching techniques in the context of facial expression recognition, while in graph matching is used for pose estimation. The other uses of graph matching are hand posture recognition and Fingerprint recognition. Image databases are another field in which graph-based techniques have been successfully employed. In this framework, finally, in a biometric system based, ear recognition, that uses a sub graph error-correcting graph matching technique.

Graph matching techniques also have been used within biomedical and biological applications. Both the biomedical applications address the problem of the correct identification of coronary arteries (artery labeling) starting from medical images, but the labeling is carried out by using different graph matching techniques. In an inexact graph matching procedure employing the A* algorithm to perform the tree search is used, while in the labeling problem is reformulated in terms of the maximal clique detection in the association graph.

10.6.2 Global Consistency

To verify the correctness of a global correspondence we can compute one rigid body transformation from all pairings and check whether each single scene feature is correctly transformed onto its corresponding model feature. To check the consistency of a local correspondence we can apply so called geometric constraints. Unary constraints are fulfilled if a scene-model pairing is locally consistent. Examples are line length, circle radius, curvature, and circumference, bounding box dimensions, area and volume. Binary constraints check whether a pairing is mutually consistent with all other pairings established at that point. The angle and the distance between two patches of the scene compared to the same relations of the corresponding features in the model can be used as binary constraints.

10.6.3 Region Adjacency Graph

In our first experiments, we used graph matching, which is one popular way used in conjunction with region oriented segmentation. The result of the segmentation step is stored in a region adjacency graph (RAG), where each vertex represents one region. Two vertices are connected by an arc if the corresponding regions are adjacent. The model information is stored in the same manner. We now search for a projection of the vertices of the one RAG onto the other which preserves the topology of the graph, i.e. two vertices (not) connected by an arc in the one RAG should (not) be connected in the other.

In other words, we are looking for a sub graph isomorphism. Of course, since we are dealing with sensor data we can not expect to find an ideal match of all vertices, therefore we have to allow for some error correction such as the addition and removal of vertices and edges. Vertices as well as edges can carry attributes to further reduce the search space by applying geometric constraints. However, since only adjacent regions are connected by arcs only they will be considered for the binary constraints. Therefore not all of the geometrical information available is used.

One problem of graph matching is the computational cost. Since the problem is NP-complete, the time generally grows exponentially with the number of vertices and edges. One way to reduce this cost is to partition the set of vertices into distinct subsets, also known as labeling. This can drastically reduce the search space and thereby save time. We have used graph matching, but have found it difficult to cope with computational cost. Because it is hard to find any sensible labeling of the vertices if all features are of the same kind (e.g. planes) we sometimes experienced worst case behavior. We were only able to match very small sub graphs (less than 10 vertices). Furthermore, adjacency is not a very stable characteristic in 3D segmentation. Problems in the alignment process and shortcomings in the segmentation both contribute to this.

■ 10.7 CONSTRAINED TREE SEARCH

A technique for creating and searching a tree of patterns using relative distances is conducted to find patterns which are nearest neighbors of a given test pattern. The structure of the tree is such that the search time is proportional to the distance between the test pattern and its nearest neighbor, which suggests the anomalous possibility that a larger tree, which can be expected on average to contain closer neighbors, can be searched faster than a smaller tree. The technique has been used to recognize Optical Character Recognition (OCR) digit samples derived from National Institute of Standards and Technologies (NISI') data at an accuracy rate of 97% using a tree of 7,000 patterns.

The task of recognizing handwritten characters, as a nearest neighbor scheme, the search technique attempts to address problems encountered in dealing with many-dimensional objects, which in this case are represented by OCR patterns. The technique is intended to be applicable not only to character recognition, but to pattern recognition tasks in general.

Pattern Insertion

Patterns are stored in a tree structure according to their relative distances for efficient searching. They are inserted into the tree by a recursive procedure starting at the root which is the first prospective parent pattern. A decision is made whether to link the new pattern directly to the parent pattern or to pass it on to the first child of the parent to which it "fits." An inserted pattern fits a child pattern if the distance between it and the child is less than the distance between the parent and the child multiplied by a constant. If the constant is S, for example, the node is passed to the child if it is within a radius of half the distance between the parent and the child patterns. Once passed to a child, the child becomes the parent for the next iteration of link checking. All children are linked to the root pattern; when set to 2, no pattern will have more than one child, i.e., the tree will be a linked list.

One feature of the algorithm is that the order of a pattern's sub tree branches is important: A new pattern is always inserted in the first titting branch (even though there can be more than one such branch). This feature allows the search of a tree which contains a duplicate of a given pattern to proceed with maximum efficiency: The duplicate will always be found on the first branch which fits the pattern. Another feature is a tree reorganization procedure which prevents excessive children from accumulating on a parent pattern. When a new child is linked to a parent pattern, every other previously inserted child is checked to determine if it should be linked to the new child instead of the parent. For each such child, the child sub tree is severed from the parent and each pattern in the sub tree is inserted at the current parent pattern. Note that they are not inserted into the new child since not all patterns in the sub tree necessarily fit there.

Pattern Searching

The purpose of the pattern search algorithm is to efficiently find patterns in the tree which are nearest neighbors of a given test pattern. Searching is done in a best-first manner, that is, the pattern whose sub tree could contain the pattern least distant from the search pattern is searched next. The essence of the search decision procedure is illustrated in Fig. 10.10.

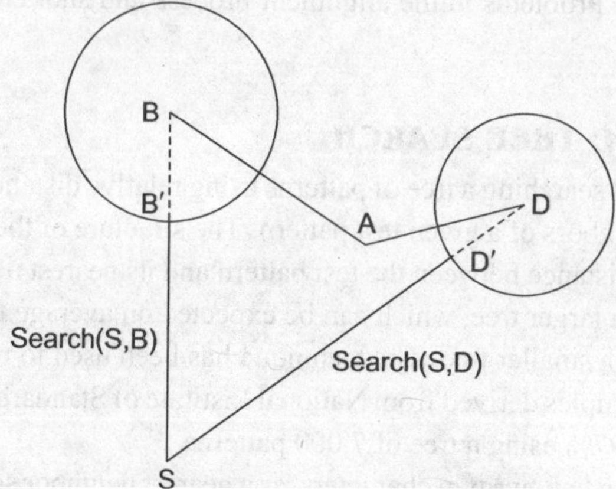

Fig. (10.10) Search database.

When the search pattern S arrives at pattern A, it must determine whether to search either pattern B or D next. It does this by calculating the least distances between S and the patterns which can potentially appear within the sub trees of B and D. These are labeled B' and D', respectively. This distance, called the search distance, is defined as follows for S and B:

Example: Because of this experience, we decided to follow the constrained tree search approach. Considering the notation as introduced above, we first start with one scene-model feature pair (fi, Fmi). For each possible pairing we find, search goes on to the next level, where a correspondence for the second feature is sought. This leads to the matching path {(fi, Fmi), (fj, Fmj)}. This search proceeds in a recursive manner. It is well-known as depth-first search. Again, the computational cost grows exponentially with the number of features. The key for finding a solution in a reasonable amount of time is the choice of the constraints used to bound the branching in the tree. For each scene feature only a subset of model features is selected as possible matches using unary constraints. At each stage of the search process we check the binary constraints of the current pairing with all pairings along the path to the root.

In the experiments conducted so far, we were not confronted with cluttered scenes. What we do have are slight deviations of the manufactured part from the CAD model. Therefore, we can not expect to find a correspondence for all model features and vice versa. This problem is increased by the difficulties in the segmentation stage where a great number of small "sliver regions" is produced which do not correspond to any model feature. To deal with this situation in the context of computation time, we first sort the scene features by size (area) and then prune the set of features to the size of the set of model features. During the search, we allow the skipping of features, i.e. if no correspondence can be found for a certain scene feature we remove this feature for the current matching path and continue with the next.

■ SUMMARY

- The problem in object recognition is to determine which, if any, of a given set of objects appear in a given image or image sequence. Thus object recognition is a problem of *matching* models from a database with representations of those models extracted from the image luminance data.
- Object recognition is a process of hypothesizing an object-to-model correspondence and then verifying that the hypothesis is correct. Generally an hypothesis is considered successful if the error between the projected model features and the corresponding image features is below some threshold, and a reasonable fraction of the object outline is covered by the image features.
- An invariant of a geometric configuration is a function of the configuration whose value is unchanged by a particular transformation. For example, the distance between two points is unchanged for a Euclidean transformation (translation or rotation).
- Clustering is the classification of objects into different groups, or more precisely, the partitioning of a data set into subsets (clusters), so that the data in each subset (ideally) share some common trait - often proximity according to some defined distance measure.
- Data clustering is a common technique for statistical data analysis, which is used in many fields, including machine learning, data mining, pattern recognition, image analysis and bioinformatics.
- The elbow criterion is a common rule of thumb to determine what number of clusters should be chosen, for example for k-means and agglomerative hierarchical clustering. It should also be noted that the initial assignment of cluster seeds has bearing on the final model performance. Thus, it is appropriate to re-run the cluster analysis multiple times.
- Statistical classification is a statistical procedure in which individual items are placed into groups based on quantitative information on one or more characteristics inherent in the items (referred to as traits, variables, characters, etc) and based on a training set of previously labeled items.
- Pattern recognition is a sub-topic of machine learning. It can be defined as "the act of taking in raw data and taking an action based on the category of the data". Most research in pattern recognition is about methods for supervised learning and unsupervised learning.
- Pattern recognition aims to classify data (patterns) based on either a priori knowledge or on statistical information extracted from the patterns. The patterns to be classified are usually groups of measurements or observations, defining points in an appropriate multidimensional space.
- A complete pattern recognition system consists of a sensor that gathers the observations to be classified or described; a feature extraction mechanism that computes numeric or symbolic information from the observations; and a classification or description scheme that does the actual job of classifying or describing observations, relying on the extracted features.
- Structural pattern recognition is based on the structural interrelationships of features. A wide range of algorithms can be applied for pattern recognition, from very simple Bayesian classifiers to much more powerful neural networks.

- An intriguing problem in pattern recognition yet to be solved is the relationship between the problem to be solved (data to be classified) and the performance of various pattern recognition algorithms (classifiers).
- Typical applications are automatic speech recognition, classification of text into several categories (e.g. spam/non-spam email messages), the automatic recognition of handwritten postal codes on postal envelopes, or the automatic recognition of images of human faces.
- Graph matching is the process of comparing two graphs by establishing a correspondence between their nodes and edges that reflect (to an extent depending on the kind of matching) the structure of the involved graphs.

Review Questions

1. Discuss the concepts of object recognition and explain the various deterministic Methods for it.
2. Discuss the concepts of Clustering, and explain various types of clustering methods.
3. Discuss the concepts of pattern recognition.
4. Discuss the types of pattern recognition and differentiate Statistical pattern recognition with Syntactic pattern recognition.
5. Write short notes on the following
   (i) Statistical pattern recognition
   (ii) Syntactic pattern recognition
   (iii) Tree Search
   (iv) Graph Matching

❑❑❑

11

IMAGE CODING AND COMPRESSION

Image compression is the application of Data compression on digital images. In effect, the objective is to reduce redundancy of the image data in order to be able to store or transmit data in an efficient form.

Image compression can be lossy or lossless. Lossless compression is sometimes preferred for artificial images such as technical drawings, icons or comics. This is because lossy compression methods, especially when used at low bit rates, introduce compression artifacts. Lossless compression methods may also be preferred for high value content, such as medical imagery or image scans made for archival purposes. Lossy methods are especially suitable for natural images such as photos in applications where minor (sometimes imperceptible) loss of fidelity is acceptable to achieve a substantial reduction in bit rate.

Compressing an image is significantly different than compressing raw binary data. Of course, general purpose compression programs can be used to compress images, but the result is less than optimal. This is because images have certain statistical properties which can be exploited by encoders specifically designed for them. Also, some of the finer details in the image can be sacrificed for the sake of saving a little more bandwidth or storage space. This also means that lossy compression techniques can be used in this area.

Lossless compression involves with compressing data which, when decompressed, will be an exact replica of the original data. This is the case when binary data such as executables, documents etc. are compressed. They need to be exactly reproduced when decompressed. On the other hand, images (and music too) need not be reproduced 'exactly'. An approximation of the original image is enough for most purposes, as long as the error between the original and the compressed image is tolerable.

Error Metrics

Two of the error metrics used to compare the various image compression techniques are the Mean Square Error (MSE) and the Peak Signal to Noise Ratio (PSNR). The MSE is the cumulative squared error between the compressed and the original image, whereas PSNR is a measure of the peak error. The mathematical formulae for the two are

$$\text{MSE} = \frac{1}{MN}\sum_{x=1}^{M}\sum_{x=1}^{M}[I(x, y) - I'(x, y)]^2$$

$$\text{PSNR} = 20 * \log10\,(255/\text{sqrt}(\text{MSE}))$$

where I(x,y) is the original image, I'(x,y) is the approximated version (which is actually the decompressed image) and M,N are the dimensions of the images. A lower value for MSE means lesser error, and as seen from the inverse relation between the MSE and PSNR, this translates to a high value of PSNR. Logically, a higher value of PSNR is good because it means that the ratio of Signal to Noise is higher. Here, the 'signal' is the original image, and the 'noise' is the error in reconstruction. So, if you find a compression scheme having a lower MSE (and a high PSNR), you can recognise that it is a better one.

The algorithms explained can be easily extended to colour images, either by processing each of the colour planes separately, or by transforming the image from RGB representation to other convenient representations like YUV in which the processing is much easier.

The usual steps involved in compressing an image are

1. Specifying the Rate (bits available) and Distortion (tolerable error) parameters for the target image.
2. Dividing the image data into various classes, based on their importance.
3. Dividing the available bit budget among these classes, such that the distortion is a minimum.
4. Quantize each class separately using the bit allocation information derived in step 3.
5. Encode each class separately using an entropy coder and write to the file.

Remember, this is how 'most' image compression techniques work. But there are exceptions. One example is the Fractal Image Compression technique, where possible self similarity within the image is identified and used to reduce the amount of data required to reproduce the image. Traditionally these methods have been time consuming, but some latest methods promise to speed up the process.

Reconstructing the image from the compressed data is usually a faster process than compression. The steps involved are

1. Read in the quantized data from the file, using an entropy decoder. (Reverse of step 5).
2. Dequantize the data. (Reverse of step 4).
3. Rebuild the image. (Reverse of step 2).

Advanced Image Coding

Advanced Image Coding (AIC) is an experimental still image compression system that combines algorithms from the H.264 and JPEG standards. More specifically, it combines intra frame block prediction from H.264 with a JPEG-style discrete cosine transform, followed by context adaptive binary arithmetic coding as used in H.264.

The result is a compression scheme that performs much better than JPEG and close to JPEG-2000. For a quick comparison, look at the famous Lena image, compressed at about 0.95 bit per pixel (25:1 compression ratio) using JPEG, JPEG-2000 and AIC:

The JPEG-2000 image has the best perceptual quality, although it tends to smooth and blur the image quite a bit, resulting in loss of detail. The JPEG image is clearly the worst, and AIC is somewhere in between. The objective quality of the AIC image, expressed as the Peak Signal to Noise Ratio (PSNR), is even higher than the JPEG-2000 image. This is because AIC preserves the details better, as you can clearly see in the hat and the feathers on the hat.

AIC is however much less complex than JPEG-2000. The AIC source code is optimized for clarity and readability, and not for speed. But the current version is already faster than most JPEG-2000 codecs around, and much faster than the JPEG-2000 reference software.

11.1 LOSSLESS AND LOSSY COMPRESSION

We have seen that image flies can be very large. It is thus important for reasons both of storage and file transfer to make these file sizes smaller, if possible. In section 1.9 we touched briefly on the topic of compression; in this section we investigate some standard compression methods. It will be necessary to distinguish between two different classes of compression methods : *lossless compression.* where all the information is retained, and *lossy compression* where some information is lost.

Lossless compression is preferred for images of legal scientific or political significance, where loss of data, even of apparent insignificance, could have considerable consequences. Unfortunately this style tends not to lead to high compression ratios. However, lossless compression is used as part of many standard image formats.

11.2 HUFFMAN CODING

The idea of Huffman coding is simple. Rather than using a fixed length code (8 bits) to represent they grey values in an image, we use a variable length code, with smaller length codes corresponding to more probable grey values.

A small example will make this clear. Suppose we have a 2-bit greyscale image with only four grey levels : 0, 1, 2, 3, with the probabilities 0.2, 0.4, 0.3 and 0.1 respectively. That is 20% of pixels in the image have grey value 50; 40% have grey value 100 and so on. The following table shows fixed length and variable length codes for this image :

Grey Value	Probability	Fixed Code	Variable Code
0	0.2	00	000
1	0.4	01	1
2	0.3	10	01
3	0.1	11	001

Now consider how this image has been compressed. Each grey value has its own unique identifying code. The average number of bits per pixel can be easily calculated as the expected value (in a probabilistic sense) :

$$(0.2 \times 3) + (0.4 \times 1) + (0.3 \times 2) + (0.1 \times 3) = 1.9.$$

Notice that the longest codewords are associated with the lowest probabilities. This average is indeed smaller than 2.

This can be made more precise by the notion of *entropy*, which is a measure of the amount of information. Specifically, the entropy H of an image is the theoretical minimum number of bits per pixel required to encode the image with no loss of information. It is defined by

$$H = -\sum_{i=0}^{L-1} p_i \log_2 (p_i)$$

where the index i is taken over all greyscales of the image and p_i is the probability of grey level i occurring in the image. Very good accounts of the basics of information theory and entropy are given by Roman |10| and Welsh |16|. In the example given above,

$$H = -(0.2 \log_2 (0.2) + 0.4 \log_2 (0.4) + 0.3 \log_2 (0.3) + 0.1 \log_2 (0.1) = 1.8464.$$

This means that no matter what coding scheme is used, it will never use less than 1.8464 bits per pixel. On this basis, the Huffman coding scheme given above, giving an average number of bits per pixel much closer to this theoretical minimum than 2, provides a very good result.

To obtain the Huffman code for a given image we proceed as follows :

1. Determine the probabilities of each grey value in the image.
2. Form a binary tree by adding probabilities two at a time, always taking the two lowest available values.
3. Now assign 0 and 1 arbitrarily to each branch of the tree from its apex.
4. Read the codes from the top down.

To see how this works, consider the example of a 3-bit greyscale image (so the grey values are 0-7) with the following probabilities :

Grey Value	0	1	2	3	4	5	6	7
Probability	0.19	0.25	0.21	0.16	0.08	0.06	0.03	0.02

For these probabilities, the entropy can be calculated to be 2.6508. We can now combine probabilities two at a time as shown in figure 11.1.

Note that if we have a choice of probabilities we choose arbitrarily. The second stage consists of arbitrarily assigning 0's and 1's to each branch of the tree just obtained. This is shown in figure 11.2.

To obtain the codes for each grey value, start at the 1 on the top right, and work back towards the grey value in question, listing the numbers passed on the way. This produces :

Grey Value	**Huffman Code**
0	00
1	10
2	01
3	110
4	1110
5	11110
6	111110
7	111111

As above, we can evaluate the average number of bits per pixel as an expected value :

As above, we can evaluate the average number of bits per pixel as an expected value :

$$(0.19 \times 2) + (0.25 \times 2) + (0.21 \times 2) + (0.16 \times 3) + (0.08 \times 4) + (0.06 \times 5) + (0.03 \times 6) + (0.02 \times 6) = 2.7$$

which is a significant improvement over 3 bits per pixel, and very close to the theoretical minimum of 2.6508 given by the entropy.

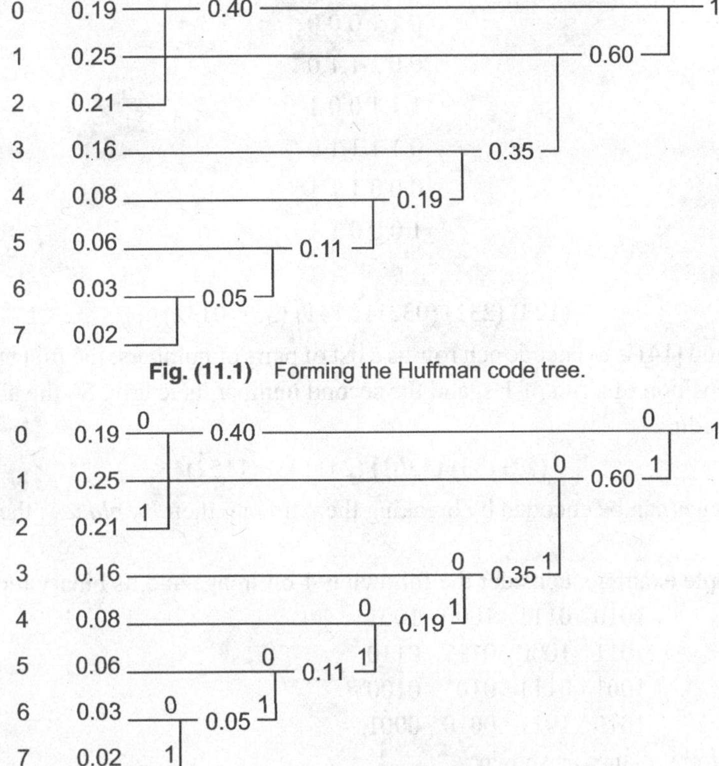

Fig. (11.1) Forming the Huffman code tree.

Fig. (11.2) Assigning 0's and 1's to the branches.

Huffman codes are *uniquely decodable,* in that a string can be decoted in only one way. For example, consider the string

$$1\,1\,0\,1\,1\,1\,0\,0\,0\,0\,0\,1\,0\,0\,1\,1\,1\,1\,1\,0$$

to be decoded with the Huffman code generated above. There is no code word 1, or 11, so we may take the first three bits 110 as being the code for grey value 3. Notice also that no other code word begins with this string. For the next few bits, 1110 is a code word : no other begins with this string, and no other smaller string is a codeword. So we can decode this string as grey level 4. Continuing in this way we obtain :

$$\underbrace{1\;1\;0}_{3}\;\underbrace{1\;1\;1\;0}_{4}\;\underbrace{0\;0}_{0}\;\underbrace{0\;0}_{0}\;\underbrace{0\;1}_{1}\;\underbrace{0\;0}_{2}\;\underbrace{1\;1\;1\;1\;1\;0}_{5}$$

as the decoding for this string.

For more information about Huffman coding, and its limitations and generalizations, see [4, 9].

■ 11.3 RUN LENGTH ENCONDING

Run length encoding (RLE) is based on a simple idea: to encode strings of zeros and ones by the number of repetitions in each string. RLE has become a standard in fascimile transmission. For a binary image, there are many different implementations of RLE; one method is to encode each line separately, starting with the number of 0's. So the following binary image:

0 1 1 0 0 0
0 0 1 1 1 0
1 1 1 0 0 1
0 1 1 1 1 0
0 0 0 1 1 1
1 0 0 0 1 1

would be encoded as

(123) (231) (0321) 9141) (33) (0132)

Another method [14] is to encode ach row as a list of pairs of numbers: the first number in each pair given the starting position of a run of 1's, and the second number its length. So the above binary image would have the encoding

(22) (33) (1361) (24) (43) (1152)

Greyscale images can be encoded by breaking them up into their *bit planes* : these were discussed in chapter 1.

To give a simple example, consider the following 4-bit image and its binary representation:

10	7	8	9		1010	0111	1000	1001
11	8	7	6	→	1011	1000	0111	0110
9	7	5	4		1001	0111	0101	0100
10	11	2	1		1010	1011	0010	0001

We may break it into bit planes as shown :

0th plane	1st plane	2nd plane	3rd plane
0 1 0 1	1 1 0 0	0 1 0 0	1 0 1 1
1 0 1 0	1 0 1 1	0 0 1 1	1 1 0 0
1 1 1 0	0 1 0 0	0 1 1 1	1 0 0 0
0 1 0 1	1 1 1 0	0 0 0 0	1 1 0 0

and then each plane can be encoded separately using our chosen implementation of RLE.

However, there is a problem with bit planes, and that is that small changes of grey value may cause significant changes in bits. For example, the change from value 7 to 8 causes the change of all four bits, since we are changing the binary strings 0111 to 1000. The problem is of course excerbated for 8-bit images. For RLE to be effective, we should hope that long runs of very similar grey values would result in very good copression rates for the code. But this may not be the case. A 4-bit image consisting of randomly distributed 7's and 8's would thus result in uncorrelated bit planes, and little effective compression.

To overcome this difficulty, we may encode the grey values with their binary *Gray codes*. A Gray code is an ordering of all binary strings of a given length so that there is only one bit change between a string and the next. So a 4-bit Gray code is :

15	1	0	0	0
14	1	0	0	1
13	1	0	1	1
12	1	0	1	0
11	1	1	1	0
10	1	1	1	1

9	1	1	1	0
8	1	1	0	0
7	0	1	0	0
6	0	1	0	1
5	0	1	1	1
4	0	1	1	0
3	0	0	1	0
2	0	0	1	1
1	0	0	0	1
0	0	0	0	0

To see the advantages, consider the following 4-bit image with its binary and Gray code encodings :

8 8 7 8	1000	1000	0111	1000	1100	1100	0100	1100
8 7 8 7 →	1000	0111	1000	0111 →	1100	0100	1100	0100
7 7 8 7	0111	0111	1000	0111	0100	0100	1100	0100
7 8 7 7	0111	1000	0111	0111	0100	1100	0100	0100

where the first binary array is the standard binary encoding, and the second array the Gray codes. The binary bit planes are :

0 0 1 0	0 0 1 0	0 0 1 0	1 1 0 1
0 1 0 1	0 1 0 1	0 1 0 1	1 0 1 0
1 1 0 1	1 1 0 1	1 1 0 1	0 0 1 0
1 0 1 1	1 0 1 1	1 0 1 1	0 1 0 0
0th plane	1st plane	2nd plane	3rd plane

and the bit planes corresponding to the Gray codes are:

0 0 0 0	0 0 0 0	1 1 1 1	1 1 0 1
0 0 0 0	0 0 0 0	1 1 1 1	1 0 1 0
0 0 0 0	0 0 0 0	1 1 1 1	0 0 1 0
0 0 0 0	0 0 0 0	1 1 1 1	0 1 0 0
0th plane	1st plane	2nd plane	3rd plane

Notice that the Grey code planes are highly correlated except for one bit plane, whereas all the binary bit planes are uncorrelated.

Run length encoding in MATLAB

We can experiment with run length encoding by writing a simple function to implement it. To make it easy on ourselves, we shall just stick with single binary images. Our output will be a single vector, giving the numbers of zeros and ones, alternating, through our image row by row. We start by putting our image into a single row. For a binary image in, this can be done with the two commands

```
L=prod (size (im));
im=reshape (im', 1, L0;
```

To find the number of beginning zeros, we obtain the position of the first 1, thus:

```
min find(im==1))
```

We append one less than this result to our output vector. It may well be that there are no further ones, in which case we have reached the end of the file, and we stop by appending the current length of our image to the output vector. We now change to looking for the place of the next zero: we can use the min(find) command again, but we first reduce our image by the zeros we have already found.

The following table shows how we can implement run length encoding:

Image	Looking for	Place	RLE output
			[]
[0 0 1 1 1 0 0 0 1]	1	3	[2]
[1 1 1 0 0 0 1]	0	4	[2 3]
[0 0 0 1]	1	4	[2 3 3]
[1]	0	*not found*	[2 3 3 1]

One more example:

Image	Looking for	Place	RLE output
			[]
[1 1 1 0 0 0 0 1 1]	1	1	[0]
[1 1 1 0 0 0 0 1 1]	0	4	[0 3]
[0 0 0 0 1 1]	1	4	[0 3 4]
[1 1]	0	*Not found*	[0 3 4 2]

Notice that in this second example, since the length of our initial run of zeros was found to be zero, we do not reduce the length of our image in the next step.

Figure 1.3 shows the implementation of this algorithm in Matlab.

```
function out=rle (image)
%
% RLE(IMAGE) produces a vector containing the run-length encoding of
% IMAGE, which should be a binary image. The image is set out as a
  long
% row, and the conde contains the number of zeros, followed by the
  number
% of ones, alternating.
%
% Example:
%
% rle([1 1 1 0 0; 0 0 1 1 1; 1 1 0 0 0])
%
% ans =
%
% 0 3 4 5 3
%
L=prod (size(image));
im=reshape (image', 1 L);
x=1;
out=[];
while L~= 0,
  temp=min(find(im == x));
  if isempty(temp),
        out=[out L];
        break
  end;
  out=[out temp-1];
  x=1-x;
  im=im(temp: L);
  L=L-temp+1;
end;
```

Fig; (11.3) A MATLAB function for obtaining the run length code of a binary image.

Now we can test this on a few images:

```
< < c=imread ('circles.tif');
< < cr=rle(c);
< < whos c cr
Name          Size          Bytes          Class
c             256x256       65536          uint8 array (logical)
cr            1x693         5544           double array
```

We can reduce the size of the output by storing it using the data type uint16: unsigned 16-bit integers.

```
< < cr=uint16(cr);
< < whos cr
Name          Size          Bytes          Class
cr            1x693         1386           uint16 array
```

Even if the original circles image was stored as one bit per pixel, or eight pixels per byte, we would have a total of

$$\frac{65536}{8} = 8192$$

bytes: still more than the run length code. So in this example, run length encoding provides a reasonable amount of compression.

```
< < t=imread('text.tif');
< < tr=rle(t);
< < whos t tr

Name          Size          Bytes          Class
t             245x256       65536          uint8 array (logical)
tr            1x2923        23384          double array
```

Again better compression can be obtained by changing the data type.

```
< < tr=uint16(tr);
< < whos tr
Name          Size          Bytes          Class
tr            1x2923        5846           uint16 array
```

Although this is not as good as for the previous image, it is still better than the minimum of 8192 bytes for the original image.

Review Questions

1. Construct a Huffman code for each of the probability tables given :

Grey Scale		0	1	2	3	4	5	6	7
Probability	(a)	.07	.11	.08	.04	.5	.05	.06	.09
	(b)	.13	.12	.13	.13	.12	.12	.12	.13
	(c)	.09	.13	.15	.1	.14	.12	.11	.16

In each case determine the average bits/pixel given by your code.

2. From your results of the previous question, what do think are the conditions of the probability distribution which give rise to a high compression rate using Huffman coding?

3. Encode each of the following binary imges using run length encoding:

(a)

1 0 0 1 1 1
0 1 0 1 1 1
1 0 0 1 1 1
0 1 1 1 0 1
1 0 1 0 1 1
0 1 1 1 1 0

(b)

1 0 1 0 0 0
0 0 1 1 0 1
1 1 0 0 0 0
0 0 0 0 1 1
1 1 1 1 0 0
1 1 1 0 0 0

4. Using run length encoding, encode each of the following 4-bit images :

(a)

1 1 3 3 1 1
1 7 10 10 7 1
6 13 15 15 13 6
6 13 15 15 13 6
1 7 10 10 7 1
1 1 3 3 1 1

(b)

0 0 0 6 12 12 1 9
1 1 1 6 12 11 9 13
2 2 2 6 11 9 13 13
8 10 15 15 7 5 5 5
14 8 10 15 7 4 4 4
14 14 5 10 7 3 3 3

5. Check your answers to the previous two questions with MATLAB. You can isolate the bit planes by using the technique discussed in section 1.17.

6. Encode the preceeding images using the 4-bit Gray code, and apply run length encoding to the bit planes of the result.

Compare the results obtained using Gray codes, and standard binary codes.

7. Write a MATLAB function for restoring a binary image from a run length code. Test it on the images and codes from the previous questions.

8. The following are the run-length encodings for a 4 × 4 4-bit image from most to least important bit-planes :

3 1 2 2 1 4 1 2
1 2 1 2 1 2 1 2 1 3
2 1 2 1 2 2 1 5
0 3 1 3 2 3 1 2 1

Construct the image.

9. (a) Given the following 4-bit image :

0 4 4 4 4 4 6 7
0 4 5 5 5 4 6 7
1 4 5 5 5 4 6 7
1 4 5 5 5 4 6 7
1 4 4 4 4 4 6 7
2 2 8 8 8 10 10 11
2 2 9 9 9 12 13 13
3 3 9 9 9 15 14 14

transform it to a 3-bit image by removing the least most significant bit plane. Construct a Huffman code on the result and determine the average number of bits/pixel used by the code.

(b) Now apply Huffman coding to the original iamge and determine the average number of bits/pixel used by the code.

(c) Which of the two codes gives the best rate of compression?

12

INTRODUCTION TO MATLAB

Before beginning with this exercise, start MATLAB. If you are new to MATLAB, you should first read the MATLAB Getting Started documentation.

You should already have installed the Image Processing Toolbox, which runs seamlessly from MATLAB. For information about installing the toolbox, see the MATLAB Installation Guide for your platform.

All of the images used in this example are supplied with the Image Processing Toolbox. Note that the images shown in this documentation differ slightly from what you see on your screen because the surrounding MATLAB figure windows has been removed to save space.

1. Read and Display an Image

Clear the MATLAB workspace of any variables and close open figure windows.

```
clear, close all
```

To read an image, use the imread command. Let's read in a TIFF image named pout.tif (which is one of the sample images that is supplied with the Image Processing Toolbix), and store it in an array named I.

```
I=imread ('pout.tif');
```

Now call imshow to display I.

```
imshow (I)
```

Fig. (12.1)

Here's What Just Happened

Step 1. The imread function recognized pout.tif as a valid TIFF file and stored it in the variable. (For the list of graphics formats supported, see imread in the Image Processing Toolbox online ''Function Reference.'')

The functions imread and imshow read and display graphics images in MATLAB. In general, it is preferable to use imshow for displaying images becauss it handles the image-related MATLAB properties for you. (The MATLAB function image is for low-level programming tasks.)

Note that if pout.tiff were an *indexed* image, the appropriate syntax for imread would be,

```
[X, map] = imread ('pout.tif');
```

2. Check the Image in Memory

Enter the whos command to see how I is stored in memory.

```
whos
```

MATLAB respond with

```
Name        Size        Bytes       Class
I           291x240     69840       uint8 array
Grand total is 69840 elements using 69840 bytes
```

Here's What Just Happened

Step 2. You called the whos command to see how pout.tif had been stored into the MATLAB workspace. As you saw, pout.tif is stored as a 291-by-240 array. Since pout.tif was an 8-bit image, it gets stored in memory as an uint8 array. MATLAB can store images in memory as uint8, uint16, or double arrays.

3. Perform Histogram Equalization

As you can see, pout.tif is a somewhat low contrast image. To see the distribution of intensities in pout.tif in its current state, you can create a histogram by calling the imhist function. (Precede the call to imhist with the figure command so that the histogram does not overwrite the display of the image I in the current figure window.)

```
figure, imhist(I) % Display a histogram of I in a new figure.
```

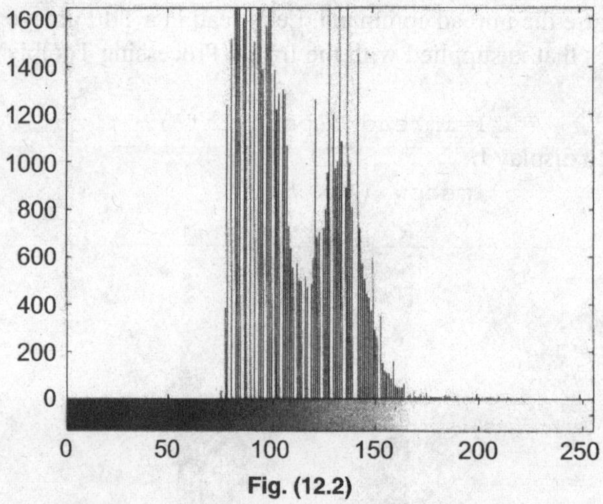

Fig. (12.2)

Notice how the intensity range is rather narrow. It does not cover the potential range of [0, 255], and is missing the high and low values that would result in good contrast.

Now call histeq to spread the intensity values over the full range, thereby improving the contrast of I. Return the modified image in the variable I2.

```
12 = histeq(I); % Equalize I and output in new array 12.
```

Display the new equalized image, I2, in a new figure window.

```
figure, imshow (I2) % Display the new equalized image I2.
```

Fig. (12.3)

Call imhist again, this time for I2.

```
figure, imhist (I2) % show the histogram for the new image I2.
```

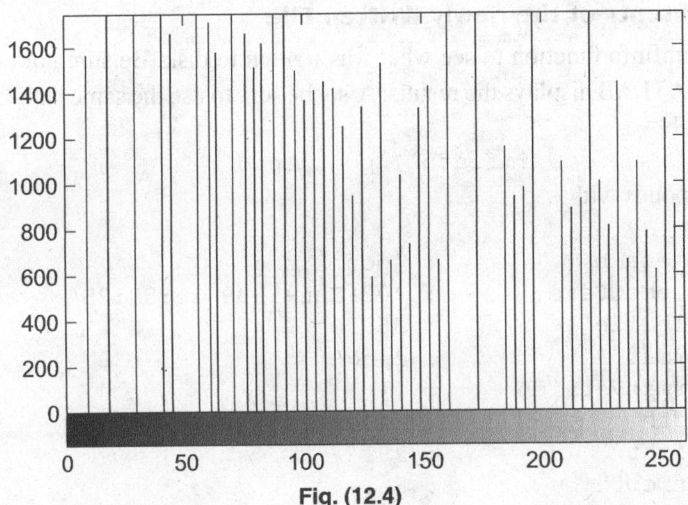

Fig. (12.4)

See how the pixel values now extend across the full range of possible values.

Here's What Just Happened

Step 3. You adjusted the contrast automatically by using the function histeq to evenly distribute the image's pixel values over the full potential range for the storage class of the image. For an image X, with a storage class of uint8, the full range is 0| *X* |255, for uint16 it is 0| *X* |65535, and for double it is 0| *X* |1. Note that the convention elsewhere in this user guide (and for all MATLAB documentation) is to denote the above ranges as [0, 255], [0, 65535], and [0, 1], respectively.

If you compare the two histograms, you can see that the histogram of I2 is more spread out and flat than the histogram of I1. The process that flattened and spread out this histogram is called *histogram equalization.*

For more control over adjusting the contrast of an image (for example, if you want to choose the range over which the new pixel values should span), you can use the imadjust function.

4. Write the Image

Write the newly adjusted image I2 back to disk. Let's say you'd like to save it as a PNG file. Use imwrite and specify a filename that includes the extension 'png'.

```
imwrite (I2, 'pout2.png');
```

Here's What Just Happened

Step 4. MATLAB recognized the file extension of 'png' as valid and wrote the image to disk. It wrote it as an 8-bit image by default because it was stored as a uint8 intensity image in memory. If I2 had been an image array of type RGB and class uint8, it would have been written to disk as a 24-bit image. If you want to set the bit depth of your output image, use the BitDepth parameter with imwrite. This example writes a 4-bit PNG file.

```
imwrite (I2, 'pout2.png', 'BitDepth', 4);
```

Note that all output formats do not support the same set of output bit depths. See imwrite in the Reference for the list of valid bit depths for each format.

5. Check the Contents of the Newly Written File

Now, use the imfinfo function to see what was written to disk. Be sure not to end the line with a semicolon so that MATLAB displays the results. Also, be sure to use the same path (if any) as you did for the call to imwrite, above.

```
imfinfo ('pout2.png')
```

MATLAB responds with

```
ans =
        Filename        : 'pout2.png'
        FileModDate     : '03-Jun-1999 15:50:25'
        FileSize        : 36938
        Format          : 'png'
        FormatVersion   : []
        width           : 240
        Height          : 291
        BitDepth        : 8
        ColorType       : 'grayscale'
```

Note. This example shows only a subset of all the fields returned by imfinfo. Also, the value in the FileModDate field for your file will be different from what is shown above. It will show the date and time that you used imwrite to create your image.

Here's What Just Happened

Step 5. When you called imfinfo, MATLAB displayed all of the header fields for the PNG file format that are supported by the toolbox. You can modify many of these fields by using additional parameters in your call to imwrite. The additional parameters that are available for each file format are listed in tables in the reference entry for imwrite.

Examle 2 - Advanced Topics

In this exercise you will work with another intensity image, rice.tif, and explore some more advanced operations. The goals of this exercise are to remove the nonuniform background from rice.tif, convert the resulting image to a binary image by using thresholding, use components labeling to return the number of objects (grains or partial grains) in the image, and compute object statistics.

1. Read and Display an Image

Clear the MATLAB workspace of any variables and close open figure windows. Read and display the intensity image rice.tif.

```
clear, close all
I = imread ('rice.tif'');
imshow (I)
```

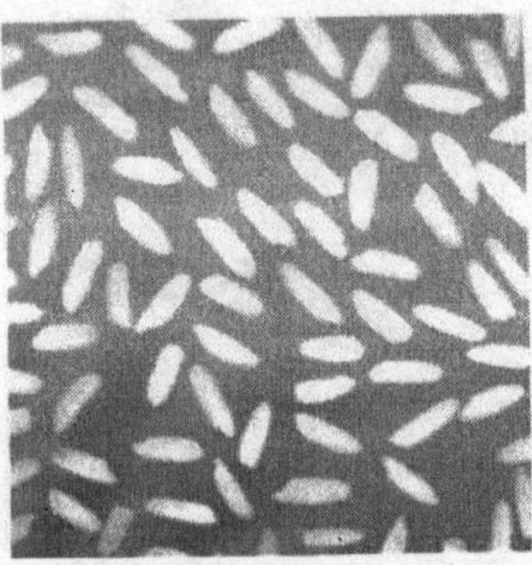

Fig. (12.5)

2. Use Morphological Opening to Estimate the Background

Notice that the background illumination is brighter in the center of the image than at the bottom. Use the imopen function to estimate the background illumination.

```
background = imopen (I, strel ('disk', 15));
```

To see the estimated background image, type

```
imshow (background)
```

Here's What Just Happened

Step 1. You used the toolbox functions imread and imshow to read and display an 8-bit intensity image. imread and imshow are discussed in Exercise 1, in ''2. Check the Image in Memory'' on page 1-3, under the ''Here's What Just Happened'' discussion.

Step 2. You performed a morphological opening operation by calling imopen with the input image, I and a disk-shaped structuring element with a radius of 15. The structuring element was created by the strel function. The morphological opening has the effect of removing objects that cannot completely contain a disk of radius 15.

3. Display the Background Approximation as a Surface

Use the surf command to create a surface display of the background approximation, background. The surf function requires data of class double, however, so you first need to convert background using the double command.

```
figure, surf (double (background (1 : 8 : end, 1 : 8 : end))),
zlim ([0 255]0; set (gca, 'ydir', 'reverse');
```

The example uses MATLAB indexing syntax to view only 1 out of 8 pixels in each direction; otherwise the surface plot would be too dense. The example also sets the scale of the plot to better match the range of the uint8 data and reverses they y-axis of the display to provide a better view of the data (the pixels at the bottom of the image appear at the front of the surface plot).

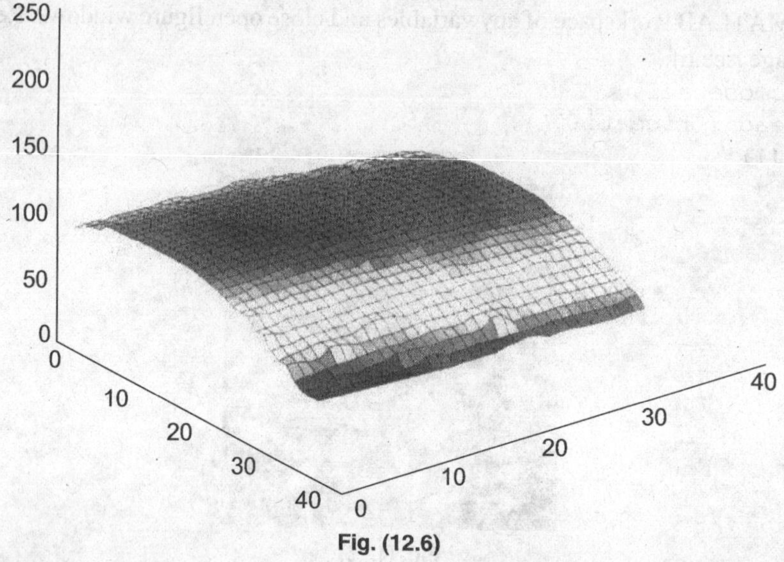

Fig. (12.6)

Here's What Just Happened

Step 3. You used the surf command to examine the background image. The surf command creates colored parametric surfaces that enable you to view mathematical functions over a rectangular region. In the surface display, [0, 0] represents the origin, or upper-left corner of the image. The highest part of the curve indicates that the highest pixel values of background (and consequently rice.tif) occur near the middle rows of the image. The lowest pixel values occur at the bottom of the image and are represented in the surface plot by the lowest part of the curve.

The surface plot is a Handle Graphics object, and you can therefore fine-tune its appearance by setting properties. For information on working with MATLAB graphics, see the MATLAB graphics documentation.

4. Subtract the Background Image from the Original Image

Now subtract the background image, background, from the original image, I, to create a more uniform background.

```
I2 = imsubtract (I, background);
```

Now display the image with its more uniform background.

```
figure, imshow (I2)
```

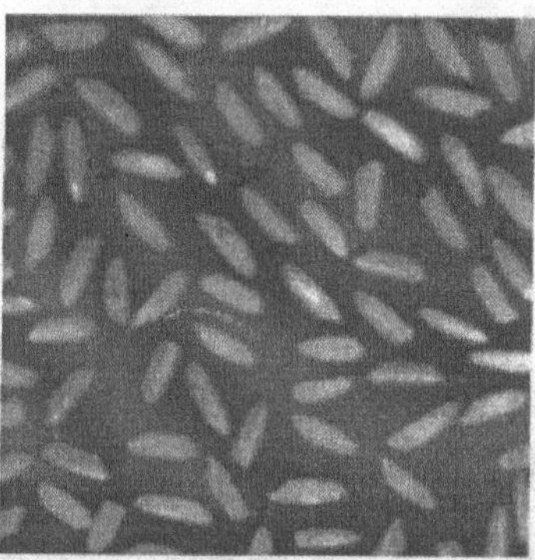

Fig. (12.7)

Here's What Just Happened

Step 4. You subtracted a background approximation image from rice.tif. Because subtraction, like many of MATLAB mathematical operations, is only supported for data of class double, you must use the Image Processing Toolbox image arithmetic imsubtract function.

The Image Processing Toolbox has a demo, ipss003, that approximates and removes the background from an image.

5. Adjust the Image Contrast

The image is now a bit too dark. Use imadjust to adjust the contrast.

```
I3 = imadjust (I2, stretchlim (I2), [0 1]0;
```

Display the newly adjusted image.

```
figure, imshow (I3);
```

Fig. (12.8)

Here's What Just Happened

Step 5. You used the imadjust command to increase the contrast in the image. The imadjust function takes an input image and can also take two vectors: [low high] and [bottom top]. The output image is created by mapping the value low in the input image to the value bottom in the output image, mapping the value high in the input image to the value top in the output image, and linearly scaling the values in between.

You called imadjust with stretchlim (I2) as the second argument. The stretchlim function automatically computes the right [low high] values to make imadjust increase (stretch) the contrast of the image.

6. Apply Thresholding to the Image

Create a new binary threshold image, bw, by using the functions greythresh and im2bw.

```
level = graythresh (I3);
bw = im2bw (I3, level);
figure, imshow (bw)
```

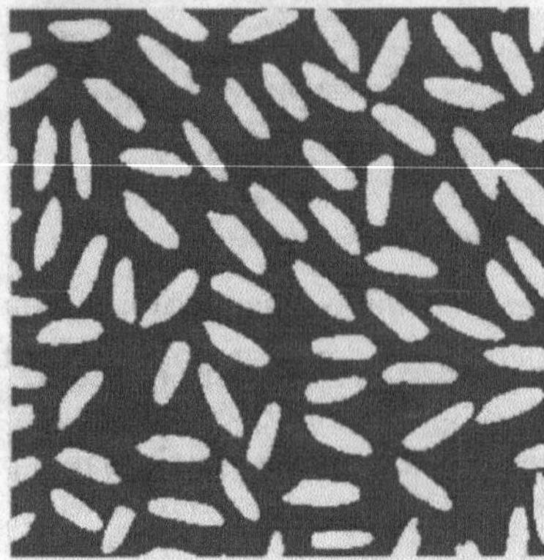

Fig. (12.9)

Now call the whos command to see what type of array the threshold image bw is.

```
whos
```

MATLAB responds with

```
Name          Size       Bytes     Class
I             256x256    65536     uint8 array
I2            256x256    65536     uint8 array
I3            256x256    65536     uint8 array
background    256x256    65536     uint8 array
bw            256x256    65536     logical array
level         1x1        8         double array
Grand total is 327681 elements using 327688 bytes
```

Here's What Just Happened

Step 6. You called graythresh to automatically compute an appropriate threshold to use to convert the intensity image to binary. You then called im2bw to perform for thresholding, using the threshold, level, returned by graythresh.

Notice that when you call the whos command, you see the expressioni logical listed after the class for bw. This indicates the presence of a logical flag. The flag indicates that bw is a logical matrix, and the

Image Processing Toolbox treats logical matrices as binary images. Thresholding using MATLAB logical operators always results in a logical image.

7. Determine the Number of Objects in the Image

To determine the number of grains of rice in the image, use the bwlabel function. This function labels all of the connected components in the binary image bw and returns the number of objects it finds in the image in the output value, numobjects.

```
[labeled, numObjects] = bwlabel (bw, 4); % Label components.
numObjects =
80
```

The accuracy of your results depends on a number of factors, including:

- The size of the objects
- The accuracy of your approximated background
- Whether you set the connectivity parameter to 4 or 8
- Whether or not any objects are touching (in which case they may be labeled as one object) In the example, some grains of rice are touching, so bwlabel treats them as one object.

Here's What Just Happened

Step 7. You called bylabel to search for connected components and label tthem with unique numbers. bwlabel takes a binary input image and a value specifying the *connectivity* of objects. The parameter 4, passed to the bylabel function, means that pixels must touch along an edge to be considered connected.

You can also determine the number of objects ina label matrix by asking for the maximum pixel value in the image. For example,

```
max (labeled (:))
ans =
80
```

8. Examine the Label Matrix

You may find it helpful to take a closer look at labeled to see what bylabel has created. Use the imcrop command to select and display pixels in a region of labeled that includes an object and some background.

To ensure that the output is displayed in the MATLAB window, do not end the line with a semicolon. In addition, choose a small rectangle for this exercise, so that the displayed pixel values don't wrap in the MATLAB command window.

The syntax shown below makes imcrop work interactively. Your mouse cursor becomes a cross-hair when placed over the image. Click at a position in labeled where you would like to select the upper left corner of a region. Drag the mouse to create the selection rectangle, and release the button when you are done.

```
grain = imcrop (labeled) % Crop a portion of labeled.
```

We chose the left edge of a grain and got the following results.

```
grain =

0 0 0  0  0  0  0 60 60
0 0 0  0  0 60 60 60 60
0 0 0 60 60 60 60 60 60
0 0 0 60 60 60 60 60 60
0 0 0 60 60 60 60 60 60
0 0 0 60 60 60 60 60 60
0 0 0 60 60 60 60 60 60
0 0 0  0  0 60 60 60 60
0 0 0  0  0  0  0  0  0
0 0 0  0  0  0  0  0  0
```

A good way to view a label matrix is to display it as a pseudo-color indexed image. In the pseudo-color image, the number that identifies each object in the label matrix as an RGB image, the objects in the image are easier to distinguish.

To view a label matrix in this way, use the label2grb function. Using this function, you can specify the colormap, the background color, and how objects in the label matrix map to colors in the colormap.

```
RGB_label = label2rgb (labeled, @spring, 'c', 'shuffle');
imshow (RGB_label);
```

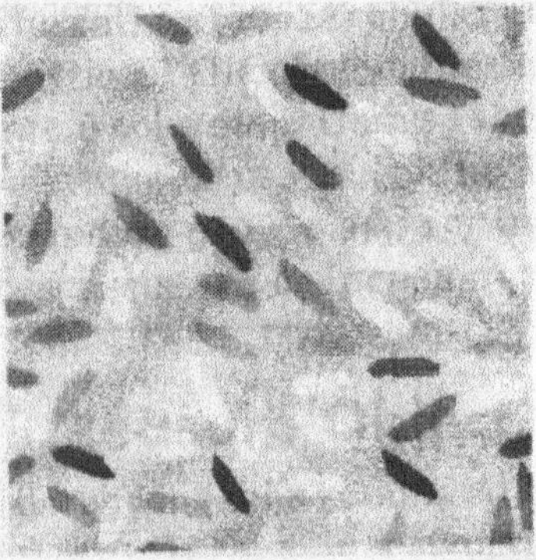

Fig. (12.10)

Here's What Just Happened

Step 8. You called imcrop and selected a portion of the image that contained both some background and part of an object. The pixel values were returned in the MATLAB window. If you examine the results above, you can see the corner of an object labeled with 60's, which means that it was the 60th object labeled by bwlabel.

The imcrop function can also take a vector specifying the coordinates for the crop rectangle. In this case, it does not operate interactively. For example, this call specifies a crop rectangle whose upper-left corner begins at (15, 25) and has a height and width of 10.

```
rect = [15, 25, 10 10];
roi = imcrop (labeled, rect)
```

You are not restricted to rectangular regions of interest. The toolbox also has a reipoly command that enables you to select polygonal regions of interest. Many image processing operations can be performed on regions of interest, including filtering and filling.

The call to label2rgb illustrates a good way to visualize label matrices. The pixel values in the label matrix are used as indices into a colormap. Using label2rgb, you can specify your own colormap or use one of the MATLAB colormap-creating functions, including gray, pink, spring, and hsv.

9. Measure Object Properties in the Image

The regionprops command measures object or region properties in an image and returns them in a structure array. When applied to an image with labeled components, it creates one structure element for each component. Use regionprops to create a structure array containing some basic properties for labeled.

```
graindata = regionprops (labeled, 'basic')
```

MATLAB responds with

```
graindata =
        80 × 1 struct array with fields:
        Area
        Centroid
        BoundingBox
```

To find the area of the component labeled with 51's, use dot notation to access the Area field in the 51st element in the graindata structure array. Note that structure field names are case sensitive, so you need to capitalize the name as shown.

```
graindata (51). Area
```

Returns the following results

```
ans = 296
```

To find the smallest possible bounding box and the centroid (center of mass) for the same component, use this code :

```
graindata (51).BoundingBox, graindata (51).Centroid
ans = 142.5000 89.5000 24.0000 26.0000
ans = 155.3953 102.1791
```

To create a new vector, allgrains, which holds just the area measurement for each grain, use this code:

```
allgraina = [graindata.Area];
whos allgrains
```

Call the whos command to see how MATLAB allocated the allgrains variable.

```
Name          Size        Bytes       Class
allgrains     1 × 80      640         double array
Grand total is 80 elements using 640 bytes
```

allgrains is a one-row array of 80 elements, where each element contains the area measurement of a grain. Check the area of the 51st element of allgrains.

```
allgrains (51)
```

returns

```
ans = 296
```

which is the same result that you received when using dot notation to access the Area field of graindata (51).

Here's What Just Happened

Step 9. You called regionprops to return a structure of basic property measurements for each threshold grain of rice. The regionprops function supports many different property measurements, but setting the properties parameter to 'basic' is a convenient way to return three of the most commonly used measurement: the area, the centroid (or center of mass), and the bounding box. The bounding box represents the smallest rectangle that can contain a region, or in this case, a grain. The four-element vector returned by the BoundingBox field,

```
[142.5000 89.5000 24.0000 26.0000]
```

shows that the upper left corner of the bounding box is positioned at [142.5 89.5], and the box has a width of 24.0 and a height of 26.0 (The position is defined in spatial coordinates, hence the decimal values. For more information on the spatial coordinate system, see ''Spatial Coordinates'' on page 2-29). For more information about working with MATLAB structure arrays, see ''Structures'' in the MATLAB programming and data types documentation.

You used dot notation to access the Area field of all of the elements of graindata and stored this data to a new vector allgrains. This step simplifies analysis made on area measurements because you do not have to use field names to access the area.

10. Compute Statistical Properties of Objects in the Image

Now use MATLAB functions to calculate some statistical properties of the thresholded objects. First use max to find the size of the largest grain. (If you have followed all of the steps in this exercise, the ''largest grain'' is actually two grains that are touching and have been labeled as one object).

```
max (allgrains)
returns
ans = 695
```

Use the find command to return the component label of this large-sized grain.

```
biggrain = find (allgrains==695)
returns
biggrain = 68
```

Find the mean grain size.

```
mean (allgrains)
returns
ans = 249
```

Make a histogram containing 20 bins that show the distribution of rice grain sizes.

```
hist (allgrains, 20)
```

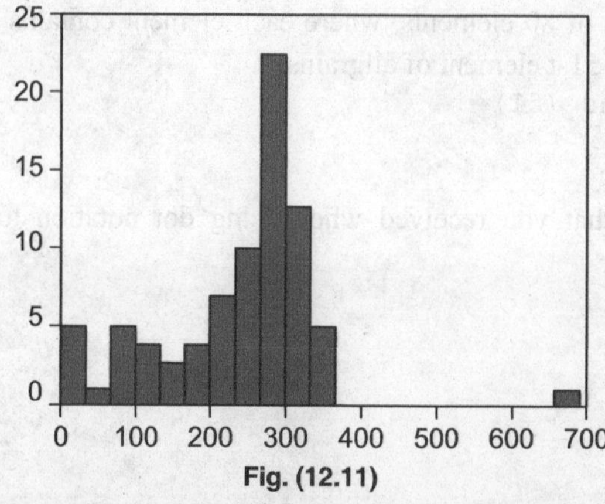

Fig. (12.11)

Here's What Just Happened

Step 10. You used some of the MATLAB statistical functions, max, mean, and hist to return the statistical properties for the threshold objects in rice.tif.

The Image Processing Toolbox also has some statistical functions, such as mean2 and std2, which are well suited to image data because they return a single value for two-dimensional data. The functions mean and std were suitable here because the data in allgrains was one dimensional.

The histogram shows that the most common sizes for rice grains in this image are in the range of 300 to 400 pixels.

Where to Go from Here

For more information about the topics covered in these exercises, read the tutorial chapters that make up the remainder of this documentation. For reference information about any of the Image Processing Toolbox functions, see the online ''Function Reference'', which complements the M-file help that is displayed in the MATLAB command window when you type

```
help functionname
```

For example,

```
help imshow
```

Online Help

The *Image Processing Toolbox User's Guide* is available online in both HTML and PDF formats. To access the HTML help, select **Help** from the menu bar of the MATLAB desktop. In the Help browser, expand the **Image Processing Toolbox** topic in the list. To access the PDF help, click on **Image Processing Toolbox** in the **Contents** tab of the Help browser, and go to the link under ''Printable Documentation (PDF).''

Toolbox Demos

The Image Processing Toolbox includes many demo applications. The demos are useful for seeing the toolbox features put into action and for borrowing code for your own applications. See ''Image Processing Demos'' in the Preface for a complete list and summary of the demos, as well as instructions on how to run them.

■ SUMMARY

- **Read and Display an Image** (User your own image)
  >>Img=imread('a:/bonermarr.tif); % Load your image from your disk
  >>imshow(Img) % Show your image in MATLAB
- **Check the Image Storage Information** (Use your own image)
  whos % See how myimg.tif is stored into the MATLAB workspace.
  % MATLAB respond with

```
Name    Size      Bytes     Class
Img     480x640   307200    uint8 array
```

Where ''Img'' – your image name; ''480x640'' – image size in pixel: ''307200'' - image data size in Bytes; ''uint8 array'' – Convert data to unsigned 8-bit integers. (This is a MATLAB function. See the online MATLAB Function Reference for its reference page.)

- **Pixel Value & Euclidean Distance** (Use your own image)

  pixval on

  This command turns on interactive display of pixel (info (x, y, and intensity) in the current image. A black bar at the bottom of the figure displays (the (x, y) coordinates for the pixel that the cursor is currently over and the intensity info for that pixel.

  If you click on the image and hold down the mouse button while you move the cursor, PIXVAL also displays the Euclidean distance between the point you clicked on and current cursor location. PIXVAL draws a line between these points to indicate the distance being measured. When you release the mouse button, the line and the distance display disappear. You can move the display bar by clicking on it and dragging it to another place in the figure.

  pixval off

  This command turns interactive display off in the current figure. You cna also turn off the display by clicking the button on the right side of the display bar.

  Img

  This command shows all pixel values in the image. If you want see the pixel value at (45, 69), just type in :

  Img (45, 69)

  If you want to see the pixel values between x = 36, …, 40, and y = 54, …, 69), just type in:

  [(36:40.54:69)

- **Image Processing**

  (1) Histogram (Use image 'pout.tif')

  imhist(Img) % Display histogram of image data.
  histeq(Img) % Enhance contrast using histogram equalization.

  (2) Edge Detection (Use image 'rice.tif')

  (a) "Sobel" has a 3 × 3 mask: h = [-1 - 2 - 1; 0 0 0; 1 2 1].
  (b) "Prewitt" has a 3 × 3 mask: h = [-1 - 1 - 1; 0 0 0; 1 1 1].
  (c) "Roberts" has a 3 × 3 mask: h = [1 0; 0 1].
  NewImg=edge9I.'prewitt');
  This command uses ''prewitt'' mask for edge detection, the new image named ''NewImg''.

  (3) Change a gray image into a binary image (Black-White Image) (Use image 'rice.tif')

  level = graythresh(Img)
  BW = img2bw(I, level);
  imshow(BW)

  The first command computes a global threshold (level) that can be used to convert an intensity image to a binary image with *im2bw*. level is a normalized intensity value that lies in the range [0, 1]. The graythresh function uses OTsu's method, which chooses the threshold to minimize the intraclass variance of the black and white pixels.

  The second one converts an image to a binary image, based on threshold

  (4) Median filter (Use image 'eight.tif')

  N = imnoise(Img.'salt % pepper',0.02);
  figure, imshow(N)

The above command add 'salt & pepper' noise on the image where 0.02 is the noise density. Then the median filter is used to remove the noise by following command:

B = medfilt2(N);

figure, imshow(B)

(5) Smoothing Filter (e.g. Low-pass filter)

I = imread('eight.tif');

J = imnoise(I.'gaussian',0.0.005);

K= wiener2(J,[5 5]);

imshow(J)

figure, imshow(K)

Note: Please repeat this problem using [3 3] and [9 9] instead of [5 5] in the third commands [1]wiener2 lowpass filters an intensity image that has been degraded by constant power additive noise. wiener2 uses a pixel-wise adaptive Wiener method based on statistics estimated from a local enighbourhood of each pixel.

- **Multiple-Image Display** (Use these commands to display multiple images in one figure)
  subplot(1, 2, 1), subimage(Img 1);
  subplot(1,2,2), subimage(Img2)
  Display multiple images in the same figure.
- **Write the Image** (If you want to store the processed image, use this command)
  imwrite (I2, 'MyNewImg.png');
  Write the processed image I2 to a disk. MATLAB recognize several file version, such as ''.tif'', ''.bmp'', ''png'', ''.jpg'', etc.

Lab Report Information

The lab report for Lab#1 is to hand in your processed images in **''4.Image Processing''** part. Please also give your own comments about the processed images, including

(1) How to determine a threshold using image's histogram;

(2) In three edge detection methods, which one or two is better for that particular image;

(3) Why the median filter is good for removing 'salt-pepper' type of noise;

(4) How the mask size (e.g., $3 \times 3, 5 \times 5$, etc.) affect the image smoothing? Why wiener filter is good a remove gaussian noise.

- Please refer to the MATLAB HELP for more information.
- Please refer to the materials that I hand out to you or go to the course website to learn the theretical stuff behind these processing algorithms.

LAB MANUALS

LAB–1

1. Introduction

The VisiQuest (formerly Khoros Pro) is visual programming environment. It is used in numerous scientific industrial applications involving image processing.

2. Getting Started

In order to start the VisiQuest program, find the VisiQuest icon on your desktop and double-click on it. You'll see the large empty window called workspace and eight pull-down menus—File, Edit, Workspace, Options, Control, Glyphs, Objects, Help.

In order to create a program, you have to draw in the workspace several blocks (functions) called **glyphs** and to connect them by wires.

2.1 Creation and deletion of a glyph

Every glyph can be accessed from the Glyph menu. For example, in order to load the image into the workspace use

[Glyphs – Input/Output – Data Files – User defined] sequence of menus.

If you want to delete a glyph, use Ctrl-B.

2.2 Creation and deletion of a connection

If you want to connect two glyphs (let's call them Source and Sink), just click on the output port of one glyph (Source) and then on the input port of the second glyph (Sink).

Note : If you have several input (output) contacts in one glyph, use the upper contact and don't use gray contacts.

In order to delete the connection click (once!) on the unnecessary wire. In a small dialog window that will appear select Delete Connection and OK.

2.3 Execution of a program

In order to execute all glyphs in the workspace click on the Run button

In order to stop the execution of all glyphs in the workspace click on the Stop button

In addition, each glyph can be executed independently by clicking on the ''window'' on its center.

2.4 Working with glyphs — several tips

''Usual'' commands : use Ctrl-C to copy, Ctrl-V to paste, Ctrl-X to cut, Ctrl-A to select all, Ctrl-Z to undo delete, Ctrl-S so save file.

''Unusual'' commands : use Ctrl-B to delete, Ctrl-D to duplicate.

Save your workspace frequently using Ctrl-S.

3. The project

3.1 Loading and display of the image

Load the image lena.jpg into your workspace

[Glyphs – Input/Output – Data Files – User defined]

and then display it

[Glyphs – Visualization – Non-Interactive Image Display – Display Image.]

3.2 Image geometrical Transformations

For image jena.jpg perform the following operations :

- Expand the image

  [Glyphs – Data Manip – Size & Region Operators – Expand]
- Shrink the image

  [Glyphs – Data Manip – Size & Region Operators – Shrink]
- Extract a region the image

  [Glyphs – Data Manip – Size & Region Operators – Extract]
- Translate the image

  [Glyphs – Data Manip – Reorganize Data – Translate]
- Transpose the image

  [Glyphs – Data Manip – Reorganize Data – Transpose]

Note : both WIDTH and HEIGHT dimensions have to be selected.

- Rotate the image

  [Glyphs – Image Proc – Geometric Operators – Rotate]
- Flip the image

  [Glyphs – Image Proc – Geometric Operators – Flip Image]

  (a possible alternative : [Glyphs – Data Manip – Reorganize Data – Flip])
- Pad the image (for example, with zeros)

  [Glyphs – Data Manip – Size & Region Operators – Pad]

3.3 Median filtering

Load and display the image jena.jpb. Obtain the image degraded by shot noise using [Glyphs – Data Manip – Introduce Noise – Shot Noise] and display the degraded image. Filter the degraded image with median filter using [Glyphs – Image Proc – Nonlinear Filters – Median] and display the result. Do you improve the degraded image? Try to apply median filter several times in sequence.

3.4 Edge detection

Load and display the image lena.jpb. Detect edges using the following operators :

- gradient [Glyphs – Image Proc – Spatial Filters – Gradient operator],
- DRF [Glyphs – Image Proc – Spatial Filters – DRF Edge Extract],
- GEF [Glyphs – Image Proc – Spatial Filters – DRF Edge Extract],
- SDEF [Glyphs – Image Proc – Spatial Filters – DRF Edge Extract].

4. Instructions for submission of the labs

Put your temporal work in the student account]/lab*/work directory ([student account] will be given to each student; * denotes the number of lab).

Put your final work in the [student_account]/lab*/checkpoint directory. Include the text file with the report (the description of the algorithms, what did you do, what parameters used, conclusions) in the [student_account]/lab*/checkpoint directory. Don't forget to write your name, I.D. and the number of lab.

LAB#1 Image Processing Lab (Tuesday, Feb. 7, 2006, E192)

Objectives :

1. To be familiar with a typical machine vision system, illumination, general functions, etc.
2. The learn how to use a Machine Vision System to take an image and store an image to a disk.
3. To learn how to use MATLAB Image Processing Toolbox to do digital image processing.

Components : A DVT 600 Vision System, a computer, a ring illuminator, a LED illumination array, and some mechanical parts.

Procedures :

1. An overall review and demonstration of the basic functions and operations of the DVT vision system— a typical industrial machine vision system.
2. Change different illumination conditions to observe how the illumination affects the quality of an image.
3. Take **an** image using the DVT system and save your image in ''xx.bmp'' or ''xx.tif'' (xx is your file name) in a floppy fisk (will be provided by Dr. Du).

Lab Report/Homework Assignment : After you take an image (for this particular lab, the image is provided by Dr. Du, see the image below), you can go to E213 to do the following assignments (if you have MATLAB Image Processing Toolbox in your own computer, you can do the assignment at home).

1. Use a 3×3, 5×5 and 11×1 low-pass filtering mask to process your image and compare three images.
2. Use a 3×3 median filter to processing your image.
3. Design an edge detector to detect the computer of the part.

In your lab report, please

(1) show all images (including the original image) you get from procedure 3;

(2) give your commands about these images. E.g. whether or not these images are improved, the designed edge detector works good or not, etc.;

(3) attach all MATLAB codes that you wrote for the image processing.

Please read attached materials before you do the assignment.

LAB–2

1. Histogram & histogram equalization

1.1 Theoretic background

For each gray level in the image (from 0 (black) to 255 (white)) we count the number of pixels colored in this gray level. The results of this counting process are displayed as a graph of number of pixels versus gray levels. This graph is called a histogram of the image.

In low-contrast images it is desired to fully utilize the available dynamic range of the displaying device. The histogram equalization tries to spread out the histogram of the original image. The mathematical description of the histogram equalization can be found in many image processing books, e.g. in [1].

1.2 The Project—Part 1 (Histogram)

Load the image lena.jpg into your workspace and then display it. Find the histogram of the image and plot its graph. In what applications can histogram be used?

Perform histogram equalization of the image lena.jpb and display the resulting image. Find the histogram of the histogram-equalized image and plot its graph. In what applications can histogram equalization be used?

Apply the aforementioned process to the image spine.gif.

2. Morphological Operations

2.1 Theoretic background

Morphology relates to the structure or form of objects. Morphological filtering simplifies a segmented image to facilitate the search for objects of interest. This is done by smoothing out object outlines, filling small holes, eliminating small projections, and using other similar techniques. We will look at the different types of operations available and at some examples of their use. We'll start with binary images and then proceed to gray-level images.

The two principal morphological operations are dilation and erosion. Dilation allows objects to expand, thus potentially filling in small holes and connecting disjoint objects. Erosion shrinks objects by etching away (eroding) their boundaries. These operations can be customized for an application by the proper selection of the structuring element, which determines exactly how the objects will be dilated or eroded.

The dilation process is performed by laying the structuring element on the image and sliding it across the image in a manner similar to convolution. The difference is in the operation performed. It is best described in a sequence of steps :

- If the origin of the structuring element conicides with a '0' in the image, there is no change; move to the next pixel.
- If the origin of the structuring element coincides with a '1' in the image, perform the OR logic operation on all pixels within the structuring element.

An example is shown in Figure 1. Note that with a dilation operation, all the '1' pixels in the original image will be retained, any boundaries will be expanded, and small holes will be filled. The erosion process is similar to dilation, but we turn pixels to '0', not '1'. As before, slide the structuring element across the image and then follow these steps :

- If the origin of the structuring element concides with a '0' in the image, there is no change, move to the next pixel.
- If the origin of the structuring element coincides with a '1' in the image, and any of the '1' pixels in the structuring element extend beyond the object ('1' pixels) in the image, then change the '1' pixel in the image to a '0'.

In Figure 2 the only remaining pixels are those that conicide to the origin of the structuring element where the entire structuring element was contained in the existing object. Because the structuring element is 3 pixels wide, the 2-pixel-wide right leg of the image object was eroded away, but the 3-pixel-wide left leg retained some of its center pixels.

These two basic operations, dilation and erosion, can be combined into more complex sequences. The most useful of these for morphological filtering are called opening and closing. Opening consists of an erosion followed by a dilation and can be used to eliminate all pixels in regions that are too small to contain the structuring element. In this case the structuring element is often called a probe, because it is probing the image looking for small objects to filter out of the image. See Figure 3 for an example of opening.

Closing consists of a dilation followed by erosion and can be used to fill in holes and small gaps. In Figure 4 we see that the closing operatin has the effect of filling in holes and closing gaps. Comparing Figure 4 to Figure 3, we see that the order of operatin is important. Closing and opening will have different results even though both consist of an erosion and a dilation.

The morphological operations described (dilation, erosion, opening, and closing) can be extended to gray-level images in the following way :

- For erosion the origin of the structuring element will be equal to the minimum of all pixels within the structuring element;
- For dilation the origin of the structuring element will be equal to the maximum of all pixels within the structuring element.

2.2 The Project—Part 2 (Binary Morphology)

- Load and display the image circles.gif. Define the disk structuring element. Set the ''Disk Diameter'' parameter to the value 6.
- Perform the erosion and dilation of the image with the structuring element.
- Perform the opening and closing of the image using erosion and dilation operations. (Don't use the Opening and Closing glyphs of the VisiQuest program because they don't work.)
- The erosion and dilation can be used to find edges of the image. Subtract the eroded image from the original one and fine the ''First'' image of edges. Subtract the original image from the dilated one and find the ''second'' image of edges. Compare between the ''first'' and the ''second'' images. Which image extracted edges better in this case?

2.3 The Project—Part 3 (Gray-Scale Morphology)

- Load and display the image orthophoto.jpb. Define the disk structuring element. Set the ''Disk Diameter'' parameter to the value 3.
- Perform the erosion and dilation of the image with the structuring element.
- Perform the opening and closing of the image using erosion and dilation operations. (Don't use the Opening and Closing glyphs of the VisiQuest program because they don't work.)

- The erosion and dilation can be used to find edges of the image. Subtract the eroded image from the original one and find the ''first'' image of edges. Subtract the original image from the dilated one and find the ''second'' image of edges. Compare between the ''first'' and the ''second'' images. Which image extracted edges better in this case? Try this for the lena.jpb as well.

3. Convolution

3.1 Theoretic background

The convolution of the image with a specified filter allows us to perform various tasks, e.g., to smooth the image (using Low-Pass filter), to extract the edges of image (using HIgh-Pass filter) and so on.

3.2 The Project—Part 4 (Convolution)

Very Important Note : Select the ''Upcast data'' property in the list of properties of the Convolve glyph.

- Load and display the image lena.jpg. Perform the averaging using 3 × 3 Average, 5 × 5 Average and 7 × 7 Average filters. What is the difference between the results? For each averaging filter from above try to find out what numbers it consists of.
- Find the horizontal, vertical and diagonal edges of the image using edge-detecting filters Sobel X, Sobel Y and 45 Degree Gradient. For each edge-detecting filter from above try to find out what numbers it consists of.

4. Appendix-Useful Operations

4.1 Common operations

Load the image into the workspace

[Glyphs – Input/Output – Data Files – User defined].

Display the image

[Glyphs – Visualization – Non-Interactive Image Display – Display Image].

4.2 Operations for Part 1

Find the histogram of the image

[Glyphs – Data Manip – Histogram Operators – Histogram].

Plot the 2-D graph

[Glyphs – Visualization – Plot Display – Display 2D Plot].

Perform histogram equalization of the image

[Glyphs – Data Manip – Histogram Operators – Equalize].

4.3 Operations for Parts 2 and 3

Define the disk structuring element

[Glyphs – MMACH – Structural Element – Disk Str. E1].

Perform the erosion of the image

[Glyphs – MMACH – dilation and Erosion – Erosion].

Perform the dilation of the image

[Glyphs – MMACH – Dilation and Erosion – Dilation].

Subtract one image from other

[Glyphs – Arithmetic – Two Operand Arithmetic – Subtract].

4.4 Operations for Part 4

Specify the filter for convolution

[Glyphs – Input/Output – Data Files – 2D Filter Kernels].

Convolve the image with the filter

[Glyphs – Data Manip – Convolusion – Convolve].

Very Important Note : Select the ''Upcast data'' property in the list of properties of the Convolve glyph.

5. References

[1] R.C. Gonzalez and P.A. Wintz, ''Digital Image Processing'', Addision-Wesley, 1987.

LAB–3

1. The Properties of the DFT transform

1.1 Theoretical background

This part consists of sequence of short demos. The purpose of these demos is to demonstrate several important properties of the DFT transform with the emphasis on the relation between images in the spatial domain and their DFT transform.

NOte. For this lab all workspaces are ready. You are supposed to analyze the results and write the reports.

1.2 The Project—The Properties of DFT Transform

(a) Images and their spectra : Load the workspace I_A.wksp. In this workspace we define and display an image of a square, calculate its DFT and display its spectral magnitude.

(b) Size modification in spatial domain : Load the workspace I_B.wksp. Change the size of the box (using ''Box Y Height'' and ''Box X Width'' parameters in the Box Projection glyph), calculate the DFT of the modified box and display its magnitude. When you expand or shrink the box, what happens to the spectrum of the modified image? Explain this property.

(c) Multiplication by complex exponent in spatial domain : Load the workspace I_C.wksp. Modify the image by multiplying it by a complex sinusoid. Change the frequency of the sinusoid (using the parameters ''Num.along Width'' and ''Num.along Height''), calculate the DFT of the modified image and display its magnitude. What happens to the spectrum of the modified image? Explainj this property

(d) Multiplication by complex exponent in frequency domain : Load the workspace I_D.wksp. Calculate the DFT of the original box image and display its magnitude. Modify the resulting DFT by multiplying it by a complex sinusoid. Change the frequency of the complex exponent (using the parameters ''Num.along Width'' and ''Num.along Height''), calculate the inverse DFT of the modified spectrum and display its magnitude. What happens to the modified image in the spatial domain? Explain this property.

(e) Rotation in the spatial domain : Load the workspace I_E.wksp. Calculate the DFT of the origin box image and display its magnitude. Modify the image by rotating it by 45 degrees (inside the box glyph). Calculate the DFT of the rotated image and display its magnitude. What happens to the spectrum of the rotated image? Explain this property.

(f) Two horizontal boxes : Load the workspace I_F.wksp. Create new image by addition of two horizontally shifted boxes. Calculate the DFT of the new image and display its magnitude. What happens to the spectrum of the new image? Explain this property.

(g) Two diagonal boxes : Load the workspace I_G.wksp. Create new image by addition of two diagonally shifted boxes. Calculate the DFT of the new image and display its magnitude. What happens to the spectrum of the new image? Explain this property.

2. Inverse Filtering

2.1 Theoretical background

Inverse filtering is the process of recovering the input of a system from its output. For example, in the absence of noise the inverse filter would be a system that recovers the input of a system from its output correctly. Suppose that the frequency response of the system is $H\,(\omega_1, \omega_2)$. The inverse filter is the reciprocal of $H\,(\omega_1, \omega_2)$:

However $H'\,(\omega_2, \omega_2)$ does not exist if $H\,(\omega_1, \omega_2)$ has any zeros. In order of stabilize the inverse filter, we introduce the pseudoinverse filter :

2.2 The Project—Part 2 (Inverse Filtering)

Load the workspace 2.wksp. Use both of the input images lena.jpg and dip.jpg. Blur the image using the Low-Pass filter. Display the original image, the spectrum of the original image, the spectrum of the Low-Pass filter, the spectrum of the blurred image and the blurred image in the spatial domain. Restore the image from its blurred modification using Inverse Filtering. Display the spectrum of the resulting image and the resulting image itself. How well you restore the original image? Explain the restoration error.

Notes : Submission is in hardcopy, 2 weeks after the lab, including images and explanations.

QUESTION BANK

1. For an image given by the function $f(x, y) = (x + y)^3$ where x, y are continuous variables; evaluate $f(x, y)\,\delta(x-1, y-2)$ and $f(x, y) * \delta(x-1, y-2)$, where δ is the Dirac Delta function.
2. For the optical imaging system shown below, consisting of an image scaling and two forward Fourier transforms show that the output image is a scaled and inverted replica of the original image $f(x, y)$.

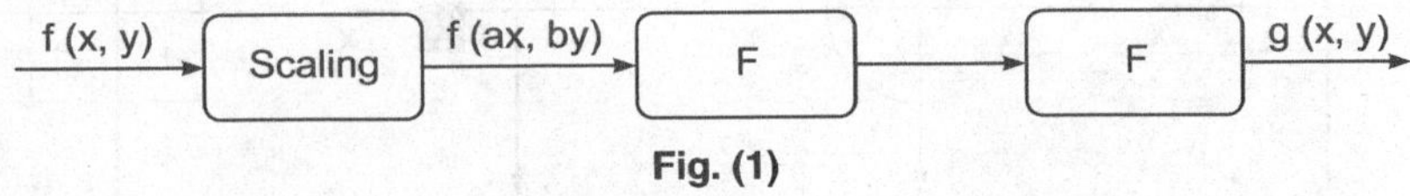

Fig. (1)

3. Three binary images (with value 1 on black areas and value 0 elsewhere) are shown below. Sketch the continuous 2D FT of these images (don't do this mathematically, try to use instead the convolution theorem and knowledge of FTs of common functions).

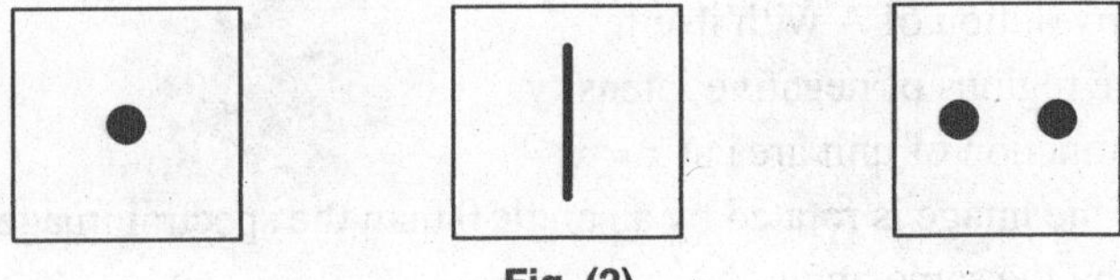

Fig. (2)

4. (a) Determine the *linear discrete convolution* of $x(m, n)$ below with each of the sampled images A, B. For each cases take the origin as the element in the top left corner. Assume outside each image pixel values are zero.

$x(m, n)$	$A(m, n)$	$B(m, n)$
1 4 1	-2	1 2 3
2 5 3	3	1 0 0
	1	

(b) Form also the cross-correlation $x(m, n)$ and $A(m, n)$.

5. (Question 3.3 from Gonzalez and Woods). A real function $f(x)$ can be decomposed as the sum of an even function and an odd function.
(a) Show that $f_{even} = 0.5\,[f(x) + f(-x)]$ and $f_{odd} = 0.5\,[f(x) - f(-x)]$.
(b) Show that $FT\,(f_{even}) = Real\,(FT\ f(x)))$ and $FT\,(f_{odd}) = iIm\,(FT\,(f(x)))$.
6. Consider the images shown on the next page (A to H). Using knowledge of symmetry properties and the convolution theorem (*not exact calculation of the Fourier integrals*), list which

images or image which have continuous Fourier transforms, $F(u, v)$ with the following properties.

(i) The imaginary part of $F(u, v)$ is zero at all u, v

(ii) The real part of $F(u, v)$ is positive for all u, v.

(iii) $F(0, 0) = 0$

(iv) $F(u, v)$ has circular symmetry

(v) The real part of $F(u, v)$ is zero at all u, v

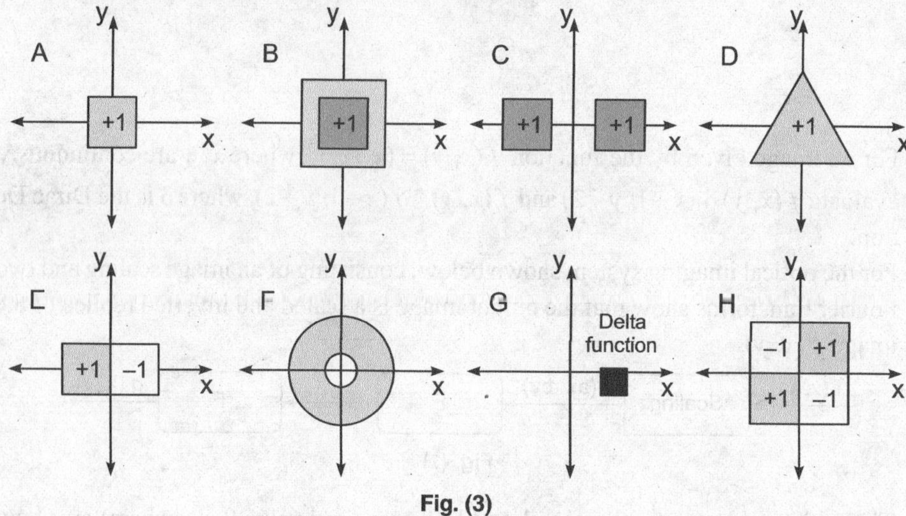

Fig. (3)

Notes : Unless otherwise stated the shaded regions have value +1, and outside the shapes the value is 0.

B - is the convolution of A with itself.

E and H have regions of negative intensity.

G is a delta function of unit area at $x = x_{x_0}$.

7. Prove that if the image is rotated by an angle θ than the spectral image (Fourier transform) is also rotated by the same angle.

8. Prove the scaling property of the Fourier transform :

$$J[f(ax, by)] = \frac{F\left(\frac{\xi_1}{a}, \frac{\xi_2}{b}\right)}{|ab|}$$

9. For each of the following linear system, determine the transfer function, frequency response, the OTF and the MTF :

(a) $y(m, n) - a_1 y(m-2, n) - a_2 y(m, n-2) = x(m, n)$

(b) $y(m, n) - a_1 y(m-1, n) - a_2 y(m, n-1) + - a_1 a_2 y(m-1, n-1) = x(m, n)$

10. An image given by the two dimensional function

$$f(x, y) = 2\cos[2\pi(4x + 6y)]$$

is sampled on an infinite grid of pixels with separation $\Delta x = 0.1$ and $\Delta y = 0.2$, in the x and y directions respectively.

We form the continuous FT of this sampled image; multiply by the ideal low pass spatial filter with cutoff frequencies at half the sampling frequency in each spatial frequency axis; and then inverse Fourier transform to obtain a reconstructed image. Determine :

(a) The spatial spectrum of the sampled image before low pass filtering.

(b) The spectrum of the image after it has been low-pass filtered.

(c) The reconstructed image.

(d) In order to reconstruct without distortion the original image from sampled data what is the maximum sizes of Δx and Δy that can used and the minimum and maximum bandwidths of the low pass reconstruction filters that can be used.''

11. A two dimensional continuous image is given by :

$$f(x, y) = \sin^2 (2\pi (ax + by))b$$

(a) Sketch the function for $a = 4; b = 4$ and $a = 1; b = 8$.

(b) We want to correctly sample this function/what is the Nyquist rate on the x and $y$axis? (as a function of a and b).

(c) Is the picture's ''actual'' frequency higher or lower then the one you gave at section b?

(d) For $a = 2$ and $b = 4$, suggest the optimal sampling grid.

(e) For $a = 2$ and $b = 2$, the image has been sampled. We want to create the image from its samples. However our new display has pixels spaced. For zero hold and 1st order hold interpolators, what will be the value of the reconstructed picture on pixels located at :

$$n, m = 0, 1, 2, \ldots$$

(f) Is there is a way to exactly reconstruct the image if the original picture $f(x, y)$ is bounded in the region $[-5:5, -5:5]$?

12. An image is samples using a HEXCOMB function, which is a function of $\delta\ (x, y)$ s, each in the center of a hexagonal covering the whole plane :

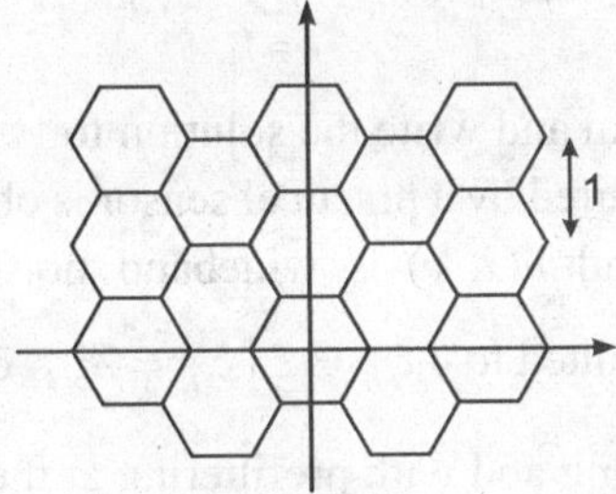

Fig. (4)

(a) Express the HEXCOMB function, using comb function or $\delta\ (x, y)$ functions.

(b) Given $g(x, y)$ which Fourier transform satisfies

Prove that sampling $g(x, y)$ using the HEXCOMB function allows a complete reconstruction, and requires less sampling points than the COMB function.

13. Given a function whose Fourier transform is given in the figure below :

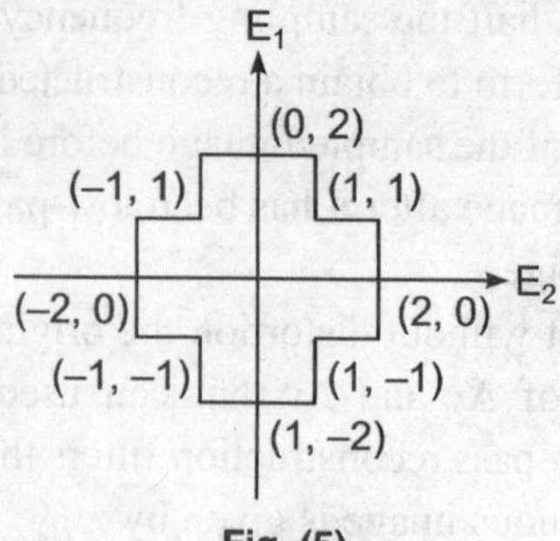

Fig. (5)

(a) This function is sampled by a rectangular grid (COMB). Find the minimum sampling resolution (in samples per meter) to allow a full reconstruction of the function.
(b) Find a different sampling grid that gives optimal sampling resolution. What is the sampling grid? What is the sampling resolution?

14. Can two monochromatic sources of different wavelength appear like the same color? Prove your answer.

15. Prove : $T_K\ (C) = \int C\ (\lambda)\ T_K\ (\lambda)\ d\lambda$

16. In this problem we show that any two tristimulus coordinate systems based on different sets of primary sources are linearly related. Let, $sssP_K\ (\lambda)ttt$ and $sssP'_K\ (\lambda)ttt, k = 1, 2, 3$, be two sets of primary sources with corresponding tristimulus coordinates $sssT_K ttt$ and $sssT'_k\ ttt$ and reference white sources $W\ (\lambda)$ and $W'\ (\lambda)$. If a color $C\ (\lambda)$ is matched by these sets of sources, then show that :

$$\sum_{k=1}^{3} a_{i,k}\ w_k\ T_k\ (C) = \sum_{k=1}^{3} a'_{i,k}\ w'_k\ T'_k\ (C).$$

Express this in matrix form and write the solution for $sssT'_k\ ttt$.

17. A bandlimited image acquired by a practical sensor is observed as $g(x, y) = f\ (x, y) + n(x, y)$ where $\xi_{x_0} = \xi_{y_0} = \xi_f$ and $n(x, y)$ is wideband noise whose spectral density function $S_n(\xi_1, \xi_2) = \dfrac{\eta}{4}$ is bandlimited to $-\xi_n ® \xi_1 \xi_n = 2\xi_f, \xi_2 ® \xi_n$. The random field $g(x, y)$ is sampled without prefiltering and with prefiltering at the Niquist rate of the noiseless image and reconstructed by an ideal los-pass filter whose bandwidths are also $\xi_{x_0} = \xi_{y_0} = \xi_f$ see figure below :

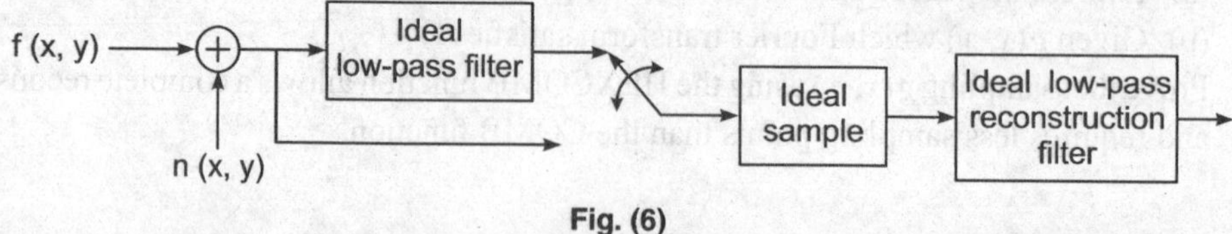

Fig. (6)

Show that :

(a) The SNR of the sensor output g over its bandwidth is $\frac{\sigma_f^2}{4\eta\xi_f^2}$ where σ_f^2 is the image power.

(b) The SNRSs of the reconstructed image with and without prefiltering are $\frac{\sigma_f^2}{\eta\xi_f^2}$ and $\frac{\sigma_f^2}{4\eta\xi_f^2}$ respectively. What would be the SNR of the reconstructed image if the sensor output were sampled at the Nyquist rate of the noise without any prefiltering? Compare the preceding sampling schemes and recommend the best way for sampling noisy images.

18. Define

Suppose the compandor transformation in the upper definition is $g(x) = f^{-1}(x)$ and $p_u(u) = p_u(-u)$. This transformation (also called histogram equalization) causes w to be uniformly distributed over the interval $\left[-\frac{1}{2}, \frac{1}{2}\right]$. The uniform quantizer is now optimized for w. However the overall quantizer need not be

(a) Let $p_u(u) = \begin{cases} 1-|u| & -1 ® u ® 1 \\ 0 & \text{otherwise} \end{cases}$ and the quantizer levels be 4. What are the decision and reconstruction levels for the input u? Calculate the MSE.

(b) Show that this compandor is sub optimal compared to the one discussed in the text.

19. (a) Show that the random variable v defined via satisfies the condition $\Pr(V ® v) = \Pr(U ® F^{-1}(v)) = F(F^{-1}(v)) = v$, where. This means v is uniformly distributed over (0, 1).

(b) On the other hand, show that the transformation

$$p_u(x_i) = \frac{h(x_i)}{\sum_{i=0}^{L-1} h(x_i)} \quad i = 0, 1, \ldots, L-1$$

gives $p_v(v_k) = p_u(x_k)$ where v_k is given by $v_k = \sum_{i=0}^{k} p_u(x_i)$.

20. The PDF of an image is given by Pr (r) as shown below. Find the transform to convert the image's PDF to Pr (z). Assume continuity, and find the transform in terms of r and z. Explain the transformation.

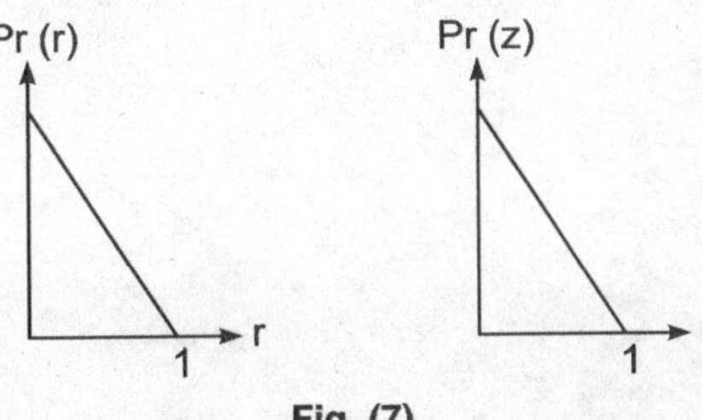

Fig. (7)

□□□